THE
AMERICAN
GAME

Also by S. L. Price

Playing Through the Whistle: Steel, Football,
and an American Town

Heart of the Game: Life, Death, and Mercy
in Minor League America

Far Afield: A Sportswriting Odyssey

Pitching Around Fidel: A Journey into the Heart
of Cuban Sports

THE
AMERICAN
GAME

History *and* Hope *in* the Country of Lacrosse

S. L. PRICE

Atlantic Monthly Press
New York

One of the first conditions of happiness is that the link between Man and Nature shall not be broken.

—Leo Tolstoy

FIRST EDITION

Published simultaneously in Canada
Printed in the United States of America

First Grove Atlantic hardcover edition: May 2025

Library of Congress Cataloging-in-Publication data is available for this title.

ISBN 978-0-8021-6473-5
eISBN 978-0-8021-6474-2

Atlantic Monthly Press
an imprint of Grove Atlantic
154 West 14th Street
New York, NY 10011

Distributed by Publishers Group West

groveatlantic.com

25 26 27 28   10 9 8 7 6 5 4 3 2 1

CONTENTS

Preamble: Splinters Rising   vii

THE OLD WORLD

PART 1: Braiding

I   The Battle of Toronto Airport   5

II   Faithkeepers   28

III   He Is Flying Over Us   44

PART 2: Bearing Up

I   The Lonely Sons of Simeon Moss   73

II   The Shadow Game   95

III   Wiggle, Please   118

PART 3: The Muslin and the Buffalo

I   Jerusalem   147

II   The Whaleness of the White   168

III   Money Ball   193

PART 4: 99 Bottles of Beer

I   Because You Killed Her   213

II   One Every Year   236

III   Builders   249

PART 5: Playing Against Type

I   We Can Do It   273

II   Strong Island   293

III The Money Game   308

THE NEW WORLD

PART 1: Nothing Without Demand

I   Tewaaraton   325

II   An Awful Roar   341

III Crops   359

PART 2: The Long Game

I   Treaty Bound   381

II   San Diego   394

III Olympia   417

Acknowledgments   439

Notes   443

Index   529

PREAMBLE

Splinters Rising

THE FIRST THING to know about entering the country of lacrosse is that you had better come primed. Curl a dumbbell. Get one of those springy grip exercisers. Gird yourself, because everyone you meet will want to shake hands, and every handshake is the old-fashioned kind. This takes getting used to. In the rest of the world, the generations raised on dad's finger-mashing, let-'em-know-you're-there handshake have all but aged out, and children of the digital age find such displays embarrassing.

I, though, had one of those dads. I became one of those dads. Yet my first days inside the sport's ambit made clear that I'd gone soft. Every man, woman, coach, parent, official and player unleashed throwback vise grips amid a startlingly warm welcome. The only way to survive was to respond in kind—battering-ram thrust, then grinningly hold on for dear life.

Because, I quickly realized, the country of lacrosse is more state of being than place. Once confined to leafy patches of Baltimore and New York and schools draped in ivy, real and symbolic, it burst those boundaries long ago, and has spent the early 21st century reveling in its status as America's fastest-growing sport and yearning to become its Next Big Thing. "We're in the process," said seven-time national champion Bill Tierney, arguably the greatest American coach ever, one afternoon in his spacious office at the University of Denver, "of going from a 'What's that?' to 'Oh, wow!'"

That was late in 2018. By then I'd been immersed for months, traveled thousands of miles to lacrosse hotbeds old and new. I'd seen enough to know that chesty ambition was just a small part of the profile, heard enough to sense that—despite occupying the North American continent for a thousand years—the sport's psyche was about as settled as an adolescent's. Each week revealed a different persona: rich, poor, Native, white, diverse, racist, empowering, retrograde, enlightened, arrogant, heroic, reverent, drunk.

Secure only in its unmatched heritage, the lacrosse I encountered toggled between thinking itself wonderful and wondering if something, at its core, was very wrong. The opinion of strangers seemed a particular fixation.

Part of this stemmed from the typical teenager yearning for popularity. For more than a century the highest expression of lacrosse was the field version found at elite American colleges—a 10-on-10 ground war featuring web-headed sticks and a hard rubber ball, the dodge-and-shoot imperative made more famous by ice hockey and basketball, and no financial future. Its lack of mass appeal was almost a point of pride. But by the time I latched on, longtime efforts to "Grow the Game" beyond boutiquity, to make it more fan-friendly, had thrown even its basics into question. Plans for a new type of professional league, complete with national TV contracts, healthcare and livable salaries, were crystallizing, along with the mission to become part of the Olympic Games. Everything—from field dimensions to length of games to ball color to team size—was open for debate.

At the same time, tensions over lacrosse's identity were bubbling into view. Though few American institutions match its record of expanding opportunity for women and recognition of Native Americans, the sport's leadership and talent pool skews predominantly white, wealthy and, at times, numbingly immune to its own progress. Indeed, a series of hostile incidents against Black and Latino players exposed a markedly raw strain of racial animus, and highlighted lacrosse's confusing popular image. On the one hand it is the most spiritual sport on Earth, a religious practice fashioned by Indigenous Americans to honor their god, heal their ailing and play in their heaven. On the other, it is the sport of Range Rovers and Vineyard Vines, a lifestyle with little on its mind beyond the right college, the next red cup of beer, and graduation into some slick-haired, big-money career.

Both are caricatures, I would learn repeatedly over the next six years, rooted in just enough truth to overshadow the variations of income, class, race and worldview layered throughout the sport. Obscured, too, is its low bar to entry: because high-level lacrosse requires neither elite speed nor great size nor leaping ability, it offers an underrated entryway—at least athletically—to all kinds.

"You have the great athletes, the Jimmy Brown with a little lacrosse stick who's going to run you over," Tierney says. "Or the little fat kid who works, throws the ball against the wall 1,000 times a day right-handed and left-handed and becomes very, very good. You have the rich kid that it's a status symbol for, the blue-collar kid who's tired of baseball and wants to hit somebody. You can do it in snowstorms, as we've done; you can do it in 100-degree weather; you can do it in California, New York. Other sports eliminate you."

And no matter their differences, all end up agreeing on one fact: the seductive tactile allure of the lacrosse stick. Outsiders tend to group this implement with baseball bat, tennis racket, hockey stick—jock gear that, even when exquisitely crafted and personalized, boils down to a favorite tool. But for the game's originators (known as "Iroquois" until, in 2021, officially assuming the Native version, Haudenosaunee), a wood stick is a sacred gift—received in the cradle and taken into one's coffin, wielded in traditional "Medicine Games" and wept over when broken. And though wood is now banned in many leagues and has long been overtaken by mass-produced versions in carbon fiber and plastic, the modern model's heft and feel, that sense of firepower and trickery begging to be unsheathed, remain irresistible. Like gun and guitar, it endows even the novice with swagger.

"The lacrosse stick," Tierney says, "is the thing that makes you special."

Though most non-Natives grow up unexposed to the Haudenosaunee game, let alone their faith, the common initiation tale hits every note of epiphany. Players of all ages and talents grow dreamy-eyed and utter abstractions: *The game took hold of me . . . I was just drawn to lacrosse . . . It wouldn't let me go . . .* In truth, they seem mystified; describing first contact is no easier than articulating the onset of love. Many were great all-around athletes, stars in more popular, more lucrative sports. Lacrosse was less a choice than conversion. They took up a stick. Soon they were sleeping with it.

In 1969, nine-year-old baseball fanatic Donnie Brown happened upon some white kids firing balls at a lacrosse goal in Baltimore's Patterson Park. He asked if he could try. "They said, 'Niggers don't do *this*,'" says Brown, who went on to become a driving force in the city's urban lacrosse scene. One offered a stick anyway: Brown spun the wood in his hands, flung a few shots. "The first time I hit that net, I knew what I wanted to do and I ain't never looked back," he says. "I was bitten."

In 1979, 11-year-old Scott Marr of Yorktown, New York, spied a new kid flinging a lacrosse ball against a schoolyard wall. Until then, his boyhood days had been consumed by football, basketball, baseball. The stick was early modern: aluminum shaft, symmetrical plastic head, synthetic mesh pocket.

He asked if he could try. Soon he was touching his stick whenever it was in reach. Soon he was toting it everywhere.

"I still have that feeling today," says Marr, the longtime head coach at the University of Albany. "It *grabs* you. I'm trying to find the words . . . but . . . you can feel it when you're in that huddle, when you're on that field, on the bus with your team: there's a real connection. Did we understand, at that time, the actual connection to the game and the Creator? Was it just being fed through us? Was it there unknown to us, but it was there and maybe that's why we gravitate towards it? There's something almost mystical about it."

I KNEW THE FEELING briefly. In the mid-1970s, a buddy playing on our school's new, short-lived lacrosse club passed on a battered hybrid—wood shaft, plastic head—and a ball. I had no real idea what to do with them. Youth sports in my Connecticut city revolved around Pop Warner football, basketball, Little League baseball and pond hockey, and their pro versions dominated weekend TV. The game's nearest enclaves, in tony Greenwich and New Canaan, might as well have been 500 miles away; I had never seen any field with lacrosse players on it, let alone one where they kept score.

Still, at 14, I liked the smooth, beveled grain on my palms, the way the hard-rubber ball rocketed off walls and garage doors, and I ran miles at night rocking a rudimentary cradle—the metronomic wrist-action that keeps the ball settled. Eventually lacrosse got tossed onto a heap of discarded teen obsessions, along with yo-yos, wrestling, skateboarding and comic books. I couldn't know that something about it had lodged, like a splinter from that thirdhand wood, under the skin. Or that, over the years, it would keep working its way out.

The first time came in spring of 1981. I had just been accepted at the University of North Carolina at Chapel Hill. In May the Tar Heels upset mighty Johns Hopkins to win their first lacrosse national championship, a shocker: even the uninitiated knew Hopkins as the sport's New York Yankees, a 39-time champion whose aura made every other program seem second-rate. UNC's feat clearly meant *something*, and—as if to emphasize the point—at the end of my first year, the Tar Heels met Hopkins in the 1982 NCAA final and won again. Still, coming after the campus emptied and long before we returned in the fall, the back-to-back titles had a spectral quality, and there was bigger game afoot. UNC football was ranked in the nation's top five. Legendary basketball coach Dean Smith won his first NCAA title. A freshman named Michael Jordan hit the winning shot.

Any contact I had with lacrosse, then, was more social studies than journalism. I lived in the prime jock dorm and worked as a weekend janitor; Sunday morning cleanup was a spectacular horror of crushed beer cans, bent window screens, used condoms, emptied fire extinguishers. Every team had boozers, but lacrosse players were renowned for quick tempers and Viking bacchanals, especially after a Saturday win. When I became a resident assistant nearby, old hands advised a gingerly approach. One RA didn't get the message: he found himself dangled high off a balcony.

There was no UNC women's team then. The men's roster was all white, and its opponents looked no different. Like fraternities and the martini-soaked lunch, the whole scene seemed easily dismissible, a niche pastime edging toward anachronism. I was sure that only mass American spectacles like baseball, football, boxing, basketball, and tennis really mattered, that in the friction and friendships crackling between Black and white and Brown, charged by TV money and the obsessive attention of millions, one could even glimpse the nation painfully—sometimes gloriously—working through its issues. Lacrosse seemed only about itself.

I did know of Jim Brown. Perhaps the greatest football player in NFL history, the frontline Black activist and one-time movie star has long been hailed as the best lacrosse player ever. But unlike Jackie Robinson's baseball career, Brown's late-1950s run at Syracuse University inspired no rush of African Americans to his favorite game; lacrosse's next Black All-American wouldn't appear for another 24 years, and his career became more a proof of the sport's indifference, a spur to pointed questions. Among them: What's taking so long? And just how relevant can a sport be when its greatest player is far more renowned in another?

So I moved on: a World Series earthquake, communist defectors, Olympics, the World Cup. In the late 1980s, noise spilled out of Syracuse about twin brothers Gary and Paul Gait and their Jordan-like lacrosse feats. I wrote for newspapers in Memphis, Sacramento, San Francisco, Miami. No one spoke of lacrosse there, ever.

Washington, DC, in the early 2000s, smack in the game's mid-Atlantic hotbed, was different. There was no avoiding lacrosse's private school network, its reputation for thickheaded entitlement, accompanied by the epithet

"laxbro"—"lax" being a shorthand term from lacrosse. But even as the carica-
ture revealed itself, its lines kept blurring. In 2005, a midfielder named Kyle
Harrison—the most celebrated Black player since Jim Brown—led Johns
Hopkins to its first NCAA title in 18 years, and became the first minority
in history to win the Tewaaraton Award, lacrosse's equivalent of the Heisman
Trophy. And then our babysitter switched sports.

She had been a superb soccer player but, after enrolling in a powerhouse
high school, found the competition—and the odds of entrée into a college
program—too stiff. But lacrosse was wide-open, she said: schools were all
but begging for players. The push to increase opportunity for female athletes, in compliance with the monumental 1972 gender equality law known
as Title IX, had made lacrosse's large rosters—and affluent demographic—
irresistible. In the previous decade, the number of women's teams at NCAA
Divisions I and II had mushroomed by 79 percent. From 2001 to 2005, the
number of lacrosse players nationwide grew by 50 percent, the game's boundaries expanded—and girls led the surge. Just three years after reviving its
program, in 2005 the Northwestern women became the first lacrosse team
outside the eastern time zone to win a national title.

Then, amid the gold rush: disaster. On March 14, 2006, what became
known as the "Duke lacrosse case" erupted: three white members of the men's
team were accused of raping a Black stripper at a team party. Duke faculty
and Durham, North Carolina, activists and national commentators quickly
conflated the accusations, laced with descriptions of some players' alleged
racial comments, into indictments of lacrosse "culture." The sport, it seemed,
wasn't just elitist; it was a boozed-up bastion of white arrogance that, in the
enflaming words of Durham, North Carolina, district attorney Michael
Nifong, spawned "a bunch of hooligans."

I was writing for *Sports Illustrated*. Nine of the 47 players on Duke's
roster were from the DC area; five, including one of the accused, had graduated from the tony Landon School in Bethesda, Maryland. On April 1, I read
this in the *Washington Post* from Landon captain George Huguely, soon to
enroll at the University of Virginia: "I sympathize for the team. They've
been scrutinized so hard and no one knows what has happened yet. In this
country, you're supposed to be innocent until proven guilty. I think that's
the way it should be."

Such measured responses gained little traction. The story's details were
too lurid, its themes basic and broad—*Race! Class! Money! Crime! Media circus!*

Trial and prison terms loomed. A gritty town and its wannabe Ivy League university were under siege: lacrosse suddenly mattered. I traveled to Durham. No one was predicting, then, that the accused would be declared innocent and the accuser a liar, and that DA Nifong would end up disgraced. Those eventualities would play out slowly, in the grind of American justice, while the nation dined on a daily feed of dark material about the team and about that night.

Duke lacrosse players had incurred more disciplinary violations on campus than any other school team. Sources in the players' camp confirmed that, indeed, one Duke player held up a broomstick during the March 13 party and suggested that it be used on an exotic dancer. Others confirmed that another white player made a comment to the two Black women during their rancorous departure, yelling, "Hey, bitch, thank your grandpa for my fine cotton shirt." The victim of assault by one of the accused, Collin Finnerty, and two high school teammates in Washington, DC, the previous November—adjudicated as the Durham rape investigation was ongoing—told police that he had been called "gay" and other derogatory names. Ryan McFadyen's postparty email to teammates described how, for the next party, he would kill and skin a stripper while gratifying himself in his "Duke issue spandex."

Explained away later as a jokey reference to the novel *American Psycho*, the email's revelation on April 5 acted, one top university official said, like "kerosene" on fire. The Blue Devils lacrosse season was canceled, head coach Mike Pressler ousted. And all the twisted rhetoric made it logical to ask if the elite college feeder system, or lacrosse's niche status, or the deep pockets required to play, produced a distinct breed of jackass—or worse. The broomstick confirmation, after all, was conveyed by lacrosse partisans not with disgust, but with nonchalance: *What's the big deal?*

Yet, generalizing about the Ugly Laxbro worked only as long as those to whom it didn't apply were ignored. Duke freshman Devon Sherwood, the team's one Black member, had felt isolated on his predominantly white high school team. "But as soon as I got to Duke, I'm out there on the field getting ready and the whole team comes out and each guy introduces himself, shakes my hand, says where they grew up. This is before I even made it," Sherwood said. "I was being recruited on campus to go into a Black fraternity, and they were trying to convince me with the idea of brotherhood. I'm like, 'I already have a brotherhood. I have 46 guys I'm really cool with.'"

Many Duke players were private school products, or raised in rich suburbs. But Duke lacrosse also tapped Long Island's oft-overlooked blue-collar pipeline, the same one that had produced Jim Brown and given decades of public school types entrée to elite institutions. Brian Loftus, the father of Blue Devils players Dan and Chris, was a retired fireman who had worked 36 straight hours at the World Trade Center after the September 11 attacks. Another retired fireman's son, Casey Carroll, was featured—top row—on a damning "Wanted"-style flyer of 43 lacrosse player headshots posted and passed around Duke's campus. He hadn't even attended the party.

"Without a scholarship I couldn't blink an eye at this place," said Carroll. "There are a lot of kids on the team with a lot of money. I come from a completely different world. I'm just grateful: now maybe I can help my family out."

By then, I knew of former Boston College lacrosse star Welles Crowther, the red-bandanaed equities trader who saved as many as 18 lives on September 11, 2001, including one woman he carried on his back 17 floors, before dying in the South Tower of the World Trade Center. I had read about Cornell's poetic All-American Eamon McEneaney, who as Cantor Fitzgerald vice president had guided 63 co-workers to safety after the 1993 attack there and then died in the North Tower on September 11. Dozens of other lacrosse players, coaches and relations died at that spot in New York that day—more than any other sport. But it wasn't until my time at Duke, in 2006, that the reason for their presence there became clear.

"Every lacrosse coach came into my house, they all had the same line— the Hopkins guy, the Princeton guy: *You're not coming to our school for four years. You're coming for the next 40*," said Brian Loftus. "And they'll tell you they own Morgan Stanley or Dean Witter: *We network . . . Going to Duke and playing lacrosse, you're going to get a job. Things are going to be good for you.*"

Over the next year, the Duke lacrosse case served up weightier insights about the relation of money to justice, the dangers of rash judgment among the self-righteous, the need to question authority in government and out. It demonstrated how one rogue prosecutor can pervert the unmatched power of the state to instill fear and ravage lives. Yet, if all that felt profound, none of it was new; I came of age amid Vietnam and Watergate, and absorbed the rape debacle mostly as a refresher. After the exonerations those big themes got shunted to some back corner of the mind, for use in the next travesty.

But I kept finding that no pro baseball, football, hockey or basketball season, no free agent negotiation, no complaint about skyrocketing ticket prices could pass without my recalling lacrosse's unique relation to money. No kid picks up a stick—and no parent funnels their kid into the sport—dreaming about multimillion-dollar contracts. But unlike love-of-the-game pastimes like softball or fencing, lacrosse does dangle a payoff: the complex network, built and lubricated by former players, that funnels graduates into careers in finance or real estate. The most storied programs are wired into Wall Street institutions like Goldman Sachs, Barclays and HSBC (and, in their day, into now-defunct powerhouses like Lehman Brothers, Merrill Lynch and S.A.C. Capital), but cross-pollination is common. Summer internships, interview patter, entrée into that crucial first job: all part of the old-boy package when you wield a stick for Princeton, Johns Hopkins, Yale, Cornell, Dartmouth, Duke, UVa.

Many players keep playing. Iterations of professional lacrosse, indoor and outdoor, have sputtered quietly for decades. But with annual pay rarely topping $60,000, the pro game has always been a side hustle; "hitting the jackpot" in lacrosse doesn't occur on the field. Hitting it in lacrosse is using a solid college career to line up a 16-hour-a-day job behind a desk staring at a computer terminal, with a decent chance to make millions. The reason so many lacrosse players died at the World Trade Center on 9/11? Lacrosse lived there.

IN MARCH OF 2009, I was reading a magazine story. Though published in the *New Yorker* and written by John McPhee—two surefire marks of importance—it was about lacrosse. I figured I'd had my fill. The time since Durham had been preoccupied with American baseball and the 2008 Olympics in China, subjects universally thought to exemplify the world's dominant power and the one rising fast. But early into McPhee's thick treatise, when I had just about decided the *New Yorker* was being willfully unimportant, I read:

> *World Lacrosse Championships have been held every four years since 1974 . . . The populationally outnumbered Iroquois hold their own in these tournaments . . . They travel on Iroquois passports . . . hold their own as a lacrosse nation . . . are the life and soul of our sport.*

I tore out the page. Ten months later, I was sitting in a hotel bar amid the gray chill of a Syracuse winter. In walked Oren Lyons—Onondaga faithkeeper, two-time All-American goalie for Syracuse University and Jim Brown's teammate—signature gray ponytail flowing down his back. Since the 1970s

Lyons has been one of Native America's most prominent voices, especially on the issue of sovereignty. His public identities neatly merged in 1983, when he co-founded the Iroquois Nationals lacrosse team.

Lyons insisted on coming to greet me, though it was late and he was nearing his 80th birthday. He pulled up in a Prius. The bar seemed a logical rendezvous, and it wasn't until I asked if he wanted a drink that I realized the mistake. "Noooo," Lyons said, looking me dead in the eye. A wave of shame rolled in: it was the first time I felt the crush of history in an exchange of pleasantries. I stammered "sorry"; Lyons smiled and waved it off. He seemed to enjoy watching me squirm.

A few nights later at the Syracuse Dome, the Nationals scrimmaged against a select group from Team USA, both working on roster-trims for the 2010 World Championship to be held that summer in Manchester, England. The affair couldn't have been more casual—no fans, no announcer, no electronic displays, and only one wry reference to centuries of bad blood. Keeping score on a whiteboard, someone on the Iroquois side had inverted the traditional labels. US VS. THE HEATHENS, it said.

That was funny, briefly. Perhaps as early as 1,100 A.D., Native Americans in North America's Great Lakes region invented lacrosse and used it to train warriors and settle disputes. In the late 19th century the white man took note, codified the rules by Victorian standards and, in 1880, effectively banned the Indigenous people from their own game. A century passed before the Iroquois, in name and fact, began seriously competing in field lacrosse again. By 2010, the Nationals had become one of the sport's four powers, on their terms: the Haudenosaunee consider themselves an independent nation. They do not recognize the US-Canadian border.

"We are *allies*," Lyons said, "of the United States."

I worked that story through the spring and, as the World Championship neared, realized I had it mostly to myself. Slim to begin with, the media bandwidth devoted to lacrosse was now swamped by murder. On May 3, 2010, University of Virginia senior midfielder George Huguely—the one-time Landon student—killed his ex-girlfriend Yeardley Love, also a UVa lacrosse player, in a drunken rage. Commentators weighed in: Every trope about lacrosse "culture" invoked by the Duke case—and muffled by the now-disbarred Nifong's disgrace—resurfaced. The sport's defenders again asked why criminal acts by basketball, football, baseball or hockey players never spark indictments of entire sports, but with far less bite. Huguely was no one's idea of innocent.

I paid little attention. Instead, I made my way back to the Onondaga Nation Reservation and the workshop of stickmaker Alfie Jacques. Most of his adult life, Jacques worked as a tool-and-dye man in Syracuse, fashioning parts for the RL 10 rocket engines that powered NASA's Space Shuttle. But at 14, he also began making lacrosse sticks with his father, Louis, and spent the next 47 years in a workshop behind his mother's house mastering the 22-step process.

It started with a walk in the woods, the felling of a hickory. Only the bottom eight to ten feet of tree flesh is flexible and strong enough to be a lacrosse stick; this was hauled home and hand-split lengthwise into eighths. After hand-carving the segments down to narrow rails with a draw shave, Jacques laid the set aside for a month to dry. Then came eight to 20 minutes in a woodfired steamer; the sticks were yanked out hot and their most pliable end—the one cut closest to the roots—got curled around a bending jig and wired fast. After eight more months of drying, the bark was planed off. Another stint in the steamer, a crank on the bending jig: the lacrosse head was shaped.

After one more pass with the draw shave and some hand-sanding, Jacques drilled holes. All that time, he had also been processing a bolt of salted cowhide—slicing off tissue and fur, soaking and slicing it into ribbony strands, drawing them through a copper sizing pipe, spinning them onto a spool. Now he laced the dried cowhide through the holes in the stick head. Jacques's finishing touch was his signature and the date burned onto each stick, along with an elaborate X logo he first doodled as a ten-year-old schoolboy.

Amid the workshop's squat, low-tech confines, it was impossible not to dwell on the sport's prehistoric reach. Baseball, football, hockey and basketball are all 19th-century inventions, the first three variants on English games, the fourth invented at a Springfield, Massachusetts, YMCA after James Naismith couldn't make lacrosse work indoors. Lacrosse, precursor of nearly every game on a rectangular patch, originated long before the United States was an idea. It emerged out of the land: A piece of wood, or a slice of deerskin stuffed with feathers, was shaped into the first ball. A tree branch was shaped into something resembling a long spoon. It likely was hickory.

After taking me, one last time, through his 22 steps, Jacques abruptly doubled back. He'd forgotten the most important part.

"You make the stick from the *living* part of the tree," he said. "You have the ceremony, and you thank the Creator for the tree that made the stick. You apologize for killing the tree, but you say, 'I'm going to make a lacrosse stick,' and the spirit from that tree is in that wood. The energy from that tree is transferred to the player who knows how to use that stick. And he does it with a good mind—not to have too much pride, not to play with anger, not to play to hurt people, but to play the game in a more spiritual manner. Nobody likes a dirty player."

When the United Kingdom refused to recognize Iroquois travel documents later in the summer of 2010, stranding the team in New York and capsizing hopes for its first world championship, a fading message could still be read on a billboard outside Syracuse: WE THE INDIGENOUS PEOPLE OWN THE WESTERN HEMISPHERE! It seemed ironic and sad, until I remembered that the Nationals players had never wavered, and US secretary of state Hillary Clinton had tried to come to their rescue, and some elders viewed the worldwide publicity snafu as a win greater than anything a tournament could provide.

Over the ensuing years, sensational details of George Huguely's behavior kept oozing out, and his trial and sentencing in 2012 led the news. But to me it all seemed less significant than the Iroquois' first-ever field win that summer over Team USA in the Under-19 men's World Championship, less meaningful than the rise of Iroquois superstar Lyle Thompson and his brother Miles at the University at Albany. I found myself fixating instead on the Iroquois Nationals' dramatic return to the 2014 World Championship in Denver, where they hadn't needed passports, and their improvement led to a bronze-medal finish for the first time.

It wasn't just that they were underdogs. Iroquois success was rejiggering the very idea of an American institution—from within. No matter that the sport's dominant strain was still overwhelmingly white and privileged, or that the International Lacrosse Federation's admission of the Iroquois in 1987 had been motivated by the knowledge that it had little choice. By accepting—and increasingly celebrating—the most ignored of minority groups, lacrosse's establishment found itself at least tolerating the Iroquois' erasure of the US-Canada border, endorsing the use of the game as spiritual practice, and cementing the continent's dark and tragic history—and its own culpability—into its narrative.

For the Iroquois, I knew, such inclusion can still feel like a deal with the devil. Lacrosse, after all, is their most enduring metaphor: White men came, saw and—bit by bit—remade the "Indian" game in their own image, mirroring the land theft and genocide that is North America's original sin. Grappling with that legacy and their enduring pain is not what a suburban kid or casual sports fan signs up for, and it's not what those scheming to grow the game in the 21st century want to dwell on.

But I wondered. Maybe it's the metaphor—and the attendant guilt— that triggers such wholesale condemnation whenever white players go bad. Maybe it's the grappling that makes lacrosse important now.

CERTAINTY DIDN'T KICK in for a while. When the 2014 death of Michael Brown in Ferguson, Missouri, regalvanized the nation's racial debate, the sport chugged along at a distinct remove. Even as demonstrations raged over the deaths of unarmed Black men at the hands of police, and the kneeling protests and outrage of college and pro athletes became cultural and political flashpoints, lacrosse's longtime inclusion initiatives and the 2016 creation of the first Division I program at historically Black Hampton University allowed for a sense of effort, if not progress.

But then, late in 2017, a majority-Black travel team, Nation United, was referred to as "convicts" in an Instagram image caption by a white opponent named Parker Underwood. Another hastily deleted post on the Instagram account of Alex Aust, All-American at Maryland and member of the 2017 gold-medal US women's National Team, dropped the N-word. Both players apologized, but the game's most prominent Black player, Kyle Harrison, declared that such incidents were not lacrosse's "only ones," said that he'd seen photos of mock lynchings sent to Black coaches and players, and called for a "serious discussion" on "inclusion, diversity and what is acceptable behavior."

That January, I headed to Baltimore for LaxCon 2018, the annual gathering that serves as the sport's reunion, convention, trade show, clinic and overall barometer. Racism was on the agenda.

"We still have the image that we're a rich-white-kid sport, and that's a big undercurrent to this weekend," US Lacrosse president Steve Stenersen said. "Is it because lacrosse is more racist than any other society or less sensitive? Is it simply because we're *more* sensitive to it? Or because we live in an incredibly polarized society?"

Later that afternoon, Stenersen sat in a conference room packed with many of the sport's major Black figures, including Kyle Harrison and his father, Miles Harrison Jr.; Chazz Woodson, former pro star and US Lacrosse board member; and Eboni Preston-Laurent, USA Lacrosse's director of diversity, equality and inclusion. Former Syracuse All-American Jovan Miller—soon to publish a post claiming knowledge of "at least 20+" times in lacrosse that players, friends and family had experienced "racial altercations"—asked the most pointed question.

"Everybody keeps asking how we get more Black kids involved," Miller said. "Why would I ever tell a Black kid to get involved in a game that he's going to be called the N-word? Parents will probably take a lot of criticism. He might get really racially charged comments to him on Instagram, Twitter—and will probably be the only Black kid on his team. Why would I tell a Black kid to play this game?"

"Nobody," Kyle Harrison observed later, "really had an answer."

The convention offered panels on everything from the psychology of boys to "trauma-sensitive" coaching to the Haudenosaunee ethos to "What Is Your Goalie Thinking?" Thousands cycled through the basement Expo Hall past demo fields; booths featuring the newest lacrosse stick, helmet, string, pad and book; a table of Alfie Jacques's gleaming sticks. The throng of players, fans and coaches radiated a peppy sense of mission; every fourth shirt commanded, GROW THE GAME. Most were white and well-fed, but the small current of Black faces never let up.

"The most diverse I've ever seen it," said Troy Kemp, former coach of the McCallie School in Chattanooga, Tennessee, and an executive director at Nation United. "I can remember coming to this thing and—I couldn't help it—*counting*. Some days I feel *super* Black, when I see the situation. And when you'd come to lacrosse? That's when you'd feel your race. But there's a power now. That room was probably 15 percent African American—customers, people walking: 10 to 15 percent. It used to be 2 percent."

Whether the majority welcomed the change was unclear. Outside the game, the culture was all abuzz about white privilege under pressure. Confederate statues were coming down across the South. Emotions remained raw from the previous August, when the deadly "Unite the Right" rally in Charlottesville, Virginia, featured torch-bearing white supremacists and neo-Nazi marchers chanting, "Jews will not replace us!" The opioid epidemic was claiming 128 lives, mostly white, a day. Census projections had whites becoming a minority in the United States within 30 years.

Two months later, a busload of white Virginia Tech women's lacrosse players was recorded gleefully chanting the N-word while singing a rap song. Only when denunciations flew did the singers—and the teammate who posted the video—realize they had crossed a red line. I recalled Stenersen's question: *Is it because lacrosse is more racist or less sensitive?* The glib response was *Yes*, but leaving it at bad groupthink seemed too easy. Because the further I moved on from 2018, the more I reported over the ensuing five years, the more lacrosse people I encountered and history I absorbed, the better I understood the game's unmatched run of the American gamut—past to present, reservation to country club, Main Street to Wall Street—and the bigger the group became. Finally, someone with firsthand experience laid it out plain.

"Lacrosse *is* America," said Chazz Woodson. "It began with the Native Americans and was taken over by white people. It's benefited people that were already privileged. It's benefited people that were not so privileged or people that got a leg up because they participated. But it's also left people behind. It's given some people horrible experiences. It's caused people to look down on the sport.

"Lacrosse really exemplifies all that America is. It can be great, but it can also be awful. Sure, there are a number of people playing it across socio-economics, race, gender. Whatever identifier you want to use: they all can be found in the sport. But ultimately it still feels like this white privileged game that only benefits a few."

Not until much later, after hundreds more interviews and research fleshed out the stark questions and entrenched dynamics exposed in 2018, did I realize I had arrived in the country of lacrosse at a crucial time. Ambitious and expanding, confronting its checkered past and trying to shape its future, the sport was rumbling toward an inflection point. The ultimate "white privileged game" had lost the luxury of functioning as a mere athletic contest; indeed, it began mirroring the tensions rising in the nation at large. Over the next three years a dozen more racial incidents would occur; fed-up minorities would demand change; the long-fraught relationship with the game's Indigenous founders would blossom into crisis. The response would reveal the kind of sport lacrosse hoped to be.

Ambition, that great American engine, proved the primary driver. By the end of 2021, lacrosse's longtime mission of returning to the Olympic Games for the first time since 1948 had become increasingly viable. For different reasons—the former political, the latter commercial—both the Haudenosaunee Nationals and the lacrosse establishment undertook all manner of reform and modernization to make it happen; after decades of clashing interests, mutual wariness and at times outright hostility, the game's two dominant elements bonded for a common goal. And it worked: in October of 2023, the International Olympic Committee admitted lacrosse as one of its five host-city sports at the 2028 Summer Games in Los Angeles.

But even with this mission accomplished, that central tension remained. IOC rules—and fear of setting a precedent for other Indigenous peoples—barred Haudenosaunee participation as a recognized national entity. And though all the game's powers, from international governing body World Lacrosse to billionaire Joe Tsai to star entrepreneur Paul Rabil, and even President Joe Biden, pledged to back the Nationals in their quest for admission, through 2024 nothing had been resolved. The prospect of lacrosse returning to the Olympics without its originators, of Americans and Canadians abandoning their Haudenosaunee peers to celebrate in the Los Angeles sunshine, loomed large.

If nothing else, the uncertainty proved that lacrosse remains a work in progress, that many of its longtime cultural dynamics were still playing themselves out. All the diversifying, enlightening steps taken since 2018 seemed irreversible but, considering the wider reactionary forces at play nationwide, who could say? Only that year's status as the dividing line between the game's past and future seemed assured. Indeed, it's fitting that the 2018 Men's World Championship took place in ancient, war-battered Israel: It was the largest and last tournament of its kind, a 46-nation festival featuring 1,000 players and a hidebound consensus on unapologetic display. It presented, day by day, lacrosse's startling contradictions, ills and greatness, and set the stage for nearly every pivotal issue in the years to come.

And, as lacrosse once did and always must, it began with the Iroquois. Stranded.

THE OLD WORLD

PART 1

BRAIDING

He has excited domestic insurrections amongst us, and has endeavored to bring on the inhabitants of our frontiers, the merciless Indian Savages, whose known rule of warfare, is an undistinguished destruction of all ages, sexes and conditions.

—The Declaration of Independence, July 4, 1776

The war's not over. Not by a long shot.

—Oren Lyons, Onondaga faithkeeper,
Iroquois Confederacy, 2010

THE BATTLE OF TORONTO AIRPORT

WOULD THEY MAKE IT? Nobody knew. The usual cheery buzz before a big-deal sporting event had given way to panic. Officials roamed the resort lobby in a panorama of shrugs, rolled eyes, pained grimaces, a pair of hands flung into the air. Random clots of twos and threes kept coalescing, only to break after a few muttery minutes when one backed out with cellphone mashed to ear. *Will they get here in time? At all?* It was an embarrassment. An absurdity. Just a day before their traditional star-turn at the Opening Ceremony, only 29 hours before their marquee showdown with the superpower United States, the Iroquois were missing.

Wednesday, July 11, 2018, just after 2 p.m. Israel Standard Time, in Netanya. A seaside city founded in 1927 and presumptuously named for New York millionaire Nathan "The Great Giver" Straus, in the unrealized hope that he'd include it in his largesse, Netanya nonetheless grew from a malaria-infested patch into Israel's seventh-largest city, an adjunct of Tel Aviv with a vacation vibe that can feel far removed from the tensions bubbling an hour south. The mere existence of such a place, so light a mood, was itself a victory, proof that even the most far-fetched dream can survive, even assume a dull maturity. Here, in the nation's 70th year, Israel was hosting one of the largest international sporting events in its history, the 13th quadrennial World Men's Field Lacrosse Championship.

Though showcasing a sport few locals knew, the walk-up had gone smoothly. Shuttle busses were running on time. Every delegation, including fledglings from Taipei, Peru, Jamaica and Uganda, had settled into their hotel . . . with one very large exception.

At that moment 5,789 miles away, perhaps the greatest player alive, Lyle Thompson, and his 22 teammates were stuck in a Holiday Inn Express outside the Six Nations Reserve at Grand River, near the Canadian town of Brantford, Ontario. Originators of the game, the third-best team in the world, deployers of dazzling stickwork and breathtaking passes, always romanticized, too long despised, now beloved and still roundly misunderstood, the Iroquois ("snakes," in the language of their early rival, the Algonquin) or Six Nations (as the British called them) or Haudenosaunee ("People of the Longhouse," as they call themselves) were waiting for the latest in a 500-year-old string of international incidents to play out.

They had been scheduled to fly out of Toronto two days earlier. It didn't figure to be a problem. This event had been in the making for 15 months. Surely the Israel Lacrosse Association organizers, Federation of International Lacrosse officials and famously strict Israeli border officials knew of the Iroquois insistence on traveling on their own self-made Haudenosaunee passports, the ones that sparked public-relations fiascos and forced them to miss FIL championships in 2010 and 2015. Surely all involved—including Iroquois management—had noted how, just a year earlier, a Nationals women's team had successfully flown roundtrip from Canada to England on Haudenosaunee passports for the 2017 World Championship. Surely all involved, in conjunction with Canadian and Israeli foreign ministries, had executed a similar plan to allow the Iroquois men to travel to Tel Aviv and back.

Stunningly: no. And now chaos ensued on all fronts—diplomatic, legal, logistical. The three-dozen-strong Iroquois delegation, already cash-strapped, scrambled to find local housing and transport. Canadian and Israeli ministers, ambassadors, immigration and justice officials, Native leaders and three billionaires unleashed a ricocheting volley of phone calls, texts and emails. At stake? Israel's image, Canada's fractious relations with its First Nations population, and the tournament's basic value. Without the Iroquois, the World Championship's marquee opening clash against Team USA—and the rare television slot on ESPN representing lacrosse's best hope of drawing casual fans—would be canceled.

Blame could be scattered widely but, at the championship's de facto headquarters, the West Lagoon Resort, nearly all irritation seemed directed at the Iroquois. Officials from the sport's decade-old governing body, the

FIL, were grumbling openly about the Native indifference to Western standards of organization—i.e., deadlines—and the fact that some Iroquois elders welcomed any passport impasse as a golden moment to showcase their claim of sovereignty. Across Iroquoia, those no-shows at the 2010 championship in Manchester, England, and the 2015 women's Under-19 World Championship in Edinburgh, Scotland, were still hailed as moral victories.

But for those trying to stage a tournament—or, like the ESPN commentators, bent on witnessing great lacrosse—the story had gotten old. Paul Carcaterra and Quint Kessenich—long-ago All-Americans at rival bluebloods Syracuse and Johns Hopkins, respectively, and the two most famous commentators in the game—couldn't wait to call the Iroquois-USA opener—and couldn't believe that it was still up in the air.

"Some of the ownership has to be on the Iroquois—that they didn't vet this thing out . . . and that, in the 11th hour, *this* is happening. It's borderline a joke, okay?" Carcaterra said. "I'm one of the biggest advocates of the Native American game. But that it's happening again? And that, after eight years, the leadership for this team obviously did not do their due diligence? If they showed up at the airport and were denied, how is all that not taken care of—priorly?"

"Months ago!" Kessenich said.

Another reason for the open irritation was the opinion that, maybe, the Iroquois were becoming more trouble than their worth. This view from the game's most influential cadre—the American lacrosse establishment, officials and administrators, as well as counterparts in Canada, England and Australia—came in qualified sentences, carefully parsed. But it was unmistakable. The vague imperative, "Grow the Game," had a concrete primary goal: the Olympics. The FIL had officially decided that becoming an official Olympic event, specifically by the 2028 Summer Games in Los Angeles, was the best path for taking lacrosse big-time. The Olympic goal was why, in May 2017, the FIL hired former United States Olympic Committee chief executive officer Jim Scherr as its first-ever CEO (and full-time employee), why it would soon rebrand itself as "World Lacrosse" and why, earlier in the year, it had invited International Olympic Committee officials to observe this championship in Israel.

Of course, the sport's leaders knew that the IOC follows United Nations guidelines for sovereign states, and the UN does not recognize the Iroquois Confederacy. Barring some dramatic rule change or exception, Olympic participation would take place without the Native Americans who many consider the soul of lacrosse, a nightmare scenario. But this latest crisis was making it easier to consider.

"After '10, the lacrosse community was feeling sympathetic and there was: 'Oh, the poor Iroquois Nationals,'" Scherr said at the West Lagoon Resort. "Now, I think the sentiment is very much: *Hey, this is largely due to their own actions and we can't have this. So either they get it fixed or we go down the road without them.*"

And yet, the thought of IOC observers assessing a lacrosse championship in which, 24 hours before opening, its No. 3 team was AWOL and its nationally televised opener was in doubt, was a horror for FIL types to contemplate. Fortunately, Olympic officials passed on their invitation. "I mean, I was having nightmares," said FIL Secretary General Ron Balls. "The IOC people would have said, 'Well, this team can't come . . . and they're ranked third, but . . . *Who ARE they?*"

IT'S A QUESTION older than America. The Iroquois are a confederation of six—the Seneca, Cayuga, Onondaga, Oneida, Mohawk and Tuscarora—of the 574 Indigenous tribal entities recognized by the United States government, all of whom represent the remains of a populace that, before Christopher Columbus, numbered perhaps as many as 18 million. Today the Navajo and Cherokee constitute the largest bands of the 6.8 million Indigenous people within US boundaries; the Iroquois, with anywhere from 30,000 to 45,000 claiming solely Iroquois ancestry and a total of some 81,000 claiming some Iroquois ancestry, rank no higher than tenth. An additional 45,000 live within Canadian borders.

Until about 1700, though, the Iroquois Confederacy was eastern North America's dominant power, ranging across a loose empire with a totality that rendered historians breathless.

"Foremost in war, foremost in eloquence, foremost in their savage arts of policy, stood the fierce people called by themselves the Hodenosaunee," wrote Francis Parkman in 1851:

> *They extended their conquests and their depredations from Quebec to the Carolinas, and from the western prairies to the forests of Maine. On the south, they forced tribute from the subjugated Delawares, and*

pierced the mountain fastnesses of the Cherokees with incessant forays. On the north, they uprooted the ancient settlements of the Wyandots; on the west they exterminated the Eries and the Andastes, and spread havoc and dismay among the tribes of the Illinois; and on the east, the Indians of New England fled at the first peal of the Mohawk war-cry.

Nor was it the Indian race alone who quailed before their ferocious valor. All Canada shook with the fury of their onset; the people fled to the forts for refuge; the blood-besmeared conquerers roamed like wolves among the burning settlements, and the colony trembled on the brink of ruin.

Though they once controlled the southern Great Lakes region and beyond—a territory, at its peak, spreading from the Hudson River to the Mississippi and encompassing swaths of present-day Kentucky and Virginia—Iroquois distinction derives less from size than political genius. The original confederacy, courted as governmental equals by France, Holland and England, was the one Native entity never subjugated, militarily, by white powers. Its uniquely binding alliance—organizing five, and eventually six, nations under "The Peacemaker" Deganawidah's "Great Law of Peace"—predated the United Nations by at least 375 years. Its representative Grand Council and matrilineal social structure provided an early model for popular governance and progressive sexual politics. Some historians—not to mention plenty of Haudenosaunee and, in 1988, the US Congress—claim Iroquois "democratic principles" as a strong influence on the US Constitution.

Splintered by the American Revolution, the confederacy nonetheless played a storybook role in the United States' origins. Onondaga chief Canassatego's widely printed 1744 recommendation that the 13 colonies unite like the Iroquois Confederacy to "acquire fresh strength and power," is said to have inspired Benjamin Franklin. "It would be a very strange thing, if six nations of ignorant savages should be capable of forming such a scheme for such a union," Franklin wrote in 1750, "and yet that a like union should be impracticable for ten or a dozen English colonies to whom it is more necessary and must be more advantageous."

George Washington's starving troops at Valley Forge were legendarily saved in 1777 after a band of Oneida trekked 250 miles with bushels of hard corn; after holding off the desperate soldiers trying to eat the stuff raw, Oneida Nation member Polly Cooper taught them how to cook corn into digestible mash, and refused any reward after the war.

"If the Oneidas didn't bring those 350 bushels of corn, you'd be English now, all the way," says Oren Lyons. "That was key. But nobody talks about it."

This sense of being forgotten, past and present, is a recurring theme for the Haudenosaunee. Steelwork on high, particularly for upstate Mohawks, provided steady work and mainstream identity through much of the 20th century. But the Iroquois suffered the chronic ills afflicting all Indigenous Americans: high alcohol and drug use, lower average income, difficulty with life away from the reservations. Since 1979, casinos operating on Native lands have made some tribes—like the Oneida of Wisconsin—and individuals fabulously wealthy, but hardly proved a cure-all. In December 2018, the US Commission on Civil Rights' 300-page report, "Broken Promises," provided a disheartening update.

"Native Americans are more likely to live in poverty, be unemployed, experience rape or abuse, and be killed by police than any other ethnic or racial group," the report stated:

> *Native Americans have 1.6 times the infant mortality rate of non-Hispanic whites, and the life expectancy for Native peoples is 5.5 years less than the national average. Native American students have the lowest high school graduation rates in the nation. The broken treaties have left many reservations without adequate access to clean water, plumbing, electricity, internet, cellular service, roads, public transportation, housing, hospitals, and schools. The often-isolated locations, lack of accurate and full inclusion in the media and in textbooks, and persistent discrimination have rendered their reality often invisible to other Americans.*

Given that disregard, the Iroquois Nationals lacrosse program exists, first and foremost, as a statement of fact. Any conversation with founder, board member, coach or player produces some variant of the message: "We are still here." To the ignorant they offer a sharper retort: "We were here first. Who are *you*?" Such exchanges officially joined the modern lacrosse conversation in November 1987, when Ron Balls picked up a phone in Stockport, England, dialed a number on the Onondaga reservation five miles outside Syracuse, and woke a dead-asleep Oren Lyons. Balls, the then-named International Lacrosse Federation's competition committee chair, informed Lyons that the ILF board had approved the Iroquois Nationals' participation in its World Championships, the first Indigenous people so recognized by an international sport. Ever since, it's been easy to think the Englishman an Iroquois ally.

But the Iroquois wonder. Their two most infamous travel dustups involved the United Kingdom. That England then accepted Haudenosaunee passports from the Iroquois Nationals women in 2017 seemed a breakthrough, but Lyons wasn't convinced. The longtime professor of American Studies still deems "the English" the Nationals' prime FIL "nemesis," and frames today's lacrosse politics as an extension of fraught Iroquois-England relations dating back three centuries. "Just cannot trust them," Lyons says. "They'll do you every time."

For his part, Balls claimed to be conflicted in Israel: "In one sense, I'd love them to win this event, and in the other I don't want them to—desperately." But, most often, he gave the impression of a man trying to ease a headache. For 30-plus years he'd been explaining one group to the other: the small, proud nation that views lacrosse and passports as vital symbols of identity, and a far larger constituency that sees only a sport and a travel document. Balls habitually called the latter group, the 59 other member nations (up from 18 in 2002, with no end in sight) "the Membership," but it often came off as a veil on his own feelings:

> The Membership viewpoint would be: The Iroquois should take away their political requests for recognition—that is for the United Nations; it has nothing to do with us. The Iroquois should be saying, "Thank you, guys, for allowing us in this sport, the only ones to be recognized by an international federation." And the Membership think, "Yes, we understand the heritage, and we love that. But all of your team do have other passports, can travel on their US or Canadian passports. Why don't they?"

The temptation to view Iroquois sovereignty as a secondary, even self-defeating, concern wasn't unusual. Even with the team dramatically stranded, no major US news outlet parachuted in to cover the 2018 World Championship; the "important" international sports news focused on France's semifinal soccer win at the 2018 World Cup in Russia and Roger Federer's loss at Wimbledon. Yet, the Iroquois trek here was more profound than either, tapping as it did the racial justice and nationhood issues resurging in Europe and the US. Here in the Middle East, of course, they had been warring over such things for centuries.

But when it comes to a narrative featuring historic displacement, epic diasporas and the fight for ancestral land, few can identify like Native Americans. After World War II, with the Nazi Holocaust fresh and ragtag Israelis surrounded by enemies, a kinship seemed obvious. But Israel's military and economic success since, along with hard-line policies toward its Palestinian populace and its ongoing "settlements" in disputed territory, transformed the country's global image. Indeed, the Palestinian comparison to Native Americans led to a bid to make common cause. On July 4, 2018, a cultural arm of the Boycott, Divestment and Sanctions (BDS) movement—the nonviolent resistance organization pressing Israel to withdraw from the occupied territories and remove the West Bank security barrier, grant full equality to Arab-Palestinian citizens of Israel and allow Palestinian refugees the right to reclaim ancestral property—posted an open letter asking the Iroquois Nationals to withdraw in solidarity from the 2018 World Championship.

"As Indigenous peoples, we have both seen our traditional lands colonized, our people ethnically cleansed and massacred by colonial settlers," the letter began. Asserting that the Wingate Institute and Netanya Stadium, where the games were to be held, stood on the grounds of Palestinian settlements wiped out by Jewish seizures in 1948, BDS paired Israeli "dispossession" with America's brutal conquest of Native territory, and ended with the hope that the Nationals would deny "Israel the opportunity to use the national sport of the Iroquois to cover up its escalating, violent ethnic cleansing of Palestinians throughout our ancestral lands."

The plea resonated with many Haudenosaunee but failed to gain official purchase; the Iroquois Confederacy responded with a letter of its own. "We said that our overall issues were more important," Oren Lyons says. "That we understand their 90-year struggle—but they should try 540 years."

Because the Iroquois had gotten word: Membership patience had reached its breaking point. Another Iroquois no-show in Israel would result in the most severe FIL punishments ever levied—a $45,000 fine and automatic exclusion from the next FIL event, penalizing the Iroquois women's and U-19 teams, and demotion of the men's team from elite to qualifier status. Combined with lost airfare and travel expenses, estimates of the long-term costs ranged as high as $500,000.

Though huge in a lacrosse context, such a hit could have easily been absorbed by wealthy nations like the US. For the eternally cash-strapped Haudenosaunee, it would have been a death blow. The Iroquois Nationals were at risk; the team had to get to Israel—or else. "We would've been done," Lyons says. "It would've been the end—absolutely."

Lacrosse without the Iroquois? Sitting in the lobby bar on July 11, Mark "Redman" Burnam could imagine just that. The head coach of the Iroquois Nationals came to Israel early, the day before his team was stopped at the Toronto Airport. He, too, was tired of the uncertainty. A member of the Nationals for 34 years, in 2010, as a Nationals assistant coach, Burnam had also arrived early in Manchester, England, too, and waited in vain for days for that team to show up. This vibe, he said, felt far worse.

Later that afternoon, the news dropped out of Toronto: the Nationals had been cleared for departure at 9 p.m. in Israel, their last chance to make the tournament in time. Burnam shrugged. Until they walked in the door, the coach said, he was counting on nothing.

NOW THE IROQUOIS' most powerful weapon kicked in. In the three millennia since David slew Goliath, few tropes have been more appealing than Little Guy versus Big. And few fit the David role better, even at this late stage, than Native Americans. But less known was the fact that just reaching that moment—with Nationals players and assistant coaches bussing a second time to Toronto to catch a flight to Israel—was itself a win. Because the Iroquois almost ended their trip before it ever began, and the reason had nothing to do with passports, or sympathy for the Palestinian cause, or chronic disorganization. It was fear.

A week before scheduled takeoff, on Tuesday, July 3, 2018, players and staff from three Haudenosaunee hubs—the reserve at Six Nations of the Grand River, in Southern Ontario; the reservation at Onondaga, five miles south of Syracuse, New York; and the territory of Akwesasne, straddling the border river separating New York from Ontario and Quebec—were just starting to pack when the Haudenosaunee Grand Council of Chiefs, the Iroquois central governing body at Onondaga, declared its opposition to the Nationals' participation in the 2018 World Championship.

Nationals officials were stunned. Instrumental in creating the lacrosse program, the Grand Council had not once, in 35 years, opposed a team trip. But the council was only reflecting the question asked by anyone boarding a plane to Tel Aviv that summer: Is Israel safe? Violence there had ratcheted to its worst level since the Gaza conflict of 2014. On May 14, the bloodiest day of border clashes between Israeli forces and Hamas-backed Palestinian protesters, a reported 58 Palestinians were killed, and more than 1,350 were wounded by gunfire. Militants in Gaza retaliated by launching more than 130 rocket and mortar attacks into Israel. On June 6, Argentina's national soccer team, citing death threats against star Lionel Messi, canceled its final World Cup tune-up against Israel in Jerusalem. On June 13, the UN General Assembly condemned both sides of the conflict. The bombs and bullets didn't stop.

Late in June, Nationals executive director Ansley Jemison had faced a hostile audience at Six Nations of the Grand River. Of the 18 Haudenosaunee territories, only Onondaga wields more clout: lying wholly within Canada's boundaries, "Six" boasts the largest and most varied population in Iroquoia (it's the only North American reserve with all six nations represented), and prides itself on combative independence. Its traditional council of chiefs meets in the hallowed Sour Springs longhouse—and, when Jemison showed up there, opposition to the Israel trip was fully baked.

The sentiment quickly spread south, to the Iroquois capital at Onondaga. Like the assembly in Sour Springs, the Haudenosaunee Grand Council there is composed solely of men representing all six nations. But their power begins with women. Each nation is divided by clan lines that represent land, water or air—Bear, Deer, Wolf; Turtle, Beaver, Eel; Heron, Hawk, Snipe— and descend matrilineally. Clan mothers nominate chiefs, monitor their work and can remove them from office. Clan mothers drove the first debate at Six Nations. And when clan mothers at Onondaga again voiced their fear at the July Council of Chiefs meeting—and others relayed that the players themselves were wary—the chiefs took heed.

Voting swung against the Nationals taking part in Israel. It was a serious threat; as administrators of the Great Law of Peace—in effect, the Haudenosaunee Constitution—the council's word is law. But the body also operates by consensus, not majority rule: a vote is binding only if all 50 chiefs reach agreement. And on that day, not all 50 were in attendance. The technicality bought time; Jemison and others from the team's 13-member board spent the next two days lobbying chiefs and clan mothers, detailing the fatal implications of FIL penalties.

For the players, the timing couldn't have been worse. Many, like stars Lyle Thompson, Randy Staats and goalie Warren Hill, had been part of the Under-19 team that upset the US, 15–13, in pool play at the 2012 U-19 World

Championship in Turku, Finland—the first time that any Iroquois field team had beaten the Americans. At the 2014 World Championships in Denver, the Iroquois men's team beat Australia twice and won a bronze medal for the first time. Like no other Iroquois team, the one assembling for Israel in 2018 was a true threat to win the title.

But just a week to go before the 2018 World Championship, few inside the community seemed to care. Warnings were coming at players from all directions: from the Sour Springs Longhouse, from clan mothers, parents, friends, coaches and the Grand Council at Onondaga. Few believed that the trip was worth the risk. Then, before the Grand Council could officially reconsider its hard-line stance, the BDS movement released its July 4 letter seeking an Iroquois boycott of Israel.

Scott Neiss, executive director of Israel Lacrosse and the 2018 World Lacrosse Championship, pressed the Iroquois to keep quiet. "I was getting a bit of a gag order from the Israeli government and folks on the Israeli side: 'Don't make any statements. Don't politicize this thing,'" Jemison recalled. "The Israelis were looking at it from the standpoint of: 'We want to honor your treaty, your spirit, your passports. We're playing *your* game and hosting it in our lands. So please come and be welcome with us.'"

Still, what was once a vague threat now felt ominously specific. If they didn't go to Netanya, the Nationals faced sporting oblivion. But if they did go to Israel, defying Palestinian wishes, who knew how harsh the reaction might be? Israelis kept saying that Netanya lay well north of any violence, but that provided thin comfort; in 2002, a Hamas suicide bomber had walked into a Netanya hotel during Passover seder, killing 30 and wounding 140 others in the deadliest attack of the Second Intifada. Deloris "Dee" Thompson, mother of the most famous Iroquois stars—Hiana, Jeremy, Miles and Lyle Thompson—was terrified, sure that her sons would be targeted.

The Nationals 13-member board left it for the players to decide: a majority voted to risk playing in Israel. The board informed the Grand Council. Concerned about both safety and the team's future, the conflicted chiefs issued a new, neither-nor resolution stating that they, too, would defer to the players. In the end, four pulled out. Jemison raced to fill their roster slots, tapping a seemingly raw high schooler, Chase Scanlan; and longstick midfielder Johnson Jimerson, who, prior to trying out for the Nationals, hadn't played organized lacrosse in seven years.

When his phone rang on Friday, July 6, Mark Burnam was just about to cancel his flight to Tel Aviv.

"Go," Jemison said. "It's a done deal."

BUT IT WAS ONLY DONE for the Iroquois. The players and coaches scrambling through the weekend to reach Toronto Airport for their scheduled July 9 departure didn't know: Israeli immigration and security authorities still had not approved the admission of the Nationals on their passports. For fifteen months tournament organizers had worked under the assumption that the Iroquois would play, and believed Israeli officialdom would welcome them. Just after winning the bid to host the games, Neiss sent government officials an explanatory missive—complete with photos of the Haudenosaunee passport—framing their participation as a public relations coup.

"We will have the ability to educate and provide hands-on experiences that will contradict the mainstream media and the misinformation about Israel that haters of our country are always espousing," Neiss wrote in his April 19, 2017, email. "We always talk about how sports transcend the hate in the world and this is an amazing opportunity for us to work with a group of Indigenous people to showcase, promote and give an experience that will reinforce our beliefs."

Neiss's interest was hardly selfless. Hosting a successful World Championship was only the 33-year-old Long Islander's latest audacious scheme, bookending his idea, in 2010, of creating Israel's national lacrosse program out of nothing. A sports nut who never played, at the age of 12 Neiss parlayed his fan website for the indoor New York Saints into a front office job; by 18, he was the team's director of operations. His first summer, Neiss drove to the Onondaga reserve for the Nations Cup championship, and became entranced by the Iroquois game.

In 2017, when Neiss corralled Dan Kraft—former Tufts backup goalie, son of billionaire New England Patriots owner Robert Kraft and an early benefactor of Israel Lacrosse—into backing his last-second bid for the 2018 World Championship, both agreed the Iroquois were a must-have. "If they don't come," Dan said, "the tournament's a joke."

But over the ensuing year, Neiss waited in vain for a hard yes from Israeli authorities—or guidance from longtime FIL officials. This seemed odd, considering the organization's recent success of the Iroquois women's team traveling on their passports from Toronto to England for the 2017 Women's World Championship. FIL officialdom, meanwhile, had good reason to think Israel was on board with admitting the Iroquois. In 2015, Israel's consul-general in New York, Ido Aharoni, assured Nationals co-founder Oren Lyons that the Iroquois would be able to travel to Israel on their passports. Neiss himself, in Israel's official bid for the 2018 World Championship, assured that Iroquois travel would be easily solved.

Still, when Nationals management blocked Neiss's attempt to consult with the officials responsible for the Iroquois women's successful trip in 2017—insisting he deal only with men's GM Ansley Jemison—it seemed an obvious time for the ruling body to broker a conversation. The FIL didn't. Neiss blamed this on lingering animosity between organization officials and the Iroquois over previous passport disputes. "They don't like each other, they still blame each other—and that's never been settled," Neiss said.

The first hard sign of trouble came early in April 2018, when Israel Lacrosse's chief operating officer, David Lasday, was told by an official with Israel's Ministry of Foreign Affairs that the Iroquois would only be admitted if Canada provided official confirmation that it would allow their return. Canada's lukewarm response, through its embassy in Israel, claimed that the "relevant ministries/agencies in Ottawa are heavily engaged with this file, but as you may imagine it is a very complex one from a sovereignty and constitutional perspective." The problem had bounced from Jerusalem to Canada's capital, putting to the test a key calculation by Nationals management.

When it comes to overseas travel, the Haudenosaunee always begin with a choice. Their population resides in both the US and Canada, but deciding which nation to exit isn't just a matter of convenience. It entails a reading, at that moment, of which is the lesser antagonist. During Barack Obama's tenure as US president, Native Americans believed they had a sympathetic ear. In 2010, the US issued a one-time waiver respecting the Haudenosaunee passports when the Nationals were stopped in New York; in early 2016, the Obama State Department hosted a ceremony in Washington, DC, reaffirming its 222-year-old treaty with the Haudenosaunee; and in one of his last major acts, in December 2016, Obama earned the applause of 30 tribal nations when he protected 1.35 million acres in southeastern Utah as the Bears Ears National Monument.

But with Donald Trump's inauguration in 2017, the air between the US and its Indigenous peoples turned chilly. On January 24, Trump reversed Obama's efforts—in solidarity with the Standing Rock Sioux—to block the Dakota Access Pipeline and allowed construction to proceed. His coining of the sneery nickname "Pocahontas" for Massachusetts senator Elizabeth Warren grated Native sensibilities; when, in November 2017, Trump repeated it while honoring Navajo code talkers at the White House, he was slammed as everything from rude to racist. That he did so—intentionally or not—in front of a portrait of Andrew Jackson, architect of the infamous 1830 Indian Removal Act, read like more mockery. A month later, Trump slashed the Bears Ears footprint to 202,000 acres—the largest reduction of a national monument in US history.

Seeking the path of least resistance, the Iroquois went north. Canada has its own brutal history with Indigenous peoples, but its current tone implied remorse. In 2015, Canada's Truth and Reconciliation Commission released a scathing, 4,000-page report detailing how, between 1840 and 1996, government policies forcibly removed 150,000 First Nations, Métis and Inuit children from their families and placed them in schools in a bid to stamp out "Indian" culture. Stories of emotional and physical abuse, rape and malnutrition were aired. Newly elected Prime Minister Justin Trudeau issued an official apology and asked "forgiveness of the Aboriginal peoples of this country for failing them so profoundly."

Trudeau also pledged a new relationship "based on rights, respect, cooperation and partnerships," but, by the spring of 2018, critics were dismissing that as mere rhetoric. Canada's relevant ministries, meanwhile, remained silent on Israel's request for a guarantee that the country would welcome back the Iroquois after the World Championship. On June 13, the now-nervous Neiss applied for the Nationals to be granted "Temporary Athlete" visas—the usual route for nations with which Israel lacks diplomatic ties. Israel's rejection came in a phone call the same day.

With all official means exhausted, Neiss informed Dan Kraft, then dug into his Rolodex and dialed anyone with pull—Ron Dermer, Israel's ambassador to the US; Dan Danon, Israeli ambassador to the UN; Netanyahu foreign affairs advisor Sara Greenberg, who played for Israel's women's national team; Netanyahu spokesman David Keyes. Neiss dropped the name "Kraft" at every opportunity. Few in Israel are more potent: Dan's father, Robert, has donated tens of millions of dollars in support of Jewish and pro-Israeli causes, including $6 million in 2016 to build the Kraft Family Sports Complex in Jerusalem.

Dan enlisted his dad's support. As backup, Neiss sent his staff scrambling for contacts to two other sympathetic billionaires with Canada ties: Israeli real estate mogul Sylvan Adams and Alibaba co-founder Joe Tsai. He also, in the face of Israeli intransigence, kept dropping the Palestinian boycott threat. *If we don't let these guys in, you're giving BDS a win . . .*

It still wasn't enough. By the time the 30-person Iroquois Nationals delegation first showed up at the El Al Airlines ticket counter at Toronto Airport on Monday, July 9, Neiss—tracking their progress from Israel—gave them only a 20 percent chance of taking off. Within minutes, those odds dropped to zero: El Al officials received official word to deny the Iroquois departure.

That's when someone from the Israel Lacrosse Association reached out to Tsai. The sport couldn't have tapped a more interested—or influential— figure. Though renowned as a co-founder and now chairman of China's equivalent of Amazon and owner of the NBA's Brooklyn Nets, Tsai's passion for lacrosse runs far deeper. Born in Taiwan, he found his social footing playing at Lawrenceville School in New Jersey, still considers being cut his senior year a devastating blow and regards walking onto Yale's team—and sticking for four years as a benchwarmer, scoring one goal—one of his great triumphs. A multibillion-dollar fortune has enabled Tsai to keep his hand in ever since: as benefactor of Yale men's and women's programs; founding owner of the indoor pro San Diego Seals and co-owner of another indoor team in Las Vegas; and backer of national teams in Taiwan and Hong Kong.

Even before the Nationals were stopped in Toronto, Tsai had been a low-key savior for the Championship. He helped resolve a bitter labor dispute between Canadian players and the national federation that had nearly resulted in Canada's withdrawal. He donated $125,000 to renovate six Netanya playing fields and another $125,000 to fund sightseeing trips to Jerusalem for every team. And as a lacrosse fiend who goes into "withdrawal" when he can't find an NCAA game to watch, and had a daughter playing at Stanford, Tsai couldn't see the game's international showcase proceeding without the Iroquois.

On July 9, Tsai dashed off a one-page email to Trudeau, urging the Canadian government to issue a letter confirming that Canada would facilitate the smooth departure and return of the team. He stressed his naturalized Canadian citizenship, how he had "personally worked" to get the Canadian team to Israel. "As I write, the Iroquois National lacrosse team are at the

Toronto airport being denied their entry to the departure gate," Tsai's letter to
Trudeau concluded. "The world lacrosse community would be extremely
grateful if your government could provide support on this urgent matter."

Robert Kraft, who had recently met with Canada's prime minister, also
forwarded Trudeau an email describing the stakes. The next available flight
wouldn't leave for two days, allowing only the slightest of margins for the
Nationals to reach Netanya in time for their opening game against Team USA.

SEEING THE JET BRIDGE door slammed in their faces, the Iroquois players were flabbergasted. Bad enough that the Grand Council, many families
and friends, and the Palestinians were against their participation, but now
Israel and Canada were blocking them. Ansley Jemison's problem was more
immediate. Suddenly, he had 30 cranky adults who needed hotel rooms for
two nights. And he had to figure out how to pay for it.

Hours passed in airport limbo. A hotel was found; a bus out of Six
Nations of the Grand River eventually came to pick them up. But the team
was stuck in neutral. With no guarantee that Israel would allow them to
travel in two days, Jemison still had to keep the team together, along with
assistant coaches Scott Marr and Lars Tiffany—head coaches at the University at Albany and the University of Virginia, respectively. Then they all
had to figure out how to fill the next 24 hours.

"Hey," Tiffany said. "We could practice."

It was a radical thought. Most other national teams had been drilling
for months; Team USA's roster had been winnowed from 48 to 23 players
over seven training weekends and finalized six months earlier. But this iteration of the Nationals had been set just the week before, and gathered for
the first time as a team at the airport. They had never practiced together.
Jemison made a call.

Six Nations offered up a field. With their head coach half a world away,
waiting aimlessly at the hotel in Netanya, Tiffany and Marr installed basic
terms for defense and offense and the players scrimmaged. "One practice,"
Tiffany said. "It forces you to do what, maybe, is the right thing and just
let them play. They know the game."

That night the Six Nations Chiefs, a power team in Canada's indoor
pro league, had a scheduled home game. Jemison made a call. The Chiefs had

had their roster temporarily plucked clean by the Nationals, so he offered the team's president a deal: *You get your players get back for tonight, in exchange for transport to Toronto airport tomorrow.* Eight Nationals then rode over to Iroquois Lacrosse Arena, and scored half the Chiefs' goals in a 10–9 win over the Brampton Excelsiors. The next morning—Wednesday, July 11— the Chiefs team bus carried the Nationals the 65 miles back to Toronto International Airport.

By then, too, all the lobbying by Tsai and Kraft and, especially, former Canadian justice minister Irwin Cotler had seemingly resolved Israel's concerns. Cotler, a renowned human rights lawyer who had counseled activists Nelson Mandela and Jacobo Timerman—and whose daughter lives in Israel— essentially brokered the final, one-time agreement to allow the Nationals to travel on their Haudenosaunee passports into Israel. Cotler also drafted the Canadian government's letter guaranteeing their return. All, at last, seemed well. The plane was scheduled to take off at 2 p.m., Toronto time.

Only one detail hadn't been accounted for. A significant number of the Iroquois delegation were also carrying US or Canadian passports. This may seem contradictory—and decidedly off-message—but is a reality when a century-long crusade conflicts with the demands of daily life. Canadian border officials, especially, have been known to dismiss the Haudenosaunee passport as a "fantasy" document. Though they don't identify with either country, many Iroquois—particularly those living in the border-flanking Akwesasne community—regularly present US or Canadian passports to streamline their "crossings."

The Nationals planned to present only their Native version at Israeli passport control. But when the two spoke by phone Wednesday morning, Jemison told Neiss that some in the delegation were also carrying US or Canada passports. Neiss's gut lurched. For 14 months he had been telling Israeli officials that the Haudenosaunee used only their own documents: How to explain the presence of others? Jemison insisted that he was being paranoid: any US or Canadian passports would be buried deep in their luggage.

The Nationals delegation received their boarding passes. Lyle Thompson, 25, with a decade of Iroquois travel woes under his belt, still was sure the team would never make it to Israel. After being questioned at check-in, the delegation passed through a second security check. Then, at the departure gate, El Al security started searching everyone's bags.

It was sometime after 1 p.m. Passengers began lining up to board. Gateway security checks aren't rare, not since 9/11, but the air crackled with a new urgency as authorities checked every Iroquois bag and scanned every laptop. The original departure time came and went. Two more hours passed, but no explanation was given. Some wondered if officials in Israel or Toronto had seen the story published that morning in Canada's *National Post*, where Lyle Thompson's comments shattered Neiss's hope for Iroquois neutrality. "What's going on in Israel and what's happened to the Palestinians is wrong," Thompson said in the *Post*. "A lot of people are relating it to what's happened to Native American people in Canada and the US, and it is similar. Morally, I want to support, and I'm going to support them in the best way I can." The piece closed with Thompson's intention to use his celebrity and social media to highlight the "subjugation of the Palestinians," and—depending on safety concerns—to visit a Palestinian refugee camp.

Every Haudenosaunee wallet, phone, hand and shoe was fabric-swabbed for explosive residue. Whether the search was for weaponry or Palestinian flags or BDS propaganda is unclear. What *was* found in the luggage of some Haudenosaunee passport bearers were US and Canadian passports. Since Canada had been the prime lobbying focus of Tsai and Kraft and Sylvan Adams, the Canadian documents didn't pose a problem. The US passports did. Virtually no legwork had been devoted to smoothing snafus on the American end. And that was enough, for the second time in three days, to stop the Iroquois cold.

When Neiss called with the news, Dan Kraft blew up. Like Neiss, for weeks Dan had been telling his Israeli contacts—and, just the day before, his father, who had then reached out to Justin Trudeau—that the Nationals used only Haudenosaunee passports. Now a waking nightmare loomed, with the family name on the line. Dan hung up on Neiss, began dialing up El Al, the Israeli government, ambassadors. His father had been a staunch supporter of Donald Trump; Dan cashed in that chit, too. He called the US embassy in Israel, recently and controversially moved by Trump to Jerusalem.

For five more hours, the plane sat on the tarmac. Bags were rummaged through and repacked. One by one, members of the Nationals delegation dribbled aboard. At least once the plane backed away from the gate, began taxiing, then returned to pick up stragglers. One of the last aboard was GM Ansley Jemison; an American passport had been found in his bag.

Eleven and a half hours later, the El Al jet landed in Israel. The players disembarked, made calls, sent out an official tweet: "We made it," accompanied by the image of midfielder Jeremy Thompson beaming and holding up his Haudenosaunee passport.

Mark Burnam still couldn't relax. Even after learning that the delegation had cleared Israel customs and boarded a bus for the hotel, the Iroquois head coach was sure that something bad would happen. He was sitting in his now-familiar seat in the lobby café at the West Lagoon Resort, afternoon sun crashing through the plate-glass windows, when the bus carrying the Nationals pulled up in front. He stared as the bus door opened. Players and staff spilled onto the sidewalk, blinking and squinting, adjusting to the sunlight.

Burnam stood up grinning. Six hours to game time.

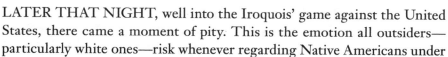

LATER THAT NIGHT, well into the Iroquois' game against the United States, there came a moment of pity. This is the emotion all outsiders—particularly white ones—risk whenever regarding Native Americans under pressure. It is a trap. "Lo, the Poor Indian!" poet Alexander Pope wrote in all sincerity in 1733, but by the mid-1800s "Lo" had evolved into snide shorthand for the very people whites were working furiously, systematically, to destroy.

When a New York sportswriter in 1869 tired of scribbling "the Mohawks" or "Indians" in his admiring account of an early lacrosse exhibition, he resorted to "the Lo's," and knew his audience would get the joke. Five years later, when the *Bismarck Tribune* set the tone for white settlers just before Lieutenant Colonel George Custer's expedition touched off the Black Hills gold rush, no one was laughing.

> *Humanitarians may weep for poor Lo, and tell the wrongs he has suffered, but he is passing away. Their prayers, their entreaties, can not change the law of nature; can not arrest the causes which are carrying them on to their ultimate destiny—extinction . . . The American people need the country the Indians now occupy . . . An Indian war would do no harm, for it must come, sooner or later . . .*

With 15:13 left in the second quarter, beneath a fading orange sky on a floodlit field in Netanya, the pity crept in. This was just after Lyle Thompson, one of the game's sublime talents and, perhaps, the greatest Native player ever, went down. Setting up on the left wing, he had lowered his shoulder and begun angling toward the crease when US longstick midfielder Michael Ehrhardt stepped in with a stonewalling check—muscling Thompson to the turf, sending his stick whirling, stripping the Nationals star of ball, weapon, dignity. "Whooooooooo!" Quint Kessenich howled on the ESPN broadcast. "That was epic."

Indeed, it seemed an emblematic instant, the point when all the obstacles—the pretournament politics and uncertainty, the two-day flight delay, the nick-of-time arrival, the lack of sleep, the disorienting jetlag, and the titanic presence of their opponent—finally swamped the Iroquois like a crashing wave. Flying on adrenaline, the Nationals had started the game with three straight goals and by the end of the first quarter held a stunning 5–3 lead. But now, in the second, the Americans were coming hard and scored two too-easy goals to make it 5–5. Thompson was on his hands and knees, groping. Surely, the inevitable fade had begun.

Given perfect conditions, military organization and seamless travel, the Iroquois would still have been vast underdogs. Not only was the US the field game's overwhelming power—winning nine of the 12 World Championships contested since 1967—it had crushed the Nationals in their eight previous meetings by a combined score of 172–63. This US squad was loaded with All-Americans, three Tewaaraton Award winners, the best faceoff man in collegiate history and, in Paul Rabil, arguably the game's best-ever professional and first-ever million-dollar player. Most important, it was a true team. Stung by its loss to Canada in the 2014 World Championship final, in late 2015 US Lacrosse hired Duke head coach John Danowski, who spent the next 30 months evaluating, selecting and bonding his roster.

In preparation for the game's mightiest, most efficient and monied program, these Iroquois, meanwhile, had practiced together once. "One day to go over clears, go over our ride, go over an offense—and we never officially put it in," Lyle Thompson said of their ad hoc workout in Toronto two days before. "Our guys don't know it like the back of their hand. We're kind of learning it. This is our first game and we're still learning our offense."

And yet, after Ehrhardt's withering check, the Nationals didn't buckle. Lyle Thompson sprung to his feet, grabbed up his stick. He looked strikingly buoyant, and even more so two and a half minutes later when, fed the ball in Iroquois territory, he unleashed a full-stride sprint up the field's right side.

Thompson crossed midfield, churned deep into the US defense, cradling furiously; then slowed and scanned for a teammate with a better angle. He might as well have been alone. American midfielder Tom Schreiber, whose play as a pro in 2018 had many anointing *him* the game's best, ran Thompson down and squared off—the only one standing now between Thompson and US goalie John Galloway.

With just one step to his left, Schreiber could have closed off Thompson's slight sightline to the goal, a channel maybe five inches wide. Thompson's stickhead waggled once, twice; what looked lazy was actually a cobra flaring its hood. Schreiber didn't step. Five inches was enough. Thompson leaned right, planted and—snap!—whipped the ball from his waist 15 yards into a hole, low between the just-late Galloway and the left post, about the size of a teacup. It was Thompson's third goal of the game, a hat trick midway through the second quarter. Nobody on the field had played close to his level.

Schreiber stared at the goal, furious. Then he gave the slightest shrug, as if to say, *Too good.* On ESPN's live broadcast, Carcaterra was asked if being "helicoptered" had woken Thompson up. "Doesn't need to," he yelled. "This guy looks at the game differently. He's got a short memory, an incredible athletic burst—and the skill of an absolute legend."

About then any sense of pity dissolved, replaced—as the clock to halftime ticked down—by a sense that something remarkable was at hand, and a question. Would the world notice? Netanya Stadium, built for soccer with a capacity of 13,610, was only about one-third filled. Lacrosse had been played in Israel only since 2011, and the country was still learning. That day's tournament preview in the *Jerusalem Post* found it necessary to include a short tutorial: "Modern field lacrosse is a contact sport in which two teams compete for possession of a rubber ball using metal sticks with mesh nets. Points are scored by shooting the ball into the opposing team's net. Different positions have different sticks . . ."

Meanwhile, though the game was being beamed live in the US on ESPN2, its timeslot—midsummer, midday on the American East Coast—promised relatively few viewers. Casual sports fans barely knew of the event's existence. "From a programming/promotional standpoint, have you heard a peep about this, while watching ESPN over the last two weeks?" play-by-play man Anish Shroff said the day before. "Had this been a bigger event, a bigger sport, you wouldn't have gotten just a little mention, a little promo on SportsCenter." To hear the ESPN broadcast team, the most publicity anyone could expect—from this tournament game or any other—was a highlight clip on the Top Ten Plays of the Week.

Yet now the Iroquois Nationals, who had never before led against an American men's field team, had absorbed the first US counterpunch and taken its second lead of the night, 6–5—after crossing six times zones and arriving just six hours earlier. The strain didn't end there. By the time the players reached their hotel rooms, it was 3 p.m., too late for a decent sleep. Then came a quick meal; another bus trip for the 20-minute ride to the stadium; then, at 6:54 p.m., the Iroquois, after declining the option of sitting out the Opening Ceremony, congregated on field for 30 minutes with 45 other nations in a draining 85-degree heat.

Once the game began, the Iroquois players weren't the only ones feeling each other out; the coaches were still learning how to mesh. Though in charge of the defense, early on Lars Tiffany found himself also running the substitution box. The last-minute withdrawals had riddled the Nationals, eternally suspect defense; Tiffany plugged holes with a converted midfielder, an untested teenager and a very rusty Johnson Jimerson. But between Lyle Thompson and his brother Miles—co-Tewaaraton winners in 2014—the oft-unstoppable Tehoka Nanticoke, Randy Staats and his rapidly emerging younger brother, Austin, the Iroquois also had, arguably, the game's most explosive offense. And with the US attack disorganized, goalie Warren Hill in good rhythm and Lyle humming, any fear about being overwhelmed died. With 3:43 left in the half, Randy Staats posted up just outside the crease and flicked in an overhand goal, extending the Nationals' lead to 7–5.

But the scoreboard, just numbers, couldn't transmit the palpable energy rising now off the Iroquois, or explain that this first half represented the Haudenosaunee's most emphatic step, in three decades, toward reclaiming their game. Ehrhardt had five inches and 35 pounds on Lyle Thompson and leveled him. Yet, with 49 seconds left in the half, on the left wing and accelerating, Thompson poked a nifty jab step at US midfielder Will Haus; this time, untouched, it was the American going down to his hands and knees. With nine seconds left in the half, the American defense broke down again, and Lyle Thompson lasered a final shot wide. US midfielder Jake Bernhardt decked a goal-rushing Nanticoke from behind as time expired, his momentum plunging him straight into Miles Thompson, who shoved Bernhardt, and suddenly Lyle and the Staats brothers rushed in and a trio of US defenders converged. Jawing and pushing ensued.

For Mexico attackman Timothy Gonzales, sitting in the stands, it was a perfect snapshot of Iroquois defiance. "They went out there like they had something to prove: that they belonged there," he said. "What they're doing in their culture by not wanting to get colonized is one of the greatest things that can happen now: to never forget where you come from, to represent who you are. And the fact that they came in—no complaints, landed, came right to the game, played? And the *way* that they played, to show everybody: *This is our sport. You guys took it from us, so we're going to give you the hardest time. It's going to take all your blood, sweat and tears to beat us.*"

Everyone knew the Nationals had to be exhausted. Everyone knew this made no sense. But even the most hard-eyed lacrosse mind was thinking: *Wait. The Iroquois could actually win this . . .*

"Listen: Our talent pool is, like, this big," Nationals assistant coach Scott Marr said, cupping his hands tightly together. Then he spread his arms as wide as possible to describe Team USA. "Their pool is this big. The fact that we ran with them and were ahead of 'em for the first time? After a 13-hour jet?"

Marr—white American, product of Johns Hopkins—shouldn't have been surprised; he coached Lyle, Miles and their cousin, Ty Thompson, at Albany from 2011 to 2015. But with the trip to Israel, he became immersed in their program, not vice versa; the opener against the US was Marr's full-body baptism, pro and con, in lacrosse the Iroquois way.

"Red Burnam kept warning me: the fight in 'em, that resiliency, is amazing," he said. "As a people: To live how they live for these last couple hundred years, and to be pushed to reservations? The white man has tried to stomp 'em out—and they just *can't*."

II

FAITHKEEPERS

OREN LYONS—SENECA BORN and Onondaga adopted, Turtle clan—is one of the most prominent Indigenous activists of the last 50 years. He has worked as a commercial artist, scholar and essayist; appeared on the classic game show *What's My Line?*; picketed with John Lennon; been honored with a clutch of humanitarian awards; and, in 2016, spoke at Muhammad Ali's funeral and addressed the UN General Assembly. But, before all that, the diminutive son of a great Seneca goalie braved the white world and wielded his own sawed-off goalie stick to a Hall of Fame career at Syracuse University. Nothing speaks more eloquently of who Lyons is than lacrosse. Nothing captures better his drive to revive Haudenosaunee nationhood, purity and pride than the Iroquois Nationals.

They were not his idea alone. Interest in rejoining the world lacrosse ranks had been percolating among the Haudenosaunee since at least 1976. In December 1980, Tuscarora stickmaker Wesley Patterson appeared at a meeting of the International Lacrosse Federation (later renamed FIL) to serve notice that they wanted to be not only "recognized as a lacrosse-playing nation," but as one "that is interested in the function of the ILF"—yet weren't ready to make a formal application. Two years later, Syracuse head coach Roy Simmons Jr., a tri-captain on Syracuse's 1957 undefeated team with Jim Brown and Lyons, suggested that his old teammate schedule the Iroquois field team in some international scrimmages.

"We don't have a field team," Lyons said. "We don't know how to play field."

One of the sadder replies in American history, at first blush it sounds odd. Over the years a steady trickle of Natives had followed Lyons's lead and played the 10-man outdoor game, most famously at Syracuse; three of Simmons Jr.'s players at that time were Haudenosaunee, including Mark Burnam. But for 50 years the Iroquois game of choice had been indoor, or "box," lacrosse—the faster, tougher six-man version created in Canada to fill off-season hockey rinks. Box's tightened confines and four-by-four-foot goals demanded creative stickhandling, crushing physicality, run-and-gun shooting. If Onondaga boys dreamed of playing competitively outside, then, it was in the reserve's open-air box arena; when Six Nations created its lacrosse league in the 1970s, indoor was the only option considered. The first Indigenous team to play as a nation, a one-time assemblage dubbed the "North American Native Warriors," finished second at "The Nations in 1980" indoor championship in British Columbia. Five months later, the ILF board agreed to include the Iroquois—but only as a non-member—in its inaugural (and soon postponed, for 23 years) World Box Championship.

Lyons's doleful statement underscored that the field game had been supplanted as the foundational Iroquois style, the prime staging ground of reserve rivalries. Haudenosaunee identification with modern field play had been, as Simmons Jr. said, "kind of snuffed out."

Initial Iroquois forays into the field game were both disorganized and disrespected. Though a bid to take part in the 1982 World Championship in Baltimore fizzled, the Iroquois presumed elite status as the game's originators and weren't shy about their intent to gain a voice in the sport's affairs. They had high-level support—most notably from Rutgers head coach and ILF vice president Tom Hayes—but much of the organization's leadership opposed granting them full membership. When Patterson showed up at that '82 Championship, a confrontation erupted with event co-chair Emil "Buzzy" Budnitz outside the doors of the Lacrosse Hall of Fame.

The moment couldn't have been more emblematic. Lacrosse's first Hall of Fame, its rudimentary Mecca, was located in a cramped room in the Newton H. White Jr. Athletic Center at Johns Hopkins University, its all-time records squirreled away in a desk drawer, the bas-relief faces of its original inductees bronzed and mounted on plaques. The field game's most storied program—and standard-bearer of the Mid-Atlantic's white, elite lacrosse aesthetic—Hopkins lacrosse happened to be celebrating its 100th anniversary. Budnitz, an all-time Blue Jays great, businessman and

Hopkins benefactor, was the establishment made flesh. Patterson, born on a
New York reservation, had been a physical education teacher and pioneering
coach for 20 years in Baltimore-area public schools before moving home to
open his wood stick factory.

Their paths crossed. Tempers ignited. Ron Balls, championship co-
chair Elmer Wingate, an ILF delegate from Canada, and Hayes hustled in
to separate them before fists flew. In the back-and-forth, according to Balls,
"there was prejudice, no doubt about it."

Lyons was undeterred. That same year he returned to Onondaga armed
with Simmons Jr.'s suggestion of an Iroquois field team, received a collective
"Why not?" from players and coaches, and landed the necessary sanction from
the Grand Council. This was, after all, a matter of state. From the start Lyons
and the Council viewed the Nationals as a way for the Haudenosaunee to revivify
their identity and push for sovereignty. As stated in a 1983 letter to the ILF by
supreme chief—or Tadadaho—Leon Shenandoah Sr.: "The Iroquois Nationals
Lacrosse Team is the official sanctioned representative of the Haudenosaunee."

Even partnered with Patterson, the program's first executive director,
and aided by Tuscarora artist and professor Rick Hill, Lyons needed more
than a year to organize management and coaching staff and raise $20,000 for
expenses; the team managed just three practices. When the newly minted
Iroquois Nationals returned to Johns Hopkins in June for "Lacrosse International '83," a four-day festival featuring all-star men's and women's teams from
the US and Canada, the far warmer welcome featured celebratory chants,
ceremonial dances and a 40-foot Canadian red cedar totem pole featuring
a turtle for the Iroquois and an eagle for the US. And once play began at
Homewood Field, the Yankee Stadium of American lacrosse, it became clear
just how estranged the Iroquois had grown from their own game.

Their first test came against Roy Simmons Jr. and Syracuse, one week
after they had beaten Hopkins in the 1983 NCAA final with one of the most
astounding comebacks in lacrosse history. The Orange scored six goals before
the Nationals could launch a shot. In the stands, Jim Brown said to Lyons:
"Your team is getting beat bad. It must be embarrassing." When Nationals
attackman Greg Tarbell finally scored the program's first-ever goal, it only
made Syracuse goalie Travis Solomon—an Onondaga—smile. "He's my
cousin," he said after. "So I let him score." Syracuse ended up taking 40 more
shots and winning, 28–5. Three days later, the Iroquois lost to Division III
national champs Hobart, 22–14.

Yet even amid that humiliation, while lacking the basic home field and locker facilities that high school teams take for granted, the Nationals envisioned an ambitious, full-circle future for themselves and their sport. Lacrosse had made appearances at the Olympics as a medal sport in 1904 and 1908, and a demonstration sport in 1928, 1932, and 1948, and a team of Mohawks from Six Nations of the Grand River—representing Canada— had won the bronze medal in the 1904 games in St. Louis. Eight decades later, Lyons began pushing for a return. "You need eight teams to have an Olympics, as I understand it, and we hope to be one of those teams," he told a reporter. "I am confident that when the day comes, when the time comes, we will be there."

The following May, the Iroquois arranged and hosted a pre–1984 Olympic Games tourney in a park 10 miles east of Los Angeles—the Jim Thorpe Memorial Pow-Wow and Native Games. Haudenosaunee runners set off west from the Onondaga reserve on a 7,000-mile, seven-week Native relay across 16 states: Oneidas and Winnebagos passing a consecrated staff to Anishinaabe in Minnesota, who passed it to the Dakota and Lakota, and onward to the Arapaho and Cheyenne, the Ute and Western Shoshone, finishing with eight different relay teams in California. The sport's four International Lacrosse Federation members—US, Canada, Australia and England—came to play. The Iroquois Nationals came loaded: Syracuse stars Burnam, Solomon and sharpshooter Emmett Printup; future Tadadaho Sidney Hill; Lyons's son, Onondaga box star Rex Lyons; and the category-defying Mikko Red Arrow, a Cherokee/Lenape midfielder who grew up on Long Island and had just earned honorable mention All-American honors for Hofstra. The Nationals played five games in blistering July conditions, losing to the sport's top three by a combined score of 54–30. But they manhandled a tossed-salad team of California All-Stars, and established their bona fides by beating England, 10–9.

At the ILF meetings in Whittier, California, Nationals leadership began intensely lobbying to join the organization. Opposition arose instantly from the US and Canada, who essentially considered Natives on their side of the border citizens, had trouble recognizing the Iroquois Confederacy as a "nation" and worried that other Indigenous people would seek similar recognition. Australia, with its large Aboriginal population, watched warily.

Traditionalists from American collegiate ranks, the sport's prestige platform, worried that the Iroquois' box style would tarnish the field game.

"It was very emotional," said then-ILF vice president Tom Hayes. "There was yelling and screaming at each other. There were people who didn't even want them voted on; fortunately they got drowned out. But there were some purists and [the Iroquois] had a history, especially in Canada playing in the box league, the Can-Am league, and some people just felt that they weren't gentlemanly enough to play with us 'preppies.'"

In 1985, the Nationals crossed the Atlantic to play a five-game goodwill tour, traveling internationally for the first time on what were, then, hand-written Haudenosaunee passports. To smooth their path, Balls had given British immigration officials proof of the Iroquois' intent to depart at tour's end. He also stressed that Lyons and the Iroquois, seeking any chance to showcase their sovereignty claim, *wanted* to be denied entry and had tipped off the British media to an airport showdown between cruel bureaucrats and sympathetic Native Americans. The briefing worked: the bewildered Iroquois sailed through passport control. Games were played, lacrosse clinics given. Intrigue with Indigenous clichés had its usual double-edged effect. Kids at an English primary school asked how the smoke got out of the Nationals' tepees, and if they still hurt people. The public paid attention in a way that it wouldn't for any other lacrosse team, but the Haudenosaunee believed that lacrosse executives liked them in traditional dress, speaking of their heritage, only when it came to hyping the game. "I'm really tired," Oren Lyons said toward the end, "of playing 'Indian.'"

In October 1985 the ILF board rejected the Nationals' first official petition to take part in the 1986 World Field Championship, citing concerns over the new program's finances and competitiveness and a strict reading of nationality. By then US opposition had faded; Tom Hayes, the most influential American pushing to expand the game internationally, was vocal in his support. "This is an original American game," he told the *New York Times* a year later. "Not to have original Americans playing it is ludicrous."

Getting on the right side of history wasn't Hayes entire motivation. He truly considered the Iroquois game a gift. Lacrosse had led him, son of a Long Island tool-and-die man, from Floral Park powerhouse Sewanhaka High into Penn State and opened up a career of purpose and world travel; Hayes was, in essence, a living counterweight to the game's brahmins in Baltimore and other East Coast precincts.

By 1986, Hayes was a decade into a Hall of Fame coaching run at Rutgers marked by top-ten finishes, a parade of All-Americans, and a blue-collar grit that Long Island aficionados still swear by, loudly. Before that, though, Hayes was an air force staff sergeant who, in 1972, was jailed for brawling in Greenville, Mississippi, with an Alabamian who slurred one of his Black airmen. The sentiment he picked up in lacrosse during the mid-'80s, regarding the Iroquois, had a similar scent. "I always felt that we should be adding countries and not worry about what color their skin is," Hayes recalled. "My parting shot to the organization was: 'This is going to come back to haunt us if we don't do the right thing.'"

But Canada remained opposed, and Australia wary that other tribal entities might want to play. The Iroquois cited the uniqueness of their status among Native nations, citing still-honored treaties with the US and Canada, lack of federal taxes paid to either, and their passport successes; they also agreed to reserve a few spots for non-Iroquois Natives on the Nationals roster. A compromise was floated: the Iroquois could join the ILF as a "competitive affiliate," with no seat on the board, but probable participation in the 1990 World Championship. In July 1986, the ILF board ratified the proposal, 4–0.

Still, the Iroquois kept pushing for full membership, with its accompanying seat on the decision-making board. In the mid-1980s, a spate of financial malfeasances forced a reshuffle of the Canadian Lacrosse Association board, and Carol Patterson, Wes's wife and head coach of Canada's first women's team, became a CLA vice president. Suddenly, Lyons said, the Nationals had someone "inside" the Canadian camp. Though Carol Patterson's influence isn't clear—even to her—old sticking points became unstuck: Iroquois players with American or Canadian passports would be given a one-time, irrevocable choice to commit to a national program; the Iroquois would be admitted as a one-time phenomenon; no other "North American Indian Nation" could follow suit.

Late on the evening of November 20, 1987, after lengthy debate, Tom Hayes moved the board to vote. According to contemporaneous notes, the US, Canada, Australia and England unanimously agreed "that the category of 'Competitive Affiliate' was not appropriate and that IN be made a full member of the ILF." Lacrosse became the first team sport to take the radical step of officially recognizing an Indigenous people. Two centuries after their demise, the Iroquois again had a seat at a table of white power.

The next morning in his hotel room, Balls dialed up Oren Lyons, asleep at his home on the Onondaga reserve. Lyons growled an earthy warning that the news had better be good, and Balls replied, "We've had the discussion, everybody's agreed: you're in the next world championships."

"My terms? Full nation, none of this 'Affiliate' stuff?" Lyons said.

Balls assured him that the Iroquois membership was unqualified, and that even Canada had pushed hard to get it done.

Lyons hung up and dialed Mark Burnam. "We're in," Lyons told the Nationals captain. "Let the boys know."

FOR THE HAUDENOSAUNEE, the breakthrough was historic, a triumph of identity; the 1990 World Championship in Perth would be their first appearance—in lacrosse circles, anyway—as a fully sovereign nation. Now all they needed was a team.

The process of assembling Iroquois players is unlike anything seen in American sports. To start, the number of high-level Haudenosaunee men's lacrosse players tops out at about 130—compared to the 130,000 available to the United States. Reaching them is not easy. Burnam, captain of the Nationals squad in 1990, detailed the steps four months before the 2018 championship:

We put it out—kind of like we're doing now: "Hey, there's going to be a tryout for the national team . . ." We do it at different reserves and different Nations. Whoever shows up? That's who we get to pick from. It's not like I go, "You're invited"—and [the players] do every single thing they possibly can to be on that team. Some guys are working, some guys are ironworkers; they're traveling, they live in California, they can't take two or three weeks off. They can't even take a weekend off because their families are depending on them to be the breadwinners.

After you narrow down, 60 of 'em are . . . world-class players . . . going to go play against the best guys in the world, currently playing or just out of college, four-times D-1 All-American. And we're talking about a guy who maybe never even went to college, just barely finished high school. We're talking about guys who trained on the weekend. We're talking about a guy who just got off climbing iron and went down and put a lacrosse stick in his hand and he's going to try out for a national team . . .

And who do we have to choose from? People think, I saw this one guy, he's Native American . . . Well, he's not Iroquois. We only get three

non-passport players. By that, I mean: You can be from any Nation, but you
have to prove that you have the lineage; you have to have the paperwork . . .
You've got to be an enrolled member of the tribe, you've got to get stuff from
the chiefs where you live. There's quantum bloodlines involved . . .

For 1990, the Iroquois' first-ever World Championship in Perth, other factors were involved. Each player needed to raise $1,200 for travel expenses. Every nation needs a flag, and the Iroquois' equivalent—eagle feathers attached to a staff—wouldn't sit well on a flagpole. Lyons and Rick Hill came up with the original design based on the Hiawatha Wampum Belt, purple and white. Mohawk artist Tim Johnson arranged the final design, and his father, Harold, manufactured the first flag in Iroquois history. Raising the flag required a national anthem: Onondaga chief Paul Waterman had repurposed the Haudenosaunee tobacco-burning song into a hymn about mindfulness, safety and the game itself. In Perth, before play began, Lyons and some players scrambled to a makeshift studio with drum and rattle and recorded a hypnotic, 90-second chant.

The morning of their opening game, Nationals executive director Sid Jamieson met with the event manager. The man, declaring the Iroquois anthem too long, asked if it could be cut back. Jamieson replied, "You're the host. Wouldn't it be more appropriate for you to snip the Australian national anthem?" The new Iroquois anthem was played in its entirety.

Anyone expecting another response hadn't been paying attention. At no point, during their decade-long trek to Perth, had the Iroquois displayed obsequiousness or waxed grateful about being admitted to the ILF. Lyons, Patterson and the players acknowledged the work of white allies, but hardly believed that the ILF had done them a favor. They felt the opposite: Lacrosse was fortunate to have them. Their presence in Australia was the righting of a titanic wrong.

"You have to understand: we're white and it's their game and they gave to us their country," said Tom Hayes. "Unless you can accept that without having any adverse feelings, you better not get involved with them."

On Saturday, July 7, the Iroquois walked on the field before their first game, heard their new anthem and saw their new flag. For 39-year-old defenseman Sidney Hill, the moment was "just overwhelming." Coming of age in the 1970s era of Native American activism, the future supreme chief of the confederacy had always questioned why he had to honor American ceremonies like the Pledge of Allegiance. He never envisioned that sports could provide an answer. "Yes, it was geared towards lacrosse, but that was: *Here We Are*—being recognized as a nation," Hill said. "We have our land— what land we have left—we have our language and culture. We're still here. We're still going."

Iroquois pride took its share of bruising in Perth. The delegation needed a $35,000 donation by the Grand Marnier Foundation of France to buy air- line tickets; its team equipment, shoes and uniforms were gifted by Brine Lacrosse. The team didn't win a game. Players visiting a park were forced to flee after being accosted by a mob of kangaroos. But in terms of setting the Iroquois template, the Nationals succeeded. They had been cleared for entry into Australia, the second country outside of North America to rec- ognize their passports and treat them like a fully realized nation. And the players left a mark.

In the inaugural game against Canada—powered by legendary twins Paul and Gary Gait, just off winning a third NCAA title at Syracuse—the Iroquois pushed the eventual finalists to the limit before losing, 18–15. Rex Lyons outplayed the Gaits with five goals and four assists. An even greater shock was caused by the sight and feel of the three Iroquois long-pole defense- men, led by Sidney Hill, wielding classic, six-foot hickory sticks. Few collisions are more feared on a lacrosse field than that of a wooden shaft striking bone and flesh. The Iroquois smelled that fear, and hacked mercilessly.

"We used to call it 'kill snakes,'" Burnam said. "If there's a snake on the ground, you don't just hit that snake. You kill that snake."

Nursing chronic tendonitis, Team USA defenseman Fred Opie was on the sideline the next day, July 8, when the Iroquois took the field against Team USA. "It was like Custer's Last Stand," said Opie, now a history professor at Babson College. "A ground ball in lacrosse is a 50–50 thing, like a loose ball in basketball; if you're going to win, you've got to get after it. When the US players would go to scoop the ball, there was no intent whatsoever from the Iroquois to pick up the ball. It was just, *Let me get a piece of this stick and a piece of your hand and a piece of your arm*. It was brutal. Like, *Whack! Whack! Whack!*"

The numbing jabs didn't stop the United States; after a tight start, the eventual champions stampeded the Nationals, 26–10. But the American field players, collegians all, were outraged by the Iroquois' tactics, typical of box play. Most had never played the indoor game. Said Burnam: "They were whining: 'You can't do that!' Don't fuckin' tell us how to play the game. We'll tell *you* how to play. A lot of our guys had little chips on our shoulder, like, *Why weren't we allowed to play in those '86 games?* So four years later we're like, *THIS is the reason why you don't want us to play, I guess.*"

The Nationals' off-field moves aimed for a different kind of impact. Media attention about the team's inaugural appearance in Perth all but forced local organizers to acknowledge Australia's own Indigenous population; the Opening Ceremonies featured a half-dozen Aboriginal people playing didgeridoos. Nationals head coach Kim Patterson and the players held a mid-tournament clinic for Aboriginal children and left behind 40 lacrosse sticks. In return, they received flutes and boomerangs.

At one point during the 1990 games, Oren Lyons presented Ron Balls with a signed print of one of his paintings, *We the Original People*, featuring Benjamin Franklin, John Adams and Thomas Jefferson at a table composing the Declaration of Independence. Hovering above their heads are spectral depictions of a hawk, the Great Tree of Peace under which the Iroquois Confederacy was originally formed and the Peacemaker, who—in this version, anyway—bears a striking resemblance to Oren Lyons. His inscription thanks Balls and calls him "friend." Balls has cherished it ever since.

THE IROQUOIS SPENT the next dozen years on the climb. Their first win at a men's field World Championship came over Japan in 1994; they finally beat England by a goal in 1998; they beat both in 2002. Four years later, in London, Ontario, the Nationals edged Australia for the first time in the preliminaries, 12–10, but lost in the bronze-medal game, finishing fourth in a field now 21 teams deep. International lacrosse was growing fast. But the Haudenosaunee's place in the game's elite, buttressed by second-place finishes at the Indoor World Championships in 2003 and 2007, was becoming inevitable.

"When you say 'Indians,' 'Native Americans'—what pops into mind? Out west, on TV, in a tepee, in a reservation, alcohol, drug abuse, drain on society, poverty, uneducated: beaten down," stickmaker Alfie Jacques said in 2010. "So to have a positive there on the world stage is such a big thing for us. We can show the world: *Look what we're doing.*"

Detractors remained: a 1998 *New Yorker* article noted an American fan, outraged after one National decked a member of Team USA at that year's

World Championship, yelling, "Get the animals out of the game!" But from the start the Iroquois Nationals were monumentally popular, and catnip to media. Mystique was automatic: Their wooden sticks and bruising play unearthed the game's roots, and their trademark single braids, anthem and names evoked emotions and associations rarely stirred by sports.

The rise of "cultural appropriation" as an academic term, one destined in the 21st century to trip into popular jargon, added another layer. Rock music had long been appropriation's handiest culprit, exemplified by Elvis Presley's success with Black Blues artist Big Mama Thornton's "Hound Dog." But the Iroquois field revival felt like appropriation's reversal even more on point; seeing the Nationals play the 10-man game against Canada or the US was like hearing Thornton in an Elvis movie. Suddenly a pastime of white elites resonated, too, with cultural shame and pride, conflicting narratives, and a palpable relief that the same "Redskins," "Braves" and "Indians" who had their identities stolen and insulted by American professional teams and universities now had a team of their own. Suddenly lacrosse—long clichéd and dismissed as a status-laden plaything—carried an explicit burden of history.

At the same time the gravitas, all that *past*, remained secondary. No one plays like the Iroquois. The Canadians, with skills also honed in the box, come closest; emblematic players of both nations can free themselves at will, pass and shoot out of the tightest of scrums, dazzle with behind-the-head or -back stickwork. But Iroquois fearlessness is a quality all its own. It's a bravery beyond physical, a kind of psychic liberation; the Iroquois are fearless because their game is free, played with an ease that no amount of drilling can replicate. "They look like they've been doing it for their entire life," said former Johns Hopkins great Kyle Harrison. "Maybe even before they were here."

US-based field play, with its bottom-line premium placed on winning, can be methodical and dull. The Iroquois shrug at turnovers, prize individual style and skill and see victory as important but hardly a necessity. That run-and-gun mentality, combined with the lack of a regimented youth-to-college pipeline, makes for unpredictable—and oft astonishing—play. Albany attack-man Ty Thompson's 2014 legendary goal against Siena—a lefty, he flipped the stick to his right and, on the move yet still casually, skipped the ball behind his back to score—was received in lacrosse circles as both revelatory and unsurprising. Such is the Iroquois way.

"Their body control is different," said two-time All-American Shamel Bratton. "How they use their stick as the release point is just really cool: stop, start, hesitation—so you almost always are on the defensive, because you don't want them to use your body weight against you. There's all sorts of craziness. And defensively it's very, very physical."

The Iroquois, in short, are a spectacle unlike any other. In 2006 Nike, the sports apparel giant famed for its edgy marketing, signed a sponsorship deal to supply the Nationals with $25,000 a year in cash, uniforms, footwear and equipment (renewed through 2028, the agreement now includes a "hefty" donation to the team's fundraising arm). The investment promised limited returns, until you factor in the psychic worth of slapping the Swoosh on a sports "brand" imbued with a millennium's worth of heroic rebellion, underclass mystique, a singular style.

Hard proof of the Iroquois Nationals' intrinsic appeal came in July 2010, when their first major passport controversy broke into view. Three days before departing New York for the World Championship in Manchester, England, the team was informed by Homeland Security and State Department officials that the United States would not—as requested by British authorities—guarantee the players' readmittance. Stuck in Manhattan, the Nationals got all the benefits of America's media capital: tabloid and *New York Times* stories, Times Square photo ops, coverage on National Public Radio. "You cannot buy that kind of publicity," then–Nationals executive director Percy Abrams said.

Hollywood director James Cameron, of *Titanic* and *Avatar* fame, donated $50,000 for expenses. Secretary of State Hillary Clinton rushed in to arrange a one-time waiver, fulfilling the British request, only to have the United Kingdom Borders Agency change tack and—citing "strengthened security measures"—declare it would not accept Haudenosaunee passports after all. "They pulled a bait and switch, and they got us," Abrams said. "Actually, that's pretty much the historical account of all the dealings between the British and Iroquois. That's how a lot of our treaties went so bad: they'd tell us one thing, and then we'd get the other when payment time comes."

Thus the Iroquois Nationals failed to play in England in 2010. FIL officials warned that the program's status was now on shaky ground. The players weren't cowed. "It is a win," said Nationals midfielder Brett Bucktooth. "We have to protect our identity. It's not only a cause for our team. It's the Haudenosaunee nation. That's who we're standing by, and that's who we are."

Four years later, the FIL was able to present a more serene picture. With the 2014 men's field World Championship staged in Denver—and, thus, Haudenosaunee passports not a point of contention—only the benefits of including the Iroquois Nationals were on display. There, in the city where Hall of Fame coach Bill Tierney had decamped to create lacrosse's newest western outpost, thousands of lacrosse fans celebrated the game's expansion and heritage, and witnessed its elite and Native constituencies advancing seemingly together. With defenders wielding wooden sticks, the Nationals beat Australia to win the bronze medal for the first time. All but the Aussies cheered.

It was a temporary peace. The Iroquois stance on passports remained hardcore—and their passports still didn't contain the security microchip required since 2009 in American and Canadian equivalents—and thus a burden for organizers. The Nationals' path to the 2011 Indoor World Championship in Prague had required 11 months of schmoozing, by a backchannel contact at the Czech Foreign Ministry, with officials in Ottawa and Washington. Their groundbreaking trip to Finland for the 2012 U-19 Worlds happened only because of inventive routing through Switzerland, a solution that nearly backfired when a visa glitch almost barred their entry into that country. Any overseas trip highlighted the trouble with fitting the Iroquois into the modern lacrosse context. The wonder is that anyone thought it could work at all.

Indeed, as they won more on the field, the Nationals exposed the limitations of athletics when it comes to answering any question beyond winning and losing. Jackie Robinson in 1947 and Muhammad Ali in 1967 used baseball and boxing as platforms for social change. But those were earthquakes; eventually their activism gave way to sport's prime imperative—excellence, performance, victory. In the Iroquois Nationals, Tom Hayes, Ron Balls and their international colleagues had absorbed a political dynamic intent on remaining permanent. The ILF of the 1980s was a small, all-volunteer organization with a four-team championship and vague visions about staging an event as broad as soccer's World Cup. Its ethos had nothing to do with addressing American wrongs. It was about expanding the market.

As the sport grew and its ambition expanded over the next three decades, the edges of its Iroquois paradox only sharpened. The Nationals overachieve and compete as hard as anyone, but their stated motivation is not supremacy.

This, for outsiders, is a puzzlement. At one level, the Iroquois players would love to be world champions. But the Haudenosaunee lacrosse ethos is spiritual, not athletic; as players, they take the field to "honor the Creator," to play with clean mind and body and spirit. Commitment to this higher calling—and the ad hoc budget and administration of the Nationals program—has made for a dismissively casual approach toward deadlines and requirements. In his first meeting as CEO with the FIL board in September 2017, Jim Scherr found the Iroquois response to his Olympic strategy bracing. "They said, 'Well, we're not going to comply with anti-doping the way other countries do,'" he said. "'We'll get our event entries in when we want to, because it's our time. We work on our time, not your time.'"

Once at a tournament, the Nationals' prime aim is trumpeting—and reinforcing—Haudenosaunee sovereignty. Any doubts about their priorities were answered whenever, passports in hand, Iroquois players surrendered the chance to compete for world titles and stayed home. En route to Israel in 2018, they were prepared to do so again. Though that crisis passed, and the Nationals made the Opening Ceremonies on time and delighted everyone with their remarkable first half against the US, the eternal tension between serving their mission and a sport's basic imperatives left "the Membership" exhausted. This became obvious a day later when FIL Secretary General Ron Balls, sitting in the West Lagoon Resort lobby, was asked what it was about the Haudenosaunee, in 1987, that convinced the game's leaders to say yes to the Iroquois Nationals.

It was a softball question, calling for a boilerplate reply, and Balls indeed spoke of the Iroquois' unique image, how it's "their game," invented 1,000 years ago and not "in England by kids in a park." He used words like "heritage" and "tradition." But before all that, Balls began with a caveat.

"Let me answer that in a moment," he said. "Let me just say this first. With hindsight? Look, 30 years later: We maybe should have said no."

THE HOLLYWOOD UPSET was not to be. If the Iroquois—with adrenaline surging, with the US back on its heels—had been able to play on, uninterrupted, maybe, riding on fumes, they could have pulled off the opening-night miracle in Israel. Instead, the Nationals went into their locker room at halftime, sat, toweled off, relaxed for the first time in days. Eyes glazed. Shoulders sagged. Ansley Jemison, the Nationals executive director and all-around Mr. Fix-It, took in the scene, his 23 players—the human version of a blackout. All energy was gone.

Because the Nationals flight had touched down so late, there had been no time to exchange currency, much less stock up on provisions. And in all their hours since at Netanya Stadium, the Iroquois had been drinking nothing but water. Jemison turned to the team's tournament liaison and thrust the little Israeli cash he had at him. "Run to the nearest gas station," Jemison said. "Grab whatever sports drinks, energy bars, fruit you see. Go!"

Fifteen minutes later, the liaison returned with two plastic bags full of Gatorade, bananas, anything he could grab. Players converged: it wasn't enough. They trudged back to the field.

Meanwhile, Jake Bernhardt's harangue in the US locker room, in which he demanded his teammates drop the "deer in-headlights" act, clearly worked: ESPN's Anish Shroff described the hopped-up pack emerging for the second half as looking "like a bear who missed breakfast." Compared to the inventive, free-flowing Iroquois and even the similarly box-raised Canadians, the methodical American style of one-on-one dodging, its top-down stress on error-free play, can seem thick-legged. But its force is undeniable, especially when roused.

Trevor Baptiste, the NCAA's all-time best faceoff man, proceeded to win five straight faceoffs; Schreiber and US attackmen Ryan Brown and Rob Pannell whirled and juked and carved open the eternally suspect Iroquois defense: after five goals in the first 40 minutes, the United States scored five straight in the next ten. By the fourth quarter the Americans had taken full control of the midfield, and things got so loose that, leading 13–8, Pannell completed an Iroquois-style pass, behind his head. The ball flew only slightly awry, but Head Coach John Danowski snapped, "I hate that shit!" Forty-two seconds later, Marcus Holman dropped in another: 14–8, USA. The pity stirred again, but only for those not watching closely.

"I saw a lot of those guys laughing—during the game," observed Mexico attackman Timothy Gonzales of the Iroquois. "Smiling—during the game. I was like, *How could you be fighting this hard, losing, and you're still smiling?* And then to realize that it's not about winning or losing: it's about that game and what it does for you. What it shows everybody."

The rest was academic. The Nationals produced one final gasp of brilliance with 11:30 to play when the 20-year-old Nanticoke—230 pounds, with a head so large that only a customized box helmet can contain it—shed defender Joel White with a cartoonish shove into the turf, then rocketed the ball in for the Nationals' final score. The US won, 17–9; on paper, it looked like every other American win. But it wasn't, and not just because, as Lyle Thompson said to a few reporters on the field after, "Twenty-four hours ago I wasn't expecting to be here."

Because then one asked him if he still planned to visit a Palestinian refugee camp. "I'm still looking into that, just looking after my own safety: I've got a family of my own," Thompson said. "But I'm someone who stands up. I want to stand up for what I believe in."

Then someone asked about the BDS movement's demand for an Iroquois boycott, the resulting divide among the Haudenosaunee. And as Thompson began to answer, it became clear that the conflicting pressures and fear of retaliation, the infusion of Arab-Israeli politics and violence, had imbued this lacrosse game—perhaps the entire tournament—with a context like no other.

"There's a lot of people looking at us coming here, and thinking it's a bad thing," Thompson said. "Even within us. And I hate that that's our look right now. I want to do something. I think if we didn't come, we're not helping ourselves and I don't know how much we're helping others, either. Because there's still a lot of people in the world that don't know what's going on—when it comes to Indigenous people, when it comes to what's going on with the Palestinian people. I didn't know about that until five days ago."

III

HE IS FLYING OVER US

THE BRAID COMES FIRST. This is not fair, athletically. When one considers Lyle Thompson, the most immediate thought should flash to his hands or vision, or the deceptive strength and quicksilver body control that creates space between himself and the most dogged defender, freeing up arms and stick for one of the deadliest shots in history. But no: jet-black, snaking two feet out the back of his helmet, whipping on his follow-through like a third arm, Thompson's braid is lacrosse's most striking personal brand. Few realize that the shorthand term, "braid," also encompasses the shaved sides of his head, the thick "Mohawk" patch growing atop and back, the grim backstory of its original name.

"Scalplock," explained Oren Lyons in 2010, when his own free-flowing ponytail was near white. "To make it easier for them to scalp you." The Iroquois braid, with its built-in handle for yanking, began as a warrior's cocky challenge. "You want it?" Lyons said. "You come and get it."

For casual spectator and lacrosse aficionado, and anyone vexed by the game's history of white appropriation, Thompson's braid makes things easy in a different way. It is a comfort. The scalplock sweep across his back is a signal that all is not lost; the Indigenous still have a grip on their game. That effect holds for his brothers Jeremy, Jerome "Hiana" Jr., and Miles Thompson—or any other braided Haudenosaunee—but to a lesser extent. Because Lyle Thompson is the best.

No Native player, in any era, ever so dominated lacrosse's prestige circuit—the American collegiate game. As a junior at Albany in 2014, Lyle totaled 51 goals and 77 assists in 18 games to break the NCAA single-season record with 128 points. Miles, his teammate and Tewaaraton Award co-winner that year, checked in just behind with 119; the next year, Lyle's 121 points pushed his brother down to number three on the all-time rankings. He is one of two men to win the Tewaaraton Award twice. His 400 career points stood as the NCAA Division I men's record until 2022, when Chris Gray reached 401 during a graduate season at North Carolina. As a professional in both indoors and field, Lyle has won championships and Most Valuable Player honors. His game has a habit of defying description.

"I don't even know if he's a once-in-a-generation: He's a once-in-a-*generations* type," said Kyle Harrison. "He's a chameleon. I hear defenders talk about this all the time, like: *There's no way to cover him* . . . Because Lyle's so skilled. He typically doesn't carry the stick left-handed—ever. Force him left, he carries it in one hand and shoots backhanded. So then try to push him the other way: now you're pushing him to his strong hand. It's just a mess."

"Such a good combination of strongest, fastest, toughest—however you want to word that," said Steele Stanwick, the 2011 Tewaaraton winner, NCAA champion and all-time points leader at the University of Virginia. "Great balance. Lyle's so deceptively strong. He's six feet, maybe 180 pounds, but when he decides to lower his shoulder or body up or go to the goal, he turns into almost like a six-four, 220-pound type guy. His skills are just off the charts in terms of passing, shooting, his accuracy, lacrosse IQ."

But overall, Lyle is best seen as the supreme expression of Thompson family values. His father, Jerome "Ji" Thompson Sr., played for the Nationals' first World Championship team in 1990; his mother's father, Leon Shenandoah Jr., was renowned for his speed. Daily backyard play honed Lyle's skills, and the mixed-bag experiences of Jeremy and Miles at Syracuse and Albany, respectively, smoothed Lyle's path to college.

For the greater sports world, rankings obsessed and recency biased, pronouncing Lyle the purest distillate of Iroquois lacrosse is tempting, especially after hearing Haudenosaunee voices chime in. But, Oren Lyons said, "I'd have a hard time. Sid Hill's grandfather, Isaac Hill, had a game leg, but I never saw a stickhandler like that. He wasn't about speed; he would go through those hard checks at a hobbled trot, but get the ball in. He was amazing. But that's just one. It's the same with Jim Brown and Jim Thorpe, each in their era. Every generation has a great player."

The memories of elders aside, Indigenous lacrosse history before 1980, field or box, remains one of sport's shadow tales, unheard by a wider world entranced by Babe Ruth, Muhammad Ali and Michael Jordan. It's only along the word-of-mouth pipeline from the New York reservations to Six Nations of the Grand River in Canada that the names get famous: Oliver Hill Sr., Ross Powless and his son Gaylord, defender Edward Shenandoah, all-around great Leroy Shenandoah. Syracuse lacrosse founder Laurie Cox supposedly called Oren Lyons Sr. the best goalie he'd ever seen; legend also had him, a star for the Syracuse Red Devils in the early 1930s, dancing the Charleston on a three-inch beam 100 feet above a steel mill floor. The Mohawk great of the early 1940s, Angus Thomas, reputedly had a shot so hard that it killed two goalies. But no one can tell you their names.

Few highlights exist, even, of Jim Brown, Lyons's teammate at Syracuse. Conventional wisdom has it that Brown never once got knocked off his feet on a lacrosse field. But at Onondaga they still talk about the day future chief Irving Powless Jr.—a 155-pound "mosquito," as Brown later described him—laid him out with a hip check. Unlike field, box lacrosse allows hitting regardless of possession; Brown had never played box before. "Of course the place went wild," said former Syracuse coach Roy Simmons Jr. "Jim was a little angry. But he caught on in a hurry, and never left his feet the rest of the day. He just destroyed 'em."

Haudenosaunee lacrosse minds, like fans of any sport, love recycling such lore. But greatest-of-all-time questions find little traction; you might get an answer, but the disinterest is palpable. Asked if she ever envisioned her sons growing up to be such good players, Lyle's mother—Dee Thompson—said, "I still don't think they are."

"The way we play, the way that my boys play this game, it's medicine for us," Ji Thompson said. "One of the first things I told them: The front of the jersey and the back of the jersey don't mean nothing. You're playing for the Creator. So you play as hard as you can. Go out there and just play and have fun, because that's the medicine that you need to communicate, that you've got to spread."

ONCE, THE CONCEPT OF lacrosse as "medicine" was as broad as the Iroquois empire. Before the 19th century, *Dey Hon Tshi Gwa' Ehs* (popularly translated from Onondaga as "They Bump Hips") or *Tewaaraton* (Mohawk for "lacrosse") was a brutal battlefield proxy used to settle tribal differences: "a game," as anthropologist and historian William N. Fenton wrote, "that anciently discharged social tensions." Massive gatherings involving anywhere from 100 to 1,000 men would contest a game over days on a field with goals spread up to two miles apart. But the fade of tribal conflict and introduction, in 1799, of the prophet Handsome Lake's Longhouse religion reinvigorated the sport's ancient role of mental repair and spiritual passage. The Medicine Games played now to help men struggling with depression are nothing new; Fenton references one staged to "cheer" Handsome Lake himself after the last of his four epochal visions, just before his death at Onondaga in 1815. After dying, the first thing an Iroquois soul does after crossing over to the "Skyworld" is grab a stick.

"You'll be playing again that day," says Oren Lyons. "And you will be the captain."

Each spring, at Onondaga, a Medicine Game is played for the health of all players, the traditional way: An unlimited number of males from seven to 70 range about; one or two feather-festooned poles jammed in the ground on opposing ends form the goals; first team to score three wins. Only wooden sticks are allowed.

"The mecca in Baltimore, or Maryland, where they make all the rules for white lacrosse, American lacrosse? We don't care what they say," said stickmaker Alfie Jacques. "We play our [Medicine] game, our way: no center line, no faceoff circle, no restraining line, no out-of-bounds in any direction, no crease, no net on the goal, no referee."

Over a year, anywhere from 10 to 16 Medicine Games take place. Any male can call for one to deal with personal strife, and only males can play; a runner contacts the players, and the food and a deerskin ball are pieced together that day. The caller usually doesn't play, but he keeps the ball. "The ball is the medicine," Lyons said.

The stick, meanwhile, carries a power that is both medicinal and metaphoric. White fans dwell on wood's antique look and feel, how it hearkens a rougher game and time, as if it's little more than a throwback jersey. "The wooden stick has always been talked about, but people don't understand that it's almost an obsession," said Rex Lyons:

Why? Because of the spiritual connection: it just consumes you. With that wooden stick, there's so much instruction: The stick is hickory. Our water comes out of the hickory tree, too; it's the heartbeat of our people, our nation, and there's a ceremony—we plant these trees and there's a real process. Water is not a resource: This is something that we respect and we replenish it and we have extreme reverence for.

And in that netting, you have the deer, which represents the four-legs; the deer is [found] on all continents, that's why he's the leader of the animals. And in the weave: That's the clans; they're all woven together. Which means you need everybody. *It's all-inclusive. Everything is connected. It's so fundamental: That stick, what it represents, comes from something that we are absolutely dependent upon. We're not superior just because we have a certain amount of intellect.*

Describing this blend of the metaphysical and the athletic is hard even for the Iroquois. Each participant's experience is wholly subjective. Subtleties, especially to confused sportswriters, can get lost in translation. Ji Thompson is adamant that it's not right to say one "calls" for a Medicine Game. He says the ball itself, being medicine, somehow "comes to" the needful man, who then organizes the game. Revealing any more than that makes Ji edgy. Describing the sensation of playing in a Medicine Game makes him grin.

"You kind of feel invincible," he says. "They say when you score one of the goals that it's going to be a good year; it's special for you to score those. Because we don't play with any gloves, and even the little kids play, and there is no rules . . . you've got so much energy."

Ji believes the "clear mind" created by the Medicine Game, not talent, is the source of his sons' success. "That energy that my boys carry when they play is that same energy. Because they don't give up. I can tell when they're hurt, and they're still out there playing. It's crazy."

Some of that is inherited. A second-generation ironworker, Ji—Mohawk, Wolf clan—had been raised on the borderline reservation at Akwesasne speaking only Mohawk. His tongue faded once he moved three hours south, in the public elementary school outside the Onondaga reservation near Syracuse. Though his parents weren't hardcore traditional, in middle school he began studying at the Longhouse and attending ceremonies. White kids sniped. Ji fought. Midway through his time at LaFayette High, he began growing his hair long. His parents didn't like it, but "when I get committed to something," Ji said, "I just don't stop."

LIKE AFRICAN AMERICANS and Latinos, the Haudenosaunee are far more varied, culturally, than white-imposed ethnic categories assume. Handsome Lake's Longhouse faith, for example, is a foundational influence in Iroquois lacrosse, reinforced by the prominence of Oren Lyons and the Thompson brothers, and a dominant reference point in tribal and mainstream media. But estimates of Longhouse adherents among the Six Nations top out at 50 percent; as an organized faith Christianity, introduced by French missionaries to the Iroquois in 1654, has deep roots. The difference is that Longhouse faith is organic, and dovetails seamlessly with the modern causes of Haudenosaunee pride and sovereignty. Unlike Christianity, it isn't walled off as a personal matter. Much in the manner of Judaism and the state of Israel, the Longhouse faith braids inseparably into almost any discussion of nationhood, politics, identity and sports. Like lacrosse, like the scalplock—it serves the larger message. *We are still here. And our traditions prevail.*

Such internal divisions among the Haudenosaunee are typical. During the American Revolution, the Oneida and Tuscarora sided with the colonists while the Seneca, Cayuga, Onondaga and Mohawk remained unofficial British allies. Centuries of wrangling with the US and Canada created two seats of Iroquois power, at the Syracuse-area reserve at Onondaga and the Ontario-area Six Nations of the Grand River. The confederacy is also split over Native America's most famous and lucrative business: casinos. Four of the six nations support some form of gambling, as well as two of the three tribes of Seneca. But the Tonawanda band of Seneca, Tuscarora and Onondaga— home of Iroquoia's traditional capital, the Grand Council of Chiefs, and its supreme leader, the Tadadaho—forbid it.

In 2005, even while pronouncing that each individual nation should decide the issue for itself—thus allowing gambling—the Grand Council declared the Haudenosaunee people philosophically, politically and "morally opposed to casino gambling and high stakes bingo within the territory of the Haudenosaunee," according to the statement signed by Tadadaho Sidney Hill. "Our Original Instructions, Great Law of Peace and Spiritual

Teachings are very clear on this matter. Our way of life is predicated upon values and beliefs that will be undermined by the greed and corruption that casinos bring."

Such a straddle seems less contradictory when the Iroquois Confederacy is viewed as an alliance, not a union of states; each nation is free to forge its own path. But it does speak to the conflicted nature—at least, tactically—of the Haudenosaunee today, and the political primacy of Onondaga. This, too, is not new. Picture a mythical bear claw slicing five vertical swaths down the center of New York state: That's the territorial map of the Iroquois Confederacy in the 16th century. Its rectangular form resembles a longhouse, with the "Western Door" guarded by Seneca, rolling east to Cayuga territory, then Onondaga, then Oneida, ending with the Mohawk in the east. Since the first Tadadaho was Onondaga, only an Onondaga can be Tadadaho. The Onondaga keep the council fire burning. The Onondaga control 14 seats in the 50-man Grand Council; no other nation has more than 10. The Tuscarora were absorbed as the sixth nation in 1722, but—another incongruity—have no formal representation at the Grand Council and must ask permission to speak.

Today, Onondaga's singular identity stems far less from structure than from attitude. No Iroquois nation is more strident in its traditionalist beliefs, embrace of the Longhouse doctrine, and refusal to brook the slightest encroachment on its sovereignty by the United States. Unlike most Native entities the Onondaga government, as it proudly states on its website, "does not pay income, sales, or excise taxes to New York State or to the US federal government, nor does it receive any of the benefits paid for by these taxes." The Onondaga also refuse to take part in the US Census; they laugh at "official" population counts—1,473 in 2000, 2,244 in 2010, 831 in 2020—for their 7,300-acre reservation. In 2015, when the US Department of Housing and Urban Development gave $6 million in housing grants to Native American groups in New York state, the Onondaga and Tuscarora nations and the Tonawanda band of Seneca turned down their shares. Offered $800,000, the Oneida did accept $200,000.

For the Onondaga, especially, that was $200,000 too much. Handsome Lake inveighed against alcohol and gambling as moral hazards, but Onondaga's opposition to the latter is also about independence. State oversight of casinos requires Indigenous nations to submit to New York–issued regulations, fines and subpoenas, and allow state officials to investigate employees and maintain a 24-hour presence on their territory. "Are you nuts, or what?" Oren Lyons says.

It's not rare to hear members of the other five nations dismiss Onondaga as too extreme. But, in the lacrosse world, no family epitomizes the challenges and triumphs of the modern Haudenosaunee experience like the Thompsons, and for Ji—a Mohawk, "hungry for a lot of tradition"—the Onondaga territory outside Syracuse instantly felt like home. His wife, Dee—Onondaga, Wolf clan—is the granddaughter of Leon Shenandoah Sr., the Six Nations Tadadaho who, in 1983, defied the US government by providing sanctuary for American Indian Movement co-founder—and fugitive—Dennis Banks at the Onondaga reservation. Three years later Ji and Dee married. Jeremy, Hiana, Miles and Lyle arrived in quick succession. The family moved to Akwesasne in 1990, and the oldest two spent their elementary years immersed in the Mohawk language program at the Freedom School. When the family returned to Onondaga in 1997, neither could read or write English.

All four received a cradle stick at birth. With Ji's time consumed by ironwork and play for the Akwesasne Thunder—a box team in Canada's Senior B division, with which he won President Cup titles in 1995 and '97—Dee was left to introduce lacrosse basics. There was only one line she could not cross. Within the Longhouse belief system, a woman's power—especially during menstruation, or "moon time"—is considered so strong that it can strip objects of their medicinal property.

"We weren't allowed to have the girls touch our wooden sticks," Jeremy said. "To us here in Onondaga, how it's a Medicine Game for the men, not the women, we took that real strong. In my family, we weren't allowed to have our mothers touch our sticks. If it was on the ground, my mom would leave it there. She wouldn't touch it. She knew, and my sister knew."

"Women do pick up a stick if they're plastic," Dee said. "I picked up their plastic sticks. But sometimes I wouldn't even pick that up, just because."

The Thompson boys played, together, all day in the backyard, where Ji built a standard six-by-six-foot goal and a plywood cover with a sharpshooter hole barely bigger than a lacrosse ball. The boys peppered it with hundreds of thousands of shots. Ji drilled them on faceoffs, dodges, picks, behind-the-back shooting, tailoring his lessons to each son's talent.

At birth each Haudenosaunee is given a name by a clan mother. It rarely lines up literally with who they become, never mind their style of lacrosse. Jeremy, an inexhaustible bull at midfield, was named *Gaä Gwa Gyehe*—meaning "the sun is leaning." The name of Hiana, a lefty marksman who works best reacting to teammates, is short for *Susquehanna*, "large treetop." Miles, slower afoot but possessing great hands, is *Giaehgwaeh*, or "he strikes the sun." Only the name for Lyle, the freeform genius, seemed to preordain greatness: *Deyhahsanoondey*—"he is flying over us."

But that didn't become evident for years. The boys had to get through adolescence first. In the late 1990s Ji was determined to keep the family close and the world—inside and outside Onondaga—at bay. Of all ethnic groups in the US, Native Americans have the highest rates of alcohol, cocaine, marijuana, inhalant and hallucinogen use disorders. Ji knew too many lacrosse talents and bright minds lost to drugs, lassitude, fear of life off the rez. He himself started drinking at 25 and stopped, during the family stint in Akewesasne, at 30. Every morning since, he has performed a small ceremony of thanksgiving to the Creator. No drinking or smoking was allowed in their Onondaga home.

"The people that we were around, that partied? We would go to birthday parties and this and that, and the booze would come out," Ji said. "We would tell them: 'As soon as the booze comes out, we're leaving.'"

"Even if they were to pull out a cigarette and smoke?" Dee said. "We would pull the kids out."

Ji never thought he could control his boys for life. But maybe bribery would get them to 18. "Get through high school without doing drugs or alcohol," he told them, "and I'll buy your first car."

There was little money to spare. In the early 2000s, Ji began building the family's two-story house at Onondaga between eight hours of ironwork, an hour commute, his own lacrosse practices and games. First came the cellar, dug out and capped off; the family moved underground, four boys in one bedroom. No running water, electricity by generator: they survived the Syracuse winters with a woodstove, ran a fridge with portable propane, stocked with deer that Ji shot himself. Night after night, he came home exhausted, ate supper, went outside, turned on the car headlights, and hand-dug the driveway out of a four-foot hill. Over the next 15 years, Ji framed and wired and built the home above their heads, 90 percent on his own. Dee and the boys hauled and drywalled and hammered.

"We kind of forced ourselves into staying as a family," Ji says:

I say the greatest thing you can give your child is your time, and there's so much truth to that. If you spend the time with them, they'll act more like you than they will everybody else. We did everything together; we went to the laundromat. There were some bad times. You can call it poverty, and most people will think of that as a negative. I don't see it. Because I've lived it, we've lived it and so many positive things have come from it.

All the things that we gave up as parents to make it better for our kids? Believe it or not, they were spoiled. They still are, I think.

When the eldest boys dropped into the public school system in LaFayette, three miles south of Onondaga, both required hours of daily tutoring. Jeremy repeated sixth grade, and was diagnosed with multiple learning disabilities. Any dreams of playing together at Syracuse died when he and Hiana, both All-Americans at LaFayette High, failed three times to score the minimum SAT score required to play Division I sports.

Miles and Lyle's academic climb was less steep, but it came with a full-immersion dunk into white America. Only 12 percent of the students in the LaFayette school system, then, were Native American. The Thompsons' conspicuously braided hair exposed them to questions, stares, ridicule. Into high school Lyle, with what he calls "an easy switch," often responded with flying fists.

Compared to his forebears, he had it easy. Both of Thompson's grandfathers had been forced as boys to attend residential schools, part of the system created in 1879 at the Carlisle Indian Industrial School in Pennsylvania by US Army captain Richard Henry Pratt, and summed up by his infamous words: "Kill the Indian, and save the man." By the mid-1970s, tens—and possibly hundreds—of thousands of Indigenous children had been run through a loose American network of more than 500 boarding schools that banned Native language, religion and clothing; forbade Indian names; and were rife with physical, psychological and sexual abuse. Canada's counterpart, which lasted from 1880 until 1996, essentially kidnapped 150,000 First Nations children to "civilize" and educate them in Christianity and Western mores. On both sides of the border, forcibly cutting the hair of Native children was considered a symbolic step, cultural murder's first strike.

"I do not recall whether the barber noticed my agitation or not, nor did I care," Luther Standing Bear, a member of Carlisle's inaugural class, said of his tears that day in 1879. "All I was thinking about was that hair he had taken away from me . . . I felt that I was no more Indian, but would be an imitation of a white man."

In effect, if not intent, Ji and Dee's parenting repudiated that history. Haircuts were about pride and love. When the boys were in need of a trim—a few inches, maybe twice a year—Dee made sure to do so only when the moon was full. "Our hair was part of who we are, but it's also a connection with another being—with the moon," Lyle said. "In Native American culture, that's one of the things that we give thanks for. We have these connections with all the beings: the winds, the trees, the animals, the sun, the moon, the stars. There's a real spiritual aspect to it, so really there was a connection from my hair to the moon."

Afterward, the clipped hair was either burned for "protection medicine," or taken outside and scattered into the air and earth. "Never once did we throw it in the garbage," Lyle said. "That was another spiritual aspect, where it was more than just hair, more than just your identity."

Each morning in the half-finished house, the Thompsons viscerally reinforced their ties, braiding each other's hair before setting off for LaFayette High and Middle School. By then the basic dynamic had shifted: Jeremy and Hiana, closest in age, were drifting apart, and Lyle and Jeremy would team up in the backyard games against Hiana and Miles.

Lyle worshipped Jeremy, had similar midfield skills; he liked to tell everyone that they were twins. Their bond grew even stronger after Jeremy shoved Hiana's head through a car window and broke his jaw their senior year, ruining LaFayette's hopes of a third state championship. The two barely spoke for a year after that. Each morning they would slide past each other, never lock eyes. Hiana wouldn't let Jeremy anywhere near his hair.

JI BOUGHT JEREMY his car under false pretenses. The eldest Thompson child had his first taste of alcohol at 14, fell in with drinkers while playing box up at Six Nations of the Grand River at 15, and managed to keep his binges secret. But once the dream of playing at Syracuse got sidetracked to Onondaga Community College, something snapped; his "bad twin," as

Jeremy calls negative impulses, overwhelmed the good. Neither his play freshman year—42 goals, 26 assists—nor winning the 2007 junior college national championship, nor patching up things with Hiana, helped. Jeremy snuck mini bottles of liquor into his room, suffered from alcohol poisoning twice, tried Oxycontin and began "smoking up."

Later that year, nearing his 21st birthday, Jeremy realized that he was spiraling fast. He asked his unsuspecting mom to ride with him the three hours up to Akwesasne, then to accompany him to a class. "It was some kind of healing," Dee says. "He spoke in front of a good 50 people and admitted that he was drinking—and I was shocked. I told him that I was proud of him for being able to realize what he was doing at a young age, trying to get help."

A year off from school, and numerous vision quests—four-day ritual fasts in the woods—were needed for Jeremy to take hold of his addiction; he returned for a second year at Onondaga Community College, won another JC national championship with Hiana in 2009. His brothers were wary. "I was at this age where I looked up to Jeremy a crazy amount and then I found out he does stuff like that, and I didn't like him," Lyle said.

"Our family's so close that we're able to learn from one another, like it was our own experience. Me and my brothers watched what Jeremy went through; we paid attention to him and to how much it stressed out my parents. So me, Hiana, Miles: we've never touched any drugs, had a sip of alcohol. It was never hard for me to say no to that."

Free of booze for nearly a year, in the fall of 2009 Jeremy finally arrived at Syracuse. It was a towering achievement, considering the alternatives. Nearly one in 10 Native Americans die of causes related to alcohol. Hiana's grades sank and he quit Onondaga Community College. In 2008 one of their teammates, Kent Squire-Hill, strangled his pregnant girlfriend and was later convicted and imprisoned for murder. Though Syracuse's campus is but 10 miles away, the psychological distance from Onondaga can be immense; Oren Lyons's partnership with Jim Brown provided a famous template, but the Haudenosaunee lacrosse pipeline flowed grudgingly. Overall, only 28 percent of Native Americans between 18 and 24 years old attend college. Only 17 percent of Native Americans attain a bachelor's degree or higher.

"We're always thinking back home is more important," Jeremy said in 2010. "That's the problem we have nowadays in getting kids off and going to college. They don't want to leave the family or the reserve, and another big part is the drugs and alcohol. They have no way of finding themselves. We don't have that connection, the role models, somebody there to direct them the right way."

Jeremy began a summer program teaching kids the Onondaga language and ceremonies at the Onondaga Nation School, tried to serve as an example. He wasn't alone at Syracuse; fellow OCC teammate and Six Nations star Cody Jamieson, as well as fellow Iroquois National Pierce Abrams, provided a Native cadre. Meanwhile, Syracuse head coach John Desko, who'd played and coached for Roy Simmons Jr. before becoming head coach in 1999—and winning five national titles over the next decade—seemed sympathetic. Upon arrival, Jeremy informed Desko that he'd miss more than a week of fall training because of a vision quest.

"I'm sitting here going, 'Whooo. Interesting,'" Desko said. "But another coach? 'Screw that, fast on your own time! Miss practice and you're done.' When he came back he couldn't practice right away. How many Division I–level places, when coaches are worried about winning and getting fired because they don't have enough wins, understand that?"

Jeremy's Division I career began with a delicious bang. Late in the first quarter of the 2010 season opener against Denver, he took just six seconds to win a faceoff, loop his stick over his opponent's head, race to the goal, fake a pass and skip the ball in for his first score with the Orange. In the stands, his younger brothers cheered. Ji stood grinning in his new college shirt, one that placed a big S on his chest. The Thompsons were a Syracuse family at last.

IN THE WORLD of lacrosse, at that time, no university came close to Syracuse's lock on Native talent. The connection traced back to the 1930s, and stars like goalie Travis Solomon, who anchored the Orange's first NCAA title in 1983, three-time All-American Marshall Abrams in the late 1990s, and 2009 national champion defenseman Sid Smith had kept it current. For at least a decade, every Orange roster had had at least one Native player. One reason: Since 2006 Syracuse has offered a free four-year undergraduate education—the Haudenosaunee Promise Scholarship—to any qualifying Iroquois student. This also gives the lacrosse program a competitive edge: A player awarded a Promise Scholarship does not count against the 12.6 scholarships allowed each Division I team by the NCAA.

Heading into Lyle's junior year at LaFayette High, 2009–2010, it had become clear that the youngest Thompson boys were lacrosse savants. Miles, a year older, was a superb attackman—95 goals and 56 assists in just 24 games the previous spring. Observers rated Lyle even higher. One play against Cazenovia his sophomore year was typical: Working the left wing, stick in his right hand, Lyle froze his defender by swinging it across his chest to his left, then behind his back to his right—all on the move—then sliced between two more opponents who, closing too late, collided comically behind him as he coiled to shoot. The goalie had no chance.

Ji made it clear that the youngest Thompson boys were a package deal: Whoever signed Miles for 2010 would get Lyle for 2011. And in October of 2009, two-and-a-half hours away at the University at Albany (SUNY Albany, the remote campus servicing 17,000 undergrads in New York's public university system)—where, since 2001, Head Coach Scott Marr had been crafting a Division I program far from the rarefied plain occupied by Hopkins, Princeton, Duke and, yes, Syracuse, dominating the obscure America East conference and getting passed over for coaching vacancies at marquee programs like Yale and Maryland—Marr was sitting in his spacious office with assistant coaches Chris Kivlen and Bill Ralph, discussing every prospect at the upcoming Turkeyshoot recruiting showcase. Except the nation's top two.

"Scottie," Ralph said to his old high school teammate. "Why are we *not* going after these guys?"

Recruiting Miles and Lyle Thompson had not even crossed Marr's mind. His program was built around Canadians and hard-nosed kids from Central New York; he had never been to Onondaga Reservation, never tried to land any Haudenosaunee. Ralph, 41 years old and fresh from coaching college club teams in Tennessee, had no experience with Indigenous talent, either. But like all good recruiters, he figured that any uninterested kid just hadn't met him yet. And Marr indulged him.

Ralph drove to Ithaca and sat in the cold and rain at the Turkeyshoot to meet Ji Thompson. Tickling the fact that many former Native players at Syracuse, Promise Scholarship and all, hadn't graduated, Ralph stressed education, and how the Albany coaching staff would work hard to ensure Ji's sons got their diplomas. He also became one of the first to pick up on the Thompson family's unhappiness with Syracuse.

To the public, all seemed well: Jeremy started every game at Syracuse, led the Big East in faceoff winning percentage his junior year and all of

Desko's midfielders in scoring his senior, earning a Tewaaraton nomination and All-American honors. But outside the family, few knew that Jeremy had lost his longtime girlfriend his junior year; inside, nobody knew that he then relapsed with alcohol. Jeremy also admits feeling frustrated by Desko's system, and left the program believing, he said, that "I got held back as a player." His younger brothers agreed.

"I remembered seeing him in high school and he was unstoppable, and he goes to college and he's jumping from first to second line and not getting a bunch of reps," Lyle said. "To me, that was, like, *I don't want to go there.*"

Over the next two years, Marr drove countless hours in the fall and spring to attend Miles and Lyle's LaFayette High games; he often was the only Division I coach in the stands. Of the elite Division I powers, only Virginia head coach Dom Starsia and Maryland's Dave Cottle showed real interest. Orange disinterest, according to Roy Simmons III, Desko's longtime director of operations, stemmed from Miles's lack of fitness and both brothers' academic struggles. The snub still stirs rage in Onondaga. But it did make for an easy decision.

"Syracuse is in my backyard, and all they did was send me one letter," Lyle said. "Coach Marr made me feel like I was wanted."

AND YET, even if Syracuse had lavished attention, it might not have mattered. Albany's weak roster promised that the Thompson brothers would play instantly. And Lyle, for one, knew that he needed to play and win and be a star—or he'd never make it academically. He'd seen his brother. Jeremy never did earn his diploma from Syracuse.

"It came down to . . . I don't know if you call it a Native American 'issue,' but it's what we do: When you see Natives go to these bigger schools, they don't stick with it," Lyle said. "And if they don't stick with lacrosse, they end up dropping out, because lacrosse is their thing, their number-one reason. That's what we're brought up on."

When Miles committed, sight unseen, to Albany in November 2009—accompanied by Lyle's verbal pledge to later join him—they were still considered flight risks. To keep it enticing, Marr went all-in on Native talent, signing their cousin Ty Thompson, Oneida goalie Edmund Cathers and Six Nations midfielder Mike Miller. It wasn't enough. Ji and Miles were both miserable at Miles's drop-off for freshman year; an hour into the trip back to Onondaga, Ji heard Creedence Clearwater Revival's "Have You Ever Seen the Rain?" on the car radio and buckled. It took everything he had not to make a U-turn.

"If I'd turned around, he would've never went," Ji says. "It was one of the hardest things for Miles to go to Albany without Lyle. There's a lot of things that he wasn't ready for."

It was no less nerve-wracking for Marr. Miles was out of shape and the team struggled in 2010, mostly because of Marr's commitment to open up the Great Danes' offense. He knew: Keeping the Thompsons happy meant allowing all the behind-the-back flair, the free-flowing play deemed "reckless" in a college lax universe that had come to prize mistake-free play. Miles made plenty of mistakes. But no matter how much fans, other parents and lax experts grumbled, Marr made no move to reel him in.

Because in reality, Marr's commitment not just to the Thompsons, but to remaking Albany lacrosse into a Native American showcase, was the result of a vision strange and intense and exceedingly personal, one that he had been waiting more than three decades to realize. One night in August of 1988, Marr—19 years old, an attackman for Johns Hopkins, number 24, part of its 1987 national championship team—broke into Baltimore's Memorial Stadium. Baseball's Orioles played there. Marr was alone. He lay down behind Seat 24 in Section 24, and—in his mind—saw a ghostly, jostling mass of Haudenosaunee men playing lacrosse in the air above the ballfield.

"A Medicine Game," Marr said. "Being played for me."

He was ill then, but didn't know it. Since June Marr had been working at a bar, selling T-shirts on the side, amassing thousands of dollars in cash, all the while churning in an extended manic episode marked by extremes of spending, emotion, energy. He barely slept. He felt almighty, tapped into the universe. The godfather of the program at Yorktown High, Charlie Murphy, had Native pictures and books all around his house, knew of the Iroquois game—maybe that planted the seed. Marr saw himself playing with ancient Haudenosaunee, meeting Pilgrims, feeling the White Man's impact.

Summer wore on, and his brain raced and Marr would clamber over rowhouse rooftops and stare at the sky. Getting inside Memorial Stadium was the final peak, the end: A watchman called police and they found Marr lying on the cement and shackled him up, notified Johns Hopkins. They were putting him in a paddy wagon when Head Coach Don Zimmerman and a couple of assistants showed up.

Then came the crash. Marr was diagnosed with bipolar I disorder, spent three months hospitalized. Doctors modulated his dosages of lithium, trying to get the right balance. Marr has taken medication ever since. The mania has never recurred. But a year after his release from the hospital, November 1989, Marr went to a parlor in Baltimore, and got the first of three Native tattoos on his shoulders, a brave with a lacrosse stick.

He told very few. But Marr felt something stir when he began as an assistant coach at Delaware in 1992, and found himself teaching the game's basics to Oneida kids at a clinic in snowy Wisconsin. He felt it again during his six years as an assistant at Maryland, whenever lacrosse's rich, white vibration became too overwhelming. He felt it strongest a few years after he took over as head coach at Albany in 2001, when he saw Jeremy and Hiana play at LaFayette High and his teenage vision blended for the first time with the Onondaga out on the field.

"Seeing the game that I knew in my head and watching them play, it was like, *Wow, it would be really cool to have* that, *be part of that*," Marr said. "Because to me that's what the game is. It's their game."

EVERY WEEKEND of Miles's freshman year at Albany was touch-and-go. Every Friday of his first fall, Miles went home to Onondaga. Every Sunday night Marr found himself praying for Miles's return. The Thompson home had its own stresses. Hoping to replace his chemistry with Miles with a pair of childhood buddies, for senior year Lyle had transferred to a high school outside Akwesasne, found himself failing a class needed for admission to Albany and pulled out. After returning to LaFayette High, he learned that his girlfriend—and future wife, Amanda, was pregnant. Though Lyle's SAT score, combined with a 2.0 grade point average, placed him just above the NCAA's minimum requirement for Division 1-A athletes, admission to Albany—along with Miles's presence—was becoming shaky. After reviewing Lyle's transcript, one admission official told Marr, "He's not a college student. He's not going to make it."

Meanwhile, between games and Amanda's pregnancy and classes, Lyle also had to prep for the New York State High School Regents exams required for graduation. None scared him more than trig. "I needed trigonometry to get into Albany," Lyle said. "Nabil is what got me in."

Nabil Akl, son of a Palestinian mother and Lebanese father and then a sophomore, invited Lyle to work with his tutor. Every couple weeks Lyle would go to the Akl home in nearby Jamesville, where the instructor and Nabil tirelessly explained theory and problems. Afterward, waiting for Ji to pick him up, Lyle and Nabil would play catch. Ji taught Nabil one of Lyle's faceoff moves, a block that ended up securing Akl a Division I roster spot.

Arriving at Albany in the fall of 2011, Lyle was distracted by Amanda and the coming baby, living far away. After giving birth to their daughter, Godehaot, Amanda moved in with Lyle in his dorm room. The baby slept in a drawer; roommate Derrick Eccles, a freshman midfielder, somehow endured. All that year, Lyle and Miles discussed transferring to Hobart or Canisius. The team finished the 2012 season with five wins and 11 losses.

Then all the angst and uncertainty began to pay off. In 2013 Marr moved Lyle from midfield to attack and ceded all offensive control to him, a trimmed-down Miles, and cousin Ty. The team's white and Native cohorts—after two years of coolness and stilted conversations—united at a February scrimmage at Cornell, when an opponent hammered Lyle with a dicey check, Albany's Jon Newhouse retaliated, and senior defenseman Anthony Ostrander bellowed in full Long Island accent, "No fuckin' *way* anybody's hittin' our brothers like that!"

Albany was primed. A week later the Great Danes opened at 13th-ranked Syracuse, near Onondaga, and it was a Thompson family affair: Miles scored the opening goal, Ty connected on a behind-the-backer to make it 4–0, Lyle flipped his sixth assist on Miles's game-winner; the trio combined for 10 goals and assisted on four others as Albany beat the Orange for the first time, 16–15, in double overtime. The upset reverberated across the sport. Syracuse had done everything right: dominated on faceoffs, outshot Albany, won the majority of groundballs. But decades had passed—back, ironically, to the days of Roy Simmons Jr.'s revolutionary run-and-gun at Syracuse—since collegiate lacrosse had seen such a freeform attack. In April, Albany traveled to Homewood Field and took down another blueblood, Marr's alma mater, 10th-ranked Hopkins, 10–9. By then no Division I team was scoring more than Albany's 15.11 goals per game. Lyle finished the season with 50 goals and 113 points in 18 games—one of only eight 100-point men in NCAA history—just one shy of the then-all-time record. The Great Danes lost in the first round of the 2013 NCAA tournament, but few doubted that a new force had arrived.

In 2014, Albany established itself as a Top 15 mainstay as Lyle and Miles broke new ground as teammates, brothers and Native Americans, becoming the first Indigenous winners and first co-winners of the Tewaaraton Award. The Great Danes upset No.1 Loyola in the first round of the NCAA tournament and nearly beat No.6 Notre Dame in overtime. Only Syracuse seemed unrattled by the onslaught. Though an Orange defenseman described Albany's attack as "controlled chaos" and John Desko dubbed its playbook "spaghetti," the Orange avenged 2013 with an overtime win in 2014, and soundly beat Albany the next four times they met.

Off the field, Marr presented a more disturbing challenge. His success in landing—and keeping—the Thompsons ended Syracuse's monopoly on the Haudenosaunee. In 2013 alone Native blue chips Zed Williams, Seneca out of New York's Cattaraugus reservation, enrolled at the University of Virginia, and Zach Miller and Frank Brown, both Seneca from Allegany Territory, committed to Denver and Hobart. The next year, Miller's best friend, Brendan Bomberry, joined him in Denver. In 2017 Six Nations sensation Tehoka Nanticoke enrolled at Albany, and in 2018 the Great Danes had their best season yet, rolling Syracuse, 15–3, in the season opener, and making it to the NCAA Final Four. The Orange, meanwhile, hadn't been back to championship weekend since 2013, the year of the Thompsons brothers' breakout.

"We still, to this day, get a lot of heat as to why the Thompsons didn't come here," said Roy Simmons III. "The best thing that happened to those guys is that they ended up going to Albany, to be very honest. Coach Marr plays a different style than we do. We used to be run-and-gun and run-and-fun and all that, and we had changed our style."

Simmons III went on to praise, at length, Marr's build at Albany and the Thompsons' success—so much that it seemed Syracuse was wholly untroubled by all those recruiting losses. Then he grinned.

"But they still didn't win one," Simmons III said. "We talk to each other, and we go, 'How many championship rings you got?' When we're feeling nasty."

THE THOMPSONS' COLLEGIATE careers were never only a lacrosse story. Jeremy's substance abuse, Miles's loneliness, and Lyle's academic struggles are classic side effects of the Indigenous collision with white culture.

And while the game provided both sides with a common bond, a mechanism for relating, it also triggered the usual, age-old ugliness.

Lyle heard opponents snarling, "Go back to the Rez," "Your parents are alcoholics"—and worse from fans in Hartford, Syracuse and New Haven. "Yale had a lot to say about my hair," Lyle said. "There was an old man that stood at the end of their field . . . He followed me and Miles and he called us 'girls,' called us 'long-haired freaks,' things that never got into my head. I can honestly say not one thing has ever bothered me."

Marr recalled Drexel fans calling them "wagon burners," threatening to cut their ponytails. "My God, it was awful," he said. And on the field, "they got the crap beat out of 'em more than any players I've ever had, literally got slashed and hit more. I had referees say to me, 'They can take it.' What does that mean? Because they're Native Americans, they can take a beating? Why is that?"

Lyle didn't complain. Some of that was shyness. In high school he ducked publicity, evaded the star's role of vocal leadership. His first years in Albany, he kept to himself; having two more children with Amanda while in college left him even more removed. But by the end, both Lyle and Miles carried themselves with a greater sense of mission. Native academic failure was not an abstraction: several Albany teammates dropped out. The brothers intended to break the age-old pattern. "We don't want to be like everyone else," Lyle said.

By senior year Lyle's presence—on the field, braid flying, and still in a classroom—reanimated the game's Native foundation. There had been past Indigenous All-Americans. Plenty of previous Haudenosaunee stars, after dropping out, had gone on to great careers in the box. But none had so dominated the premier showcase of NCAA competition, or crossed over to become a nationwide idol for white prep school kids. None had injected the game's Native element, long ghettoized as an exotic historical feature, so spectacularly into its mainstream.

"What [Lyle]'s done with the Tewaaraton and his brothers and his family is, he's validated the greatness of it," Denver head coach Bill Tierney said in 2015. "And what I love about it is, these guys are graduating, and when they talk, they're talking about their families and their culture. To me, it's brought lacrosse back full circle. We're going back to our roots through a young man who is just so talented and so dynamic that it's reawakened us to something that has been there for a long, long time."

Lyle and Miles graduated in 2015 with matching degrees in sociology, a sign of what's possible. Years later, pushing for Albany to establish a
Native scholarship like Syracuse's Haudenosaunee Promise, Marr reminded
an Albany vice president of admissions that his people didn't think Lyle
Thompson could survive college.

"Well," Marr said, "he graduated with a 2.8, and had three of his kids
while he was here. The fact that we gave him the opportunity—not to do
the schoolwork—but to be in this environment, to be around education,
he's helping so many kids get to that same level. He's the most high-profile
person to ever come through here. The fact that he suffered and had to get
through the schoolwork? That helped him grow. From when he first started
to when he left? He's such a different person."

IN THE FALL OF 2016, the Cleveland Indians were on pace to win the
American League pennant. The use of Native American symbols by college
and pro sports teams had been long decried, but that summer's eruption of
Black Lives Matter protests in US cities all but guaranteed that the club's
Indigenous nickname and cartoony logo of "Chief Wahoo" would be tar-
geted. It also highlighted the ongoing insult of an NFL team called the
"Redskins"—a pejorative deemed "contemptuous" by Webster's Collegiate
Dictionary as early as 1898 and, for some 20th-century activists, redolent
of the practice of white authorities paying for scalps and other Native body
parts—playing in the nation's capital.

In mid-September, with Cleveland heading toward the playoffs, Lyle
Thompson posted a photo of himself wearing a hoodie with the word CAU-
CASIANS in Indians-style script and Chief Wahoo with his feather replaced by
a dollar sign. This made Ji nervous. But Lyle, at 24, was the most celebrated
Native athlete in North America, with a ready-made platform and 54,000
Instagram followers. He asked his dad: "If not me, who?"

"It's dehumanizing," Lyle said of such mascots. "And what I've learned
is, through Blacks, Natives, colored people: When there's something to
be talked about, something to complain about? It's the thing to do, to use
your voice.

"I find 'Redskins' the worst one. I hate that the Redskins play the Cow-
boys on Thanksgiving; people don't understand what Thanksgiving even is.

People don't understand what a 'Redskin' actually is, what 'redskinning' means, what it was in history. I'm not going to argue with anybody; I'm just going to hope you understand. The name is what gets me. The place is what gets me."

Meanwhile, a more basic conflict had been brewing for months near the Lakota and Dakota peoples' Standing Rock Indian Reservation in North Dakota. On July 25, 2016, the US Army Corps of Engineers approved the placing of a section of the $4 billion Dakota Access oil pipeline beneath a Missouri River reservoir just north of the reservation, known as the Lake Oahe crossing. Native scholars and activists contended that pipeline construction and leakage risked damage to sacred sites and contamination of the reservation's water supply. Both sides filed lawsuits. In mid-August a protesting crowd halted construction. In early September, activists confronting three working bulldozers were subjected by private security personnel to physical force, chemical agents and biting dogs.

Clips from protesters' live feeds began popping up on Lyle Thompson's Facebook timeline. His audience there were mostly Native family and friends. Seeking a bigger audience, Thompson shifted to Instagram, where his broader following included "a bunch of lacrosse people who had no idea."

By September, thousands of activists had assembled on the northern border of the Standing Rock reservation—the largest gathering of Native Americans in a century. Hundreds of Indigenous nations, and non-Native allies, formed a sea of tents, Lakota tepees, modern wigwams, yurts, cars and campers across three main protest camps named Sacred Stone, Oceti Sakowin and Rosebud. In October, Lyle retweeted the support of Senator Bernie Sanders and actor Jaden Smith. The number of arrests at Standing Rock rose to 140. In November, Lyle retweeted updates, videos of protester crackdowns, his support of the Cleveland Indians' loss in the World Series. Nike's N7 Fund, which had contributed millions to Indigenous youth sports since 2009, proclaimed him the public face of a newly launched "Spirit of Protection" line.

It didn't seem nearly enough. November was Native American Heritage Month, and thousands of his people were camping and marching and fighting in the bitter North Dakota cold. "I had to be there, I had to feel it," Lyle said. "I wanted to witness what was happening—not so that I could tell the story, but more so for myself." And he thought, *I'm going to do a Medicine Game. These people need that kind of energy.*

On the afternoon of November 20, Lyle, Amanda and their three kids piled into a rented sport utility vehicle packed with 18 lacrosse sticks, a tent and luggage at their home on Six Nations of the Grand River outside Brantford, Ontario. Up front was Lyle's cousin Bill O'Brien, along with Scott Marr. On the other end of their journey that night, Standing Rock police attacked protesters with tear gas, rubber bullets and water cannons in subzero temperatures; 26 people were hospitalized and more than 300 reported injuries. En route Lyle's mom, grandmother and friends kept calling, warning them to turn back.

They pressed on, over 1,345 miles, to the makeshift campgrounds at Sacred Stone near the confluence of the Missouri and Cannonball Rivers. The place was dark, starlit, when they arrived. A communal bonfire blazed, ringed by a jumble of mostly Native faces—a couple hundred strangers from all over. Some had heard of Lyle Thompson. He stood and made a short speech, announcing the carload's support, his desire to hold a Medicine Game.

They stayed a few hours, decided against trying to put up a tent in the dark, drove an hour north to a Bismarck hotel. The next morning Thompson's group returned to the Six Nations campsite, where a white banner hung on the longhouse-shaped tent: THE HAUDENOSAUNEE SUPPORT OUR WESTERN BROTHERS. WATER IS LIFE. A lacrosse field was marked by a makeshift sign nailed to a knobby tree branch, reading RESERVED FOR THE CREATORS GAME. Sticks were distributed, teams formed; Medicine Game rules were explained. Some men had played lacrosse. Some had never picked up a stick.

Marr, a 48-year-old white man, was granted a rare dispensation to play. With no conventional goals to aim for, the RESERVED sign and its tree-branch post became the lone target for both sides: hit sign, score goal. First team to three wins. The intention was to play one game in the endless, slicing wind, but after a few minutes of jostling and yelling and laughing, no one wanted to stop. The first game was extended to five. Then two more games to five were played. The whole thing lasted no more than an hour.

Lyle spent the rest of the day conferring with tribal elders and Standing Rock activists, mixing with other nations' people, doing interviews. He told one reporter that he thought "the Native American are being completely disrespected," and that he was done being quiet. "If it's something I believe in and something I care about, yeah, I'm going to speak on it. I have the right to and I have a bigger stage, and more people can hear what I'm saying." They drove away that evening expecting to return, but a National Guard roadblock the next day diverted the SUV too far east. Marr took the wheel. Within a few hours they had left North Dakota behind.

"What I learned? Stand for what you believe in. See more of our people," Lyle said. "That's one thing I'm definitely going to do: take action and experience that."

After they left, thousands more poured into Standing Rock for Thanksgiving and nearly doubled the protest crowd. When, 10 days later, the Army Corps of Engineers announced a decision to delay work on the Dakota Access Pipeline, it smelled like victory. But, in January 2017, the newly minted Trump administration reversed the decision and fast-tracked construction; four months later, the oil began to flow. Every day over the next four years, nearly 500,000 barrels of crude gushed through: south from the Bakken oil fields, under Standing Rock's water supply, running on into Illinois.

The protests, the road trip, the Medicine Game: All of it seemingly accomplished nothing. But for Scott Marr, too, Standing Rock remains pivotal. Never before had he been so immersed in Native life. Never before had he taken a public stand, or protested a wrong.

"It had a purpose," Marr said. "We play games, and what's the purpose? Winning. This wasn't a winning or losing situation. This was a healing situation, an opportunity for the earth to grow, to be a part of something much bigger than yourself, a community for the whole earth . . . Water is life: If we don't have water we're in trouble, and the fact that big-time oil and big-time politicians don't understand that? You know why? Because they're not going to be affected. It's very frustrating in our society that we don't think of each other on a human level, but there's separations, there's classes, it's *You're down here and I'm up here.* I just don't buy into that."

Sometime during their journey, Marr asked Lyle to design him another tattoo. Recalling how Marr had always halted practice whenever a hawk flew overhead, Thompson penciled a minutely detailed sketch of a fearsome bird placing a lacrosse stick into the upraised hands of a grateful brave, a gift from the Creator to humans. Marr didn't wait long. The image now covers ten inches of skin atop his right shoulder blade.

TWENTY MONTHS AFTER the trek to Standing Rock, Lyle Thompson logged in to his Instagram account, typed a direct message and hit send. It was July 8, one day before the Nationals' originally scheduled flight from the Toronto airport to Tel Aviv. By then, the Palestinian call for an Iroquois boycott of the 2018 World Championship seemed a dead issue. The Grand Council had left the decision up to the Nationals, players had decided to participate and every official Nationals comment since had lined up with Israel's plea for neutrality. But Thompson was still uneasy.

The BDS movement's claim of common cause resonated, especially when coupled with the assertion that the tournament's two venues sat on Palestinian villages "ethnically cleansed" by Israeli forces in 1948. And the days since had brought harsh criticism in Haudenosaunee media. Mohawk radio host John Kane, with shows in Seneca territory and New York City, slammed the team for "honoring Israel with our presence in light of their behavior over the last three or four months," and said the decision never should have been left to players with little grounding in geopolitics. "It should be the ambassadors, the diplomats and the leadership," Kane said, "that say when and where we should subject our athletes to play."

He had a point. The Nationals' most prominent star knew nothing about the Palestinian cause before deciding to go. So at the last minute, packing and heading to the airport, Thompson reached out to his high school teammate and trig tutor, Nabil Akl.

Thompson typed in a direct message:

Excuse my ignorance, but I'm trying to dig into some information since I'm heading to Israel. I think I remember you telling me stories on your parents and how they met. And was wondering if Israel is of any connection to your family line. I'm trying to find out 1) how safe Israel is and 2) the history of Israel and Palestinians. The Palestinians have been urging the Iroquois to withdraw from the games . . .

Akl, then a law student at Syracuse, had already decided not to watch Thompson or anyone else play in Israel. Born in Syracuse and raised Christian, he is a son of Middle Eastern tumult. His father, Wuhid, grew up in Beirut amid the run-up and fallout of the 1967 Six-Day War and arrived in America at 23 with no money. His mother's family fled Jerusalem for Jordan after the Zionist bombing of the King David Hotel in 1946, and in 1957 emigrated to the US.

Akl responded to Thompson:

Israel is generally safe for Americans considering Americans can go
back there and do whatever they want. But for Arab people, it's not
as safe of a place. Israel has currently quarantined Palestinians in
limiting their food and water that go to these certain areas. It's basi-
cally slowly killing the Palestinian people . . .

Whereas Israel is funded by the United States, so they have
state-of-the-art weapons, bombs and things in their power. It is sad
that the world really turns a blind eye to the killing of innocent
people . . . similar to the Native Americans getting forced out of
their lands with no recourse . . .

Nabil relayed how his grandparents' homes were seized by the Israeli
military, how the Israel court system controls the land through laws, how
the outgunned Palestinians have little hope of redress.

Thompson replied:

Damn, that's much better info than we were receiving from some
of the people from the other side. So is this an ongoing war or more
of a protest by the Palestinians like Standing Rock? Why is this not
known? Palestinians don't have a network to create media via social
media? Or is there an American/me who wouldn't see it?

Akl wrote:

It's an ongoing struggle and it's disgusting to see what's happening.
The reason that people don't see it is because a lot of . . . networks
don't show this information. They're not going to show information that's . . . going against the Israeli side if US supports Israel.
I think that's just common sense.

"I don't hate Jewish people," Akl insisted in 2020. "It's not the Jewish
religion that causes issues; it's the Zionist people. I definitely think that the
solution should lead towards independent states, to Palestine. People deserve
to live off the land that they live on, and to be treated like human beings.
Everybody deserves that right of humanity."

Akl never tried to convince Thompson to sit out the 2018 World Championship. "This is their Medicine Game," Akl said. "I'm happy that they reached out, at least, to get the information. That showed me that they were making a conscious decision, an understanding decision, and going into it with education. That was big: I knew that they understood what was going on. Because, I guarantee you, a majority of other people from other teams had no clue."

NETANYA STADIUM WAS almost empty. Fifteen minutes after the Iroquois Nationals' opening night loss to the United States, Lyle Thompson's teammates had all headed to the bus. But even with legs jellied by jet travel and two hours of harrying world-class defensemen, he was still standing on the scrubby grass, taking questions, processing out loud his support of the Palestinian people. He mentioned Nabil Akl.

"He educated me," Thompson said. "He let me know what it's like here, and the history he knows. I talked to more than him, talked to a lot of people, just to get an understanding."

Maybe it was the lighting, or the late hour. But though he was just 25 years old, an athlete in his prime, Thompson looked 10 years older. He was asked if he ever wished that he didn't have to speak on matters like pipelines or the Middle East's forever war, wished that lacrosse, for once, could just be about sports.

"I don't think it's *ever* just about sports," he said. "I think it's about what's morally right for the earth, for all the people and all the beings of the earth, whether it's human beings or the living beings, our trees. That's what our culture's about: showing respect. And I try to do my best to live that. I don't want to just be someone who talks it. I want to walk the walk."

PART 2

BEARING UP

OMAR: . . . You go to Edmondson, right? You was ahead of me. You was the first brother I ever seen who play that sport with a stick—uh, what's it called?

BUNK: Lacrosse, man . . . I was All-Metro attack. Those prep school boys used to pee themselves when they see ol' Bunk coming at 'em.

—*The Wire*, season 1, episode 7, "One Arrest"

I

THE LONELY SONS OF SIMEON MOSS

B Y NOON OF THE second day—Friday, July 13—the proceedings in Israel assumed an entirely different feel. All the drama surrounding the Iroquois' last-minute arrival—the security concerns and Opening Ceremony jitters, that clash of two historic enemies—was gone. The US and the Iroquois both had the day off. Lacrosse action downshifted from Netanya Stadium to six sunbaked fields, outside town, at Israel's Wingate Institute for Physical Education. It felt like some giant hand had turned the tournament volume knob to low.

This sudden relaxation became more disconcerting as the weekend unwound, because the outside world was only getting louder. Ninety minutes south of the 2018 World Lacrosse Championship, during the weekly Friday border protests in Gaza, an Israeli officer was injured by a grenade flung across the barrier fence from the Gazan side. An unarmed 15-year-old Palestinian boy climbing the fence was shot and killed; dozens of Gazans were injured. Both sides steeled for a new cycle of violence.

But in Netanya hotel staff and tournament personnel reassured lacrosse players and coaches and families that the violence was far away. Tourists trooped out the resort door armed with towels and sunscreen. Hang gliders tilted over the streets and sand and scalloped Mediterranean Sea. Organizers insisted that the day's schedule would be played.

Early in the afternoon, Mexican attackman Timothy Gonzales and his teammates arrived after a half-hour shuttle bus ride along the Coastal Highway, past nondescript block buildings, rocky berms and scrubby fields, for the day's first game against Greece on Wingate 2. Only a few hundred spectators—mostly family and friends—were wandering past the low-slung architecture toward the stands. Indeed, though billed as Israel's "National Institute for Sports Excellence," training ground for nearly all its top athletes and coaches since 1957, Wingate in mid-summer gave off the lethargic feel of a college campus after finals. And in the coming days its scrubby fields, dim lighting and one temperamental scoreboard would lay out the truth of the 2018 Field Lacrosse World Championship: It was more sport festival than sports Armageddon.

The top six teams in the elite "Blue Division" (US, Canada, Iroquois, Australia, England and Scotland) viewed winning as a matter of national honor. But everybody knew the other 40 had no chance; for FIL officials this was, above all, a "Grow the Game" event—a chance to reward fledgling nations and inspire new ones. Any significance would come in retrospect, in hope that 2018 became the moment world lacrosse entered adulthood. For 28 years the game had been expanding, adding members from Asia, South America and Africa. All were welcome. Competition was secondary. But for the next World Championship, in 2023, all but the top six would be required to vie for a spot via regional qualifiers, and the field would be slashed from 46 teams to 30.

Israel 2018, then, was the last lacrosse championship to feature so great a bonanza of novelty teams, those beneficiaries of instant goodwill and loosey-goose requirements. Along with the rule allowing four members of any 23-player roster to be non–passport holders of that country, FIL's guidelines allowed two additional players to be dual passport holders, deferred to each nation's—often minimal—passport requirements and left room for what FIL vaguely termed "a further exception."

In other words, the tournament was swarming with ringers: usually American born, good enough to play for an NCAA program but not Team USA, often with little real-life connection to said foreign land. "When I was taking the team from Greece, I was thinking that I'm going to actually find people from *Greece*," said an Israeli tour guide charged with squiring lacrosse delegations around Jerusalem. "You know, the original people. But it appeared that all of them were Americans. When I took the Scotland team, half of the group were Americans. Same story about Hong Kong."

Little was expected here of Chinese Taipei, China, Croatia, Hungary, Luxembourg or Peru, but the ringers on Jamaica, the Philippines and especially Puerto Rico made every opponent nervous. Somewhere in between fell a rookie like Greece, with its May/December goalies—a 16-year-old high schooler and the 48-year-old, Oscar-winning producer of *12 Years a Slave*— but enough high-level pedigree in its lineup to be dangerous.

Such roster stuffing seemed alternatively comical, cynical or wholly justified by the sport's stated need to appear increasingly "international"— especially to Olympic officials. As in the Olympics, the presence of such teams lent the proceedings charm and grit, and trumpeted lacrosse's appeal. Many ringers were obscure, aging grinders with two or three World Championships under their belt, with no chance of medaling. Yet their hunger to keep playing thrummed with an almost childlike desperation, palpable in any sampling of the flood of GoFundMe campaigns to pay their way to Israel.

"Help me get a plane ticket out there," read the plea of 29-year-old Timothy Gonzales of Mexico. "This is my last year playing elite lacrosse and this has been a dream of mine to play in the World Games since I was very young . . ." Gonzales' goal was $2,500. Friends, family and ex-teammates chipped in $2,831, in case he needed a nice souvenir.

IT IS FOR SUCH PLAYERS that Tom Hayes, the American coach who lobbied long and hard for lacrosse's international push, coined the phrase "the stick is magic." The way cradling syncs with the rhythm of your breathing and pumping legs; the heft of a ball in deep webbing; the rare moments when one melds savvy with firing fast-twitch muscles to dodge and flinch through a web of harassing sticks, knees, elbows to score: "magic" captures all that for Timothy Gonzales. But it still doesn't sum up the game's impact on him, because he tried to kill himself once, and got very close to trying again. The second time, lacrosse saved his life.

Gonzales was 12 at the time. He knew where to get a gun. He had written goodbye notes, and knew he could do it because he'd tried once already at seven, dragged a razor blade across a wrist; he had been bleeding out in a $16-a-night flophouse room in San Luis Obispo when his brother found him and called 911. Most suicide cases, Gonzales said, decide too late that it's all a mistake. But his seven-year-old self didn't regret it—not then on the grimy floor, not in the hospital when he heard the doctor telling his mother about

the vein he'd missed, not once in the five years after. So when the thought
struck him again, at 12, it didn't feel dramatic.

"I was going to shoot myself, 100 percent," Gonzales said. "Everything
was prepared. I knew exactly what I was doing. It was going to happen. I was
ready to just say, 'I'm done.'"

He was born in Southern California. His father, Jesse—a Mexican
immigrant who claimed descent from ancient Aztecs and worked as an
electrician—and mother, Pamela—white, tangled forever in drugs and crime,
who spent, Gonzales said, "roughly about 18 years of my life in prison"—
never married. His dad insisted the boys wear their hair in braids, and left
when Timothy was five. The family moved to San Luis Obispo, bounced in
and out of homelessness. When Timothy turned 10, an aunt came to take
both boys and their little sister, Ashley, to her home in West Los Angeles;
for years, no one revealed that their mother had gone to jail. In the sixth
grade, feeling abandoned, neglected, bullied because of his hair, Timothy
spent a lot of time plotting his death.

In the seventh grade at Paul Revere Middle School, a kid showed up
toting a lacrosse stick and let Timothy roll it around in his hands. Before
his next soccer practice, Gonzales went early to watch the lacrosse team. He
began attending those practices, learned the rudiments: Something shifted.

"The moment I started playing, I had zero thoughts of depression,"
Gonzales said:

> *I wouldn't think about what I was going through . . . All I cared about*
> *was playing the sport and the way it made me feel. During lacrosse I was*
> *genuinely happy, and it's still like that to this day . . .*
>
> *I started doing research and reading up on the Iroquois and how it*
> *is the Medicine Game and how you're not doing it for wealth, for money,*
> *for fame. You're doing it for the ancestors, for the land. And it changed me*
> *because I was like,* Maybe this is what I'm supposed to do.

Gonzales cracked Revere's roster in eighth grade, never scored, then
played four years—five foot seven, 120 pounds, hair flapping atop his
shoulders—on the nascent program at tony Palisades High, thriving under
the intense tutelage of former Santa Clara star Scott Hylen, who later co-
founded Argentina's national team and coached the Swiss. Gonzales went

everywhere with his stick, retaped and slept with it before every game. "Timmy was tiny," Hylen said. "He'd get knocked all over the place, but he'd never stay down long."

Senior year, Gonzales became one of Pali's leading scorers and the Dolphins reached the 2008 sectional semifinals. One Division III college showed interest, Carthage in Wisconsin, but he needed money. Gonzales graduated, began his career as an emergency medical technician, played for the Hollywood Stars and the Chiefs in Southern California's high-level club circuit.

Work forced a slow breakup. By 2016 Gonzales was toiling full-time as an EMT, sometimes 19 hours straight, and not playing at all. Depression set in. That July, he grudgingly traveled to a one-off field tourney in Lake Tahoe, where the Mexico team invited him to Mexico City to try out for the 2018 World Championship squad. Gonzales was torn. This would be Mexico's third World Championship, and roster rules tightened after the first: 60 percent of a team's players must be domestic, living full-time in the country. Gonzales was 27 and didn't even speak Spanish. He figured he had little chance.

Instead, Gonzales's tryout week in the summer of 2017 was pure joy, capped by an invite invitation to join the team. Among the most welcoming was Mexico attackman Andres Axkana Patraca, a 25-year-old who grew up playing soccer and American football. In 2009, while studying math at Mexico City's Instituto Politécnico Nacional, Patraca stumbled upon the school's newly formed lacrosse club. Like Gonzales, he felt his mind altered and slept with his stick. "I decided," Patraca said, "this was going to be my life." Like Gonzales, he immersed himself in Iroquois lore, made Haudenosaunee friends on Facebook and, throughout Mexico's run at the 2014 World Championship in Denver, pumped Lyle Thompson's father, Ji, for insight and advice.

But the lessons didn't truly take until Patraca buttonholed Ji in the wake of an 18–10 loss to Italy, lambasting himself because he hadn't been good enough; the defeat was surely his fault. Ji disagreed. "You were *there*," he said. And when he repeated that, something clicked; Patraca felt, for the first time, the Iroquois way. "Just by being there and giving my best in the field and doing my best before the game and after the game with my teammates: that was the most important part. Not *I scored four goals!*"

Mexico finished 23rd in Denver in 2014, and Patraca—the program's future president—spent the next four years transfusing Ji's words, the Iroquois mindset, into the program. "He has no idea the impact that he had made in lacrosse in Mexico," Patraca said.

STILL, DESPITE THAT INFLUENCE and the fact that Mexico's coach, Andrew Haas, was Hawaii born and Virginia bred, there was no mistaking the team's ethnic pride—its burgeoning Mexican-ness—in Israel. This was by design. Haas lived and based the squad's training in Mexico City, tailored its style to reflect Mexican assets like quickness and grit, tried to make the 2018 World Championship a uniquely Mexican experience. He even pushed his US-based players—Spanish speaking or not—to learn the national anthem, "*Mexicanos, al grito de guerra*" ("Mexicans, at the shout of war").

Standing on the sidelines of Wingate 2 before the opener, Patraca glanced around. With no recorded music to hide behind, most of his teammates were singing loudly. Even Haas was trying his best. When Greece's national anthem, "Hymn to Liberty," played, Patraca made a point to watch. "Their whole team was quiet," he said. "That was a big difference for us: It was a really big pride that we have for Mexico after singing the national anthem."

Such displays are hardly the clearest gauge of patriotism, and in Greece's case likely measured proximity more than pride. Aside from American-born players like Gonzales, Tufts graduate Ernie Melero (who wouldn't get the "*al grito de guerra*" lyrics down until tournament's end) and Arizona State midfielder Tlaloc Orozco-Cohen, its mostly homegrown roster had been hearing Mexico's national anthem forever. Greece had just one player born and raised in Greece, and barely: Introduced to lacrosse 18 months before at a high school outside Thessaloniki, coached over Facebook Messenger for a year, against Mexico 17-year-old midfielder Elias Zacharopoulus would be playing his first competitive lacrosse game. Ever.

The rest of Greece's players came of age in the US. On paper, Greece had been an official FIL member for only a year; Mexico was the veteran. But most of Mexico's players on Wingate 2 picked up lacrosse at colleges like Patraca's Politécnico Nacional and Universidad Autónoma Metropolitana, while the Greeks on field for the opening faceoff—nearly all products of American lacrosse hotbeds, youth travel teams and coaching clinics—hardly carried themselves like rookies. Attackman Joe Boulukos, 34, had been a three-time All-American at Cornell and a 2006 Tewaaraton nominee. Others played for powers like Loyola and Tufts and Bucknell. Attackman Nate Lewnes (All-American at the University of Maryland, Baltimore County, where in 2016 he averaged a nation-leading 3.91 goals per game, and scored 10 in one loss to No. 5 Albany) scored first; from the start the Greeks controlled the pace, and pounced on every loose pass or hasty shot. At halftime Greece held a 9–4 lead, and on the ESPN broadcast, the contest was looking downright routine.

Down on the field, though, the tone had grown progressively nasty. Early into the first quarter, Timothy Gonzales checked into the game and wasn't sure he heard correctly. "You guys swim across?" a Greek player said to the Mexico attackman. "I know you're used to swimming because you're wetbacks."

Ever since, Greece's players had been deriding his braids by calling Gonzales "Pigtails" and "Pocahontas." He also heard "a ton of racial slurs toward the other players, like, 'Oh, give them the toothbrushes to go clean the floors.'" Patraca claimed that—starting in the third quarter—"at least three times," he and the rest of the Mexican bench heard Greek players dropping racial slurs on the field, including at least one "fucking beaners." Coach Haas didn't hear slurs from the sidelines, but said his players complained the entire game about the Greek team's "racial comments."

"You cannot insult us as a nation at a tournament like that," Patraca said. "We were on fire. We were really, really angry."

Early in the third quarter, Mexico's defense stiffened and cut Greece's lead to four; if the players had kept their composure, they could have chipped further away. But they didn't. Greece responded by playing even better. And, according to Patraca, their slurs intensified. "We were playing awesome, playing as a team," he said. "And that made us lose our mind and actually lose the game, because we couldn't focus anymore."

Timothy Gonzales's breaking point came with 7:03 left in the fourth quarter. After cutting into the crease to dig out a rebound, Gonzales—at the exact moment he flipped a behind-the-head score to cut Greece's lead to 13–7—found himself leveled by Loukas Sotiropoulos-Lawrence, a 16-year-old sophomore defenseman and linebacker from Maryland's Severn School. Sotiropoulos-Lawrence stalked away. Down on his hands and knees, amid a milling group of four Greek players, Gonzales heard someone say, "Stay down, beaner. All you're good for is making tortillas."

Tempers spiked when the clock hit zero. Mexico midfielder Derek Knute bull-rushed Greece midfielder Nicolas Ioannou into the end of the Greek bench. Greek players swarmed Knute; his Mexican teammates rushed in to pull him away. Meanwhile, Ernie Melero—alone—confronted a scrum of seven Greek players at midfield, looking for the one who'd slurred Gonzales. Most didn't want to hear it. According to Team Mexico, two Greek players were singularly gracious: Jordan Korinis, Melero's former Tufts teammate, and Anthony Katagas, the 48-year-old movie producer/goalie who placed a hand gently on Melero's shoulder during the scrum, hugged Gonzales and six other Mexico players in the traditional handshake line and was heard saying, "We thought you were going to come back and trounce us; we were scared; you're a good team."

Two Greek players later said they recalled no unusual tension with the Mexican team, nor any of their teammates uttering racial epithets. The five-man crew officiating the game, led by head referee Mark Buckley, never warned or penalized the Greek players or coaches during or after the game; Buckley and chief bench official Steve Luxion said they heard no slurs. That doesn't mean the alleged slurs didn't occur. Luxion said the contest was the "most heated" he had called in Israel, but an official must hear any offending words directly—in real time, not as a complaint after the fact—for a penalty to be assessed. Greece players could well have been muttering out of earshot. Buckley said cultural ignorance may have blunted the officials' sensibilities; not until years later did he actually learn that "beaner" was a derogatory term for Mexicans. "It could well have happened," he said of Mexico's account. "Players talk to each other. We are only at three points on the field."

Maybe Mexico's players and coaches should have complained louder that day, or more often. If any aspect of that game against Greece is undisputed, it's that they left the field beaten, feeling vaguely helpless. "I was very surprised at the refs: like, nothing really happened," Melero said. "It was just, like, *This is it: you can just be a little racist towards us, and there's no consequences to that.*"

SUCH INACTION seemed out of character, if only because—as an institution—the sport had taken very public pains to welcome people of color. Since 2003, US Lacrosse, through initiatives like its BRIDGE and First Stick programs, had poured millions of dollars into introducing the game to low-income urban communities nationwide. The early 2000s also saw inner-city lacrosse programs spring up in Baltimore, Denver, Dallas, Chicago, Oakland and, most prominently, New York. In 2011 Simon Cataldo, a special education teacher at Frederick Douglass Academy, aimed straight at the cultural Mecca of Black America and launched Harlem Lacrosse.

And on paper, it worked: US Lacrosse's Urban Lacrosse Alliance had since expanded to 76 programs serving 9,000 kids a year nationwide. By 2017 the Harlem initiative—featuring a teacher/coach embedded full-time in underserved middle schools—totaled 19 schools and 1,000 students in New York, as well as "Harlem" chapters in Boston, Baltimore, Los Angeles and Philadelphia. Some youngsters went on to play for elite prep schools, earned scholarships to the likes of Tufts, Hobart and the University of Virginia, part of a demonstrable shift: In 2008, 92 percent of the men and women playing Division I lacrosse were white. By 2024, that figure had dropped to 82 and 83 percent, respectively.

If nothing else, this seemed to signal that the sport's boom—from 2001 to 2018, overall lacrosse participation in the US grew by 227 percent*—hadn't escaped the notice of minority populations. The NCAA's Black lacrosse bloc in that time ticked up only slightly, from 2 to 3 percent, but by 2024 its pool of Latino, Native American, Asian/Pacific Islander or mixed-race players since 2008 had more than doubled to 13.6 percent.

Yet from the perspective of minority players, that hardly alters the big picture: A 45-man college roster that once featured one Black player now might have one Black, two Asians and one Latino. The game's essential whiteness holds. It is cited as a foundational factor anytime racial incidents occur, including after Mexico said it heard slurs on Wingate 2. "I don't think it's a lacrosse issue," said Ernie Melero. "There's assholes all across the board, in any sport you get into. It's just a little more prominent in lacrosse. There's just, I feel like, a lot more racism because it's such a white space."

---

* After hitting an all-time high of 2.1 million in 2017, the total of US lacrosse participants held steady at 2-plus million through 2019. Amid a general drop in team sports participation caused by the Covid-19 pandemic—and a dramatic rise in socially distanced sports like pickleball—lacrosse participation dropped to 1.8 million in 2020, a level maintained for the next two years. In 2023, total US lacrosse participation rose 5.5 percent to 1.98 million.

Since the first Lacrosse World Championship in 1967—14 national teams, 341 players in all—the United States men's field lacrosse team has featured a player of color six times. All were Black. The first, defenseman Fred Opie in 1990, had many friends and former teammates on the roster, and heard not a single racial comment directed at him (or Native American opponents) during their eight-month stint together. Indeed, throughout the trip to Perth and the team's title run there, none of the management or players once referred to Opie's singular and historic status.

"I knew all those guys, but it was one of the most lonely times I've ever felt in my life," Opie says. "Being the only Black guy on the team? Lonely. Because I didn't share a lot with my teammates, off the field, culturally."

Kyle Harrison, one of the sport's biggest stars, played on the 2006 and 2014 national teams but felt no such isolation. The lone US Black player in Israel, faceoff specialist Trevor Baptiste, seemed equally at home. This may be due to the empathetic tone set by US head coach John Danowski, a supportive club teammate of Chuck Sherwood, Duke's first Black player, in the late 1970s. Or the example set by famously progressive midfielder Paul Rabil, who not only parlayed a savvy social media approach to becoming lacrosse's first million-dollar player, but was—even in Israel—busy laying the groundwork for his new US pro lacrosse league.

It helped that Baptiste, like Harrison, was central to US hopes. Though the youngest American—and, at 22, the only one playing straight out of college—Baptiste made an immediate impact in the opener against the Iroquois; his dominance at the faceoff X keyed the US's second-half surge, and his final stat line—17 of 19 faceoffs won against Nationals star Jeremy Thompson—highlighted one of the great World Championship debuts. Yet it came as no shock: At the University of Denver, Baptiste became only the sixth player in history named first-team All-American four times, and set new NCAA career records for faceoff wins (1,158) and winning percentage (.714).

Of course, it's possible that none of Baptiste's white teammates or opponents harbored racist or ignorant impulses—or just knew to keep them quiet. Baptiste learned early how closely the sport could mix bad and good: Two years after he picked up the game in Roxbury, New Jersey, after a win as an eighth grader, Baptiste says an opponent sneered at one of his white teammates, "The only reason you won is because you got that nigger." That teammate had to be held back from assaulting the offender. Other white teammates, angry and worried on his behalf, cried. "It was, like: *Wow, these guys have my back*," he said.

Starting in the early 2000s, as collegiate field lacrosse slowed to a possession-obsessed—and, some argue, duller—game, the faceoffs taken before every quarter and after each goal became central. Coaches chased players with mastery of the position's base moves—clamp, jam, razor and quick rig. A new lacrosse player was born: the FOGO, a.k.a. "faceoff: get off," whose main job was to win the brief, joint-grinding battles for leverage, pass the seized ball to a teammate and exit the field as soon as possible.

Baptiste was a scoring midfielder throughout high school, lightly recruited. But to Denver coach Bill Tierney, his physique, vision and skill added up the greatest FOGO yet. In his first game against defending national champion Duke, Baptiste won 25 of 34 draws and the Pioneers won 13–7. The last game of his freshman year, he and Denver won the 2015 NCAA championship. "I don't know if lacrosse was meant to be dominated that much by one single specialized position," says midfielder Max Seibald, the 2009 Tewaaraton Award winner and Baptiste's teammate with the Major League Lacrosse Boston Cannons in 2018. "But he took it to that level."

Indeed, as a total package, there has never been a lacrosse player quite like Baptiste. Even with lacrosse authorities loudly pushing changes—a 90-second shot clock for college, a faster-paced version for the Olympics—sure to deemphasize faceoffs, he worried little about his place in the game.

"I'm happy with it," Baptiste said. "I think I'm doing what I'm really good at. If I could dodge like Rabil, I'd be doing that. If I could shoot like Ryan Brown, I'd be doing that. But I can't—or I don't—so I faceoff like myself. That's my strength."

AMERICAN LACROSSE'S first response to players of color was containment. There had been no strategizing beforehand by a white authority figure, like Brooklyn Dodgers owner Branch Rickey with Jackie Robinson, and virtually no notice taken at the moment, in 1939—that defenseman Simeon Moss became the first Black man to play for an American university. Moss played for the Rutgers junior varsity his sophomore year, and sparingly for the varsity only part of his junior year before quitting. Fifty-eight years later, he claimed that Rutgers coach Fred Fitch once benched him solely because of his race before a 12–0 loss at the University of Maryland in College Park.

"The only thing that I know about anything that had to do with discrimination," Moss recalled in 1997, "was when I was on the lacrosse team."

Fitch could well have been leery of grating his host's segregationist nerves, then a common consideration for visiting Northerners. On April 4, 1941, Harvard University's lacrosse team, 18 members in all, arrived at the US Naval Academy in Annapolis, Maryland, and sallied to the dining hall for lunch. Among them was Lucien Alexis Jr., the New Orleans–born, Black son of a 1918 Harvard grad. The sight of Alexis triggered instant alarm: The officer of the watch was notified, the mess hall emptied. At dinner, Harvard's lacrosse team—against all academy custom—was forced to eat in a private room.

At the time, the armed forces of America were still seven years away from desegregation. Just 2.3 percent of navy personnel were African American, all enlisted men, and all but six bore the lowly rank of steward's mates— or, as the Black press dubbed them, "seagoing bellhops." Citing a fear of race riots, Navy's athletic director and then the academy superintendent, Rear Admiral Russell Willson, demanded Alexis's removal: America's midshipmen could not take the field with a "colored man."

The race riot threat was a canard. Just the day before, after some initial resistance, Alexis competed in Harvard's game at the University of Maryland in College Park; neither that school's president, coach nor players had objected. Ignoring that intelligence, Willson demanded that Harvard coach Dick Snibbe bench Alexis or Navy would have to forfeit the game. A hater of segregation, Snibbe refused. Willson phoned Harvard athletic director William Bingham; Bingham wired Snibbe an order to place Alexis on that night's train to Boston and play on. "We were guests of the Naval Academy," Bingham said, "and had no choice in the matter."

Within a week a campus petition decrying "Jim Crowism" and demanding that the Harvard Athletic Association never again support discrimination had 600 signatures, including one from the godson of President—and Harvard alum—Franklin D. Roosevelt. Politicians, labor unions and the NAACP weighed in; the senator chairing the subcommittee on naval affairs vowed to investigate. On April 17, First Lady Eleanor Roosevelt wired a message to the Harvard Council for Democracy in Education, archly skewering both Willson and Bingham.

Two days later, Harvard's team bus—with Alexis aboard—arrived in West Point for its game against Army. Waiting Black cadets provided a strikingly warm welcome. The college's Athletic Association then reversed its stance, with Bingham announcing that the Crimson would no longer tolerate racial discrimination during athletic contests with other colleges.

The commander- in-chief had been paying attention. Historians list the Harvard lacrosse brouhaha as a factor when, the following month, Roosevelt made perhaps the first official call for affirmative action in government-ordered factory work and, in June 1941, issued his historic executive order prohibiting racial discrimination in the defense industry. On September 6 Roosevelt expanded his scope, ordering all government departments and agencies to take immediate steps to end racial discrimination, particularly against Black people, and review all employment practices "to assure me that in the federal service the doors of employment are open to all loyal and qualified workers regardless of creed, race, or national origin."

Thus began the long, intermittent campaign to kill off federally mandated racial policies. In 1948 Harry Truman desegregated the US armed forces. On June 3, 1949, Wesley A. Brown became the first Black man to graduate from the Naval Academy.

In 1953, the year that 17-year-old Jim Brown graduated from Long Island's Manhasset High School, the hard color line had been all but dissolved in professional baseball, basketball and football. Lacrosse's complexion was still white. Not officially: Perhaps the game's first Black player, Ontario's Albert F. Lewis, starred for the Cornwall club in the late 1880s and was described as "the only colored man who has ever played lacrosse on a champion team in Canada." And not completely: A few Native Americans, most lasting only a year or two, could be found at select universities, and Brown was not the sole African American playing public school lacrosse on Long Island.

But the rosters of the elite Division I college teams—Johns Hopkins, Maryland, Army, Navy and Princeton—were heavily populated by wealthy, mostly private-schooled, and all white men. When Brown first took the field for Syracuse as a sophomore in the spring of 1955, he was doubly unique. Beyond being the only Black player, at six foot two and 207 pounds, he was also the biggest, strongest and fastest man at play. In football he had

had a breakout season, but not overwhelming. Lacrosse was another story. Though the Orange finished 6–4 his sophomore year, Syracuse coach Roy Simmons Sr. saw enough to anoint Brown "America's best lacrosse player" and "the finest midfield man I've ever seen."

His reasoning was self-evident: Already no one could stop Brown, and that would be their best chance. By his senior year Brown was 25 pounds heavier, and hadn't lost a step. "At that time, maybe, 175 pounds would be the biggest player you'd have," said Simmons Sr.'s son, Roy Jr., Brown's Syracuse teammate and future Hall of Fame coach. "But Jim Brown's the fastest player I've ever run against, at 230 pounds, and he's ambidextrous with his stick work, which was very unique for that time; so he *controlled*. He'd just run at you and if you got in the way, he ran you down."

Brown, of course, became a Hall of Fame running back for the Cleveland Browns in the 1950s and '60s, perhaps the best football player in history. He was also endowed with a freakish versatility, matched in American history only, perhaps, by Sac and Fox football star and Olympian Jim Thorpe. Prior to Syracuse, Brown had never thrown a discus; during his freshman spring, he broke the school's varsity record three times. When not twice earning All-American honors carrying a football, Brown kicked extra points, averaged 13 points in two years of varsity basketball and, in between tyrannizing lacrosse games, popped over to star in the occasional track meet.

To this day, the rumor persists that Brown used a shorter stick than rules allow, or bulled about clenching the webbed ball against his chest like a newborn—no cradling, no stick movement at all. Brown later joked sarcastically about this, but no contemporaneous account mentions that complaint by opposing coach or player; the claim that the sport, in response, instituted a "Jim Brown rule" seems empty (the injunction against clutching—Rule XI, Section 2, F (2)—was enacted 16 years after his last game).

Roy Simmons Jr. finds the notion absurd. College contemporaries raved about Brown's over-the-shoulder passes and faceoff dominance; his one-handed, underhand "shovel" shots, left or right, rocketed with the force of other men's two-handers. At Syracuse Simmons Jr. later coached the Gait and Powell brothers, all legendary for their touch. Brown, he said, "was the best stickhandler we ever had."

Yet, for most of his college career, the totality of Brown's genius flew beneath even the sport's radar. One reason was structural. College sports, especially non-revenue types like lacrosse, mostly played a regional schedule, and Brown's reputation had never been tested in lacrosse's prime hotbed. "People down South had never seen him play," Simmons Jr. said. "We didn't play Hopkins or Duke or Virginia or Carolina. We played Rutgers and Army and Cornell." Brown's spring schedule also involved a unique juggle of football practice, lacrosse games and track events; when, in his junior year, Syracuse made one of its periodic lacrosse forays to Baltimore, Brown didn't go. Some cited his reluctance to travel below the Mason-Dixon Line. The official excuse was that he needed to train for the upcoming 1956 US Olympic Trials, where Brown finished fifth in the decathlon.

Without him, Syracuse lost its opening three road games that season at the University of Baltimore, Navy and Maryland by a combined score of 61 to 20. He met the team coming back for its game at Harvard, scored two goals and assisted a few more; Syracuse won, 24–4. The following spring, with no football to distract him, Brown racked up 64 points, a nation-leading 43 goals and arguably the greatest end to a college athletic career. On May 18, 1957, after a two-year absence from track, he won the high jump and discus and took second in the javelin to prove the difference in Syracuse's dual-meet win over Colgate. Then—with no time to change out of his track shorts— Brown picked up a lacrosse stick and tallied a goal and three assists to seal the Orange's first win over Army in 23 years and its first undefeated season since 1924.

Still, Syracuse's schedule was considered weak—hence it lost out in the US Intercollegiate Lacrosse Association voting for the 1957 national championship to undefeated Johns Hopkins—and Brown's football reputation made him easier to underrate. His first and last chance to win over the elites came June 7 at the North-South All-Star Game at Hopkins's Homewood Field, against a Southern team populated by greats from Virginia and Washington and Lee, Maryland's All-American goalie, and a midfield anchored by three members of the national champs from Hopkins. None, it turned out, were in Brown's league.

"He put on a show for the people down there that think they invented the game," Simmons Jr. said. Before 6,500 fans, Brown won nearly every faceoff, scored three times in the first quarter, led the North to a lead it never lost, showed off a full repertoire of drives and passes and finished with five goals and two assists—all in the first half. "He scored one goal underhanded with his right hand, one overhanded with his right, one underhanded with his left, one overhanded with his left," the elder Roy Simmons recalled in

1984. "There was nobody like him . . . I coached this game for 46 years, and Jim Brown was the greatest lacrosse player I ever saw."

The day after the North-South game, the *Baltimore Sun*'s William Tanton—four years removed from his own Johns Hopkins playing career and soon to become the dean of American lacrosse writers—described Brown's career-ending "blaze of glory," fans being "left in awe" and "shaking their heads in disbelief" at his performance, the game's leaders conceding him the all-time title. Legendary Johns Hopkins coach Bob Scott, three weeks removed from the first of his seven national titles, had been in the stands that day, too.

"Jimmy Brown was a man among boys," Scott said in 2002. "He looked like a college senior playing against the best 10th graders . . . Hopkins had three senior midfielders playing against him for the South in that All-Star game—Jerry Bennett, Dick Steele and Carl Muly—and they couldn't stop him. He was just so superior with his size and speed and stick work."

Scott retired from coaching in 1974 as the sport's gold standard. Simmons Jr., who coached Syracuse to six national championships himself and retired in 1998, considers his perspective—which takes in his father's playing and coaching career, starting in 1924, and ranges all the way to 2024—better than anyone's. "I played with Jim and I played with other greats, and I've coached the best there is in the history of lacrosse," Simmons Jr. said. "Of course, in my mind he's the greatest."

COMPARING ON-FIELD SKILL across eras is a slippery task. Variables like training and equipment advances, quality of opponent and recency bias, ensure that generations will forever debate Jim Brown's quality against stars old and new. But 60 years later, there's no doubt that he remains the sport's Babe Ruth: its mythic figure, the lacrosse player non-lacrosse fans know best, with a presence made even more towering by its incongruity. Unlike Jackie Robinson during his historic rookie season, Brown wasn't an excellent Black athlete mixing in with equally talented whites. He was a Black man, in an openly racist era, emphatically dominating a sport of elite whites.

At the time, if only because lacrosse coverage rarely strayed from game reports, this fact declared itself obliquely. Tanton's laurel-crowning account, for example, refers to Brown as the "giant Negro athlete." Though a relatively benign example of the day's racial caricatures (in 1965, *TIME* magazine described Brown as a "fire-breathing, chocolate-colored monster"), it is striking. Studies and anecdotes detailing a tendency by white people to subconsciously assign more size—and menace—to Black men are legion. Brown was indeed bulky, but hardly the only six-foot-two man at Homewood that day; he wasn't, like exact contemporary Wilt Chamberlain, more than seven feet tall. But in lacrosse, his Blackness made him bigger.

In a sense, it does still. With each decade that passed after Brown, at 21, stepped away from the game forever; with every new lacrosse initiative into minority communities and every vexed comment about the slow growth in Black players; with any new report of friction felt by Black, Native and other players of color; with every incidence of racial invective from white fans and players that persisted deep into the 21st century—his lacrosse experience seemed even more of a marvel. Not because of the obvious visual: a Black man mastering a space of uniquely resilient whiteness. Rather, lacrosse's Jim Brown paradox lies below the surface, in the unpredictable personalities of game and man. It lies in the fact that Brown, a proud, militant, uncowable Black athlete— one of the 1960's most prominent activists, racial antennae forever on high alert—didn't just endure a sport with a long history of racism. He loved it.

Brown never once reported a racial incident while involved with lacrosse in the 1950s, on or off the field, growing up on Long Island or during his time at Syracuse. Not that they didn't happen: Roy Simmons Jr. says he heard plenty of abuse when they were on the field together, which Brown answered by scoring. After an opponent from Rensselaer Polytechnic Institute called him the N-word his senior year, he piled up six goals and two assists.

The one time he came close to admitting racism in a lacrosse space concerned his final game. Wary, indeed, of playing anywhere in the South, Brown later conceded that he had initially balked at traveling to Baltimore for the 1957 North-South All-Star Game that sealed his legacy. But he heard not one harsh word there, in city or stadium. Afterward, he received more congratulatory notes than he would in any other sport. Lacrosse, Brown always said, was his favorite.

"It's like a special fraternity, and there's not much racial pressure or racial emphasis," he said in 2005. "It's a sport that you play only because you love it."

Though a Northern school, Syracuse during Brown's time was barely integrated; in an enrollment of nearly 19,000, only about 30 students were

Black. The school's racial history featured the twisted walk of Wilmeth Sidat-Singh, who in 1936 became one of the first Black quarterbacks only because Syracuse administrators designated him as "Hindu," then banned him a year later from playing a game at the University of Maryland when his race was revealed in a Black newspaper. Sidat-Singh's death at 25, while flying with the Tuskegee Airmen during World War II, made little impact on the Syracuse mindset. In 1953, Manhasset lawyer Kenneth Molloy—a former Orange lacrosse All-American and Brown's prime advisor in high school— approached Syracuse officials on his behalf, but, Molloy later recalled, "they did not want [B]lack athletes."

Only after Molloy threatened to quit as chair of an ongoing fundraising drive did their attitude change. Lacking a football scholarship, forced to walk on, as a freshman Brown found himself the only Black player on the football team, and essentially segregated: assigned to a different dorm and lesser dining hall than the white players, with less meal money. He was repeatedly warned by coaches and teammates to avoid the path of a previous Black quarterback, Avatus Stone, who had dated a white woman.

Syracuse head coach Ben Schwartzwalder, a hard-nosed West Virginia native and much-decorated veteran of World War II, initially wanted to move Brown from running back to end. Brown refused. Another coach encouraged him to focus on punting. Brown was sure his skin color was the reason, and mentally dismissed the Syracuse football staff: *Okay, you racists . . . fuck you.* In practice Brown was known for sleeping or skipping drills he found useless, and in the year before he proved himself astonishing, Schwartzwalder would've been happy to see him leave. "I was tired of him," he said of Brown. "But I was told by people that I had to take him back."

The springtime shift from football to lacrosse was like moving from night to day. Practice was fun. Brown enjoyed his coaches and teammates. While dating "a pretty white co-ed" his senior year, he felt some campus hostility, but in Syracuse lacrosse circles nobody said a word. "One afternoon we hopped in my convertible, big red Pontiac," Brown wrote decades later. "I put down the top, drove to [Archbold] Stadium where I had a lacrosse game. All the fans were out on the road. We drove real slow, parked my car. I walked my girl to her seat in the bleachers, gave her a kiss, went down to change. Stands were so quiet you could hear time crawl."

The difference boiled down to the authority figures involved, and one in particular: Roy Simmons Sr. Syracuse's head lacrosse and boxing coach had already proven his color-blindness in 1954 when, after Syracuse beat a formidable Onondaga squad, he invited its goalie—a 25-year-old former army paratrooper named Oren Lyons Jr.—to play for him. Simmons Sr. was also one of Schwartzwalder's assistant coaches (and the man who, in 1936, had encouraged Sidat-Singh to play football), and, Brown said, "the only encouraging voice" he heard from the Syracuse football staff.

"The greatest man I have ever known," Brown once said. "Roy treated me so well during my first season in football that I went out for lacrosse purely because of my affection for him. He's the kind of guy you never want to let down. He was the reason I stayed in school."

Eventually Schwartzwalder gave Brown a scholarship, and the two men arrived at a mutual—if wary—respect. Schwartzwalder's racial legacy ended up an odd mix. His regime allowed plenty of room for the era's bigotry, but he coached Black players when many white coaches wouldn't and, when Syracuse traveled to play Texas Christian University in the 1957 Cotton Bowl, endorsed a small stand against racist custom. Until then, Black players weren't allowed in Dallas hotels and visiting teams housed them with local Black families. Syracuse, though, insisted on booking its hotel out of town. Brown stayed with the team, scored three touchdowns in the Orangemen's 28–27 loss and was named the game's Most Valuable Player. By the time he graduated in 1957, Brown became convinced that his struggles at Syracuse forced racial enlightenment upon Schwartzwalder's program, and he helped recruit halfback Ernie Davis, who in 1961 became the first Black player awarded the Heisman Trophy.

To Brown's contemporaries, perhaps the most eloquent statement on his college career came far from any athletic field. In 1963, after breaking all of Brown's rushing records and becoming the Cleveland Browns' number-one draft pick, Davis died of leukemia at 23. Fifteen hundred people crammed into the First Baptist Church in Elmira, New York, for the funeral service, and 3,000 more stood outside. President John F. Kennedy sent a telegram praising Davis's character and inspiring life. Teammates and staff from Syracuse University, as well as the Cleveland Browns and other NFL teams, flew in to pay their respects. A procession 300 cars long flowed from the church to Woodlawn Cemetery.

Afterward, Brown was walking with some Cleveland teammates when he spotted Schwartzwalder and Roy Simmons Sr. standing together. "Guys," he said. "I want to introduce you to my favorite coach."

Schwartzwalder heard, looked over, visibly paused. Brown brushed past and led his football friends to Simmons Sr. The Syracuse lacrosse coach, touched but embarrassed, found himself shaking hand after hand, struggling to say something to defuse the awkwardness. But Schwartzwalder had already walked on.

JIM BROWN KNEW the routes he didn't take. With 40 other mainstream universities dangling scholarships, he was one of the first Black athletes offered a broad choice of American higher education. He also could have opted for the well-trodden path of his forebears—a historically Black university. If not for the maneuverings of Ken Molloy (who lied to Brown about receiving his scholarship from Syracuse, then quietly raised the money to pay for his freshman year), the unrecruited Brown would never have suited up for the Orangemen. And the idea of Black men and women, united in betterment, always held its appeal.

After college, Brown's vision of Black progress played out like a projection of his independent, prickly—at times, intimidating—persona. He had no interest in accommodating white authority, opposed Martin Luther King Jr.'s policy of nonviolence and, though under intense pressure, refused in the late 1960s to disown the militant Nation of Islam. By the time he retired from pro football at 29, in 1966, he also shared Booker T. Washington's opposition to integration; Brown had become convinced that the road to "Black Power" lay in "Green Power," the development of Black businesses and wealth.

While against forced segregation, Brown believed integration only diluted Black economic growth and power, and looked to follow the example of politically strong ethnic blocs like "Koreans and the Jews and the Japanese." In 1966, with other Black businessmen, activists and athletes, Brown founded what became known as the Black Economic Union with offices in Cleveland and Los Angeles. The organization eventually spread to eight cities. The Kansas City branch alone, still in existence, has invested nearly $60 million in the community since opening in 1968, developing more than a thousand housing units and nearly 721,000 square feet of commercial and office space.

By then, Brown had left lacrosse far behind. There was little talk about growing the game—racially or geographically—in the 1960s, and he devoted his energies to pro football, acting and activism. Indeed, it could often seem as if he had never played the sport at all. Because Jim Brown, in the lacrosse sense, was self-contained. He did not, like Jackie Robinson in baseball, spark a steadily growing influx of Black talent. He did not, like tennis stars Venus and Serena Williams in the early 2000s, immediately inspire a wave of young African American players and fans to embrace a largely white game.

"I'm sure finances and exposure had a lot to do with minorities not playing," Brown said in 1993 of lacrosse. "The great black athletes wanted to get into the money sports."

Lacrosse's leaders also showed little interest in them. Alabama's bellwether football program is infamous for its failure to integrate until 1971, but Brown's favorite sport proved only marginally better. No African American played lacrosse in the Atlantic Coast Conference until Maryland midfielder Len Spicer in 1970. As the state's prestige private institution—founded by an abolitionist with Quaker roots—Johns Hopkins seemingly operated with greater latitude: On April 1, 1966, 21 years after the school admitted its first Black undergraduate and nine years after Brown's reve-latory performance at Homewood Field, Blue Jays head coach Bob Scott casually announced that Joe Carlton, a pre-med sophomore defenseman from Grambling, Louisiana, and Don Bosco Prep in Ramsey, New Jersey—who had never played before coming to Homewood—would be taking the field for the Blue Jays.

But neither Scott—nor the *Baltimore Sun*—publicly noted the ground-breaking color of Carlton's skin that day; nor after Hopkins's subsequent loss at Princeton; nor after Carlton became the first to hold Navy's All-American sharpshooter, Owen McFadden, scoreless; nor anytime publicly during Carlton's three seasons at Homewood. When, during an away game in Charlottesville, Virginia, Carlton's race did become an issue, he wasn't even aware.

On April 15, 1966, the team bus stopped at a restaurant outside Char-lottesville for lunch, and the players disembarked. Scott and two managers went inside to make sure it could accommodate the large party. "Mr. Scott, you don't have to worry," the man in charge said. "We'll prepare a nice meal for your Black player and serve him in the bus. We don't serve Black people in this restaurant."

Scott came back fuming, neck and face crimson. "Get on the bus!" he said. "Hurry up!" On board, Scott snapped that the reservation had been botched, and shut down the discussion.

"Nobody knew what happened," said Joe Cowan, Johns Hopkins All-American attackman and Carlton's teammate. "And the reason is because Bob Scott did not want to humiliate that young Black man. He'd never say anything about it."

Carlton, who became a doctor of neurology at a Montreal hospital, has never spoken publicly about his lacrosse career at Johns Hopkins. Cowan's most vivid memory occurred during the final game of Carlton's college career, May 18, 1968, when Johns Hopkins beat Maryland, 10–8, to win the national championship at Homewood Field. Midway through the second quarter, after Carlton ran on field, a Maryland defender "started to yell, 'Hey, they put the [N-word] in the game!'" Cowan recalled. "I didn't know what to do. Anyway, that's the end of the Joe Carlton story. Isn't that horrible?"

For a long time, lacrosse's knee-jerk defense for its overwhelming whiteness boiled down to quality, and on the largest scale that appeared true. Unlike baseball, a sport in which the Negro Leagues daily presented proof of African American interest and excellence, there was no large, organized, parallel group of elite Black lacrosse players, championed by white and Black media, demanding by word or deed to be allowed in.

Instead, lacrosse's onboarding of early Black talent resembled nothing so much as absorption. Converting football, soccer and hockey players is one of the sport's time-honored practices, even at America's greatest program. Joe Carlton never played high school lacrosse and came to Johns Hopkins as a basketball player. A decade earlier Ernest Bates, who in 1955 became the first Black football player in Blue Jays history, had also been wooed. "They wanted me to go out for lacrosse because I was fast," Bates said in 1999. "But . . . football took a lot of time and I was worried about my grades. So I didn't do it." Hopkins wasn't seeking statement-making Black stars; its first efforts at integration focused on raw athleticism. Those in charge wanted their progress to come one player at a time—and quietly.

But elite African Americans were available. Right outside Hopkins's door, in fact, a group waited with sticks in hand. It had taken them a while to understand: If Black people wanted a place in lacrosse, they were going to have to make it themselves.

II

THE SHADOW GAME

O NE SUMMER SATURDAY morning, Dr. Miles Harrison Jr. gave a tour of the mounted pictures, newspaper articles, plaques and lacrosse memorabilia mounted along the basement walls of his Pikesville, Maryland, home. He stopped below a team photo. "This was the North-South All-Star team in '71," he said. "You can find me there easily: just looking at the skin. I'll be tied forever to Jim Brown, who was the first African American to play in the North-South All-Star game. Who was number two? Me. But nobody remembers number two."

Harrison also admitted he wasn't sure of his facts; indeed, two Black men after Brown played in the North-South Game before him. But in a larger sense, he was correct. Miles Harrison was the second Black pioneer at lacrosse's oldest All-Star event, because he was the first selected from an historically Black college. And that's because no Black college ever fielded a lacrosse team before Miles Harrison and his friends decided to create one.

It was a passion project. Harrison would become the third in the family's line of doctors, part of what W. E. B. Du Bois dubbed Black America's "Talented Tenth," but he was also the fastest kid in school. In the mid-1960s, when Black quarterbacks were rare and Black swimmers rarer, Harrison started for two winning years as Forest Park High School's QB and swam the butterfly and 200 individual medley. Sophomore year, he picked up a lacrosse stick for the first time. Two years later, he was Forest Park's leading attackman and an all-Maryland Scholastic Association honorable mention.

In truth, Harrison's trailblazing was also a matter of timing. He attended Forest Park during peak "white flight," a tense and violent era when white populations nationwide emptied out of American cities and public schools. During his four years at Forest Park, Harrison estimates, enrollment flipped from majority white to majority Black—and the coaches still needed athletes. By 1967 Black people in Baltimore proper—many, like Harrison, introduced to lacrosse by football coaches looking to keep their players fit—had taken to the sport in growing numbers; 15 of his 17 Forester teammates were African American. In the Maryland Scholastic Association's premiere "A" Conference, predominantly Black lacrosse teams at Edmondson and City College high schools consistently held their own with private school powers Gilman, McDonogh and St. Paul's.

Dartmouth showed interest in Harrison, but he wanted to stay close to home: Johns Hopkins seemed logical. Harrison's academics alone made him worthy, and in spring of Harrison's senior year, 1967, someone on Bob Scott's staff invited him for a recruiting visit. It didn't seem earthshaking; Joe Carlton, the year before, had already crossed the team's racial barrier. Harrison gathered on campus with a few other out-of-town recruits, chatted with Hopkins All-American Joe Cowan, sat down for a nice lunch. Waiting for him, marking his seat, was a drinking glass with a small piece of paper inside. The words MILES HARRISON, FOREST PARK were inked above the Johns Hopkins University seal. He made sure to take it home. He has it still.

"Held onto it, thinking: *This is going to be a start of something big*," Harrison said. "But beyond that one moment, nothing else happened."

Perhaps Hopkins simply lost interest. Maybe Scott or a staffer spotted flaws during Harrison's senior season or found someone better; such is the way of recruiting. But the insidious nature of that era's racism lay in its myriad gradations, the way it left so much room for the demoralizing second-guess. Did some Hopkins administrator or alum decide that its sporting jewel wasn't ready to field more than one Black player? Or any Black men capable of becoming stars? As Harrison's son Kyle, the Johns Hopkins great, says, "Folks that look like him didn't really end up at places like that at that point."

Miles Harrison didn't dwell on such questions. He itched to get on the field. His uncle was a vice president at nearby Morgan State University, the historically Black college founded in 1867 and located in northeast Baltimore. Harrison thought he might play on the Bears' formidable football team, until his size and a bout of mononucleosis convinced him that he stood no chance. Soon after, Harrison and City College high school star Val Emery began agitating for a lacrosse program, energized whenever they bumped into another Baltimore public-school star overlooked by big-time programs: Edmondson's Wayne Jackson, Dickie Hall and the fearsome Stan Cherry; Patterson High's Joe Alex—another All-MSA defenseman, and Morgan State's first-ever white football player.

Morgan State was then a hotbed of activism. Though America's first Black college team grew amid the 1968 assassination of Martin Luther King Jr. and two successive summers of urban riots, societal impact wasn't much discussed. Players just wanted to play. "People continue to ask, 'How'd you guys know it was *time*?'" Harrison said. "Nobody knew it was time. Nobody had a *vision*."

Indeed, the most prominent voice on racial implications belonged to Howard "Chip" Silverman, the Bears' white, Jewish head coach. Since he was the only administrator with lacrosse experience, the assistant dean of Morgan's graduate school was pressed into presiding over the program's first meeting in the fall of 1969 and remained in charge until 1975. "The team has a lot of pride," Silverman told Baltimore's *Evening Sun* after its first-ever game on March 24, 1970, a respectable 10–6 loss to Amherst. "The boys want to show people that blacks can play lacrosse and play it well."

For so unconventional a team—the budget provided only 10 sticks; players smoked on the sideline before opening faceoffs—Silverman proved a perfect match. Irreverent, ever quotable, he'd seen every kind of street hustle from his days working, as the *Evening Sun* called it, "a swaggish clothing store" squat in the center of Baltimore's drug trade. He also had no qualms about raiding Morgan State's football roster, running out future Oakland Raider Raymond Chester in that inaugural season until Raiders head coach John Madden, fearing for his player's health, demanded that Silverman pull him. A few years later he dragooned seven-foot-one basketball star Marvin Webster, installing the "Human Eraser" at defense before his coach found out. One of the town's original "Diner Guys," Silverman ended up being an unlikely bridge between Baltimore's Black community and its provincial—and fading—white ethos.

He also knew just enough about lacrosse to explain the basics to novices filling out Morgan's roster; more accomplished heads like Harrison, Jackson and Ben Kimbers took care of strategy. Their first season, as a club team, the Bears went 4–3, beat the Johns Hopkins freshman team, lost 12–9 to Maryland's "B" squad and played its best game in a 12–8 loss to rising Division II power

University of Maryland, Baltimore County. A *Baltimore News-American* photographer captured Harrison scoring a goal against UMBC with his signature jump shot: at the apex of a 36-inch vertical leap, midsection level with three defenders' heads. "Look where the helmets are," he said, tapping the framed print on his wall. "Looking at my *waist*."

Less frequent were the opponents who snarled the N-word: it usually only happened once. "As soon as one of them called one of us that, the game changed," Harrison said. "We just turned into *Excuse me?*—and went after them. So why're you going to do something to make the dog bite you a second time?"

None of those incendiary moments seized the national spotlight. Unlike Muhammad Ali's resistance to the military draft in 1967 or the black-gloved protest of USA track stars Tommie Smith and John Carlos at the 1968 Summer Olympics, Morgan State lacrosse never broke out as a cultural flashpoint. Home crowds at Hughes Stadium were rarely more than paltry. Indeed, only one student on campus, activist Clarence "Tiger" Davis, seemed to invest the Ten Bears with a larger mission. "That team was an extension of the civil rights movement and the fight for equality," said Davis, who went on to serve 24 years in the Maryland House of Delegates. "That's why I followed the team. It was important what they did. Their response to the racism was to play harder, and get in some good licks."

In 1971, Morgan State lacrosse's first year as a varsity sport and Miles Harrison's senior year, the Ten Bears won nine games and lost five. Harrison finished with 22 goals and 16 assists for 38 points, just a handful behind teammate Wayne Jackson, the nation's highest-scoring midfielder—and better than anyone playing for Johns Hopkins. Coming off their 35th national championship, the Blue Jays won just three games and—perhaps most painful—found themselves conspicuously ignored when the NCAA announced the field for its newly created Division I lacrosse tournament.

IN ITS 11-YEAR span as a varsity entity, starting in 1971, the Morgan State Bears were an unqualified success. Chip Silverman expanded his recruiting to Long Island and the team became a Division II force, ranking in the top 10 four times, producing All-Americans and reaching the playoffs twice, occasionally beating an elite name like Harvard or Georgetown. In 1972, perhaps the most diverse game in lacrosse history occurred when Syracuse—backboned by Six Nations stars Freeman "Bossy" Bucktooth, a late-20s Oliver Hill and his cousin Ron Hill—visited Morgan State at Hughes Stadium. Silverman privately dubbed the physical and bloody contest, marred by fights and racial insults, the "Ultimate Affirmative Action Bowl."

"The Indian players called the blacks 'wool heads and Brillo tops,'" Silverman wrote in his book *Ten Bears*, co-authored with Miles Harrison, "while the Morgan blacks referred to the Indians as 'Spics, Tonto, and Crazy Horse.'"

Syracuse won, 17–13. Morgan's Wayne Jackson made the most lasting impression, his four goals and single-handed dominance on faceoffs all but announcing him as Jim Brown's first true lacrosse heir. "He's a superman," Syracuse head coach Roy Simmons Jr. said after. "Jimmy had a better stick, but Wayne's a helluva athlete."

But Morgan State's signature moment—the cinema-ready breakthrough that prompted state proclamations of honor in 1990 and ensured a permanent exhibit in the Lacrosse Hall of Fame—was its win over Washington and Lee University. In 1975, the private school in Lexington, Virginia, named in honor of the slaveholding Founding Father and the Confederacy's supreme icon, was a Division I lacrosse power that hadn't lost a home game in four years or a regular-season game in two. The year before, W&L beat Morgan State by 12 goals. With two of its All-American defensemen returning, the smart money was on more of the same.

But on March 8, 1975, the Bears traveled to Lexington, Virginia, and caught the Generals napping, overcame a three-goal deficit at halftime to win, 8–7. Silverman's prize Long Island recruit, Dave Raymond, paid off with two key goals. Morgan's five-foot-three, white two-time All-American goalie, Courtenay Servary, stopped 25 shots. The lone W&L player to vex him, Donnie Carroll, had a chance to tie in the final seconds, but Servary snagged the lunging attempt. The whistle blew. Other Bears hurled their sticks in the air and danced. Servary dropped to the ground, hyperventilating so badly that he passed out.

Before their bus pulled out for the ride home, Washington and Lee head coach Jack Emmer made a point of climbing aboard. "That was no upset or fluke," the future Hall of Famer said. "You guys are a great team."

It took a while for the world to catch on. After the *Baltimore Sun* buried a short piece deep inside the next day's sports section, the *Evening Sun* waited another 10 days before admitting that it had underplayed one of American sports' great upsets because it had been distracted by the Atlantic Coast Conference basketball tournament.

Only lacrosse's tiny Black network was instantly abuzz. A day after the upset, one of Raymond's close friends from Long Island walked into the Duke lacrosse locker room in Durham, North Carolina, "tooting my horn," said Chuck Sherwood. The Blue Devils were due to face Washington and Lee in just three days. Sherwood, a goalie, was both Duke and the ACC's first Black lacrosse player. "See, you guys?" he said. "Morgan State's a Black school and they beat Washington and Lee's behind! You're telling me we can't go up there and compete against them?"

Washington and Lee crushed Duke, 23–2. But the magnitude of Morgan State's upset didn't truly emerge until months later, when Emmer's Generals snapped Johns Hopkins's 27-game home winning streak to reach the 1975 NCAA semifinals and ended the season just two games shy of winning the Division I national title. By the end of that year, when Silverman retired, no one could question that he and his players and program had achieved what Althea Gibson and Arthur Ashe previously achieved in tennis, what Jim Brown achieved alone at Syracuse, what no one in lacrosse before had dared to try en masse.

"We proved," Silverman said, "that the Black athlete could play an elitist white sport."

Yet, in Black Baltimore, the phrase "elitist white sport" would have puzzled some, given how the infusion of Black talent into lacrosse at public schools had trickled down to the street. Born in the McCullough Projects before moving to Edmondson Village at five years old, Lloyd Carter was given his first stick by his older brother in 1968 and grew up surrounded by the game.

"In a four-block radius, I would say 90 percent of the guys in my area played lacrosse. We all played and all were good," Carter said. "It wasn't a white sport. It's what we did in our neighborhood. I never even assumed it was a 'white sport' until I was at Morgan and realized, *Yo, we're the only Black team*."

Literally right next door, local schools like Johns Hopkins, Maryland, UMBC and Loyola ignored the Black players in Baltimore public schools. Though an all-state attackman, Carter's only offer upon graduation in 1976 was a full-ride academic scholarship to George Washington University in DC. "That opportunity was never placed in front of us," he said. Nobody was getting recruited. That's the truth. "It wasn't a negative, *Let's march! 'We Shall Overcome'* thing. It was just the reality . . . Where I grew up, I played with some of the best lacrosse players I've ever seen. One of my best friends, Anthony Newby? Just phenomenal with the lacrosse stick. He went to Edmondson, played club ball, but he never got recruited to play college. It's just two different societies. They don't see us as . . . you know."

EVEN IN THE AFTERMATH of the Washington and Lee win, its told-you-so apex, the Morgan State program was in trouble. Cutbacks in the athletic budget loomed. Silverman, who spent most of his $1,500 salary on equipment and player meal money, retired after the 1975 season. Though the threat of extinction never lifted over the next six years, lacrosse's Black pipeline kept pumping. Donnie Brown, the kid "bitten" by lacrosse at Patterson Park, played for Bears legend Val Emery at City College High and went on to ensure that Morgan State didn't go down without a fight. During Brown's senior year, 1981, the Bears beat Division I pillars Villanova and Notre Dame in one three-day span. He scored three goals in the March 20 win over the Fighting Irish, including the game-winner 90 seconds into overtime. But his most vivid memory of that final season had nothing to do with heroics.

On the afternoon of May 6, 1981, minutes before the de facto Division II semifinals against crosstown rival Loyola at its field off North Charles Street, nobody knew that the game would be Morgan State lacrosse's last. But all year Brown had been hearing of lacrosse programs around the city shutting down, each loss reminding him of what he'd come to love: how lacrosse lent him an identity, humbled him, gave him confidence and credibility and a common language when rubbing elbows with Baltimore's network of white elites.

Brown did something very unlike him before the final game against Loyola, huddling up his teammates to kneel and say a silent prayer. For a moment, all the chatter and shuffle at Loyola's Evergreen campus seemed to go quiet.

Please, God, Brown begged. *Keep it alive. Send somebody to make sure lacrosse survives here in Baltimore.*

Loyola beat the Bears that day, 25–8. In the fall of 1981 Morgan State unceremoniously dissolved its lacrosse program and left players like Lloyd Carter, the junior out of West Baltimore who scored twice in the program's finale, on their own.

Months after the last game, Brown was bartending at the downtown Hyatt Regency, drinking and smoking on the corner of Carolina and

Lafayette, when he got hit by a bad feeling. Mass layoffs had carved away nearly a third of the 18,000 jobs at the Bethlehem Steel Plant at Sparrows Point. Drug culture was seeping everywhere: pistols flashing, 15-year-olds carrying too much cash. He enlisted in the army that July, sure that he'd be leaving Baltimore forever. But the news followed him to basic training: a childhood friend from East Baltimore murdered, a young mother gunned down in his old neighborhood's first drive-by. Brown's eight-year hitch took him to Arizona, Texas, California, Hawaii, South Korea, Japan, Thailand. The farther away, he figured, the better.

Still, to each new stop Brown brought his two lacrosse sticks. "You always run into another player," Brown said. "Basic training in Fort Jackson, one of my drill sergeants was a lacrosse player. When I got to Fort Huachuca, Arizona, I met a guy from New Jersey who had a stick, couldn't wait to find somebody to play catch with. When I went to Hawaii, there was a lot of officers up at the Italian family day picnic and I brought my sticks out. Oh, that was gold."

IN THE MID-1980s, the air surrounding lacrosse seemed aswirl with change: Johns Hopkins's domination had been broken, the Iroquois Nationals were emerging and former UNC co-captain Steve Stenersen—the nonprofit Lacrosse Foundation's executive director—had come home to Baltimore with a bent for new, even subversive, ideas. The city needed any and all.

In November 1983, a 14-year-old boy named DeWitt Duckett was shot in the neck and killed at Harlem Park Middle School in West Baltimore. His death caused a national sensation when police—erroneously, as revealed decades later—alleged that Duckett had been murdered for his Georgetown basketball jacket. Local revulsion centered on the fact that his was the first homicide ever in a Baltimore city school, a sign that the wolf had crossed a sacred threshold. A horrified human resources manager at Westinghouse, Earl King, reached out to Harlem Park with an offer to create educational incentives, donate computers and send its own engineers into classrooms. King, who played at Gettysburg College, also kicked in thousands of dollars for a lacrosse program.

Harlem Park's principal, Stanley Holmes, was sure there would be no interest. But King convinced school volunteer Earl Banks to coach. Two hundred kids, most with no lacrosse skills, showed up for tryouts in the winter of 1984. Before a crowd of 1,500, Harlem Park's team won its first game by six, finished 7–1–1 for the season and drew an average of 800 fans in a neighborhood that accounted for one-third of Maryland's murders. Player participation was tied to grades. Attendance went up. Grades followed.

The next two springs, 400 children showed up for tryouts. Kids in Harlem Park dropped basketballs and footballs and dubbed a new street game "Ghetto Lacrosse": hit the tree with a can and score. In 1988 Stenersen—fresh off declaring that "lacrosse is no longer a sport played only by Indians and preppies"—applied for a $134,000 grant to expand the program to low-income areas throughout Baltimore County. The Baltimore City Middle School Lacrosse League was born. Trophies for the highest grade-point average were handed out at halftime of the title game; attendance and promotion rates spiked. Five more local schools instantly signed on, and an additional seven in ensuing years; the league has existed, under various titles and authorities, ever since. Copycat programs began in Hartford, Connecticut; Newark, New Jersey; and Wilmington, North Carolina.

Though players, coaches and officials at lacrosse's elite level remained overwhelmingly white, groundwork for a more inclusive future appeared to be laid. An all-Black midfield, the "Soul Patrol," keyed four high-scoring Division III national championships for the Hobart men from 1984–87, and a sprinkling of Black players were now found on Division I rosters at North Carolina, Virginia, Loyola and Syracuse. The first Black head coach in Division I, Tina Sloan Green, led Temple's predominantly white women's team to national titles in 1982, 1984 and 1988.

"There was a parochialism that was present in the game in the 1950s, '60s and '70s," Stenersen crowed to the traditionalist's hometown paper, the *Baltimore Sun*, in 1993. "There was an old guard, 'The Lords of Lacrosse,' that just didn't want the game to grow. But the sport has gone through a renaissance, nearly doubling in participation from the 1980s to the 1990s. I think that period of parochialism is over."

MUSTERING OUT of the US Army in 1990, Donnie Brown had a homesick wife and the thought that he should keep her happy. They returned to Baltimore. The marriage didn't last; Baltimore and lacrosse did. Brown came upon his younger brother, Kenny, trying to play one day and the sight broke his heart. "I was like: *There's no way you be my brother and be that horrible*," Brown said.

Coaching Kenny led to a reunion with his Morgan State linemate, Joe "Flaky" Fowlkes—the first Black man, in 1977, to lead the nation in scoring; first to grace the cover, in 1978, of the NCAA lacrosse guide; now coach at Lombard Middle School. By then, Fowlkes had turned Lombard into the preeminent power in the nascent Baltimore City Middle School Lacrosse League.

Donnie Brown was all-in. He spent the decade establishing himself as the area's lax godfather, founding a program at Diggs-Johnson Middle School, taking over as head coach of Baltimore County's Woodlawn High, running club teams, serving as middleman between STX and inner-city high schools whenever the manufacturer had surplus gear to unload. Amid all that hustle, he began to understand: The God he begged on Morgan State's last day was listening. "I think what I'm doing is answering the prayer that I prayed," Brown said. "Whether I wanted to be or not."

By the early 1990s, 800 minority kids had cycled through Baltimore's middle school league, but few developed into even small-college prospects. At lacrosse's highest level, the percentage of Black men and women in Division I college lacrosse remained stubbornly low—below 2 percent—compared to 92 percent white, and the remaining 6 percent Latino, Native American, Asian/Pacific Islander, or mixed race. The pipeline was clogged. Fresh eyes figured out that the blockage involved money.

Lloyd Carter, the last Morgan State player to score before the program was killed off, had spent his first 18 years after college away from the game, moving up the ranks of the Baltimore Fire Department to deputy chief. When his son, Lantz, began playing, Carter reconnected with old Morgan teammates Donnie Brown and City College (H.S.) coach Anthony "Merc" Ryan in the middle school league. Then, in 1999, Morgan lacrosse pioneer Wayne Jackson, athletic director at Baltimore's Northwestern High, asked Carter to be his new head coach, and he hit the new reality of scholastic sports head-on.

Coming of age, Carter and other inner-city kids had spent their Baltimore summers butting heads and sticks with elite high school and college talent from Johns Hopkins, Princeton and Maryland in the 550-player, non-profit Hero's lacrosse league. In the ensuing decades, with college admissions increasingly competitive and athletics seen as a golden ticket, hopping onto the merry-go-round of youth travel clubs and recruiting showcases had become near mandatory. The lacrosse version cost anywhere from $5,000 to

$10,000 a year. All the elites played for travel teams; Carter's Northwestern kids sat idle. And all over Baltimore city and county, he watched one good Black player after another go unrecruited, promising careers ended too soon.

The most galling case was Shawn Medlin, Northwestern's high-scoring attackman in 2000 and 2001. When Carter first met Medlin—great smile, but no bigger than five foot six—he expected disappointment. Then Medlin flicked his stick, unleashed a few quicksilver dodges: Carter couldn't stop himself from exclaiming, "Oh, my god." He had seen Wayne Jackson. He played with plenty of Baltimore studs and college All-Americans. Shawn Medlin remains the best lacrosse player he's ever seen. "He had everything," Carter said. "Speed, quickness, left hand, right hand, IQ. He ended up being, like, the leading scorer in the state."

It didn't matter. At the end of his senior year, at the 2001 Maryland State Lacrosse Coaches Association All-Star Game, the *Baltimore Sun* was still referring to Medlin as "little-noticed." The contest featured blue-chippers bound for Division I-A programs, including Kyle Harrison, soon to be the most famous Black player in Hopkins history, a private school product who had grown up accessing the travel teams and showcases that college coaches flocked to. Yet, that day Medlin outplayed him and everyone else, scored three goals and was named the game's offensive Most Valuable Player. He ended up playing community college lacrosse in Catonsville.

"They just ignored him," Carter said. "Nobody gave him a look. I said, 'This cannot happen again.'"

Late in 2001 Carter and Merc Ryan founded Blax Lax, Inc., a nonprofit program aimed at inner-city high school and college players. By 2003, a Blax Lax adult club was playing in the final of the Howard County Summer League; in 2004, organized under US Lacrosse's new BRIDGE initiative, Blax Lax featured winter camps, a Baltimore City senior All-Star showcase for college coaches and a "Runn and Gunn" summer league. Its pirate-like logo—hovering over the phrase STIX IN DA HOOD—featured two crossed lacrosse sticks and a silhouette of Shawn Medlin's head, baby dreadlocks flying.

In 2005, while still coaching at Northwestern High, Carter also began the still-unrealized quest to revive Morgan State's varsity program, co-founding and coaching the school's low-level club team. He had come to realize: even with programs like Blax Lax, waiting for mainstream colleges to come calling was a fool's game. Three decades had passed since the founding of Morgan State lacrosse, but little had changed.

"Because Morgan was gone, kids weren't getting recruited," Carter said. "Even after that type of career, they would put their stick down. Because they had nowhere to go."

———————⟨⟩

GROWING UP, Kyle Harrison possessed all the great athletic assets: a 39-inch vertical leap, hand-eye coordination, liberating quickness. But perhaps his most valuable tool was the handicap he lacked: Harrison never thought he didn't belong. Surrounded by whites, he didn't know that the game was considered "white" and could feel hostile to someone with dark skin. When it mattered most, at the point in a boy's life when such news can curdle interest, Harrison had no idea. "My dad played lacrosse," he says. "He's Black."

American sports has many hallowed tropes, but none more enduring than father and son playing catch. It's particularly relevant to a low-pay, low-visibility sport like lacrosse, which abounds in stars brought into the faith by obsessed fathers, grandfathers, uncles and—increasingly now—mothers. Born in 1983, Kyle is one of the few African Americans with generational bona fides. His dad is Miles Harrison Jr. "Big poster of him wearing number 18 in his office," Kyle says. Their home was strewn with sticks. They played catch.

The future Hopkins star, future Tewaaraton Award winner, future president of Baltimore's Charm City Youth Lacrosse nonetheless came to the game almost incidentally. His father, preoccupied with a thriving practice in general surgery and an assistant professorship at the University of Maryland Medical School, didn't push it. Kyle dreamed of becoming the next Michael Jordan, with soccer as a backup. Halfway into his prep career at Friends School of Baltimore, Kyle liked picking up a stick but "lacrosse was my worst sport," he says. "By far."

An overwhelming week at Five-Star basketball camp told Kyle that North Carolina wouldn't be calling. Then Harrison put up All-American lacrosse numbers against name private schools his junior year, and was invited to the Top 205 showcase for the area's best players. His heart still lay on the hardwood; Harrison showed up at Loyola wearing AND1 basketball shorts below his knees, bristling with crossover moves cribbed from NBA stars. His stick and shooting skills were raw, but Harrison dodged and juked around everyone. "I don't know his name," a coach said that night. "But there's a kid in AND1 shorts that no one on the field can cover."

The instant the recruiting window opened in early July, then–Hopkins lacrosse coach Dave Pietramala offered Harrison an all-but-free ride. The only North Carolina school interested in him for basketball was Davidson, not UNC. He was now committed to lacrosse, and falling in love.

"No sport in America has our history: that's the first thing that draws you in," Kyle said. "But when you get down to tangible things, lacrosse seems the best sport available. If you're an athlete, it combines the best parts of all the other sports we love: the physicality of football, the X's and O's of hockey—and offensively, if you understand pick-and-rolls, all these things from basketball. I *popped* because I was so good at basketball. It was just on turf, and I'm holding the ball in a stick.

"The last reason I love it: we are one of the few sports left that it comes down to who works the hardest. I'm six one: I couldn't play hoops. Football? Ain't happening. You could be overweight, underweight, skinny, tall, slow, whatever: but if you're willing to put the time in with your stick and understand the game, you can be an All-American. You can play professionally. And if you're the top-end athlete? You can put it all together and you can be just dominant. You can be the best of all time. You can be Jim Brown."

Harrison remembers no altercations or slurs at Friends, or after he graduated in 2001 and started playing at Hopkins—or, for that matter, in any NCAA, professional or international lacrosse space his entire career. "I was just super lucky," he said. "I mean it: my close friends—Jovan Miller, Chazz Woodson, Shamel and Rhamel Bratton—a lot of these guys have been through and seen some awful things, and for whatever reason I've been lucky in that. I've never had a confrontation on a field where someone said the N-word to me or something racial."

Perhaps because he arrived at Homewood Field already one of the nation's best midfielders, started every game and grew into the era's best overall player, nobody wanted to give Kyle Harrison extra motivation. Still, Miles recalls one white club coach benching his uninjured son for so long that white parents asked him why. "Think about that," Miles replied. "You know the answer to that question." And whenever a rap song played and some white teammate bellowed lyrics featuring the N-word, Kyle found himself debating—even as he was putting on jersey and pads: *Should I say something here?*

"That's so uncomfortable," Kyle said. "Because what would be the best way of explaining? Like: *I know said person isn't racist . . . but he's obviously uninformed if he doesn't get the weirdness of doing that.* And it's just so much a deeper conversation than I have time for before going out in the field to play a game."

Miles never forgot that, back in the 1960s, he'd have great performances for Forest Park High—a few touchdowns, three or four goals, a big win—and his own father would open the next day's newspaper hoping for a nice write-up. Instead, there'd be a photo and story detailing some white Gilman kid's two-goal day, and the sight of his dad sagging. Three decades later with Kyle, he had reflexively steeled himself for more of the same, but the world had changed. Most important, Johns Hopkins wanted his son. And, from Kyle's junior summer on, more than just Pietramala and staff. Bob Scott—Hopkins's seven-time national champion coach, the legend who had recruited and then ghosted Miles in 1967, was the first voice to alert Pietramala to Miles Harrison's son. It all happened so fast—Kyle committed in December of his senior year—that Miles never thought to buttonhole Scott and ask about his own recruiting saga in the 1960s.

It would've been easy, at any time over the next four years, for Kyle to charge his narrative at Homewood as redemptive—a mission, even. That wasn't the Harrison way. Father and son left Miles's recruitment unspoken, except inside the home. The Christmas before his first season, Kyle told his dad that he'd be wearing number 18 at Hopkins, "in honor of the first person from our family," Kyle said, "that was recruited there and should've worn that number there."

UNLIKE JIM BROWN, playing in a bubble of one, Harrison's college career unfolded amid lacrosse's first notable crop of Black stars: Princeton's Damien Davis, UVa's John Christmas, Maryland goalie Harry Alford, Army attackman John Walker, Brown's Chazz Woodson. But, as an immediate starter for the sport's most storied program—albeit one trying to overcome a 14-year title drought—Kyle set the tone for Black players everywhere. Eighty-two seconds into his first game in 2002 as a freshman, at No. 1 Princeton, he scored his first goal; he later popped in another and Hopkins won. Two weeks later, in his first home game against archrival and then-No.1 Syracuse, Harrison scored and Hopkins won.

During his career, the Blue Jays went 55–6 and never lost at home. Still, leadership—not scoring—proved to be Kyle Harrison's sweet spot. The natural right-hander sent an early message by spending his entire freshman summer shooting only with his left, drilled endlessly to make himself one of the best faceoff specialists in Hopkins history and became the sport's ultimate playmaker. The only complaint by Blue Jays coaches concerned his ego, or lack thereof; Harrison needed prodding to take over a game. But after the Blue Jays endured their third straight crashout at the 2004 Final Four, he typed a team-wide email pledging to change. Indeed, in 2005 Harrison emerged as the Jordanesque force of his dreams, shaking off regular double- and triple-team defenses to lead the team in scoring, assists, example and timing. And with Hopkins's unbeaten record teetering against Navy, he exploded with a career-high five goals, including one to tie the game in the final seconds of regulation and one to win it in overtime.

"He didn't score all that many points," Paul Rabil, then a freshman, said of Harrison's senior season. "What jumps out, to me, is that all his goals were either the first goal of the game, the icebreaker, or the game winner—and that is unique. I'm not sure there have been any Tewaaraton winners whose stat lines looked like Kyle's. He won ground balls, played defense and offense, but he didn't set NCAA records. That speaks to his presence on the field."

Off the field, Kyle's sense of history also matured. As a child, he absorbed his dad's lacrosse career as just another part of family lore. Then Miles published his 2001 book *Ten Bears*, re-sparking talk about trailblazing Morgan State. Then his dad's old teammates kept showing up in the stands, cheering him like one of their own.

"It wasn't until I'd have a big game at Hopkins and there'd be 12 of them standing there to give me hugs afterwards—that I started putting it together," Kyle said. "Not only how supportive they were of me. But, really, how everything they went through back then . . . I was the product of it. I started to understand how proud those guys were. The look on their face was almost like: *It was worth enduring what we had to go through in order to have this happen.* Because without that? If they didn't stick it out and do what they did, I wouldn't have had the opportunity I had. I felt that."

Nothing captured that progress better than the 2005 NCAA semifinals in Philadelphia, when Harrison, John Christmas and Henry Alford led their teams into championship weekend before a crowd of 45,275. At halftime of the Duke-Maryland clash, John Walker and Harrison were named first-team Division I All-Americans—the first time two Black men earned the honor in the same season. Then Harrison asserted his preeminence. In the second

semifinal, after making little impact while Virginia scored four straight goals
to take a 7–6 lead, the Blue Jays captain charged out of a 46-minute lightning
delay and scored to tie matters, 7–7; his best friend, Benson Erwin, went
on to tally the game winner in overtime for the 9–8 win. Two days later,
Kyle scored twice in the championship game and Hopkins edged a hungry
Duke squad, 9–8. The triumph completed Johns Hopkins's first undefeated
season since 1984, and ended the longest title drought in program history.

A few days later, Miles and Kyle attended a celebration barbeque at the
Chesapeake Bay home of a former Blue Jays star. The buzz from Hopkins's
43rd national title was still fresh, and the subsequent awarding of the 2005
Tewaaraton Award to Kyle—the only Black man, and Johns Hopkins player, to
win it—kept the congratulations coming. The hundreds of alums and parents
and coaches and players gathered for a presentation. Bob Scott, now 75 years
old, called Miles; his wife, Wanda; and Kyle up front. The crowd fell quiet.

Scott opened by speaking about Kyle's greatness. Then the old coach
pivoted, said that Kyle was like so many: he started playing lacrosse because
his dad played. Someone passed Scott a handful of shimmery blue cloth.

"What we'd like to make you understand is your son means the world to
Hopkins," Scott told Miles. "He restored credibility to the Hopkins lacrosse
program. And we understand how much an integral part in that you were, and
we've looked at your accomplishments through your book, and understand
that you were an elite player. Because of that, we feel like you should be in
the Hopkins family. And we're going to make you an honorary Blue Jay."

Scott handed the bundle to Kyle's father. Miles held it up by the shoulders, let one end drop, revealing to the applauding crowd a Johns Hopkins
lacrosse jersey with the number 11, the first one he wore in 1971 during
Morgan State's inaugural varsity season before switching to 18. Signatures
covered the front. Kyle's read, "I love you, Dad."

Scott locked eyes with Miles. Neither had ever spoken about what did
or didn't happen with one Black lacrosse player's recruitment in 1967, and
they didn't speak about it now. But both men's eyes filled with tears.

A few weeks later, Miles was visiting the Hopkins lacrosse office.
Waiting for him was a framed montage: photos of his playing career, of his
moment with Bob Scott and the jersey, all of it under the title "Honorary
Blue Jay Miles Harrison." On the back, 18 signatures were scrawled, all of
them Hopkins royalty. Seven-time national champion Bob Scott. Two-time
All-American Homer Schwartz. All-American Jimmy Greenwood. Three-

time All-American Dave Pietramala. National champion and North-South All-Star Seth Tierney. And his son.

KYLE HARRISON'S HEROICS in the spring of 2005 clearly represented a symbolic leap forward for Black lacrosse, but the resultant payoff—gilding on the lily—sealed his career as a mark of racial advancement.

At the time, even with the lacrosse boom cresting, only a handful of players could make a good living off the game. Between the newest iteration of the professional field game, Major League Lacrosse, which ran from May to August and paid average annual salaries of $18,000; the indoor National Lacrosse League, with its November–April season, and yearly salaries topping out at $25,000; and camps and equipment endorsements, a half-dozen stars earned annual incomes well into six figures. This elite featured two sets of transcendent brothers: Syracuse alums Paul and Gary Gait; and Casey, Ryan and Mikey Powell. The rest side-hustled to night practices and weekend games after full-time work as brokers, bankers, Wall Street traders, teachers, coaches.

Kyle Harrison's emergence from Johns Hopkins in 2005 was a textbook example of the right man at the right time. With his way paved by Mikey Powell, whose college pyrotechnics alerted corporate America that lacrosse could smack of alternative cool, Harrison ticked all boxes for marketers looking to hook young, urban and Black fans enthralled by the NFL and NBA. STX, a Baltimore-based gear maker, signed him for what one source estimates at close to $100,000 annually to what would end up being a career-long deal; Harrison's K18 line of lacrosse gear is now used by more than 60 college programs. Nike followed with its first sponsorship of a lacrosse player: within three years, Harrison's annual earnings edged toward $1 million. Between his dazzling MLL career and self-founded LXM pro tour, Harrison mainstreamed the sport like no other; in 2013, Beats Electronics customized headphones for select celebrities, including singers Lady Gaga and Justin Bieber, soccer star Wayne Rooney, NBA stars LeBron James and Kobe Bryant—and Kyle Harrison.

He gave as much as he got. Harrison became Exhibit A for whites eager to demonstrate the sport's diversity, a seemingly pain-free example of what, for a Black athlete, lacrosse could be. But he was, indeed, "super lucky." Contemporary Chazz Woodson followed a similar path, starting with a father who had played in college and an elite private education in Norfolk, Virginia. But unlike Harrison, Woodson grew up acutely conscious of navigating two worlds: the blue-collar, majority-Black town of Norview where his family lived, and the predominantly white Norfolk Academy where he went to school from first to 11th grade.

Even small moments, like arriving at a rec football practice with lacrosse stick in hand, provided a jolt. "I got some odd looks," Woodson said. "I was the only private school kid. I was the one that spoke 'proper English.' I was the one that seemed white. How did I manage that? I busted my ass as an athlete, and that was usually the equalizer. If I could hit as well, or run as fast, all of those walls fell down. Otherwise I was going to be the dorky, white/Black kid."

Woodson also felt himself at a remove from his white teammates. "I didn't live in the same neighborhood with any of the kids I went to school with," Woodson said. "I distinctly remember in lower school trying to fig- ure out how all these kids knew each other, already, at Norfolk Academy. It didn't take long to realize brothers, sisters, parents were in the same fields or grew up in the same neighborhoods or went to the same college. I was used to being the lone wolf, the outlier, and it was never a major issue to me. But in hindsight, how many other outliers are there . . . that don't get the same attention or don't get the same opportunities?"

Arriving at Brown University in 2001, Woodson had a chance to dictate his environment. As a lacrosse player, he could have followed the easy path of eating, studying and partying entirely with his overwhelmingly white—and welcoming—teammates. But he was wary of the impulse that Fred Opie calls,

> a real tragedy—and not a lot of people talk about it: Black folks who get into the game are trying so hard to be accepted as insiders. And they try to the point of repressing their own culture, assimilate to the point where the only thing culturally that says "African American" about them is when they have a holiday meal with their relatives. They grow up in an environment where they're one of the few Black folks, but don't keep a Black consciousness.
>
> They take on a lacrosse consciousness—from who they marry, to who to hang out with and what they do. It's unfortunate that to be a lacrosse player means you have to take on this different identity. I know that, because I went through that. I've seen that you're accepted in the lacrosse community if you assimilate.

To feed a hunger to connect with his heritage, shed the weight of being so many white people's one Black friend, Woodson consciously broke away from Brown lacrosse. After practice and games, he plugged into the campus's African American community, humming with political and artistic speakers and programming that had nothing to do with sports. It helped, especially when Brown's liberal reputation and Ivy League pretentions proved no barrier to ugliness.

Near the end of the first quarter of one game, an opponent "called me a nigger," Woodson said. "I had to make a choice at that moment. This is where the way I was raised came into play, because I know it's always the second person that gets caught. I also know how it looks if—all of a sudden—I, the lone Black guy on the field between two teams of 35, 40 guys, go off and start a fight. There's a very good chance that it could work out horribly for me. I knew that, one, I had to temper my reaction, and two, it was important to pull myself aside, calm down, and get back to playing. So I pulled myself out of the game. Because I could feel myself. I knew I was going to lose it and do something crazy."

Another time, after a road loss and a long bus ride home, a drunken Brown teammate was stumbling outside the bus. "He caught me looking at him while everybody's trying to help him and he's like, 'What are you looking at, you fucking nigger?'" Woodson said.

> *Again, everything in me said,* Just punch this guy in the face. *Because, one, what is he going to do? And two, what is anybody else going to say about it? They're all standing there. They heard it.*
>
> *But I also know: What if I get brought up on some kind of charge? I'm at Brown University. I can't fail: that's not an option. I can't get kicked out. It goes back to pros and cons, and not reacting the way you normally want to react. To this day, I don't have a clue if he remembers it or knows. Nobody ever said anything around me about it. There were two or three guys trying to help him. There were no coaches around, but I don't know if anybody said anything to a coach. I don't know if they ever brought it up to that kid himself. I have no idea. I didn't bring it up.*

IN APRIL 2006, with the head coach fired and the season canceled and the alleged rape of a Black stripper by three members of the Duke lacrosse team morphing into America's latest cable-TV staple, a Black elementary school gym teacher flew from his home on Long Island to Durham, North Carolina, to save the program. Careers and reputations were crashing. Loud voices were calling for Duke men's lacrosse to be terminated. Chuck Sherwood couldn't have that.

"It's important for two reasons," Sherwood said on Mother's Day 2006, on the eve of the Durham County grand jury's decision to indict one of the team's co-captains on rape and kidnapping charges. "Playing lacrosse was very important to me. And when I look at it from a historical standpoint, being the first Black player to play there, that's the contribution I made. I don't want it to go away."

Sherwood wasn't wrong to worry. Every debate that conflated the alleged crime with the Duke players' wealth or whiteness or family status or alcohol consumption, every recounted drinking infraction or legal misdemeanor or disgusting act or word, seemed to also indict the sport they played. Duke's president, Richard Brodhead, had appointed committees to investigate the team's culture and history. The school paper had published a full-page ad, signed by 88 faculty members and titled "What Does A Social Disaster Sound Like?" that made the lacrosse case emblematic of racial and sexual oppression. Students, neighbors and activists marched in front of the now-infamous "lacrosse house" banging pots and pans. A poster featuring 43 Duke players—outlaw, WANTED style, under the banner PLEASE COME FORWARD—was plastered around campus.

Unlike the O. J. Simpson murder trials, where the sociological underpinnings of football were barely referenced, early commentary on the Duke lacrosse case framed the stripper party, the Duke players' loathsome comments and the alleged rape as near-logical expressions of a milieu marked by arrogance and clannishness. Duke history professor Peter Wood, a former Harvard player who once coached the Duke women's club team, recalled being jarred—while teaching a 2004 Native American history class populated by at least 10 Duke players—by a collective attitude he described as "a great sense of privilege, or a great sense of immunity, or a great sense of 'Screw you.'" When, in one subsequent class evaluation, he read the anonymous comment "I wish all the Indians had died; then we wouldn't have to study them," Wood was sure the writer was a lacrosse player.

Writing from Baltimore, the game's capital, *Sun* columnist David Steele compared the Duke situation to that of the 2001 St. Paul high school's boys' team, whose season was canceled after a player videotaped a bout of sex with an underage girl and screened it for two dozen teammates. "Entitlement is at the heart of the issue and at the heart of the fury this incident and its handling has inspired," Steele wrote. "It's not just about college athletes getting in trouble; it's about lacrosse players. It's a sport of privilege played by children of privilege and supported by families of privilege."

Locally and nationally, media coverage of the Duke case quickly made the leap from cultural to criminal. Though the three players renting the house where the party took place submitted immediately to police interviews and the taking of DNA samples and offered to submit to a polygraph test—and 46 team members submitted to DNA tests a week after the party—*Raleigh News and Observer* columnist Ruth Sheehan accused every player of a cover-up and called it no coincidence that Tom Wolfe, in his novel *I Am Charlotte Simmons*, "chose lacrosse players as the most vile players in his depiction" of college life. A *Sports Illustrated* headline, "Blue Wall of Silence," also implied stonewalling above an essay that described a team "living by their own set of rules," with an attitude "coming from a sense of entitlement and lack of accountability."

Few commentators emphasized the notion that no one stepped forward to corroborate the rape accusation because no rape actually occurred. *USA Today* sports columnist Christine Brennan wrote that Duke lacrosse players were "giving us all a whole new definition of the word 'teamwork,'" and enlisted the reinforcing bona fides of Mike Eruzione, the hero of the legendary 1980 US Olympic hockey team:

> *"Put it this way: I wouldn't want to be associated with a teammate who possibly committed a crime like this," Eruzione said. "Why would you want someone like that as a teammate? Why aren't kids speaking up right now? I'm surprised with something of this magnitude that they're not. It's one thing to have a code of honor with teammates, but that code of honor goes out the window with something like this. The team has to separate itself and say, 'Hey . . . you did it. We can't protect you in something like this.'"*

The *New York Times'* Selena Roberts followed two days later with a column implying erroneously that none of the team had cooperated with the investigation, equating the program to a street gang enforcing omerta, and describing Duke's lacrosse team as "a group of privileged players of fine pedigree entangled in a night that threatens to belie their social standing as human beings."

All those opinions, of course, took their cue from District Attorney Michael Nifong's immediate and oddly public certainty of the players' guilt. By early April, inconsistencies in the accuser's account crept in, and defense attorneys released crime lab results indicating that none of the 46 players' DNA had been found on or in the accuser or her belongings. Yet the 55-year-old district attorney, running in his first election, declared he would pursue the case anyway. It wasn't his last baffling act. At an April 12 candidate forum in Durham, with 46 lives hanging in the balance, Nifong wore an enduring smirk and quipped, "I thought everybody was here because they liked me." He also wound up one answer by yelling, "I am not going to allow Durham in the mind of the world to be a bunch of lacrosse players raping a Black girl in Durham!"

Chuck Sherwood found all such depictions unrecognizable. He graduated Duke in 1975 with an economics degree and a then–program record of 583 career saves, and never heard a racial remark from teammates. His youngest son, Devon, was just finishing his freshman year, playing goalie for the Blue Devils like Chuck and—like his dad—the sole Black player on the roster. That fact, with its inference that little, racially, had changed for Duke lacrosse in the intervening decades, lent the Sherwoods unique perspective. In the weeks after the March 13 party, Black strangers found Devon on social media and accused him of betraying his ancestors. Black friends asked, "Are these teammates racist? Have they ever come across that way to you?"

Each time, Devon said no. He also said that Duke's head coach, Mike Pressler, treated him with warmth and firm guidance, that Duke was a great improvement on his time playing at Long Island's Baldwin High School. His new teammates laughed and cheered when Devon, a fan of poet Langston Hughes and rap, freestyled a song before the Maryland game featuring every name in the locker room. "I was again having fun with lacrosse for the first time in a couple years, largely due to the guys, the way they treated me," Devon said:

> I was the only Black player on the team and I always was aware of that—but they let me be me. I didn't look like the stereotypical lacrosse player: I dressed differently; this was the hip-hop era when everything was baggy, and I was looking like that. But I could show up to the practice facility and be

*my authentic self, be accepted and embraced for my differences. Even though
I was a walk-on freshman, my voice was—even before the scandal—well
received. It didn't have to be that way. But I was fortunate enough to have
that, and I owe that to the leadership on that team.*

Devon had been at the infamous party, witnessed his teammate prof-
fering a broomstick for use on an exotic dancer, but did not hear anyone
thanking a Black dancer's "grandpa for my fine cotton shirt." On Mother's
Day 2006, long before the accuser's tale had been discredited, Devon stressed
that, the day after news of that racist language emerged, two seniors sought
him out in the weight room to assure him, "We would not ever, ever do that."

At the time, amid the cacophony of condemnation raining down on
all things Duke—and lacrosse—Devon sounded naïve. But his older, wiser,
pioneering father, too, found the caricatures bewildering, and their combined
testimonial was one of the first signs that the public take on Duke lacrosse
"culture" was dangerously skewed. When Chuck and Dawn flew to Durham in April 2006, lacrosse parents were complaining that Duke president
Richard Brodhead refused to meet with them. Brodhead didn't refuse the
Sherwoods. At their meeting, Chuck stated that he represented 300 alumni,
every ex-player along with every current parent. He told Brodhead it would
be "an absolute shame" to abolish the program, spoke of its 100 percent
graduation rate, the future businessmen and doctors and lawyers that it was
creating that very moment.

Brodhead gave no hint of his plans. Only later—after the fraud was
exposed and the players cleared; after the accuser was revealed as a liar and the
prosecutor disgraced; after the faculty was exposed as foolish and the administration as weak and the university settled with the three accused players for
$20 million apiece—did others hear what Chuck and Devon Sherwood had been
saying all along. The Duke lacrosse case was a 13-month cultural trainwreck.
Father and son were two of the few to emerge unscathed, if not stronger.

Still, one issue—forgotten amid the three players' exoneration—was
never fully settled. Late in 2006, with the "thank your grandpa for my fine
cotton shirt" comment one of the few allegations against the Duke lacrosse
team confirmed by sources and never denied, Devon conceded in a national
TV interview that "if it is in fact true, it's disgusting." Fifteen years later,
he still couldn't be sure that those two seniors who insisted they "would not
ever, ever do that" were being honest.

III

WIGGLE, PLEASE

O N APRIL 12, 2007, North Carolina Attorney General Roy Cooper took the extraordinary step of declaring the three Duke players innocent— not merely "not guilty"—and dubbed the soon-to-be disbarred and jailed Michael Nifong a "rogue prosecutor." The ensuing round of recriminations and soul-searching, so often involving uppercase buzzwords like "Rush to Judgment," "Presumption of Innocence," "Political Correctness" and "Sensational Reporting," would reverberate in academic, legal and media circles for years. Yet, even as the exonerations restored personal reputations, the case's impact on the sport's image would end up, essentially, a wash.

In the scandal's first months, the media and nearly everyone else outside America's lacrosse bubble assessed matters with a tone that that presumed the players' guilt for something. Riding in tandem was a palpable expectation that the case would lay out lacrosse's white and wealthy aesthetic, its booze-soaked bonding, as foundational ills. It didn't. The rape case was a fraud, and so proved nothing. Any disgust about racial slurs or the proffered broomstick was neutralized by the innocence of the accused and Nifong's malpractice. When the rape case was thrown out, so was the case against lacrosse. A stigma remained, gut-felt and vague. The sport was off the hook.

On the field, of course, the immediate costs were wrenching. Edged by Johns Hopkins in the 2005 NCAA final, the players saw their quest for Duke's first national title derailed. Coach Mike Pressler, whose vindication came too late to land him a job at alma mater Washington and Lee, had his career detoured to Division II Bryant College in Rhode Island. Of the three accused players, David Evans graduated, and Reade Seligmann and Collin Finnerty transferred to Brown and Loyola, respectively. The program's greatest hit came in recruiting; four of Duke's commits for 2006, including third-ranked Scott Kocis of the Huntington High Blue Devils, opted to play elsewhere.

Still, most of Duke's roster—including six All-Americans—returned the following season and the team made it to the 2007 NCAA championship game. Three years later, the Duke men's team won its first national title. Competitively, the most immediate effect was a momentum lost, the championships never won. The most intriguing is less obvious, though it involves two of the greatest Black talents ever, and might have altered one of the most dispiriting chapters in lacrosse history. Because, growing up on Long Island, Shamel and Rhamel Bratton wanted to play for Duke.

When the Duke case erupted, the Bratton twins were juniors at Huntington High and already considered the nation's top prospects. Whether Shamel and Rhamel would've thrived in Durham in the aftermath of the rape scandal is impossible to say. But, if nothing else, their careers certainly would have been less ironic. In the fall of 2007 the brothers sidestepped the situation in Durham and enrolled at the University of Virginia, where they would live through perhaps the darkest period ever experienced by a college lacrosse program. Two UVa lacrosse players would die and another would start serving a 23-year prison sentence for murder. The Brattons' careers would arc from astonishing achievement to ultimate humiliation, expose an alcohol-infused culture more extreme than anything proven at Duke, and highlight the game's racial dynamics far more directly than a disputed clash between white players and two Black strippers ever could.

Not since Jim Brown had one Black player, never mind two together, engaged the game with so blatant a sense of ownership. Superb all-around athletes, as high school sophomores Shamel and Rhamel won a Long Island football championship—with future Duke opponent Zach Howell at quarterback—and as juniors led Huntington to a county basketball title. As seniors, they were simply the best lacrosse players on any field they stepped. Rather than being intimidated by the game's overwhelming whiteness, they saw it as an advantage.

"All my brothers were like, 'These Black kids are going to get to specialize in one sport and play against a bunch of *white* kids!?'" Shamel said. "So I'm thinking we'll be fine—as freshmen. I had no doubt in my mind."

Coach Dom Starsia's Virginia program—then-winners of three national championships, including the NCAA's first undefeated titlists in 2006—daunted most newcomers. But at Huntington High, the Brattons led one of the most talented lacrosse teams in Long Island history to two straight Class B state titles and a 63-game winning streak. Shamel (older by 30 minutes, left-handed, more assertive) rang up 153 goals and 53 assists in 64 games; right-hander Rhamel totaled a marginally less spectacular 123 goals and 61 assists. Before the twins played a minute for the Cavaliers, they were dubbed lacrosse's "Boy Wonders" by the *New York Times* and featured twice on the cover of *Inside Lacrosse*; the second time had them posed beside new UVa teammates Bray Malphrus and Adam Ghitelman behind the headline "Best Recruiting Class Ever?"

"In the end," Kyle Harrison predicted in 2007, "I think people will be talking about Shamel and Rhamel Bratton as two of the best players to ever play our sport."

Talent was only part of the equation. Harrison's off-field earnings hinted at the mainstream appetite for an upper-middle-class Black lacrosse player, but—as Venus and Serena Williams had already proved—nothing matches the buzz created when two dynamic, inner-city African American siblings dominate a niche white sport. With depictions of Duke entitlement still fresh, the Brattons imbued the game with street credibility, urban edge— not to mention the impression of expanding economic diversity. "You want a can't-miss story?" a top college coach told *Inside Lacrosse*. "Jump on their bandwagon ASAP."

Echoing the Williams' youth in Compton, California, the Bratton narrative began amid the rough-edged Crown Heights section of Brooklyn. Their mother, Lois, worked as a nurse's aide. Just after Shamel and Rhamel entered elementary school, Lois and their father, Reginald, divorced, and Lois felt Crowns Heights' drug and criminal influences pressing close to home. When the twins were six, Lois hurriedly—and, "under," Shamel said, "a very heavy threat of violence"—moved them and two older brothers out to Huntington's working-class pocket, Huntington Station.

Two years later, at a June birthday party for fellow twins Ryan and Joe Askerberg, Shamel and Rhamel, then rising fourth graders, picked up lacrosse sticks for the first time. Lois signed them up for an indoor rec league; Zach Howell's dad, Jay, was the coach. It didn't feel like a big step: Shamel and Rhamel were already mixing in elementary school with the mostly well-off white kids from tony Huntington Bay. The two shuttled from there to Crown Heights' dodginess to blue-collar Huntington Station; slept over at the Howells' and joined their family vacations on Hilton Head, South Carolina; bonding all the way into high school with hard-core athletes like Zach and the Askerbergs and Sam Cutrone.

By then, Sam's father, Frank Cutrone—a two-time All-American at Johns Hopkins—and Jay Howell, who played at Gettysburg, had pegged the twins as lacrosse savants. Later, after Duke had been ruled out, they remembered the way UVa lacrosse wasn't overshadowed by a legendary basketball or football program, how the athletes seemed like one big fraternity. Also, Starsia had a history of cultivating Black talent, from defenders Tommy Smith, Mark Dixon and Woody Moore in 1994 to John Christmas and Will Barrow, one of the nation's premiere short-stick defensive midfielders.

The Brattons knew Barrow. Though no offensive star, his dogged handiwork and speed—peers voted him the fastest player in the nation—were instrumental in Virginia's 17–0 run to the 2006 national title. Like them, Barrow was a multisport Long Island kid good enough to draw football scholarship offers from powers like Michigan State, Maryland and Wisconsin. Like them, Barrow made a choice outsiders wouldn't understand. As high school freshmen, Shamel and Rhamel had watched him, three years their senior, practicing at Hofstra University for the 2004 Empire Challenge, the Long Island–New York City high school football All-Star Game. Barrow was named Most Valuable Player that year, but what stayed with Shamel was the sight of him doing football drills in UVa lax shorts.

Kyle Harrison knew Barrow back then. He put him up at Johns Hopkins for his recruiting visit. They battled a few times, the last during Hopkins's lightning-delayed 2005 NCAA semifinal win over Virginia, when the Cavs' defense bottled up Harrison like few others. "Really athletic, hard worker, skilled in between the lines," Harrison said. "He had a chance to be great."

Asked if he knew what went wrong, Harrison said, "I don't, really. It was a weird time in Virginia lacrosse history. That couple of years in there, it just seemed like thing after thing was happening."

THE BRATTONS' FRESHMAN year at UVa panned out almost as planned. Shamel started at midfield in 2008, struggled with his shot but piled up enough statistics—14 goals and four assists—to serve notice. Rhamel, a reserve midfielder, finished with 10 goals and six assists. They produced just one fraternal fireworks show: against Johns Hopkins on March 22, 2008, Rhamel scored twice and Shamel racked up a hat trick and the assist on the game-winning goal in overtime. A small milestone was reached midway through the third quarter, when the brothers joined with Will Barrow to form the first all-Black offensive midfield in Division I lacrosse history.

Thirty seconds later, Rhamel fired a 12-yard laser to score. The moment passed. There was no announcement in Charlottesville's Klockner Stadium, no notice taken by ESPNU's white commentators, no mention in postgame reports. Neither Starsia nor his staff were consciously seeking to make a racial point, and neither the Brattons nor Barrow was conscious of the history until afterward. But the Black lacrosse community noticed.

"There's major significance here," said longtime coach Ryland Huyghue, who in the late 1970s became Long Island's first Black prep All-American:

> There are less than two percent of African Americans playing the sport of lacrosse. It shows the sport has no color boundaries and that anyone of any background can play the sport and play it well. It also shows that the coach is looking at them as athletes whom he has confidence in to get the job done.
>
> The media should be all over this . . . It wasn't a tragedy like the Duke scandal. Why do we always have to hear the bad things that happen? Why can't we, for once, hear about something good and meaningful?

While signaling growing diversity, UVa's Black midfield highlighted oft-overlooked variations within Black America. The Brattons and Will Barrow hailed from different worlds. Shamel and Rhamel hewed to the Hollywood-ready type served by programs like Harlem Lacrosse: single mother, working class, plagued by urban pathologies. Barrow emerged from a Black middle and upper-middle class that, since the end of legal segregation in the 1960s, had expanded past easy pigeonholing. Just as one-size-fits-all—and often white-dictated—labels like "Latino" can't account for deep distinctions between Mexicans, Argentines and Puerto Ricans, the term "Black" does no justice to the differing perspectives of Southern descendants of slaves, Nigerian immigrants—or South American-born, prep school-educated bankers like Will Barrow's father.

Will Barrow picked up a lacrosse stick for the first time as a freshman at Baldwin High. His love for the game was instant and oddly pure. No matter that his wide receiver skills produced ego-boosting hits of scoring glory and big-college recruiters, or that his father and mother, Rita, tried steering him toward the riches of an NFL career: Will wanted to play college lacrosse. And just as he preferred the subtleties of playing cornerback to wide receiver, Will had no interest in being a star. He loved grinding at lacrosse's least glamorous position, defensive midfield, the one noticed mostly when something has gone wrong, the one charged with stopping the other team's stars and igniting—but rarely finishing—the fast-break goals that draw all the cheers.

George Barrow couldn't understand it. He kept urging his son to be selfish and score, but Will would only laugh and say, "Dad, you know nothing about lacrosse." And while George became self-conscious whenever the family turned out to be the only Black faces at recruiting showcases, Will never seemed to notice. During the recruiting process George and Rita dug into each program's history of diversity, consulted Kyle Harrison and Johnny Christmas and Chuck Sherwood. George pushed hard for Hopkins. Will decided on Virginia. There, as in high school, he never complained of isolation or the slightest discomfort or a single racial incident. He seemed content.

As senior co-captain and a preseason first team All-American, Barrow set the 2008 team's hustling tone, dug up a career-high 28 groundballs and chipped in seven goals and three assists. Virginia finished 14–4 and made it to championship weekend in Foxborough, Massachusetts, before losing in the NCAA semifinals to Syracuse in double overtime. The bitter end had bright spots: The Brattons scored a goal apiece to seal their freshman campaign, and Barrow capped his career with a first-quarter hint that he had been capable of the spectacular all along, running coast-to-coast and single-handedly taking on five Orange defensemen with a furious juke-and-drive to tie the game, 2–2.

"He was really humble, like my wife," George said. "Whether it was a great lacrosse game or a great football game, he rarely talked about it. I would talk about how proud I am of him: *The team had a great game, you had a great game*—and he just said, 'Thanks, Dad' . . . I never got it. Because no one would describe me as humble."

Shamel, too, was overjoyed. From the start Will had taken the twins in hand, folded them into the Cavs' cadre of Long Islanders, looked after him like an older brother. "He was one of my close friends," Shamel said. "I don't think I ever heard the word 'no' come out of his mouth. If you asked him to drive you somewhere or asked advice, he always said yes or 'I can't do it right now, but let's figure out a time.' Every time I would text or ask him something, it was always 'Yes. What can I do for you?'"

Barrow's relationship with his coach was chillier. Throughout his 24-year career at Brown and Virginia, Dom Starsia famously made "connections" with star and scrub a priority; as a father who openly, tearfully publicized the challenges—and joys—of raising intellectually disabled twin daughters, he signaled warmth, an open door. Many players responded. Not Will. "A little bit standoffish for me," Starsia said. "When we had to deal with each other, it was more like he *had* to do it."

Starsia's best chance to make headway came during Barrow's junior year. According to Starsia—and confirmed by two others close to the situation—Barrow and his girlfriend, a player on UVa's women's team, had a "volatile relationship" that flared at one point because of another man. "So we were talking about it," Starsia said. "I was saying to him, 'You may not love her as much as you think you do, if you guys set each other off all the time . . .'"

But the issue fell off the radar, at least between coach and player. Barrow's college eligibility ended with the 2008 season. He was drafted 11th in the Major League Lacrosse draft by the Chicago Machine, played five games as a pro, scored three goals. In the fall of 2008, he returned to Charlottesville to complete a bachelor's degree in sociology. On November 9, 2008, Barrow and his co-captain, Ben Rubeor, traveled with 150 of Starsia's former college players to the Grand Lodge in Hunt Valley, Maryland, to fete their coach's induction into the Lacrosse Hall of Fame. That touched Starsia. Maybe he had forged a connection, after all.

On Friday, November 21, Barrow volunteered at a lacrosse camp with teammate Max Pomper in Charlottesville. Teammates had always found Barrow to be outgoing, smiling—"a happy guy," as Shamel Bratton said. Pomper and Barrow had grown up 20 miles apart on Long Island. Their fathers were close. At the clinic, Pomper said, "Will was fine, his regular self."

George Barrow, too, noticed nothing unusual. When the two spoke by cellphone around 12:30 p.m., George was walking to lunch from his office at JPMorgan Chase in midtown Manhattan. Will was still getting over a case of mononucleosis, complaining about difficulties in his Spanish class. "Do you need me to come down and talk to the professor?" George asked. No,

Will assured his dad, he'd take care of it. In two days Will would be home for Thanksgiving break. "I'll see you Sunday," George said. As always before hanging up, they both said, "I love you."

Later that Friday night, Shamel was walking out of a Charlottesville bar when he happened to pass Will. The twins had made plans to drive home with him Sunday to Long Island, but Shamel planned to be out late Saturday night, too. "Yo," Shamel said, still walking. "Text me exactly what time. Text me when to wake up."

November 22 was a football Saturday in Charlottesville, the streets and shops filled for a noon game at Scott Stadium against Clemson. On football Saturdays UVa lacrosse players wake up late, hang out with friends. Shamel was accustomed to texting with Barrow at least once a day. Toward evening, he began to wonder why he hadn't heard a word. Weren't they leaving the next morning? Then his phone rang.

It was George Huguely. Shamel liked that, unlike the quick-to-offend DC/Baltimore guys on the UVa squad, Huguely could take the razzing of Long Islanders and give it right back. But they weren't close. A phone call was weird . . .

Shamel swiped his phone to answer. Huguely was crying.

"He's gone," he said. "Will's gone."

"What?" Shamel said.

"He's gone, man."

Shamel said, "What?" one more time. The words "gone" and "what" and "Will" suddenly seemed foreign, meaningless. All he knew was that Huguely lived near Will.

"I hung up the phone," Shamel said, "and booked it out of my apartment to get to the street where they lived."

LATER THAT EVENING, sometime around 8 p.m. on November 22, officers of the Baldwin Police Department arrived at the Long Island home of George and Rita Barrow; Will's 18-year-old brother, Trevor; and his 11-year-old sister, Sabrina. Their words hit the family like stones. That morning, Will, 22, had been found dead in his apartment of an apparent suicide. George's first reaction was that the Charlottesville authorities had it wrong, that it was all some stupid mistake.

There are those, like Starsia, who believe that Barrow and his former girlfriend had a titanic argument. Some speculated that Barrow was desperate to keep her attention. "I guess it was a tough night," George said. "They had a fight, they broke up, he couldn't get a hold of her. And I don't know, he just short-circuited—that's the only explanation I could think of. It just must've been a tough night and then into the morning, and he just short-circuited."

Others dispute that. "Obviously some kind of relationship thing was going on," Shamel said. "But he didn't seem, in my eyes, the type that a relationship could put him through *that* much." Even George, speculating about the couple's tough night, deems any fight or breakup "an irrelevant data point." As a triggering event it still makes no sense. "People break up all the time," George said.

Some figure that Barrow had been drinking, perhaps to excess, perhaps supplemented by an illegal substance. George Barrow insists that postmortem examinations found no drugs or alcohol in Will's system. As far as he knows, Will didn't suffer from depression, never sought treatment for mental health issues, and never suffered a concussion playing football or lacrosse—the kind that might have led to the erratic behavior associated with chronic traumatic encephalopathy (CTE). Wondering about such factors, too, strikes George as a waste of time.

"I've never asked any of those questions," he said. "I've never asked any questions ever. The only emotion I have is I miss him. That's it. I know I'm unique in how I deal with life and deal with issues. We certainly talk about it in my family and I talk about it with my best friends and they always ask me, like, 'How have you been able to continue to function, even a week or a month after it happened?' Partially because of my faith. More importantly, it's because I just love him."

In 2008, the CDC reported 36,035 suicides in the United States and approximately 666,000 more reported hospital visits for nonfatal self-inflicted injuries. Suicide was the nation's 10th-leading cause of death and the third-leading cause among young people. Older white males composed the largest demographic bloc, Black females the smallest; Black males fell midway between. The ripple from one suicide is estimated to intimately affect an average of six people. There's no "typical" reaction. Will's mother and siblings and grandmother, the rest of the Barrow family and friends, all absorbed the blow differently.

Even after two hours of speaking about Will Barrow's life and play and sensibility; about the thrill in his son's voice—the happiest moment of his career—when he learned he'd be starting for Virginia for the first time; about even his manner of death, George sounded happy to go on forever. It was only when the conversation shifted to goodbyes that something broke.

"It's been . . . it's been great," George said. He began to cry, but wanted to be clear: He was feeling only joy. "It's given me a chance to talk about William," he said. "I love talking about him. I love it." By the end his sobs were coming with every breath.

WILL BARROW'S LAST game in a Virginia uniform came at a good moment for the sport. The Duke case did nothing to slow America's lacrosse boom: despite—or, perhaps, because of—two years of unseemly publicity, in May 2008 NCAA men's lacrosse participation was up 28.5 percent; more than 60 games had just been broadcast nationwide; and the sport's premier event opened on Memorial Day weekend with the loftiest of imprimaturs. Most knew New England Patriots coach Bill Belichick as the dry-as-dust winner of Super Bowl titles, but any mention of lacrosse made the ex–Wesleyan player visibly giddy. Belichick's three children played. Belichick scouted high school talent for fun. And Belichick had lobbied hard, as part of Boston's organizing committee, to bring the 2008 NCAA men's championship to the Patriots' Gillette Stadium for the first time.

Some 48,224 fans turned out on a perfect 70-degree Saturday, May 24, for the Division I semifinals. Those with an eye on diversity saw growth; at times during the Virginia-Syracuse game, four Black players were on the field. While that reflected the 2 percent mark for African Americans (4 percent, overall, for people of color), in Division I, their backgrounds signaled an encouraging trend. In the home of the NFL's then-premier dynasty, it seemed telling that Barrow, the Bratton brothers and Syracuse midfielder Jovan Miller had once been high school football stars recruited by top Division I programs.

More striking, the double-overtime thriller confirmed that lacrosse's pipeline of Black players, long marked by stand-alone examples—from Jim Brown to Wayne Jackson to Chuck Sherwood to Navy's Syd Abernethy to Fred Opie to Kyle Harrison—was now producing in bulk. The Brattons generated the most hype, but over the next four years Miller would prove more accomplished; never had such great Black talent clashed on the sport's biggest stage. Years later ESPN's race, sports and culture website, The Undefeated, would publish a photo of that high point: Shamel Bratton shooting, Jovan Miller trying to stop him. Headline: "The Dream (or Fantasy) of Black Lacrosse."

Though he went on to win two national titles at Syracuse and was twice named All-American, Miller's career mixed in a bit of nightmare. Unlike the Bratton twins, who had Will Barrow to guide them and each other to lean on, Miller was the sole African American on the 2007–08 Syracuse roster. He had been raised to question the system. His father, Jeffrey, spent 30 years teaching in the Syracuse school system, and his mother, Delbra, grew up in segregated Mississippi in the 1950s. Jovan found it odd that schoolbooks didn't teach the racial history his parents taught at home. He found it even odder when, in seventh grade, after lacrosse tryouts at West Genesee Middle School, a coach told Jovan that he had great potential—and that some parents had asked, "Why is that Black kid on the team?"

"I was really confused because I thought that the whole operative was to get the best team out there," Miller said. "So the best player would play—not their being Black or white. That was an eye opener. I think he was trying to tell me, *Get prepared: More than likely, this is going to be your reality as long as you play this game.*"

At Christian Brothers Academy in Syracuse, Miller heard opponents call him the N-word. In one game—encouraged by a white teammate and their coach and his father in the stands—Miller refused to play on until a fan yelling, "What's up, my nigger—?" was ejected. He experienced nothing like that in college. Indeed, on paper, few had a better run: Miller was a mainstay on the last two of Hall of Fame head coach John Desko's five NCAA champions, and the program's first Black All-American since Jim Brown. Yet years later, before Desko's retirement in 2021, Miller said, "My nephew is 13. He loves Syracuse lacrosse. If things stay the way they are—based on what I know, and based on who is still there—he will never go to Syracuse. Ever."

Miller didn't accuse Desko of racist language or acts. His stance arose from Desko's halting response to racial remarks, especially a 2013 exchange involving a Black former teammate and longtime Syracuse defensive coordinator Lelan Rogers. Factoring in his own experience, Miller believed the sensitivities of all Syracuse players—regardless of race—were secondary to the program's need to win. They were all just cogs. But as Syracuse's lone Black player his freshman year, he felt such alienation doubly.

Once, in October of 2007, Miller and his new teammates were stretching after a run, discussing an upcoming Halloween party. Talk turned to costumes. One of Miller's roommates joked that he should dress up as "Radio," a mentally impaired Black man who served as a mascot for a Southern football team in a popular 2003 film of the same name. The team laughed. Miller felt the pressure to grin and let the moment pass. "Don't you fucking laugh," he said, instead.

"So now it's awkward," Miller recalled. "Because now this ain't lacrosse play. It's about me being a Black man on this team. And now you've disrespected me and now I'm hot as fire. Players are walking in and it's still quiet. Everyone's like, *Oh my God.* Like: *What just happened?*"

Miller said he then walked into Desko's office and relayed the incident, threatened to "put my hands" on his roommate, demanded that the problem be addressed. Desko listened. In a subsequent study hall, Miller confronted the roommate and asked for an apology. "Whatever, dude" was the reply. The other freshmen in the room laughed. Miller got angrier. He called his father, who called Desko: Jovan refused to return to practice until he received an apology. A day passed, and Desko—without Miller present—addressed and castigated the players. Miller rejoined the team. "I end up changing roommates," he said. "Never got an apology."

In the ensuing years, Miller said, he had many supportive white teammates, even allies, on 50-man rosters featuring Iroquois stars like Sid Smith, Cody Jamieson and Jeremy Thompson. In his sophomore year another Black player, Joe Moore, arrived; Hakeem Lecky and Drew Jenkins doubled Syracuse's African American contingent to four for Miller's senior season. But Miller never got past being "that one little dot" in his freshman team photo. "I had to find a way to be comfortable, even in the midst of being on an all-white team," he said.

Miller knows his experience doesn't hew to Syracuse's progressive image: the program of Jim Brown and Oren Lyons, with an unparalleled history of Native American players and today's Haudenosaunee Promise Scholarship program. But as Jeremy's teammate in 2010 and '11, he witnessed the Thompson clan's unhappiness, and wasn't surprised when Miles and Lyle played elsewhere.

On paper, ironically, nothing about the program had changed; under Desko, during Miller's final years there, Syracuse lacrosse was boasting perhaps the most diverse Division I rosters in the country. But the numbers, the reputation, weren't enough. Miller's unease never dissolved.

"Yes: SYRACUSE is still across our chest," he said. "But was it a safe haven for us? I would say: not exactly."

———————

PLAYERS OF COLOR FACE a delicate task trying to fit into a locker room, earn and keep playing time, establish and maintain a chemistry with teammates—all while safeguarding their dignity. There's pressure to minimize physical and mental bruising in service to maximal goals like championships and a college degree. There can be a creeping suspicion, especially in the early days with a new white coach, when singled out.[*]

"Here's the number one thing that happens: When a player [of color] makes a mistake and the coach corrects him, there's a 'BECAUSE' clause in the back of their minds that says, *Is he harder on me . . . BECAUSE?*" observed Troy Kemp, a Black man who coached for 24 years at private, majority-white McCallie School in Chattanooga, Tennessee, winning eight state boys' lacrosse championships. "But if I make the same comment to an African American kid? That's gone. Not to say that I made a better decision, but it takes away the perspective that can potentially be negative. You want a player with a clear head."

The player of color engages in an unsettling calculus whenever he or she enters a typical lacrosse space. Even Devon Sherwood, who felt unqualified acceptance from white teammates at Duke, picked up on it. In 2011, Sherwood's thesis for his master's degree in liberal studies at Duke, "Give Me a Sporting Chance: Accessibility to Sport: African Americans and the Game of Lacrosse," spared little in its depiction of the game's racial dynamic:

> *In lacrosse, due to the dominating numbers of white athletes, the black lacrosse player often plays the role of the token. Taking this into account, the possibility of a black lacrosse player experiencing a sense of cultural marginality is probable.*

———————

* Out of the 77 NCAA Division I men's lacrosse programs in 2024, only Hampton University had a Black head coach; of the 129 Division I women's programs, five had Black coaches.

With the large white population within lacrosse, some of whom may belong to upper class society, a social standard has developed within the sport where the ethos is based upon white culture. Presently, the fear that some black athletes have concerning lacrosse is they may be accepted on the team, but not regarded as full members of their teams due to the white-dominated culture within the sport.

This is similar to the roles African Americans teammates [sic] played on their teams in various sports in the 1940s and early 1950s. As a result, the black athlete may assume the role of an outcast within a team.

Though he arrived as a freshman in 2010 at a Syracuse with Jovan Miller and Hakeem Lecky on the roster, African American midfielder Drew Jenkins later called his years as a role-player at Syracuse "a nightmare." Early in his junior season, Syracuse defensive coordinator Lelan Rogers, who is white, used the term "colored" when describing an opposing player during a film session. Jenkins asked for an apology but said Rogers brushed off his request (Rogers has maintained that he apologized "right away"); then Jenkins demanded one twice more during a later practice. That failed, but Rogers eventually apologized to Jenkins and the team, and in an interview with the *New York Times* called his action "wrong" and "inappropriate." But his explanation, during a 2013 interview with the newspaper in Desko's office, revealed something of the psychic landscape players of color experience. Regarding his use of the term "colored," Rogers said, "I didn't mean it in a bad way. I meant it in a good way."

Sitting next to Rogers, who also left the program in 2021, Desko said, "Sometimes I think you find it confusing if you have to call someone an Afro-American or have to describe somebody . . . I am sometimes myself confused on what is appropriate and what isn't."

Jovan Miller's outspokenness places him at one extreme on the spectrum of those navigating lacrosse's white space. Years of social media attacks have made it clear that he is, indeed, regarded by some as the sport's "angry Black man." But, like few others, he ended up exposing both the awkward growing pains of a sport seeking to shed its rich, white, suburban reputation, and the cost of calling it out. After a second All-American season and graduation in 2011, Miller was selected eighth in the Major League Lacrosse draft. He made a quick transition to the pro field game, and in 2012 became one of the sport's most popular figures, scoring 21 points (13 goals and six assists) in

14 games for the Charlotte Hounds and earning a spot at the MLL All-Star
Game. Then, on October 25, 2012, Miller—along with the two other Black
players in the MLL, Kyle Harrison and Chazz Woodson—learned of a new
marketing push by manufacturer Warrior Sports, the main financial force
behind the MLL and its official outfitter. To promote its "Dojo" training
shoe, Warrior had rolled out a campaign on Twitter and wall posters and
its website, aided by MLL partnership promotions on the league's social
media platforms. "Tag #NinjaPlease," went the slogan, "to Win a pair of
Dojos."

Founded in Michigan in 1992 by former Princeton lacrosse All-
American—and MLL co-founder—David Morrow, Warrior had long traf-
ficked in in-your-face ads and slogans. "You'd call up and sometimes they'd
giggle at you and say, 'Ah, we're just being edgy,'" said David Gross, commissioner of Major League Lacrosse from 2004 to 2017. Bolstered by a partnership with athletic shoemaker New Balance, in 2007 Warrior acquired
Brine Lacrosse to become the sport's dominant brand. All MLL teams were
required to wear Warrior uniforms.

For Miller and other Black players, Warrior's use of the phrase "ninja,
please"—a derivation of the skeptical African American retort "negro, please"
and "n-word, please"—set off alarm bells. It was one thing for African- and
Asian-Americans to sub in "ninja, please." But a white-led company toying
with a racial slur in a bid for street cred was the corporate version of a white
player singing the N-word in a rap song. At best, it was wildly presumptuous. At worst: appalling.

"Looking back now, I didn't expect to be 'Kaepernick, 10 years before,'"
Miller said of San Francisco 49ers quarterback Colin Kaepernick, whose
practice of kneeling during the national anthem in protest of police brutality in 2016 drew the ire of President Trump and, effectively, ended his NFL
career. "My intent was just: *You can't fool me. There's a whole bunch of people
that don't get it—but I do. It's not slick. It's not funny.*"

The next day, October 26, Miller responded with a tweet: "be offended."
He also met on a conference call with 10 other Black lacrosse stars, including Shamel Bratton, Harrison and Woodson. The group coalesced around
the idea of signing a collective letter of protest. Miller says that he wanted
to go further, proposing that he, Harrison and Woodson—the three MLL
players—refuse to play until Warrior pulled its campaign. The response was
lukewarm. "I'm not going to knock anybody: not everybody's Jovan Miller,"

Miller said. "I was definitely serious about it. The other two, when we got off that phone call, sounded like they weren't coming off their assignments to write a letter."

Later that day, Chazz Woodson issued a statement on his Facebook page that read, partially:

> . . . I came to the decision that as a Black man, and as a professional lacrosse player, I couldn't sit back and NOT say anything when a campaign, from such a large and influential lacrosse company, says to the Black community - overtly or not, and in so many different ways - that . . . well, what you (the Black community AND ANYONE who is offended by or uncomfortable with the use of the word nigga/nigger) think or feel does not matter . . .
>
> . . . I think it reflects poorly on the lacrosse community as a whole. To the outside eye, if this is the type of message that's being put forth AND/ OR accepted in the lacrosse world, then why do I want to involve myself or my kid with this community?

Within the week, Miller offered to give away—and pay to ship—his Warrior equipment on Twitter, saying, "I can't let something so backwards be in my house or on my hands or feet in a sport I love." Alone, he threatened to quit the MLL unless Warrior's "#NinjaPlease" campaign stopped. Hateful and racist responses filled his Twitter feed; Miller reposted them. But combined with Woodson's more measured objections, the stand worked. US Lacrosse issued a statement condemning Warrior. MLL commissioner David Gross pressed the company to retreat.

"When you look at the sport of lacrosse, you've got to be realistic," Gross said:

> Because there is a degree of racism in the game. At that time, there definitely were situations: We had a team that we were about to sell, and I was having dinner with the prospective buyer the night before we were going to close on the thing, and the buyer said, "You know what I love about the sport? You don't pay the kids too much money in the MLL. If you did, all the white players would lose their jobs to Black athletes."
>
> I didn't even know how to react. I couldn't believe someone was thinking this way, but even more I couldn't believe someone would actually say it out loud. So, as politely as I could, I said I don't think we're the right

fit for each other and can't do this, and I had to go back to our owners and say, "Yeah, the deal fell through." But that wasn't the only time I'd ever heard a comment like that in the game of lacrosse.

So for Jovan's antennae to be up on something like "#NinjaPlease"? He had reason.

Four days after Miller went public, Warrior's marketing head called him, apologized and issued a statement apologizing to "anyone who was offended." The company halted the #NinjaPlease campaign, deleting all references to it online. Major League Lacrosse removed all references on its channels. In the aftermath, Miller apologized "to just about everybody" for causing a "rift" in the sport. He agreed to return to the MLL. But the experience left him bruised, not least because Miller felt abandoned in the thick of the controversy by his two fellow Black pros, Harrison and Woodson.

"Kyle and Chazz and I had to work through that," Miller said in 2020. "I definitely felt they left me out to dry. Because nobody else's career got altered. Mine got altered from that decision. I believe I'd still be playing lacrosse and be on somebody's roster right now had that not occurred. For all the coaches, GMs, whatever, it made me look 'difficult.' That was the word I heard the whole time: he's a 'rabble-rouser,' a 'troublemaker'—all the stuff that you've probably seen on Colin Kaepernick—that was Jovan Miller. *Who is HE? He needs to be grateful*: That was me."

The difference in Miller's career pre- and post- #NinjaPlease was day and—if not night—a decided dusk. In 2012, his MLL jersey had been a top seller, and he received the most votes from *Inside Lacrosse* magazine readers for Personality of the Year. In 2013, he wasn't even nominated. That may be because Miller played only five out of 14 Hounds games in the summer of 2013; after being used sparingly early in the season, scoring four goals, he was placed on the Hounds' practice squad. "They, all of a sudden, just stopped playing me—I wasn't even dressing," Miller said. Finally, on July 9, Hounds managing partner and president Jim McPhilliamy pulled him aside. "I wrote it down. It was one of the most powerful things that ever happened to me," Miller said. "The owner says to me, 'I'm not supposed to tell you this: You should probably think about playing in another league.' Obviously, at the time, there was no other professional outdoor league. Translation: *You're not playing here again.*"

Miller was traded at the end of 2013, didn't play at all in 2014, went off to study in Great Britain. He was picked up in the MLL's supplemental draft in 2015, got stuck on Chesapeake's practice squad, played a bit for Ohio and then settled in with the Florida Launch for the next three years. Overall, Miller appeared in 31 total games after the #NinjaPlease controversy, but never again played like a star.

Gross said that—as far as he knows—Miller's marginalization was due to friction with Charlotte head coach Mike Cerino over his play, and neither was MLL-directed nor had anything to do with #NinjaPlease. Cerino agreed, saying that he and Miller disagreed over playing philosophy, but that he never was told by owner or league to freeze him out of the lineup.

Miller doesn't buy it. He's convinced he was blackballed, though his term for it is more pointed. "White-balled," Miller said, "if we're going to keep it real. My career didn't turn out the way I wanted it to. But look, as long as history doesn't repeat itself, I'll be good. And the best way I can do so is by talking about everything to help the next group, whether the next crop be Black kids, white kids, whoever. To make sure these actions are not repeated. Yeah, I love the game, but by far the most important thing is to understand that the game is still the game. It's the people that ruined it."

MORGAN STATE'S VARSITY lacrosse program ended in 1981. But the vision of Miles Harrison and Val Emery—an elite program by and for Black lacrosse players—never died. It refired when Howard University upgraded its women's club team to varsity in 1998, or anytime a talented cadre of Black kids coalesced at programs like Harlem Lacrosse or Charm City, or any time a team began at a public school like Washington, DC's Wilson High, or in those rare moments when multiple Black men appeared on a Division I field. In the spring of 2015, it flashed on Thomas Stallworth, standing on the sidelines at a game somewhere north of San Diego. He was watching his son.

Christian Stallworth, then a freshman with Sante Fe Christian School in Solana Beach, had been introduced to the game by close friend Isaiah Dawson. Both are Black; Dawson, a year older, would emerge as one of the nation's top recruits and play at Harvard. Christian fell in love with lacrosse. Yet soon enough, during school and club play, his father picked up something that he didn't at first understand. "I watch my son play with this . . . *nervousness*," Thomas said. "And he's maybe the only one African American kid on the lacrosse field."

Thomas knew how jarring that could be. Growing up he never experienced that kind of isolation: not when competing in football, basketball and track for predominantly Black St. Martin de Porres High in inner-city Detroit; not at his historically Black college, Florida A&M. Then he entered the US Navy. "Went to flight school: *huge* culture shock," said Lieutenant Commander Stallworth. "If I bumped into another Black pilot in the squadron, the running joke was: 'Hey, did they mess up the count? What are *you* doing here?'"

Stallworth recalled one commanding officer's roundtable, featuring a dozen "highly educated, upper-middle-class white males and two African American men, one African American female," on ethics and inclusion. When someone asked about diversity in the officers' mess—the relaxed social atmosphere of a wardroom—some white officers responded that they "don't see color." Stallworth raised his hand. "How many African American pilots do you know, personally?" he asked. "I challenge you to name five, not counting me." None could.

Stallworth's point: "It's not a question of whether *you* see it," he said. "The *only* African American guy? *He* sees it. He feels it—all the time. As a squadron, anytime we do a social, we go to McGuire's Irish Pub. *Well, did it ever dawn on you I don't like Irish music or beer?* But if I don't go, I am 'non-sociable'—and that hurts my career. And if I do go, I have to be uncomfortable. Not only that, I have to fit into *your* metric. I can't dress how I normally dress, I can't speak how I normally speak. That's not malicious. It's a social construct that African American men and minorities deal with, whether it's at the executive levels or prep schools or sports."

After watching Christian's anxious play, Stallworth compared lacrosse notes with Brian Dawson, Isaiah's father. Over the next year and many discussions, they kept coming back to the same thought: "There's obviously more of us who play this game," Stallworth said. "What if we put 'em all on the same team? Would it change the way this sport looks?"

They weren't the first to propose an elite, all-Black club team. A few years after graduating in 2005, Kyle Harrison and Chazz Woodson and other Black players spitballed the idea of forming a Black national or world program on the order of the Iroquois Nationals. Instead, in October 2013 Woodson and Harrison launched the Sankofa (Ghanian for "Go back and get it," i.e., use the past to enhance the future) Lacrosse Alliance, a union of African American college and pro lacrosse players committed to hosting clinics, sparking interest among young Black athletes and staging exhibitions against national and college teams. By 2016, when a partnership with US Lacrosse cemented its emphasis on ground-level development, the exhibitions were an afterthought, and the spirit of Sankofa had found a vessel even more on point.

On May 5, 2015, Hampton University announced it would become the first historically Black college since Morgan State to field a men's varsity lacrosse team.

MIDWINTER, 2011: Lloyd Carter received a phone call. The deputy chief was heading into his office at the Baltimore City Fire Department Headquarters, wearing his full uniform of badge and tie and peaked hat—"chiefed up," as he likes to say. He looked at his cellphone: didn't know the area code, didn't answer. Carter ambled into his corner office, sat down at the desk. Glanced again at the phone. He had a minute. He tapped the strange number.

A woman answered, Verina Mathis-Crawford. Carter didn't recognize the name, but her first words came across accentless, corporate; he assumed she was white. The woman started talking about her son, Michael, and lacrosse, but Carter knew the game and its players; his son Lantz was about to start playing at Salisbury University. Michael Crawford wasn't a name Carter recognized. Ms. Crawford spoke of how Michael had attended Hampton University; how Michael had fallen in love with lacrosse at his Connecticut boarding school and missed it his first three years at Hampton; and how in his senior year, in September 2010, Michael had written a proposal to the Hampton administration to establish a club program there. She proofread it.

Halfway through the call, Verina Mathis-Crawford told Lloyd Carter how Michael came home over the latest Christmas break, 21 years old, went upstairs to his Brooklyn bedroom on December 28 and didn't come down. No one knew that he had an enlarged heart. When Verina went to get her only child for dinner, he was dead.

At that point, Carter could hear Verina Crawford crying on the other end of the phone. Tears began rolling down his cheeks and chin. He still doesn't know why he interrupted her then. He was busy. By the end of the year, Carter's 28-year career with the Baltimore City Fire Department would be effectively over and he would sue the Baltimore mayor, city council and its fire department for $3 million on the grounds of racial discrimination. Normally, by this point, he would just give the stranger a contact for US Lacrosse, or pass her off to Donnie Brown. Instead, he asked a question.

"Ms. Crawford, you believe in God?" Carter said.

"Yes," she answered.

"God had you call the right person."

It was as good an explanation as any. A month after Michael's death, Verina Mathis-Crawford had been scanning old emails when she came upon her son's proposal. She thought about Michael's dream, and idly googled "black" and "lacrosse" and "coach." Carter had stopped coaching Morgan State's barely supported intramural team in 2008, but he had just spoken at LaxCon about diversity. His name—and phone number—topped the search results.

Carter agreed to hold a general interest meeting at Hampton, and a few weeks later made the five-hour drive to the campus. Fifty students attended. A couple weeks later, he drove down again for the first practice. Three students showed. Carter rolled out the balls anyway, dubbed the three captains and spent the next two years commuting from Baltimore to Hampton on weekends for practices and games. His office was a small dorm room. Verina rented an apartment in Newport News. Together they badgered school officials for help and practice space and hustled for grant money. In 2013 Carter moved to the area, ramped up the team from intramural to club; by late 2014 they thought they'd gained the support of Hampton's visionary, controlling and oft-mysterious president, Dr. William Harvey, for the move to varsity. But no official word came.

In May 2015, Carter was standing before a roomful of students, teaching an emergency medical training class at a nearby community college, when his phone rang. It was Arthur Johnson, who years earlier founded a Philadelphia-based program for inner-city Black players after being called a racial slur at a lacrosse party. "Congratulations," Johnson said. "They just announced Hampton is going Division I. And you're the coach."

Carter sent the students out into the hall. He didn't want them to see him crying.

As a signal of Hampton's intent to raise its profile—and land more students, African American or not—the new lacrosse program was an instant success. But it was also handicapped by the same dynamic that had sapped overall HBCU enrollment in the postintegration era. The best Black students and athletes now had their pick of America's best universities and athletic programs—flush Division I schools, like Yale or Alabama, that shine like gold on a résumé or recruiting report. Meanwhile, in its first two years, Hampton lacrosse had zero scholarship money to offer.

Even given a year's head start, Carter landed no coveted recruits and entered the Pirates' inaugural Division I season in 2016 with a collection of the untested, the unexceptional and the wholly inexperienced. Five of his club players quit. Five of his remaining players were decent. The other 15 had to be taught basics that the typical D-I player learns by sixth grade. So when, on February 13, 2016, Hampton lost its varsity opener to tiny Roberts Wesleyan College, 20–3, Carter was happy. When the Pirates lost their remaining four contests by a combined score of 80–17, he didn't mind. "My goal that first year was not to get shut out," he said. "Every game when we scored our first goal, I would just say, 'Thank you, Jesus.'"

In truth, the season's lone win came before it began, when ESPN came to town. The sports broadcasting giant had never before covered a Hampton sport. But its personnel spent days conducting interviews for the opening game and then, for two hours, provided live national coverage from every angle, marbled with archival footage of Morgan State's Ten Bears and an interview with Jim Brown. Told that such publicity for a university was priceless, President Harvey agreed.

With Michael Crawford's vision and Verina's help, Carter had built something unmatched even by his beloved Morgan State. The Bears, after all, were only Division II, and they never appeared on national TV. At one point that week, an ESPN commentator remarked that if Hampton lacrosse ever became "successful," it would surely inspire a Disney movie. Carter laughed.

"Well, where's the Disney movie?" he said. "Because this *is* successful. I don't care if we never win a game. We've done it. We're a Division I program."

FOUR MONTHS LATER, June 28, 2016, Stallworth and Dawson's idea of "changing the way the game looks" debuted at the Adrenaline Summer Invitational in Downington, Pennsylvania. "Nation United" was, indeed, a mix of 23 rising collegians and high school seniors, some committed to colleges like Syracuse, Notre Dame, UNC and Harvard. But not all were African American. Across the previous year, as the two men brainstormed and planned and signed up head coach Chazz Woodson and coaching director Troy Kemp, something unexpected happened. Early concepts like an African American version of Team USA, the Sankofa mix of new and veteran players, and Stallworth and Dawson's original all-Black club team had been discarded.

In their place was a twice-yearly demonstration of what is possible. Inverting lacrosse's usual racial demographic, 20 of Nation United's 23 rising high school seniors and college freshmen on that first team were Black—and three were white. Six months later, at the team's second tournament appearance in Wesley Chapel, Florida, 16 players were Black, five were white and two were of Latino or Asian descent. A general guideline had been set: No more than 75 percent of the players could be Black or Latino or Asian. Whites were encouraged to apply. Christian Stallworth's "nervousness" would be addressed not by walling it in, but by replanting the garden.

"We're pulling the best kids that we can find, and rostering them together to show what we believe lacrosse really should look like," Woodson said. "Because there are people who don't believe it should look that way."

Of the 13 games played against elite clubs from the US and Canada in its inaugural year, 2016, Nation United won 11. In July 2017, both Nation United men's teams—rising college freshmen and rising high school seniors—won the program's first championships at the Inside Lacrosse Recruiting Invitational. Driving home after, Kyle Harrison was struck by the different feel, a flash of Morgan State 1971. He rang up his father and said, "I feel like I just saw a team of *Me's*, at 14 years old, play lacrosse."

The Nation United style, Harrison noted, was looser, a bit "angry," with enough improvisational flourishes—what Troy Kemp calls "wiggle"—to make it seem uniquely African American. "Fast-paced, athletic, up and down the field, get after it on the defensive end, on the offensive end they'll embarrass you: they're going to dodge and try to put you down," Harrison said. "More skilled than I was, but the same athleticism . . . There was so much energy and excitement and pride that I never got to feel in high school—the formative years of being comfortable. It would've been nice to be on a team with the guys that look like you."

Familiarity remains only part of the mission. From the start, Nation United was built to be the Black lacrosse pipeline's refinery, its elite empowerment zone. All players are expected to have high lacrosse IQs, college-bound transcripts and an eagerness for community service. Some require financial help, but mix with legacy or private schoolers who grew up nowhere near the inner city. Those who can afford Nation United's price tag—anywhere from $450 to $1,550 for a camp or tournament, not counting shoes, stick, helmet and pads that run anywhere from $250 to $1,000—pay it. In early 2018, Nation United added an elite women's program.

The founders aren't shy about their lofty aims—participants aren't called players, but "ambassadors"—and early on Nation United's standards and success, not to mention media attention, had a way of grating on long-standing urban programs. "Like, *Oh, you guys got all the rich kids, got all the shine and sponsorship, and we're down here grinding*," Kemp said. "And we're, like: Don't let the suit fool you, baby. We came for the same thing. But what we did is figure out *how* this thing works. And we're using a wrench instead of trying to turn the screw by hand. We're not any better. We just learned."

In 2018, some of that gap was bridged when Kyle Harrison was named president of Charm City Youth Lacrosse in Baltimore. Within months, the organization partnered with Nation United to create a new travel team, "Charm Nation," stacked with the program's best high school players. Nation United also leveraged its coast-to-coast profile to address needs overlooked by the white lacrosse world. Its "NationWorks" career development program linked financial donors with players for internships, mentoring and job prospects (in 2023, Harvard grad Isaiah Dawson was hired by Morgan Stanley). Its "Incident Report" served as a database for racial friction at all levels of lacrosse. Rising talent and established stars, aided by social media, connected like never before.

But even as Nation United provides clinics and camps, even as it provides a space to compare notes on referees who excessively flag Black or Latino players for fouls, or the coaches who stack minorities in defensive positions, its founders push to expand its reach. Hence the handful of white ambassadors on every NU roster.

"The way I look at it, you have the ignorant, the willfully ignorant and the malicious," Stallworth said. "Our goal is to educate the ignorant."

The point, then, isn't to merely showcase diversity, but to have Black and white players live it—and carry it back home. So the next time one hears a teammate spewing the N-word in a rap song, or—as one white NU alum in Texas experienced on day one of high school practice—slurs against

Mexicans, they won't stare at the ground. They'll push past the hostility and awkwardness, push back against the ignorance, maybe even change the culture of that team forever.

"That's what it takes: intent," Stallworth said. "What we're breeding with the non-African American players on our team is *the intentional*. They're going to intentionally have these conversations. They're going to intentionally, when they see something, speak up."

MIDWAY THROUGH THE FIRST weekend of the 2018 World Championship in Israel, Mexico head coach Andrew Haas got a bad feeling. His team had Saturday off after losing its first two games, a chance to rest and revive, but he sensed only demoralization. Hangover from the Greece game? Shock at facing world-class competition? Haas couldn't say. By the time of their next contest, Sunday against South Korea, lacrosse felt like the least of their concerns.

"Before we stepped on the field, there was something going on, emotionally, with a lot of the players," Haas said. "I didn't hear them saying, 'Everybody's talking trash to us' or '[Everybody's] calling us "beaners" or "wetbacks."' But it showed."

Mexico lost to South Korea, 9–6. The team's mood worsened. The Mexican players,—especially the Americans based in Los Angeles—concede that "chirping"—insulting chatter during play to break an opponent's focus—is a widespread, time-honored tactic, and usually given wide latitude. But Greece's behavior felt like a line crossed, and it was only the most brazen example of an emerging pattern. Timothy Gonzales said that he also heard racial slurs from Latvia's players in their opening game—and now again from South Korea's players. Ernie Melero said—and Haas confirmed—that other Mexico players "definitely" complained about being slurred by teams besides Greece.

After the loss to South Korea, Haas called a team meeting, giving everyone a platform to vent. That seemed to work: Mexico won its next four games, only to be whipsawed again in a tournament-ending, 9–6 loss to Bermuda.

"Bermuda was horrid," Gonzales said. "The first time I checked into the game, [a player] for Bermuda—this big white guy—looks at all his defenders and goes, 'Hey, double-team this wetback, he's their best scorer.' I remember laughing, because right after he said that I scored."

Not since high school had Gonzales and Melero been subjected to such invective. To have it surface at a World Championships—from mature adults, and ethnicities themselves subjected to racial stereotyping—was a shock. "During a lacrosse game," Gonzales said, "I have never dealt with racism more than what I did in Israel." Crushed by the experience, two of his Mexico teammates ended up quitting the sport for good.

Despite all that, Gonzales said that he "couldn't be more thankful" to play for Mexico, to meet and compete against those athletes who treated him with respect. His love for lacrosse remains undimmed. "I don't think anything anyone says or does could change the way I feel about this sport," Gonzales said. "I have such a connection with what it did for my life; nothing can ever change that. I plan on playing this sport until I can't move anymore."

PART 3

THE MUSLIN AND THE BUFFALO

". . . out of the fullness of our apostolic power, by the authority of Almighty God conferred upon us in blessed Peter and of the vicarship of Jesus Christ, which we hold on earth, do by tenor of these presents, should any of said islands have been found by your envoys and captains, give, grant, and assign to you and your heirs and successors, kings of Castile and Leon, forever, together with all their dominions, cities, camps, places, and villages, and all rights, jurisdictions, and appurtenances, all islands and mainlands found and to be found, discovered and to be discovered towards the west and south."

—Inter Caetera, "The Doctrine of Discovery,"
Pope Alexander VI, May 4, 1493

". . . the Indians had no individual rights to land; nor had they any collectively, or in their national capacity; for the lands occupied by each tribe were not used by them in such a manner as to prevent their being appropriated by a people of cultivators. All the proprietary rights of civilized nations on this continent are founded on this principle. The right derived from discovery and conquest, can rest on no other basis; and all existing titles depend on the fundamental title of the crown by discovery."

—Johnson v. McIntosh, Chief Justice John Marshall,
March 10, 1823

"Under the 'doctrine of discovery' . . . fee title to the lands occupied by Indians when the colonists arrived became vested in the sovereign—first

the discovering European nation and later the original States and the
United States."

—City of Sherrill, New York v.
Oneida Nation of New York, Footnote 1,
Justice Ruth Bader Ginsberg, March 29, 2005

I

JERUSALEM

ONE OF SPORT'S fundamentals—so basic that it's barely mentioned—holds that nothing is more valuable to the athlete than sleep. Any sleep at all is what the 23 members of the Iroquois Nationals were hoping for when they boarded a bus huffing outside Netanya's West Lagoon Resort Hotel early Sunday morning, July 15. After their draining gauntlet into this 2018 World Lacrosse Championship, they had one day off to adjust to the seven-hour time difference. Then, visibly jet-lagged, the Iroquois fell into a three-goal hole Saturday night against England on Wingate 4 before scoring 12 unanswered goals and winning, 18–7.

On paper, with the next game against Australia set for 8:15 p.m. Sunday night, that morning looked to be an ideal time for rest. Nationals management had a different idea: The team would rise early, travel two hours south for a noonday "Coexistence Practice" with Israeli and Palestinian children, then take a walking tour of Jerusalem in the scorching afternoon. It made no competitive sense. Tehoka Nanticoke, Jeremy Thompson, Frank Brown, Randy and Austin Staats, Brendan and Tyson Bomberry, a dozen other large men, all heavy lidded, tried desperately to retrace the fragile trail leading back to slumber. Heads tilted against window glass. Eyes slammed shut, mouths soon gaped.

Then, with a resounding *click* and *thump!* the bus's speaker system jerked to life. From up front a tour guide, peppy and cheerful, introduced herself: ex–Israeli army, native-born. Over the past week she had squired many of the 45 other visiting lacrosse teams, busloads of Christian, Jewish,

even some Muslim players, all eager and wide-eyed. Her stilted English
was loud. She seemed oblivious to Haudenosaunee exhaustion, and saw no
reason to soothe nerves.

The tour guide opened with the events of the last 24 hours: Israeli jets
targeted Hamas sites in Gaza; Hamas personnel launched 174 retaliatory
rockets and mortar shells back into Israel, wounding three; Israeli warplanes
responded with the largest daytime airstrike in four years, hitting 40 Hamas
sites with 50 tons of explosives and killing two; Egypt brokered a brief ceasefire; Hamas forces, claiming the ceasefire applied only to rockets and mortars,
launched a stream of incendiary kites, balloons and condoms into Israel. She
held up a copy of the day's *Jerusalem Post*. "I have a newspaper here," she said.
"You can see some of the pictures."

The players didn't know that the conflict was centered 90 minutes away
from the day's destination. They did know they were heading south, getting
closer. From the back a voice yelled, "Let me off the bus!" The tour guide
moved on to geography, describing how Israel borders Lebanon, Syria, Jordan
and Egypt, and the players began to understand. She wasn't going to stop.
Sleep was slipping away. She brought up the only aboveground freshwater
source in the country. "The Sea of Galilee," she said. "Some of you guys
more familiar, because of the story in the Bible."

At that, another player from the back answered, flatly: "No."

That "no" hinted at what—there on that Israeli highway—made the
Haudenosaunee unique. This went beyond the diplomatic coup they achieved
by having, for the first time, 25 Iroquois passport holders admitted by a
nation unequaled in border security; and beyond the fact that, in George
Washington's day, American "Indians" were thought to be descendants of
the Ten Lost Tribes of Israel (whose return, in some Mormon and Jewish
quarters, would signal the coming of the Messiah), and the news of two
dozen Iroquois slouching toward Jerusalem would have caused a galvanic
religious stir.

What made the Haudenosaunee truly singular was that—unlike the Mus-
lims, who claim Jerusalem's Dome of the Rock as the site where the Prophet
Muhammad ascended into heaven; or the Christians, who claim its Golgotha
as the place of Jesus's crucifixion and its Holy Sepulchre as the site of burial
and resurrection; or the Jews, who claim its Western Wall as the remaining
edge of Temple Mount where once, in the confines known as the Holy of
Holies, the Ark of the Covenant was stored and God himself was believed to

be present—in short, unlike the billions of people who view Jerusalem as the center of their spiritual universe, or the millions in lands surrounding who claim it as the ultimate historical prize, or the thousands of pilgrims visiting that day, the Haudenosaunee approached the city with no obvious sense of mission.

Indeed, considering Jerusalem's centrality in Roman Catholic dogma, the principles animating centuries of missionary and settler abuse, Haudenosaunee feelings toward the place are conflicted at best. Pope Alexander VI's 1493 papal bull, the "Doctrine of Discovery," justified (and justifies still, according to Justice Ruth Bader Ginsberg's 2005 Supreme Court opinion) to all explorers and kings the seizing of lands not inhabited by Christians, and provided spiritual and legal cover for colonization and the genocide wrought upon Indigenous people in the Western Hemisphere, Oceania, Africa and Asia. By 1600, perhaps as many as 56 million Native people in the Americas were destroyed—with an untold number uprooted or enslaved—by the diseases or violence of European settlers sure that they were doing God's work.

This is not to say that Christianity, as a faith, has no hold among the Haudenosaunee. Churches stand today in most reserves and a substantial percentage of Six Nations citizens—perhaps as many as half—count themselves as devotees. "We've got a lot of Christian Indians," said Onondaga faithkeeper Oren Lyons. "Our system is: We can't tell you what to believe or what to say or what to think. Just behave yourself. Don't impose on somebody."

But Haudenosaunee leaders are some of the loudest voices in the pan-Indigenous call—begun by Shawnee/Lenape scholar Steven Newcomb and Lakota spiritual leader Birgil Kills Straight in 1992—to revoke the Doctrine of Discovery, and their most famous creation grew out of the same impulse. From the start, the Iroquois Nationals men's lacrosse program was formed not only to reclaim a vital piece of Haudenosaunee culture and recharge the fight for sovereignty, but to serve as a vehicle for traditionalist values and the Longhouse faith codified in the early 19th century by Seneca prophet Handsome Lake. Players aren't required to be members of the Longhouse but agree to represent elements of Longhouse belief. This may be why no Iroquois National, unlike many American athletes, publicly thanks Jesus Christ for his play. But regardless of faith, all Nationals players readily speak of lacrosse as "medicine," extol the virtues of the Medicine Game, take part in the traditional pregame tobacco burning ceremony and, during warmups, screech in unison to signal to the Creator their intention to play for his amusement.

Here is one of many hazy spots on the border between religion and culture: you don't have to be a Longhouse adherent to find its intent and practices attractive. Scholars have long noted Quaker influence upon the prophet Handsome Lake's visions (one features a meeting with Jesus) and precepts, and the Christian lore (including a virgin birth) surrounding the earlier prophetic figure Deganawidah "the Peacemaker," who, after arriving in an otherworldly white stone canoe sometime in the 15th century, founded the Iroquois Confederacy and endowed it with the Great Law of Peace.

Some arch-traditionalists find such Christian elements disturbing, if not entirely counter to the Peacemaker's intent. But to hear Nationals attackman Lyle Thompson—who, along with his brother Miles, opted out of the Jerusalem tour because of safety concerns—sometimes the two seemingly opposed faiths merge. "I did want to go," Lyle Thompson said of the Holy City:

> I wanted to experience that. Because I haven't touched a bunch of different religions, and I know that place has a connection with part of our history, too.
> As part of the Peacemaker's journey, which is part of our history: we're told that he was able to switch. The Peacemaker—he's got a name, but we're not supposed to say his name—when he did his duty and created peace within this land, he said, "I'm going to go across the ocean and try and do it there." There's paintings of the stone canoe that he was able to make float, and he went across the ocean—and we're told that that's him: he was able to shape-shift.

Asked if that means, to his understanding, that the Peacemaker was also Jesus, Thompson says, "Yes. What we're told is that he went to Jerusalem, came back as an actual person where he didn't have the powers. He just had his voice, to be able to teach. They killed him over there. That's the story of the Peacemaker."

UP FRONT, IN A SEAT close to the tour guide, Ansley Jemison wasn't chasing sleep. He was getting ready. He had a speech to give to a few dozen Israeli Jewish and Arab kids, and the 42-year-old executive director of the

Iroquois Nationals wanted it to answer a question. For weeks, amid all the wrangling and snafus getting to Jerusalem, Jemison had found himself thinking: *What* are *we going for?*

The stock answer—sovereignty, reinforced by traveling on the Haudenosaunee passport—didn't seem enough, which was odd. Sovereignty is a Jemison family affair. Since 1994 Ansley's father, Seneca artist and historian G. Peter Jemison, has presided over the annual ceremony commemorating the Treaty of Canandaigua, the November 11, 1794, document upon which most Haudenosaunee claims stand. Negotiated when the US still saw Great Britain as an existential threat—and Indigenous Americans last wielded strategic clout—the pact proclaimed "perpetual" peace between the US and Six Nations, and guaranteed the latter "free use and enjoyment" of their territory. It was signed by President George Washington and 50 Six Nations sachems—including eminences Handsome Lake and Red Jacket— and endorsed by Quaker mediators. It experiences a revivifying jolt each year on the lawn of the Ontario County Courthouse in Canandaigua, New York, where American elected officials, Iroquois chiefs and Quaker dignitaries join Pete Jemison and hundreds more to view a reproduction of the fading parchment, and wonder about its relevance.

"The Treaty of Canandaigua is significant today because it recognizes— in the way, I think, few other treaties do—nationhood for the Six Nations," says New York historian Michael Oberg, author of *Peacemakers: The Iroquois, the United States and the Treaty of Canandaigua, 1794.* "That the treaty is still recognized and commemorated publicly today at a ceremony in which federal, state and representatives from the Society of Friends are all present, I think, contributes or confirms that lasting significance of the treaty."

But three years later, in 1797, the US revealed its narrow view of Haudenosaunee "nationhood" by exacting a huge cession of mostly Seneca lands at the Treaty of Big Tree. More chunks of Canandaigua-guaranteed Seneca holdings were taken in 1826 and 1838, while ravenous purchases of Iroquois tracts by New York State, in clear yet unpunished violation of federal law, completed the conquest. At Canandaigua in 1794, the Haudenosaunee still owned the western end of the state; 50 years later, they owned almost none of it. Onondaga lost 95 percent of its territory; today it controls 7,300 acres. By 1919, Oneida holdings that once covered six million acres had been reduced to 32.

"In practice, the United States has been pretty faithless in recognizing the Treaty of Canandaigua and enforcing it," Oberg said. "Nonetheless, it's there. And the language is black and white, on paper."

Though the US has violated or broken some 368 treaties with Native tribes, the Iroquois have nonetheless honored their side of the bargain (free and undisturbed passage for US citizens through their lands, via wagon road or today's highways) and believe Canandaigua is made of stronger stuff. Invocation of the treaty in the 1960s forced Congress to pay out $15.5 million after the US Army Corps of Engineers seized and flooded 10,000 acres of Seneca land to build Pennsylvania's Kinzua Dam. And on February 22, 2016, the State Department under President Barack Obama hosted a treaty renewal—in Haudenosaunee terms, a "polishing" of "the covenant chain"—in the Indian Treaty Room in the Eisenhower Executive Office Building adjacent to the White House. The ceremony included 50 tribal leaders and at least five federal officials; in her remarks, US Deputy Secretary of State Heather Higginbottom called the Treaty of Canandaigua one of the earliest acts of US diplomacy, and "a contract based on shared interests between two sovereign entities."

Haudenosaunee leaders had brought the George Washington Covenant Belt, the wampum commissioned by President Washington and presented to the Six Nations chiefs in 1792. Composed of nearly 10,000 purple and white beads crafted from clam and whelk shells, the six-foot-long piece features 15 figures—13 representing the original states, plus George Washington and the Six Nations Tadadaho—all holding hands. That day in 2016, their modern counterparts—clan mothers, chiefs, Higginbottom and two other US officials—stood together holding the belt. Camera shutters clicked.

Perhaps more important to the Haudenosaunee, at the end of her remarks, Higginbottom handed thick folds of white muslin, wrapped in plastic and a gauzy white bow, to Six Nations representatives. She was following the treaty's Article 6, which states that the US will pay out, "yearly forever," $4,500 worth of "clothing, domestic animals, implements of husbandry, and other utensils." In 2016—as in the 229 other years before and since—payment was made.

The form of the annual settlement has varied. Early on, the animals and utensils evolved into more basic supplies, and the inclusion of coarse, flowered cotton gave the "Calico Treaty" its enduring nickname. Sometime in the 20th century the payout evolved into its present form: More than a third—$1,800—is carved away for the 16,567 members of the Oneida Nation of Wisconsin. The remaining $2,700 of the allotment is sent to five of the Six Nations in New York in the form of medium-grade muslin; the Mohawks, who had just one representative at Canandaigua in 1794 and are not mentioned in the treaty text, receive nothing. The amount of cloth fluctuates with the price of cotton. Early on there was enough to provide each citizen with multiple pieces of clothing, which over time shrank to a set of bedsheets, then a pillowcase or two. In 2001, the New York Oneida were getting just four inches apiece. In 2019, the Seneca allotment ended up about three feet long.

Normally, there is no ceremony. Sometime each autumn, a box or two of muslin arrives at the central administrative office of each nation. They are packaged plainly, with no mention of the treaty. Sometimes the muslin is delivered by the US Postal Service, sometimes by a private concern like FedEx. "It comes in a truck," said Oren Lyons, "and they dump it out in the middle of the night."

Distribution is made by the federal Bureau of Indian Affairs. For the Wisconsin Oneida, an official in the BIA's Midwest regional office fills out a form for the Office of Trust Services to transfer the $1,800. The Oneida then distribute it on a per capita basis; in 2009, that meant payment of about 11 cents apiece. For the Oneida of New York and the four other nations receiving muslin, in late October an official in the BIA's Eastern regional office—now in Nashville—fills out a requisition form and contacts a New York fabric store. Based on the population of the five nations in 1794, the official figures each nation's allotment, and provides the distributor with the appropriate yardage and six FedEx labels for delivery.

Some Haudenosaunee are notified of the muslin's arrival by newsletter. Some pick up their annuity at a community picnic, or wait for it to be mailed. "Me being Seneca, I can go to the Seneca Nation clerk's office and ask to have the treaty cloth, my one yard, allotted to me," Peter Jemison said. "We have an annual Fall Festival and sometimes they'll be set up there with the bolts of treaty cloth, and you identify yourself by name, your Seneca Nation ID, and they cut off a yard of this treaty cloth and hand it to you."

The official US stance on the 574 recognized Native American tribes within its borders, established by Supreme Court Justice John Marshall in 1831, is that they are "domestic dependent nations": i.e., independent political entities subject to paternalistic oversight by US authority, with full power over tribal affairs but no ability to establish relationships with foreign nations. Westward expansion prompted further legislative assault via the

Indian Appropriations Act of 1871, which ended the US policy of treating tribes like independent nations, and the Indian Citizenship Act of 1924, which automatically made Native Americans citizens. The Haudenosaunee rejected that bill, and the citizenship, as an unwanted replacement for treaties like Canandaigua. When the US tried to reverse its longstanding policy of cultural assimilation with the Indian Reorganization Act of 1934, the Haudenosaunee—with 74 other tribes—rejected that, too.

"It's about implementing our sovereignty, it's about being self-determined and all of these things that we've been saying since the beginning of time, since our European brothers came over here," said Rex Lyons. "We didn't put the Canadian border there. They said—like, geographically—that we don't represent a nation. Oh yes, we do. Not under your terminology, but ours."

Hence the importance of travel, by either lacrosse teams or individuals: Each time the Haudenosaunee passport is accepted by a new foreign nation (even better, a US ally) like Israel, the Iroquois view it as support for their position. In the same vein, no matter all the US violations, each payout of cloth reaffirms that the treaty has not been broken. Haudenosaunee sovereignty lives.

"For the United States to deliver all this muslin to a tribe every year: it *is* coming through on treaty promises," said Raina Thiele, White House Tribal Affairs liaison from 2014 to 2016, who is Dena'ina Athabascan and Yup'ik, two of Alaska's Indigenous peoples. "Which is pretty unique, but it should stand out as an example of what the US government should have been doing all along. That's why, symbolically, it's really important."

But nationalists like Oren Lyons suspect that US officials view the cloth *only* symbolically. The US originally voted no when the UN—in an otherwise near-unanimous vote—passed the nonbinding Declaration on the Rights of Indigenous Peoples in 2007. And two years later, a leaked diplomatic cable from the US embassy in Ottawa stated: "The inherent right of self-government does not grant a right of sovereignty in the sense of international law, and does not create sovereign independent aboriginal nation-states."

Thus the Haudenosaunee insist that the treaty is neither symbol nor ceremony, but fact. Of all the Native tribes and nations confronting the US across the last three centuries, their identity derives still from forcing the US to abide by it. Similarly, since 1980, when the Supreme Court ordered a $102 million settlement for the US's treaty-shattering, 19th-century seizure of the Black Hills, the destitute Great Sioux Nation (encompassing the Lakota and Dakota peoples) of South Dakota—arguing that their sacred land was never for sale—has refused payment. By 2021 the Black Hills settlement, placed in trust, had ballooned to nearly $2 billion. Such heroic stubbornness matches the Haudenosaunee in quality, if not kind: Until the US returns to the Sioux their sacred land, it won't be honoring its original commitment. The comparatively worthless $4,500 annual payout to the Haudenosaunee, on the other hand, means that it is.

And since the Haudenosaunee take the definition of "treaty"—a formally concluded and ratified agreement between two nations—literally, the muslin can't be dismissed as some charming artifact. The muslin means dignity. The muslin, in its tiny way, refuses to let the giant off easy. Former slave Frederick Douglass—in the second most historic event in Canandaigua history—famously said in his 1857 speech there: "Power concedes nothing without a demand. It never did and it never will." The Haudenosaunee vow to make this demand, forever.

"At one point [in 1948], the United States government came to us and said, 'Why don't we just give you a lump sum of money and that will be the end of this giving of treaty cloth?'" Peter Jemison said. "We said, 'No, we don't want to do that. We want you to continue your commitment annually to provide this cloth.' We don't care if it gets down to the size of a postage stamp. It's the principle. The principle of this is: The United States is being forced to meet its word, to continue to provide this as a term of a treaty that was made between the Six Nations and the United States."

Once distributed, the muslin's uses run the gamut. Some pieces go unclaimed, or pile up forgotten in closets, or become rags. Some people make embroidered pillow shams; some families combine their allotments for larger pieces. Since passage of the 1990 Native American Graves Protection and Repatriation Act, which provided for the care of Indigenous remains and sacred objects, the muslin has wrapped Haudenosaunee remains returning to their homelands. Peter Jemison, whose eclectic works can be found in collections like New York's Whitney Museum of American Art, used treaty cloth as canvas for at least two paintings, and incorporated a smaller piece in a photo collage. Most famously, Mohawk artist Carla Goodleaf Hemlock employed muslin issued in 2009 to create a "Treaty Cloth Shirt" complete with wampum shells, the hand-holding figures of the George Washington belt on the sleeves and—on the back—summations of the Canandaigua treaty's articles written in black Sharpie.

Steeped in family and treaty lore, Ansley Jemison embraced lacrosse at all-white Canandaigua Academy with a depth his teammates couldn't know. He played for the Nationals junior team, appeared in four Final Fours with Syracuse from 1996 to 1999, drifted the next six years through various jobs. Purpose returned when he returned to the game. Ansley was the Nationals general manager when they pulled out of the 2010 World Championship, the Haudenosaunee's most public stand on sovereignty in a generation. In 2012, he was an assistant coach with the U-19 field squad that became the first Iroquois team to ever beat Team USA outdoors on grass. "That was 'the Shot Heard round the World' for the Indigenous people," Jemison said. "We got one back, baby!"

For his wedding in 2014, Jemison commissioned one of his father's colleagues to handcraft a traditional ribbon shirt, replete with wampum beads and deer antler buttons at the wrists. The fabric was an easy call. He got married in Canandaigua treaty cloth.

SOLIDARITY WITH First Nations, everywhere, had been an Iroquois Nationals constant since their moving clinic with Aboriginal Australians during their first World Championship in 1990. But that impulse for the 2018 World Championship was short-circuited when the BDS movement accused the Iroquois of hypocrisy and their Israeli hosts implored them to steer clear of politics. At first, Jemison was stumped. The Nationals' mission in Israel couldn't just be about winning games. In the Haudenosaunee heart, winning isn't really the point.

Finally, just days before heading to Toronto Pearson International Airport, the words came to him: *Dish with One Spoon*. Jemison had been studying up on Haudenosaunee wampum belts, the beaded representations of Six Nations treaties and belief; "Dish with One Spoon" is how Natives refer to a 1701 agreement between the warring Haudenosaunee and Anishinaabe to share hunting grounds. The Great Law of Peace broadened the phrase to a philosophy meaning all nations sharing the land, using resources judiciously, and consuming the bounty amiably: Disagreements arise, but you can't spill blood with a spoon.

He commissioned decals and T-shirts for players and coaches, dirty gray with the Dish symbol emblazoned in purple. "Here's the cradle of three major religions," Jemison said. "Maybe this game can be a message and a healing. Because we couldn't do any kind of political statements, I put on the chest of all our players and on the back of our helmets the Dish with One Spoon—as sort of a peaceful protest, but also a reminder that we can all eat from the same place and not harm one another and leave enough for everybody else."

The Nationals' bus rolled off Highway 1 for its first stop: the Kraft Family Sports Campus in northwest Jerusalem. At its glitzy opening on June 20, 2017, the $6 million, 25-acre complex seemed mostly a signifier of its benefactor's clout in America. Only New England Patriots owner Robert Kraft could have induced NFL commissioner Roger Goodell and 18 Pro Football Hall of Famers—including Jim Brown and Joe Montana—to jet to the Middle East to ribbon-cut a training facility.

But locals understood the new complex as something far deeper: Kraft's part in celebrating in June 2017 the 50th anniversary of the reunification—or, according to most, illegal occupation of half—of Jerusalem. The then-76-year-old billionaire emphasized the point, in Hebrew, in his welcoming words to a crowd of 400, recalling how Israel's victory in the 1967 Six-Day War wrested East Jerusalem, the Old City and the Wall from Jordan's control. Israel's annexation of East Jerusalem—and 1980 declaration of the unified city as its capital—remains perhaps the most violently knotted issue in the Israel-Palestine conflict; the UN General Assembly and Security Council have repeatedly condemned the annexation as a violation of international law. Israel's offer of citizenship to East Jerusalem residents has been widely refused. On that June day—six months before President Trump announced the move of the US embassy from Tel Aviv—there were no foreign embassies in the city.

None of that was mentioned by Goodell or the Hall of Famers. Nobody dwelled on the dark side of Israel's founding, though reminders—like the site of Deir Yassin, where at least 107 Palestinian inhabitants, including women and children, were slaughtered in 1948—weren't far away. The stated hope was that Kraft's three new athletic fields—including Israel's first fully marked American football field, complete with goalposts—would provide a platform for coexistence. "The fields bring people from all tribes," Jerusalem mayor Nir Barkat said. "Muslim, Christian and Jewish alike."

And then, the Haudenosaunee. The Nationals' delegation emerged from the bus, coaches and managers full of pep, players stretching and blinking.

Sticks weren't needed yet. Some 40 kids from the youth program of Hapoel
Katamon F. C., a second-division pro soccer team, were waiting. The first
fan-owned team in Israeli Premier League history, Hapoel was known more
for its social mission than its prowess. Founder Shai Aharon had declared his
team a beacon of anti-violence and anti-racism, which sounded overheated
until contrasted with Beitar Jerusalem. An IPL mainstay, Beitar was the only
club never to field an Arab player, and its right-leaning fanbase made the
point clearer by screaming, "Death to Arabs!" Meanwhile, Hapoel played
all races and religions, middle-class and dirt-poor, from East Jerusalem and
West. It organized monthly neighborhood games between mixed teams of
Jews and Arabs, and once adopted a team of disabled youth when officials
learned they were being bullied.

That day's Hapoel group consisted of kids aged 10 to 14, Israeli Jews
mixed with about a dozen Palestinians. The Iroquois Nationals lined up
facing them on the football field; a whipping wind blended with the traffic
hum from nearby Highway 1. Jeremy Thompson and another player held up
a purple-and-white Haudenosaunee flag. With Israel Lacrosse chief operating officer David Lasday translating English into Hebrew, Ansley Jemison
began by pointing out the flag's symbol of the original Five Nations, told of
the Peacemaker's metaphor when first proposing the Iroquois Confederacy:
one arrow alone is easily snapped, but five arrows together are unbreakable.
"It's easier if you come together as a group, protect each other," Jemison said.
"It's very important to overcome your differences."

Jemison then revealed the narrow cloth in his hand: a replica of the
Dish with One Spoon wampum. He mimed scooping food with an invisible
spoon from an invisible bowl into his very visible open mouth. "Everybody
in the world is eating from the same dish," he said.

He held up the wampum belt wide in his hands for all to see, tas-
sels fluttering. He mentioned that, like Judaism, Haudenosaunee culture is
matrilineal. "Our women are very important: those are our leaders," Jemison
said, eliciting *oob*s from the crowd. "Women are the ones who teach the
men how to serve the people." He translated lacrosse's Native name—They
Bump Hips—and more laughs erupted when coach Mark Burnam surprised
Lasday with a gentle hip-check.

Near the end of his eight-minute talk, Jemison used the word "Haudenosaunee" for the first time—and something remarkable happened. Lars
Tiffany changed. For the entire presentation, the Nationals' assistant

coach had been standing at the far edge of the delegation, restless and
fidgety: weight shifting from leg to leg, hands dropping one minute to his
hips, then into his pockets, then behind his back. But now Tiffany stiffened.
He removed his purple baseball cap, widened his stance and clasped both
hands behind his back. None of that was required. None of the players followed suit. The other two dozen members of the Iroquois delegation still
had their eyes on the kids or Jemison, and every other purple cap stayed
firmly in place.

For the following two minutes, as Jemison spoke and Lasday translated and the pitiless sun beat down on his expanding scalp, Tiffany stood
at attention. This wouldn't have been notable, but for the fact that Tiffany
is American, and white, and the head lacrosse coach at the University of
Virginia. More to the point, Tiffany's star has been rising so fast that many
believed him the best young lacrosse coach in America, a perfect candidate to
coach Team USA. It was a bit puzzling to see him standing with the Iroquois
at all, let alone absorbing Jemison's final words like a prayer.

"The most important thing is that this is our delegation of our best
athletes, our best young men, and we're here with a message of peace,"
Jemison said. "We don't consider ourselves Americans, we don't consider
ourselves Canadians. We consider ourselves Haudenosaunee, because we
have treaties with those countries. It's a nation-to-nation relationship. We're
the Indigenous people of North America."

By the time the kids started applauding, Tiffany's hat was back on his
head. The line of players and officials relaxed. Then he blended back in with
the rest of the Iroquois, honoring a treaty all his own.

ONCE, OREN LYONS was mulling the conflict between white and Indigenous cultures when he said a curious thing. He was then, in 2010, 79 years
old—a lifespan in which the Onondaga faithkeeper had taught history, lived
it daily and made more than his share—and entitled to take the long view.
Still, his words came out of nowhere. "Left to our own devices," he said, "we
never would have made an airplane."

Deep into a different topic, Lyons didn't elaborate. His punctuating
chuckles range—even in the same breath—from derisive to delighted, and he
deftly deploys deadpan quips to keep white interlocutors off-balance. After

the Nationals' inaugural field game in 1983, the lopsided defeat to Syracuse, Lyons told a writer from *Sports Illustrated*, "We should have offered them Manhattan." In 2015 with pen hovering above the contract to extend their sponsorship deal, he turned to Nike chief executive officer Mark Parker and said, "When we sign this contract, we get our land back, right?" Nervous laughter ensued.

After many conversations it became clear that Lyons's airplane remark, in a tone neither light nor sardonic nor, for that matter, woeful, drifted from some deeper thought. He wasn't pinpointing a weakness so much as highlighting opposing ideas of progress. Western civilization and its conquests, of course, rode in tandem with a fetish for innovation and speed, horse to train to automobile to jet, with each advance representing another step of estrangement from the land. But Lyons's choice of words wasn't accidental; to him Indigenous America's lack of aeronautic skill was about a relationship with the earth so intimate that one would look up at the great machine— engines spewing befouling chemicals, turbines grinding up stray birds—and wonder: *Who needs such progress?*

This is not to say that Lyons is off the grid; he has flown tens of thousands of miles himself, traded in his Prius for a gas-powered Subaru, and is happy to pick up the phone. But maintaining connection with Mother Earth by ceremonially burning tobacco or using a wood lacrosse stick or bow-hunting deer remains a Haudenosaunee imperative. Clan remains as vital a marker of identity as tribe. The Thompson brothers' further self-labeling as deer (Jeremy), wolf (Hiana), hawk (Lyle) and bear (Miles) is not, like the naming of sports teams, metaphorical. It's a declaration of kinship. In the same way, though the game's origin story is spiritual—after making people on earth, the Creator invented lacrosse as one of the games in which to battle his evil twin, Sawiskera—its oft-repeated legend of inclusion features a showdown between Animals and Birds, related—as in this tangent delivered by former Nationals head coach Sid Jamieson to a roomful of non-Indigenous coaches—with utmost gravity:

> *The Animals are the bear, the deer and the turtle; and the Birds are the eagle, the hawk, and the owl. The eagle flies down and meets the bear; they decide it's a one-goal game. As the birds are in the tree, here come these two creatures climbing up the tree and the birds say, "What are you doing?" And they say, "We want to play in the game, but the Animals told us we're*

too small." So the Birds talk, and the consensus is that they should be able to play—but they have to be birds.

One animal is the squirrel. So the Birds stretch his skin, throw him out of the tree: he's now the flying squirrel; and since he can fly, he can play. The other one is a mouse. Eagle flies down, snips off some leather off the drum, flies up and they attach it to the legs in the back and throw the mouse out of the tree: the mouse can fly; the mouse now is a bat. And bats are nasty-quick.

So the Animals decide to send a huge turtle out for the faceoff. The Birds agree the best thing to do is to have the flying squirrel go do faceoff. And, we all know, faceoffs are huge. There's a cloud of dust and the turtle has crept on top of the ball, but the squirrel is a digger. He digs the ball out, takes a couple steps, jumps, flies up to the tree and passes the ball off to the hawk. The hawk now is soaring, and the deer is chasing the hawk, but the deer is never catching the hawk. It's not going to happen. Eventually the deer is totally exhausted; he's out, done, can't participate anymore.

So nighttime approaches and the owl is on top of the tree and the bear thinks he's going to sneak up the tree and get the ball. The owl says, "Hey, I can see at night; you're wasting your time." And with that the bear says, "Okay," and went back to his den. So the birds are getting together at the top of the tree, having a conversation, saying, "Since we have the ball, what's the best way to score? We need to get the ball into the bear's den to win the game."

So the eagle flies out of the tree, and each time he flies out the bear tries to cuff him out of the sky. The eagle flies back to the top of the tree and the birds come up with a great game plan, executed fantastically good . . . the birds decide to take the mouse—which is a bat now—put him on the eagle's back; he's going to fly over the top of that bear, and each time the bear reaches up to cuff him out, the eagle is going to turn over, release the bat; bat's going to fly between the bear's legs and deposit the ball in the bear's den. That's it: the game is over.

As faithkeeper, Oren Lyons can detail all the complex narratives and practices in Haudenosaunee cosmology. He rhapsodizes about the virtue of hickory and deerskin over "tupperware" lacrosse sticks not out of fogeyism, but out of the belief that a player with wood in hand personally recharges their symbiotic relationship with nature. Perhaps his most popular painting, *The Great Tree of Peace*, under which the original five-nation Iroquois Confederacy was mythically formed, features the Peacemaker and Onondaga helpmate Hayenhwatha and key animals spread throughout its branches and roots.

Despite being the most famous explicator of Haudenosaunee ways, Lyons is extremely wary of speaking about spiritual practice with non-Natives. Part of this is because he is not authorized by the Onondaga chiefs to do so, part because details like the Peacemaker's actual name and incarnations are rarely spoken about even by the faithful. Traditionalists also haven't forgotten the time in 1959 that American critic Edmund Wilson gained access to a Seneca religious ceremony and wrote about it in the *New Yorker*. Lyons often blocks seemingly innocuous questions by insisting that he must "be very careful," and his hospitality has limits. When asked whether lacrosse is mentioned in the Iroquois national anthem, he refused to answer, saying, "It's not even your real business anyway."

THE EARLIEST RECORD of European contact with the game—and its naming as "lacrosse"—came, in 1636, in the form of godly condescension. The French Jesuit missionaries penetrating Huron territory (then southwestern Quebec) of course dismissed Indigenous spiritual practices. But the use of ball-and-stick marathons as medicine for everything from illness to foul weather seemed particularly misguided.

"Is this not worthy of compassion?" wrote Father Jean de Brebeuf that year in his report on Native villages on the southern shore of Georgian Bay:

> *There is a poor sick man, fevered of body and almost dying, and a miserable Sorcerer will order for him, as a cooling remedy, a game of crosse. Or the sick man himself, sometimes, will have dreamed that he must die unless the whole country shall play crosse for his health; and, no matter how little may be his credit, you will see then in a beautiful field, Village contending against Village, as to who will play crosse the better, and betting against one another Beaver robes and Porcelain collars, so as to excite greater interest.*
>
> *Sometimes, also, one of these Jugglers will say that the whole Country is sick, and he asks a game of crosse to heal it; no more needs to be said, it is published immediately everywhere; and all the Captains of each Village give orders that all the young men do their duty in this respect. Otherwise some great misfortune would befall the whole Country.*

The hooked stick's resemblance to a bishop's crozier has made for a tidy etymological legend, too good not to repeat. But even missionaries might have noticed that French sportsmen, then, had been calling any curved stick-and-ball game "crosse" for more than a century. Such vagueness and counterclaim, colored by the moment's tribal and colonial conflict, is typical of early lacrosse lore. For example, the account of the massacre at Fort Michilimackinac, bristling with Indian perfidy and British stupidity, couldn't appeal more to an American public conditioned to regard both as enemies.

On June 4, 1763, two years after the British took possession of French trading posts in the French and Indian War, the Ojibwe (then called Chippewa in English) and Ozaagii (Sauk) tribes invited the three dozen redcoats inside Fort Michilimackinac—overlooking the Mackinac Straits, in what is now Michigan—to watch them play *baggatiway*, the name for lacrosse among Great Lakes tribes. This was a celebration, they said, of King George III's birthday. Though an Indian attack had been feared for more than a year and he had been recently warned of specific plans to kill him, Michilimackinac's commander, George Etherington, didn't find the offer strange. He and his soldiers trooped out to watch.

Four to five hundred Ojibwe and Ozaagii men took the field. Each team scored twice, and then a seemingly errant ball went flying through the fort's open gates. "Nothing could be less liable to excite premature alarm than that . . . having fallen there, it should be followed on the instant by all engaged in the game . . . all eager, all struggling, all shouting, all in the unrestrained pursuit of a rude athletic exercise," recalled British fur trader Alexander Henry. "Nothing, therefore, could be more happily devised . . . than a stratagem like this."

The ruse, fifth in a series of attacks on British forts that became known as "Pontiac's War," worked perfectly. "Then throwing their ball close to the gate, and observing Lieut. Lesley and me a few paces out of it," Captain Etherington recalled, "they came behind us, seized and carried us into the woods."

Hundreds of players threw down their sticks; grabbed tomahawks, war clubs and knives; and rushed into the fort. Henry saw "a crowd of Indians within the fort furiously cutting down and scalping every Englishman they found." Mass butchery, rife with mangling, shrieking and the drinking of blood, followed. "They found their squaws, whom they had previously planted

there, with their hatchets hid under their blankets, which they took, and in
an instant killed Lieut. Jamet and fifteen rank and file, and a trader named
Tracy," Etherington recalled. "They wounded two, and took the rest of the
garrison prisoners, five of whom they have since killed."

Along with the 21 British soldiers tortured and killed, another dozen
were taken captive. The Natives controlled the fort for the next year.

Michilimackinac turned out to be a minor skirmish in the three-year
war. But the ambush has become a major part of the sport's white narrative,
a Kiplingesque tangent few can resist. Oddly, when lacrosse was introduced
in England by a tour of Canadian-backed Iroquois in 1867—just as the final
war on the Indigenous population in the American West hit high gear—the
Michilimackinac debacle was falsely retailed to the British public as victory.
History may well be written by the victors, but that doesn't mean the losers
don't try.

Lacrosse's North American birthplace has never been pinpointed.
Virtually all the continent's Indigenous peoples engaged in ball games for
medicine or the training of warriors or to settle boundary disputes, and the
development of web-headed sticks made for regional variants. The southeastern Cherokee played a two-stick version called "little war"; Great Lakes games
featured a roughly 30-inch-long shaft topped by a small circular pocket; the
Haudenosaunee in the northeastern woodlands wielded the four- to five-foot
staff and larger head recognized as the modern game's forebearer. Early balls
were wood or animal matter wrapped in deerskin. The field had no boundaries. Games could last all day.

French explorers in the 17th century described Sioux playing as far
west as the Mississippi River (hence the city of La Crosse, Wisconsin), but
current consensus traces the game's origin to Eastern Algonquins ranging
somewhere between Lake Champlain and the St. Lawrence River—what
is now upper New York and southern Ontario and Quebec. The vagueness
allows both the US and Canada to claim the game, geographically, but the
idea that the Algonquins invented lacrosse and passed it to the Huron and
Haudenosaunee doesn't sit well with the latter. After all, one theory has the
Iroquois emerging prehistorically as an Algonquin offshoot, then displacing
them in the 17th century as the dominant regional power. Which tribe first
picked up the stick can't be known.

Oren Lyons is certain the Onondaga invented the longstick game—
"Right here," he said, sitting with his son in Firekeepers restaurant on the

nation's reserve outside Syracuse. Situated in the geographic center of the original Five Nations, the Onondaga were charged by the Peacemaker with tending the fire of the confederacy, keeping it forever lit. As Haudenosaunee capital and home of the Grand Council and the burial place of Handsome Lake, the Onondaga Nation considers itself the caretaker of traditional values, spirituality and pride. "Here's how fundamental lacrosse is to the Haudenosaunee. When you're a male and you're born, you're one of three things: You're a speaker, which means you speak the languages and do the ceremonies; or you're a singer of the songs that you need for the ceremonies; or you're a lacrosse player," Rex Lyons said. "That's why those crib sticks are there: so even before you can walk, you have a lacrosse stick in your hand. And you're buried with your lacrosse stick. It's not a casual thing. It's a part of our culture, our cosmology, our creation story."

By the time of the American Revolution, exposure to the white man's guns, germs and alcohol had eroded Haudenosaunee independence and strategic clout; after smallpox devastated the Onondaga in the winter of 1776–77, the council fire—for the first time in history—was covered, and the confederacy broken. Allied with Great Britain in its continental victory over France in 1763, each of the Six Nations was now free to choose sides. The Oneida and Tuscarora sided with the Americans; the Mohawk, Seneca and Cayuga took up arms with the British; the Onondaga claimed neutrality, though its chiefs and warriors fought with both.

In 1778 a series of brutal British and Iroquois raids on frontier settlements sparked a response from George Washington, the Virginia general who prided himself on an Indian nickname, inherited from his great-grandfather but soon fully earned: *Conotocarious*, Town Destroyer. Over the spring and summer of 1779, Washington's personally directed campaign against Iroquoia, carried out principally by General John Sullivan, sent 4,469 soldiers on a mission of "total destruction and devastation" of more than 50 Native settlements in New York, beginning at Onondaga.

On April 21, 558 Continentals descended on the confederacy's capital, killed 12 and captured 34, torched 50 houses and the village stores of corn and beans, and butchered all horses and livestock. Though Colonel Goose Van Schaick claimed a tidy operation, Iroquois narratives claim that Continental soldiers murdered babies, raped and killed female prisoners. Washington stated only that the operation brought "the highest honor" to himself and the army.

The Sullivan campaign sent the Haudenosaunee scattering from their demolished villages—some 5,000 freezing and starving refugees swarmed the British fort at Niagara alone—and American independence ensured that few would ever return. Without consulting or even mentioning the Six Nations, in 1783 Great Britain ceded all lands under its control, including most of the Iroquois' New York territory, to the US in the Treaty of Paris. New Seneca settlements sprung up in western New York, with a council fire lit at Buffalo Creek. Thousands of Iroquois streamed over the border to the lands south of Montreal; both sides of the St. Lawrence River at Akwesasne; and present-day Ontario, where the British rewarded loyalist Mohawks, led by war chief Joseph Brant, with a 675,000-acre reserve at Grand River.

There, too, a council fire was lit. Within two years, Grand River's population, representing all Haudenosaunee nations and a mix of other Native tribes, stabilized at a few thousand. Meanwhile, south of the Canadian border a series of forced treaties—Fort Stanwix in 1784 and Fort Harmer in 1789—along with the quick retaking, in 1797, of Seneca land supposedly restored by the Treaty of Canandaigua, sealed the US grab of nearly all Haudenosaunee territory.

Widespread depression and dissipation among the remaining Iroquois sparked Handsome Lake's anti-gambling, anti-alcohol visions in 1799, and it's easy to read the mass embrace of his preaching—*Gaiwiio*, or "Good Word"—as a response to a demoralizing sense of loss. By 1829, the number of Native Americans in the original 13 colonies had dwindled to 16,093.

"I have met the last of the Iroquois; they were begging," Alexis de Tocqueville wrote, in *Democracy in America*, about his travels in 1831. "All of the nations I have just named once reached to the shores of the [Atlantic] ocean; now one must go more than a hundred leagues inland to meet an Indian. These savages have not just drawn back, they have been destroyed."

Or forcibly displaced. In May 1830, President Andrew Jackson signed into law the Indian Removal Act, effectively seizing the ancestral lands of southeastern tribes like the Choctaw, Cherokee and Seminole and, by the early 1840s, evicting thousands of Indigenous people to federal lands west of the Mississippi River. "They have neither the intelligence, the industry, the moral habits, nor the desire of improvement which are essential to any favorable change in their condition," Jackson said in his 1833 address to Congress. "Established in the midst of another and a superior race, and without appreciating the causes of their inferiority or seeking to control them, they must necessarily yield to the force of circumstances and ere long disappear."

The template for the policy and its infamous "Trail of Tears" had been carved out a decade earlier in New York. Squeezed out of their lands by white settlers and promised a 6.7-million-acre tract—quickly whittled to 500,000— in the 1820s the Oneida began emigrating to Wisconsin; they established a reservation near Green Bay in 1838. The original Iroquois Confederacy in the US was now fully dismantled, in fact if not in mind.

As a result, the Canadian enclave known as Six Nations of the Grand River emerged as a new de facto capital of Iroquoia. Mohawk leader Joseph Brant's ambition to forge an alliance with western tribes, though unrealized, for a time produced a momentum, a hope, unfelt by those left behind. The wheel of history turned: War refugees had nudged the Haudenosaunee center of gravity northward. They brought their lacrosse sticks.

II

THE WHALENESS OF THE WHITE

WHITE WANT, BY THEN, followed a familiar pattern. Terms like "colonialism," "empire" and "Manifest Destiny" were just grandiloquence for a hunger that boiled down to *They came, they saw, they*—after that one breathless pause, F. Scott Fitzgerald's "transitory enchanted moment"—*had to have it.* The explorer begat the missionary, who begat the trader, pilgrim and farmer, and then, on August 27, 1860, a 19-year-old lacrosse goalie named W. George Beers. He was standing on the Montreal cricket grounds, and facing something commensurate to his capacity for wonder. Under the eye of the Prince of Wales and thousands more, in a game tied 2–2, Beers was desperately trying to fend off shots from a dazzling team of Mohawks.

"The playing on both sides was determined and excited," Beers recalled, "and ended in a dispute: Baptiste, of Caughnawaga, the Indian captain, having picked up and held the ball with his hand at a moment when the whites had a clear chance of carrying it into the Indian goal. The match was awarded to the whites."

Neither Beers nor his older teammates seemed surprised by Baptiste's odd gambit in what was billed a "Grand Display of Indian Games." Perhaps it was typical. The Mohawks, from the nearby Caughnawaga reserve, had been staging exhibitions in Montreal since 1834, played their first game against whites in 1844 and manhandled all challengers for the following decade. Perhaps such disputes were common, and Beers and his friends decided they had had enough.

Beers had joined the Montreal Lacrosse Club at the age of 13. He would later emerge as an accomplished dentist and nationalist, but both occupations were preceded by his precociously self-assured drive to make field lacrosse a Canadian institution. And he wanted the game his way. Two weeks after the 1860 exhibition for the Prince, Beers wrote up a foundational pamphlet establishing basics like field dimension, number of players, ball composition and stick specifications. Rule number three begins: "Throwing the ball with the hand is prohibited."

Whether seen as a refining of lacrosse or as outright theft, Beers's codification was a presumptuous move for a white man of any age, though welcomed by his peers. MLC had combined with another Montreal lacrosse club for the "Grand Display," amid a growing Canadian fascination. Indeed, the nation's early interest in lacrosse—at a time when US policy called for forced displacement of all Eastern tribes to the West—highlighted a subtle difference between Canadians and Americans.

Though just as imperious, Canada's history with Indigenous people was leavened by memories of the British-Iroquois alliance and respectful treatment by the French. In 1877, after defeating Custer at Little Bighorn, Sioux chief Sitting Bull and 5,000 followers sought refuge in Canada. "We are British Indians," he said, holding up a century-old silver medallion given to his grandfather during the American Revolution on behalf of George III. "Our grandfathers were raised on British soil." Sanctuary was granted, and the inspector who met Sitting Bull at the border became the only white man he ever trusted. But Canada ultimately denied the Sioux a reserve and food. After four years of increasing neglect, they returned to America.

There, Sitting Bull and his people collided again with a culture far more hostile and far less intrigued by Indigenous methods of play. Beers saw lacrosse as Canada's answer to cricket in England and viewed Natives with a racialist—and to modern eyes, obliviously racist—mix of reverence and dismissal. The Indigenous game, with its emphasis on endurance, dodging and mesmerizing stickwork, was good only for them. "We may wish for the hereditary sagacity of the Indian, who plays mainly by instinct . . ." Beers wrote in a typical assessment. "But the Indian can never play as scientifically as the best white players, and it is a lamentable fact, that Lacrosse, and the wind for running, which comes as natural to the red-skin as his dialect, has to be gained on the part of pale-face, by a gradual course of practice and training."

But, he declared, "sensible, thoroughly civilized people cannot, and should not, play Lacrosse exactly after the manner of the Indian. The fact that they may beat the pale-face is more a proof of their superior physical nature, than any evidence of their superior science. They play on the old principle of war . . . and obey no arrangement of any kind . . . The Indian village game was not intellectual enough for the whites, and needed systemizing."

Yet, bemoaning the comparative roughness of the white game, Beers tried to credit Native Americans with moral superiority, if only in lacrosse. Watching a Native game in the Caughnawaga—now Kahnawake—reserve south of Montreal, a "gentle savage turned to us and said, in broken English: 'You can't play lacrosse like that. You smash heads, cut hands, make blood. We play all day; *no hurt, except when drunk.*'"

But Beers's respect had strict limits: The Native game was for whites to control. The uniting of four colonies into a single dominion on July 1, 1867, is considered modern Canada's birthday; that same month, Beers published his expanded rules of field lacrosse—the technical basis for his nickname, "The Father of Modern Lacrosse." Rule IX, Section 6, declared, "No Indian must play in a match for a white club, unless previously agreed upon." When the National Lacrosse Association of Canada was formed two months later, it adopted the slogan "Our Country and Our Game."

Despite cricket's greater popularity, Beers campaigned tirelessly to make lacrosse the "National Game of Canada," to the point of propagating the fiction—lasting until 1964—that Parliament had declared it so in 1867. And partly because of his magical thinking, by the end of that year, some 80 lacrosse clubs had sprung up, mostly around Ontario and Quebec. At the same time, hoping to cash in on the white world's paradoxical fascination with the "noble savage," Mohawk and Six Nations teams embarked on tours in France, the US, Ireland and Britain. The first departed in that month of Canadian firsts, July 1867—18 players from five of the Six Nations, led by Caughnawaga Mohawk Jean-Baptiste "Big" Rice.

"The Indians looked very smart dressed in their blue and red drawers," claimed one report on a match at London's Beaufort House in Walham Green, "the chiefs of each side being distinguished by feathers in their cap and other ornaments." Lacrosse clubs soon formed in London, and the English Lacrosse Association was founded. During a Beers-organized tour in 1876, 13 Caughnawaga played a team of 14 white Montrealers, or "Canadian Gentlemen Amateurs," in a private display for Queen Victoria at Windsor Castle.

Though happy to conduct "war dances" and wear "Indian" regalia for the sake of box office, a Mohawk player named Jean-Baptiste Aiontonnis also pushed back against Canadian presumption. "We hope you come and look upon us playing *our own great game* of La Crosse in England against the pale-faced young men of Canada," he said in a pregame speech to the Queen, "who now play *our game* like us."

Victoria's sole response, from her diary: "The game . . . very pretty to watch. It is played with a ball, and there is much running."

By then, club lacrosse in Canada was afflicted by gambling, fears of match-fixing, increasing violence and under-the-table payments for ringers. In 1880, the sport's ruling body, the National Lacrosse Association, added "Amateur" to its name and banned professionals from membership or championship play. No teams were more obviously professional than the cash-strapped Indigenous players, who negotiated hard for their cut of gate receipts: Beers's Rule IX, Section 6 had reached its ultimate expression: For official league competition, lacrosse's highest expression, Canada barred the Iroquois from their own game.

That didn't mean that Natives stopped playing field lacrosse, either as a Medicine Game or in exhibitions against white teams; in fact, their tours to US cities expanded. And though the International Lacrosse Federation's decision to recognize the Iroquois Nationals in 1987 has been celebrated as the game's authority righting a century-long wrong, a team of Mohawks (playing under a Canadian flag) finished third behind Canada and the US at the 1904 Olympics in St. Louis, and played—and lost—in an American qualifying tournament for the 1932 summer games in Los Angeles.

Still, the 1880 ban did mark a turning point. Key actors in the early legitimizing—and marketing—of the game, the Iroquois and other Indigenous players were officially ghettoized just as Beers's version was taking root among white people in Canada, then in the United States. Iroquois disengagement from the modern field game had begun. Lacrosse had passed its own Indian Removal Act.

Few noticed. The ban came amid a supreme existential crisis for Indigenous peoples in the US, where imperious debate ("[C]olonize and improve them," Secretary of the Interior Alexander H. H. Stuart stated the choice in his 1852 report to Congress, or "exterminate and kill them off.") had tipped toward chilling consensus. "I don't go so far as to think that the only good Indians are the dead Indians, but I believe nine out of every 10 are," future president Theodore Roosevelt said in an 1886 lecture in New York. "And I shouldn't like to inquire too closely into the case of the tenth." Hunters had all but destroyed the buffalo population on the

Great Plains, under a quasi-official US policy of eliminating the prime Indigenous source of food and warmth and, thus, its cultural will. "Kill every buffalo you can!" advised one post–Civil War army colonel. "Every buffalo dead is an Indian gone."

America completed its seizure of the Black Hills and its gold in 1877, the same year that the great Sioux warrior Crazy Horse—who wore, famously, an Iroquois shell necklace—surrendered and was killed in prison, his people herded onto reservations. In 1879, Richard Henry Pratt opened the most famous of the residential schools, Carlisle, with its stated mission to kill Native identity at the root.

Oren Lyons has a name for all that:

> *That's ethnocide, cultural genocide. That's a process. That was deliberate. They took children away from their parents. Can you imagine? Do you have any children? Imagine somebody come into your house, take your children and going to keep 'em. What would you do?*
>
> *In the 1870s, they tried to kill everybody and couldn't do it, so then they said,* Well, let's make 'em Americans. *So, in 1924, they sent the Indian Citizenship Act to make everybody American:* That'll get rid of them and then they won't have a claim to land. *Everybody didn't know that, but Six Nations did. Six Nations said,* No, thanks, we're going to remain who we are. *That's why we have passports today.*

THE FIRST HAUDENOSAUNEE passport was issued on July 28, 1921. It was carried by the Cayuga chief Deskaheh, speaker of the council at Six Nations of the Grand River, on a desperate mission. The year before, Canada had amended its ever-amended Indian Act to compel Indigenous children into its residential schools and force Canadian citizenship on any Indigenous people—both in repudiation of 150 years of history. The Iroquois, especially those descended from the original Loyalists at Grand River, considered themselves British allies since King George III had called them precisely that. And the Iroquois' ongoing exercise of free passage across the border, guaranteed by the 1794 Jay Treaty between Great Britain and the US, ratified that alliance daily.

Deskaheh, aka Levi General, took his case to the Court of St. James. In September he sailed to London to present a petition for sovereignty and justice to King George V, and was summarily told to take it back to Canada. Two years later, on behalf of the world's oldest league of nations, Deskaheh traveled to Geneva hoping to address the new League of Nations; one account had him cutting a "figure of romance, as he strides through the streets in full war regalia." His petition to have the League rule on Haudenosaunee independence made for "heroic and pathetic reading," reported the *Guardian*. "It is easy to regard this claim to nationhood by a remnant of the Iroquois and the others as humorous, but one hears that the red men by the Great Lakes are in grim earnest."

Deskaheh remained in Geneva more than a year, lobbying for an audience that was never granted. He returned home exhausted in early 1925 and, six months later, died at 52. Yet the failed missions established a visceral precedent; Great Britain and Switzerland admitted Deskaheh under his Haudenosaunee passport, the first countries to recognize its validity. A template for cultivating public opinion had been created. Newspapermen had smirked, but around the globe they published the Haudenosaunee story: *We are still here.*

Oren Lyons grew up in lockstep with the modern Iroquois independence movement, its battles fought mostly in courts and newspapers. In May of 1925 his great-uncle Jesse Lyons, an Onondaga chief and former lacrosse player at Carlisle, led a delegation to Washington, DC, bearing eight Iroquois wampum belts—including the one marking the original confederation in 1550 and each subsequent treaty with Europeans and Americans, all unseen by white men since George Washington's day. The *New York Times* ran a story. Five years later, on March 5, 1930, Oren was born in the New York village of Gowanda, hard by the Cattaraugus reservation, the oldest of seven. His Wolf clan mother gave him the name *Joagquisho*, which translates as "Sun Rays Making Path in the Snow."

He recalls a chief coming through the front door of the family home in Onondaga on June 14, 1935, to instruct Oren's father how to vote on the 1934 Indian Reorganization Act. The heart of President Franklin D. Roosevelt's "Indian New Deal," the IRA was a progressive piece of legislation designed to reverse the federal policy of assimilation and promote Indigenous culture, self-governance and education. The IRA could be applied only with tribal approval; 172 other tribes voted to accept it. "Tomorrow you're going to be there," the chief told Oren's dad. "And vote no." Distrustful of US motives and wary of any increase in federal oversight, Onondaga and the rest of the Six Nations voted no, overwhelmingly.

Oren Sr. worked construction but was mostly a wrecker, and often took his son along as he dismantled decrepit houses and buildings in the Syracuse area. Nights, Oren Sr. played in goal for field games at Onondaga, and in the box for the Onondaga Red Devils once they got started in 1933; Oren watched his father repair sticks and pads by candlelight. The two played on the same Onondaga field team during World War II, Oren 11 years old and his father giving him only one bit of advice: *Watch the ball, not the man.* At 13, scrambling in the piles of the Onondaga Nation dump, Oren found an art kit, paints and brushes, and began daubing away. He never intended to follow his father's path.

"I started out in the field, and then on one trip we had a rain day; waiting for the rain to clear, our goalie went out into a bar and got drunk," Oren said. "So they said, 'Your dad was a goalie; you get in there.' I've been in it ever since."

By then the game had effectively split in two, offering divisions by country, style and status. George Beers's hope to make field lacrosse Canada's national game faded early in the 20th century, overtaken by ice hockey and even baseball, leaving hots pots only around Montreal, Southern Ontario and British Columbia. "Can Lacrosse Come Back?" the national magazine *MacLean's* wondered, in 1929, and mourned where it had gone: "If Canada has rejected its offspring, the sportsmen of the United States have generously afforded it board and lodging and a chance to grow."

Reversing the Iroquois migration a century earlier, in the post–Civil War decades a southward flood of Canadian immigrants introduced the game to working-class Irish across New England and New York. With Queen Victoria's approval of the 1876 exhibition still fresh, the American upper crust signed on; one month later, the Westchester Polo Club staged games between the same teams at its athletic festival in Newport, Rhode Island. The first intercollegiate lacrosse game was played between New York University and Manhattan College in 1877; teams formed at Princeton, Columbia, Yale and Harvard. Montreal-born John Flannery moved to Boston in 1875 and three years later led his lacrosse club to the US's first intercity lacrosse championship—over a New York opponent, before a crowd of 40,000—on Boston Common. Seven weeks later, Baltimore got its first taste when a track-and-field team returned home from a multi-sport competition in Newport bearing new lacrosse sticks. The city's first intraclub lacrosse game, in November 1878 at Newington Park in northwest Baltimore, drew a few hundred fans. A year later, Flannery, the "father of American lacrosse," created the US National Amateur Lacrosse Association.

Ironically, Beers's vision of a rugged Canadian game imbued with English-inspired amateurism and "gentlemanly" values, characterized by passing and "scientific" strategies and teamwork, would now realize its greatest expression in America. In 1881, Harvard beat Princeton to win the first intercollegiate championship, and within five years Boston had more than two dozen lacrosse clubs. Gritty early adopters found themselves edged aside. "Some of these organizations," observed a Boston alderman, "are made up of people who do not care to associate with some people who [would] like to be members." Founded by Yale grads, the wealthy and influential Crescent Athletic Club of Brooklyn fielded its first team in 1893, further cementing the sport as an emblem of the nation's intellectual and power elite. In 1911, President William Howard Taft, with New York's governor and mayor, would stop by to watch Crescent lacrosse beat Montreal Athletic Association, 6–3.

Johns Hopkins played its first game against the Druid Lacrosse Club in the spring of 1883, disbanded, reconstituted for good in 1888 and won its first national championship three years later. In 1904 Hopkins coach Bill Schmeisser organized the Mount Washington Lacrosse Club in that affluent northwest Baltimore suburb, a powerhouse of Blue Jays alums working in finance, medicine and law that would eventually succeed Crescent A.C. as the sport's premier club. Ivy League schools, along with Navy and Hobart, all made an early mark on the college game. But by the late 1920s, Johns Hopkins had won 21 national titles; established a feeder system in Baltimore's private schools and its two largest public high schools, City College and Polytechnic; and stood as the lacrosse paragon for the country. Aptly, when lacrosse appeared as a demonstration sport in the 1928 Olympic Games in Amsterdam, the United States did not send a continental all-star team. It sent Hopkins.

Four years later the sport arrived at a decision that, in retrospect, was a crossroad. The 1932 Olympics in Los Angeles would again feature lacrosse as a demonstration sport, and for a time its international officials hoped to include an Iroquois national team—coached by Onondaga chief Jesse Lyons. Opposition from the US and Canada scotched that. Instead, Six Nations took part in an eight-team elimination tournament for the right to represent the US, and quickly lost to a New York club. Worse, the Haudenosaunee had their lacrosse bona fides questioned beforehand by Hopkins head coach Ray

Van Orman, who, according to the *Baltimore Sun*, "declared the Indian teams he had seen were not in a class with the college twelves, and that he had not expected their request for a play-off position to be granted."

Coming 50 years after the original ban of Native Americans, the Olympic snub was a decided setback. If allowed to play, Chief Jesse Lyons would have been able to point to his team's presence in Los Angeles as an Iroquois statement of sovereignty on the order of Deskaheh's passport and his wampum-laden trek to Washington, DC. If allowed to play as an Olympic nation in 1932, the Iroquois detachment from the field game might well not have become so extreme. The lacrosse establishment might not have taken another 50 years to embrace the game's founders and denounce the ban. The mission to return both lacrosse and the Iroquois to the Olympics—now aiming for 2028, in Los Angeles—might not have taken nearly a century.

Johns Hopkins won the 1932 elimination tournament, then beat Canada's All-Stars in a three-game series to claim the Olympic title. But Van Orman's disdain for the Iroquois was not universal, and not every program smacked of elite prep school. Syracuse coach Laurie D. Cox built his first team in 1916 out of his forestry students, and tried to play a field game with Onondaga every year, sometimes twice. In 1919, Cox hired Onondaga's Ike Lyons—another of Oren's uncles—as an assistant coach. In 1930, Cox convinced Onondaga star Clinton Pierce to become the first Indigenous player for Syracuse; in one of his last acts before retiring in 1932, Cox personally named him an All-American.

Pierce was an outlier. Few Natives, then, left the reservation for mainstream college, and fewer still graduated. And though Medicine Games never stopped, the secular discipline of field lacrosse in Iroquoia faced new competition. Once the owners of the Montreal Canadiens and Toronto Maple Leafs hockey teams launched their box lacrosse circuit in the summer of 1931, the field game in Canada all but disappeared. Ice hockey's conquest of the Great White North was complete by then, and when "boxla"'s creators chopped team size from field's 12 players down to seven (and after game reforms in 1933 reduced field teams to 10 men, seven down to six), walled them within a melted rink's oblong, sanctioned cross-checking and encouraged fighting, the intention became clear. Boxla made hockey a year-round affair. Canadians loved it.

For Iroquois players, the new lacrosse came as a salvation. Pro box had no ban on Native players, required no forays into the alienating world of American universities and provided needed income. Men from Caughnawaga, Akwesasne and Six Nations of the Grand River populated newly formed teams in Montreal, Toronto and British Columbia in the early 1930s, and broke into the US market on the all-Indigenous Buffalo Bowmans. An American box league ranged from Toronto to Baltimore. A tryout for the Syracuse Red Devils—where Oren Lyons Sr. took up residence in goal—drew 70 Native Americans, aged 8 to 69, and one white man. The Rochester Iroquois, starring Six Nations Mohawk Harry Smith—a.k.a who would become the actor Jay Silverheels, who played Tonto in television's *The Lone Ranger*—served as a pride point for that city's booming Haudenosaunee population during the Great Depression.

Pro box's popularity also helped recharge the Iroquois Confederacy. Onondaga and Akwesasne built outdoor boxes; clubs sprung up to represent the Seneca, Tuscarora and Mohawks and drew from reservations at Cattaraugus, Allegany, St. Regis and Akwesasne; four teams served Six Nations of the Grand River alone. Intra-reservation rivalries were created; old hatreds and bonds were rekindled between Six Nations men who otherwise might never have met. Indeed, in its very violence and speed and emphasis on individual play, its place as a manly proving ground, box was deemed far closer in spirit to the original game than anything dreamed up by Beers or Van Orman.

In contrast, proponents of the American field game—starting with Syracuse coach Laurie Cox—condemned box lacrosse as mere bloodsport. Collegians ignored it or, in the manner of suburban hoopsters visiting inner-city playgrounds, ventured to outdoor Native boxes—dirt surface littered with stones, splintery boards topped with chicken wire—for a dose of underclass grit. "I was out of my element, a white boy playing college ball in the field, and went down to the reservation where I didn't belong and wanted to play their game their way," said Roy Simmons Jr. of his first taste of the Onondaga box in the late 1950s. "But I wasn't tough like that."

Quickly, Simmons found that the extended cradling or slow jog he could indulge in field left him bloody. Quickly, he learned to take the spittle launched from Native women in the stands as gestures of respect. "Every Sunday I went out there," he said. "I'd carry the ball and purposely go over to spitting distance . . . and said, 'Goddammit, I hope they hawk a big gob on me today.' You felt like a gladiator in there."

ONE AFTERNOON in the late 1940s, Simmons's future co-captain at Syracuse, goalie Oren Lyons Jr., 18 or 19 years old, was feeling unusually good in the Akwesasne box. All game he had held off a legend: Mohawk Angus Thomas, first time playing after serving a long ban for killing a goalie with a rocket-shot to the neck, with word that his notoriously heavy ball had also killed another. But Lyons—young and cocky—had been "anxious to play him, test this guy out," and was blocking most everything Thomas fired his way. And Onondaga was winning.

With about eight minutes left, Thomas came racing toward goal with ball on stick. Lyons wore no face mask, but his chest was encased in the armor of two baseball chest protectors, reinforced underneath with a wad of sliced fan belts. When his younger brother, an Onondaga defenseman charged with slowing the onslaught, blocked his view, Oren yelled, "Get out of my way, Lee!"

Thomas wound up, fired the ball underhand. Lyons heard its sizzle, felt it crack his side, fell. He needed 20 minutes to catch his breath. Three ribs were broken; instead of a bruise, the ball's force had left Oren's skin pure white. But Thomas didn't score. "You're going to be a good goalie," he told Oren after.

Lyons got away from the game for a time, boxing and boozing. In keeping with the Iroquois sense of alliance with the US—the confederacy made its own declaration of war on Germany in World War I, never rescinded it, and added Japan and Italy to Nazi Germany for World War II—during the Korean War many Haudenosaunee, including 20-year-old Oren and Lee, joined the army. Oren served in the 82nd Airborne as a machine gunner. During his last jump at Fort Bragg, 3,000 feet up, his parachute failed to open and he awoke dangling from a branch of blackjack oak, leg broken. His unit left for Las Vegas without him, parachuting through the mushroom clouds of nuclear tests. Years later, when hearing of comrades ill with symptoms consistent with radiation exposure, Lyons recast his terrifying plummet as a lucky break.

After mustering out Lyons returned to Onondaga, and stepped back into net. In May 1954, with Lyons in goal, the Onondaga box team was riding a three-year winning streak when it hosted Syracuse. The annual exhibition game served as a telling gauge of the fading Iroquois' focus on field: the Orange had won the previous eight meetings by a combined 116–29. After Roy Simmons Sr.'s team won again, 15–8, he asked Onondaga's 24-year-old goalie if he'd ever consider enrolling at Syracuse.

Lyons lacked the basics of proper English grammar and spelling, but his skill in goal—and paintings of boxers, lacrosse players and clan animals—provided a way in. Simmons Sr. had him admitted through the university's fine arts department. The walk from reservation to campus was still rare; Clinton Pierce's trail was three decades old. "I was the second Indian to play at Syracuse," Lyons says. "Very few Indians went."

There was nobody on campus like him. Apart from being Indigenous, Lyons was a veteran, older than most, living with his girlfriend, Beverly, in a university apartment and the father of a daughter, Lonnie. He fought for Simmons on the Syracuse boxing team in 1955, got stopped in the last second of the second round of a 139-pound bout in the Sugar Bowl against Louisiana State. His artwork appeared in the school newspaper. Math was a problem. An English professor tutored him; in the end Lyons graduated with, he said, "a legitimate C" average. One day in the spring of junior year, 1957, Lyons got married in the morning and teamed with Jim Brown to win a lacrosse game in the afternoon.

In goal, Lyons was even more unusual. Though defending the field game's six-by-six-foot goal, the man newspapers delighted in calling "little" Oren Lyons set up like a goalie in front of a four-by-four-foot box goal: stick held vertically, often with just one hand. The stick itself was cut down to the length of a camp skillet's, anywhere from six to eight inches. "Just about long enough to get his two hands on the handle, and unique to look at, because most goalies like—for the leverage to clear the ball—at least 30 to 40 inches," says Roy Simmons Jr. "So it wouldn't get stuck in the net, and he'd swing it both ways. He played ambidextrous. Very wide head."

In his first season in 1956, Lyons set a collegiate record with 274 saves—his 21-save-per-game average still stands as the school record—and Syracuse finished 8–5. The next year, with him and Simmons Jr. as co-captains and Jim Brown unleashed, Syracuse finished 10–0. Lyons was named All-American and, after Syracuse went 6–3 his senior year, was so honored again. Roy Simmons Sr., in his 26th year leading the lacrosse team, called his goalie "the best I have ever coached."

Despite the accolades, Lyons held no illusions about the white world's regard. Nothing, really, had changed. Throughout college, he always returned to the reservation. Days after graduation in 1958, he was fishing in a canoe with an uncle then on the Council of Chiefs, who said, "You've been to college and must know a lot. You must know who you are, then."

"I'm Oren Lyons," he said, but his uncle responded, "That's all?" He then tried his Native name, then tribe and clan. Still: "That's all?" Finally, Lyons gave up.

"See that pine over on that shore?" the elder said. "You are the same as that pine, Oren, no different. You see where the roots go, finding the earth? That's how your roots are, too. You got old roots that go back a long way. Old roots, that's who you are . . . The earth where they go in: that's your mother."

THE LESSON STUCK, even when Lyons moved with Beverly and Lonnie to the distracting wilds of New York City. He landed work at the Norcross Greeting Card Company and soon was overseeing hundreds of artists; his 1960 appearance on the TV gameshow *What's My Line?* opened with the host joking about his Native name. Many were the weekends he drove the five hours hours back to Onondaga, clearing his head with a shotgun hunt or a ceremony at the Longhouse.

In 1965, Lyons's clan mother approached him about serving on the Grand Council. Problem was, the open seat belonged to Onondaga, and under the matrilineal system the mother's bloodline prevails. Thus began a seven-year process, from his application to renounce Seneca citizenship, to his "condolence" into the council as faithkeeper, to the Seneca Nation's official release, to his adoption by the Onondaga Nation. The marriage broke up. His role in Native America's burgeoning protest movement was expanding fast.

Though the Six Nations reserve in Canada often rivaled the Haudenosaunee capital as a political force, in the 1960s Onondaga effectively reasserted its primacy. Traditionalist leaders like Tadadaho Leon Shenandoah (great-grandfather of Lyle Thompson) and Irving Powless Sr. set a newly aggressive tone, and Lyons's unmatched feel for white culture and media savvy made him Onondaga's most effective young voice.

"I was a runner for the nation," Lyons said. "What happened with me, in particular, is I went to university and I got to speak the language of our [white] brother very well—way better than I speak my own language, actually . . . So the whole Six Nations depended on me, a lot, and then I realized that other Indian nations depended on us, too. It kept broadening out and I kept understanding that I'm speaking, finally, for all the Native people at times."

Lyons came of age in a US riven by protests and street-level unrest. The American Indian Movement (AIM), begun in 1968 by Russell Means and Dennis Banks of the Lakota and by Vernon and Clyde Bellecourt of the Ojibwe, was the most extreme version of what came to be known as "Red Power." Its effective launch came in late winter of 1969, when a fast-expanding amalgam of Indigenous people—fronted by "United Indians of All Tribes" spokesman Richard Oakes, a former Akwesasne Mohawk steelworker—began a 19-month occupation of the decommissioned prison on Alcatraz. Years of pan-tribal activism ensued—with Oren Lyons often in the thick of it.

On November 1, 1972, a conceptually peaceful, highly disorganized, AIM-led caravan of protesters from 200 tribes in 25 states—including Onondaga, Mohawk and Tuscarora—arrived in Washington, DC, to end a cross-country demonstration dubbed the "Trail of Broken Treaties." Bearing a list of 20 demands that included the abolition of the Bureau of Indian Affairs and return of 110 million acres of Native land, the participants soon realized they had no place to sleep. Meetings had been set up between "Trail" leaders and Nixon administration officials by BIA Commissioner Louis Bruce, of Oglala Lakota and Mohawk descent—Onondaga born and Akwesasne raised—who, during his three-year tenure, had managed some striking reforms. Lyons was part of a group from Six Nations "assigned," he said, "to oversee" AIM's activities in DC.

The first night, 700 protesters were given shelter in a rat-infested church in a poor Black neighborhood. The next day, some 350 Natives—including elders, women and children—descended on BIA headquarters on Constitution Avenue in search of accommodations. Talks disintegrated when police in riot gear tried to clear the building. Protesters barricaded the entrance. What began as a civil rights demonstration, then a housing negotiation, swiftly devolved into an occupation of a federal building. For the next week, police surrounded the building; snipers aimed from a roof across the street. A pinned-up banner outside read, NATIVE AMERICAN EMBASSY.

On Monday, November 6, with the 1972 presidential election two days away, Lyons returned from a weekend spent reporting to the Grand Council at Onondaga. "The place was barricaded, there were seven kinds of Washington police lined up, one right after the other: it was chaos," he said. "And then we went into the building and there was all the men all painted up, getting ready."

A sudden shutdown of phone lines seemed to signal a coming government attack. Native occupiers, smeared with war paint, fashioned spears out of knives and broken furniture. Molotov cocktails lined the stairs. After someone yelled that the building was going to be blown up, a Cheyenne and Muscogee reporter, Susan Shone Harjo, saw AIM leader Russell Means on the building's front steps, lighting the long fuse on a gas-filled bottle.

"It's a good day to die," Means said.

Cooler heads stepped in. One was Oren Lyons.

"I could smell gasoline; they had the place lined up to set it on fire and go outside and fight to the death," Lyons says:

> *He's looking at me, all painted up . . .*
> *I said, "Russ, what are you doing?" He said, "We're getting ready to fight. Fight to the death" . . . I said, "Don't you understand what's going on here? We're working this through. This is just the first skirmish. There's going to be more. Where you going to be if you've all fought to the death and the second one's coming? . . . Put that stuff down."*

Hank Adams and Francis Boots—Sioux and Mohawk, respectively—led the push for a peaceful resolution, and Lyons helped convince AIM leadership to allow moderate Natives, including grandmothers and youths, to front negotiations with the government. That night, a settlement was brokered: The Natives agreed to leave, and the US agreed to respond to a 20-point list of demands and pay travel expenses home. "We've got people without money, got to fix their cars: people coming down with no spare tire, running on balloon tires, no treads," Lyons said. Somehow, $66,650 in small bills was procured. The cash was doled, and the broken caravan rolled out.

Red Power reached its peak—in messaging, if not results—during the siege of Wounded Knee in early 1973. Led by AIM's Russell Means and Dennis Banks, some 200 Oglala—Lakota—seized the quintessential site of Native American loss and white atrocity on the Pine Ridge Reservation in

South Dakota. For 71 days they held it, despite the starvation tactics, guns, armored vehicles and 130,000 rounds of ammunition wielded by 1,000 federal agents, disguised military personnel and National Guardsmen. Gunfire was a constant. Two Native men died; 17 were wounded; a Black pacifist who came to aid the Natives clashed with AIM security and disappeared forever. A U.S. Marshal and FBI agent were seriously wounded.

In March, after declaring itself sovereign on the order of the Iroquois Confederacy, the Lakota asked the Haudenosaunee for help. Lyons led a delegation of 14 to Pine Ridge and delivered a statement of support from the Grand Council of Chiefs. The delegation stayed four days. Two months later, Lyons and two Haudenosaunee chiefs traveled to Washington, DC, to apply pressure to the ongoing negotiations, meeting with Massachusetts Senator Ted Kennedy. A few days later, May 8, the siege ended.

The confederacy's presence and Lyons's reading of the Grand Council's statement, upon arrival at Wounded Knee, provided the siege with necessary context. Starting with a reassertion of Six Nations sovereignty, he reiterated the binding power of US treaties and endorsed Lakota nationhood. He spoke of the irresistible might of the US and its responsibility for any violent tactics by Native activists. He positioned "Second Wounded Knee" as the latest battle in a 500-year conflict, spoke of Native lands seized for power dams and ransacked for timber and coal, Native water polluted by industry. He spoke, that is, less to the Lakota present than to white Americans beyond, finishing with a reminder:

We have not asked you to give up your religion for ours.
We have not asked you to give up your ways of life for ours.
We have not asked you to give up your government for ours.
We have not asked you to give up your territories.
Why can you not accord us with the same respect? For your children learn from watching their elders, and if you want your children to do what is right, then it is up to you to set the example.

During his four days at Wounded Knee, Lyons looked past the current siege and wondered about American culture, private property, human nature, selfishness. "This is the fence system of the United States," he said then. "The white man says, 'This is mine.' Indian says, 'This is ours.' That's the two ideologies: this is the conflict. We must be concerned for the welfare of all human beings. When we function on that level and concern ourselves with the welfare of coming generations we can all move in the same direction. The Creator has made us all brothers and we should be of one mind."

SOMETIME IN THE second half of 1973, a white ex–US Marine and wealthy restaurateur named Bradford Tiffany opened the front door of his 250-acre former dairy farm off Cherry Valley Turnpike in LaFayette, New York. Oren Lyons was standing there. "So," Lyons began. "What do you do with those buffalo?"

"What took you so long?" Tiffany replied. "We've been waiting for you."

Five years earlier, before his newly purchased property had been fully fenced, Tiffany had achieved a boyhood dream by buying 17 buffalo—"American bison"—at $600 a head from the National Bison Range in Montana. In 1969, he bought 22 more of the still-endangered species; by 1971 his herd had multiplied to 71—the largest buffalo enclave east of the Mississippi River—and was doing brisk business selling hides and breeding stock. The year Lyons knocked, Tiffany had already offloaded two dozen calves to ranches in New York, North Carolina and Canada.

By the late 19th century, North America's buffalo numbered no more than 1,000; the Smithsonian Institution counted 85 free-ranging bison in the entire US. Though dime novels and movies popularized the decimation as a Western phenomenon, the original population of 60 to 200 million buffalo ranged as far east as the Appalachians and western New York State. An 1806 account written by Briton Thomas Ashe had buffalo frequenting the salt licks around Onondaga Lake, outside Syracuse, and included a description by one of the region's first settlers of a herd of 300 bison—amid a swarm of 10,000—crushing his cabin, and his own work killing "six to seven hundred of these noble creatures, merely for the sake of the skins." Though Ashe's narrative has been dismissed as exaggeration, if not pure fiction, within a few decades bison bones and a skull were being unearthed in the region, and later in the graves and refuse pits of Indigenous settlements.

Haudenosaunee proof lies in tradition: The ancient buffalo medicine society at Onondaga, still active, performs a medicine-invoking ceremony, or "dance," that predates the white man's arrival and features an imitation of the muddy beast stamping and wallowing to ward off flies. Someone's ancestor saw that firsthand. "They were here," Lyons said. "It's a spiritual relationship: We call them the buffalo nation. They have leaders and responsibilities."

In ancient Haudenosaunee cosmology, all animals—and all manifestations of the natural world—are considered equal members of Mother Earth's family. This is why any hickory cut for a lacrosse stick or deer hunted for dinner are thanked for their sacrifice, why senseless tree cutting or trophy hunting causes such offense. When, some 300 years ago, the bison—*Dege-ya-gih*—became the first of the Haudenosaunee brothers-in-spirit to disappear, Onondaga elders foretold their return someday.

No one envisioned Brad Tiffany as the man to make it happen. The son of a Binghamton, New York, butcher, during the Korean War Tiffany dropped out of high school to load bombs on an aircraft carrier, brawled constantly and twice lost private's stripes for disciplinary reasons. "It was him against everybody—and he could take 'em on," Lyons said. Upon returning, Tiffany earned his diploma and enrolled in Cornell's vaunted hotel and restaurant management program, only to drop out to work full-time at hotels and restaurants. In 1962, partnered with his brother, Dar, and a friend, Brad opened the first Scotch N' Sirloin in his hometown. His mom made cheesecake, his dad handled butchering and the place became the first in the continental US to boast a salad bar. By the late 1970s, the family opened and controlled Scotch N' Sirloins in Buffalo, Rochester, White Plains, Boston, Scranton, Pennsylvania, even San Juan, Puerto Rico. Sometimes, the Syracuse location served buffalo chops.

"My dad was always saying, 'Sizzler, Outback Steakhouse: Those are knockoffs. People stole this concept,'" Lars Tiffany said. "In the mid-1970s they were making *so much* money, he and the partners. This is embarrassing: My dad found a check underneath his car seat one day and he's like, 'Oh, $2,200. Holy cow. Forgot to deposit this.' Then he goes to the bank, and it's $22,000."

Though Brad's buffalo fascination had more to do with the beasts than the Natives, he long wondered why the Onondaga hadn't approached him. Once they did come, with the stated goal of breeding up their own herd, members of the National Buffalo Association cautioned Brad that the Indians would only shoot and eat them. And once negotiations began, the Onondaga remained cagey. When Tiffany offered 10 head for six breeding seasons, on the condition that the Onondaga fence 200 acres of the reservation and return him 11 buffalo at term's end, the Onondaga refused to sign. "They wanted," Brad said, "no part of a piece of paper."

But Lyons kept coming by the Tiffany home to chat, and invited Brad's family for ceremonies at the Longhouse. Five-year-old Lars, the eldest of three boys, found himself exposed to the traditional religious ceremonies and festivities. He didn't see any other white faces. His earliest lacrosse memory is being on the reservation, awkwardly firing three-shots-for-a-quarter at a box goal.

Months of oft-heated talks at the Longhouse yielded Brad a taste for sassafras tea, but no deal. In the fall of 1974, against every rule of negotiation and his own near-pathological terror of being fleeced, he loaded 10 buffalo onto a truck for the short ride to Onondaga. Buffalo are smart, mean when cornered, and can weigh more than a ton. In the day's chaos, a stray made it onboard. "Eleven got on the truck; it was supposed to be 10," Lars said. "Try to get one off? You probably lose all of them." Watching them roll out, all Brad could think was *There's no contract . . .*

At noon on New Year's Day, 1975, Lyons returned to Tiffany's door with Tadadaho Leon Shenandoah, Chief Vincent Johnson of the Buffalo Medicine Society, and other Onondaga chiefs with their version: a treaty, hand-painted by Lyons onto a stretch of deerskin four feet tall and three feet wide, framed in hickory branches and featuring figures representing the chiefs, 11 buffalo, Lars, his mother, Faith, and younger brother Hudson; though Peter had been born in 1971, Lyons mysteriously represented him by depicting Faith as pregnant. Six wintry silhouettes represent the six-year term. Brad is depicted shaking hands with Shenandoah. The treaty was one of only a half dozen struck by the Onondaga in the 20th century, and one of the few ever fully honored by the white man. Despite that, the moment warranted no immediate notice; three years passed before the *New York Times* wrote an article, and then *Parade*, the widely circulated national weekly, splashed the story on its cover with the headline "The Treaty That Brought the Buffalo Back."

Both accounts emphasized the fulfillment of ancient prophecy. "It's a spiritual feeling," Onondaga chief Irving Powless Jr. said then. "With the coming of progress and the pushing of our animals back into smaller areas, not only the buffalo but our other brothers, such as the deer and the bear, are being pushed into small places so that they are disappearing. To have them return to us: it's a feeling that you can't explain. But it's good to have our brothers back."

From the start, the Haudenosaunee framed their reunion with the buffalo as a litmus test for a planet besieged by pollution and the churn of industrialization. "The Indian, like all of our brothers—the wolf, the bear and the eagle—are hard pressed for survival," Oren Lyons said then. "Our fate may indicate the fate of the continent and of the people who live here, [because] the principle of equality of all life is a natural law that extracts its own retribution upon violation."

The first two calves in Onondaga's new herd were born in 1975, followed by three more in the spring of 1976 and four in 1977. By then Brad Tiffany was showcasing the deerskin treaty in a place of honor in his home, and had come to see the Onondaga buffalo as one of his proudest legacies; after the six-year treaty term expired, the Onondaga responsibility to return 11 buffalo to the Tiffany ranch dissolved. Brad did not go into detail, but left his wife and family with the impression that he had, uncharacteristically, freed the Onondaga of their debt.

"This was a different side of my dad that didn't usually come out," Lars recalled. "He started to really appreciate the connection to the buffalo with the Native Americans, and he really liked Oren . . . And he always said later, 'I kind of like it, too, because if I ever change my mind, I could go back into the buffalo business.'"

Indeed, for Brad the beast represented nothing greater than hard work. Though the wealthiest man in town, he charged into ranch life with macho marine abandon, repairing splayed fences, hopping recklessly into the corral to nudge bison toward the squeeze chute for inoculations. One bull pinned him between its horns—tips stuck in the planks just long enough for the man to wriggle free; another flipped Brad nine feet up in the air. Young Lars might have gotten awestruck by the sight of a newborn calf, blood-orange and steaming in a snowy pasture, but the family concern was meat. It was just product out there, raised for cash or slaughter.

Until, one day, it wasn't. Lars was 9 or 10 years old. The squeeze chute closed too tightly on a bellowing cow, suffocating it to death, and he watched as a tractor backed in and the chained carcass was dragged to the swing set in front of the house where he played and hung from the top. Then came the knife, the disemboweling, blood and steamy viscera slithering into dirt. Even more shocking was the sight of his so-tough father, witness to thousands of dead animals in his 46 years, broken. "Crying and crying and crying," Lars said.

As the oldest Lars soon grew into one of his dad's foremen, leading his brothers in clearing and salting burdock weed, chopping trees for barn repairs, dispatching the annual buffalo for the family freezer. But that day's horror never lifted.

"It really bothered me, killing the animals," Lars said. "I loved the role: I can remember, in snowstorms, looking out and wanting to walk out to make sure the fences were good, that they were safe. There was something about being with animals, and making sure they're safe, that felt really great. Whereas slaughter and eating flesh and eating the body of an animal just repulsed me. I wanted out of the death cycle."

BRAD TIFFANY'S TIES to the Haudenosaunee faded with time. Visits from Oren Lyons became rare as the push for pan-Native unity went global. In 1977, 50 years after Deskaheh's futile mission, Lyons traveled amid a delegation of 12—all bearing Haudenosaunee passports—to Geneva for the first-ever United Nations conference on "Discrimination Against Indigenous Populations in the Americas." Some 165 representatives from North, Central and South America gathered in the UN's Palais des Nations to begin the 30-year work toward the 2007 Declaration on the Rights of Indigenous Peoples. Along with Tadadaho Leon Shenandoah, Lyons also pushed the Haudenosaunee principle of decision-making based on the impact seven generations hence, the confederacy's role as stewards of the earth.

"I do not see a delegation for the four-footed," Lyons chided the assembly on the first day of the 1977 conference. "I see no seat for the eagles. We forget and we consider ourselves superior, but we are after all a mere part of the Creation."

His life filled with conferences, interviews, lectures. Lyons taught college classes, wrote essays. He led an Iroquois delegation of peace-talk observers to Bogota, Colombia, in 1985; testified before Congress in 1987; occupied an hour of Bill Moyers's national television airtime in 1991; addressed the UN General Assembly in New York to a standing ovation in 1992. Meanwhile, his shepherding of the Iroquois Nationals, from concept to reality, gained more attention from sportswriters than anything he ever did as a goalie.

Still, amid that external goodwill, trouble developed in Iroquoia. While Lyons was reinvigorating his people's primacy in Native affairs under a unified banner—the *Iroquois Nationals!*—the confederacy was cracking anew. In 1988, the federal government enacted the Indian Gaming Regulatory Act, allowing high-stakes bingo halls and casinos on reservations and tribal lands, subject to federal law and state taxes. Tribes nationwide seized upon the industry as economic salvation; by 1996, 177 different ones were operating 240 gambling venues, and "Indian gaming" was a $3.5 billion industry.

The Six Nations split over gambling, bitterly: traditionalists versus modernizers, old chiefs versus new militants known as the Warrior Society, strict nationalists versus those seeking more nuanced relationships with the US. Factions formed. Families stopped speaking. Bullets and fists flew; in 1990, a shootout in Akwesasne between pro- and anti-gambling Mohawks killed two. Eventually, the Mohawk, Oneida and two of the three federally recognized Seneca tribes—Seneca Nation in New York, and the Seneca-Cayuga in Oklahoma—embraced gambling. The Onondaga, Tuscarora and New York's Cayuga and Tonawanda band of Seneca, citing varying combinations of Longhouse teaching (Handsome Lake inveighed against alcohol and gambling), independence and suspicion of US motives, opposed it.

The right of each nation to govern itself without interference allows such division. Nevertheless, the policy statement issued by Tadadaho Sidney Hill on behalf of the Grand Council in Onondaga made the standoff between theory and practice an official fact of current Haudenosaunee life:

The Haudenosaunee is philosophically opposed to casino gambling and high stakes bingo within its territories. Gaming is predicated upon fostering greed and unrealistic visions about striking it rich. There is a reason why casinos are constitutionally banned in New York State. In the past, casinos corrupted the people. New York has chosen gambling as a way to generate income for itself and we feel that this is socially irresponsible.

The Haudenosaunee is morally opposed to casino gambling and high stakes bingo within the territory of the Haudenosaunee. Our Original Instructions, Great Law of Peace and Spiritual Teachings are very clear on this matter. Our way of life is predicated upon values and beliefs that will be undermined by the greed and corruption that casinos bring. The culture of casinos would violate the principles and values that we have inherited from our ancestors. Casino culture destroys the social, cultural and spiritual fabric of our people, and will lead to more serious disruption of the overall health and welfare of our people.

The Haudenosaunee is politically opposed to casino gambling and high stakes bingo within the territory of the Haudenosaunee. The gaming compacts, as currently structured, represent a serious violation of our collective rights. The compacts deliver jurisdiction over our people and lands to New York

State. You should be well aware of our position that New York State does not have any civil or criminal jurisdiction over the Haudenosaunee or our territory. The gaming compacts violate this most basic of sovereign principle . . .

Or, as Oren Lyons put it, voice rising: "In order to open a gambling establishment, we'd have to *get permission* from the US federal government. Are you nuts? Then we'd have to get permission from the state, which would be really nuts. We told people, 'Do you know what you're signing?'"

Soon enough, the hard-line stances by the Tuscarora and New York Cayuga would soften. Onondaga's position remained non-negotiable. "We don't take gambling money, period," Lyons said. "That's been our mantra, all the way through."

THE GRAND COUNCIL was always open about its use of lacrosse as a political tool to advance Longhouse ethics and Haudenosaunee sovereignty. Yet from the day, in June 1983, that the Iroquois Nationals played their first field exhibition—and Lyons began his push for Olympic participation—the universally sympathetic coverage on television and in mainstream publications always came framed as a sports story. Few understood that reclaiming the Creator's Game, using Haudenosaunee passports, and receiving IOC recognition were but means to a greater end. Since 1945, the Iroquois had been campaigning for membership in the United Nations. The goal involved more than a shiny nameplate.

Fred Opie, the first Black man to make the US national team, was standing among teammates on the field during opening ceremonies at the 1990 World Championship in Perth when Lyons invited him for a private chat. Named by his activist parents after abolitionist Frederick Douglass, the former Syracuse defenseman knew of the old man's friendship with Jim Brown, and figured he'd been tapped because of the logical alliance of African Americans and Native Americans as marginalized peoples. Out of all the Americans in Australia, Lyons looked to explain himself to only one.

"Do you know why we're here?" Lyons asked Opie in his hotel penthouse the next day. "To establish our sovereignty so that we can take different nations that have essentially violated our sovereignty by acts of criminalism over the years before the United Nations and get this addressed."

Opie had just started on his master's degree in history at Shippensburg University, coaching and working on the side at Gettysburg College's Intercultural Advancement Center. "I later realized that this was the same tactic of Malcolm X," he said. "Oren said, 'We want to be recognized before the UN to take the United States before the UN for human rights violations.' I don't think people knew at that time that that's what the Iroquois were strategizing. I considered it a privilege to be there, and witness that."

Opie's stint with Team USA felt, in the end, oddly polite. No one in team management—publicly or privately—acknowledged his groundbreaking status. He didn't speak of it with any teammate, nor was he interviewed about it in the weeks before, during or after the 1990 World Championship. Perhaps this was because he wasn't much of a factor; Opie played in five of the six US games, including the 19–15 win over Canada in the final, but never scored. And a five-team lacrosse tournament is nothing like the Olympics. Opie never expected to receive even a fraction of the attention paid to track star Jesse Owens at the 1936 Summer Games in Berlin, or the black-gloved protests of Tommie Smith and John Carlos in the 1968 Olympics.

Still, in the sport's collective silence, it seemed to Opie that lacrosse was saying that his breakthrough—the very Blackness that defined him daily—didn't matter. Only once, during that meeting in a Perth hotel with Oren Lyons, did he feel important. "I felt," Opie said, "like a Tommie Smith." He felt seen.

THOUGH OREN LYONS'S time in Perth was dominated by the Haudenosaunee mission, his son's presence at the 1990 World Championship marked a personal milestone, the braiding of generational paths. Unlike his father, Rex went to Syracuse in 1981 right out of high school; devoted more to his guitar and punk rock band, he bristled at college lacrosse's "entitlement" aura and lasted half a semester. Instead of NCAA glory in goal, Rex found high-iron work as a glazier and Haudenosaunee fame as a sharpshooter with Onondaga's box team and the Rochester Knighthawks. He also inherited Oren's wit: the name of his most successful band—White Boy and the Wagonburners—was a smirk in 4/4 time.

As a young man, Oren struggled to get free of alcohol. Rex, too, was plagued by booze—plus his era's cascade of narcotics and stimulants.

"I was pretty much a garbage head," he said. Cocaine became his drug of choice: smoking, snorting and injecting it, then dealing it so he could buy more.

"At one point everybody gave up on him but me," Oren said. "Me and his dog."

Father and son weren't unique. The US Indigenous population has suffered disproportionately from alcohol's ravages since first contact, and the modern flood of narcotics and hallucinogens into mainstream America only compounded the scourge. Native Americans today report higher substance abuse and addiction rates than any other ethnic group: in 2023 nearly 20 percent reported binge drinking in the previous month; 25 percent reported substance abuse in the previous year; nearly 37 percent reported using any illicit drugs. Victim-blaming—via the discredited theory about Indigenous susceptibility to "firewater"—once enabled the continent's conquerors to deny culpability. Today, scientists attribute the Native substance crisis to personal and cultural trauma.

"You're spiritually bankrupt," Rex said.

His demons hit him young. His father's stature undermined his self-esteem. The music scene offered endless drugs and drink. Only lacrosse provided ballast: after another cycle of rehab, Rex would get clean for months and play box or for the Nationals. He made his debut in Perth in 1990, appeared in the '94 and '98 World Championships, for a time was the program's career scoring leader. "That saved my life," Rex said. "Most drug addicts, their health breaks at some point. Everything gives out. But I played at such an intense pace that I was able to counterbalance a lot of the self-destruction things I was doing in the off-season."

Still, the drugs nearly won, killing off nearly all that mattered: appetite, marriage, relationship with his mother and children, the heat and lights in his home. When Rex showed up at his mom's house at 4 a.m. to say goodbye forever, she said that his sons needed him alive. That registered. Then Oren kept coming by to feed him in bed, repeating, "I need you to sit up, one more time. One more time." That jolted Rex into giving life one more shot. After two more years of therapy and struggle, on December 7, 2002, he declared himself sober. He says he hasn't used since.

Each morning now begins with a prayer to the Creator. He still calls himself an addict. He's sure he can help other Natives enduring the same. "I'm like tempered steel," Rex said. "I kept going through the foundry and I come out on the other side. You can't break me."

III

MONEY BALL

A S A VARIANT on a very old story, drug abuse in the late 20th century couldn't compete with the unprecedented onset of Native gambling. The Oneida launched Wisconsin's first lottery in 1988 and signed its first gaming compact with the state in 1991; the New York Oneida opened Turning Stone Casino in 1993; Akwesasne Mohawk Casino opened in 1999, and Seneca Nation followed with the first of three New York casinos in Niagara Falls in 2002. By 2011, the Indigenous gaming industry was producing $27.1 billion in annual revenue (growing to $41.9 billion in 2023), a transformative windfall that kept proving itself, daily, to be no panacea for Indigenous despair.

The Onondaga Nation decided to offer an alternative. In early 2012, Oren Lyons phoned then–FIL president Stan Cockerton to say that the Haudenosaunee capital wanted to host the 2015 World Men's Indoor Lacrosse Championship. No Indigenous people had ever staged a global sporting event; Cockerton wondered if they were up to the task. But in its greatest leap of faith since recognizing the Nationals a quarter century before, on September 2012 the federation awarded the confederacy the games.

Locking in Syracuse's massive Carrier Dome and Onondaga's utilitarian 2,000-seat arena for the competition was easy. Construction of the event's signature venue went down to the wire. But in September of 2015, five months after groundbreaking and just days before the first game, Onondaga opened its new, 40,000-square-foot field house at a cost of $6.4 million. That's small change for a casino, but in place of craps the Onondaga offered pride and competition. Instead of air-conditioned slots, they offered a structure both airy and rooted, a tribute to the surrounding stone and wood. Taking in its majestic beamed ceiling from field level, one gets the cozy sensation of sheltering under a flipped canoe.

Lacrosse love prompted then–Patriots head coach Bill Belichick to chip in $50,000 for the event, but Onondaga claims of purity only went so far. The field house—and the additional $3.75 million needed to stage a 10-day, 13-team event—were financed mostly by the same 24-hour, tax-free tobacco shop that provides much of the nation's operating income. Yet as a statement of purpose, a show of competence and—especially—a piece of sovereignty theater, the venture's success was undeniable. Jim Brown, visibly hobbling, flew in from Los Angeles to give his blessing. Former US vice president Al Gore showed up at the welcoming buffalo feast and said, "I'm rooting for the Iroquois."

Once within the Onondaga Nation's 9.3 square miles of territory, fans and family at the World Indoor Championship experienced few reminders that they had stepped into another country. There are no signs pointing to Onondaga's small lacrosse Hall of Fame, the headstone of Handsome Lake, or the high meadow home of Onondaga's buffalo herd. Visiting players, however, received a jarring reminder when they found themselves processing through Haudenosaunee passport control. Eleven of the delegations—including England, Germany, Israel and the United States—took part in the expected role reversal, viewing the Iroquois stamp in their passports as a badge of cool, if not honor. Only Canada's players, coaches and officials refused to present their documents. And then pointedly refused to say why.

This occurred at a delicate time in Canada's relationship with its Indigenous population. Seven years earlier, the Ottawa government began reckoning with the ravages of its 110-year residential school policy by appointing a National Truth and Reconciliation Commission. More than 7,000 survivors testified. Records revealed that at least 54 children died at one of the longest-running schools, the Mohawk Institute on the reserve at Six Nations of the Grand River—home of many Iroquois Nationals, past and present. Just three months before the 2015 World Indoors, the commission released an executive summary that officially labeled the school system "cultural genocide" and called for a "multi-generational journey" of reconciliation throughout Canadian society.

Yet, Canada's refusal to present passports at Onondaga was hardly a shock. After all, Canada had questioned Iroquois nationhood and cast the lone "No" vote—unlike the US, England and Australia—when the Nationals first applied to play in the 1986 World Field Lacrosse Championship. And though US attitudes and practices were historically more hostile, in the 21st century Canadian authorities proved to be more openly dismissive of Haudenosaunee sovereignty claims, citing examples like the Mohawks at Akwesasne who refuse Canadian citizenship and don't recognize the US-Canada border, but received $390 million in Canadian federal funds from 2001 to 2010.

"It's a stretch to claim all the benefits of the Canadian nation-state—her institutions, her tax regime, her social welfare programs, her security—and yet pretend one is independent," said Mark Milke, a director at the Fraser Institute, an independent research institute in Canada in 2011. "It's a bit like a 13-year-old who says, 'I don't owe anything to my parents, they can't tell me what to do, yet I'm under their roof.'"

Canada's Custom Act lists the Haudenosaunee passport as one of 71 "fantasy passports"—along with defunct countries and territories countries like British Honduras, and something called the "Principality of Vikingland"—that it does not recognize. Enforcement varies. Just two weeks after the 2015 World Indoor Championship, Tadadaho Sidney Hill and two Mohawk colleagues were pulled off a Peru-bound jet and detained for days in Bolivia; there, someone with the Bolivian foreign ministry told them that the Canadian government had pressed Peru to reject their passports. Only the intercession of a US official—and new routing through Miami, on Haudenosaunee passports—enabled them to return home.

With the diplomatic air thus charged, Canadian lacrosse officials had their own reasons to be annoyed at Onondaga. Since 1930, the men's game had been divided into two spheres of influence: the US dominated field lacrosse and Canada dominated box, beating the Iroquois in all three World Indoor finals contested since 2003. But now Canadian field players were increasingly seen on American college rosters, and Canada was still reveling in its upset over the US in the 2014 World Field final. Yet the current narrative fixated on the Iroquois: winners of their first field bronze medal at that 2014 championship, now welcoming the game's two superpowers with the feistily possessive slogan "Lacrosse Is Coming Home."

So, however how scintillating Canada's play at the 2015 World Indoor Championship, the lacrosse was always going to feel secondary. The Iroquois' first game, a 13–9 win over the US, thrummed with about as much symbolism as a sporting event can carry. And in a statement of priorities, Tadadaho—and former Nationals defenseman—Sidney Hill missed the Iroquois' semifinal win over the US to lead a delegation to New York in a vain attempt to confront Pope Francis and demand the rescinding of the Catholic Church's Doctrine of Discovery, the 1493 papal bull that justified explorers' conquest of Native lands.

Tendered an invitation to join other North American spiritual leaders at a multi-religious service at the September 11 Memorial and Museum at Ground Zero, Hill was under the impression he would be able to speak to the pope personally. He brought literature about the Doctrine and a gift of wampum for Francis. But upon arrival at the event, Hill not only learned that he would not be allowed onstage ("We weren't recognized," he said, "as a national religion like the others"), but was made to leave his sacred Gustoweh—the ceremonial Tadadaho headdress—outside because its decorative antlers represented a security risk. When Hill left the auditorium after the hour-long service, he found the sacred and symbolic Gustoweh abandoned on a table.

Wary of being reduced to a political prop—and of setting what Ottawa clearly perceived as a dangerous passport precedent—the Canadian lacrosse delegation at the 2015 World Indoor Championship seemed intent on pushing back on the Haudenosaunee narrative. The chairman of Canada's national team program, Dean French, conceded that his country needed to better educate its children on Indigenous history. But even after Canada beat the Iroquois Nationals, 12–8, in the final, his irritation was palpable.

"We hear a lot this week about how it's the Haudenosaunee game—and it is. We respect that," French said. "But Canadians invented the box lacrosse rules. We invented the box lacrosse game. It's our game. Sometimes people need to speak up for that, too."

THE 2015 WORLD INDOORS represented a triumphant culmination of all Wes Patterson and Oren Lyons had envisioned in 1980. It was also the end of an era. Since the mid-1990s Onondaga had been providing the bulk of the

Iroquois Nationals' budget (anywhere from $50,000 to $200,000 annually), backing what was essentially an Onondaga-led program celebrating Onondaga traditionalist values. But after spending at least $10 million to host the Worlds, the Onondaga declared its bankrolling days done. Going forward, the other Haudenosaunee nations would need to contribute much more.

That meant, of course, a loosening of Onondaga control. Rex Lyons glimpsed the future before the 2015 World Indoors, when he traveled to the other five nations seeking cash. "It was challenging to go there and say, 'We all agree we love lacrosse. That's how we need to approach this. It can't be pro-tobacco, [pro]-casino. It's got to be pro-lacrosse and pro-Nation, and—in order for it to be healthy—it can't take a political position,'" Rex said. "And I ran into some opposition."

Among the Iroquois, Onondaga's hard-line resistance to gambling was becoming increasingly lonely. The Cayuga, who began buying back their lost New York lands in the early 2000s, reversed course in 2003 and had been fighting ever since to win court approval of its casino operations in Union Springs, New York. The only other anti-gaming holdouts were the Tonawanda band of Seneca and Tuscarora—but Tuscarora was hardly solid. The majority-Christian nation had been bitterly divided on gambling since 1987, when 28-year-old dissident Joe Anderson added a 400-seat bingo hall—with $1,100 per game payouts—to his discount gasoline and tobacco store on the nation's 5,700-acre reservation outside Niagara Falls. The Grand Council in Onondaga condemned the operation and tribal leaders eventually shut it down, but Anderson opened another high-stakes bingo parlor in the 1990s. It didn't last. But as he grew wealthier and more influential over the next two decades, his ambition to open a full-blown casino on Tuscarora land became an open secret.

For the Onondaga, especially, Anderson personified a new destabilizing force. A nephew of Wallace "Mad Bear" Anderson, the Tuscarora activist famed for cultivating white media, Joe Anderson deployed cheeky irreverence as a weapon. Self-made and ever grinning, one of the militant Warrior Society's early spokesmen, he styled the old guard as defeatist frauds, "Baptists" in chief's clothing who hid Christian beliefs behind Longhouse custom. He insisted that his bingo profits created the very jobs, housing and recreation facilities that tribal leaders couldn't. By 1995, he was running a small empire of "Smokin' Joe" gas stations and smoke shops in western New York, manufacturing his own cigarettes and gas blend, selling jewelry, sneakers and as much as 40 million gallons of fuel yearly. "Tradition is nice," he often said. "But that and 50 cents doesn't buy you a cup of coffee."

Soon after expanding into land and real estate development in downtown Niagara Falls, Anderson got his hands dirty. In 2003, he gifted Niagara Falls mayor Vince V. Anello a series of no-interest loans totaling $40,000 during an election campaign—payoffs, critics said, that resulted in many favors, including Anello's recommendation to grant Anderson a 30-year no-bid lease on a downtown pedestrian mall. Anello eventually faced federal charges of public corruption, pleaded guilty to the unrelated crime of improperly collecting a pension and served 10 months in federal prison. Anderson pleaded guilty in 2008 to one count of scheming to deprive citizens "the honest services of an elected official," cooperated in the Anello investigation and, in 2011, was slapped with a $50,000 fine.

After that, Smokin' Joe seemed to mellow. Though he still openly hoped to open a casino—and perhaps become Tuscarora chief—Anderson's public profile had edged closer to the mainstream. Or vice versa: During the summer of 2018, the state of New York was closing a deal with the 59-year-old Anderson to buy his downtown Niagara Falls real estate for $25 million.

The loss of Onondaga funding, meanwhile, began to tell on the Iroquois Nationals. Long-unaddressed dysfunctions in administration, not to mention the enterprise's basic handicaps, could no longer be papered over. "It's just the size of it, the scope," Rex Lyons said then. "We have a small pool of players, and we have a small organization trying to run this extremely high-level thing. We don't have the financing. We don't have the organization. USA Lacrosse has got six-figure people, and that's their job. We're trying to get there but, being sovereign, we have a hard time setting up a 501(c)(3), getting funding; we have to have [a donation site called] 'Friends of Iroquois Nationals.' All these logistics come into play that keep us always trying to catch up."

Nothing highlighted the program's vulnerabilities like the 2018 World Championship in Israel. Nike provided $25,000, but funding pleas to the other Five Nations came up short. The Seneca Nation pledged $40,000, the Mohawks chipped in, but Tuscarora, miffed that the original roster included no Tuscarora players, refused to donate at all. That opened the door to private benefactors like Mohawk millionaire Curt Styres, the owner of the pro indoor Rochester Knighthawks, given control of the program for the 2019 Indoor World Championship. It also pushed Nationals general manager Ansley Jemison, just two weeks before opening night in Netanya, to call Smokin' Joe Anderson.

He had already been helping quietly. Anderson had never stopped paying one of his former employees, Nationals head coach Mark Burnam, even after he left New York in 2015 to run the IMG Lacrosse program in Florida. And during tryouts in 2018, Anderson's outfit had donated boxfuls of Iroquois Nationals training shirts to raise money. When Jemison called seeking help paying for the team's airline tickets, Anderson pledged $25,000. Then Jemison learned that the Seneca Nation's $40,000 wouldn't come until after the tournament. Even as the team was loading up for the Toronto airport, it wasn't clear he had enough to cover the cost of the team's flight. Jemison called back Smokin' Joe, who wrote a $51,000 check for the tickets.

"That's the least I could do," Anderson said. "I mean, the Thompsons are heroes. Our community needs heroes, real heroes—not a businessman, not a rich man. Lacrosse is important. The Iroquois Nationals are important . . . They really are."

With that, Anderson essentially rescued the Nationals—and became fully enmeshed. His 19-year-old son, Liam, a non-playing student at Cornell who had played for Burnam at IMG, filled one of the roster's last-second vacancies. Smokin' Joe accompanied Burnam on the flight from the US to Israel, bristling with ideas. He offered to finance marketing efforts, provide free retail space in dozens of his stores to supercharge the "Iroquois Nationals" brand, give the Nationals use of his attorneys for guidance on upgrading the Haudenosaunee passport to post-9/11 standards. He even backed efforts to open Iroquois consulates in other countries. In return, Anderson said, he wanted nothing.

Charged by the Grand Council to operate the program as a platform for sovereignty, pride and Longhouse values, not professional sport, the Nationals board of directors—led by Oren Lyons—had long resisted such offers from businessmen. Yet now a pro-casino, anti-traditionalist force had become intricately involved. Anderson certainly didn't hide his presence in Israel; the FIL even honored him and his contributions, on field, with its prestigious Spirit of Lacrosse Award. But few on the Nationals board learned of Joe Anderson's major financial role until after the tournament was over. Health concerns had kept the 88-year-old Lyons from traveling with the team to the Middle East. And, it seems, the Nationals co-founder and Onondaga faithkeeper was left strikingly unaware.

Four months after the 2018 Championship, Oren was sitting at a table at Firekeepers Restaurant, next to his son, Rex. The two were then told of Smokin' Joe's $51,000 donation for flights—as well as the figure of well over $100,000 that he claimed to give the program in 2018. Rex, a rising Nationals board member, admitted that he learned of Anderson's contributions after the fact. Oren seemed baffled. "Nobody knew," he said. "I'm just finding out."

Rex admitted that depending on a rich man's largesse had its dangers, starting with a sudden change of mind. But Oren's eyes flashed, mouth setting in a tight line. He wasn't interested in whether Joe Anderson could be trusted, or had matured, or whether his donations came directly from gambling income. The news that the Iroquois Nationals, in one of its great crises, had placed itself in Smokin' Joe's hands was an alarm bell ringing.

"If I knew that he was putting . . . how much money did you say? I would've said no. Absolutely: I would've said no," Oren said. "I think I have to step in stronger than I've been. If there's a vacuum, people move in."

LARS TIFFANY KNOWS better than anyone: He could have been your typical suburban white boy. He could have been like many a rich man's son, grown up softer than his hard-ass dad, oblivious to the force that comes closest now to being his religion. He also knows that his story would be more delicious if he could say that the buffalo led him to the Onondaga, and lacrosse, and the coaching life. But his route was hardly that dramatic. Everything he is and has can be boiled down to lines on a map.

Not far from the southeastern edge of Brad Tiffany's buffalo ranch, in LaFayette, lies the boundary with the town of Fabius, and archrival Fabius-Pompey High School. Had his father made their home just a half mile away, Lars would have enrolled at Fabius-Pompey, which had no football or lacrosse team and no significant cadre of Native students. He might have played baseball, grown up to be a veterinarian. "I was that close to never playing lacrosse," he said. "Talk about being born in the right place at the right time."

LaFayette's rightness didn't stem just from proximity to the Onondaga Nation. It was a matter of attitude. In 1960, Carl Weist, a young science teacher—and former Dennison lacrosse player—troubled by the hostility between white and Indigenous students at LaFayette High, started a boys' team to find common ground. The program became a fountain of championships and stars like the Bucktooth and Thompson brothers. Nearly as important, the LaFayette High team was successful enough that it spawned a feeder team in the junior high that employed eager sixth graders as managers. In 1979, Lars Tiffany was one of them.

Between visits with Joe Solomon—the Onondaga boy who would become his lifelong best friend—and family trips to the Longhouse, Lars had seen enough kids whipping lacrosse balls in Onondaga's outdoor box to be intrigued. Joe's older brother, Travis, soon to star in goal at Syracuse, was the most famous athlete he knew. Freshman year, he joined the Solomons on the Syracuse fan bus to the 1983 NCAA championship at Rutgers, where Travis anchored the 17–16 upset that toppled Johns Hopkins and established the Orange as a modern power. That clinched it.

Slotted into the entry position for athletes lacking speed and stick skill—long-pole defense—and backed up by Joe Solomon in goal, Tiffany managed a fine career at LaFayette High. Onondagans composed about a quarter of the student body, and more of the lacrosse team. Tiffany's closest friends were white guys like Tim Papa and Chris Volan, and Natives Jake Lazore, Brad Powless and Solomon. They didn't talk about the mix: it just *was*. Fall was for football, winter for basketball, everybody joking and playing and winning together. Then came spring and lacrosse, and Tiffany would feel a shift in attitude. Onondaga kids didn't obsess over lacrosse titles and trophies. They didn't play tight, didn't worry about turnovers; they shot at will. And win or lose, afterward the question was always the same. *When's the next game?*

During lacrosse season, Lars got the feeling—from Joe and his family, from the Onondaga boys and their parents—that he was accepted, part of the tribe. He knew that he wasn't—sensed, even, that it was wrong to think so. But his friends allowed it. "There was always something different with this sport, why we painted our faces and ran around war-whooping," Tiffany said. "Like, we *became* Native warriors, for a couple of hours on that lacrosse field."

His true baptism occurred in the summer of 1985, when—at 17—Lars became the first white man to play for the Iroquois Nationals. No one thought it a major moment. The Haudenosaunee, still reviving their field bona fides, were short on long-pole defensemen for an exhibition in Ottawa. Lars was recruited last-minute and, with Joe Solomon and Mark Burnam, climbed in the flatbed of Travis Solomon's pickup truck for the rattly, 200-mile trek north. Nobody recalls the final score.

In February 1986, Brown lacrosse coach Dom Starsia came to the Solomon home at Onondaga to recruit Joe. Iroquois players were not unheard of at Brown: one of Starsia's closest friends there in the early 1970s, a Mohawk named David White, introduced him to the Akwesasne box with a fight-filled game against a team from the other side of the St. Lawrence River. Regardless, Joe Solomon decided to attend the Naval Academy. At the end of his visit, Starsia had asked Joe's dad if he knew of other promising locals.

"Lars Tiffany," Bo Solomon replied. "He's pretty good, and no one's really talking to him."

Starsia's Hall of Fame career, then, was just blooming: Brown had won the 1985 Ivy League championship and he had been honored as Division I Coach of the Year. Tiffany played three years for him, co-captained and led Brown to its first-ever NCAA playoff win in 1990, establishing a lifelong bond. Over the next 15 years he became one of Starsia's most prominent alums, crafting first-rate defenses at W&L, Dartmouth and Penn State and bearing all the traits—Ivy-educated, upbeat, quotable—coveted by college presidents. His quick lift of Stony Brook into the Top 20 in 2005 made him one of the American game's bright young things. Two years later, with Starsia an established winner at Virginia and lending a strong endorsement, Tiffany became Brown's head coach.

All along, he maintained a shadow career with the Haudenosaunee, reinforced on a level he wouldn't know about for decades. Indeed, the final, unwritten corollary of the treaty between the Tiffany family and the Onondaga was forgotten by all except the man it helped most. In 1990, Onondaga chief Vincent Johnson, the Buffalo Society member who helped present the treaty and oversaw the herd for more than 40 years, was sitting in a trauma ward at Crouse-Irving Memorial Hospital in Syracuse. His son James, a former lacrosse defenseman and US Marine, was lying in a coma, neck broken in a freak cycling accident, paralyzed permanently from the waist down. In walked the head nurse: Faith Corwin, Lars's mother and now Brad's ex-wife.

"Vince," she said. "Don't you recognize me?"

He stood, crying, and they hugged. Faith oversaw James Johnson's care for the next five months; he emerged from the coma after two. Chief Johnson considers this no coincidence. Her presence at his moment of need, their connection via the buffalo, was strong medicine. "We say the buffalo are our protectors," he said.

In August 1993, Lars was teaching biology and coaching at a private school in Pebble Beach, California, when the Nationals called: they needed some long poles for a three-game tourney with clubs in Santa Barbara. Tiffany rustled up a club teammate and took the field under the fake name of Luke Warmwater. Two years later, Tiffany played a season in the box with Onondaga A.C. of the now-defunct Iroquois Lacrosse Association. In 2006, he was head coach for the Nationals' festival field squad at the World Championship in Ontario. There, in a game against an in-your-face elite team from California, he was struck hard by the divide he straddled—the opposing vibes of white collegiate "laxbros" and the Indigenous game.

"It's so different," Tiffany said. "We lost, but the amount of showboating and trash-talking, hooting and hollering, was just unsettling. I could see then that was disrespecting the game, not playing the way it's supposed to be played . . . It infuriated our men so much." But in the moment, Tiffany froze. If it had been his college team, at halftime he would've used the insults to whip the players into a frenzy. But the Iroquois? He wasn't sure how a *Go-Fight-Win!* speech would go over in a program dedicated to lacrosse as the Creator's Game.

Finally Travis Solomon, his 46-year-old goalie, pulled Tiffany aside. "You know," he said, "it's okay if you incite the Mohawks."

THE BUFFALO WORE Brad Tiffany out, eventually. Too many broken fences, too many bulls busting loose and tearing up neighbors' foliage, turf, stone walls; one winter, the snowdrifts were so high that the beasts simply walked over the eight-foot fence around their enclosure. In 2001 Tiffany sold his herd and moved away. But his legacy grew with every buffalo calf born at Onondaga, and in the bond his eldest forged with the people and their game.

When Oren Lyons asked him to join the Nationals as an assistant coach for the 2018 World Championship in Israel, "I felt like I was being called home," Lars Tiffany said. "Like: *Alright, you've been out in the world, you've learned, you've grown. Now it's time to take what we sent you out there with and bring it all back, and help us.*"

His first night in Netanya, in the aftermath of the Nationals' opening night loss to Team USA, Tiffany was leaving the stadium when his phone buzzed. It was Lyons, calling from Onondaga thousands of miles away. "I knew I would get a very measured report," Oren said. Tiffany told him about the players' tired legs, the confused substitute box, the inspired first half. He stayed measured until the moment they hung up. "I just float after I talk to him," Tiffany said.

The matchup against his countrymen caused him no conflict. Though proudly American and the son of a US Marine, Tiffany desperately wanted to win. A part of him also hoped that his time with the Nationals prevented any future association with the US team. "I truly am an Iroquois National," he said. "I want to coach the Iroquois Nationals. That is the national team that, if they invite me and want me, I would love to spend my every four years with. The USA team could ask me to be head coach, and the Iroquois could ask me to be assistant coach: I would choose to be the Iroquois assistant. These are the people I grew up with."

EVERYONE IN NETANYA said that they loved the Iroquois. Everyone said they loved the new members percolating at the 2018 Men's World Field Championship—nine nations participating for the first time—and how impressed they were by upstarts like Puerto Rico and the Philippines. But while all the nods to Native heritage and a global future served the urge to make lacrosse bigger, everyone knew that nothing had changed. Not at the top. Lacrosse was still a bipolar world, dominated by the United States and Canada. The tournament's primary mission—as always—was to provide the field of battle, a platform for the national teams' deliciously mutual dislike, and build to the inevitable showdown.

On Sunday, July 15, the teams—both winners of their first two games—tromped onto the Wingate Institute's soggy showcase pitch, colors popping in the buttery Mediterranean light: Canada in deep scarlet, Team USA in vivid white, the grass a glowing emerald. The stands were maybe half full, but back in North America, half a million lax fans had this date circled. Since its start in 1967, only the US and Canada have won the World Field Championship. America won seven of the first eight. The next-door neighbors spent the early 21st century trading titles, but Canada's 8–5 upset in the 2014 final in Denver seemed a momentum shift. Stepping off the team bus this night, US head coach John Danowski—64 years old, winner of three NCAA titles at Duke but participating in an international game for the first time—felt a "heat" between opponents that he had never experienced before.

Part of it was the American need to avenge that lackluster loss at home in 2014, and part the fact that, having won two of the last three, Canada was feeling particularly chesty. Also, it was virtually impossible to declare one roster better than the other. "Imagine the '92 Dream Team," said US faceoff specialist Greg "The Beast" Gurenlian, of the legendary US Olympic basketball team. "Imagine they split the team in half: both teams can beat the other on any given day. That's what it's like for us. Yeah, they play completely different, they're different types of people. But they are our mirror image. We look at them as our evil twin, they look at us as their evil twin."

To the Haudenosaunee, of course, both countries reek of bad history, the arrogance of successful thieves. From George Beers in 1869 declaring lacrosse Canada's "national game"; to the first white lacrosse clubs; to American universities; to the international game's early lords, who ignored the Iroquois for their first 20 years; lax authorities on both sides of the border—while evoking Native mystique—repeatedly invoked their Doctrine of Discovery. "They robbed our game from us," said four-time National Neal Powless. Field lacrosse evolved into a white, elitist pastime, emblematic of old-boy connections and amateur purity. And though many US and Canadian players and coaches today speak reverently of Native heritage and talent, the Creator's Game, the Native impression remains: They fight over stolen goods. America and Canada play the Appropriators' Game.

Still, any meeting between the US and Canada is a fan's dream game, the highest expression of field lacrosse—its 46 all-stars a distillate of countless hours lost to wallball, at least a decade of merciless competition, and generations of families immersed in a feeder system of costly clubs and costlier universities. In Israel, the eyes and reflexes of Canada goalie Dillon Ward, the playmaking mind of USA attackman Rob Pannell and fast-twitch explosiveness of Ryan Brown, the box-bred bravado of Canada attackmen Curtis Dickson and Jeff Teat—all promised individual fireworks. Yet the pregame vibe was aggressively matter-of-fact. More than half the players on the field were over 27. Two were pushing 40. Heirs of a British ethos that viewed sport as preparation for war, modeling Western values of organization and professionalism, Teams USA and Canada were lacrosse's mature machines. They alone had mastered the drill.

Indeed, the vast gap between the two elites and the rest of the field was on stark display. While Canada and the US coolly prepped for their opening faceoff, the No.3 Iroquois Nationals were just now arriving—exhausted, ill-fed and late—at the Wingate Institute for an 8:15 p.m. game against Australia. Four times a World Championship runner-up, the Aussies were now the Haudenosaunee's prime rival for the bronze medal. But with that morning's clinic at the Kraft Family Sports campus and their draining tour of Jerusalem, the Nationals had made the tough task even tougher. Then the team's 5:30 p.m. pregame meal never happened, because Nationals management wrongly counted on the hotel's usual buffet. Sunday nights, the restaurant was closed.

Since Teams USA and Canada expected to meet again in the final, most figured to that night's pool play to be a probing, throttled-back affair. But two minutes in, after Pannell sealed a languorous possession with a barely contested goal to make it 1–0, it became clear that only the Americans got that memo. The Canadian players were trash-talking, delivering stinging checks and message hits at every chance. After US attackman Paul Rabil fired his first shot, defenseman Tyson Bell delivered a cross-check so fierce that he snapped his own stick in two.

Some venting of Canadian rage or frustration made sense: A month earlier, nobody knew if they would even be in Israel. For months, the Canadian Lacrosse Association had been in a standoff with its top national team players, who had long paid most expenses and were demanding increased health insurance and a resolution of tax issues. The CLA refused. The players went on strike. A plan to use replacements fizzled. Faced with the humiliating prospect of a World Championship without the defending world champion, FIL threatened Canada with fines and sanctions, and a last-minute compromise was cobbled. Rosters, travel arrangements, gameplans and mindsets came scrambling together.

Meanwhile, the Canadian squad had been death-haunted for years. For every game, jerseys with the numbers 17, 18 and 35 were draped over the backs of empty chairs next to Canada's bench. The first and last belonged to goalies from their 2006 World Championship field team, Chris Sanderson and Kyle Miller, who died of cancer at the ages of 38 and 31, in 2012 and 2013, respectively, and to whom Canada's 2014 world title was dedicated. The enduring memorial speaks, in part, to the singular importance of that 2006 title, which announced Canada's return as a field power. Sanderson's impact was particularly profound. In 2010, while suffering from brain cancer, the former UVa product came back to lead Team Canada to a silver medal—and was named the 2010 World Field Championship's top goalie. He remains the Canadian lacrosse standard "in more ways than people can even understand," Canada faceoff specialist Geoff Snider said. "Chris took six months off chemotherapy to play in 2010. He did that to be physically ready to play, and ultimately gave up time with his wife and daughters."

After twice rupturing the same Achilles tendon in 2016, Snider, 37, figured his playing days were done. But in November 2017, Dave Huntley, Team Canada's longtime architect and coach, offered him a place on the 2018 national team as coach or player. Sanderson's example left him no choice. "If I come over here and rupture the other one, then I'm a happy guy: at least I honored Chris and his sacrifice," Snider said. "That's the culture within this organization. This team is something worth fighting for."

Snider learned that, too, from Dave Huntley, the pioneer of Canada's field renaissance. In the mid-1970s, Huntley led the first wave of Canadian players into US colleges and universities, became an All-American midfielder, won two national championships at Johns Hopkins and keyed Canada's fluky run to its first World Field Championship in 1978. He was Canada's assistant coach when it won a second title in 2006, head coach for the silver medal run in 2010 and program director for Canada's third field championship in 2014. Huntley sided with the players in their contract battle with the CLA. There wasn't a player or coach or official with the 2018 team whom he hadn't mentored or helped.

On December 18, 2017, seven months before Canada began the campaign for its fourth title in Israel, the 61-year-old Huntley was coaching at a lacrosse clinic in Delray Beach, Florida, when he collapsed and died of a heart attack. The decision to drape his number 18 upon an empty chair here was automatic. So too, when asked about his decision to wear number 18, were Snider's tears. "Dave was one of those guys who saw more in me than I saw in myself," he said. "He pushed me to be a better leader, a better person, a better man, a better teammate. It sucked losing him, a lot."

But, in truth, the best tribute came between the lines. Huntley always insisted that Canada's blue-collar box mentality could thrive in field: the make-'em-pay slashes; the repeated pick-and-rolls and tight-elbowed shots; even the late blindside hit on American Matt Danowski in the crease after he scored to make it 3–1, USA; had become field staples. Twenty-two of the

23 men on Canada's roster had played at US colleges like Cornell, George-
town, Bucknell, Ohio State and Vermont. Attackmen Curtis Dickson and
Kevin Crowley were then the all-time leading scorers at Delaware and Stony
Brook, respectively. Midfielder Wesley Berg had attended the University of
Denver, where his 39 NCAA tournament goals stand second only to Gary
Gait, the Canadian who followed Huntley's trail to the US and became
arguably the greatest lacrosse player ever.

Snider—barrel-chested and thick-necked—jawed from the start at
Gurenlian, goalie John Galloway and anyone else in USA white who came
within earshot. During his time with UDenver and the indoor pro Calgary
Roughnecks, Snider earned so indelible a rep as a brawler that it was semi-
startling to see him flip a nifty, behind-the-head pass to Ryland Rees for the
goal that cut the US lead to 4–2. His instigating also spread like a contagion,
and though the Americans maintained the two-goal lead at halftime, each
possession was marked by what Rabil called "the back-and-forth, the mind
games and the chippiness, the trash-talking." Three minutes into the second
half, US midfielder Kevin Unterstein hammered his shaft into Jeff Teat's
face mask; Teat retaliated with a stick to the back of the neck. A cluster of
pawing, shoving players was yanked apart.

Early in the fourth quarter, Snider began complaining that the Americans were illegally checking with the stick's butt end, and the once-flowing US
offense sputtered. Berg lunged across the crease to score; Teat tied matters,
9–9; and, with 5:03 to play, midfielder Ben McIntosh gave Canada its first
lead. The Canadian strategy—sand in American gears—seemed to pay off
until Danowski's 32-year-old son, Matt, playing in his farewell tournament,
responded with a rising underhand to tie it, again, at 10–10 with three minutes
to play. Everyone in the place readied for a classic finish.

Once an unstoppable scorer, Rabil—also 32 years old, and playing
in his last World Championship—had spent the night setting up younger
teammates. Now, with 73 seconds left, he tapped an old spring and bulled
toward Tyson Bell, unleashing a 360-degree spin so tight that Bell slipped and
sprawled. After nearly falling himself, Rabil dropped a steadying left hand on
the grass and, in one fluid motion, rose to fire an overhand rocket into the
high right corner of the goal. 11–10, USA. When Gurenlian beat Snider in
the ensuing faceoff, the Americans only needed to run out the final minute
with a bit of keep-away.

But then Snider bellowed to Randy Mearns, Canada's head coach, "Check his stick!" A whistle blew once, then urgently, nine times in all. Gurenlian ran to the sideline, handed over his implement. In 35 years of coaching field, Danowski had never witnessed a stick-check, nor did he remember any when he played at Rutgers in the 1970s or at Long Island's East Meadow High.

Still, stick-checks aren't unknown in pro lacrosse, and Rule 75.3 of the FIL field rulebook decrees a three-minute penalty for a violation. Faceoff men are nearly always the target because their stick heads and pockets— mashed repeatedly, with mammoth torque, against ground and opponent— get bent grotesquely out of shape. A gnarled head or stretched pocket often clutches a ball tighter than a legal one, making it nigh impossible to dislodge, thus becoming a faceoff man's best friend. And one of lacrosse's unwritten laws holds that, with all face off sticks compromised to some degree, to call for a stick-check is bush league.

Snider had broken that law. Rabil, helmet off and shaking his head, was the picture of appalled. Now came a startling bit of theater: One ref stood onfield with arms outstretched, presenting Gurenlian's stick like a soiled baby, while another unfurled a tape measure to check its overall length and width, then the length of the head, then the depth of the pocket. Next a ball was produced and dropped into the pocket. The ref lifted the stick to forehead level, then flipped it upside down. The ball—in a legal pocket—should drop like a rock. Instead, Gurenlian's ball defied gravity, pinched in his webbing as if crazyglued.

The crowd roared in surprise. The ref flung a yellow flag for an illegal stick. With 61 seconds to play and a chance to tie, Canada would have a man advantage. Gurenlian entered the penalty box, disgusted and resigned. "They were desperate, so it's a smart play," he'd say after. "It's just so frowned upon. It must've killed their coach to do it, because it's embarrassing but what are you going to do? It's within the rules."

Yet, the tactic backfired. The Americans interpreted Canada's move as panic and retook the field oddly cocky. Though Canada won possession and parked itself in the US end, though it pried open the US defense enough to launch two fine shots, they skittered wide. On Canada's final foray, with 19.8 seconds left, American defenseman Joe Fletcher's headlong rush at attackman Mark Matthews on the right wing forced a high, flailing shot to nowhere.

Team USA goalie John Galloway gathered the ball in, chased by three red jerseys, and scurried into a corner. Time expired: on TVs scattered across the lower 48, ESPN's announcer could be heard yelling, "The US survives!"

After, Danowski gathered the players around him on the grass. He was thrilled to the point of babbling. "I've never been in a game like this," he told them. "Physical, guys getting thrown to the ground, cross-checking, all sorts of shit happening—and it was great. You held your own, you didn't whine."

He left unsaid what Rabil, Gurenlian and six other veterans on Team USA know: the lack of whining was new. Four years before, in Denver, the US had cruised through the early rounds only to dissolve against Canada in the 2014 final. "When things didn't go our way? We rolled over, and started going palms up—blaming the ref, blaming each other," Gurenlian said. This time? "We took body punches, we responded and the sideline never changed."

Now the state of lacrosse's top three was coming into focus. Cool intensity would mark every Team USA performance from here on. Nearby, on Wingate 4, the tired and hungry Iroquois Nationals were romping to a 16–9 win over Australia—proof that, despite all the obstacles, they had recovered fast. And Canada, of course, was not pleased. That night its players threw everything they had at the Americans. They were tougher, meaner, more inspired, more motivated, more conniving—and still lost.

The following day, July 16, brought no solace. If anything, with the Haudenosaunee up next, Team Canada's mood was even more strained. At one point Nationals coach Mark Burnam stepped into the hotel elevator with Canada's coaching staff, some of them old friends, and tried to catch someone's eye. He was met with silence. They all stared at the ceiling.

"I don't get it with Canada," Burnam said later. "I know these coaches. I'm the most competitive guy in the world, but still I'm like, *Did you guys forget this was a game? This is not the end of the world. It's not a war, thank God.* I don't know: it's a weird vibe when I see stuff like that."

PART 4

99 BOTTLES OF BEER

In America I have seen the freest and best educated of men in circumstances the happiest to be found in the world; yet it seemed to me that a cloud habitually hung on their brow, and they seemed serious and almost sad even in their pleasures.

—Alexis de Tocqueville, *Democracy in America*, 1831

I

BECAUSE YOU KILLED HER

ON TUESDAY, JULY 17, 2018, Max Seibald was sitting in the lobby of a Netanya hotel, parsing stereotypes. He knew the American game's image. His celebrated college career had coincided with lacrosse's darkest era: as a Cornell freshman in 2006, Seibald played in Duke's last game before the rape accusations erupted, and his last win as a senior came against a Virginia team that included George Huguely. Eight years later, in his last tournament before retirement, the 30-year-old midfielder still heard plenty about white entitlement. "It's always got that stigma: it's a 'Northeast,' 'rich,' 'Ivy League' sport," Seibald said. "And on some levels, it's earned that."

Seibald grew up affluent, too, in Hewlett, Long Island. But in leading Cornell to two Final Fours, the 2009 Tewaaraton Award winner earned a reputation for relentless work and selflessness off the field. As a pro he was a five-time Major League Lacrosse All-Star and earned an MBA at New York University, volunteered with City Lax and hustled his own camps into virgin territory like Minnesota and Nebraska. After World Championship stints with the US team in 2010 and 2014, Seibald joined Israel's team to reconnect with his heritage. His dad's father's parents met and married in Netanya in 1954: Ending a near-perfect career there seemed the perfect finishing touch.

As Seibald recounted his life, he clearly saw himself as a living retort to the broadest lacrosse caricature: clad in baggy shorts and half-calf socks, loud and dumb, with a helmet of hair crunched under a backward ballcap. "The worst is the 'laxbro,'" he said. "That signifies: *I didn't work hard to get where I am, I'm just a surfer bro who's disrespectful, a stoner, escaping* . . . And that is exactly who I'm not. If someone chooses to think that of me because I play lacrosse? Fine. I can prove you wrong."

But lacrosse had earned that stigma, too. A month before the 2018 World Championship, the NCAA released the results of its quadrennial substance use survey—conducted in 2017—of 23,000 student athletes. Out of all college sports, men and women lacrosse players self-reported the highest levels of binge drinking (69 and 57 percent, respectively) and use of cocaine (22 and 6 percent) and marijuana (50 and 34 percent). The percentage of lacrosse men using cocaine at least once in the previous year had doubled since the previous survey, in 2013, and increased 600 percent among women. Men's lacrosse was also tops—17 percent—among the 11 sports surveyed in use of narcotic pain medication, both with and without a prescription, and women's lacrosse, at 12 percent, was ranked fourth in the list of 13 sports surveyed.

The previous two NCAA surveys revealed similarly high findings about alcohol and marijuana, with lacrosse having "substance use rates that are notably higher than other sports," as the 2014 executive summary stated. Taken as a whole, the numbers suggested a best of times/worst of times split: from 2001 to 2018, when a 227 percent participation growth earned lacrosse the label of "America's fastest-growing sport," America's best players were self-medicating more than any other college athletes. Yet there were few signs of alarm in the days leading up to the 2018 World Championship, and the common response in Israel was skepticism about the NCAA's latest findings. When Seibald said that he hadn't seen or even heard about the 2018 survey results, it felt like the preface to another dismissal.

Instead, he nodded and said, "I 100 percent—probably—would stand by that. Two kids in my class at Cornell have passed due to drug-related . . . overdose."

Asked why he thought lacrosse players would be more apt to use, Seibald said, "There's two ends to it. One is money: You can afford some of these drugs. Two is the painkillers. Most of my teammates started with an injury— *Here's a bunch of Vicodin!*—then it goes to Oxys [OxyContin pills], then to heroin. It's been all too close to me, people that I played with in college . . . One was a heroin overdose after a couple stints in rehab . . ."

That was his freshman roommate, John Decker, a fine athlete from Philadelphia who suffered a knee injury in high school, underwent multiple surgeries and couldn't play a minute of lacrosse for Cornell his sophomore and junior years. He escalated from prescription to street drug use, underwent two stints in drug rehabilitation, lost his longtime girlfriend. His parents found his body. Decker, 30, died on January 16, 2016.

"And one," Seibald said, "happened last week."

LACROSSE PLAYERS LIKE to party. This is a truism with a history: alcohol has forever been a part of the men's college game. Some argue that it's impossible to fully separate the sport's history of booze consumption from that of booze consumption in private schools and country clubs, or booze consumption among college students, or booze consumption in America overall. But there's a reason that, after the repeal of Prohibition in 1933, the first college athlete suspended for drinking was a lacrosse player. There's a reason that, 79 years later, a lacrosse mother warned newcomers in the *Baltimore Sun*, "You will see alcohol. Lots of alcohol . . . If your child tells you that his lacrosse teammates don't drink, he is lying to you. And if you believe it, you are lying to yourself. You are not smart enough to outsmart the secret drinking plans of a lacrosse team."

Booze consumption is a fact of lax life, transcending age, class, race—even the fiercest of rivalries.

"Maryland guys go down to play lacrosse at Charlottesville and, win or lose, you're out Saturday night and are like, *Why are the Maryland guys out with Virginia guys?*" said former UVa midfielder Shamel Bratton. "It's part of the culture, the camaraderie. We kick each other's asses on the field and we all have a bunch of drinks off the field."

Dom Starsia remembers. Long before his Hall of Fame coaching days at the University of Virginia, Starsia was a New York City cop's son finding his feet in the Ivy League, a football player new to lacrosse. Sophomore year, the coach's declaration of a no-alcohol rule set off a scramble: players made sure to stock up on beer on the way home. "Alcohol and lacrosse have gone hand in hand since my days at Brown in the '70s," Starsia said in 1999. "Whether it was postgame celebrations or just in general, there was something about the sport and alcohol."

Brian Holman remembers. Long before heading out in 2016 to build the game's westernmost Division I program at the University of Utah, long before his years as an assistant coach at North Carolina and Johns Hopkins, Holman was a freshman goalie under Johns Hopkins head coach Henry Ciccarone. In 1980, the legal drinking age in Maryland for beer and wine was 18. Freshmen everywhere were drinking plenty. But on the lacrosse team, it was encouraged—from the top down.

"When we rode back on the bus from away games? The first thing Chic did was pull over and go to a liquor store, and there were three cases of beer on the bus," said Holman, a three-time All-American goalie for the Blue Jays. "So we'd already had two beers before we got off the bus, by the time we got back. Then we'd go out to this party, and that party, and I look back on it and I'm like, *That was bad.*"

Overall, the high rates of substance abuse appear to have little effect on lacrosse players in the classroom. Indeed, academic achievement—or at least the attainment of a bachelor's degree—is an even more prevalent pursuit. With graduation rates topping 90 percent, men's and women's lacrosse regularly rank at or near the top of all NCAA Division I sports. The jarring combination allows for a broad range of interpretation. The most benign plays into lacrosse's self-image as a "work hard/play hard" pastime populated by overachievers; a more critical eye sees it as another example of the sport's Jekyll-Hyde identity, the sense that lacrosse's positive and negative traits are forever at war. "So in one part, we're going, *Yeah! ESPN has us on and it's cool and we're going places!*" said Hall of Fame coach Bill Tierney. "But the next is *We're a bunch of drunks and drug addicts . . .* How does that happen?"

One reason is that, when freshmen first arrive, they're met with a culture that long modeled alcohol consumption not merely as the classic college lubricant, but as central to what a lacrosse player *is.* Throwing back beers postgame was not just a way to socialize; it was a team-building test as revealing as a self-sacrificing check. "Everything that happens off the field—the bonds—are made for success on the field," said Josh Offit, an All-American midfielder at Duke from 2010 to 2013:

> *Do we take it too far sometimes, on the partying side? The national survey would say,* Look: there's a cultural issue here. *But what it's stemming from is the expectation that you can party all night, wake up and go kick ass on the field tomorrow. And if you can't do that? Then you're not fit enough to play.*

There is a difference between off-season and on-season. During the off-season we were leading the parties. During the season, we only drank one night a week after games, but we were leading the charge and making up for the week that we weren't drinking—in one night.

Of course, substance use is a problem larger than any sport. Overall, significant blocs of men and women surveyed in the general full-time college population reported binge drinking (26.8 percent of men and 29.3 percent of women in 2022, respectively), as well as the use of cocaine (1.3 percent and 0.5 percent), marijuana (21 percent and 20 percent) and other illicit drugs (4.1 percent and 2.2 percent). America and lacrosse *both* have a problem. But with the 2023 NCAA Substance Abuse Survey again revealing that the percentage of college lacrosse players using and abusing remains strikingly higher than that of the general population, it seems clear that the sport's culture can act like an accelerant.

No one can say exactly when illegal narcotics joined alcohol as a recreational substance of choice for athletes, but it no doubt tracked the seep of drug use into the general population in the 1960s. Tierney saw plenty of it as a player at Cortland State in the early 1970s. Before the 1986 overdose death of Maryland basketball player Len Bias highlighted the dangers of cocaine, Holman witnessed its marriage with booze. "It just bred on each other," he said. "The hard-charging, cocaine-induced '80s of lacrosse? That was everywhere. So, yeah, it's a black mark—and it is true, 100 percent."

Yet, despite decades of polling data and anecdotal evidence, there has been little serious study devoted to the reason for lacrosse's outsized incidence of substance use. Self-reported surveys lack scientific rigor—and can encompass everything from one-time experimentation to full addiction. But the repeated results, every four or five years, increase their credibility. "It certainly is concerning," said Dr. Margot Putukian, chair of US Lacrosse's Sports, Science and Safety Committee from 2009 to 2019.

Some blame the longtime lack of a uniform drug-testing policy for "non-revenue" sports like lacrosse. Certain schools can't—or won't—afford the cost of a rigorous, department-wide testing regime, and rely on the NCAA's once- or twice-a-year random testing program, which is applied after a 24-hour notice. Before moving to Princeton in 2004, Putukian ran Penn State's drug-testing program: all sports three times a year, and football players weekly. Princeton officials asked about replicating it. But the president of the Ivy League told her there was no real appetite. To this day, neither the Ivy League nor its individual schools, which include lacrosse powers Cornell, Brown and Yale, have their own layer of drug testing.

Tierney coached at Princeton from 1988 to 2009, then Denver until his retirement in 2023. He preferred Denver's policy: players were tested monthly, without warning. It defused peer pressure; players could blame testing for their refusal to ingest, and not lose social cachet.

Still, neither the method nor degree of deterrence answers the question: *Why lacrosse players?* Some posit that the game's rough-and-tumble attracts risk-taking personalities. Others wonder if it's because they have little to lose. Unlike their counterparts in football, basketball, hockey or baseball, no lacrosse player jeopardizes a multimillion-dollar professional contract by using. American college lacrosse remains the game's peak; pro lacrosse has traditionally averaged a five-figure income, at best. "There's no incentive," Offit said. "A college basketball player? They're not going out because they need to get drafted. The NFL? If they're not working out 24/7, they're getting run over by Alabama, and they're not going to make it at the next level. Lacrosse? The next level is sitting at a desk and making money, generally speaking."

Eventually, all discussions on the subject turn to parents. Like the general population of high schoolers, lacrosse players grow up in a feedback loop of societal norms and media-fueled clichés about college life, compounded by generations of lacrosse mores reinforced, for years before graduation, at countless games and club events and showcases. The high school lacrosse universe is nearly as alcohol soaked, notably among its adults. One of the game's traditions is the postgame "tailgating": families and friends gather under a tent or in a nearby parking lot, players and coaches show up after showering. Food is consumed, alcohol flows.

"I think, historically, that the norm was created," said Virginia head coach Lars Tiffany. "So for those young players whose parents played and [who] have grown up with going with their parents to lacrosse games and in the parking lots and going to club lacrosse games, it's *When's the beer party?* A good friend of mine, fellow captain at Brown, had his epiphany when his 11- or 12-year-old daughter after a lacrosse game said, 'So, now we go to the beer party.'"

There, behind the parked cars or in families' leafy backyards, is where lacrosse's substance abuse habit formed and got reinforced year after year. "It's cultural. We've bred it," said Brian Holman, who, during his five-year stint at Utah, banned alcohol for both players and parents at all lacrosse functions. "Why do we have team tailgates after every event in lacrosse? No other sport does this. Why do we have to? And you go there, the parents are drinking. Half of them are shitfaced by the time we get there. That's not good."

ON PAPER, FEW SPORTS looked healthier than lacrosse as the aughts came to a close. The Duke rape debacle, paradoxically, seemed only to boost the game's popularity: From 2006 to 2011, the NCAA's Division I-men's championship weekend drew its biggest crowds, including the all-time mark of 52,004—for a semifinal lineup in Baltimore that included Duke—in 2007. Sales of lacrosse gear were growing faster than those of any other sport. Participation at the youth and high school level had tripled since 1999. Recognition of lacrosse by US high school associations had risen 70 percent: there were now more high school lacrosse teams than ice hockey teams.

Amid all the upbeat data, a troubling trend surfaced. In January 2009, Hobart midfielder Warren Kimber IV, 20, died after overdosing on alcohol and the painkiller oxycodone at a lacrosse party. Seven months later, former St. Mary's High and Towson University midfielder Drew Pfarr, 27, killed himself while undergoing treatment for substance abuse. In February 2010, former University of Massachusetts attackman Kevin Glenz, whose seven-year addiction began in college with OxyContin, died of a heroin overdose at 27.

Combined with the findings in NCAA drug and alcohol surveys, the drumbeat of deaths indicated that lacrosse's substance-use problem had edged into alarming territory. In one regard, the sport was only tracking a national trend: From 2005 to 2015, the percentage of overdose deaths from heroin in the US tripled. But instead of presenting lacrosse—in the time-honored image of athletics as a "clean" pastime—as an alternative to drug use, the news about lacrosse culture seemed anything but. "Should we view these as random, unrelated tragedies or the aching confirmation of an emergency too critical to ignore?" wrote longtime Bates lacrosse coach Peter Lasagna in *Inside Lacrosse*. "Do people with influence care enough to tackle this immense, complex, dark side of the heritage of our game?"

Lacrosse's excessive drinking, meanwhile, never stopped. A prime spot was in Charlottesville, at the University of Virginia. On top of the usual fraternity excesses, UVa's boozing reputation had been reinforced for a century by "secret" undergraduate drinking societies like Eli Banana and T.I.L.K.A., whose membership often overlapped with the men's lacrosse roster, and traditions like the "fourth-year fifth," wherein seniors guzzle a fifth of liquor—nearly 20 shots—to celebrate their last home football game. From 1990 to 1998 alone, 18 UVa students died of alcohol-related deaths. As a "public Ivy," one of the few schools that could match Princeton, Cornell and "hidden Ivy" Hopkins in prestige and resources, "Mr. Jefferson's University" was a magnet for great players; Tierney says that no program landed more talent from the early 1970s to 2010. Yet the Cavaliers won just three national titles in that span, and got tagged as underachievers. Rivals retailed the easy conclusion: Too often, the sleeping giant was sleeping one off. At UVa, the party seemed more important than the winning.

This was odd, considering that its head coach had been voicing concern about alcohol abuse in lacrosse for more than two decades. After his hiring in 1993, Dom Starsia preached constantly about the dangers. "I always thought alcohol was an issue here," he said in 1999, after issuing a dictum limiting the team's drinking to one night a week. His top worries were never recruiting or playing Maryland. They were the keg-party fight, the stomach pump in an emergency room, the dorm room torn apart in a drunken fury.

"It's what I lived with all the time: the fear," Starsia said. "It dominated my life. What I first and foremost *don't* miss about coaching college lacrosse is those phone calls that we used to get for kids being in, getting in, a jam."

Often, Starsia felt as if he was the only one who cared. Early one season, before his first NCAA championship in 1999, a Virginia player was arrested for drunk driving. Starsia kicked him off the team. Halfway through the season, after his team asked to have the player reinstated, Starsia did so only on the condition that he not consume alcohol. The player agreed. Three weeks later, his father approached Starsia. "Dom," said the dad. "Can you please let the kid drink? So he and I can share, postgame?"

Starsia refused, but the question was revealing. Though he was tough on police matters like a DUI, word had it that Starsia wielded a looser hand when it came to "lesser" incidents like underage drinking or public urination. He was known as the ultimate player's coach, a caring uncle type who imparted valuable life lessons. "Dom does things differently," said Steele Stanwick, an all-time UVa great and team captain in 2011. "He kind of trusts kids to do the right thing and trusts the players to kind of govern themselves, in a lot of ways." And as long as Starsia won—UVa made the Final Four 13 times under him, and he left in 2016 with the most career victories, 375, of any Division I coach—that approach was considered an asset.

Starting in the late 1990s at UVa, Starsia's coaching prime coincided with the ever-widening expansion of sports as the preeminent entity on many Division I campuses, powered by television rights fees and sharp annual spikes—in a time of otherwise low inflation—in the cost of a college education. Top football and basketball programs, whose success fueled admission applications and alumni donations, became known as a university's "front porch"—for good and ill. Titles for non-revenue sports like lacrosse or soccer added to the overall luster, but their main job was to avoid embarrassment. Bad news—like the Duke rape scandal—had outsized power to destroy a university's image.

Still, UVa lacrosse players graduated. Starsia's gut philosophy held sway. Starting in 1999, he empowered his teams to establish the details of each season's alcohol policy—essentially, when it was okay for them to drink—reasoning that they'd more likely follow rules they set and policed. The majority went on to be productive citizens; a minority fell short; a few failed spectacularly. But, Starsia said, not once in his 24 years on campus did any administrator—including longtime athletic director Craig Littlepage—complain to him that the program was out of control, or call for a crackdown on its culture.

The first opportunity presented itself in late 2008, after Will Barrow committed suicide. But Barrow was no longer a Virginia lacrosse player then, and those closest to Barrow, in their endless pain, have never felt cause to blame the sport, the school or the coach for what happened.

"I have a lot of respect for the leadership at UVA, and for me it all starts with Coach Starsia: he's a terrific guy," George Barrow said. "It's a championship program, that's it: winners. What happened to William, what happened with George Huguely—and there were several other instances—that's at every program. Those were isolated situations, tied to personal responsibility."

THE LAST MORNING of Yeardley Love's life—May 2, 2010—was a day to remember. It was designed as such. For lacrosse at the University of

Virginia, "Senior Sunday" always serves as the season's coda, the sweet and low-key finale of a weekend dedicated to the program's departing "fourth-years." But this one thrummed with a rare sense of satisfaction: The day before, 13 senior men had been honored before their last regular season game at Klockner Stadium, then crushed Robert Morris University to finish 14–1 and seal the nation's No. 1 ranking. The NCAA tournament, perhaps a national championship, loomed. Drinks flowed afterward, Saturday night–style.

Senior Sunday's pace was different. The graduates rode 30 miles outside Charlottesville, to Wintergreen Resort, for the traditional round of father-son golf. Come brunch time, the remaining underclassmen from the men's and women's teams—their striking cross-pollination powered by community, athletic and sometimes intimate bonds reaching back to high school—meandered into Boylan Heights, an upscale burger bar in a downtown area known as the Corner. Around noon, Love and a roommate, fellow UVa women's lacrosse player Caity Whiteley, arrived from their apartment just down the street.

"We were drinking pitchers of beer at this bar on Sunday, all day, hanging out, waiting for the seniors to come back from the golf thing," Shamel Bratton said. "Then we'd all get together with them, kind of like the last hurrah. Not necessarily a hurrah, but another one of these Sundays that remind you that they're leaving."

In the two years since receiving George Huguely's phone call about the death of Will Bratton, Shamel hadn't grown any closer to him. His relationship with Yeardley Love was similar: friendly but not deep. But all the men's and women's players knew, in varying degrees, that Love and Huguely—both 22—had a tempestuous relationship. They also knew that Huguely was a bad drunk, even by UVa standards. Seven other Cavalier players on the 2010 roster had been charged during their careers with alcohol-related infractions, but Huguely's glaring decline on the field (he played minimally in his final game against Robert Morris, and turned the ball over twice), and four-times-a-week benders were impossible to ignore. As that season progressed, friends discussed something virtually unheard of in lacrosse: holding an intervention. It never happened.

In truth, George Huguely V had been a problem for a while—for family, friends, the sport's image. His full embrace of the "laxbro" persona provided a one-man rebuttal to anyone insisting lacrosse wasn't overpopulated with rich, boozed-up rockheads. Indeed, hoping to undermine the idea of his client as calculating murderer, defense attorney Francis Lawrence would later gloss over Huguely's intelligence—he was, after all, on track to graduate from one of America's top universities with a degree in anthropology—and paint him as the cliché's embodiment. "He's not complicated," Lawrence said. "He's not complex. He's a lacrosse player."

Early on, anyway, Huguely's flaws seemed more a result of nurture than nature. He grew up rich and spoiled. "George Huguely had no constraints," said Josh Offit, who, in 2006, played on the same midfield line with Huguely at the exclusive Landon School in Bethesda, Maryland. "He came from a background where he never heard 'No.'"

One of Huguely's great-great-grandfathers co-founded a Washington, DC, lumberyard and building supply firm—Galliher & Huguely—that, over the next century, provided ensuing generations fine homes in Montgomery County, Maryland, memberships in exclusive country clubs, the leisure time to pursue yachting and golf. His father, George Huguely IV, reportedly had little in the way of ambition or restraint. *Washingtonian* magazine described him as a "party boy" who sustained a posh lifestyle with million-dollar loans from his dad and a liquidated trust fund. He and George V's mother, Marta, divorced when their son was in elementary school.

By sophomore year at Landon, Huguely had honed a rakish, attention-seeking persona. During a football game he vowed to make a big play—in exchange for a kiss from an assistant coach's fiancée—then, after quickly intercepting a pass, walked off the field and demanded her phone number. As a senior, Huguely was Landon's best lacrosse player, a high school All-American renowned for envelope-pushing pranks. Landon's longtime head coach, Rob Bordley, described him as "upbeat."

That didn't last. At UVa, Huguely never emerged from a secondary role on the lacrosse roster, allowed his six-foot-two, 209-pound body to go slack. He hosted teammates at the family beach house in North Carolina or on his father's 40-foot yacht, the *Reel Deal*. Sometimes his father came along; players knew George IV as a regular at tailgates and team parties in Charlottesville. But by Huguely's junior year, things began to sour. In November 2008, a policewoman in Lexington, Virginia, named Rebecca Moss, found him stumbling into oncoming traffic and advised him to get a ride or face arrest. Huguely unleashed a spew of racial and sexual epithets at Moss and another female officer, screaming, "I'll kill all you bitches." After tussling for a few minutes and ending up on the ground, Moss resorted to subduing him with a taser. Huguely was so intoxicated that he remembered neither the incident nor, more remarkably, the 50,000 volts coursing through his body.

Six weeks later during winter break, Huguely argued with his father and a cousin on the *Reel Deal* a quarter mile off the coast of Palm Beach, Florida, then jumped into the ocean and refused to return. Another boat brought him to shore. George IV filed a domestic abuse complaint. UVa officials said they didn't know of either incident; university policy required Huguely to self-report them to Starsia. He did not. Nevertheless, his reputation was dimming; rather than keep repeating "Fuckin' Huguely" in disgust or dismay, teammates took to calling him "Fuguely."

While Huguely's volatility didn't intrude on the lacrosse field, by the spring of 2009 his increasingly combative relationship with Love had become a fact within the UVa lacrosse social whirl. That February, a teammate named Gavin Gill walked Love home after a victory party downtown. Huguely later barged into Gill's room while he slept, said, "Sweet dreams, punk," and sucker-punched him in the face. Both met with Coach Starsia, downplayed it as a minor scuffle and apologized. No discipline was levied.

On February 27, 2010, University of North Carolina midfielder Michael Burns and a teammate were at a party at Huguely's apartment when they heard a woman's voice screaming, "Help me!" from Huguely's bedroom. Burns was chatting with some Virginia lacrosse players; he looked at them for a cue of how to react. The UVa players shrugged it off. Burns bolted to the bedroom, opened the door. Huguely was laying on his bed, on his back. Love was on top of him. Huguely's arm was around her neck, choking her. "I can honestly say his hand was on her neck," Burns would later testify.

At the sight of Burns, Huguely released Love and rolled over to face the wall. She rushed out of the room crying, told Burns she was scared that she couldn't breathe. Nobody reported the matter to police or UVa officials. Huguely sent Love a letter of apology. "Alcohol is ruining my life," he wrote. "I'm scared to know that I can get drunk to the point where I cannot control how I act."

Burns's presence in Huguely's room—as well as on the witness stand during trial—opened a window on college "hookup" culture, with its slack interpretations of dating and romance and near-impenetrable rules on commitment. Huguely, it turns out, was also in an "on and off again" relationship with one of Love's sorority sisters. Love became suspicious. On April 27, Love, who had been drinking, angrily confronted Huguely when she found him and teammate Tim Fuchs with two female lacrosse recruits in Huguely's apartment. Love hit Huguely on the face and body with her hands and purse, scattering its contents, losing a camera and cellphone in the flurry.

Burns, who met Love in 2009, had hooked up with Love the night of the choking, and they resparked a sporadic sexual relationship over the spring of 2010. A few days after the purse incident, she texted Huguely about it. On April 30, he sent an email back:

"A week ago u said u would get back together with me if I stopped getting so drunk then u go fuck burns attack me and in the midst of the attack say burns is fucked me better than you. That is so so fucked up on so many levels. I should have killed you."

"you should have killed me?" Love replied. "youre so fucked up."

She showed the email exchange to her roommates, and talked about it with friends. Nobody reported the matter to police or UVa officials.

ON THE MORNING of May 2, 2010, George Huguely was drinking by 9 a.m.—tee time for the daylong father-son golf gathering for lacrosse seniors at Wintergreen Resort. It was a quasi-official event for the men's program. Alcohol was certainly not forbidden: They were all adults, and Huguely was of legal age and playing with his dad. Young George became so drunk that he was unable to play the final holes. A restaurant dinner with his father and two teammates was cut short because the others were embarrassed to be seen with him. Combined with his imbibement the night before, after UVa's season-ending win, later courtroom testimony estimated that Huguely consumed 44.5 drinks over a 30-hour period.

Looking back a decade later, Starsia still couldn't see how he could've controlled that dynamic. "Huguely was with his dad the whole freaking day. He just drank all day: That's an issue," he said. "I implore the parents to help out here. If your father said to you, 'Hey, stop drinking,' it might have an effect.'"

Love, a senior midfielder from Cockeysville, Maryland, was not a star for the UVa women. Standing five foot six and weighing 115 pounds, she was a bit small for Division I lacrosse, though terrier tough, and her warm, generous nature made her near-universally beloved. While Huguely was out golfing and drinking, Love was drinking, too. She and roommate Caity Whiteley remained at Boylan Heights for three hours until about 3 p.m., went home to their 14th Street apartment to study until 6 p.m., then returned to the burger bar for a birthday party that lasted until 10 p.m. Whiteley later described Love that night as "kind of drunk, but not so out of control drunk." Her blood alcohol level was around .14, nearly twice the legal driving limit in the state of Virginia. They returned to the apartment. Whiteley went out again. Love went to bed.

That was about 10:50 p.m. Huguely had sent Love a flurry of unanswered messages from his apartment building next door. At about 11:45 he walked the 70-plus steps it took to get to Love's apartment and entered. Love's bedroom door was locked. Huguely kicked it open. She was in her bed, set against a wall, wearing underwear and, according to Huguely, a T-shirt. Love shrank from him, pressing herself against the wall. Huguely tried talking, then grabbed Love by the shoulders and shook her repeatedly. Her head hit the wall again and again; her nose began to bleed; soon they were struggling on the floor. At 11:50 p.m., a downstairs neighbor heard a "very, very loud" slamming sound from Love's room. Huguely stood, threw Love's body on the bed, grabbed her laptop and walked out.

Whiteley and a UVa tennis player, Phillippe Oudshoorn, entered the room at about 2:15 a.m., Monday, May 3, and found Love's body face down and blood on her pillowcase and sheets. Her right eye was blackened and swollen shut; her face was mottled with blood. She had bruising on her cheek, cuts on her lips and inner cheek from her own teeth. Bruises the shape of fingerprints were found on her hands, buttocks, forearms and thighs. She wasn't wearing the T-shirt. After dissecting her brain and finding multiple contusions, the local medical examiner determined cause of death as blunt force trauma to the head.

At 7 a.m., Huguely was picked up by police. He did not know that Love was dead. Uncharged, believing that he was speaking only about a possible assault on Love, he agreed to waive his Miranda rights. At 7:52 a.m., in a narrow, white-walled interrogation room at the Charlottesville police station, detective Lisa Reeves and a colleague began questioning Huguely. Reeves's demeanor was patient, understanding, as if she just needed Huguely to explain a few things about their tumultuous history, his drinking and state of mind the previous night.

And Huguely obliged, for the first 46 minutes, eagerly relating how he shook Love, and about her head hitting the wall, and her nosebleed and their wrestling. In minutes he would be cuffed and charged with Love's death; in August 2012 he would be found guilty of second-degree murder and sentenced to 23 years in prison. But it was there in that little room, nine hours after his last binge, that life as Huguely once knew it came to an end.

At 8:38 a.m. Reeves glanced at her colleague, turned to Huguely and abruptly said, "She's dead. You killed her, George. You killed her."

For a moment, Huguely didn't speak. He showed no sign of being drunk still.

"She's . . . dead?" he said.

"I think you knew that already," Reeves said.

"No, I did not," Huguely said. He put his head down, placed his hands on his face. "She's dead? How the fuck is she dead?"

Reeves answered instantly—all warmth and patience gone, steely and sharp as a razor.

"Because you killed her, George," she said.

THE DEATH OF YEARDLEY Love shattered the spring of 2010 for UVa's men and women lacrosse players. It also ravaged the university's image and raised a familiar set of questions. Huguely's privileged background, the sport's link to alcohol and entitlement, again came under fire from the nation's commentariat. Yet, compared to—and perhaps because of—the overreaction of the Duke administration four years earlier, the official response in Charlottesville was pointedly measured. The faculty did not, en masse, indict the school's lacrosse culture. Neither team's season was canceled. The head coach was not forced to resign.

Part of this, certainly, was due to Dom Starsia's three NCAA titles, as well as his palpable humanity. Starsia and his wife, Krissy, arrived in Charlottesville in 1993 with twins, Maggie and Emma, who had been born with a "developmental delay" that, as he described it, rendered them forever "like seven-year-olds." Yet he and Krissy were early adopters of the need to normalize life with special-needs children; Starsia always called his daughters a "blessing," and the two were constants at practice and UVa basketball games. Meanwhile, in the weeks before Huguely's crime, everyone around the program knew that Starsia was facing a looming loss. His father was dying.

Dominic Starsia, 86, had been living in a spare bedroom at the Starsia home since February, after the cancer metastasized. He rallied some in the spring. After that final regular-season win over Robert Morris on a gorgeous Saturday sealed UVa's No. 1 ranking, Starsia went home in the early evening and stepped into the spare bedroom. "Way to go, Dom," his dad said.

"The last words he spoke," Starsia said.

The next week was a blur: Huguely jailed and media swarming and all the players broken and shocked and crying. Sometime overnight Thursday, May 6, to Friday, May 7, Starsia heard his father stir and went in to sleep next to him. Later that morning, when Dom was in his lacrosse office, Dominic died. Nonetheless, in processing the murder, the afterburn and bewilderment and mourning, the fact that one of their own was responsible, the hunkered-down men's team expected the 58-year-old Starsia to set the tone.

"Humility and gratefulness, respect for everyone around you: we went through these life-altering experiences that no one could ever fathom, from Will Barrow to Yeardley, and that was the example he showed us," said Adam Ghitelman, a junior goalie at UVa in 2010. "That was the example: staying in the moment, and understanding that lacrosse is the Medicine Game. And it was for us. Practice was, at times, the only solace we had—and Dom was there leading us. Who knows what he was going through, off the field in his office, with the administration, the media? And he's stepping on the field and still . . . You want to teach kids about toughness? About strength? Well said is great. But well done is better. That was Dom for us."

Surrounded by inquiring students and parents, enmeshed in a horrific narrative dissected nationwide on message boards, television and news sites, the men's and women's lacrosse programs became even more insular. No one knew Yeardley or George better; no one but them could know their shock and grief. It was like Will Barrow's suicide, only worse: Two lives destroyed this time. And each new revelation reinforced the fact that, unlike Barrow, the warning lights on George Huguely had been flashing long and bright yet nobody had been perceptive or brave enough to put up a hand.

On May 15, after attending his father's funeral in New York, Starsia returned to Charlottesville for the men's first game back after Love's death, a matchup with Mount St. Mary's in the first round of the 2010 NCAA tournament. There was a moment of silence. Players wore warmup T-shirts with ONE LOVE printed on the back, then jerseys with a black-and-white patch featuring Love's initials. No. 1 Virginia won, 18–4. Players spoke of the contest as solace, a way to forget. The Associated Press described their dominant play as "business as usual."

The next day, 13 days after Love's death, the women's team played its first NCAA tournament game against Towson University. They wore warmup T-shirts emblazoned with ONE SQUAD. ONE HEART. ONE LOVE," and black patches on their jerseys reading, LOVE. Brittany Kalkstein and Caity Whiteley had known Love since they were six-year-olds in suburban Maryland. Kalkstein scored the winning goal to break an 11–11 tie and Whiteley—who discovered her roommate's body—scored an insurance goal to help seal the 14–12 win. After, the women held up placards with Love's number 1 on it. The sound system played Cher's "Believe," with its ever-repeating line *Do you believe in life after love?*

Drained and dispirited, the UVa women ended their tournament run the next week in Chapel Hill, losing to North Carolina, 17–7. The next day, the UVa men beat Stony Brook by a goal to move on to the 2010 Final Four and a semifinal meeting with Duke. That was the week Krissy Starsia also complained of chest pains and Dom rushed her to a Charlottesville hospital; the diagnosis was intense anxiety. Everyone's nerves were shot.

Before, during and after Duke's thrilling 14–13 win in Baltimore, there was no avoiding the obvious: Bound by catastrophe, the two elite programs also stood as avatars of the sport's most notorious traits. Duke's march that year to the national championship was framed as the final closure on the discredited rape scandal, but also reconjured the 2006 program's undisputed excesses. And the relentless reporting on UVa culture and Huguely's descent made it easy to think that, in the years since, lacrosse had learned nothing.

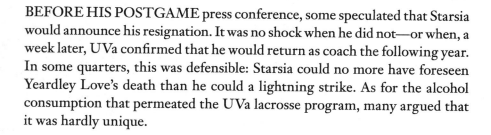

BEFORE HIS POSTGAME press conference, some speculated that Starsia would announce his resignation. It was no shock when he did not—or when, a week later, UVa confirmed that he would return as coach the following year. In some quarters, this was defensible: Starsia could no more have foreseen Yeardley Love's death than he could a lightning strike. As for the alcohol consumption that permeated the UVa lacrosse program, many argued that it was hardly unique.

"Just firing me," Starsia later acknowledged, "was not going to solve the problem."

Others argued, quietly, that it would be a good start. The head coach sets a college program's tone, is paid well and receives disproportional credit whenever his players achieve, score, graduate and win. With that comes a commensurate responsibility for their failures, losses and crimes, not to mention the matter of optics. Firing a head coach is the surest way to "send a message"—especially to rich alumni and the media—that the university understands that "enough is enough." That was the knee-jerk Duke response in 2006 with head coach Mike Pressler—an overreaction that, while panicky and precipitous, unquestionably improved the program's reputation.

For those concerned about the sport's image, a hard-line stance in Charlottesville seemed the only response. Starsia now had two blights on his record, lightning strikes that nonetheless seemed to indicate something wrong with UVa lacrosse culture. Certainly Sharon Love, Yeardley's mother, thought so in May 2012, when she filed a $29.45 million civil lawsuit against Starsia, assistant coach Marc Van Arsdale, athletic director Craig Littlepage and the Commonwealth of Virginia, alleging gross negligence. A year later, the suit was quietly withdrawn. But for some in the game, the sentiment lingered: *Shouldn't someone pay a price? Doesn't Starsia have to go?*

The dean of US coaches, Bill Tierney, declined to address Starsia's case, except to say, "No one could ever blame a coach for a kid killing a young woman. That was so far away from Dom and what Dom is all about."

But in general, Tierney believed, a head coach should be held responsible for his team's culture. "I've had a weird experience," he said in 2018, while coaching at Denver. "I've been coaching 44 years, 37 in college, and for the first time this year I had to demand that a family put their son into rehab. Who am I? I had no right to do that. But I know that if a path is bad, and that kid gets killed or kills—and I knew he had a drinking problem? Sorry: You're gone. And maybe culpable. It's a scary profession in that way."

DOM STARSIA WAS A superb coach. After winning two Ivy League titles and two Division I Coach of the Year awards at Brown, he moved to Charlottesville in 1993 and proved the right man at the right program at the right time. Virginia hadn't won a national title since 1972 or even reached the NCAA tournament quarterfinals since 1988, yet bulled its way to the quarterfinals in Starsia's first season. The next year, they fell just short of a national championship, losing in the NCAA final in overtime by one goal. In an era dominated by Hall of Fame coaches like Syracuse's Roy Simmons Jr. and Tierney, Starsia built UVa into the sport's new power. The Cavaliers soon dominated the Atlantic Coast Conference, won NCAA titles in 1999 and 2003—and then got even better. In 2006, UVa crushed opponents by an average of eight goals, became the first Division I men's team to go 17–0, and Starsia won his third national championship.

Yet, in 2011, he exceeded all of that. Leading a program shadowed by death, riven by controversy and enduring withering scrutiny, Starsia pulled off the greatest coaching job of his career. By all rights, that UVa men's season should have hurtled off the track any number of times. Instead, the Cavaliers careened to the most remarkable athletic triumph in school history.

On paper, the Cavaliers headed into the spring of 2011 loaded with All-American talent—led by first-team midfielder Shamel Bratton, brother Rhamel, Steele Stanwick and goalie Adam Ghitelman—and ranked second in most preseason polls. Any concern about the team's psyche in the wake of Love's murder seemed to have been answered by its subsequent run in 2010 to the NCAA semifinals, and 11 of that squad's top 12 scorers were back. Meanwhile, the intensified scrutiny demanded that the program be on its best behavior, a ratcheting back on the ethos that had encouraged—if not spawned—George Huguely.

"If we didn't change the way we conduct ourselves on and off field, it would have been blatantly disrespectful to the Love family," senior defense-man Bray Malphrus said that May. "It would have been pretty much spitting on her grave if we didn't take a sober look at the program."

Though Starsia stuck by his long-held stance that players must set the team's alcohol policy, everyone knew that the slightest offense would be magnified. Before the season, the team met and agreed to what Malphrus called "the strictest, most stringent rule since I've been here." According to Shamel Bratton, UVa lacrosse players usually embargoed drinking 24 or 48 hours before a game. But for 2011 the team restricted itself to just one night of alcohol consumption: Saturday night. If a player broke the rule, he would be suspended for the next game.

As the team's most decorated player, its biggest star, a senior, Shamel seemingly put his full weight behind the new policy when he announced it to the rest of the team. Months later, after a confounded Starsia reminded him of that fact, Shamel replied, "I never intended that for me."

So cavalier a response explains, perhaps, why Starsia conspicuously didn't select Shamel as one of that season's co-captains. Bratton says he understood that a hard-line rule was inevitable: Love's murder had reset the state of play. Yet when Starsia began insinuating that even one sanctioned night was too much, that "we'd rather you not be out," to Shamel and Rhamel it smacked of posturing.

That the Bratton twins willfully refused to see the need for a lower profile, especially from star players, speaks to their immaturity and failure as leaders. But the pressure rankled: As the program's most prominent Black faces, Shamel said, they were being asked to bear a disproportionately large burden. And though the program had been through a tragic, gut-wrenching event, as products of lower-class Brooklyn, the twins still knew family and friends on the streets. Sirens and sudden death weren't, for them, all that rare.

"Good or bad or indifferent, you kind of got to live through it," Shamel said. "You kind of hurt through it. We probably should be talking to a professional about it—rather than going through another extreme."

So it was that the Bratton twins—face of the 2011 UVa program, symbols of Black progress, lacrosse's best hope yet to break loose of its too-rich/too-suburban/too-white image—decided to ignore the team's self-imposed alcohol policy. They weren't alone in breaking team rules that year: Adam Ghitelman was suspended for the season opener against Drexel, and attackman Nick O'Reilly joined the Brattons in at least one transgression. But the twins were the policy's most vocal critics, and pushed to soften it with a revote. In February, the weekend before the Cavaliers' second game against Mount St. Mary's, Shamel and Rhamel drove to North Carolina's Outer Banks with a few teammates and consumed alcohol. Questioned the following Monday, Shamel and Rhamel refused to give up their teammates' identities. Under the rule, both expected to be suspended for the Mount St. Mary's game; they had, in fact, timed their escapade so that, if caught, they wouldn't miss a pivotal matchup at Stony Brook.

Starsia, instead, suspended the twins for Stony Brook. That exacted maximum pain: The Stony Brook game was the Brattons' last scheduled college appearance on Long Island, a final homecoming anticipated for months by family and friends. The punishment felt arbitrary, personal. But, according to Shamel, far worse was the fact that, when explaining his reasoning, Starsia didn't say that he had to take a tough stand, that Love's death demanded it. Instead, Starsia only said that he didn't want their suspensions to be "a distraction" for Mount St. Mary's. The twins traveled to Stony Brook anyway, hoping for a last-minute reprieve. When their family learned they wouldn't play, they were outraged.

UVa still broke out to a 7–1 start, losing only on the road to Syracuse, and seemed to be holding together. Then, on March 26, after losing by a goal at Johns Hopkins, the team boarded the bus for the trip back to Charlottesville. One of the Brattons' brothers brought them beer to take along—it was a Saturday, after all—and a handful of players joined in drinking in the back of the bus. After the team unloaded, Starsia confronted the Brattons.

Shamel and the others were technically in the right; under the alcohol rule the twins couldn't be punished. But Shamel also knew he was pushing his head coach, hard, in front of the team: Their power struggle was now out in the open. And soon after, word reached Starsia that Shamel had admitted to previously breaking the rule by drinking at a fraternity party a few weeks earlier. Thus, Starsia suspended him a second time, for the April 2 ACC opener against Maryland.

UVa lost to the Terrapins, 12–7, badly and at home. The team was spiraling downward. Three weeks later, after the Cavs lost their fourth game in five at Duke, Shamel, Rhamel, Ghitelman and his brother Jacob were excused from Monday's practice to attend a funeral on Long Island for the mother of Maryland player Ryan Young. The Ghitelmans made it back to campus on time. The Brattons did not, and then missed Tuesday's practice as well. The next day, Shamel was kicked off the team and Rhamel was suspended indefinitely.

Press reports had the UVa players voting the twins out. But Shamel said he never heard that, and Steele Stanwick—a co-captain and the 2011 Tewaaraton award winner—said the endgame was more complicated. The four UVa co-captains had met and decided that Shamel had to go, but before they could meet with Starsia, Stanwick said, a coach informed them that the decision on both brothers had been made. "It ultimately came from the coaches," he said.

The timing seemed catastrophic. UVa's offense now had a massive hole: In the first 13 games Shamel, the all-time points leader for a UVa midfielder, had racked up 20 goals and 8 assists; Rhamel tallied 17 goals and 5 assists. The team's best defender, Matt Lovejoy, was injured and out for the season. Stanwick was ailing from a sore calf muscle and a sprained foot ligament. And a weekend showdown with powerful Penn, in the regular-season finale, loomed.

But the next day, Malphrus—co-captain, future Army Ranger, hyper-intense—went to Starsia. "We're with you," he said. "We're ready to go."

Starsia had no idea how that would translate to the field. Desperate, he doubled down on the zone defense he'd been tinkering with—for the first time in his career—and he and assistant Craig Van Arsdale scrapped the team's run-and-gun offense, handed Stanwick the ball and had him run the attack from behind the goal. Experts predicted disaster. Stunningly, the Cavaliers played their most complete game of the season to crush Penn, 11–2. Then, seeded seventh in the NCAA tournament, the Cavaliers came from behind to squeeze a first-round win over Bucknell in overtime, and beat Cornell by two to reach the Final Four in Baltimore.

"Just trying to get from game to game at that point, kind of limping in," Stanwick said of the run. "The coaches were scrambling, trying to get from day to day, but some of the young guys were so young and new, almost too dumb to realize the magnitude of the situation. We just had great leadership and, so, quiet confidence . . . It was unprecedented, in a lot of ways, for us to win that thing."

And for the first time, the conversation around UVa—the ultimate blue blood, a "public Ivy" with every advantage—shifted. Now, though still stocked with blue-chip players, the Cavaliers had become the ultimate sports cliché. They had "responded to adversity." They showed "heart." It took a murder, dissension, the expulsion of two stars, but they were now—of all things—underdogs. The switch to zone defense, meanwhile, exploited some of the era's most unappealing on-field qualities. It was the lacrosse version of winning ugly. With no shot clock and stalls rarely called, then, a disciplined team could slow and snarl up a high-octane attack like Denver's. "The zone," Ghitelman said, "was their kryptonite."

By the time UVa beat Tierney's Denver Pioneers in the semifinals, 14–8, people began using the phrase "addition by subtraction" whenever the Bratton name came up. But the team's misbehaviors hardly ended with the twins' departure. Cavalier attackman Colin Briggs, who scored five goals in the 9–7 win over Maryland in the NCAA final, was suspended from the semifinals for breaking a team rule. Nick O'Reilly, who chipped in a goal and four assists, was suspended the next year for the entire season.

Shamel and Rhamel traveled to Baltimore that weekend to support their friends and teammates. They sat in the stands and cheered for the co-captains who had lobbied for their expulsion, cheered the coach and fans who had moved on without them. Rhamel has since expressed regret for some of his actions during the 2011 season; Shamel remains more blasé. He knew he was going to be drafted early in that year's Major League Lacrosse draft, would have a chance to play that summer in Kyle Harrison's barnstorming LXM Pro Tour. He had already moved on. "It's almost better," he said in 2019, "that I wasn't a part of it."

Everyone's takeaway was different. Some teammates appreciated that the Bratton twins showed up and gave their support. And while Starsia never saw Shamel after the championship, his wife never forgot bumping into him later that day. Their eyes met and Shamel burst into tears and pulled Krissy Starsia into a full and deep hug. "I'm so sorry," he said.

It took months—years, really—for the larger implications to reveal themselves. Once bristling with hype and possibility, Shamel and Rhamel Bratton disappeared into the pro game and had little impact. College is lacrosse's prestige platform, and their time ended not with a glorious bang, but in ignominy. The Bratton twins never won an NCAA title. They helped lead UVa to three Final Fours, but will be remembered most for the one they missed.

"It's heartbreaking," Stanwick said. "I'm not close with them now, but I was friends with them, and to watch that unfold is, in a way, tragic. I wanted more for them. Big picture, they could have been great role models and great examples for African Americans looking to get into the sport. You know what I mean? We need more diversity."

II

ONE EVERY YEAR

O N NOVEMBER 1, 2011, the Center for Disease Control and Prevention officially declared death by overdose of prescription painkillers—opioids—an "epidemic" in the US. The accompanying report cited more than 40 deaths daily from the use of drugs like Vicodin, OxyContin and methadone. No strata of the population were immune (though Native Americans were nearly 50 percent more likely to suffer fatalities); one in 20 people in the United States age 12 and older—roughly 15 million people—reported using prescription painkillers nonmedically. And by then, coaches and parents nationwide had begun to realize that high-achieving athletes, particularly in contact sports, were prime candidates. They weren't starting in college.

The path for young athletes, just as in the general population, often began with pain, injury, a doctor's eagerness to prescribe—and, thus, endorse as safe—opioids for relief. Over the previous decade, prescriptions for pain medications in America had more than quadrupled, in large part because of aggressive—often criminal—marketing practices by drug manufacturers like Purdue Pharma. Male high school athletes were twice as likely to be prescribed painkillers and four times as likely to misuse or abuse as peers who didn't participate in sports. And by senior year of high school, some 11 percent of male and female athletes in 2013—more than twice the number in the general population—were using a narcotic like OxyContin nonmedically. Not all became addicted. But many leapt with the rest of the general population into the epidemic's second wave from 2010 to 2013, finding a cheaper, more potent high in heroin.

No sport, class, region or race proved exempt to the resulting rash of athlete abuse, though the incidence of injury in contact sports like football, hockey, lacrosse and soccer—and the risk-taking personalities such sports reward—likely increased their numbers. But as participants in a non-revenue niche sport, in careers that barely had a chance to get started, most of lacrosse's victims received limited attention.

On Long Island, Kings Park High star Thomas Ventura dreamed of playing college lacrosse, but began shooting up heroin as a high school senior in 2008 and died of an overdose in 2012. Huntington Beach High attackman Tyler MacLeod, 18, overdosed on heroin and died in California in 2012, early in his senior year. Alex Bement was a sophomore defenseman at Penn in 2011 when he became addicted to opioids. He dropped out, entered a seven-month rehab regime, recovered enough over the next nine years to coach high school in Colorado, resurfaced with a Division II club team, landed a girlfriend and a steady job. In 2019, Bement overdosed in Washington, DC, and died. He was 27.

Only Timmy Brooks, rich and handsome, generated national attention. A self-described addict and alcoholic, the Haverford School attackman was supposed to star on the University of Richmond's inaugural team in 2013 but injured his shoulder, dropped out and soon was co-running a drug ring—the "Main Line Takeover Project"—that peddled cocaine, ecstasy and marijuana to kids in Philadelphia high schools and colleges. Brooks pleaded guilty to five counts of dealing marijuana and in 2015 was sentenced to 9 to 23 months in jail.

While the growing drug scourge among athletes was by no means limited to lacrosse, the sensational nature of Brooks's fall, coupled with the growing substance use as revealed in widely reported NCAA substance abuse surveys, made it easy over the ensuing decade to broaden the sport's stereotype. Laxbros weren't just boozers. "Lacrosse," Princeton head coach Matt Madalon told US Lacrosse magazine in 2019, "is notoriously an alcohol- and drug-use sport." Whether the darkening image had anything to do with lacrosse's slowing growth rate in participation (3.5 percent in 2015, down from 16.7 percent in 2004), or the seven straight years of declining attendance at the Final Four, is unclear. Neither Yeardley Love's death nor the spate of drug casualties sparked any official acknowledgment—let alone systematic study—of the game's link to substance use.

Starting in 2013—as overdoses from prescription opioids were beginning to level off—medical authorities noted a spike in overdoses involving the synthetic opioid fentanyl, illicitly manufactured and consumed with heroin, cocaine and illegal pills. The surge was attributed to user ignorance, at least at first; considered 50 times more potent than heroin and 100 times more potent than morphine—$10, according to the *New York Times*, "kept you high all day"— fentanyl was being laced into illegal street drugs in wildly varying amounts, often without user knowledge. Sourced in China, produced in Mexico, ordered on the internet, delivered to homes via the US Postal Service, fentanyl swiftly overwhelmed law enforcement. From 2015 to 2016, the total amount of fentanyl seized by US border agents rocketed from 32 kilograms to more than 270.

No street drug in American history has ever been deadlier. Only two milligrams of fentanyl—the equivalent of two small grains of salt—can kill a human being, whether inhaled, swallowed or absorbed through skin. In March 2015, the Drug Enforcement Agency issued a nationwide alert calling fentanyl a threat to public health and safety. Between 2013 and 2017 more than 67,000 Americans—more than the total dead in the wars in Vietnam, Iraq and Afghanistan combined—died from synthetic opioids, the majority from fentanyl. Fentanyl was part of the drug cocktail that killed Prince in 2016, Tom Petty in 2017, Anaheim Angels pitcher Tyler Skaggs in 2019. Fentanyl is what killed lacrosse's Alex Bement.

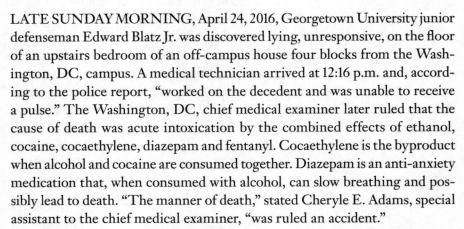

LATE SUNDAY MORNING, April 24, 2016, Georgetown University junior defenseman Edward Blatz Jr. was discovered lying, unresponsive, on the floor of an upstairs bedroom of an off-campus house four blocks from the Washington, DC, campus. A medical technician arrived at 12:16 p.m. and, according to the police report, "worked on the decedent and was unable to receive a pulse." The Washington, DC, chief medical examiner later ruled that the cause of death was acute intoxication by the combined effects of ethanol, cocaine, cocaethylene, diazepam and fentanyl. Cocaethylene is the byproduct when alcohol and cocaine are consumed together. Diazepam is an anti-anxiety medication that, when consumed with alcohol, can slow breathing and possibly lead to death. "The manner of death," stated Cheryle E. Adams, special assistant to the chief medical examiner, "was ruled an accident."

Eddie Blatz was 21 years old. Fifteen hours earlier he played in Georgetown's final home game, an 8–7 loss to Virginia. It was the program's Senior Night, marked by a pregame ceremony at Cooper Field and a sellout crowd.

Though ranked as high as 12th nationally in preseason polls, the Hoyas had won only two games in a disappointing 2016 campaign. For much of it Blatz, a celebrated, six-foot-five, 215-pound product of Long Island powerhouse Garden City, had been limited by injury. But he seemed to be finishing the season stronger; he started in the Hoyas' final four games and played extensively against the Cavaliers.

Media coverage of Blatz's death was remarkably light. Only *The George-towner*, a community newspaper with a readership of 50,000, came close to reporting the circumstances, with unnamed sources stating the cause as a possible overdose due to "a combination of prescription drugs and alcohol." In large part, perhaps, this is because the Blatz family declined to speak about his death, and university officials, coaches and Blatz's teammates, along with fellow lacrosse players and childhood friends, were determined to respect their privacy.

But Ed Blatz was beloved, and not only because he was one of the great all-around athletes in Garden City history (a three-sport captain, All–Long Island wide receiver and owner of the school's career reception and touch-down records, who also led the lacrosse team to two state championships), but because he was also funny and never talked about himself. "Eddie brought light to any situation he was in," recalled Garden City teammate Justin Guterding. "He just brought joy to everywhere he was and every situation. He wanted to make everyone else happy."

Many of Blatz's former teammates and opponents from Long Island had moved on to prominent roles at high-profile programs, and felt compelled to honor him. Maryland defenseman Tim Muller, a childhood friend from Garden City, learned of Blatz's death just after lunch that Sunday, lay on his bed for hours and nearly left for home, but instead decided to play in that night's win over Ohio State, "for him." For each game in Maryland's ensuing run to the 2016 NCAA final, Muller played with Blatz's name and number stickered onto the back of his helmet.

Guterding, then a junior attackman at Duke, learned of Blatz's death via a phone call on his way to practice, and broke down sobbing. He played in Duke's ACC subsequent semifinal against Notre Dame in a mental fog, produced one of the worst games of his life until 40 seconds into overtime, when he lasered in an overhand to give the Blue Devils the come-from-behind 10–9 win. Guterding had never scored an OT game-winner; he instantly flung away his stick and thrust a finger up to the sky. *For you, Eddie.*

The story ricocheted across Lacrosse Nation. "Everyone knows that that wouldn't have happened without Eddie: He was laughing down at me," Guterding said. "That was huge—not only because we won, but it was huge for my community. I had people texting me that I hadn't heard from in a long time. But they knew Eddie."

The cause of Blatz's death—and the toxic factor of fentanyl—was never published in a major news outlet or aired on radio or television. But within lacrosse circles and the Georgetown neighborhood, word quickly spread. Speculation had it that one or two other Georgetown students, one or both on the lacrosse team, also needed medical treatment after drug use that night. On May 4, 2016, a source quoted in *The Georgetowner* said that one student had also been taken to the hospital and another was "revived by paddle defibrillator." (Multiple sources since confirm that at least one was another lacrosse player.) The paper's editorial headlined "Cause of Student Death: Swept Under the Rug?" spoke to the lack of coverage.

"Georgetown University is so tight-lipped on this," *The Georgetowner*'s unnamed source asserted, "as it is a clear demonstration of the complicit conspiracy within the quasi-elitist lacrosse community-culture cover up—just as are all schools, coaches, parents and players where the self-ordained immunity to rules violations and consequences tolerate the norm of 'good boys from good families' allowed to historically and chronically abuse drugs and alcohol. You needn't be so disappointed in just Georgetown. This overlooking of the root cause of the problem is systemic and ubiquitous in lacrosse."

The editorial closed by saying that Blatz's death should be used to shine a light on student problems with substances, because "drug abuse or alcohol abuse survive in the dark, not so much in the light."

Though its reporting was not definitive, *The Georgetowner* had the basics right. Yet it was entirely alone. The wave of national coverage that engulfed the Duke rape case and the murder of Yeardley Love was not repeated. Most conspicuously, the *Washington Post*—staffed by reporters with close connections to the school and neighborhood—printed only one brief paragraph about Blatz's death the next day, but nothing on its aftermath or the numerous Blatz memorials the following year. For the 2017 season Guterding and Muller—along with players at Lafayette, Boston University, Furman, Harvard, Vermont and Richmond—changed their uniform numbers to Blatz's high school or college number. This prompted heartfelt coverage in newspapers and publications dedicated to lacrosse, mentions of Blatz's sudden death and, always, an oblique phrase about its underreported cause. Publicly, the players involved refused to discuss it.

The silence was contagious. Though many within the lacrosse community knew the reason, though the tragedy was the latest horrifying sign of an ever-growing cancer, no one in the American lacrosse hierarchy took it as a spur to action, or the chance to issue a clarion call about the immediate dangers of fentanyl. Six years earlier, Bates's coach Peter Lasagna had posited that lacrosse's substance-related deaths were "confirmation of an emergency too critical to ignore," and asked: "Do people with influence care enough to tackle this immense, complex, dark side of the heritage of our game?" The answer, after the death of Yeardley Love, was no. After Eddie Blatz, the answer was still no.

In Washington, DC, too, Blatz's death faded fast. Few off campus noticed when, in the following semester, fall 2016, Georgetown University asked all student athletes to complete on-line courses on alcohol and drug use and attend a mandatory substance abuse seminar. Or when—in a rare, mid-school-year policy shift—Georgetown athletics announced, in December 2016, a new, far more stringent drug- and alcohol-testing regime to take effect in the spring of 2017. In addition to the mandated NCAA drug-testing program for all varsity athletes, Georgetown would now subject its athletes to randomized, year-round testing for alcohol and recreational drugs. Though athletes interpreted this as a response to Blatz's death, neither his name nor the lacrosse team nor the specific danger of fentanyl was referenced.

In February of 2017, the Georgetown men's team returned to the field. Despite the previous year's calamity and 2–12 record, Kevin Warne returned for his fifth season as head coach. Warne told the student newspaper that even as the team would play to honor Ed Blatz, they had spent the fall "building culture," that "the whole vibe is just a lot different, and it's very exciting as we move forward." Warne did not detail the particulars of the old vibe, but neither the second player who, according to multiple sources, received medical treatment the night of Blatz's death, nor the player who—with two companions—discovered his body and called 911, were on the roster.

In October 2018, the DC Office of the Chief Medical Examiner confirmed its ruling of acute intoxication featuring alcohol, cocaine and fentanyl. In response, Justin Guterding emphasized that the Eddie Blatz he had known since middle school used no drugs and suffered from no addiction. That's why the news "was a complete shock," he said. "That was the worst part about it. It's not like we were trying to get him help. It was nothing along those lines. It was just that he made a bad decision and it turned out for the worst. It's a nightmare situation, but that's just the truth."

Guterding wore Blatz's number 14 the rest of his college career, and graduated from Duke in 2018 as the NCAA's career leader in goals. He carried that number into the pros, switching to Blatz's Georgetown number, 22, only when 14 wasn't available. Five years later he was still waking up to photos of his friend on the wall, still wearing three wristbands in memoriam, still mourning. Blaming Georgetown, the drug supplier—anyone else—for Blatz's death might provide comfort. But he can't.

"Absolutely not," Guterding said in December 2018. "Maybe he was hanging out with the wrong guys. Maybe he made a stupid decision, and he just paid for it. Which I hate saying, but it's just the way it is. People know that one bad decision can end your life. It can impact your life. It can change the way you live forever."

Blatz's death made him more grateful. But lacrosse's collective silence had its effect: Guterding didn't think Blatz's death had changed the sport, or its attachment to alcohol and drugs. "You heard about the kid at Lafayette," he said. "Same thing." On September 11, 2017, Lafayette freshman McRae Williams died of blunt-force head injuries after passing out drunk at a lacrosse team day party.

"You do hear, unfortunately, too many stories . . . like, you hear one every year," Guterding said. "Guys are going to have their fun and guys are going to act the way they want to act. I don't think you're really going to change anything there. It's a huge part of the culture, and it could impact *more* people, but the majority of the time, it doesn't—until it does. Which has happened to me—and to plenty of other people, too. It has to happen to you, for you to realize that you can't do some of these things and not pay for them."

THE GEORGE HUGUELY hangover hit UVa lacrosse much like Ernest Hemingway's famous progression of bankruptcy: "gradually, then suddenly." For two years Dom Starsia and his staff had managed to keep the men's program focused amid the ongoing investigation, murder trial and sentencing, following up its surreal national championship with a perfectly respectable— and drama-free—2012 season before losing in the NCAA quarterfinals to

Notre Dame. Only recruiting revealed the wobble in the walk: The national title won in 2011 didn't prompt its usual bump; indeed, UVa's next few hauls were conspicuously lean. Starsia figured that wary mothers were telling their boys, "You're *not* going to Virginia."

From 2013 to 2016, the Cavaliers won just one regular-season Atlantic Coast Conference game, twice lost badly to Johns Hopkins in the first round of the NCAA tournament and twice missed the tournament outright, retreating from prominence just as ACC archrival Duke was ringing up back-to-back national titles. Starsia had never had a worse stretch as a head coach. Calls for his ouster—minimal after Love's murder—gathered steam.

Ironically, during this time Starsia pulled off one of his most gratifying coups. On paper, there was no reason for Seneca attackman Zed Williams to be interested in UVa. Aside from the traditional Haudenosaunee path to Syracuse, the success of the Thompson brothers had established another Indigenous-friendly option at the University at Albany. Williams grew up fiercely close to his five brothers and two sisters on the Cattaraugus reserve outside Buffalo, and no one from Six Nations had ever played in Charlottesville. Though enamored with Native culture and history, Starsia had landed only one Indigenous player, Muscogee midfielder Justin Giles, two decades earlier.

Still, he had to try. Williams was a wonder: six foot two, 185 unstoppable pounds. After becoming a high school starter in eighth grade—and totaling 74 goals and 28 assists—he tore up New York and national scoring records, and would end up shattering the career schoolboy marks of Lyle Thompson and Casey Powell. The UVa coach's first glimpse came in 2011, Williams's sophomore year at tiny Silver Creek High, when the midfielder played every minute and scored five goals in a loss to Cazenovia in the state semifinals.

On his first home visit, Starsia learned two facts that would make Williams an outlier at UVa. No one in the family drank alcohol, and no one had earned a four-year college degree. Zed hadn't cracked 1,000 on the SAT test, and had shown little interest in college. But Starsia loved his eager unselfishness, his humble habit of picking up litter, and the two took a walk. Williams had also been recruited by Syracuse coach John Desko and his staff, but their message was all about Orange success—all lacrosse, all the time. "I knew, and my parents knew, I needed more than that," Zed said. "I needed someone who was going to take care of me off and on the field; I needed that guidance." Starsia kept asking about Zed's life. Lacrosse barely came up.

When he left for Charlottesville in the summer of 2013, few figured that Zed Williams would be there long. Homesickness was only one reason. Williams was in no way prepared for UVa's academic level and pace. He had never watched television. He had no idea how to write, as he puts it, "a proper email." He didn't understand that his habit of avoiding direct eye contact, common in many Native societies as a sign of respect, would be taken by some professors as rudeness. With only an outdated flip phone to help navigate the first weeks on campus, he found himself constantly lost and late.

Williams barely survived freshman year, his performance so dismal that the team's new academic advisor, Heather Downs, tearily told Starsia that winter, "I don't see any way this can work out." UVa placed him on academic probation, but when Williams rejected the suggestion of summer school, Starsia didn't press. Only a push by family, and his determination to prove naysayers back home wrong, sent Williams back for sophomore year. Starsia's son, Joe, a UVa assistant, shepherded him through study halls, kept tabs on his grades. Needing just to pass a fall statistics class to stay eligible, Zed earned a C: It felt like the biggest win of the year.

In the lacrosse space, Williams felt only a bit less adrift. His teammates knew each other from the prep school and club circuits; he was raised in the Native box galaxy. The athleticism that once enabled him to dominate high school wasn't enough to overcome his low field IQ. He didn't know most basic drills. His idea of clearing was to run the ball upfield. But from the start his UVa teammates bristled with tips on everything from writing essays to offensive tactics. Perhaps more important, for four years they supported Williams's refusal to drink alcohol.

"That wouldn't have worked if it wasn't for Starsia," Williams said. "Once I came on campus they were all very welcoming and didn't pressure me to do anything. Even though I didn't drink, I hung out with them. They were all very nice to me. Though it took a while to get on a personal level, once I hit that level with them, I learned to love these guys—and I trusted them. They were like my family now."

In lacrosse terms, Williams's college career was something of a disappointment. Though twice named honorable mention All-American, he never became the spectacular force once predicted, the next Lyle Thompson. Starsia didn't care. Not a summer or holiday break passed without the UVa staff worrying that Williams would drop out. Few, if any, of Starsia's players overcame more academic hurdles or worked harder, all the way to the end. Zed's father, Daniel, died of diabetes in April of his senior year. Six weeks later, in the spring of 2017, Williams graduated—on schedule—with a bachelor's degree in drama from the University of Virginia.

"I wouldn't have graduated from that college if he wasn't there," Williams said of Starsia. "He's one of the best human beings and with the best heart. The way he led and saw life and cared about people: that's the kind of person I aspire to be. It wasn't business with him. It wasn't lacrosse with him, or winning championships so he could keep his job. He actually cared about not only me as a kid, but what I was going to get out of it and bring back to my community and my family and my children one day."

Starsia, too, counts Williams's graduation as one of his most satisfying achievements—more than any of his four national championships. But it didn't happen when he was head coach. On May 2, 2016—ten days after beating Georgetown in Ed Blatz's last game, two days after UVa finished another losing season with a 19–11 loss to his protégé at Brown, Lars Tiffany—Starsia was back at his Charlottesville office at 7 a.m., working out on the elliptical machine. The phone rang. It was UVa athletic director Craig Littlepage.

"We want to make a change," Littlepage said. "Think about it."

Starsia was mystified. The recent years of losing had been brutal, but didn't he have four national titles? Wasn't his most recent recruiting class bristling with blue-chippers, the best sign yet that the program—and lacrosse parents—had finally moved on from George Huguely? The next day, Starsia called Littlepage with an offer: Give me one more year. If you're not happy after that, I'll retire.

Littlepage wasn't budging. Incoming talent would help, but the upperclassmen were a study in lassitude. "When we were with Starsia and we were losing, the players didn't care," said Zed Williams. "I'm not saying everyone—a couple guys were pissed—but people didn't care. *Whatever: let's go party, or let's go drink.*"

When word circulated that UVa wanted to fire its legendary coach, the uproar from former players and alumni forced Littlepage to backpedal. The athletic director tried to take Starsia up on his original offer of one more year, but now Starsia demanded a new three-year contract. UVa refused. Conflicting reports about his future made the confusing mess public. After three weeks of turmoil Littlepage made it official: Starsia was gone. No official cause was ever given.

Few believe that Starsia would have been fired had he still been winning championships. But over the next month, as UVa zeroed in on hiring his replacement, it became clear to at least one man what the administration believed was needed. Dynamic, demanding, recent success at an elite academic institution: all desired qualities. But the new coach also had to tackle the plague that stained the school still.

"I was asked about that by Craig Littlepage through the interview process. Sort of: *Can you be a tough sheriff?*" said Lars Tiffany. "Essentially— my own words—what I heard was, *We need to change the relationship with our men's lacrosse team and drugs and alcohol.*"

Littlepage insisted that he wasn't that specific, but "it's true that we were looking for a higher level of accountability."

Meanwhile, a striking reminder of the worst-case scenario went public. Throughout the failed appeals of his conviction for second-degree murder, George Huguely maintained that Yeardley Love's death was a drunken accident and that he was guilty of no more than negligent manslaughter. For six years, Yeardley's mother and sister, Sharon and Lexie Love Hodges, maintained that an enraged Huguely beat Yeardley to death. Indeed, they founded the high-profile One Love Foundation to publicize the scourge of relationship violence and filed a wrongful-death civil lawsuit against Huguely, seeking $30.45 million in damages. In 2022, a Virginia jury finally awarded the two women $15 million and agreed that Huguely's "willful and wanton" misconduct resulted in Love's death—verbiage that Sharon took as further affirmation. "It was to make a point that, in fact, it was intentional," she said after. "It wasn't an accident."

Yet, on June 3, 2016, the Huguely family had found itself joined in its legal struggles by the unlikeliest ally: Sharon Love. At issue was whether the Huguelys' insurance company, Chartis Property Casualty, would pay out a $6 million homeowner's policy for damages incurred in the Loves' upcoming civil trial. Chartis, citing a policy exclusion triggered by Huguely's criminal conviction, argued that it should not; the Huguelys, contending that George's intentionality had not been proven, contended that it should. Opposing Chartis's bid for summary judgment in a Maryland civil court, Love filed a 30-page "interested party" brief that backed George Huguely's version of a drunken accident, stating, "There is a wealth of information—much of which was never even introduced during Mr. Huguely's criminal trial—supporting the Love's [*sic*] contention that Mr. Huguely's conduct on the fateful night of May 2, 2010 was negligent and not subjectively intentional."

The seeming flip could well have a been a tactic to ensure the maximum punishment—exacted by a higher amount of damages. Indeed, a federal judge ruled in 2017 that Chartis did not have to pay out the $6 million, and the Loves were eventually awarded half of what they sought. But its immediate effect was a brief agreement between distraught opposing parties that, while the exact nature of George Huguely's violence could never be known, the effects of his alcohol abuse were clear. Love's motion painted a detailed picture of the 30-hour, 45-drink binge in Charlottesville that preceded Yeardley's death, and quoted a medical expert's opinion that, by then, Huguely was "so intoxicated that he lacked the capacity to form the specific intent to hurt Ms. Love and . . . so intoxicated that he lacked the capacity to be aware that he was committing any crime."

Love's motion also, in its narrative of sloppy imbibement from apartment to restaurant to bar to apartment to golf course, subtly showcased the enabling behavior of Huguely's parents, friends and teammates, not to mention the town's restaurant and bar staff. No one in town, on his team, in his family, saw fit to cut George Huguely off. And, while it was true that he represented a homicidal one-off, the most extreme example, anyone hearing about it again six years later recognized that many of the same elements remained in play.

Tiffany, for one, felt that Littlepage had issued him an urgent mandate. "So I came in, essentially, with a zero tolerance for drugs," he said. "From a macro level, the sport needs to be fixed. The only place I could really attack is here in Charlottesville, Virginia, though. So we're going at the micro level."

LARS TIFFANY WAS HIRED on June 21, 2016, and—in one sense—his transition into Virginia's head coaching position couldn't have been smoother. All parties have Dom Starsia to thank for that. Despite the pain over his firing, and a bitterness that led him to cut off all communication with many once-trusted colleagues, Starsia set all bitterness aside when dealing with his protégé.

In early June, when UVa was fixated on poaching Notre Dame coach Kevin Corrigan, Starsia was the first to suggest that Tiffany apply for his old job. Their subsequent phone calls, with Tiffany seeking advice on how to get his name in the mix, felt "a little weird," Starsia said, "a little awkward"—but he got through it. Then, after Tiffany was hired and needed somewhere to live his first month in town, Starsia put him up in his home. Krissy found that weird. Starsia insisted, and provided a room for new assistant coach Kip Turner, too. And when Tiffany needed a place to hold the orientation barbeque for freshmen that August, the one held for decades in Starsia's home, the one featuring Starsia's last-ever batch of recruits, UVa's ex-coach said, "Why don't you just have the barbeque here?"

Tiffany's introduction to sheriffing proved more jarring. On August 12, he received a phone call from UVa's All-American goalie, Matt Barrett. He had just been arrested after Ocean City, Maryland, police—answering a noise complaint—noticed him using a credit card to cut white powder. Barrett first told police the substance was Adderall, then allegedly admitted it was cocaine. Tiffany kicked him off the team.

Starsia has never accepted the idea that his program needed an overhaul. Barrett's arrest was enough to convince Tiffany. "The culture of Virginia lacrosse at the time," he said, "was a disaster." The new coach soon found the athletic department's seemingly tough drug-testing regime, which conducted random tests on a dozen athletes three times a week, was no deterrent. Within his first 18 months as coach, Tiffany found himself confronting another player for cocaine use and two others for marijuana use.

"Fellas," he told a cadre of players early on, "I'm almost apologetic because you weren't recruited to become a part of the culture that we're creating now. I'm sorry. If you want to go somewhere else, I'll sign the transfer papers."

But Tiffany wasn't sorry, and the faux-apology tone didn't last. It wasn't long into his first fall before he was confronting players in a way that Starsia rarely did. "He flipped the switch a lot more, and when he yelled he flipped out," said Zed Williams, a senior that year:

> *You didn't want to see him do it, especially on you.*
> *When Lars came in he just said how it was:* Everyone's trying out. *We had a two-week period where we all tried out, and one cut was a senior who was on the team for three years. Another was a junior on the team for two years. If you weren't in shape and you didn't come back to school prepared, you were going to get cut. That helped me in the long run:* This is how the professional is. You gotta get the job done and keep performing and put the work in. Perform well or you're gonna get replaced.

III

BUILDERS

O N THURSDAY, JULY 19, 2018, between semifinals at the 2018 World Championship in Israel, Brian Holman showed up in the VIP section of Wingate 1. Head coach of Division I's new men's team at the University of Utah, the farthest outpost yet in lacrosse's push westward, Holman had just flown in to watch his son, US star Marcus Holman. Gaunt, 58 and gray, Holman's professorial mien already made him stand out in a fraternity prone to beefiness. That he had spent his 15-year coaching career as an unpaid volunteer assistant, yet now was charged with building a program seeded by a $10 million endowment from Brazilian-born, Utah-raised airline entrepreneur David Neeleman made Holman even more striking.

No doubt the risks scared off coaching candidates who—on paper, anyway—were more qualified. When, in 2016, Neeleman unveiled his plan to elevate Utah's club team to varsity for the 2019 season, the school's athletic director was opposed, travel costs seemed prohibitive, and there was no guarantee that the tycoon's backing wouldn't dissolve with a recession. No top assistant wanted to lose two years coaching club, much less in virgin territory like Salt Lake City. Fired Virginia coach Dom Starsia turned the job down. Holman himself said no, twice, before taking the leap.

Still, Utah's choice of Holman was less radical than it seemed. Despite its elitist image, the American game's most dramatic growth has been disproportionately pioneered by strivers from blue-collar households. Indeed, out on the field at that moment, watching warmups, was US head coach John

Danowski, the self-described "turnpike guy" who redeemed Duke and tipped into place as a lacrosse power. Heading toward the gate was Iroquois assistant coach Scott Marr, architect of the new force at Albany.

"I went to school with a couple kids with money," Marr says. "My roommate, we got into a fight one night: He was calling me a 'piece of shit from Yorktown,' 'cowfucker,' this and that. That's the downside of our game: the perception that we're all *that* guy."

The rich irony, literally, is that Marr—like Holman and so many of the sport's agitators—cut his teeth at Johns Hopkins, bastion of the Baltimore style and home base for the lacrosse establishment. Call it another measure of greatness: Lacrosse's premier name has long produced the tools of its own diminishment. The first was Howard "Howdy" Myers, who, after winning his third straight national championship at Hopkins, bolted for Hofstra in 1949. Dubbed "a modern-day Johnny Appleseed" by the *New York Times*, Myers transformed Long Island into lacrosse's next great hotbed. Out of that emerged Richie Moran, son of a shipyard worker, who built the Cornell dynasty that cracked the old-line stranglehold with NCAA titles in 1971, '76 and '77, the last with a win over Hopkins in the final. Moran's Sewanhaka High teammate was Tom Hayes, son of a Floral Park tool-and-die man, who became the earliest and most aggressive American voice pushing lacrosse's lords to recognize the Haudenosaunee and expand the game worldwide.

But the most intrepid of Myers's progeny may be Bill Tierney, who forged a new dynasty at Princeton with six NCAA championships in the 1990s, then moved to the University of Denver and, in 2015, made it the first Division I school west of the Mississippi to win a national title.

The son of a Rheingold beer truck driver, Tierney was born in 1951 and raised in Levittown, the segregated, cookie-cutter development on former Hempstead farmland. He picked up lacrosse for the first time at Division III Cortland State, won a national championship, spent the next decade coaching in Long Island high schools. After a head-turning head coaching stint at Rochester Institute of Technology, in 1985 Tierney joined Johns Hopkins as Don Zimmerman's defensive coordinator. He lasted three years. The rest of the 10-deep staff (most programs had, maybe, two or three assistant coaches) were Homewood alums. Accent, background, terminology: Tierney never quite fit.

"I was 'head assistant'—but I really wasn't," he said. "Those guys were tough. When I left Hopkins, we had just won the national championship;

I think people knew I was going to get out at some point, but I didn't matter to them much. Because I wasn't a Hopkins guy."

BY THE LATE 1980s lacrosse's first pioneer power, the template for every far-flung program to come, had risen 300 miles south of Baltimore. Its mastermind was a Hopkins guy. Willie Scroggs played midfield for three straight Blue Jays national championship teams from 1967 to 1969 (and was an all-conference defensive back in football) and, during a six-year run as an assistant coach, won two more. But, with an air of Zen cockiness and an upbringing—and name—straight out of Dickens, he was also like nothing Homewood had ever seen.

Scroggs was raised in the rowhouse neighborhood of Waverly in inner-city Baltimore. His grandfather was a boxer known as "Handsome Harry." His Japanese mother, Helen, had two boys by another man when his father, Willard, met her while an army MP at Pearl Harbor during World War II. Willard returned to Baltimore and became a corrupt and alcoholic cop; in 1953, five months after being accused of extorting hush money from a numbers runner, he was fired from the Baltimore Police Department for shaking down an 82-year-old pharmacist for $3,000.

Willie was six then. By the time he was in sixth grade, his parents had split up. Helen left the house at 5 a.m. each morning to stitch London Fog raincoats at Baltimore's famed Meadow Mill complex, and developed tuberculosis; during his middle school years, an aunt moved in while his mother recovered in a sanitarium. On the night of December 10, 1961, Helen was at home on Old York Road entertaining a man named Harry Fujiwara when Willard, 43, smashed the glass on a door and broke in wielding a .38-caliber revolver. "He came to the house to kill my mother with a gun," Willie said.

Willie was 14. His father hit his mother in the face and clubbed Fujiwara over the head. Willie and his brothers wrestled the gun away. His father was covered with blood; Willie began screaming and crying that he had to get to a hospital. When Willard refused a ride, Willie walked him a few blocks up the street to Union Memorial.

"I hardly saw him after that," Scroggs said.

Wiry and tough, five foot nine and 150 pounds, Willie starred as a football and lacrosse player at nearby City College high school. He'd scan the stands: his father never showed. George Young, future general manager of the Miami Dolphins and New York Giants, was head football coach. Willie loved him. Sophomore year, Helen got him a summer job at the raincoat factory as a bundle boy, hauling 20 coats at a time from one end of the sewing floor to the other. Junior year, he landed work cleaning the playground at his old elementary school, swept up hair at Joe's Barbershop. For eight years, through high school and college, he parked cars at nearby Memorial Stadium for Colts and Orioles games.

Scroggs wanted to play football for Ohio State, but after he scored five goals on private school power Boys Latin to open the 1965 season, Bob Scott invited him to a recruiting weekend at Johns Hopkins. Helen didn't like it; she wanted Willie to work. When he went off to college anyway, she made him pay rent. Life at Homewood was a comparative wonderland: In autumn Scroggs played sterling defensive back for the middling football team; come spring he stepped into lacrosse's rarified air. Stick wizards like Charlie Goodell, Jerry Schnydman and Joe Cowan milled about; the team lost three times in three years; "Catch Us If You Can," by the Dave Clark Five, blared daily in the locker room. His father never showed. Each year before the first home game, there was an alumni smoker—dinner and drinks—and all these Hopkins legends, the names the current team grew up worshipping, would be introduced and he knew he was part of something golden.

After graduating with a degree in history, Scroggs worked three years as a teacher and coach at Gilman. The private prep school had none of the racial and economic mix he knew at City College: First day of class, a seventh grader called him "Willie," and Scroggs threw him to the floor and said, "It's Mister Scroggs to you." On his first day as head junior varsity lacrosse coach, Scroggs's father died somewhere in West Virginia. His uncles and aunts promised to chip in on funeral costs, but Willie, cash-poor, ended up paying the whole $2,000. He never spoke to them again.

Like nearly everyone who had contact with Hopkins coach Bob Scott, the seven-time national champion, Scroggs calls him "a wonderful human being." When, in 1972, Scott offered a place on his staff, it felt like an anointing. All his life Scroggs had studied older men, teachers, coaches, the decisions they made and the way they handled crises; he desperately wanted to be a head coach. After Scott retired in 1974, Scroggs was 27 and thought—despite just one season of experience—he might get the job. Instead, Scott became athletic director and chose the more seasoned Henry "Chic" Ciccarone as his successor. Scroggs became Ciccarone's assistant, in charge of defense and scouting opponents.

It wasn't the last time he would feel slighted. In 1976, when Princeton's head coaching job opened, Scroggs asked Scott for a letter of recommendation. After saying yes, he instead wrote a glowing letter for eventual hire Mike Hanna—a Hobart product who coached one year at Hopkins. When confronted, Scott told Scroggs, "You didn't want that job at Princeton."

After that, he applied for every head coaching job: Penn State, UPenn, Delaware. His strained dynamic with the flinty, superstitious Ciccarone, meanwhile, became icy in 1977 when Scroggs called his boss out on what he believed were questionable administrative practices: Ciccarone "essentially fired me," then took him back. The tension hardly bothered the players. After losing their only regular-season game to No. 1 Cornell, attackman Mike O'Neill and the Blue Jays halted the Big Red insurgency with a 13–8 win in the 1978 NCAA final. Ten days later, North Carolina hired the 31-year-old Scroggs as head coach. Neither he nor Ciccarone was sad to part ways.

The absence didn't hurt Hopkins. Henry Ciccarone proved to be the program's perfect transitional figure, embodying its heritage and the lunchpail edge needed to keep it alive. Son of a tailor who arrived in America penniless, made suits for presidents Franklin Roosevelt and John Kennedy, and died a multi-millionaire, Henry graduated from Maryland's exclusive Severn School, crazy competitive, joined the marines for two years, then began an All-American career at Hopkins. Junior year, he made off with his fraternity's grocery money to elope in Las Vegas.

Ciccarone could be jocular and warm, but his program was a combustible blast furnace, fueled by stratospheric expectations. By the 1970s lacrosse excellence had become as central to the Johns Hopkins brand as Nobel Prizes and medicine. Its campus housed the sport's Hall of Fame. Its greatest coach, Bob Scott, literally wrote the book on the game—*Lacrosse: Technique and Tradition*. Its self-regard was limitless. "Would you rather be Babe Ruth in Yankee Stadium?" Ciccarone said when recruiting blue-chipper Jeff Cook, who was also considering Virginia. "Or [then Baltimore Orioles minor leaguer] Terry Crowley in Rochester?" In other sports the Blue Jays competed in Division III; only in lacrosse did Hopkins compete in Division I. Only because of lacrosse did its homecoming weekend fall in the spring. Only for lacrosse did its crowds act as greedy as Alabama football fans, counting up the day's goals and then chanting, "We want more!"

Anything but a national title was considered failure. Ciccarone's screaming clashes with opposing coaches—especially true threats like Cornell's Richie Moran—and game officials imbued the lofty program with a darker persona. Armed with Mike Federico's stony goaltending, four-time All-American defenseman Mark Greenberg's shutdown genius and the scoring of Mike O'Neill, Canadian import Dave Huntley, and Cook, in 1979 Ciccarone recharged the Blue Jay mystique, unleashing Hopkins's first undefeated and untied season in 38 years, and then—with his son, Henry Jr., aboard—beat Virginia, 9–8, in 1980 to become the first program in the NCAA era to win three straight Division I titles. Hopkins rolled into the 1981 final riding a 22-game winning streak, with every reason to believe they would win number four.

But Scroggs had been busy, too. The program he inherited at Chapel Hill in 1978 was a Bizarro World version of Hopkins; that year's player revolt against head coach Paul Doty had resulted in 14 suspensions, 11 reinstatements and no sign that men's lacrosse could ever thrive. UNC lacrosse had already died once, in 1954, and its resurrection 20 years later had done little to spark interest on campus or around the state. Not one high school in North Carolina played lacrosse. Scholarships at UNC were being slashed from 13 to 9. And because head lacrosse coach wasn't a full-time position, come off-season Scroggs worked as assistant business manager in the athletic department, in charge of tickets, security and fire marshals at Tar Heel home football and basketball games.

None of that slowed him. Soon after arriving Scroggs headed back north, intent on larceny. His alma mater and Maryland had long divvied up the best Baltimore recruits, with cost no factor; though it didn't offer "athletic scholarships," Hopkins's system of targeted aid erased tuition bills for top talents. But with a beautiful campus and starting jobs to dangle, in 1979 alone Scroggs picked off five of the *Baltimore Sun*'s 12-man All-Metro first team—Calvert Hall goalie Tom Sears, Loyola midfielder Peter Voelkel and defenseman John Haus, St. Paul's midfielder Bill Ness and St. Mary's attack Michael Burnett—plus honorable mention Towson attackman Dave Wingate. "With one or two more recruiting years like that," said the *Evening Sun*, "Scroggs will soon have UNC at the top." The next year, he poached Baltimore area Player of the Year Andy Smith; by 1981, 17 Baltimore stars had migrated to Chapel Hill.

None were more important—or coveted by Ciccarone—than Sears, the son of a Sparrows Point ironworker who had been long fixated on UNC. To keep costs down, Scroggs took uniforms home and washed them himself. Seeing that ROTC made $3,600 to clean Kenan Stadium after football games, in the fall of 1980 Scroggs wangled away four of the home dates, and had his team show up 6 a.m. Sundays in the cold and rain to blow, sweep and hose down the grunge. Some players came directly from drinking on Franklin Street; Scroggs considered their suffering a positive, mostly. Informed of the stadium duty, future Hall of Fame goalie Larry Quinn decided to commit to Hopkins.

Scroggs allowed players freedom but not selfishness. His noted reserve, accentuated by full beard and thick glasses, kept people off-balance. He liked that. "I've never met anybody like Willie," said Sears, who often found himself alone with Scroggs at the UNC training table. "I'd sit and have lunch with him for 20 minutes, and neither one of us would say a word. Nothing. You know how unnerving that is as a sophomore, and it's your coach, and you're thinking, *Should I say something—should I NOT say something?* But when he did say something, it was usually pretty profound. I've never had a better coach."

Asked, 40 years later, if he finally has come to know Scroggs, Sears laughed. "I don't know that anybody really knows him," he said.

REALIZING THAT, like the era's "Showtime" Los Angeles Lakers, he had the shutdown defenders necessary to run a relentless, even reckless, fastbreak, Scroggs's favorite practice gambit was a drill called Scramble: Fling a ball on field and let the man-up offense and man-down defense run. "Play like the Indians play," he'd say. The Tar Heels resembled Hopkins during warmups, but not when the clock started. "Those guys were power brokers, one-on-one; they were more 'settled offense,'" said Peter Voelkel, a three-time All-American midfielder. "We were run-and-gun. We wanted to push the ball."

In Scroggs's second year, the Tar Heels reached the Final Four and lost to Virginia in double-overtime, but realized that they were good enough to win. The next fall, 1980, when Hopkins and its three straight national titles came to Chapel Hill to scrimmage, Scroggs sat his top talent and played possum. He wanted to beat them when it mattered.

The Tar Heels' rampage through the 1981 season was like sport's version of Sherman's March—in reverse. Behind Sears's goaltending, daring and steady, North Carolina slashed through the sport's heartland: Virginia in Charlottesville, 11–6; Towson and the University of Baltimore by the combined score of 34–7; and then, in an exhibition on March 28 in Baltimore, the legendary Mount Washington Lacrosse Club by a gasp-inducing score of 19–10. "For one of the few times in its long and distinguished history," the *Sun* wrote, Mount Washington's "many former college All-Americas . . . not only looked like old-timers, but played that way, too." Noting the Tar Heels' "overpowering speed and quickness," the newspaper called UNC's performance "a warning to Johns Hopkins."

Though Sears—while making 25 saves—severely sprained his left ankle, Scroggs didn't disagree. The next day he went to Philadelphia to see if Dean Smith's basketball players could beat Indiana to become the first UNC team—in any sport—since 1957 to win a national championship. They couldn't. Groggy from his all-night drive home, Scroggs arrived at practice and said, "Guys, they had their chance. Now it's up to us."

With unbeaten Maryland next and Sears's injury revealing UNC's one vulnerability, Scroggs's calm made little sense. The previous fall, after his backup goalie abruptly quit, Scroggs had no choice but to hand Gary Waters—an athletic, practice-only midfielder with one season of high school lacrosse experience—a goalie stick, and spent weeks pelting him personally with thousands of balls. UNC's all-time record against Maryland was 0–17. Waters's game experience consisted of one fall scrimmage. Now the Hagerstown product headed home to face the 11-time national champions in College Park, sensing little confidence from his teammates. But Scroggs never mentioned the circumstances, issuing his usual terse command in the locker room: "Okay, get your gear on. Let's go out and kick the shit out of these Maryland boys."

Waters stopped 20 shots and North Carolina won, 13–12, in double overtime. Sears missed the next game, and Waters picked up 11 saves in a 22–5 runaway over Duke. It is upon such unlikelihoods that good teams gain a sense of destiny; after Sears's healthy return, the Tar Heels galloped into the NCAA tournament hungry and loose. The day before hosting the Syracuse Orangemen, attackman Chris "Rocky" Mueller pumped out nine one-handed push-ups to mark the season's wins, then pulled an orange out of his jersey for all to stomp. UNC won 13–6 in heavy rain. For the semifinals three days later against No. 3 Navy, Mueller dieseled 10 push-ups, then pulled out a toy battleship for all to smash to bits. Before 6,000-plus home fans, North Carolina scored nine times in the fourth quarter for a runaway 17–8 win.

After its last practice before meeting Johns Hopkins in the 1981 final in Princeton, New Jersey, Mueller polished off 11 one-handers, pulled out a wind-up plastic Blue Jay, and tried stomping it—but missed. The bird kept hopping. Everyone knew the game's epic implications, stuffed within a family affair: both teams undefeated, opponents who had grown up playing together, Scroggs the Oedipal stalker coming for Daddy. Even his assistant coaches, Zimmerman and Michael O'Neill, were Hopkins alums. "It's not going to be easy," Scroggs said, "to kill that Blue Jay." The howling players converged, crushing the toy beneath their feet.

Poised to win its 40th national title, Hopkins came in looking its usual dominating self. Winners of 22 straight games—and 47 of its previous 48—the defending three-time champions had been ranked No. 1 all season and, in attackman Jeff Cook and midfielder Brendan Schneck, boasted the game's two best players. But it had also been a year of subtle erosion. After temporarily deafening a Syracuse player the year before, the tradition of firing a short-barreled cannon after a Hopkins score at Homewood had been silenced. Graduation had riddled Hopkins's Hall of Fame defense, and sophomore goalie Brian Holman, Ciccarone's second choice after Sears, enrolled there only because his older brother had insisted.

"I never felt comfortable at Johns Hopkins University," Holman said. "I always felt like I was out of place there. I never felt like the coaching staff had a lot of faith in me."

The night before the final, Scroggs cadged a ride from the Lacrosse Foundation's annual reception back to his Princeton hotel in the back of a pickup truck. With him was old teammate and buddy Joe Cowan, still a Hopkins assistant—and the trophy presented to the winners of the national championship. The two mock-tussled—"You want it? I'll take it"—and laughed. The next morning, May 30, the head coaches and officials gathered at Palmer Stadium for the mandatory pregame meeting. As required, Scroggs presented his official roster. But Bob Scott—with Johns Hopkins's official roster—was stuck in traffic. "Does that mean they forfeit?" Scroggs joked. Ciccarone was not amused.

Later, when Hopkins and North Carolina walked out of their locker rooms into the sunshine for the 2 p.m. faceoff, a then-tournament record crowd of 22,100 filled the stands. Scroggs looked across at the milling Hopkins contingent: former colleagues like Cowan, Jerry Schnydman, his favorite assistant Fred Smith, Dennis Townsend, Ciccarone. Scroggs's face was its usual inscrutable mix of beard, squint and tight grin. He got their attention. Up went his middle finger.

Befitting its place in the lacrosse firmament, Hopkins opened with two quick goals and entered the third quarter leading, 8–7; North Carolina was chasing nearly all game. Early on Scroggs scrapped his man-to-man defense and slowed Hopkins with a harassing, gambling zone ride—in basketball terms, a full-court press. Cook nevertheless scored six goals, Sears and Holman played essentially to a draw, and in the end it took some weird mojo to decide the national championship. Twice, at the end of the first and third quarters, the referees disallowed last-second Hopkins goals by ruling that time had expired—calls that, especially at Homewood Field, usually went the other way.

Peter Voelkel scored UNC's third straight goal to finally even the score, 11–11, with 8:21 left to play, and things got stranger still. A minute later, Cook fired a bouncer that clearly seemed to fly past Sears's stick into the upper left corner of the goal. Instead of stopping, though, the ball kept flying beyond the field. The referee waved off that score, too, which seemed logical until the protesting Hopkins players pointed to a hole in the net, and Blue Jay Joe Ciletti shoved his right arm through to demonstrate. Sears said afterward that it felt like a score. Scroggs agrees that it should have been a goal. But the refs had no access to the TV replay: the call stood.

Hopkins sagged, Carolina surged. Backup midfielder Doug Hall streaked in with a breathtaking finish to give the Tar Heels their first lead, and 40 seconds later sophomore attackman Michael Burnett flipped a low, no-look backhand—Haudenosaunee style—to make it 13–11. Ciccarone went haywire. His sideline tirade with 4:19 to play resulted in a one-minute penalty for unsportsmanlike conduct, forcing Hopkins to play down a man at the worst time. Then, with UNC inbounding on the Hopkins end, Ciccarone's decision to pull Holman—leaving the goal wide open—backfired when Carolina easily scored again. Schneck and Cook unleashed two astonishing displays in the final minutes to make it 14–13, but time ran out. The greatest run in Hopkins lacrosse history was over.

Publicly, Ciccarone couldn't have been more gracious. He called Scroggs a "good friend" and a "class person," and refused to criticize the officials for the three disallowed goals. "I personally take the blame for the loss," he said.

"I should never have gotten that penalty. But I guess it took a Hopkins man to come back and beat us."

Behind the locker room door, though, the loss dropped like a bomb. "It was devastating," Holman said:

> *First of all, we're losing to who? Second of all, it's Willie. And Willie's not a blue-blood. Willie's public school, immigrant, mom was Japanese; Willie was the antithesis of a Hopkins guy. He and Chic did not get along, even when he was there. So him leaving—and then beating us? Whoa.*
>
> *Chic couldn't handle it. It was almost an affront to them . . . Not so much Chic, but a lot of our staff guys had this air to them, like, they sort of invented this game. And for them to lose a national championship under the circumstances—getting penalties, and it wasn't pretty, then getting screwed by refs when we're typically the ones getting the ref's calls? It was like the world just shifted around.*

Bitterness over the loss rippled through the Homewood community. Johns Hopkins's dominance had bred a world of enemies, making paranoia an almost logical leap. Ciccarone was convinced that the mutual loathing between him and referee Bob Schlenger factored into the three rescinded goals. And the Ciccarone family was not alone in believing that some had it in for the Blue Jays.

"Nobody wanted Hopkins to win four in a row, and they did everything that they could to have Hopkins not win that game," said Mark Greenberg, nearly 40 years later. Asked who "they" was, Greenberg replied, "The lacrosse community as a whole. As Hopkins players, we were always sitting on the pedestal. We were everybody's biggest game; it was the defining moment of their season. So I'm talking about *everybody* but Hopkins. But I understand it. Maybe it was better for the game that way."

But more than Hopkins losing, it was the Tar Heels' win that lacrosse minds took delight in. Cornell's run in the late 1970s signified a challenge to the old guard, but the New York Ivy League school expanded the game's reach within domains already occupied. Scroggs's work in North Carolina proved that lacrosse could root and thrive in hostile terrain—basketball-mad North Carolina, and at a public land-grant university, no less. "The same old teams were winning all the national championships. The game was too small, too close, too inbred," Baltimore's *Evening Sun* columnist Bill Tanton, a former Hopkins attackman, wrote a week later. "Lacrosse is spreading. Finally. Hallelujah!"

ANY DOUBT ABOUT that ended the next year. North Carolina again went undefeated, edging Johns Hopkins in overtime during the 1982 regular season at Homewood, and put on a defensive clinic in the NCAA final in Charlottesville, Virginia, to again beat Ciccarone, Holman and the Blue Jays, 7–5, for its second straight national championship. This time there was no conspiracy talk: UNC was just better. It would take a decade for the sport to take root in high schools in Durham, Charlotte and Raleigh, but Scroggs kept blazing the trail, pushing his record against his alma mater to 4–0 with another overtime win during the 1983 regular season, then running into the NCAA semifinals for another meeting with Johns Hopkins.

For that one day, the world seemingly shifted back on its axis. Ciccarone's Blue Jays beat North Carolina 12–9, setting the stage for an expected and restorative championship win over Syracuse. The Orangemen had only defeated Johns Hopkins once before, in 1922, then spent the next 50 years stewing over the Blue Jays' superiority complex. In 1957 Roy Simmons Sr.'s best team, led by Jim Brown, Oren Lyons and Roy Simmons Jr., went 10–0, only to have the USILA's committee vote the 8–0–1 Blue Jays national champions; by the time Simmons Jr. took over for his dad in 1971, Johns Hopkins didn't even bother with Syracuse anymore. When he asked head coach Bob Scott if he could bring his team to Baltimore for a mere scrimmage, Scott demurred. His team, he said, would get more out of playing against themselves.

"That sat with me," Simmons Jr. said. "Man, I'll never forget that."

Scott wasn't wrong. Syracuse wasn't very good in 1971, and would not appear in the NCAA tournament for another eight years; in their return clash in the 1980 semifinals, Ciccarone's Blue Jays romped to an 18–11 win. But Scroggs had proved that anything was possible, and by 1983 Simmons Jr. had assembled an offense so frenetic it made the Tar Heels look slow. And once Syracuse handily disposed of Maryland in the other semifinal, Simmons Jr. made clear that he wasn't anything like quiet Willie Scroggs.

At the time, tradition called for both teams and staffs to gather for a friendly banquet on the eve of the NCAA final—a usually tame affair marked by bland food and even blander speeches by the coaches. But on this night, in a room near the Rutgers campus, Ciccarone said a few clipped words before Hopkins players met with what one called "a completely different animal." Though the son of a coach and a Syracuse captain himself, Simmons Jr. hardly smacked of the breed populating lacrosse—or any other sport. After his dream of becoming a veterinarian ended up a degree in fine arts, he became an accomplished sculptor of found objects and liked to describe his teams as "collages" with "a physical jell not unlike the visual jell in my art." He spoke in a meandering and soft-toned flow so offbeat that it was hard to know if he was being playful, serious or insulting.

For the Blue Jays, it was the latter. Simmons Jr. stood and began by saying how thrilled and grateful he was to finally be able to play "*John* Hopkins," and—just in case anyone missed it—made a point of sarcastically repeating the error more than once. "That's a real no-no. You never call them 'John' Hopkins: it's 'Johns' with an S," Simmons Jr. said. "That's like calling someone 'Hey boy,' you know? And, really, I saw a grimace from Chic particularly, like he was ready to get up and swing. He was a very temperamental and high-strung guy."

Simmons Jr. then punctuated his ramble with a painterly prediction that, the next day, the sky that dawned "Blue Jay blue" would end in an Orange sunset. His players gasped. And once they realized that he was predicting a win, the Hopkins contingent was furious. "I can't remember word for word what he said the night before the game," recalled one of the Blue Jays stars. "But we were all like, 'We're going to kick their ass.'"

Backstopped by Holman's stiff goaltending, the Blue Jays smothered Syracuse's attack and led 8–4 at the half. Instead of letting his players cool down in the locker room, Simmons marched them over to the scoreboard so they could stare at it under the blazing May sun. That seemingly backfired; halfway through the third quarter Hopkins led 12–5. Everyone thought it was over, until Holman saw second-string defenseman Steve Dubin celebrate on-field by tossing his stick in the air. *Uh-oh*, the goalie thought.

He still wasn't ready for what happened next. Longpole defensemen at midfield—especially those who haven't scored all year—are supposed to unload the ball quickly. Instead Syracuse co-captain Darren Lawlor bolted for the goal, froze the stunned Hopkins defense with a pass-fake and flipped a bouncer through Holman's legs. Then Mike Powers—a transfer from Hopkins—scored. The Blue Jays' response widened the lead to 13–7, a twig snap that triggered the avalanche: Over the next eight minutes, Syracuse scored eight unanswered goals. Hopkins then scraped together two to tie the score at 15–15, but its confidence and aura were gone. With two minutes to play, Ciccarone's son, All-American midfielder Henry Ciccarone Jr., lost his shoe in a scramble along the sideline; he and the rest of the Hopkins midfield stopped in expectation of a whistle. None came. Syracuse attackman Brad Kotz glanced around, took a pass and glided unchallenged through the disorganized defense to score his fifth goal and seize the lead for good. Chic Sr. raged at the ruins. In the greatest comeback in the history of the NCAA championship, Syracuse won its first, 17–16.

Afterward, Simmons Jr. was down on the steamy Rutgers field exulting when Bob Scott, Hopkins athletic director, approached to offer congratulations. "I think you're good enough now," Scott said with a smile. "I guess we'd better start playing one another again, shouldn't we?"

In the 40 years since, Hopkins and Syracuse have met every year but one. That was hardly the only change triggered by the upset. The following October Henry Ciccarone Sr., whose sideline demeanor had grown increasingly combustible (he would die of a heart attack, at 50, in 1988), resigned as head coach to run a beer distributorship. Scott had a successor in place. Sensing that North Carolina's back-to-back titles were as much a commentary on his program as theirs, he had already lured Scroggs's offensive coordinator, Blue Jays alum Don Zimmerman, back to Homewood the year before. Zimmerman became head coach.

At the time, the revamp seemingly revived Hopkins's primacy. Fortified by the wondrous netminding of Holman's replacement, Larry Quinn, the Blue Jays went unbeaten in 1984 and avenged themselves upon Syracuse in both the 1984 and 1985 NCAA title games. They lost to Scroggs and UNC in the 1986 semifinal, but then rode goalkeeper Quint Kessenich's heroics to beat Cornell for their 42nd national championship in 1987. Still, the opponents revealed this Blue Jay era as more a last gasp than counterrevolution; the durability of the Big Red, Tar Heel and Orange challenges spoke to the permanence of lacrosse's spread. Hopkins wouldn't win another national title for 18 years—its longest-ever drought—and only two over the next 37 years.

Yet the name still held enormous sway, especially for—of all people—Willie Scroggs. To most, he was the man who had broken lacrosse's boundaries, taken down the sport's giant. "Hopkins was the mecca," said UNC alum—and Baltimore native—Peter Voelkel. "They were the best. It was great satisfaction to know that we didn't go the traditional route. We took our risk, and we beat 'em. And I really do believe that was the start of the growth outside the traditional Virginia, Cornell, Maryland, Hopkins. Who even thought about North Carolina in lacrosse? Our success propelled the game to grow its footprint. Willie is the architect."

"It never seemed to leave Maryland," said Roy Simmons Jr. of the game then. "It never went west, until Willie went down to Carolina and started it there, then it spread and now, my God, it's coast to coast and north to south and Canada."

But at his core, Scroggs remained the kid from a broken home in Waverly who sat in the stands at Homewood Field when Jim Brown unleashed his legendary performance in the 1957 North-South game, the kid who grew up to win five national titles with his hometown school. When Ciccarone retired in 1983, Scroggs couldn't understand why Johns Hopkins never contacted him about the position. It stunned him to later hear that Bob Scott—for the second time in Scroggs's career—was telling people that he had turned down the job. When his mother asked why, Scroggs replied with the only logical conclusion: "They didn't want me, Mom."

Of course, his uneasy relationship with Ciccarone guaranteed that Scroggs had someone in-house who was cool to his candidacy. But by leaving Hopkins and then becoming so dramatically successful against Hopkins, Holman believes, Scroggs had also crossed an unwritten line in the Hopkins ethos. The illogic is overwhelming, and many Hopkins folk scoff at the idea. After all, no one at the school thought Zimmerman a traitor for working as Scroggs's top UNC assistant. Scroggs himself found the notion silly, on its face, even as he recounted his other Hopkins snubs.

The last came in 1994, when Scott announced his retirement as athletic director. At the time Scroggs was no longer coaching and had been working as an assistant AD in Chapel Hill for 14 years. He didn't wait for a call. This time he applied for Scott's job, and received only an impersonal card in response. An interview was eventually set up. His daughter was enrolled at Hopkins then. But Scroggs felt like an afterthought during the day he spent on campus, starting when his first interviewer showed up a half hour late. A few days later, he received a call telling him that Hopkins had hired his friend, Tom Calder. A few years later, Joe Cowan asked Scroggs why he didn't want the AD job. Scott, Cowan said, had told him that. And Scroggs again found himself mystified.

Looking back at the age of 74, in 2021, Scroggs shrugged and said that everything worked out for the best. His close friends from Hopkins remain close. The move to North Carolina placed him in an office next to his future wife—10-time national champion field hockey coach Karen Shelton, and mother of their son, Will—and enabled Scroggs to carve out a unique place in lacrosse. He called himself lucky. In so many ways, Hopkins made everything possible.

And on his end, at least, he figured out one small, clean way to keep his dignity and show his love.

"I'm proud that I was a football guy there," Scroggs said. "When I give money back to Hopkins, what little money I give them, I always designate it for the football program."

WHEN SYRACUSE ARRIVED as the game's upstart power in 1983, the effect was akin to the moment, in an Olympic relay, after the baton was handed to Usain Bolt. North Carolina had been fast. The Orangemen cranked the pace to unprecedented levels. "It was like they dropped 'em out of the sky," Holman said. "We had never seen lacrosse like this."

Until then, American collegiate play was mostly a precise, coach-dictated affair: a half-field game consisting of careful probes for weakness—sometimes for minutes-long stretches—in search of the highest-percentage shot. Errors were sins, turnovers death. Simmons Jr.'s teams, by contrast, were invariably described as free-flowing, run-and-gun, loose and flat-out fun. This was by design, fueled by a bit of desperation: Syracuse's coach felt he had no other choice.

After Simmons Jr. took over for his father in 1971, the Syracuse program was underfunded, had no scholarships and was chronically ignored by the lacrosse prospects in Baltimore. He spent the decade recruiting castoffs from other programs and local high schools like West Genesee and LaFayette. And over time he enticed, and kept, his players by liberating them and made his hands-off approach common knowledge. "The only coach who thinks X's and O's are hugs and kisses," Simmons Jr. described himself. Which, of course, was its own kind of genius.

Though it seemed an amplification of North Carolina's strategy, Simmons Jr.'s approach reached further back. Unlike Scroggs, whose idea of playing "like the Indians" was based on hearsay, Simmons Jr. had played with Native Americans at Syracuse and after, absorbed their game's brutal flow and freedom in the Onondaga box. He was close to Oren Lyons, knew of the Medicine Game. And he had actual Haudenosaunee players like Greg Tarbell and goalie Travis Solomon and midfielder Mark Burnam pushing to keep their style alive. "It's 40 seconds: get the ball, you got to get a shot off," said Burnam, the 2018 Iroquois Nationals head coach. "That's how we play. That's how we've always played. Sometimes, to a fault, we're not patient enough, but that's exactly how Syracuse started playing."

It wasn't all hugs. Simmons Jr. had top assistant John Desko, trained in West Genesee's methodical system, to work up actual X's and O's. He demanded his teams be in top physical shape to endure the high pace, and justified the mission mathematically: Unleash 60 shots a game and you're bound to score 20. But the freedom to freelance and fling behind-the-back passes inspired improvisations the game's old guard couldn't abide. "It caught everybody completely off-guard," said Roy Simmons III, who played and coached for his father. "They were flabbergasted by the fact that we didn't care about turnovers; we didn't worry about anything. Sometimes even three defensemen were running down the field leading the fastbreak and leaving middies behind. Just: Go. Go. Go."

Though the results were undeniable, so undisciplined a stampede offended the Johns Hopkins sensibility. Bill Tierney's first task as a Blue Jays assistant in the spring of 1984 was a scouting report. "So," came the first question from the staff. "Is Syracuse still playing 'spaghetti'?" Larry Quinn's Hall of Fame goaltending talent ensured it didn't much matter; Hopkins beat the Orangemen 13–10 for the 1984 national championship and kept them corralled the next few years. But once British Columbia's Gary Gait, often described as the greatest player of all, arrived with his twin brother, Paul, in 1987, Syracuse became unstoppable—and anything seemed possible.

The next year, Gait invented his historic leaping score—the soon-outlawed "Air Gait"—from behind the goal, cementing the Carrier Dome's brand as the mecca of lax creativity. By 1995 Simmons Jr. had racked up five more national titles, upstate New York was established as a prep hothouse, and the coach's open-range style had become industry standard. When Dom Starsia, whose early Virginia offenses were hardly high-octane, retooled and trampled Syracuse, 15–7, that year, Simmons Jr. took it as a compliment. "Roy," Starsia said afterward, "I finally beat you at *your* game."

In the process, though, the sport that forever held itself apart as a fount of amateur purity found itself stepping, thigh deep, into the muck of big-time collegiate sports. First, during the 1992 season, Syracuse lost three scholarships after an NCAA investigation found the program had given out "excessive" financial aid from 1988 to 1991. Then, just before departing for the trip to College Park, Maryland, where Syracuse would beat North Carolina 13–12 (on, yes, a fast-break goal with eight seconds to play) for the 1993 national championship, Simmons Jr. learned that his 1990 Orangemen—undefeated, six first-team All-Americans, one of the greatest teams of all time—would be stripped of their national title for breaking NCAA rules. The organization found that Simmons Jr. had personally loaned one player $40; that Desko had guided him into a class guaranteeing an A; and that Simmons Jr.'s wife, Nancy, had cosigned a car loan for Paul Gait's wife, Katherine.

Then and now, Simmons deemed the initial investigative reporting by a Syracuse newspaper a hatchet job, the infractions minor and the NCAA "evil." The NCAA punishment hadn't been announced when Syracuse won Simmons Jr. his fifth title, but he already knew the NCAA would be demanding the 1990 trophy back. Standing on the field of Byrd Stadium in College Park, elated and bitter, he accepted the 1993 trophy from an NCAA representative and asked whether it came with postage stamps—in case he needed to return that one, too.

In truth, Simmons Jr. declared that he would never return the 1990 national championship trophy. It soon disappeared from its display case in the Ernie Davis room at the Carrier Dome. The NCAA demand for its return remains active, and the organization continues to regard Syracuse's 1990 championship as illegitimate. The trophy's location is a mystery. Rumors have it buried with Simmons Jr.'s father, or his late wife. He denies both. He denies any knowledge of its theft, and does not care that few believe him.

"Well, the Friends of Syracuse Lacrosse are guilty of taking it," Simmons Jr. said. "I don't know how they got it, and I don't know where it is. And that's my answer to the NCAA."

LARS TIFFANY CAME of age during Syracuse's big bang. He road-tripped as a high school freshman with Travis Solomon's family to the 1983 NCAA final at Rutgers Stadium and thrilled to the Orangemen's colossal come-

Engraving of a match between the Iroquois and Canada in 1876.
Penta Springs Limited / Alamy Stock Photo

Future NFL Hall of Famer Jim Brown,
who excelled at four sports at Syracuse
in the late 1950s, is still regarded as one
of lacrosse's all-time greatest players.
Courtesy of Syracuse Athletics

Johns Hopkins head coach Bob
Scott, winner of seven national
championships, during his inaugural
season, Baltimore, 1955. *Courtesy of
Johns Hopkins Athletics*

Iroquois Nationals defenseman, and future Tadadaho, Sidney Hill (13) and Nationals co-founder Oren Lyons (far right) at the Jim Thorpe Memorial Pow-Wow and Native Games, Los Angeles, 1984. *Courtesy of Upstate Lacrosse Foundation*

Rex Lyons, former all-time scoring leader of the Iroquois Nationals, and father Oren Lyons, Onondaga faithkeeper, Indigenous activist, and Nationals co-founder, Baltimore, 1998.

University of Virginia head coach Lars Tiffany, Oren Lyons, and the Onondaga-Tiffany Buffalo Treaty, Syracuse, New York, 2024. *Courtesy of Lisa Moore, Onondaga Historical Society*

2005 Tewaaraton Award winner Kyle Harrison with father Miles Harrison, Jr., mother Wanda, and sister Kia, Washington D.C., 2005. *Courtesy of Johns Hopkins Athletics*

Kyle Harrison, after Johns Hopkins beat Duke, 9-8, to snap an 18-year national title drought, Philadelphia, 2005. *Courtesy of Johns Hopkins Athletics*

Teammates Paul Rabil and Kyle Harrison celebrating Johns Hopkins' 43rd national championship, Philadelphia, 2005. *Courtesy of Johns Hopkins Athletics*

Northwestern head coach Kelly Amonte Hiller, program pioneer and winner of lacrosse's first Division I championship outside the Eastern Time Zone. *Courtesy of Northwestern Athletics*

Northwestern great Selena Lasota, who, in 2021, left Team Canada to play for the Haudenosaunee Nationals. *Courtesy of Northwestern Athletics*

Northwestern head coach Kelly Amonte Hiller celebrates with her team after breaking an 11-year title drought to win her eighth NCAA championship, Cary, North Carolina, 2023. *Courtesy of Northwestern Athletics*

Former Princeton and University of Denver head coach Bill Tierney, winner of seven NCAA championships, including the first by a school west of the Mississippi River. *Courtesy of Denver Athletics*

Haudenosaunee Nationals head coach Lars Tiffany and Nationals co-founder Oren Lyons at the 2023 Men's World Field Lacrosse Championship, San Diego, 2023. *Courtesy of Ahmed Gaber*

Duke and two-time Team USA head coach John Danowski, after Duke's overtime win over Penn State in the NCAA tournament semi-final, Philadelphia, 2023. *Nat LeDonne, Duke Athletics*

Roy Simmons, Sr. (1931–1970) and Roy Simmons, Jr. (1971–1998) created perhaps the greatest father/son coaching tandem in lacrosse history, combining to win 543 games for Syracuse. Roy Jr. expanded the family legacy by winning six NCAA championships. *Courtesy of Syracuse Athletics*

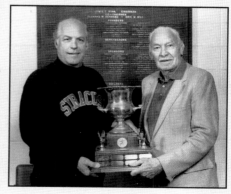

Lyle Thompson with mother Dee Thompson, San Diego, 2023. *Courtesy of Ahmed Gaber*

Haudenosaunee Nationals attackman Lyle Thompson, two-time Tewaaraton Award winner, San Diego, 2023. *Courtesy of Ahmed Gaber*

Haudenosaunee Nationals head coach Lars Tiffany and midfielder Jeremy Thompson, World Championship faceoff drill, San Diego, 2023. *Courtesy of Ahmed Gaber*

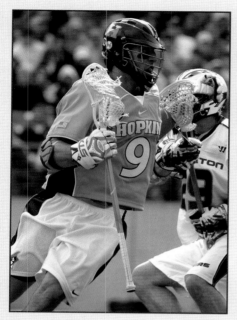

Duke defenseman Casey Carroll, 29, during win over Syracuse in his return season after serving in the Army Rangers, Durham, North Carolina, 2014. *John Williams, Duke Athletics*

Paul Rabil, all-time Johns Hopkins great and future co-founder, in 2018, of the professional field Premier Lacrosse League. *Courtesy of Johns Hopkins Athletics*

Duke and Team USA attackman Brennan O'Neill, during Duke's NCAA tournament quarterfinal win over Michigan in which he tallied six goals and one assist, Albany, New York, 2023. *Nat LeDonne, Duke Athletics*

The first Black All-American at Syracuse since Jim Brown, in the 21st century midfielder Jovan Miller was part of a prominent wave of African-Americans in the college game that included Brown's Chazz Woodson, Army's John Walker, and Virginia's Shamel and Rhamel Bratton. *Courtesy of Syracuse Athletics*

Haudenosaunee attackman Austin Staats, who led all scorers at the 2023 World Lacrosse Championship, San Diego, 2023. *Courtesy of Ahmed Gaber*

Haudenosaunee Nationals midfielder and captain Jeremy Thompson, pregame meeting with Team USA at the 2023 World Lacrosse Championship, San Diego, 2023. *Courtesy of Ahmed Gaber*

Here completing his legendary—and later NCAA-banned—"Air Gait" shot, Syracuse superstar Gary Gait tops many lists as the game's all-time greatest player. He later became a coaching force in the women's game at his alma mater and then, in 2021, became head coach of Syracuse's men's team. *Courtesy of Syracuse Athletics*

back over Hopkins. Thus affirmed, Tiffany and his white and Onondaga teammates at nearby LaFayette High played as if wired: every third pass dropped, every chance to shoot taken. Shots flew like Iowa hail. Then Tiffany went off to Brown and Syracuse kept winning and he plugged in with post college stints with Onondaga A.C. and the Iroquois Nationals, all the time certain: Freewheeling, remorseless lacrosse—Haudenosaunee, Roy Simmons Jr. lacrosse—was the ideal.

But Newton's Third Law has few better showcases than sports, and Syracuse's action soon had its equal and opposite reaction. In 1987, Hopkins assistant Bill Tierney left Baltimore to take over as head coach at Princeton. The program was a relic: Its last national championship came in 1953; it had never appeared in the NCAA tournament; it had won only three games in two years. Tierney won two games his first season, six his second. While telling his players they could win national titles, he knew he'd go nowhere trying to replicate his Hopkins defenses with second-rate talent, no matter how brainy.

Though zone schemes were often used situationally, most recently by Willie Scroggs, man-to-man had forever been the sport's basic defensive set. Tierney's attempt to merely fake a zone while at Hopkins had gained little traction; when, in 1987, he submitted the four-page plan that later transformed the game to head coach Don Zimmerman, it came back in 30 minutes with the red-inked response: "This Will Never Work." Then again, Hopkins didn't need a radical overhaul; it was still winning big. Princeton, Tierney realized after his first two years there, was a different matter entirely.

In 1990, Tierney scrapped Princeton's man-to-man defense for an intricate, ever-shifting system of slides—essentially, double-teams and switches, abetted by traps—that minimized the Tigers' lack of talent and athleticism, and confused the hell out of opponents. As if taking the reins from soon-to-retire Princeton basketball guru Pete Carril, his offenses bucked prevailing trends and emphasized discipline and precision. In a sense Tierney was taking issue with Simmons Jr.'s base equation: Over time, the team with the fewest turnovers, not the higher amount of shots, would win. Syracuse told lacrosse to go fast. Tierney hit the brakes.

Princeton's 1990 season was bookended by Jekyll-Hyde road games against Johns Hopkins. The Tigers lost their season opener at Homewood Field, 20–8, but gradually settled into Tierney's new system and made the NCAA tournament for the first time. Then they returned to Homewood and shocked the Blue Jays in the first round, 9–8, becoming the third new power in the decade to announce itself by taking down the king. Two years later, Princeton won 13 games and—with offensive sets typically running two to three minutes—methodically ground up Roy Simmons Jr. and Syracuse, 10–9, in double overtime to win the 1992 national championship. Over the next six years the Tigers won four more titles and Tierney's "Princeton defense" spread. New Jersey became lacrosse's new beachhead.

Tiffany, just starting his career as a defensive assistant, was dazzled. When, at a 1997 coaches convention, Tierney finally felt secure enough to reveal his secrets, he scribbled as fast as he could. "Bill was *managing* the game," Tiffany said. "He was the ultimate lacrosse manager—and, I still believe, the greatest lacrosse coach ever in the history of our sport. He understood the rules and within them created a different style. He taught team defense. Instead of it being all about *you have me; don't get beat*, all of a sudden there were slide packages and communication and changing the slide package at the end of the first quarter to throw off the offensive coordinator who thought he was getting into a rhythm. He completely reinvented the way you look at the game. He revolutionized the way the game was coached and played."

Johns Hopkins, meanwhile, was flailing. Tierney's 1990 win at Homewood—only the second time ever that the Blue Jays had exited in the NCAA's first round—ensured the end of Zimmerman's time as head coach. It had been only three years since he'd won his third national title. Hopkins alumni still couldn't see the new era dawning, and the school's lacrosse priority looked far less charming when the titles stopped. Bob Scott offered Tierney the job at $65,000 a year. He had then won just one NCAA tournament game at Princeton, yet in a telling measure of the position's waning appeal, opted to stay put.

"We knew we were going to be pretty good—and we had just *beaten* Hopkins," Tierney said in 2018. "Why would you want to take a job at the place you beat? Well, 44 national championships, the history, all that stuff. But that was it."

Scott instead hired UPenn coach Tony Seaman, Hopkins's first outsider in 43 years. He lasted eight years, never made it past the NCAA semifinals, got fired in 1998. Hopkins again pursued Tierney, but the words of a Princeton dean had lodged in his head—*It will never be your program*—and he again said no. And later, when Johns Hopkins couldn't win big and changed coaches or thought about it and ran at him a third and fourth time, Tierney's conclusion didn't change. He liked building from scratch. Johns Hopkins once might have landed arguably the best coach lacrosse ever produced, but its aura had become too establishment, too massive, too crushing.

"I'm fearful of that," Tierney said. "Maybe I'm just like I was in Levittown, when my buddies could drink 10 beers and I could only drink two— maybe I was a little afraid of that. Maybe I was a little afraid to live up to that Henry Ciccarone, Bob Scott, Don Zimmerman legacy—and it was better for me to do okay on my own. Then I turned into being pretty good."

PART 5

PLAYING AGAINST TYPE

Forever alive, forever forward,
Stately, solemn, sad, withdrawn, baffled, mad, turbulent, feeble, dissatisfied,
Desperate, proud, fond, sick, accepted by men, rejected by men,
They go! they go! I know that they go, but I know not where they go,
But I know that they go toward the best—toward something great.
                    —Walt Whitman, "Song of the Open Road"

I

WE CAN DO IT

A LONG WITH THE men's 2018 Men's World Championship, the Israeli organizers staged all-but-unnoticed tournaments for youth, over-40 and women's club teams. The latter had a midweek game set for noon. Women have contested their own quadrennial world and annual NCAA championships since 1982. It's also true that women's lacrosse—which, more than almost any sport, differs greatly from its male counterpart—has flourished despite spending most of its time overshadowed. When the world thinks about lacrosse, it thinks first of men—Jim Brown or Gary Gait or old paintings of Native braves or laxbros on a tear. Men still draw the biggest crowds and the most attention, and bear the heaviest weight of history. And yet, the impact of women upon the sport has been outsized, dramatic, wholly at odds with their relative obscurity. When it comes to American lacrosse growth in the 21st century, women have done the heavy lifting.

From 1998 to 2018, the number of NCAA women's teams on all levels leapt 151 percent—from 201 to 505—and nearly doubled in Division I from 60 to 115. In the same span, the number of men's teams grew an impressive 104 percent—from 186 to 380 overall—but only expanded in Division I from 51 to 71. (By 2024, the men would add two more Division I programs, and the women 12.) While the men's game looked on jealously, women's varsity programs took root at D-I flagship universities in Sun Belt targets like Florida and Arizona State, and coveted Pacific Coast spots like Stanford, UC Berkeley and the University of Southern California.

"I wish the men's sport the same success as the women's, actually," said former Duke midfielder Josh Offit, whose sister, Mickie, played at Florida. "Men's lacrosse, in the US, is still predominantly a Northeast sport—aspiring to be at the level of women."

In Israel, the women's game was held a few blocks in from the sea, at a small stadium usually occupied by one of Netanya's pro soccer clubs. There was no security, and no spectators. With the coastal breeze cut off by a wall of high-rises, the sideline temperature was suddenly 15 degrees hotter.

The home team, Barak Netanya (the Netanya Lightning, with canary-yellow jerseys accented by cartoon bolts and a small flag of Israel), played L. C. C. Radotin, a top European club from the Czech Republic. Though the locals had three Division I ringers from the US, Radotin dominated from the start—and the difference from the men's game was instantly clear. Play was freer, ever flowing, all passing and breakaway speed. Recent NCAA rule changes had added a 90-second shot clock and ended the infamous "freeze-tag" element (for more than a century, in a strict following of George Beers's written rules, players had to stop cold for every penalty whistle), but checking was still illegal and birdcage helmets non-existent. Instead of scrabbling in the dirt like groundhogs, the women's faceoff—or "draw"—remains a stylish toss-up between two opposing sticks: ball flung high, in John McPhee's indelible phrase, "as if on the jet of a fountain."

Radotin won, 11–5. The women milled through the postgame handshake line then posed for photos in a cheery mix at midfield. Everyone seemed driven, upbeat, self-contained: The celebrated men's championship happening nearby felt momentarily like the afterthought. Even in that empty, dusty stadium, the Girl Power was palpable.

Anyone in women's lacrosse knows they are riding a great wave. While the men's mission depends on selling the culture on lacrosse's coolness, women wield the force of hard numbers and law. In the late 1990s, equal percentages of men and women attended postsecondary institutions. Now nearly 60 percent of all college students are women; women are also more likely than men to graduate, and to earn master's and doctoral degrees. Part of that shift is due to Title IX, the 37-word segment of the 1972 Education Amendments Act that overhauled academia in areas ranging from college admissions to teaching positions to academic majors to the handling of sexual harassment—and, most dramatically, women's sports. According to the 1979 policy interpretation issued by the Department of Health, Education and

Welfare, Title IX required that any institution receiving federal funding provide "equal opportunities in athletic programs," and apply the "equal" to scholarships, tutoring, training facilities, staffing and publicity. "The governing principle," it stated, "is that male and female athletes should receive equivalent treatment, benefits, and opportunities."

Once the effort to exempt college football—with its massive budgets and rosters—and high-revenue sports like men's basketball from Title IX failed in 1978, the need to "level the playing field" by expanding women's sports became a fact of academic life. In 1972, some 300,000 American women played high school and college athletics; today, the total tops 3 million. The sports with the highest participation then were track and field, basketball and volleyball—and remain so today. But Title IX's galvanizing effect was seen most clearly in soccer. From 1981, the first year the NCAA offered championships at all three levels, to 2023, women's soccer grew *1,515 percent*—from 1,855 players on 80 teams to 29,959 players on 1,035 teams. Only outdoor track has more college participants.

If only because of saturation, soccer's growth rate slowed by the turn of the century. Title IX's second wave lifted up women's lacrosse. With rosters averaging around 24 players, in 1997, for the first time, there were more Division I women's teams than men's. Over the next two decades, the gap would only grow—20 . . . 31 . . . 44—and spawn not a little bitterness. Because even as Title IX made the women's game irresistible, it rendered Division I men's lacrosse (and its average 40-player rosters) vulnerable. When administrators began slashing marginal programs for men, like wrestling, to adhere to the new guidelines, men's lax teams found themselves endangered, even dropped. Athletic directors passed on adding the male version of America's hottest sport: The numbers didn't work. At lacrosse's showcase level, men's growth slowed to a comparative crawl. Title IX had supercharged women's lacrosse, but handicapped the men.

"We're stalled," said former Georgetown assistant Howard Offit, a three-time national champion at Johns Hopkins and advisor for Team Israel, in 2018. "We just added Cleveland State and Utah, but it's very slow. NC State should have a team. Why doesn't any SEC school have lacrosse? How about Stanford?"

The Barak Netanya team exemplified the contrast. Its coach, Janna Kaufman, grew up in Atlanta and played three years for Division III Goucher College, and was readying to take over as Israel's head women's coach. Attacker

MacEllen McDonough was introduced to the game from a Hopkins alum in California, became a star in Colorado Springs for Air Academy High and—after considering the D-I programs at UC Davis, Fresno State and Colorado—joined Jacksonville University's four-year-old team in 2014. Following the path laid by many of Israel's American transplants, McDonough combined her 2018 birthright trip with an internship at the men's World Championship. She planned to remain, coach kids and play for Israel.

San Diego State defender Julia Masias—half Sephardi Jewish, half Ute—gave up soccer and cross-country to start playing lacrosse as a sophomore at Eastlake High School in Chula Vista, California. Within months, she became adept enough to start for the varsity, and so taken with the sport that she started, with her brother, a relatively low-cost ($425 per season) club team to introduce local minority kids to the game. She had no thought of playing college ball. But she kept practicing and emailing Aztecs head coach Kylee White, who had taken the program into Division I only four years earlier. After Macias enrolled in 2016, White invited her to try out. She was the only walk-on to make it. White even gave her some money.

She, too, first came to Israel on a birthright trip, and had just signed up to coach Israel's U-19 team. Like every young female player and coach in lacrosse, these women were the children of possibility. Title IX put sticks in their hands. But their expectation that the game could thrive in far-flung California, Colorado and Georgia, Israel and the Czech Republic, owes everything to the example and standards of perhaps the greatest builder—male or female—in lacrosse history. That woman's nickname is "Killer."

LACROSSE FIRST CAME to white women in America the way it came to white men: via historical bankshot. Both versions began with the Haudenosaunee along both sides of the US-Canada border, the scattering of the Six Nations and George Beers's vision of a model Canadian pastime. But unlike the men's game, which then migrated south with job-seeking Canadians, the women's version crossed oceans. The 1876 Windsor Castle exhibition between Caughnawaga natives and Montrealers, where Queen Victoria declared herself amused, sparked interest in Great Britain, and the teams' 62-game tour across the Isles in 1883 proved galvanizing. After attending what she described as a "wonderful game, beautiful and graceful," Louisa Lumsden, a former headmistress at Saint Leonards School for Girls in St. Andrews, Scotland, suggested it to her successor. In the spring of 1890, the first matches between the school's boarding houses—and, seemingly, women anywhere—were played.

"Whether the game on the whole has proved successful may be doubted but at least we have advanced so far in its mysteries as to get a good and exciting game in the field with teams of eight and they lasted one hour not including a ten minute interval in the middle, after which goals were changed," reported the June 1890 issue of the *St Leonards Gazette*. "The game was close and fast but the play rather wild and far too much on the ground."

Even in its first incarnation, the women's game differed from the men's: played in dresses, with no physical contact and no hard boundaries, closer in spirit to badminton than to anything dreamed by the Caughnawaga. It soon spread to other British private schools. Clubs formed in London. American graduates steamed home to New England and the Mid-Atlantic region to teach physical education: In 1926 Rosabelle Sinclair introduced women's lacrosse to the Bryn Mawr School in Baltimore—and to the United States. Seven decades later, she became the first woman inducted into the Lacrosse Hall of Fame.

In 1941, the first intercollegiate women's lacrosse game in America was reportedly played between Sweet Briar and the College of William and Mary. As a measure of how seriously the sport was taken, neither the local newspapers nor the colleges posted any accounts; the final score is unknown. Even more than the men's version, the female version of lacrosse had cycled back to North America as a near-unrecognizable cousin of the Haudenosaunee pastime, another vehicle for a white upper class that still took cues from the British. Like all women's athletics in the mid-20th century, it was considered a novelty, wholly distinct from its male counterpart, with a constant chauvinistic reassurance of its "feminine" features.

The dismissal of women's lacrosse as little more than a helpmate received its most patronizing portrayal in the April 23, 1962, issue of *Sports Illustrated*. For many in mainstream America, this served as an introduction: The cover—for the only time in the magazine's 70-year history—featured a lacrosse player, Johns Hopkins attackman Jerry Schmidt, under the headline "The Tough Game." The story contained an authoritative primer on lacrosse's Native origins and rules, elementary descriptions of play and avowal of Hopkins's place atop the elite universe of collegiate men. Then, near the end, it pivoted:

> *Lacrosse is a game for girls, too. . . . The girls' game prohibits contact, which enables them to forgo the armorplate and appear fetching, except for the goalie, who is uniformed like Yogi Berra.*
>
> *Molly Schmidt, a pretty blonde Baltimore debutante who married Jerry Schmidt, played girls' lacrosse but found it boring and much prefers watching her husband's team in action. Raised in a lacrosse tradition, she comes from a large family of lacrosse players and devotees. Her uncle, Howard Myers, is the head coach at Hofstra.*
>
> *The Schmidts occupy the third floor of her family's home in fashionable Guilford. There is always a family turnout for Jerry's games; Molly has missed only one—a football game last fall, the day she had Ann Austin, their 5½-month-old daughter. Hopkins teammate Bobby Mayne's wife isn't allowed at the games because he says she makes him nervous. But Molly Schmidt sits near the Hopkins bench and cheers mightily. She has had dreams of Jerry winning the scoring championship.*

The dawn of Title IX a decade later provided the chance for Johns Hopkins to replicate its rule at the highest level of women's lacrosse. It didn't happen. In 1976 the Blue Jays women began a 23-year run as a successful—at least, by any other school's standards—Division III program, reaching five Final Fours but winning no national titles. Meanwhile, women's Division I emerged as a more porous ecosystem than its male counterpart, dominated early by public universities like Maryland and Penn State, enabling quick climbs by upstarts like Delaware, Massachusetts and New Hampshire. It also felt more daring: In 1974 Tina Sloan Green, the first Black woman to play for US national teams in both field hockey and lacrosse, was named head coach at Temple, the public university in inner-city Philadelphia.

Sloan Green's tenure spoke less to the sport's enlightenment than to her own drive and ability, and to Temple's rare institutional commitment to the advancement of Black coaches. Quietly, she set the school's standard. While also coaching field hockey and badminton, her overwhelmingly white lacrosse rosters—led by scoring machines Marie Schmucker and Gail Cummings—went on to reach 10 straight Final Fours and win three Division I national championships in the 1980s—207 games overall—before Sloan

Green retired in 1992. No Black lacrosse coach, male or female, has matched her achievements since.

"It's a disappointment," Sloan Green observed three decades later. "The bottom line is, you can't change the color of your skin. It's a visual thing. So until we deal with the fact that color makes a difference—and has made a difference, past and present—there's not going to be any change. You say [many people] haven't heard about [my record]: Why? Because I'm Black. If I had been a white coach and did all this, it'd have been out there, right? And being Black—and a female, too? I don't know. I have hope for the future, because hopefully the academic piece and the social piece will all come into play and bring about real change."

Temple faded as a lacrosse power by the turn of the 20th century—and has since never made it past the first round of the NCAA tournament. Under head coach Janine Tucker, the Hopkins women finally moved up to Division I in 1999, but administrators and alums seemed content with rarely advancing past the NCAA tournament's first round—and never reaching the Final Four. Tucker, unlike any male lacrosse coach at Hopkins no matter his success, held on to her job for 29 years. Disinterest in replicating the mens' stature made it easier for locals, even Baltimore's premier lacrosse family, to shrug off Home-wood's gravitational pull. All eight Stanwick children grew up to play Division I lacrosse; two of the four brothers—but none of the sisters—attended Hopkins. In 1997, Sheehan, the oldest, set the tone by opting for Georgetown. Wick and Coco followed her there, and Covie Stanwick attended Boston College.

Now an ESPN lacrosse analyst, Sheehan said that what attracted her most to the Washington, DC, school was the chance "to be part of building something." The Hopkins women would always be overshadowed in a city and tradition dominated by Hopkins men. "Baltimore is still a hot spot," she said in 2020. "But some kids really want to go away. When USC started a team, they got a lot of Baltimore girls."

Sheehan became Georgetown's all-time leading scorer, the catalyst of its rise. She ended her career by losing in the 2001 NCAA final, by one goal in triple overtime, to Maryland. It was the Terrapins' seventh straight national championship. By then, Maryland's women were well on their way to becoming the equivalent of the Hopkins men—the sport's dominant power, its standard of excellence. Head coach Cindy Timchal would go on to become the winningest women's coach in Division I history and launch the varsity program at Navy, but her most striking coup came in 1994, when she convinced superstar Gary Gait to sign on as assistant coach at Maryland. There simply was no precedent, in any American male sport, for its greatest player to work for and coach women.

"I was pretty skeptical," said Kelly Amonte Hiller of seeing Gait for the first time her sophomore year. "Like: Why does this guy want to work with us? Is this a joke?"

Timchal wasn't trying to make a splash. And anyone figuring that Gait was just marking time before a men's job opened (he ended up assisting for seven seasons, spent the next 14 years as head coach of the Syracuse women's team, then succeeded John Desko as Syracuse head men's coach in 2021) found themselves impressed. Until then, Amonte Hiller had divided her time at Maryland equally between soccer and lacrosse. Gait's tutelage made her a lacrosse player first.

"Once Gary started coaching, it was over," she said. "Whether it was the women's stick, how to string it, how to shoot, how to fake, how to play with your teammates, he was *always* innovating. I just became another level of passion."

KELLY AMONTE'S DRIVE made her easy to teach. Her grandfather, Rocco, immigrated from Italy and worked the coal mines of western Pennsylvania. Her father, Lewis, worked construction in Hingham, Massachusetts, until a massive heart attack in his 30s forced him to retire. The family survived on disability payments, Lewis's shifts at a local ice rink, wife Kathy's babysitting fees. The four Amonte kids were remarkable athletes, but needed full scholarships for every club team and school. Kelly's older brother Tony went on to star for the Chicago Blackhawks. Midway through her time at Thayer Academy—a high-end, Boston-area private school—he signed his first NHL contract, and Thayer administrators tried to withdraw her aid.

Raised in the shadow of Title IX, Kelly grew up playing ice hockey, basketball and soccer, intent—like so many girls—on being the next Michelle Akers. Lacrosse started her freshman year at Thayer, where she ran circles around her coach, a member of the US national team, and earned the nickname "the Kneebreaker." Come summer, she worked at a day camp and nights waitressing at Jake's Seafood in Hull. By then the college soccer boom had hardened recruiting, and made increasingly expensive clubs and camps a prerequisite for exposure. Just being a high school All-American didn't cut it anymore.

"My parents couldn't afford it, so I never played high-level soccer," Amonte Hiller said. "I never got recruited because I wasn't at the club tournaments." She did attend one US Lacrosse event—for individuals, not teams—only because it was held in nearby Connecticut, and became one of the top recruits in the nation. After she committed to Maryland, the soccer coach invited her to walk-on. Amonte started out as a reserve forward, then set Maryland's single-season scoring record as a freshman and was named All-American. The following spring, she racked up the first of four All-American lacrosse campaigns. Opponents took in her merciless sharpshooting and blank expression and called her "Killer"—but never to her face. Junior and senior year, Amonte led Maryland to the 1995 and 1996 NCAA titles and was named back-to-back national Player of the Year.

Still, she had never wanted to leave home. Fiercely close to her family, after graduation Amonte headed back to New England. She bounced between assistant coaching gigs at Brown, the University of Massachusetts and Boston University, camps and lessons, thought about becoming a professional triathlete. She met and married Harvard men's lacrosse assistant coach Scott Hiller, a four-time All-American at UMass and member of the 1994 US team. Settling in Boston was the plan.

Then Amonte Hiller started getting inquiries from Northwestern University about becoming head coach of its reviving program. The Evanston, Illinois, school had tried varsity women's lacrosse in the 1980s. With no scholarships and few home games, even Cindy Timchal couldn't make that work: She left after nine seasons and the team folded in 1992. The new push was a clear Title IX play, with no talk about winning Big Ten titles or national championships. Northwestern's lone NCAA title had come in men's fencing in 1941. They dangled a starting salary of $45,000.

Hiller insisted she fly out for an interview, and she was sold. At 26 Kelly moved west, transitioned the team from club to varsity, experienced a crash course on paperwork, budgets, compliance. The team shared its practice field with the marching band. She recruited for the first time in her life, targeting second-tier talent from Long Island and Massachusetts. Most thought she was calling from Northeastern.

Hiller joined his wife in 2001 and became a volunteer assistant. One afternoon in the fall of 2001, Kelly was at practice when she noticed identical twins dodging with ease through an intramural flag-football game. A week later she saw the same twins, Northwestern sophomores Ashley and Courtney Koester, jogging fast on Sheridan Road. A week after that, when she saw them walking near her office, Amonte Hiller pulled over her car, ran up and said, "Excuse me! Do you know what lacrosse is?"

The Koester twins did not, and had no interest. Courtney had quit basketball after her freshman year; neither wanted to dedicate themselves to varsity sports. But Amonte Hiller emailed a heartfelt missive detailing her philosophy, then gave them sticks to fiddle with over Thanksgiving break. They came back converts. Nineteen women played that first spring, 2002. To make up for the lack of stick skills, Kelly installed an obnoxiously in-your-face pressure defense. During the opener, the twins were still asking if they were allowed to go in the crease (they weren't); Courtney scored three goals in the 15–2 win over Marist. The Wildcats finished the 2002 season with five wins and 10 losses.

Amonte Hiller had told her first recruiting class that they would win a national championship. It sounded daft. The second recruiting class heard the same. "And I'm like, *I believe you*," said Lindsey Munday, a three-sport star out of northern New Jersey. "The biggest reason why is her. All of us were like that: *Tell us anything, and we will do it*." As the talent improved, Amonte Hiller moved the less-skilled twins out of the midfield, made them the spine of her defense. The Wildcats lost to Hopkins but improved to 8–8 in 2003. Few saw them coming: In the run-up to the 2004 season, Northwestern cracked neither the coaches nor the media's preseason Top 20. *Lacrosse Magazine*, the voice of the US game, added three bubble teams and Northwestern wasn't one of those, either.

But after losing early, the Wildcats ripped off 13 straight wins, defeated names like Penn State, Notre Dame and Johns Hopkins, finished 15–3 and reached the 2004 NCAA quarterfinals before falling to Virginia. The sport's radar was, finally, on high alert. Preseason polls for 2005 had Northwestern No. 3; preseason All-American lists featured Munday, midfielder Kristen Kjellman, goalie Ashley Gersuk and the Koester twins. But nobody would believe the Wildcats belonged up there with East Coast royals Virginia, Princeton, Duke and Maryland until they proved it. So they did. Northwestern beat North Carolina and Duke, crushed Hopkins, beat Princeton in the quarterfinals and then traveled to Annapolis and avenged themselves upon Virginia, 13–10, in the 2005 NCAA final to finish 21–0 and become the first lacrosse program—men or women, at any level—from outside the Eastern Time Zone to win a national championship.

Some dismissed that as an aberration. Four straight national titles followed, but an aura of mystery remained. Chicago was alien terrain, and Amonte Hiller's roster was loaded with names from Ohio, New Jersey, Massachusetts. Timchal's titanic roll at Maryland had recharged the Mid-Atlantic region as the sport's hotbed, but Northwestern's upstarts had no part in it. "We were so used to seeing a certain kind of player—girls who I grew up playing with and against," said Virginia midfielder Brittany Kalkstein, an All-American who lost the three games she played against Northwestern from 2007 to 2010. "But Northwestern, I didn't really know any of the players. It was an unknown: a different style of play, a different type of athlete. And sometimes the unknown is intimidating."

With the success of North Carolina coach Anson Dorrance's "competitive cauldron" in the 1980s, women's soccer became the first sport to shed "femininity" and embrace the no-prisoners competitiveness once reserved for men. The rock upon which Dorrance built that philosophy was April Heinrichs, who had been Amonte Hiller's soccer coach at Maryland. Amonte Hiller brought that soccer mentality to lacrosse as a player, then transplanted it as a coach in Evanston. She also took a page from the men's game to install a system of rotating shifts in the midfield, pitting endlessly fresh legs against gassed—and outwitted—opponents.

Soon other teams, including Maryland, started running lines like the men's game. But none was as relentless as Northwestern, nor seemed more delighted to run up the score; the opponents who faced the Wildcats after their three losses from 2006 to 2008 got thrashed by a combined tally of 54–18. Amonte Hiller tapped into a new and edgy vein in the women's game, one the established powers and regions struggled to define. When her players wore flip-flops to the 2005 team's midsummer visit to the White House, observers couldn't decide whether they were being self-confident or irreverent. When, in 2008, Northwestern became the first women's lax program to play in shorts, people wondered whether it was a feminist statement or mere practicality.

To opposing coaches, the symbolism mattered far less than the way Amonte Hiller aggressively stretched rules and tradition and territory. Before her, few women's coaches recruited high school sophomores or offered scholarships to juniors—a practice that helped spur ever-younger recruitments and led the NCAA to impose new age restrictions in 2017. From the start, Amonte Hiller cheekily set up girls' lacrosse camps in Massachusetts and Long Island—opponents' turf—where she met many future Wildcats while they were still in elementary school. Both practices were legal, justified by Amonte Hiller as the best way to build a program from scratch. But that didn't stop Northwestern's nickname, "the Evil Empire," from spreading across lax message boards or characterizations of her as a singularly "polarizing" figure. When *Lacrosse Magazine* named Amonte Hiller its 2008 Person of the Year— normally the occasion for a warm-and-fuzzy portrait—the accompanying piece was headlined "Killer Instinct."

She was the sport's ultimate disrupter, with a success so unexpected and total that it still defies comparison. Howdy Myers and Bill Tierney were already coaching legends when they set out on their pioneering missions to Hofstra and Denver: Their efforts, so far, have yielded one national championship. Timchal crafted the Maryland dynasty, but the program she inherited at 37 had already won a title and been threatening dominance for a decade. Even Willie Scroggs, the template, had the advantage of working at an NCAA power.

Amonte Hiller landed in a sports desert at 26 and had it blossoming by the age of 30. Her first star, Kirsten Kjellman, became the first two-time Tewaaraton Award winner in lacrosse history; her second star, Hannah Nielsen, became the second. Only three goals prevented Amonte Hiller from beating out UCLA coaching icon John Wooden, who won a record seven straight NCAA basketball titles: After Northwestern's consecutive championships streak ended at five in 2010, with a 13–11 loss in the NCAA final to Maryland, Northwestern rebounded with 21 wins and beat Maryland in the 2011 NCAA final. Then Amonte Hiller won her seventh national championship in 2012.

By then, few were questioning her methods, except to ask: How do we replicate them? Coaches and administrators pilgrimaged in to query Kelly and Scott on practice plans, program-building, camps—some of them, even, from the men's game. When Marquette started its Division I team in 2011, new coach Joe Amplo made Evanston one of his first stops. After Maryland tried to lure Amonte Hiller away in 2007, Northwestern locked her up with a raise and five-year contract, and antsy programs looked to the next best option: clones.

In 2010 the University of Massachusetts hired 28-year-old Angela McMahon, Northwestern class of 2004, as head coach. A month later,

Mount St. Mary's announced the hiring of 26-year-old Wildcats assistant Lindsey Munday, class of '06—who lasted three months before bolting for Southern Cal. In 2012 Sarah Albrecht, class of '06; former Northwestern assistant Alicia Walker-Weinstein; and Ann Elliott, class of '07, took charge at New Hampshire, Boston College and Colorado, respectively. Division I schools were snapping up even more Amonte Hiller disciples as assistants. But the most spectacular gauge of how Amonte Hiller rewired the game's sensibility came in July of that year, when Hofstra announced 22-year-old Shannon Smith—fresh off leading Northwestern to its 2012 NCAA title and graduation—as its next head coach. Smith acted like this was perfectly normal. And the lacrosse world barely blinked.

WHEN THE TITLE IX boom hit American lacrosse full force, the effect was giddying. It indeed seemed to help everybody: adding jobs, sparking equipment sales, offering athletic girls a fresh empowerment zone and Black lacrosse a new foothold. While bids to revive Morgan State's defunct men's program went nowhere, in 1998 Howard became the first historically Black university to reincarnate the Ten Bears spirit—as women's varsity. But the boom's core contained a paradox, one that decoupled the women's game from its Native roots. Haudenosaunee women were commanded not to play. The game that had otherwise become a muscular advance for female equality was not, according to lacrosse's originators, a game for females.

This wasn't always the case. Soon after the formation of the Iroquois Nationals in 1983, Carol Patterson, the wife of co-founder Wes Patterson and a pioneer coach of girls' lacrosse in Baltimore County and western New York, pushed for a comparable program that could, eventually, compete in the recently created women's field World Championship. As both the Nationals treasurer and head coach of Canada's first women's field team, Carol Patterson was uniquely connected: In 1984, after an invite from a Canadian tournament, the hurriedly organized, inaugural Iroquois women's team played its first tournament in Montreal. And though Wes Patterson and co-founders Rick Hill and Onondaga faithkeeper Oren Lyons had originally envisioned only a men's team, all three backed the formation of the Iroquois women's program.

But they were not the final authority. Along with its function as a symbol of sovereignty, the men's program had been sanctioned by the Grand Council at Onondaga as a vehicle of conservative Longhouse values—to which women wielding lacrosse sticks were increasingly seen as a threat. In contrast to white norms that historically inveighed against female sports participation, this was not a matter of supposed female fragility. It was about female power. The belief that a woman's touch—especially during her menstrual cycle, or "moon time"—can strip a hickory lacrosse stick of its medicine remains strong to this day, and had long discouraged women's play. The emergence of so-called plastic sticks in the 1970s offered a way around that taboo. When public high schools in New York State began adding girls' teams in the 1980s, Haudenosaunee girls from nearby reservations began signing up.

But none hailed from the traditionalist Onondaga, or the equally conservative Seneca Nation at Tonawanda. Objecting to the fact that many girls played with sacred hickory sticks and risked their important matrilineal roles by exposing their uteruses to injury, these influential blocs barred female play, while seemingly tolerating the new phenomenon elsewhere as a tribal variant—like casinos—within the Six Nations confederacy. The Iroquois Nationals made that position untenable. From the start the program had been a political, cultural and spiritual statement about the Haudenosaunee as a whole, controlled by the Tadadaho and other influential Onondaga chiefs. When, in 1987, the Nationals women's program asked for funding and sanction from the Grand Council, clan mothers representing Onondaga and the Seneca at Tonawanda voiced opposition. When the team planned an exhibition in Syracuse, clan mothers vowed to lie on the field in protest. Clan mothers possess final word in Haudenosaunee matters. The exhibition was canceled. The Nationals women's program disbanded, and remained so for the next 18 years.

"My heart broke into a thousand pieces," said Kari Miller, an original member of the Nationals, 20 years later. "That was my opportunity to go traveling and play the game I loved. We got a taste of it, then it was taken away."

Yet the program's erasure did not end lacrosse for Haudenosaunee women, so much as fracture enforcement along barely visible lines. Location mattered. The Onondaga in New York represented hard-line opposition, but at least one Onondaga chief at Six Nations of the Grand River in Canada adopted a tolerant stance. Pete Sky, a stickmaker and strict Longhouse adherent, didn't object when his wife, Gloria, a Cayuga clan mother, and daughters joined pickup games, nor when his 16-year-old granddaughter, Tia Smith, took part.

Still, before 1995 organized girls' lacrosse in Six Nations was unheard of. When a teenaged Smith first learned that a Seneca cousin from the Cattaraugus reserve near Buffalo played goalie for her high school team, she was astonished. "I just grew up watching the guys play," she said. "I was dumbfounded. I never thought that I could *actually* play."

Fortified with good genes—Smith's other grandfather was Canadian Lacrosse Hall of Famer Roger "Buck" Smith, and her younger brother, Sid Smith, became an All-American defender at Syracuse—Tia embraced the family business. Two years after starting, she made an elite Ontario junior team; in 1999, at 19, she tried out for Team Canada. The first Six Nations winner of the 2002 Miss Indian World beauty pageant, Smith showed up for one New Mexico appearance with a knot on her forehead and a black eye, residue of her defense work for Brock University. Wearing the crown hurt.

Soon after, Smith began a relationship with Iroquois Nationals great Gewas Schindler and became pregnant. Their oldest daughter, Kimaura, was a year old when the movement to revive the Nationals women's program began in 2005. Pressure had been growing on opposed clan mothers from all angles: More Indigenous girls were playing in high school and college; the explosion in NCAA programs had broadened scholarship chances; even conservative parents wanted their daughters to play. In everything but the Medicine Game, non-natural sticks had replaced wood. And the first generation of Haudenosaunee players, once heartbroken, had now raised healthy, lacrosse-minded girls.

In 2005 a new team was organized for the Cup of Nations festival for under-18 girls. Because the initiative had yet to gain tribal approval, it competed under the name "First Nations." In 2006 the traditional council at Six Nations of the Grand River sanctioned the program, but as the Haudenosaunee—not Iroquois—Nationals, and that July the International Federation of Women's Lacrosse Associations embraced its 11th member nation. In 2007, Tuscarora goalie Amber Hill set the Syracuse season record for saves—under the Orange's new head coach, Gary Gait—and became the first known Native American woman to appear in the NCAA tournament.

Tia Schindler—she and Gewas married in 2010—served on the executive board and as assistant coach when the Haudenosaunee Nationals made their debut at the 2007 U-19 world championship in Peterborough, Ontario. They won their inaugural game, 15–7, over New Zealand and finished the tournament in fifth place. In 2009, the Haudenosaunee women traveled to their first World Championship in Prague and finished 11th. By then Schindler had three children and thought her playing days over. Four years later, at 32, she suited up as a defender for her first World Championship in Oshawa. The improved Nationals won six games and finished seventh.

"I remember being so emotional, representing my own people," she said. "At that time I had two daughters, so that's been my motivation. I just wanted them to have a place to play. It's about giving girls the opportunity to represent the Haudenosaunee and represent that pride in who they are."

By then all traditional objections, at least officially, had been resolved. "As long as the women don't want to play in the men's game—and certainly not the Medicine Game," Oren Lyons said in 2010, "it's alright."

Yet a vocal bloc, young and old, remained adamant that women should not touch any stick, no matter the composition, and attacked players on social media. The return home from competitions sparked a mix unknown to male Nationals: congratulations and smiles from some, silence and shunning from others. That, along with the program's late start, might explain the Haudenosaunee women's comparatively lesser accomplishments. Indeed, the best Indigenous player of her generation grew up oblivious to such opposition, on the other side of the continent, with no connection to any of the Six Nations.

Selena Lasota, daughter of a fisherman and a hair salon owner, grew up off Canada's west coast on Vancouver Island. Her introduction to lacrosse had nothing to do with the Native bloodline inherited from her father; her older brother, Bryson, played. The community didn't offer girls' lacrosse. When she was nine—in a move that would horrify the Onondaga—her mother, Lisa Sharpe, signed Selena up for a boys' box league. From then until her sophomore year of high school, Peewee to Bantam to Midget leagues, she aged up with the same team of boys in both box and field. In terms of physicality, box compares to ice hockey and boys' field is a festival of body blows. Selena was the only girl out there.

Her teammates—and their parents—never objected, and went full force at opponents who tried to bully her. "I didn't really need to be protected," Lasota said. In a Bantam game against Victoria, one guy took every loose ball as an opportunity to level her; Lasota took it until he cracked her helmet with both fists. "I hip-tossed him," she said. "You know in judo when they have you by the neck and, like, throw you over their hip? That's what I did." In Midgets, a pair from Saanich razzed Lasota about her hair, quieting after she glared and scored twice. Scoring—a lot—was her thing.

Selena was 13 the first time her father, Steve, took her to work fishing tuna in the waters off Haida Gwaii archipelago. Elite players usually spend summers drilling on the wall, playing club. Her middle and high school summers entailed two-week voyages in the North Pacific, the only girl in a crew of four, sleeping top right in the bow bunkroom. Every 5 a.m. unleashed the 16-hour cycle of set-and-haul: clipping five dozen traps onto a rope up to a mile and a half long, playing out the lines unspooled by the hydraulic engine, dragging in the previous day's catch of, hopefully, 1,300 wriggling pounds of halibut, tuna or black cod. Then, processing: One of the crew beheads the fish, two scrape them clean. Skin ravaged by the salt and scales and icy water. Hands constantly cramping. One night she woke terrified because her right arm had gone dead.

Selena's parents divorced when she was a baby, and she grew up with her mother and stepfather in Campbell River. Steve Lasota identifies through his mother as Katzie First Nation, a Vancouver-area Indigenous group with a fishing tradition. But Selena credits exposure to the people and traditions at her mom's home, near the Kyuquot settlement by Campbell River, for activating her sense of heritage. That this dovetailed with the Creator's Game lent her, onfield, "a different feeling of strength."

In the fall of 2012, Selena began her junior year of high school. She had just aged out of boys' youth lacrosse and won the 2012 Midget girls' box national championship with Team British Columbia. A coach suggested she try out for Team BC's U-19 women's field squad. That meant a drive-and-ferry jaunt across the Georgia Strait to Vancouver, 10 hours roundtrip but worth it. There was no one on the field like her. Shaped by box's cramped dimensions and angles, Lasota flashed behind-the-back passes, long-range rockets and a ball control unfamiliar to those limited by a lifetime wielding the shallower pocket allowed in women's sticks. And she never backed down.

Lasota played her first-ever field lacrosse game under women's rules in mid-November, at the 2012 President's Cup recruiting showcase in Naples, Florida. Four thousand players came in that weekend, all but one trying to impress 430 college coaches. Lasota was still learning the basics, leaning toward staying in Canada, maybe playing soccer. She didn't know someone had tipped off Danielle Spencer, Northwestern's first-year assistant. Spencer took in a game, the only coach in the stands, then called Amonte Hiller. Lasota knew nothing about the school or program. A month later, she committed to Northwestern.

By the time Lasota arrived in Evanston two years later, the gears in Amonte Hiller's dynamo were starting to slip. It took a while to notice. In the 2015 opener, Lasota announced herself by scoring four goals, including the game-winner in overtime, and two assists in the Wildcats' comeback win over Lindsey Munday's fledgling program at USC. Lasota went on to set Northwestern's freshman record with 69 goals in 21 games, but the Wildcats lost seven games, including two to Maryland, and missed the Final Four for the first time in a decade. Things got worse the following season: Lasota slumped to 50 goals in 2016 and Northwestern went 11–10, got beaten by USC for the first time, by Maryland twice again, then limped out of the second round of the NCAA tournament after a shocking 15–3 loss to Notre Dame.

It felt like undeniable proof: *We're not a powerhouse anymore*, Amonte Hiller thought. *Our history's over.*

Or, everyone else had just gotten better. Opponents were replicating Amonte Hiller's model, recruiting more sharply, accessing strategies and ideas unshared before the internet. Meanwhile, Amonte Hiller's dazzling start had created a monster that demanded only one result: national championships. The notion that anything else was failure had set in with her and Scott, the coaching staff, even the university that never set out to build a dynasty in the first place. Communication between coaches and players curdled. Players were urged to have more of a "killer instinct," and the only acceptable reaction to a loss was graphic sadness or silence or rage. No one dared make a mistake.

It all went against Lasota's lacrosse roots—and the Haudenosaunee approach that reflected her own. She saw it like a circle: Native stars like Randy Staats and the Thompson brothers, especially in the box, play with a freedom that leads to creativity that leads to joy, and none of it has anything to do with the score. Before landing in Evanston, Lasota never once played to win a game. Life in Amonte Hiller's cauldron activated her competitive side, "but I lost a lot of my personal values in the first two years in thinking I should be crying after a game," she said. "Because I'm an important player on the field—and if we lose, I need to be visibly upset. I totally lost myself with that."

The loss to Notre Dame in the NCAA tournament proved a turning point. "That summer, I was like: *We need to do something different*," Amonte Hiller said. "*This just can't happen*." After digging through old notes from her first season in Evanston, she, too, realized she had grown harder, lost touch with her players, in the drive for results. She wasn't sure of the fix, but easing up and reaching out seemed key. Northwestern produced an equally mediocre season in 2017—finished 11–10, nearly missed the NCAA tournament, then lost to Stony Brook in the second round. And then, just in time, the program's malaise began to lift.

Lasota had spent most of the 2017 season sidelined by a broken foot, mulling a transfer. An end-of-season meeting with Amonte Hiller cleared some of their tension, but only a love of teammates and Northwestern's campus life brought Lasota back the following September. Amonte Hiller, meanwhile, had doubled down on the need to blow open communication lines because the players "just perceived *everything* coming from us as pressure," she said. "We needed them to understand: No. We're proud of them. We need to get together and work hard to create the culture and the environment of passion."

When fall ball began, Lasota found herself facing a "completely different" head coach, more laid-back with her staff, more trusting with her players—and far less critical. "We had more of a relationship," Lasota said. "It felt unifying, in some weird way."

In 2018 Northwestern responded with its best season in five years, finished 15–6 and advanced to the NCAA quarterfinals before losing to No. 2 North Carolina. Lasota unleashed a record-tying, 22-goal tear in the Wildcats' three-game run through the tournament, finishing with career highs in goals, points and assists, while raising her teammates' level. It wasn't just that the Wildcats needed to be ready at all times, in traffic, for her behind-the-back feeds. Or that she expanded the attacker's range with fierce cannonades from 25 feet out. "Selena changed the entire sport with the way she shoots," said teammate Lindsey McKone, but Lasota also set an example on defense. "She was sprinting all around until the 30[-yard line] to ride. A lot of great players shoot and score and do all these tricky things, but the gritty details—that's where she stood out. She will put in the hard work to become the best teammate on the field."

McKone grew up amid wealth, attended a high-achieving private school in Houston, went to Northwestern to excel. Lasota tempered that. Her attitude and gratitude about lacrosse itself "made the game feel more important in some way—and not just the game, but every day at practice," McKone said. "We are all freakishly competitive people and want to win. But you do think about more of the moments and the memories over the wins and losses. She brought a lot of that to Northwestern."

IN THE LAST DAYS OF 2018, the outside narrative on Amonte Hiller's program had not budged much. Six years had passed since her last national championship, four since Northwestern had appeared in a Final Four. Under head coach Cathy Reese—her former Terrapins teammate—Maryland had reclaimed its role as the sport's flagship, winning three more national titles to raise its total to an unmatched 14. The Evil Empire was dead. Fewer pilgrims came to pick Amonte Hiller's brain. At 44, she couldn't recall the last time another university had tried to hire her away.

"No, I'm not a winner right now," she said. "So I guess I've got to prove myself again. I like this. I've got to prove myself, every day. It's good. It's a good place to be."

Her voice had a facetious edge, and she laughed like one who knows the flimsiness of labels like "winner." She recalled Selena Lasota's passion, their similar backgrounds, the restorative mindset that had taken hold, and believed herself in the coaching sweet spot—legend counted out, legend become underdog—and was sure she had learned in the losing more than anyone suspects.

"We haven't gotten the results yet," she said. "But I *know* it's coming."

II

STRONG ISLAND

T HE US MEN'S TEAM isolated itself for the 2018 World Championship 15 minutes down Highway 2 at Herzliya's Shefayim Kibbutz, though not in the rustic manner that the name implies. The socialist spirit that animated Israel's founding dissolved long ago and the kibbutzim ideal of mass dining halls, equal pay and lifetime security is dust. Shefayim, one of the nation's richest and largest, boasts a water park and shopping mall. The low-slung three-star hotel housing the Americans could cost well over $200 a night.

Clearly, Team USA found the accommodations agreeable. The Americans went undefeated in their first six games, including a 14–5 pasting of Australia in the semifinals that ensured another showdown with Canada. More important, their gritty cohesion stood in marked contrast to the whiny persona of the second-place finishers in 2014, an upgrade due almost entirely to the touch of John Danowski.

At that point, the 64-year-old head coach didn't need a world title to confirm his status as one of the game's all-timers. Winner of three NCAA championships at Duke and a participant in nine Final Fours, Danowski notched his 376th victory in 2017 to pass Dom Starsia and become the career Division I leader. Amid the 2006 rape debacle, with the sport's image flambéed daily, Danowski assumed control of a program with arguably the highest—and worst—national profile in lacrosse history. He spent the next decade providing a one-man hedge against depictions of laxbro entitlement, real and exaggerated, and a template for handling its ills. His 2015 appointment to Team USA was as much an endorsement of who Danowski is as of what he does.

"One of the best men you'll ever meet," said USA attackman Jordan Wolf, a four-time All-American and 2014 Duke graduate. "He knows how to make you a better person, and as I go on in my business career or family life, I'll always turn to him for advice. He's just so big on doing the right thing, even things that are so little."

Bill Tierney calls Danowski the lacrosse version of Phil Jackson, the NBA coaching great whose approach encompassed Zen Buddhism, Lakota spiritual practices and a missionary zeal for deep reading. After North Carolina's Marcus Holman scored during one of the rivalry's epic contests, a heated 18–17 win in the 2013 ACC semifinals, he was passing the Duke bench when he heard a voice. "Marcus, what a *great* shot that was," Duke's head coach said. "Great play."

Holman screamed, "Don't talk to me!" He didn't know: Danowski actually meant it.

For Danowski, seeking the Duke job in the summer of 2006 made perfect sense. Parents and players trusted him like no other outsider: His son, Matt, was then a junior attackman for Duke. Like them, Danowski had raged and worried that his son would be randomly accused; like them, he had stressed over the prospect of huge legal bills. Meanwhile, in 2006 the native Long Islander managed the greatest season in his 21-year coaching career at Hofstra, reaching an unprecedented No. 2 ranking amid dizzying highs and lows. After one win, he chased a camera crew asking about the Duke scandal out of the building. Every few days he knelt in a back pew at St. Kilian's church in Farmingdale, praying "that it would all go away."

For Duke, the job description was more amorphous. The three accused players wouldn't be exonerated for months, and the stain from the team's otherwise racist and boorish remarks showed no sign of fading. For the first time, officials tacitly acknowledged that the sport's norms—and even more, its popular image as rich, entitled and wedded to alcohol—were serious dangers. A decade before Lars Tiffany was charged with cleaning up UVa, Danowski sat for an interview with Duke's search committee and was peppered with questions about team culture, off-field behavior, discipline. No one asked about recruiting or even lacrosse.

"Not once," recalled Danowski during Team USA's off day at the kibbutz. "Somebody made a joke at the end—I think it was the AD, Joe Alleva—

said, 'So, what kind of offense d'you like to run?' And everybody laughed around the table, because they knew that was unimportant."

In time, it would become obvious that his predecessor, Mike Pressler (who went on to coach Team USA to a redemptive World Championship in 2010), had been unfairly forced out. But the goal was change for change's sake, and it was instantly clear to Duke officials that Danowski offered a break from Pressler's hard-charging style. It helped, too, that Danowski was the first coaching candidate, in any sport, to show familiarity with Duke's course catalogue, and had a master's degree in counseling and college student development. "We needed more of a guidance counselor, at that point, than a coach," said Duke goalie Devon Sherwood. "He was like our team rabbi."

Throughout Danowski's first academic year at Duke, 2006–2007, amid ongoing legal wranglings and the constant static of outside criticism, he regularly sat his players down on the grass for a round of venting. He would ask, "What's pissing you off today?" one day, and "What makes you happy?" the next. Eleven years later, at a kibbutz thousands of miles away, nothing had changed: Danowski presided over a daily team meeting on the sun-beaten grass, everyone on plastic lawn chairs, where he prodded the US players to speak, bond, laugh and publicly promise their teammates their best.

Keeping the Duke players in line, socially, was easy that first 2007 season. Duke won 17 games and surged to the 2007 national championship game before losing, 12–11, to Johns Hopkins. Though Danowski stressed all year that winning couldn't provide redemption, he knew his players felt it would be the perfect answer to all their critics. "I wanted to deliver that for them," he said. "I did feel like I failed."

Scars remain. Danowski hates how the rape accusations made his son Matt forever suspect adult authority—professors, administrators, media, parents. But he understands: In those first years, aside from interim athletic director Chris Kennedy, he said, "We trusted no one." In the fall of 2008, a Duke vice president phoned to say that Matt had been seen throwing a beer during a tailgate at a Duke football game. Danowski's son was on crutches, nursing a foot injury. Danowski procured security camera footage: A beer was seen flying over Matt's head, but his son had thrown nothing.

Ever since, the reputation of Duke lacrosse has been pristine. There have been no reports of criminal acts or heinous excess. But the mistrust of his bosses endures.

"That person still works there," Danowski, in Israel, said of the vice president. "So I'm still leery because I hear the stories—and I don't hear half of it. But we work really hard not to give them any ammunition—and they have none on us. I mean, they've got *none*."

THE RISE OF John Danowski to the top of the American game—late in 2018 he was reappointed to an unprecedented second term as head coach of the US men's national team—was also a triumph for a playing style, an attitude and one very mouthy worldview. Call it the Long Island School of Lacrosse.

In its first iteration, the sport took root on New York City's great extremity in the 1880s—just after the completion of the Brooklyn Bridge—with every intention of following the upper-crust model blossoming in Baltimore, Boston and elite East Coast colleges. Brooklyn's Crescent Athletic Club served as the early hub for local high school teams eager to take up its gentlemanly pastime. But the Great Depression ended Crescent A.C. and World War II ravaged scholastic funding and interest; by 1945 the number of Long Island high schools bristling with wood sticks had dwindled to three—Manhasset, Garden City, and Sewanhaka in Floral Park.

The solution—a blueprint for every panicky New York sports owner to come—was simple: Find the biggest name and buy it. In February 1950 Hofstra, a 15-year-old commuter college in Hempstead, offered Johns Hopkins head coach Howdy Myers—39 years old, and fresh off his third national championship—the titles of athletic director, head football and lacrosse coach and a pile of money. "The opportunity is such," said the lifelong Baltimorean, "that I cannot afford to turn it down."

The venture began in tragedy. In April Myers moved north to assume lacrosse duties and run spring football practice, leaving behind his wife, Anne, a prominent 38-year-old socialite; their 16-year-old daughter, Dorsey; and 5-year-old son, Howard Jr., in the wealthy enclave of Guilford. At 1:45 p.m. on November 8, the day after checking out of Baltimore's Seton Institute, a psychiatric hospital, Anne leapt from the midpoint of the 29th Street Bridge and plunged 100 feet to her death. The children moved north. Myers remarried. Dorsey attended Hofstra for two years, and wed one of her dad's players.

Myers coached Hofstra lacrosse for a quarter century, won eight conference titles and the 1955 Class B (now Division II) national title, was named
Division I Coach of the Year in 1970, made the Hall of Fame. But his legacy
rests on his work broadcasting the game islandwide. Determined to re-create
Johns Hopkins's prep pipeline, Myers gave clinics and talks to hundreds of
area public schools, cajoled administrators into starting programs, endorsed
former players as coaches. A decade after Myers arrived, in 1960, 10 Long
Island high schools had lacrosse teams. By 1975 the number approached 100,
an unmatched schoolboy cluster buttressed by middle school and summer
leagues, top-ranked clubs like Long Island A.C., and rec programs for kids
as young as eight.

And nowhere was the mix more eclectic. The talent pool that produced
Jim Brown included the sons of cops and electricians and train conductors,
mid-island Irish and Italians and Slavs who couldn't make Manhattan rent, a
current of working-class striving that diluted lacrosse's high-end cocktail—
and made for a different taste. Natives say that you can pick up the Long Island
essence anytime blue-chip factories Manhasset and Garden City renew their
historic rivalry, dating back to 1935. A rawer version is the dreamchild of New
York police officer Ronnie Kloepfer, a Sewanhaka High grad and Division II
national champion at Adelphi, who was killed in the line of duty on September 11, 2001. Six years earlier, Kloepfer founded the NYPD's lacrosse team,
always in the hope of a showdown with its brethren at the New York Fire
Department. Three months after 9/11, the first game in the series was played
in his honor. At least once a year since, the NYPD-FDNY lacrosse game has
been played to raise money for the families of first responders and veterans.
Both teams are stacked with Long Islanders, and it's always a little war.

One afternoon in Israel, a strong whiff of the Island wafted about the
stands at Wingate 4. Ireland was in the process of thumping Italy, 15–7. Corey
McMahon, a 21-year-old Cortland State attackman who grew up in Linden-
hurst, New York, was moonlighting for the Irish and, with three more goals,
buttressing his place among the World Championship's leading scorers. His
father, Tim, retired after 32 years in the FDNY, had lost six colleagues from
his firehouse in Bedford-Stuyvesant on September 11, 2001, when terrorists
obliterated the World Trade Center. His older son, Kieran, had played Division II ball in Pennsylvania, but, as a New York City police officer, couldn't
get time off to play in Israel. "I'm under the Brooklyn Bridge, on patrol,"
he told his dad over the phone the night before. "Man, I wish I was there."

Since 1970, when *Sports Illustrated* certified the sport's new power center in a piece titled "They're Not Going to Like It in Maryland," American lacrosse has been largely divided into two genially hostile—and caricatured—camps. The kingdom labeled "Baltimore," which stood less for the city than for the triangle of Johns Hopkins, Maryland, Navy and all old-boy points surrounding, teemed with third- and fourth-generation talents rich in agility, polish and mesmerizing stickwork. The upstart labeled "Long Island" bristled with public-school toughs who took up lacrosse to keep fit for football—and played like it. The bruising Long Islanders considered the Baltimore boys soft. Their coming, meanwhile, hit the game's patricians like Vandals on the outskirts of Rome.

"There is a 'thug' mentality, so to speak," says Howard Offit, who won his third national championship with Johns Hopkins in 1980. "We learned very quickly you'd better be as tough, or tougher, than they were. As you're getting up, they're jabbing you with the butt of the stick, telling you about your mother and your father—a lot of trash-talking."

Exceptions abound—players from Long Island public schools like Garden City can flaunt ski trips and Range Rovers with the snootiest, and Baltimore privates produce more than their share of brutes—and the lines blurred further as the game grew less physical and expanded nationwide. Today the split is more a matter of class and mindset. A "Baltimore" type can come from private schools in DC, Virginia and any other expensive institution along the East Coast. "Long Island" could describe any New York public-school scrapper from Buffalo to Westchester. But the stereotypes endure.

No one is more Long Island than Danowski. Even with the Mediterranean sunburn, he retains the hangdog mien of a commuter on the LIRR, and his booming New York accent betrays a lifetime of talking over traffic. His US assistant coaches Joe Amplo and Seth Tierney, who coached under him at Hofstra, are fellow "turnpike guys"—a nod both to Hempstead Turnpike, which slices through campus, and to working-class values: hard work, self-sacrifice, a code that can't be measured in dollars and cents. Jordan Wolf worked in finance in Manhattan after graduating, and saw Danowski's face anytime he passed on taking the subway. *If Coach D saw me taking a cab right now*, Wolf thought, *he'd kill me*.

Pay-to-play is at the heart of Danowski's biggest gripe about today's game. It irks him that the world Howdy Myers created, a Long Island of multi-sport athletes and town summer leagues that provided free coaching, pads, helmets and gloves, has been overwhelmed by exclusive travel teams and clinics that can easily run $10,000 a year. "This is America: I don't begrudge anybody for running a club program and making money," he said in Israel. "But the amount of money that people are paying is absurd. I hate that concept that it's just a rich kid's sport, a white kid's sport. And to the outside observer, it still is—and actually becoming more so than ever, more rich, because of the club thing. They just had 'the World Series of [Youth] Lacrosse,' in Denver, for under-13-year-olds, with two Long Island teams. These people, families, are paying to go to Denver? I mean, what are we *doing*?"

Maintaining that stance—and identity—at an $86,000-a-year university isn't easy. Even years after taking over at Duke, Danowski could still be heard vowing that he was done with "these private-school kids" and would only recruit Long Island grit. He never did; private-school kids were key to his NCAA titles in 2010, '13 and '14. But the hometown pull persists. His own father, Ed Danowski, son of a Polish immigrant who farmed cauliflower and potatoes on the east end of Long Island, was a former champion New York Giants quarterback and head coach at Fordham—assisted by future legend Vince Lombardi—in the early 1950s. But John grew up watching his dad later teach physical education and coach at the junior high in East Meadow, and drive a carful of kids home whenever they missed the bus.

John excelled at quarterback, led East Meadow High to county championships, found himself recruited by the Ivies. The Danowskis couldn't afford them, and Rutgers offered a full scholarship. Overwhelmed as a junior by football, fall and spring, lacrosse and chemistry and physics classes, he quit football. "I regret it to this day," Danowski said. "I never achieved any of those things that I'd hoped for—and I just felt very embarrassed about the end of my career. I wasn't going to allow that to happen to the guys that I coach. Somehow that did drive me, without knowing that it was driving me: *I'm not going to let what happened to me happen to you.*"

In lacrosse, he played against type: Attackmen live to score. Danowski's gut impulse was generosity; he set Rutgers single-game (13) and season (54 in 1973) record for assists that, 50 years later, were still unmatched. "Most unselfish player I've ever had," said Tom Hayes, Rutgers's head coach from 1975 to 2000.

Soon after Danowski took over at Duke, opposing coaches began noticing a different tone from the Blue Devils. Gone were the amped-up warmup drills, complete with leaping chest-bumps and roaring meant to intimidate opponents. Gone were the gratuitous cheap shots that Pressler never seemed to notice, and the aura, as then–North Carolina assistant Brian Holman later described it, "of that whole 'party-hard, tough guy, F-you' mentality." But sanding down that edge took nothing away from the team's grit. Holman said that in his eight years with the Tar Heels, Duke was almost always mentally tougher, which made for a jarring paradox.

Both programs had players with "Baltimore"-style skills. But public UNC after 2008 reflected the personality of Baltimore-born, private Loyola Blakefield–educated head coach Joe Breschi, while private Duke radiated Long Island. The arch rivals played 19 games in Danowski's first 12 years: Duke won 15 of them.

"We had this saying: 'We Finish in Front'—finish in front of the goal and we don't mind getting hit," said Justin Guterding, who graduated in 2018 as Duke's all-time leading scorer. "Carolina guys fade behind the net and make the play look cool, stick it in the corner and don't want to get hit: We would always joke about that. But we did really feel that, and that's why we have an edge on them. We're a bit tougher and we want it more than they do. They'll make the SportsCenter plays, but we'll make the plays that win the game."

LIKE NOTHING ELSE, the Duke rape saga and killing of Yeardley Love cemented the idea of "lacrosse culture," and fueled public chatter about its worst excesses. The steadying presence of a coach like John Danowski couldn't alter that. Players are lacrosse's lifeblood. Only players themselves could reset a popular image gone seriously askew.

Casey Carroll, whose epic, All-American career as a Duke defenseman encompassed the program's fall and revival and triumph, didn't set out to reveal a better strain of lacrosse culture. In the spring of 2006, he was one of the 46 Blue Devils asked to give DNA samples to Durham police. Carroll, a junior, wasn't too worried. Out for the season with a knee injury, he had spent the night of the party with his girlfriend, Erin Hathorn, a Duke soccer player from Durham. On March 23, he and his teammates entered a Durham police lab with jackets over their heads to hide from a news photographer. He was swabbed in the mouth, stood shirtless during a fruitless search for fresh bruises or scratches. A rubber-gloved female officer probed his torso, found three 12-year-old chicken pox scars and announced, "We have something here."

Though the first in his family to go to college, Carroll didn't seem unusual then. Seventeen of his teammates also came from Long Island, and three others were sons of firemen. He rehabbed his knee and rebounded in 2007 with the best season of his career, anchored Duke's redemption campaign—capped by its one-goal loss to Johns Hopkins in the NCAA final—and was named first-team All-American. He graduated with a degree in history and visual arts, and glittering options. An extra year of eligibility, granted by the NCAA because of the cancellation of the 2006 season, offered another run at a title. Lacrosse's lucrative job network dangled a good job in finance.

Instead, Carroll—at the height of America's wars in Iraq and Afghanistan—enlisted in the US Army. He wasn't looking to make a statement. Serving was always the intent. Carroll's grandfather had been in the military; his father, Peter, served in the navy during Vietnam; both of his older brothers had gone navy, too. Casey was just beginning his junior year at Baldwin High when 9/11 immolated Lower Manhattan. His dad had just retired with back trouble from 30 years in the New York Fire Department, but counted many friends among the 343 FDNY personnel who rushed in and died. Casey decided to enlist, then got derailed when Syracuse, Notre Dame and Duke dangled offers. No one in his family, ever, had the opportunity for that kind of education.

Though the sport is often linked with words like "entitlement," lacrosse's embrace of military values like self-sacrifice, duty and honor rivals—perhaps even exceeds—that of any other sport. This stems, in part, from the service academies' early success; from 1932 until 1971, when the NCAA held its first lacrosse tournament, the Naval Academy and West Point, along with Johns Hopkins and Maryland, dominated the college game. In lieu of playoffs, each year a committee from the US Intercollegiate Lacrosse Association decided the champion. Army won or shared eight national titles from 1923 to 1969. That year, the NCAA's outstanding player award was renamed to honor Lt. Raymond Enners, an Army lacrosse player killed in action in Vietnam in 1968. Navy's 17th championship in 1970 was its last, but it has since reached the Final Four eight times and, led by defenseman and soon-to-be SEAL Brendan Looney, lost the 2004 final to Syracuse by one goal.

Their postgraduate commitments, of course, ensure that all Navy, Army and Air Force players end up in uniform. But military tradition also runs deep in civilian schools. For more than a century, the goal nets at Hopkins's Homewood Field have displayed service flags with gold stars to honor the 11 Johns Hopkins players who died serving during World Wars I and II and Vietnam. More striking still, during an era when military service had been marginalized, many non-academy stars volunteered during the wars in Afghanistan and Iraq, and vied for elite assignments. The Hopkins contingent includes a Navy SEAL, two marine officers and a member of the Army Special Forces. Of the eight Duke players who entered the military during Danowski's first 11 years, three became SEALs, three marines and one a Ranger. Syracuse captain Rorke Denver, who played on two national champions hip teams, served a decade with the SEALs before becoming a senior training officer at its infamous training school, Basic Underwater Demolition/SEAL, in the late 2000s. Four years after graduating in 2010, Rutgers captain Tad Stanwick joined the navy and graduated from BUD/S. Twelve hours after winning the 2011 national championship, Virginia captain Bray Malphrus drove to an army recruiting center—NCAA trophy buckled into his passenger seat—and signed up.

But the one player Carroll most identified with was Army Sgt. Jimmy Regan. A fellow Long Islander from Manhasset and Chaminade High, the Duke midfielder graduated in 2002 and turned down a job with financial services giant UBS and a law school scholarship at Southern Methodist University to enlist. "If I don't do it," he asked his fiancée, "who will do it?" Regan then passed on Officer Candidate School to become a Ranger, machine gunner and fire team leader, and served two deployments apiece in Afghanistan and Iraq. The two men never met. Just before his senior season, early in 2007, Carroll acquired Regan's contact information, but Regan went overseas before they could speak. On February 9, he was killed on patrol in northern Iraq after an improvised explosive device ignited near his vehicle. He was 26.

Within minutes of hearing the news, Carroll again decided to enlist. Ten weeks later, Duke hosted Army, and Regan's parents—James and Mary—and fiancée attended the game in Durham with members of his platoon. When Carroll told Ranger Tyler Hansen of his plan to honor Regan by following his path, Hansen gave him his phone number. Carroll held on to it through basic training, then Airborne School at Fort Benning, Georgia. A few days before entering the Ranger Indoctrination Program, or RIP, he called Hansen. "Alright," Hansen said. "We'll keep an eye out."

Half of all who enter RIP wash out. For the next four weeks, Carroll endured a regimen of physical and psychological testing marked by grueling marches, little sleep and the culminating excruciation of "Cole Range," a four-day stretch marked by stark hunger, soaking wet clothing, and freezing conditions that Carroll would not discuss. Predicting survivors was impossible: Some scrawny specimens proved leather tough, some former Division I football players were among the first to break. When Carroll emerged, intact, Regan's comrades had arranged to transfer him into their own Ranger unit—2nd Platoon, Company C, 3rd Battalion. Faced, for the first time, with stepping into his hero's actual footsteps, he asked himself: *Who the fuck do you think you are?*

During his four-and-a-half-year hitch, Carroll hit all of Regan's marks—the four deployments, the 60-day Ranger School gauntlet of even more intense training to become a team leader, the rank of sergeant and fire team leader. During his tours of Iraq in 2008, and Afghanistan in 2009, 2010 and 2011, his platoon raided terrorist strongholds and destroyed many; during a two-month stretch in 2010, the 3rd Battalion suffered men killed and wounded daily. Carroll was never injured, but friends died.

Meanwhile, lacrosse's casualty list only grew: In April 2007 Marine Corps Lieutenant Travis Manion, Looney's best friend at the Naval Academy and an all-league player at La Salle College High outside Philadelphia, was killed by a sniper in Iraq's Al-Anbar province. In May 2009 former Air Force lacrosse captain Roslyn Schulte, an intelligence officer serving in Afghanistan, was killed by an IED. In September 2010 Brendan Looney died in a Blackhawk helicopter crash in Afghanistan. He was buried in Arlington Cemetery next to Manion.

Understanding why the military likes lacrosse players isn't hard. Generally, the sport produces smart, strong cardiovascular outliers adept at processing ever-shifting opponents at high speed amid chaos and constant harassment—"the skills and mindset," says Rorke Denver, "that could be useful on a future military assault raid."

Two of every three SEALs candidates fail. In the late 2000s, a navy study found those most likely to stick were former wrestlers, triathletes, water polo, rugby and lacrosse players. Football and lacrosse often share the same talent pool, but the latter prizes lean power over bulk, good for hauling a

90-pound pack, or an injured comrade, long distance across rough terrain. Also, the average Division I men's lacrosse roster, like a platoon, numbers about 40—historically considered the ideal size for unit cohesion.

The military's attraction to lacrosse players, on the other hand, can seem jarring, especially considering the higher-paying and safer jobs available to non-academy grads. But the traditional lacrosse community, which has passed the game down for generations, skews more conservative than the elite universities at the game's forefront. Patriotism—especially for the 9/11 generation—factors in. Like the military, lacrosse people are dedicated to a dynamic activity thick with history, distinctive mores and nomenclature, and believe outsiders get them wrong. Carroll acknowledges that the game has plenty of rich kids, and players do think they're special. But he's sure their perceived arrogance is less a function of wealth than a confidence the game itself creates, the kind that the SEALs and Rangers demand.

"It's one of the more humbling sports, because you physically get beaten down," he said. "When you get hit, it doesn't matter what school you went to: It hurts. But with that comes the same kind of pride you see in the military or firemen. When you self-select to those more aggressive sports, you end up feeling much more self-assured and more alpha male. That translates into, I think, a lot of the lacrosse players walking around like they're hot shit."

On the afternoon of May 31, 2010, Memorial Day, when John Danowski and Duke won their first national championship by beating Notre Dame, 6–5, in Baltimore, Carroll was 10 time zones east at Sharana, a well-outfitted Forward Operating Base set on a rise in southeastern Afghanistan, resting between missions. He stayed up through the night in a recreation room tracking the game on a community computer, constantly hitting refresh on the ESPN webpage. When C. J. Costabile scored the winning goal just five seconds into overtime, Carroll felt neither regret for the two title games he played in and lost, nor a sense of closure on the rape debacle. What he liked best, in fact, is that—seven redshirt seniors aside—those Blue Devils were mostly untouched by the scandal, freed of pressure to prove a point. He pumped his fist and whooped.

He had no thought, then, of playing lacrosse again. He didn't pick up a stick for nearly five years. But by the time Carroll mustered out in February 2012, he had canvassed Duke coaches and administrators: Military service preserved his original extra year of NCAA eligibility. Carroll knew enough about veteran troubles readjusting to civilian life. What better way to downshift from the unmatched purpose and adrenaline high of Ranger duty? D-I lacrosse had every element except guns and terror.

"The names on the jerseys were going to be different from when I'd last been there, but I knew the caliber of guys," he said. "My dad, as a fireman, it didn't matter that he'd been out of his firehouse for 5, 10, 15 years: he'd always go back. It wasn't the same guys, but it was the same personalities and ball-busting. Coach Danowski takes such painstaking effort in crafting a culture that I knew, going back there, that it was going to be the same group of awesome guys that would welcome me—and I'd get to have a lot of fun."

In the fall of 2012, Carroll began classes full-time at Duke's Fuqua School of Business, paid for by the GI Bill and the supplemental Yellow Ribbon program, and by Erin's earnings as an elementary school teacher. She gave birth to their first child, Patrick, that September. Carroll was 27. The practice field was across the street from class; his teammates called him "Old Man." Hearing the freshmen retail wide-eyed recaps about the weekend's keggers or women, he found himself nodding, smiling: *Yeah, I was you once.*

Those first months, Carroll got by on muscle memory, and wondered if his timing and quickness would ever return. Then in January, two weeks before Duke's 2013 season opener—and just minutes after realizing, *I got it. I'm back*—he planted his left foot during a one-on-one drill, turned and blew out the anterior cruciate ligament in his left knee. His season was over. Carroll still tried to contribute. Duke's first game would be played on the anniversary of Jimmy Regan's death, and freshman Deemer Class, a blue-chip midfielder from Loyola-Blakefield in Baltimore, had been issued Regan's number 10. Carroll buttonholed Class in the locker room a few days before. He recounted Regan's personal impact, and urged him to write Regan's parents.

"I could just see it in his eyes, the way that Casey spoke," Class said. "Casey was an amazing—gentle, but respected and firm—leader, and when he said it, it became this huge privilege to understand the reverence of wearing that number. It became special. It became an honor."

Carroll spent the 2013 season rehabbing and, once again, missed playing on a national championship winner when Duke picked up its second NCAA title. The injury had created yet another season of eligibility, but an intense summer internship with Wells Fargo in Charlotte undercut his fitness, and the final year of grad school ate up energy and time. Erin, pregnant with their second, asked the obvious: *Maybe time to hang it up?*

"But at the end of the day, she was so supportive," Carroll said. "Millions of former athletes out there say, 'What I would do for one more day out there with the guys . . .' If the opportunity's there to do something special, why give that up?"

On February 8, 2014—a decade after first enrolling at Duke, and 2,447 days since after his last collegiate game—Carroll, now 29, ran out in Duke's Koskinen Stadium for the season opener against Jacksonville. The Blue Devils won. He played nearly every minute, led the defense with five groundballs and forced three turnovers, was named ACC Defensive Player of the Week.

Carroll never did regain that full confidence. His knee ached. A hip flexor injury slowed him. He was usually the team's third-best defenseman. But he started all but one of 18 regular-season games as Duke went 15–3, racing out of the locker room—past Regan's framed jersey—to spell Erin or grind through assignments for the final semester of his master's degree. He addressed the team before every big game, including its 19–11 win over Johns Hopkins in the NCAA quarterfinals. Sometimes he choked up speaking about his Ranger buddies, stressing the profound importance of working together. Chemistry in both his worlds formed out of the same elements: exhaustion, time, stifling proximity, a terror of letting comrades down. Like the military, Carroll said, "sports help you figure out who's who."

Injuries, military, age, circumstance: There was nobody in American sports like him. During Duke's run to the 2014 national championship game in Baltimore, Carroll's 10-year odyssey became a dominant, tidy and—with the final set for Memorial Day—irresistible storyline. "Perhaps no one," said the *Baltimore Sun*, "would fit better on Monday's stage than Carroll." And then the impossible happened: Seven years after losing his seeming last shot at an NCAA title, the 29-year-old former Army Ranger came back to the same field and won, anchoring the Duke defense in an 11–9 victory over Notre Dame.

Carroll's first reaction was typical: He wasn't happy with his play. For his entire athletic life, he had felt detached from any result. Now, after all he'd seen and lived, how could a game really matter? He hugged teammates and wandered about seeking a feeling that wouldn't come, even after picking up his two sons in the emptying grass. Then, on the field, Carroll saw Jimmy Regan's parents. He still can't talk about this without choking up.

"Hugging them . . . they are always so special," he said. "My path had obviously been so parallel to his, and I can't ever fully appreciate the size of the heart it takes to have that—but they never made me feel, in any way, that I needed to do anything for their benefit or their son. But he's the reason I became a Ranger. And holding my kids there, and now having that perspective of being a father myself . . . it's every parent's worst nightmare. Seeing the strength that they carried through: That's where the cracks started forming in the walls I'd built up."

III

THE MONEY GAME

CHAMPIONSHIPS SHOULD NOT be a morning event. In the biggest American sports, they're not even an afternoon event anymore, except in old-time mentions of TVs wheeled into childhood classrooms. We have grown accustomed to our Super Bowls, NBA and Stanley Cup Finals and World Series at night. This is prime time—when most are watching, when the cost of a 30-second commercial spikes, when crossover stars are born and casual fans buy in. A championship is every athlete's dream. But a championship at night has the chance to become a cultural moment, the ultimate money game.

Yet, faceoff for the 2018 Men's World Field Championship final at Netanya Stadium was set for Saturday morning at 10 a.m. People griped. But for organizers, the fact that this was the tournament's most jarring element meant victory. The largest sporting event in Israel's history had been no more dangerous or frightening than any other 10-day string of games held under a sun-bleached sky. There were no visible BDS protests, no Iroquois gestures of solidarity, no incidents or detonations. The day before, a 20-year-old Israeli soldier, the first in four years, was killed by sniper fire on the border with Gaza; Israeli planes and tanks attacked 60 Hamas targets and killed four Palestinians; a shaky ceasefire was now in effect. As promised, it all felt far away.

Organizers also had no choice on game time. The venue, the shuttles, any labor and lights—all had to shut down before sundown. Then began Tisha B'Av, the saddest Sabbath on the Jewish calendar, dedicated to mourning at least five historic calamities through fasting and a suspension of enjoyable activity. Hence, the sparse and still-yawning crowd's subdued air, and the deflating knowledge that few back home would watch: Live coverage in the US aired in the graveyard slot of 3 a.m., EST.

Very quickly, none of that mattered. Canada's Geoff Snider beat Trevor Baptiste on the opening faceoff, the US scored two early, Canada responded with four straight, the US scored two: the first half was exactly the fierce, probing back-and-forth expected from equals. Canada goalkeeper Dillon Ward was near impermeable; attackmen Curtis Dickson and Jeff Teat were lacrosse savants. US sharpshooter Ryan Brown and attackman Rob Pannell couldn't be contained; many called midfielder Tom Schreiber the best player alive. Both teams dominated everyone but each other. This was their sixth straight meeting in the final. It was like watching twins wrestle.

Still, too often Team USA flailed in the crease, proved a step slow, waved sticks as the Canadians scored unpunished. Motivated by its testy loss a week earlier in the stick-check game, Canada again played sharper, more aggressive, and took a 6–4 lead into halftime. Emotional fuel seemed the difference. All tournament the Americans had been—publicly, at least—*anti*-mission, dismissive of the most basic sports motivator: In 2014 Team USA lost lamely to Canada on home soil. "I said from the beginning: it's not about '14," said Paul Rabil, one of eight holdovers from the 2014 US team. "The only sport where you defend your title is boxing. The roster's changed. So what's that about, to come in this locker room and make it about that game? No one will ever 'take' 2014 back. You have to turn the page."

Yet when they retook the field for the third quarter, that cool American aura was gone. Team USA's will—and defense—stiffened. Ryan Brown and Marcus Holman each scored to even things midway through, but it was the men bodying up, giving no ground, who mattered more. For the period's full 20 minutes, including an exhausting, five-minute and 21-second stand on the final possession, Team USA held Canada scoreless—and no one was more responsible than long-stick midfielder Michael Ehrhardt. A six-foot-five, 220-pound Long Islander out of the University of Maryland, Ehrhardt, 26, had been a fury all tournament—hoovering groundballs, neutralizing the opponent's big gun. He yard-saled Lyle Thompson on Opening Night. He cracked Canadian star Josh Byrne so hard in their group game that it sent his helmet flying.

Now, with the cauldronic conditions at a noontime 95 degrees and the
Canadians coming again and again, Ehrhardt was everywhere: stripping Teat
and scrapping to win possession; flattening Ben McIntosh and then, from
behind, deflecting his shot on a near-sure breakaway; chopping the ball, in
one final, desperate lunge, out of Teat's grasp as time expired; unleashing a
gladiatorial roar to send the rivals, tied at 6–6, to the fourth quarter.

That sequence was the clinching reason Ehrhardt was named the tournament's Most Valuable Player, and equaled any heroics in big-money sports.
As the highest expression of lacrosse's corporate connection, that vaguely
Victorian mix of amateurism and establishment wealth that has long made
the game unique, he also represented a breed that has all but disappeared
from the American scene.

Because lacrosse was Ehrhardt's side hustle. He was in Israel on vacation from his full-time career as vice president of business development
at First Nationwide Title Agency, a Manhattan title insurance operation
that services commercial and residential real estate interests nationwide.
All tournament Ehrhardt had been checking in with clients, answering and
forwarding emails, and was even prepared to break away to check on a client's hotel development, 21 miles south, in Jaffa.

A two-time All-American at Maryland, Ehrhardt graduated in 2014 with
all the credentials to play pro lacrosse but little incentive. Drafted seventh
overall by the Charlotte Hounds of the now-defunct Major League Lacrosse,
he signed up to play a 14-weekend summer slate that promised $7,000, travel
expenses and no benefits. "More of a glorified summer league," Ehrhardt
said. He spent the rest of the year working camps and clinics, figured that
even endless hustle would net him only about $30,000. Real estate sounded
better. Ehrhardt's mother knew the wife of First Nationwide's founder. He
put on a suit and started there in January 2015.

Thus began Ehrhardt's career, one of millions in the post recession
gig economy, as a gig athlete. Fifty hours of the week were devoted to woo-
ing clients, traveling to cities like Atlanta, Los Angeles, Washington, DC,
closing deals, entertaining into the night. The rest of the time he was a pro
lacrosse player—and his own coach, general manager and trainer. Mornings,
he would wake at 5:30 to lift weights or run or head downtown to Battery
Park, where former Team USA defender Mitch Belisle drilled a pack of fellow
former D-I stars at his 75-minute lax Breakfast Club. On Fridays during the
MLL season, Ehrhardt headed to the airport for Charlotte or some other

city, ate, went to practice, played Saturday night, then scrambled Sunday morning to fly back to New York.

Through it all, Ehrhardt perpetuated one of lacrosse's most enduring archetypes: the Finance Bro. Under that term sits many a non-finance field—real estate, insurance, technology—but the basics entail expensive suits, exhausting office work and the toting of lacrosse gear at odd hours onto subway cars and jets. For nearly a century such a life has been the sport's most tangible post college payoff, compensation for the pro game's meager salary, capstone of the game's hoariest cliché.

An alternative path began to emerge in the mid-2000s, when Kyle Harrison attracted enough mainstream sponsors to play full-time. Then his former Hopkins teammate Paul Rabil—after a post grad year in commercial real estate—grasped the potential of social media in a Facebook fan page, created a nexus of direct fan engagement with instructional videos and branded his stardom; in 2013 Bloomberg.com declared him lacrosse's first "million-dollar man." Many tried following his example. A few, like Max Seibald and Rob Pannell, generated solid six-figure incomes. But, as Seibald emphasized in Israel, the subset of lacrosse stars that drew mainstream sponsors like Nike, Red Bull or Wheaties consisted of "less than 10 guys." The average guy, he said, "is *not* making a living playing lacrosse."

Most were still like Ehrhardt: low-profile talents who saw more security, income and, most important, health care coverage in conventional white-collar jobs. They also felt a jealous twinge at the sight of a gleaming NFL facility or hearing about some pro hoopster's personal cook or trainer. Not a day passed that Ehrhardt didn't imagine life with lacrosse as his sole occupation, how much better he might have been. Then another email would ping in—client emergency—and he would get back to work.

Fed up with the real world/MLL shuffle, Ehrhardt had planned for the summer of 2018 to be his last as a lacrosse player. Early on, he had been low on the US depth charts. But guided by US assistant Tony Resch, also his coach with the Hounds, in 2017 Ehrhardt locked in on mastering the long-stick middie position and rededicated himself with a fervor he hadn't felt since college. Named to Team USA in January, he then cut out alcohol, dairy and sugar, and dropped 20 pounds. The idea was to peak at this World Championship and walk away. It seemed like the perfect ending.

But by the final day in Israel, the first rumblings of a revolution in the game's economics were starting to be heard. After failing in their attempt to buy—for $35 million—and reform the MLL in 2017, Rabil and his older brother, Mike—sons of a paper salesman and Catholic school art teacher—scrambled all year to build a new pro league: locking up big-name investors, meeting with television executives, creating a target list of the game's biggest stars. The short-term plan included a tripling of salaries, health care and unprecedented exposure on network television. The long-term aim? To make a life like Michael Ehrhardt's obsolete.

DEMAURICE SMITH, executive director of the National Football League Players Association from 2009 to 2023, knows plenty about networking. A graduate of UVa law school, he spent two decades cultivating beltway contacts as an assistant US attorney, Justice Department counsel to future attorney general Eric Holder, and corporate attorney at DC's weighty white-shoe law firm Patton Boggs; indeed, his connections with political and corporate power were a major selling point in his 2009 campaign for the NFLPA job. But he found lacrosse's old boys pipeline a wonder to behold.

"I have never seen anything like it," Smith said.

Smith grew up in the DC area, played football at Riverside Baptist School in Prince George's County, Maryland. He knew zero about lacrosse until his son, Alex, took it up in seventh grade at the St. Andrew's School in Potomac, remained wary of its party-hard reputation and overwhelming whiteness, flinched at compliments couched in racial code words like "fast" and "raw." Alex became a star, earned a scholarship to the University of Hartford and eventually played for Maryland. But his dad's eye-opening moment occurred near the end of high school.

"This guy comes up to me," DeMaurice recalled, "and says, 'Hey, you're De Smith!' I was thinking, *Oh, we're going to have another conversation about football.*"

Instead, the man brought up Alex's breakout game sophomore year, a six-goal, two-assist romp against his own son's team at archrival Maret. Then he got to the point: "Me and my friends here work in finance/real estate," he said. "When the time comes for your son, I want you to know that he can pick up the phone and call us anytime."

"Sort of *weird* coming from a parent from another school, right?" Smith said. "I was like, 'What are you talking about?' And he goes, 'Everybody who's in the lacrosse world around here is either in finance, real estate, business, banking. He seems like a great young man: I just wanted you to know that he's got a line to pick up—because that's what somebody did for me when I was playing.' It was astounding to me."

As with playing styles, the distinction between the Mid-Atlantic and New York schools of the lacrosse network has grown blurry in the 21st century. But the southern version, forever flush with Hopkins, Maryland and Naval Academy grads, began 120 years ago with the embrace of the game in old-money Baltimore redoubts like Mount Washington and Guilford, and spread over generations through private schools and family businesses centered on money and property. Atop it sat America's oldest and biggest investment firm, Alex. Brown & Sons, founded in Baltimore in 1800 and energized for the last three decades of the 20th century by former Princeton faceoff whiz—and eventual CEO—A. B. "Buzzy" Krongard.

Krongard is a legendary figure in Baltimore lacrosse. He is not just a Hall of Famer and Team USA captain who rose from bottom-feeding associate in the investment banking department to $4 million-a-year CEO, but a former marine captain and rumored CIA operative who went on to become executive director of the Central Intelligence Agency. He is also an expert scuba diver who, on a $100 bet at the age of 55, swam out from under a protective cage off Australia and punched a great white shark in the jaw. "If the shark was going to kill me," he said, "what more elegant way to die?"

In 1964, Krongard—son of a tailor, raised in a rowhouse—had sold off his wife's family business, was seeking work and playing for the Mount Washington club team. At least a dozen of his lacrosse buddies were at Alex. Brown. "They just said, 'Why don't you come to Alex. Brown?" Krongard said. "I knew so many people there. You couldn't ask for a better network. The only problem is, we weren't the only investment bank. And the other investment banks had lacrosse players also."

Blue Jays Hall of Famer Mark Greenberg joined a local mortgage banking firm after graduation in 1980, recruited alums like Brian Holman and kept up the practice when he founded Equity Mortgage Lending six years later. "A great pipeline," Greenberg said. "I hired I don't know how many teammates and lacrosse players."

All are part of a cozy ecosystem that St. Paul's coach Mitch Whiteley once described as Baltimore's "lacrosse mafia." Befitting its location, New York's version (the "Wall Street lacrosse mafia," so dubbed by *Bloomberg*

Businessweek, a publication owned by former Johns Hopkins intramural player Michael Bloomberg) is less forgiving and far more famous. The celebrification of Wall Street titans and traders in the "Greed Is Good" 1980s established the Finance Bro as a type, elevating the marriage of lacrosse and go-go Manhattan to a mind-meld. Both prize smart team players with a work hard/ play hard mentality and hefty egos. Both offer an adrenalized experience of exacting labor, orgasmic payoffs and the constant threat of failure. By 2008, the pairing had become so predictable that the *Wall Street Journal* dropped what it called an "old" joke: "The only way to get a job on Wall Street is to have high test scores or play lacrosse."

Bill Tierney estimates that more than 140 of his Princeton players, from 1988 to 2009, entered Wall Street careers. Business executive Howard Offit, the Johns Hopkins faceoff man who graduated in 1981, says he knows "hundreds" of ex-players who ended up working in Manhattan's finance sector. S.A.C. Capital became a Hopkins haven after 2004, when former Blue Jays attackman—and future Chief Operating Officer—Sol Kumin came aboard. Perhaps the best bird's-eye view comes from former Georgetown All-American Kyle Sweeney, the former Maverik Lacrosse COO who co-founded the Gotham Lacrosse summer league in 2007. "Thousands," he said. "I know definitely over a thousand people that work in finance and play lacrosse." Before collapsing in the 2008 financial crisis, firms like Bear Stearns, Turnberry Capital Management and Lehman Brothers Holdings, Inc.—and survivors like Goldman Sachs, Citigroup and Credit Suisse First Boston—dominated the league's 16 men's teams. The crash forced roster-jumping and name changes (Lehman became Barclays), but the Tuesday night games at Columbia didn't stop.

William Lewis played at Harvard, became the first Black managing director at Morgan Stanley in 1988, and in 2004 began a 17-year career at Lazard as co-chairman of investment banking. "When I'm looking at résumés, if I see any reference to lacrosse on the résumé—I don't care where—I'm circling that and I'm pulling that résumé out of the stack," he said. "There is something about that person that I want to know more about. That's just the way the world is."

One of Wall Street's most powerful Black executives, Lewis is just as realistic about its enduring racial dynamic. "There is nothing close to black power on Wall Street. Period. Full stop," he once told *Fortune*—and he doubts any increase in Black lacrosse players will change that. Indeed, the limits of Wall Street's lacrosse network stem from the fact it merged two white and wealthy subcultures. The mixing of "elite" candidates with elite corporations has created an even more top-heavy phenomenon—a network dominated by elite Division I schools. Lacrosse does provide common ground for players from less prestigious universities and lower NCAA divisions and an HBCU like Hampton. But the pipeline in is not nearly as seamless.

"The money is not in being a player. The money is in what happens next," said Hampton University head coach Chazz Woodson, who graduated from Brown in 2005. "What's the job you get? What's the career you land in? Who are the people that you now have connections to that you didn't before? We talk about that a lot as a sport, but it's not true for everybody."

In the same way that college football teams list alumni making millions in the NFL, lacrosse coaches woo recruits—and parents—with visions of a lucrative career. They aren't talking pro lacrosse. Instead, Georgetown and Hopkins hype their autumn team trips up I-95 to connect upperclassmen with ex-Hoyas or Blue Jays on Wall Street. Princeton and Virginia push their hundreds-deep databases of helpful former male and female players. Dartmouth might mention its ties with Goldman Sachs, Duke will speak of all its alums at Morgan Stanley, but the overall thrust is about a Street-wide "sprinkle." Because of Vice Chairman Brian Reilly, a former Yale captain, Barclays' Manhattan office often has more than a dozen Yale alums on its floor, with Dartmouth and Princeton sprinkled in.

With internships and postgrad job interviews a given, and the contacts so rich, for decades the Wall Street pipeline generated a near-irresistible pull: even the uninterested were sucked in. "When I got to Duke, I didn't even know what 'finance' was," said three-time All-American Deemer Class, who graduated with a degree in sociology in 2016. He had an internship after his junior year at Barclays, rotating for 10 weeks among the sales and trading desks. A year later, he yearned to play pro and try out for Team USA, but Barclays offered a position as an investment-grade bonds sales analyst. Class started work near the end of his first season of MLL with the Atlanta Blaze: first man in on the sales desk at 6 a.m., 12-hour days, bolted meals, a few nights out a week courting clients.

At first, he loved it all—parsing market and client data, formulating trade ideas, pitching. His first bond sale felt almost like a goal; the first few trade ideas that hit almost felt like wins. "That's why so many lacrosse guys go into finance: it's the next best thing," Class said. "You're competing against other salesmen, trying to make a sale, trying to make a trade. That's the thrill. That's the rush." But the 65-hour workweeks took an instant toll. Class could all but feel his legs weakening as he finished out the 2016 MLL season, and over the next year found no way to wedge in three-hour workouts. During the 2017 season, he was benched and traded, played in just three games; at 24, Class felt his prime slipping away. Barclays was paying him more than $100,000 a year, but the thought of turning 30 behind that desk was a horror. His MLL salary for 2017 would be $8,500. Class quit Wall Street.

On paper, it looked like he had jumped into the unknown. But Class had picked up on shifts in the lacrosse landscape his last two years at Duke, when Instagram got hot and Duke highlights went viral and high school kids across the country weighed in on his moves. After graduation he and Johns Hopkins great Ryan Brown teamed up, as RBDC Lacrosse, to stage a few successful shooting clinics. Both realized that the market had changed since they were young, that Rabil's success had exposed possibilities. Lacrosse parents were now willing to spend thousands a year for individual or small-group coaching with an All-American from Duke or Hopkins. And because of social media, the ability to brand and post content, to connect with kids and parents—and their money—had never been easier.

In the year after leaving Barclays in July 2017, Class held boys' and girls' clinics in 26 states, served as assistant coach for the McDonogh School's top-10 boys program, revitalized his pro career in Atlanta with a 24-goal season, landed a Division I assistant's position with the women's team at Southern Cal. He loved the teaching, loved how playing proved and promoted all he taught, loved the control. In 2018, attendance at MLL games fell for the eighth straight year, down to an average of 3,619 per game. But Class's personal lacrosse business was growing.

Among the game's top players, a new calculus started playing out in real time, shrinking the old breed. Including Michael Ehrhardt and fellow Breakfast Clubber Jordan Wolf, who left Wall Street after four years to go to business school, only six of Team USA's 23-man roster in 2018 held down full-time office jobs. The rest, like Class's business partner Ryan Brown, had opted for the mix of coaching teams or clinics or camps, courting sponsors, playing MLL and/or indoors with the National Lacrosse League. The hustle remained. But it had become easier to resist the call of the Finance Bro.

"I haven't had a regret," Class said in 2018. "I am much happier, and have made and am making more money than my first- and second-year salaries (at Barclays) would have been. The trajectory of a finance career is bigger, no question. But the problem is, you don't know how big. It's very bonus-dependent, market-dependent, very career- and bank-dependent. Banks can bust. I was like, *I need to do this now, when I don't have as much to lose, and see what I can do.* And it's paid off."

THE FINAL 20 minutes of USA vs. Canada in Israel began in mystery, the great spectator hope. Team USA's epic third-quarter stand, punctuated by Ehrhardt's howling fist pump, killed off Canada's edge and made prediction foolish. Matched step-for-step in talent and will, battered together by the unrelenting sun, the Americans and Canadians walked out for the fourth quarter all but wearing each other. Then Curtis Dickson scored early to make it 7–6, Canada. Tom Schreiber struck two minutes and forty seconds later to tie it again. Everyone in Netanya Stadium sensed that victory in the 2018 World Lacrosse Championship would come down to the infinitesimal, the barely seen: a half step gained or lost, a slip of the grip.

An eternity of probing ended when Mark Cockerton—son of Stan, the Canadian great who scored the championship game-winner against the US in 1978—beat John Galloway with an overhand drive to make it 8–7. With 4:10 left to play, given the pace, the lack of a shot clock in international play, and the fact that the US's Trevor Baptiste won the faceoff but lost the ball, it was a lead Canada had every reason to think would hold. Instead: mystery and controversy forever.

Ten seconds later, Canada lost possession when it was penalized—wrongly—for an offside violation. The Canadian sideline erupted, but not for long: Lacrosse allowed no possibility of video review. A minute later Ryan Brown's underhand rocket, rising from his ankles, tied it again 8–8—and suddenly, oddly, everything started bending the American way. Baptiste beat Snider in the most important faceoff yet. Matt Danowski fired an errant pass—but Canada was whistled for pushing on the ensuing loose ball scramble. With 12 seconds left, the US began its final assault, just-missed on three shots; with 3.6 seconds left, all signs pointed to overtime. Then Pannell snatched up the ball and spotted Schreiber, left side, hurting goalward. He threaded the ball, calmly, between four red jerseys.

Schreiber took the feed just outside the crease, high and to his left. Every field coach would demand, in that situation, that the stick be in his left hand: It was in his right. "I've gotten yelled at a few times for that," Schreiber would say later, "but I guess it paid off this time." He stepped, drew the stick across his face, flicked his wrists. It was, ironically enough, a shot developed long ago in Canada for such cramped moments, a box-style finish called a "twister." Ward was helpless. The ball hit the net, officially, with one second left. 9–8, USA.

Canada's bench erupted. Head coach Randy Mearns screamed at officials, pointing to the clock on the stadium scoreboard. That read two seconds left at the time of Schreiber's score. ESPN2's broadcast registered 2.6 seconds left. The clock at the official scorer's table recorded one second left. Mearns was sure—and broadcast video confirmed a clear discrepancy—that after the first of the three final American shots, play began but at least three seconds passed before the stadium clock began moving: Regulation time should have expired. He wanted the goal disallowed, the game sent into overtime.

The referees conferred and quickly ruled that Schreiber's shot occurred before time expired at the scorer's table. "This," Quint Kessenich said on ESPN2, "is an international incident."

After one last faceoff, the horn sounded: The US team converged into a scrum of grins, hugs, flag-waving. If these were the Olympic Games, the clearly dodgy finish would instantly have been compared on American TVs to the US basketball team's still-controversial loss to the Soviet Union in 1972. Instead, it was a blip on the cultural radar, flashing and disappearing at 5:30 a.m., EST, on a July Saturday morning, ignored by major news dailies and fated to be reported—if at all—in blogs and briefs and agate type. Most outrage was confined to the moment.

Boos rained down from the confused crowd in Netanya Stadium. As the Americans were awarded their gold medals, a chant of "Can-a-da!" began. When Ward was announced as the tournament's outstanding goalie, someone yelled, "Give it to the timekeeper!" Mearns, Curtis Dickson and Mark Cockerton, drained and empty-eyed, were hustled into the interview room. All remained perplexed by the finish. "Chaos, pretty much," Mearns said. "It felt to us that there was nine seconds on the clock and the play started and the clock didn't move for four seconds, and then all of a sudden it went on and went on and went on. And Team USA took a shot and there was four seconds, and we're like, 'How come we're not already at zero? . . . Is there two, three different timers? I don't know.'"

As for the phantom penalty that forced the fatal turnover, Mearns said, "We didn't feel that we were offside. We were up a goal and had the ball; we're pretty good at holding, too—so I don't know what happens with that. We'll watch the video. Were we offside or not? I don't know . . . but at the end of it? Team USA made a play, had the ball last, and they scored. So kudos to them and congratulations."

Happy Team USA people entered next. Players and coach said little about Canada's outrage or time confusion, but no one deemed the complaints sour grapes. "It's a shame that the game had to end that way," Schreiber said. "But for a couple plays either way, we could've lost one or both games," Danowski said. "We're grateful that we did win." Four days later, FIL announced that its video review confirmed Schreiber's game-winner, "with time still on the clock," and conceded—sheepishly—that the errant offside call against Canada "could have been made in error."

In other words, the athletes and their supremely riveting contest revealed an administration still not ready for prime time, a case of growing pains. During Canada's press conference, a moment occurred that reinforced how lacrosse is still a sport like no other. Usually, given the contentious ending, the gutted losers would have spent the whole time replaying the final seconds, spewed bitterness and stalked out. Instead, someone asked about the new countries playing lacrosse, and Curtis Dickson talked about Uganda and the Olympics and the bright future.

"I'll add to that," Mearns said, beginning a soliloquy about the game's "amazing" growth, its expansion to Indoor and U-19 World Championships, the booming women's game and the need to keep the expansion going. "Because at this point?" Mearns said. "I certainly know that if you're going to try to play in the NLL, you're not getting paid $7.5 million to be the number one draft choice. I wish it was, because Curtis would be a millionaire. Mark would be a millionaire. I'd probably be a millionaire, and that would be cool. I would be really, really happy to be."

That sparked laughs: In lacrosse, money is never far from mind. A few hours later, though, the bar and terrace tables at the West Lagoon Resort were filled with edgy, disgusted Canadian players, families, coaches and empty bottles. Everyone had seen a replay by now: With four Canadians set in the defensive end, the offside call was clearly wrong. A championship had likely been taken from them. Mearns was passing through the lobby toward his room, grinning sadly and repeating—"*You* were offside!"—to nearly every Canadian he passed.

At the elevator, someone approached and Mearns's face and neck flushed and he snapped, "You saw the film." Then he stepped in. As the doors slid shut he was still mumbling: "But, no . . . We were offside . . . we were offside . . . we were offside . . ."

THE NEW WORLD

PART 1

NOTHING WITHOUT DEMAND

Those who profess to favor freedom, and yet deprecate agitation, are men who want crops without plowing up the ground. They want rain without thunder and lightning. They want the ocean without the awful roar of its many waters. This struggle may be a moral one, or it may be a physical one, and it may be both moral and physical, but it must be a struggle. Power concedes nothing without a demand. It never did and it never will.
— Frederick Douglass, Canandaigua, New York, August 4, 1857

In our play we reveal what kind of people we are.

— Ovid

TEWAARATON

O N OCTOBER 22, 2018, Paul Rabil announced the launch of the Premier Lacrosse League, aflush with radical intent. Unlike the Major League Lacrosse model, with nine teams anchored in nine cities, the PLL planned a six-team, 12-city tour resembling pro tennis, golf and Formula 1. Unlike the MLL, still struggling for exposure on second-tier cable channels, the PLL boasted a multi-year partnership with broadcast giant NBC. Most striking, for the players, the PLL base salary of $25,000 was three times the MLL average (and topped the indoor NLL average of $19,000) and included benefits like health care and an undisclosed equity stake in the league.

At the same time, the original PLL lineup served as a referendum. MLL defectors who voted with their feet included 10 Tewaaraton Award winners and 86 former college All-Americans—stars like Tom Schreiber, Duke all-timers Deemer Class and Myles Jones; Canadian legends like Curtis Dickson and Brodie Merrill; the African American honor roll of PLL co-founder Kyle Harrison, Chazz Woodson and Jovan Miller; and 19 members of the 2018 world champion US team, including MVP Michael Ehrhardt. Though not enough to make Ehrhardt quit his day job, the PLL compensation package was a striking start.

"I was ready to hang up the cleats," Ehrhardt said. "But Paul provided us with this incredible opportunity that I never thought we'd ever have. There were big investors behind us, a TV deal. And we took a leap of faith."

Indeed, the PLL's financial backing was as impressive as its player pool—and the most public flex yet by lacrosse's "Wall Street" fraternity. "That pipeline is a bit of the Kevin Bacon [Six Degrees of Separation] game: you know a guy who knows a guy and get your foot in the door," said former NFLPA head DeMaurice Smith, one of eight members on the PLL's initial advisory board. "So when Paul starts this new lacrosse league? It's just . . ." Smith opened his hands slowly, like a magician. "*funded*. Never seen anything like it."

This wasn't due solely to Rabil's reputation as a visionary who had cashed in on lacrosse's potential, or fluency with jargon like "non-endemic" and "monthly actives." He and his brother, Mike, the new league's CEO, had rejiggered enough aspects of the continent's oldest game to make it feel—on paper—like something fresh. Ten yards had been cut from the middle of a typical lacrosse field, and 28 seconds from the 80-second college shot clock. Gone was the community-based, all-for-the-team ethos of the NFL, NHL and collegiate lacrosse. In its place was a barnstorming, star-centric festival featuring tight uniforms, sexy team names like "Whipsnakes," in-game interviews and seven-camera broadcasts.

One of the first to see the PLL as a compelling bet was Fortress Investment Group managing partner Drew McKnight, a former All-American attackman at Virginia and part of an early group of investors that pledged around $3 million. Soon aboard were former Hopkins players Jon Marcus and Sol Kumin, the latter now co-president of Leucadia Asset Management, and then–New England Patriots wide receiver Chris Hogan, who captained his lacrosse team at Penn State. The initial round of funding, led by The Raine Group's managing director Colin Neville, a former Yale attackman, included Blum Capital, the Chernin Group and Creative Artists Agency, whose head of sports—and future PLL board member—is former Cornell attackman Mike Levine. As if to demonstrate the lax/finance bond in real time, the PLL also revealed that Tom Schreiber, a Princeton grad who moonlighted as a partner in a venture capital firm, would join its front office as a financial analyst.

But the moment of ultimate fusion arrived four months later, when lacrosse's supreme Finance Bro gave his blessing. On February 12, 2019, Alibaba co-founder and Brooklyn Nets owner Joe Tsai—former Yale player, $10.2 billion net worth, the 154th-richest man in the world—was announced as lead investor in the PLL's second round of funding. Beyond filling the new operation's sails heading into its inaugural season, the news boldfaced a fact that had been forming for months. Taiwanese by birth and Canadian by choice, Tsai was now the most powerful figure in the game.

Tsai himself wouldn't put it that way. He describes all his lacrosse roles—Yale benefactor, San Diego Seals owner, financial muscle of the Olympic mission—as labors of love. Certainly, his is an obsession unmatched by basketball or e-commerce: During the Covid pandemic of 2020, Tsai set up a three-by-three-foot lacrosse goal in his La Jolla kitchen. He's sure the game helped smooth his early days in a strange land. Tsai's father, Paul, co-founded one of Taiwan's most influential law firms. Sent at 13 to New Jersey's elite Lawrenceville School in the late 1970s, Joe was fast enough to play football and good enough in lacrosse to get cocky. Getting called "chink" by opponents didn't shake him. Getting cut senior year was a wound he never forgot.

"One of the most devastating things in my high school career—or my entire career," Tsai recalled. "Nobody likes to face rejection. Nobody likes to be told that you're not quite good enough to make this or make that. I wasn't angry. I was maybe upset and frustrated for a couple of days and then I started to reflect, *What I could have done better?*"

Assuming he'd be on the team again, Tsai had slacked off, didn't practice enough, let his conditioning slide. "So to this day I actually thank coach Marshall Chambers for cutting me," he said. "Because I learned so much from that experience: Never take anything for granted."

Going on to make the Yale team as a walk-on, and sticking for four years, remains a point of pride. Teamed with the likes of future Barclays chair Brian Reilly—and future Maryland attorney general Doug Gansler, who broke Tsai's kneecap in a collision freshman year—Tsai rarely saw the field. The one time a close friend from Taiwan saw him play was in 1986, senior year against Georgetown. Tsai scored, falling down, in a 17–4 win. It took years before he could admit to his friend that was his lone collegiate goal.

Tsai met Alibaba co-founder Jack Ma in 1999, got in on the ground floor at a $600-a-year salary, and eventually became the corporation's executive chairman and second largest shareholder. In 2015, well before setting his sights on NBA, soccer or NFL football teams, Tsai was approached in Hong Kong by two representatives of the Federation of International Lacrosse. The FIL's skeletal, all-volunteer administration had spent the previous 20 years welcoming all comers, 43 new countries in all. More were coming. Its annual operating budget, according to then-president Stan Cockerton, topped out at $80,000.

Tsai offered concrete help. During the 2016 men's U-19 World Championship in Coquitlam, Canada, he met over dinner with Hayes, Cockerton, board member Ron Balls, and others. All figured on a getting-to-know-you affair, with the hope of gauging Tsai's support for FIL's still-amorphous plan to make lacrosse an Olympic sport. He was way ahead of them. At first mention of the subject, Alibaba's chairman said, "I'm all-in on the Olympics."

Tsai then asked about the FIL's vague strategy to hire the organization's first executive director. The rough plan was to get $50,000 from US Lacrosse, maybe some chip-in from other countries, and hope that they could somehow gather enough to create a $100,000 position for one year. Tsai told them that wouldn't be nearly enough and—on the spot—guaranteed FIL $250,000 a year for 10 years. He also told them that they'd need to expand their international development budget—and pledged another six-figure sum to that end. The FIL delegation was stunned; sitting down, Hayes was worried about paying the dinner check. After, Cockerton said, "You've never seen so many grown men cry." With Tsai's commitment their future as a worldwide sport, and financial health, assumed a concrete dimension.

If Hayes needed any more proof of Tsai's commitment, it came during that 2016 U-19 tournament, after a game meaningless to the rest of the world. Taiwan and Mexico were both winless, yet their meeting evolved into a lunatic and emotional, seven-overtime 8–7 win for Taiwan. Tsai's sister knew the program's founder, who happened to live in their mother's building in Taiwan; Tsai was one of its financial backers. He was on the Taiwan sideline, with his two sons, when the winning goal scored and the players converged in joy. "You know what a dogpile is?" Hayes recalled. "Joe's right on top of it. When you see something like that, you know the guy's genuine."

Tsai can imagine a scenario where some version of pro lacrosse in America matches its winter sibling—ice hockey—in popularity, and players make millions solely through playing. "I'm baffled why the NHL is so big, because it's really a Canadian sport," he said. "You have teams in LA and Arizona, Florida, Texas; I mean, they've never seen ice in their life and they're crazy about hockey. I think lacrosse can be as big. Historically, lacrosse has never had people savvy enough to present the sport in a way that's friendly to fans until the PLL came along, until Paul Rabil. They have revolutionized the way lacrosse is viewed."

But this revolution has limits. As an NBA owner, one who knows what rock star fame in athletics looks like, Tsai sees no way for lacrosse to reach the stratospheric attendance and viewership levels of football, basketball or baseball, to break beyond sport into the realm of pop entertainment and culture. The equipment is expensive and, unlike football, rarely paid for at public schools. The game is hard for young kids to learn and enjoy, doesn't lend itself to the pickup play that fuels spectatorship, and is nowhere close to a formula for attracting "non-endemic"—non-lacrosse-playing—fans. NFL stadiums and NBA arenas are filled with men and women who've never picked up a basketball or football. Lacrosse is watched by lacrosse people.

Tsai plans to keep pumping his money in, though, because he is one of them: hooked on the game and convinced of its greatness, eager to attract a mass audience while doubting—cheerily—that it ever will. "I'm afraid probably not, in my lifetime," Tsai said. "It'll always be kind of a niche sport."

THERE'S NO SHAME in being a niche product. Tennis, track and field, and swimming have churned along quite profitably in that space, edging into the cultural mainstream with the occasional Grand Slam sensation and regularly scheduled Olympic Games, sometimes sparking a "boom" for a decade or two before receding back into the arms of hardcores. In 2018, lacrosse felt the first hint of such an ebb. After years of explosive growth and hitting an all-time high of 2.1 million participants in 2017, the American total stalled and would remain there for the next two years. The abruptly flat graph line looked like the first traces of a ceiling.

Yet atop the game, the feeling of momentum only increased. In October 2018, the admission of Ecuador and Ukraine to the Federation of International Lacrosse expanded the total of lacrosse-playing nations to 62—a 233 percent rise since 2002. In November, the dream of becoming an Olympic sport—and participation at the 2028 Summer Games in Los Angeles—received its first official encouragement when the IOC granted provisional recognition to the FIL. "I can't think of a more significant milestone in the sport's history," FIL vice president and US Lacrosse CEO Steve Stenersen said at the time.

The move opened a spigot of IOC funding for the FIL and a three-year process toward full recognition, but its greatest effect was messaging: Lacrosse was now officially on the Olympic radar. A plan was already in the works to create a smaller, faster, Olympics-friendly version of the game. The next step would be a first-time demonstration of it for men and women at The World Games—a quadrennial festival for non-Olympic disciplines and, since 1984, a gateway for the entry of nine sports into the Olympics—in 2021 in Birmingham, Alabama.

Yet there was no mention of the Iroquois Nationals in the IOC announcement, nor any acknowledgment that the IOC doesn't recognize the sovereignty of the world's third-best lacrosse nation. Four months earlier in Israel, FIL CEO Jim Scherr had acknowledged that exasperated FIL members were ready to "go down the road without them"—the Nationals—and made it clear where the Iroquois stood on his list of priorities.

"They need to understand," Scherr said. "We're going to go down this Olympic pathway as our number one driver as an international federation. Because it drives our mission: to grow and protect and steward the game on a global basis. There was uniformity in the desire for this sport to be in the Olympic Games. The athletes want it, the coaches want it, the member nations want it, the fans want it. So we're going to do it. Now, what I understand our federation's position to be is: We are not going to abandon the Olympic vision if the IOC says, 'The Iroquois are not going to be participating in the Olympic Games.'"

Scherr added that the game's originators were vital, and that the FIL would press the IOC to make an exception and allow them to play. But the Federation of International Lacrosse's intent seemed clear. If admission to the Olympics came at the expense of the Iroquois, so be it.

The same week of the IOC announcement, Lyle Thompson didn't seem worried. Thompson rarely does. "The Iroquois Nationals will always be there," he said. "We will always be—whether we're part of the Olympics or not. We will have exhibitions. They'll create a Cup for us to play Canada and the US. It'll still be a big deal . . . for us.

"The Olympics is a long shot. I'd love to play on the world stage, and I want to say, 'I played in the Olympics.' But if you're going by Olympic rules, it's not going to happen—and I'm fine with that."

Then, two months later, some white men said something awful. On January 12, 2019, at the Wells Fargo Center in Philadelphia, Thompson, in his fourth season with the Georgia Swarm of the pro box National Lacrosse League, was cradling the ball near midfield with just under four minutes left in a 13–11 road win over the Philadelphia Wings when public address announcer Shawny Hill boomed, "Let's snip the ponytail right here!"

Sitting out the game in the stands, Wings attackman Justin Guterding couldn't believe his ears. "It was disgusting," he said. "Even if it had nothing to do with his heritage, even if it was just he had long hair, you're an announcer. It's not like you're a fan or saying something 'cause you're drunk. He fully knew what he was doing. That was the worst part."

Thompson hadn't heard Hill's comment in the moment, but he was already primed. Earlier, while heading to the locker room at halftime, he had heard a man yell, "Cut your hair!" During the third quarter came another male voice: "So are you going to cut your hair? Or do we have to scalp you?" After returning to the bench, Thompson learned what Hill had said.

He hadn't been so angered on the field since high school. The game ended; his teammates, Native and white, hugged him in solidarity; and that night Thompson tapped out a pair of tweets describing the incident in a tone closer to puzzlement. Three minutes later Brendan Bomberry, speaking for himself and the five other Haudenosaunee on the Swarm roster, defined it more starkly:

```
your in game announcer's comments toward my teammates,
"let's snip the braid," was disgusting and a reality
for my ancestors when they were forced into Christian
residential schools.
```

Though a reckoning over the erasure of Native identity has been roiling Canada since the government's admission of cultural genocide in 2015, at that point scant attention had been paid south of the border. For much of the decade, American culture and its sports-industrial complex had been engaged in debates over immigration, the #MeToo movement, equal pay, gender and presidential politics, as well as a Black civil rights movement explosively recharged by the death of young men at the hands of police. Sensing that an unrecorded slur might have been easily dismissed, Thompson said, "I'm glad it's happened at the professional level—with 13,000 people in the stands—and it being televised."

But the reaction came fast, furious and more comprehensively than for any previous racial incident in lacrosse. Within 12 hours both teams, US Lacrosse, the NLL and two of lacrosse's preeminent white stars—Paul Rabil and Tom Schreiber—tweeted out sweeping condemnation of Hill's words. Kyle Harrison, the greatest Black player since Jim Brown, called the incident

```
Embarrassing and disgraceful. We're not nearly as far
along as we think we are. Damn shame," adding, in refer-
```
ence to Thompson's number, `We're all rockin' with you, 4.`

Hill apologized, saying that his words reflected a "lack of knowledge on heritage and history." The Wings fired him the next day. The team also announced an immediate launch of diversity training for all employees, with a focus on Native traditions. An Iroquois flag decal was slapped on every NLL helmet, joining the American and Canadian flags already there. Subsequent in-game videos at Wells Fargo Center featured Seneca defenseman Frank Brown's thoughts on the incident, a reminder of Native lacrosse history and players of all ethnicities declaring, "We fly together."

In one sense, this was classic corporate damage control: Mainstream media—not to mention the NLL's sizeable bloc of Native American talent—were now paying attention. Throughout the spring, Thompson took every opportunity to inform reporters and social media followers about the braid's symbolic power, his pride, his pain. When the Wings and Swarm met again on April 20 in Atlanta, both teams wore Lyle-designed BACK THE BRAID T-shirts featuring a silkscreened ponytail. "It's tough for me to say this was a bad thing that happened, because so much good came of it," Lyle said.

Indeed, for the first time lacrosse leaders and commercial interests made racial tolerance and inclusion an institutional imperative. In April STX, the iconic lacrosse manufacturer, unveiled its #DrawTheLine campaign, featuring stars of all skin tones demanding that lacrosse people speak up against racist incidents on field and around the game. The same weekend of the braid incident, US Lacrosse, which had been developing a "cultural competency" platform on bias, microaggressions and social class since a spate of racial incidents against African Americans in late 2017, launched its online course for coaches, parents, officials and athletes. Heading into its inaugural training camp that May, the new PLL, guided by Director of Player Relations and Diversity Inclusion Kyle Harrison, made that course mandatory for players and pledged to make "ongoing dialogue" central to the PLL experience. The following month the NLL did the same, and expanded the requirement to coaches, front office staff and league personnel.

"This has brought the lacrosse community together in awareness, on another level, outside of just Native Americans," Thompson said. "It's making sure those things don't happen inside the game, outside the game, around sports. It's really created a movement."

BRAD TIFFANY NEVER was an easy man to read. Like many in his Depression-era cohort, the ex-marine and buffalo rancher was what later generations would term "emotionally distant"—tough, demanding, not given to displays of affection. Still lifting weights into his 80s, in 2017 he bought a working farm outside Charlottesville, near his oldest son. Lars was in his first year of coaching UVa. When he tried to end one chat with his dad by saying, "I love you," Brad became upset. "Stop saying you love me," he said. "Show it. Do it."

Lars began to figure that one out after his father died, following a stroke, on January 28, 2019. The following week, Lars, his two younger brothers and two dozen family members traveled to Binghamton, New York, for the memorial service and dinner; with the ground frozen, burial had to wait for spring. Lars had forgotten about Brad's repeated promise of a late Christmas present. Everyone was milling about the restaurant parking lot, beginning goodbyes, when his best friend from Onondaga interrupted.

A year earlier, Brad had asked Joe Solomon for help acquiring a traditional hickory longpole for Lars's 50th birthday. But stickmaker Alfie Jacques couldn't complete it until a few months later, and then Solomon didn't dare entrust the six-foot artifact to the US mail. For months after, Brad kept calling Joe to ask, "How are we going to get it to him?" Now Joe pulled the gleaming stick from his truck and told the story. Wide eyes, gasps, tears: "It's like a gift from the other side," Lars said finally. "How did my dad give me a gift at his own funeral?"

In time, Tiffany would understand this as the last note in a lifelong theme: Love is an action. Though a classic meat-and-potatoes guy, after Lars declared himself vegetarian in 1991, Brad spent hours whipping up special meals: cauliflower, rigatoni, a prideful "Tofu Tiffany." Nothing spoke to his regard for the Onondaga as loudly as the buffalo grant, but 44 years later Brad wanted to do more. He was working to endow an educational foundation for Onondaga children when the stroke hit.

For Binghamton in February, it was an unseasonably warm day. The cluster of Tiffany family in the parking lot thrummed now with a bit of awe, a sense of propriety. Some suggested that the gift be preserved, mounted on a wall, encased in glass. But the Haudenosaunee believe a wood lacrosse stick to be a living entity, medicine from the Creator. "No, no, no," Solomon said. "This stick was built to be played with."

Lars knew. He had witnessed Longhouse ceremonies when young, took part in the Nationals' tobacco-burning ritual; lacrosse laced with Haudenosaunee spiritualism is his one abiding faith. After taking over at Virginia,

Tiffany tried not to harp on his Onondaga influences and vegetarianism but did install the same guilt-free blitz that he and offensive assistant Sean Kirwan revived at Brown: the style played by the Natives at LaFayette High, the flying circus Lars saw at Syracuse in the 1980s, the attack that propelled Brown to its second-ever Final Four in 2016. The Cavaliers hit the ground sprinting in his inaugural game in 2017, won 16–15, and by mid-season seemed even faster. "We're going to give you an ulcer," Tiffany warned after another barnburner, 19–18 in overtime, over Cornell early that season. "And we're not going to slow down."

The turnovers that most American coaches considered cancerous, Tiffany turned into a plus. Now an intercepted UVa pass was not something to rage over, but a chance to gleefully trigger their 10-man ride—essentially, a full-court press—and expand the Creator-pleasing positivity. It was needed. Despite the abstinent example of Seneca senior Zed Williams, Tiffany still had his hands full trying to clean up his team's behavior. A lacrosse-only carveout from the UVa athletic department's three-strike drug policy enabled him not only to permanently flush a player after two violations, but to exile him for the entire academic year after just one. Four players found to use cocaine or marijuana were booted.

To discourage the traditional Saturday night drinking blowouts, Tiffany moved the Cavaliers' toughest practice day of the week—packed with intense weightlifting and conditioning drills—from Mondays to Sundays. He referred to his team as "men." He began "Cultural Thursdays"—weekly team meetings dedicated to assigned readings, the airing of grievances, mutual support. "It was intense and crazy, because he came in really hot," said UVa midfielder Ryan Conrad, a sophomore then. "He cut a bunch of people, stripped everyone's numbers. Frankly, I loved it."

After Tiffany shifted Zed Williams from midfield to attack, he produced his best season in Charlottesville; the Cavaliers finished 8–7. In 2018, Virginia improved to 12–5, won its first ACC game in six years, made the NCAA tournament. Inspired by his time in Israel with the three famously sober Thompson brothers, Tiffany returned that fall intent on curbing the program's attraction to alcohol. As always, Virginia was loaded with talent: Midfielders Dox Aitken and Ryan Conrad, scoring machines Michael Kraus and Matt Moore, goalkeeper Alex Rode. As always, its greatest challenge came off the field.

A near tragedy set the tone. In August of 2018, as students were still trickling into Charlottesville for the fall semester, 10 underage UVa lacrosse "first-years"—or freshmen—were drinking in a downtown bar when a male and a female player fell off a balcony onto the landing below. The female was hospitalized; the male, according to Tiffany, limped away. Subsequent testing netted four more men's lacrosse players for alcohol use, and the full attention of athletic director Carla Williams. "We were now on double-secret probation," Tiffany said.

The players, including those over 21, voted to refrain from alcohol for the 2019 season. Parents were asked to refrain from drinking at postgame tailgates. "It wasn't easy, frankly," said Conrad, then a senior and one of the team's tri-captains. After losing two of three games to open the season, including a fourth-quarter collapse at home to High Point, the players met. Some wanted to ditch the no-drinking rule. "People were like, 'What's the point? We're not winning anything,'" Conrad said. "We had to right the ship a bit and say, 'Trust the process. Dedication and more work and drinking less is definitely not going to hurt.' There was a bit of an epiphany. We got the buy-in, and that's what pushed us over the top."

In early April, another UVa player—who had reeked of alcohol during an early season weightlifting session—was kicked off the team after being arrested for public intoxication. But this occurred during an eight-game stretch when the team's maturity, and a more controlled offensive tempo, were paying off: The Cavaliers beat Princeton, Syracuse and Johns Hopkins on the road, along with North Carolina and No. 7 Notre Dame. They had won virtually all "character" games (three in overtime and five of six decided by a goal) and risen to No. 4 in the national rankings.

On April 13 a streak-snapping, 12–7 loss at Duke proved pivotal. No Cavaliers drank that night; UVa won its next two games by a combined score of 46–11. Every player then doubled down on the agreement to swear off alcohol for the rest of the season, and the Cavaliers went on to beat UNC and Notre Dame to win the ACC Championship. "Absolute validation," Tiffany said.

By then, too, the entire sport was speaking more openly about substance abuse. Timmy Brooks, the former Haverford attackman and drug dealer who was released from jail in 2015, had famously gotten clean and was finishing an All-American career at Cabrini University with a Division III national championship. In 2019 UVa student Shea Megale, daughter of former Cavaliers player Larry Megale, published the book *American Boy* about her brother Matt, who had died at 26 of an overdose. Larry Megale and former teammate Kevin Corrigan, head coach at Notre Dame, then organized the first annual American Boy Fall Brawl in Centreville, Virginia, with Colgate and Princeton, to raise money and awareness about drug abuse and treatment. Timmy Brooks was a featured speaker.

Over the next four years, American Boy Fall Brawls would become a fixture of the lacrosse calendar, featuring 29 college teams, including UVa, Ohio State, Marquette and Penn State. Combined with the national alarm (in 2021, overdose deaths in America, most involving fentanyl, rose to a record 108,000), the increasing dialogue seemed to have some effect. In the NCAA's 2023 Abuse Survey, both men and women lacrosse players would report a significant drop in cocaine use (from 22 and 6 percent, respectively, in 2017 to 7 and 2 percent in 2023). Though lacrosse men would again lead all sports in the use of narcotic pain medicine, stimulants and marijuana, the amount of those using the latter would drop from 50 to 38 percent. And though its binge-drinking cadre still nearly doubled that of the general student body, lacrosse also would drop just behind ice hockey as the sports leader in alcohol abuse; in 2023, 61 percent of men's lacrosse players and 48 percent of women would report engaging in binge drinking—down from 69 and 57 percent, respectively, in 2017.

When Lars Tiffany brought his father's gift back to Charlottesville before the start of the 2019 season, he didn't intend for it to become a touchstone. But the stick became part of his profile, propped near the desk, a fixture in his hands. After weightlifting and a long film session, Sunday's light scrimmages were intended as "a healing," Tiffany said, his version of a Medicine Game. And he began awarding his hickory longpole to the player, that week, who best represented the program's values.

"It meant a lot," said defensive midfielder Matt Dziama, one of 2019's honorees. "That stick is a representation of the way the game should be played: with compassion, with toughness, with grit and skill—the Creator's Game. Meeting Zed Williams and learning more about the Native American culture opened my eyes up more about the way the game should be played."

During the 2019 NCAA tournament, Tiffany's Haudenosaunee talisman became a key element in Virginia's narrative. The longpole was on the sideline in Charlottesville when UVa sailed through its first-round win over Robert Morris. Tiffany warmed up with it on field before the Cavaliers met Maryland in the quarterfinals and erased a five-goal deficit to win, 13–12, then displayed it prominently at the postgame press conference. Two days later, Lars was in Binghamton to attend his father's delayed burial, a ceremony marked by full military honors and a 21-gun salute. He brought his stick.

Brad's gift then traveled to Philadelphia on Memorial Day weekend for the Final Four. The stick resonated as a symbol of grief, lost fathers, carrying on. But Betty Lyons—Onondaga, Snipe clan and president of the American Indian Law Alliance—cried the first time she saw Lars with it because "he was telling the world: This is where this game came from. This game is as meaningful to him as it is to us—which is unusual to see. He listened to the origin story of lacrosse, and he not only heard it: He felt it. Him growing up with us, he understands what it means."

Virginia hadn't beaten Duke in nine years. The Cavaliers trailed their semifinal the entire second half until attackman Ian Laviano tied it up with 15 seconds to play in regulation, then scored again in the second overtime to win 13–12. Monday's championship game was less tense: UVa pummeled defending champion Yale with a lacrosse master class. Moore scored four goals, Kraus scored three, Rode finished with 13 saves. The Cavaliers fended off Yale's one serious surge in the third quarter by forcing seven turnovers and scoring five goals. Tiffany won his first NCAA championship, 13–9.

For the American game, there is no bigger platform. The 31,528 fans at Lincoln Financial Field saw Tiffany on the field beforehand, flinging a ball around with his wood stick. A nationwide TV audience had been told its story. Reporters in the victory press conference heard his tribute to the Onondaga. Winning ensured that Brad's gift would become lacrosse lore, a reminder and a message: *The Haudenosaunee are—must be—central to our game.* Five months after a white man in Philadelphia insulted Native Americans by calling for the cutting of Lyle Thompson's braid, a white man came to Philadelphia and celebrated—in deed and words—lacrosse's unpayable debt.

THREE DAYS LATER, the 19th annual Tewaaraton Award ceremony was held in Washington, DC. If Virginia's run to the 2019 NCAA championship represented the most heartfelt blend of lacrosse's elite white culture and its Indigenous roots, the state-of-the-art confines of the Smithsonian Institution's $199 million National Museum of the American Indian presented the institutional version.

"Tewaaraton" is the Mohawk word for lacrosse. In 2000, when members of DC's University Club decided to honor the year's best male and female collegiate players and lacrosse's Native American heritage, they made sure to gain backing from both US Lacrosse and the Mohawk Nation Council of Elders. Iroquois Tadadaho—and former Syracuse attackman—Sidney Hill presented the trophy featuring a stick-wielding Mohawk warrior to the first male winner in 2001. The Tewaaraton Foundation's first college scholarships for Haudenosaunee high schoolers were awarded in 2006. When in 2009, the ceremonies shifted to the five-year-old limestone edifice on the National Mall—the first national museum dedicated exclusively to Native Americans—it only furthered the impression of a bifurcated sport edging toward singularity.

Indeed, the air at the 2019 Tewaaraton Award reception the night of May 30 hummed with mutual regard. Since 11 of the night's 12 honorees and finalists were white, it made sense that the milling crowd of family, friends and teammates, expanded by locally based coaches and officials, revealed few Black, Latino or Native faces. Still, Onondaga stickmaker Alfie Jacques was seen finishing up a traditional lacrosse and stickball demonstration. Lars Tiffany—now the Native stick's most prominent booster—found himself swarmed by congratulations. Selena Lasota—fresh off leading Northwestern back to its first Final Four in five years, and the first female Tewaaraton finalist of Indigenous descent—was there grinning with her family.

The ceremony began with the Haudenosaunee Thanksgiving Address, delivered by eight-year-old Mohawk Hohnegayehwahs Mitchell. One of the boy's grandfathers was a Mohawk faithkeeper, the other a lacrosse stickmaker. The program contained Mitchell's short, self-penned bio: "I was raised a traditional Longhouse person. The game of lacrosse is part of our religion. Even we use it in our ceremonies and I take part in medicine games that are played at the longhouse. I enjoy playing lacrosse and hockey. I also smoke dance at various powwows within the confederacy."

Decked out in traditional feathered headdress and ribbon shirt, with a grin as wide as a carved pumpkin, Mitchell was clearly thrilled to step onstage. "Now the time has come," he began in Mohawk, with the words translated behind him on a giant screen: "Our ancestors have laid this responsibility down, for me to speak about this matter. So now it is, I will carry our words as far as I am able. Let your minds be long [have patience] with these words."

Then, for another four and a half minutes, Mitchell continued the litany of gratitude, first for the chance to gather, then to Mother Earth, the Waters, Fish, Fruit, Food Plants, Animals, Trees, Birds, the Sun and Moon, the Four Winds and "Our Grandfathers the Thunderers," the Stars and the Creator. Each stanza detailed the respective qualities of each and ended with the repeated coda "Now we are of one mind."

Watching the words translated on a big screen, the crowd sat respectfully throughout and gave the boy rousing applause. The ceremony lasted 100 minutes, full of testimonials to the finalists' grit and talent, and ended with the men's and women's Tewaaraton Awards going to Loyola attackman Pat Spencer and Maryland goalie Megan Taylor. Hohnegayehwahs Mitchell then returned to recite the same Thanksgiving prayer. Again the words "NOW WE ARE OF ONE MIND" flashed onscreen 13 times, and at the end many in the mostly white crowd stood and cheered. For that moment, at least, it was impossible to think of lacrosse's ancient and modern strains as anything but unified.

But in the months after the Tewaaraton ceremony, the Iroquois Nationals found themselves operating amid a troubling silence. Officials from the newly rebranded FIL—now called World Lacrosse—were in the final stages of selecting teams for the organization's most public step in the campaign for Olympic recognition: the 2021 World Games in Birmingham, Alabama. There, World Lacrosse would unveil its newly contrived, Olympic-friendly face, a pared-down six-on-six field discipline demonstrated by the top eight men's and women's teams. As the planet's No. 3–ranked men's field team and No. 2 indoor team, the Iroquois Nationals had every good reason to believe they would be invited.*

---

* To prevent confusion concerning lacrosse and the label "World," three distinct entities are referred to. The quadrennial lacrosse World Championships, such as those held in Israel in 2018, are run by World Lacrosse, the international governing body that, as the previously named FIL, recognized the Iroquois as a national entity in 1987. The World Games are a separate quadrennial competition run under International Olympic Committee auspices, involving non-Olympic sports that sometimes are elevated to the Olympic Games. Lacrosse was contested for the first time, by women only, at the World Games 2017 in Wroclaw, Poland, but because the Iroquois are not recognized by the IOC as a sovereign nation—and don't have a National Olympic Committee—they were not eligible to participate.

The first indication that they would not arrived in August, at the 2019 U-19 Women's World Championship in Peterborough, Ontario. World Lacrosse also held its General Assembly meetings, attended by Iroquois officials. There was plenty of talk about Birmingham 2021, but not a word about the Nationals playing. "It was really deliberate," Rex Lyons said later. "Why wouldn't you bring that up? Because they were afraid, and they knew we were going to push back." In September the Iroquois reaffirmed their lacrosse stature, finishing second to Canada—after a 9–7 semifinal win over the US—in the men's 2019 World Indoor Championship in British Columbia. World Lacrosse officials were there. Again, nobody spoke to the Iroquois about the World Games in Birmingham.

By that November, World Lacrosse had begun issuing invitations for Birmingham to eight countries—led, of course, by the US and Canada. The Iroquois men had not received one. World Lacrosse had not reached out to explain why. Lars Tiffany was not conflicted. "If the Iroquois aren't a part of it," he said, "I have very little time and attention towards it. Partially because it seems like US Lacrosse spearheaded the creation of a game that doesn't exist. Why do we have to come up with a hybrid version? We already have a 6-v-6 game: It's called box lacrosse, and it can be played outdoors. Why not use the box lacrosse model? Oh, wait a minute: *The US isn't dominating in box lacrosse. The Iroquois and the Canadians are.* So it doesn't seem right to me. It smells a little."

Disturbing him most, though, was the prospect of a body without a soul. "Lacrosse without Native Americans? I don't know if I can imagine it," Tiffany said. "Because it loses so much. It loses everything, really."

Three weeks later, December 4, 2019, World Lacrosse and The World Games 2021 Birmingham Organizing Committee announced the participating 10 nations for the men's and women's lacrosse competitions. Lesser powers like Australia, Japan, Germany, Israel, Great Britain and Ireland were listed. There was no mention of the Iroquois Nationals, and no explanation why.

II

AN AWFUL ROAR

FIFTEEN MONTHS BEFORE the Covid-19 virus metastasized across the globe, Oren Lyons was already dreading it. All his life, the 88-year-old faithkeeper had emphasized the Haudenosaunees' role as steward of the earth, the responsibility to consider one's impact seven generations ahead. But man's despoiling of nature now felt increasingly irreversible, and the Iroquois Nationals co-founder saw a future marred by enveloping drought, mass migration and water wars, a cycle of degradation beginning with the human body.

"The first things are going to be pandemic; the pandemics are coming," Lyons said. "We're just half a step ahead of it now. There's terrible times coming."

ON MARCH 12, 2020, the same day that the National Hockey League suspended its season and Major League Baseball halted spring training, the NCAA canceled its basketball tournaments and all spring sports. The college lacrosse season was barely a month old—with defending Division I champion Virginia off to a 4–2 start—but, in a broader sense, the stoppage couldn't have come at a worse time. Because, absent the usual clamor of game scores, the news of lacrosse's latest racial controversy now stood alone.

On the morning of March 8, after Amherst's men's lacrosse team lost at Tufts, 25–15, three of its white players—including one co-captain and a former high school All-American—chanted, "N——! N——! N——! Goodnight, n——!" outside a Black teammate's dorm room. The Black player emerged and then, reportedly, punched one of the offending players. The school's administration swiftly condemned the incident. Head coach Jon Thompson, who benched the three white players for Amherst's final game against Endicott on March 10, then issued a public statement condemning their racist language as "revolting." That was not the end of it.

Long considered one of the nation's elite colleges, Amherst was a rising lacrosse power; the seventh-ranked Mammoths had appeared in their first-ever NCAA Division III final in 2019. Now previous incidents involving the lacrosse team—first reported by the campus newspaper, the *Amherst Student*—circulated nationwide: a December 2018 party when a swastika was drawn on an unconscious player's forehead and circulated on players' social media, a series of transphobic comments made by other players. On March 20 Amherst president Carolyn Martin—along with its athletic director and faculty dean—issued a statement to alumni citing the "N-word" incident as "only the most recent in a list of deeply troubling cases." Jon Thompson was fired. The college placed the team on probation, and banned it from postseason play in 2021.

Overshadowed by the greatest mass health crisis in a century, any discussion of lacrosse's race problem figured to fade. Then, on May 25, 2020, a Black man named George Floyd, stopped for allegedly passing a counterfeit $20 bill, died in Minneapolis after a white policeman knelt on his neck for eight minutes and 46 seconds. Bystander video of the murdered Floyd gasping, "I can't breathe," hit social media. Outrage that had been building since the February killing of unarmed Black jogger Ahmaud Arbery in Georgia by three white men, and the fatal shooting in March of Breonna Taylor in her apartment by Louisville police, broke across cultural lines. At least 15 million people braved Covid to hit the streets in protest—and some rioting—over the summer. Activists and media reinvigorated the term "Black Lives Matter" for what quickly became one of the largest social movements in US history. America's eternal racial question again became central, applied to seemingly every institution: Who are we now?

Lacrosse was not immune. Within two weeks of Floyd's death, Southwestern Lacrosse Conference president Matt Holman, a Black former Syracuse midfielder and San Diego State head coach, began a 14-part, weekly online Zoom series, *Overtime: A Candid Discussion of Racism in Lacrosse*, featuring a rotating panel of Black, white, Native American and Latino figures from in and around the game. Holman grew up in Summit, New Jersey, one of two Black players on his eighth-grade team, always outnumbered in high school and college. Knowledge of a Native American ancestor provided quiet fortification.

"It was my sport," Holman said during the second *Overtime* episode. "It's not a lily-white sport, even though lily-white people think they own it." The regular public forum helped ensure that, in 2020, lacrosse was subjected to a racial accounting unlike any in its history—sustained, detailed and refreshed by events in real time. On June 2, Marquette University rescinded the admission of an incoming women's lacrosse player after learning that she had posted racially offensive comments on social media.

At first, lacrosse's professional flank seemed untouched by the fray, even a source of good news. A month earlier, on May 6, Paul Rabil's Premier Lacrosse League had been the first pro sport in America to announce its return from the pandemic with a two-week, self-contained "bubble" tournament in July. Instead of scrapping the fledgling operation's second season, Covid had given the seven-team PLL an opening to position itself as sport's agile innovator, not to mention a savior of network programming. The tournament would help fill the titanic programming hole left on NBC by the postponement of the 2020 Summer Olympics in Tokyo.

Behind the scenes, racial issues threatened to undermine all that. After conferring with PLL star and Director of Player Relations and Diversity Inclusion Kyle Harrison, the Rabil brothers had released a five-point statement on June 1 that condemned "the senseless deaths of George Floyd, Breonna Taylor, Ahmaud Arbery and many others"; condemned systemic racism; pledged to stand with the PLL's Black players, families and friends; promised to call out racist jokes and behavior; and supported legal action and ballot reforms. "We stand united in our belief," it concluded, "that Black Lives Matter."

Paul Rabil had envisioned the statement as a dramatic step toward "unwinding," as he put it, the sport's image as a bastion of "elitism and exclusivity." Indeed, it lined up with the sustained messaging of players, teams and leaders in the NBA and WNBA, the leagues that produced the most forceful and effective response to Floyd's death, as well as the sentiment of Black lacrosse players. The statement also reflected—at that moment—widespread sympathy for Black Lives Matter among whites; 60 percent of

white Americans polled in June expressed some or strong support for the
BLM movement. Many prominent white lacrosse players followed suit.

"The time is now. We can't wait any longer," said longstick midfielder
Kyle Hartzell, a member of the 2018 World Championship US team, during a filmed interview on June 8. "We can't have another incident like this
happen." When the PLL's bubble play began, he said, players needed to
signal—perhaps with GEORGE FLOYD or BLACK LIVES MATTER printed on every
jersey nameplate—full support. "We need to make our message heard and
we need to continue this message," Hartzell said. "It cannot stop. And I'm
going to make it my duty to not let it stop."

But sometime between George Floyd's death and the beginning of
the PLL bubble tournament on July 25, the lacrosse conversation changed,
and any hope of a unified stand vanished. Instead of refashioning the sport
under a progressive banner, Rabil's alignment with the Black Lives Matter
movement—and, especially, his push to have every player in 2020 display
BLM uniform patches—only showcased and sharpened the sport's sociopolitical divide.

"There was a ton of really difficult—but positive—conversations that
happened around lacrosse about race," Harrison said later. "It was uncomfortable for a lot of folks, but it was necessary. And I think we're better off
for it, and more prepared to handle difficult discussions than we were before
that happened."

At issue, ostensibly, was the dual nature of the phrase "Black Lives Matter."
Its founding impulse—a social media hashtag, #BlackLivesMatter, created by
activists Alicia Garza, Patrisse Cullors and Opal Tometi in 2013 in reaction to
the acquittal of the white killer of Black Florida teenager Trayvon Martin—
expressed a self-evident truth, and soon became shorthand for action against
racism, police brutality and anti-Black violence. But during the supercharged
summer of 2020, the movement's foundation, the Black Lives Matter Global
Network—colloquially referred to simply as "Black Lives Matter"—became a
focus of contention and anger by some. Critics—mainly from white, right-wing
sources but also including prominent former NFL lineman Marcellus Wiley,
a Black man raised by blue-collar parents in Compton, California—lit into
the founders' self-declared "Marxist" leanings, the BLMGN's stated aim to
"disrupt" the nuclear family structure and its call to defund police departments.

Combined with news reports of near-daily demonstrations and attendant violence, the revelations led to a quick erosion of white sympathy for

BLM nationwide: Between June and September, the percentage of white Americans saying they supported the Black Lives Matter movement dropped from 60 to 45 percent; among those who leaned toward or were members of the Republican Party, support plummeted from 37 to 16 percent. And by mid-July, it was clear that Rabil had a problem. Only 13 of the PLL's 154 players who would play in the 2020 bubble were African American, and sympathy for BLM in his mostly white constituency was tracking the national trend.

No one personified the erosion better than the 35-year-old Hartzell. In his public statement in June, the Dundalk, Maryland, native had not only vowed to display support for BLM on his uniform, but pledged to correct his lifelong lack of awareness about racism and Black history. Floyd's death had clearly been a revelation; Hartzell seemed the very picture of "woke." But sometime within the next 50 days, he became one of the original three PLL players to declare that they would not wear the BLM uniform patch. The spark was hearing Wiley in late June on a Fox Sports program critiquing the declaration on the Black Lives Matter Global Network website: "We dismantle the patriarchal practice. We disrupt the Western-prescribed nuclear family structure requirement." Hartzell then visited the BLMGN's website, saw that Wiley's reference was accurate and factored in that two of his best friends were police officers. Soon after, he made his decision.

In the weeks leading up to the players' arrival in Salt Lake City on July 19 for pretournament training camp, questions and objections to the BLM patch circulated among white players and their families. Mass calls were organized on Zoom to discuss the issue. Blacks like Kyle Harrison, Trevor Baptiste and Jules Heningburg tried to convince objectors that, in the BLM patch, they were seeking only "allyship": support for the core sentiment of the phrase "Black Lives Matter"—not of the BLM foundation—a basic endorsement of their Black lives.

Discussions became heated, and sometimes edged into dangerous territory. Friendships frayed. Some ended. "Very charged times," said Heningburg, co-founder and president of the PLL's Black Lacrosse Alliance, which had been formed just weeks before. "I can't say that the way people were acting at that moment was representative of who they actually are, and definitely there was: 'I don't agree with that organization.' Definitely there was: 'I have a cousin who's a police officer; it's really hard for me.' But then there, definitely, were other things said about Black people from certain areas and not great socioeconomic backgrounds versus other Black people, and perspectives on that that were being shared that were very insensitive and, I would say, just ignorant."

The Black Lacrosse Alliance afterward described the white players' position as "stark opposition" and the talks as marked by "a reciting of prejudiced speaking points throughout." Along with Team USA star Michael Ehrhardt, Hartzell led the discussion for white players opposed to the patch—and admits that some of them made "dumb" comments. He remains emphatic that he, like most white Americans, needs to educate himself more about slavery, "how wrong that was," civil rights, policing and today's Black experience. He learned much from his aggrieved Black peers. "It was a difficult time," Hartzell said. "But it was way more difficult for them than it was for us."

To the then-24-year-old Heningburg, son of a Black father and white mother, opposition to the BLM patch didn't necessarily make a white player racist, so much as confusing. The big picture had dissolved in the details. "I have a very close friend who would have taken a bullet for a Black person or anyone else—but he wouldn't wear the patch," he said. "How do you digest that?"

What began as an expression of support for Black pain and fear seemed, now, to have morphed into a matter of protecting white sensibilities. The white objectors kept pointing to the PLL's insistence on BLM as its sole social messaging choice for uniforms—at the same time the NBA was offering its players 29 options, including BLACK LIVES MATTER, I CAN'T BREATHE, and ANTI-RACISM. Some threatened to quit if forced to wear BLM. Word spread about players tearing BLM patches off their jerseys. Paul Rabil's nascent league, suddenly, felt as combustible as any other corner of America.

"We have, like, players who want to fight each other and everyone is now pointing at me as the bad guy," Rabil said at the time. "This is not a racist discussion; this has become a political discussion. That's how fucked up our country is."

Officially, the PLL's original support of BLM did not change. Its Black players were fully backed in their expressions of grief and defiance, as well as the founding, during those pre-bubble weeks, of the Black Lacrosse Alliance. But what happened among players was a decided setback for Rabil's vision of progressive unity. The vast majority of white players visibly supported their Black peers, and, according to Harrison, even some politically opposed to the BLM patch quietly reached out. But of the 141 whites in the PLL's 2020 bubble, some two dozen—including Hartzell, Michael Ehrhardt and fellow

Team USA stars Jake and Jesse Bernhardt—took the field without BLM patches on their jerseys. Tellingly, at a time when Black athletes in every sport were baring personal stories and justifying political and social positions, none of those opposing white players publicly explained their objection to Black Lives Matter—the phrase or the foundation or the patch. The league never issued a statement explaining why its once-mandatory expression of support had become voluntary. NBC's coverage highlighted the league's— and some white players'—support of BLM, but there was no mention of contentiousness. Only social media posts by the PLL's Black players, a week after the 2020 PLL bubble championship ended, ensured that the episode did not go wholly unnoticed.

"Why must the Black players justify their decision to wear a 'BLM' patch, yet not those players who opted not to do so?" the Black Lacrosse Alliance asked in a statement released August 17. "This double standard is a microcosm of the minority experience in our sport and beyond."

Attempts by PLL's diminishing rival, Major League Lacrosse, to address the charged racial climate were even more ham-handed. On July 2, the MLL had announced its plan to stage a six-team, nine-day quarantined tournament in Annapolis beginning July 18—the weekend, notably, before the PLL tournament. Upon arrival, the MLL's only Black players—Isaiah Davis-Allen, Chad Toliver, Mark Ellis and Kris Alleyne—decided to make a statement by standing alone or together at midfield, hand over heart, during each game's national anthem. Lacrosse media took note, and a photo of the league's biggest star, Lyle Thompson, with BLM written on his helmet strap, gained wide circulation.

But the "MLL Four" soon discovered that the league photographer wasn't shooting their demonstrations, and MLL social media feeds were not posting messages of support or sharing player posts on the matter. No explanation was given, no policy had been announced. The players felt ignored. Frustration among the MLL Four reached a breaking point, Toliver said, on July 23, after an MLL employee told him that the league's leadership—led by commissioner Alexander Brown—had banned any publicity relating to racial protests. That led the four, after recruiting representatives from the MLL's all-white Players' Council, to burst in on a meeting later that day featuring Brown, Chesapeake Bayhawks president Mark Burdett and MLL coaches. The scene devolved into shouting, some tears, accusations of lying, and the coaches, too, demanding answers.

The clash did spark change. Soon after it ended, Brown posted a tweet admitting his "candid, and at times, painful discussion" with the players, and pledged his support. Over the next few days the MLL commissioner also lauded the players in interviews and posts for igniting dialogue; ESPN networks began featuring profiles of the Black players and broadcast footage of their anthem display. Many white peers encouraged the four protesting players. But the aftertaste varied. Toliver, who grew up poor, the son of a single mother in Atlanta, and attended Rutgers on a full scholarship, completed his second MLL season that summer. He hasn't played since.

"This game changed my life, and now I get to a level where I'm like, *this* is really what this is like behind the scenes? This culture hasn't changed," Toliver said. "I used to love this game. I still do. But I don't love what comes with the game. The professional level and the political side of lacrosse has truly broken me."

Yet Major League Lacrosse, itself, was the most prominent casualty of lacrosse's Covid-19 summer. Since 2018, the Rabil brothers had been draining the 20-year-old operation of its talent, stature and value. Three teams folded. Then, in contrast to the PLL, the MLL's ill-conceived bubble tournament resulted in a rash of Covid cases and cancellation of both semifinals; the moneymen began to flee. Only two MLL owners remained when the Rabils, who three years earlier had dangled $35 million, called with a $1 million buyout offer. By the end of 2020, the PLL had swallowed the MLL whole.

Davis-Allen, an All-American and national champion at Maryland, was the sole member of the MLL Four to move into the new league. Toliver admitted that he was not at Davis-Allen's level, but said that, before the 2021 season, four PLL coaches contacted him about tryouts. Perhaps they were just casting a wide net; Toliver never heard another word. Soon after, a coach showed him one PLL colleague's text: "I heard he was bad for the locker room." Toliver suspected that was because of his hard-line questioning of the motives of some in PLL leadership.

Still, Toliver felt more disillusioned by the coolness of some of his fellow Black players in the PLL, including his one-time idol Kyle Harrison and Heningburg, his former Rutgers roommate. Heningburg denied that the Black Lacrosse Alliance froze Toliver out, and said that "bad blood" between the two leagues complicated matters. Mark Ellis put it more starkly: He was told that the PLL—in its effort to break the MLL and replace it as lacrosse's pro outdoor league—pressured its Black players to ignore the MLL Four's demonstrations.

"Black lacrosse is very small," Ellis said. "Chad played with Jules, Isaiah played with them, so before we go into the bubble, we're having these conversations with Chad, with Kyle, with Trevor, and we get to the point where we're in the bubble and text messaging back and forth and someone brought it up, 'Why aren't they supporting us and posting us?' Then we got the weird answers from some of the Black players: 'Oh, we can't do this, we can't do that . . .'"

His relationship with the game, too, would never be the same. Ellis went on to be a conditioning coach at Princeton and Northwestern. "Put it this way: I had an offer to play in the PLL and I didn't," he said.

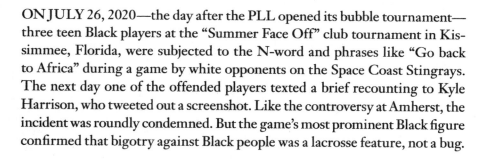

ON JULY 26, 2020—the day after the PLL opened its bubble tournament—three teen Black players at the "Summer Face Off" club tournament in Kissimmee, Florida, were subjected to the N-word and phrases like "Go back to Africa" during a game by white opponents on the Space Coast Stingrays. The next day one of the offended players texted a brief recounting to Kyle Harrison, who tweeted out a screenshot. Like the controversy at Amherst, the incident was roundly condemned. But the game's most prominent Black figure confirmed that bigotry against Black people was a lacrosse feature, not a bug.

> "I get texts/DMs/emails like this almost weekly at this point," Harrison commented in his tweet on the player's text. "This [excrement emoji] has to stop man."

One of Matt Holman's repeat guests on his *Overtime* sessions that summer was Mexico women's coach Daniela Eppler, a former midfielder at the University of Virginia. Eppler grew up in Baltimore's upper-middle class, the daughter of a Mexican mother and American dad; she suspects that her last name and Anglo features shielded her from early profiling. Though she always felt less naïve than her white UVa teammates, Eppler was stunned to hear the string of insensitive, coded or flat-out racist episodes described on the Zoom panels. And near the end of an August 5 episode titled "The Denial," you heard her heart all but break.

This came after Karen Healy-Silcott, a former Black star at Syracuse in the early 2000s, had spoken about how she and four Black teammates were greeted by one visiting team's bus flying a banner declaring, BEAT GHETTO LAX. Tia Schindler, the Cayuga pioneer of the Haudenosaunee women's program, acknowledged that "there isn't anything that I haven't heard, derogatory toward Native people, in my life," and spoke of the biased refereeing her teams receive, and the fact that, when her daughter moved to an all-white club team, she fielded questions about living in a tepee. "It's hard raising little brown kids in a world," Schindler said, "where they're always going to be seen as a troublemaker or whatever."

"Just based on conversations I've heard over the past few weeks," Eppler said, "if I had a child who was Black or Indigenous, I don't think I would send my kid to play lacrosse, honestly, right now, with the way that the community is. I just want to know what other people's take is on that."

Even for this diverse crowd, the idea seemed stunning. No one responded. Eppler kept going.

"What can we do to change the hostile environment that, I think, is so prevalent?" she asked. "Especially starting at the youth level, and then following through: The Mexican national team, the men's team, were called 'beaners' at the World Cup in Israel. Some of those players don't even want to play lacrosse anymore. That happens at all different levels. It's a huge problem. I don't think it's unique to lacrosse, but I think there's a high, high prevalence of that happening."

COMMON SENSE DICTATES that a sport's tint matters: The darker it is, the fewer racial incidents occur. It seems hardly coincidental that basketball and football, which on the Division I college and professional level are dominated by Black players, and major league baseball—59.7 percent white, 30.2 percent Latino, 6.2 percent Black in 2023—rarely report racial slurs by white players. The diversity issues in those sports focus mainly on overwhelming whiteness in management and the coaching ranks.

Conversely, a sport like ice hockey (whose players and fans skew even whiter than lacrosse) has long reported racial incidents at all levels, with Black players subjected to slurs from teammates and coaches, from fans during games and on social media. "Players Against Hate," an initiative started by a Black Washington, DC, hockey dad after his 13-year-old son had been subjected to "monkey sounds" and other racial hazing from opponents during a 2019 game, launched an online portal for the reporting of racial altercations in youth hockey. In its first year, 2021, the database compiled nearly 100 reports.

Yet, in one key sense lacrosse differs from hockey. Though the number of Black players in the North American game remains small at 4 percent, the overall white grip on lacrosse has loosened; from 2008 to 2023, the percentage of white men and women in Division I lacrosse declined from 89 to 83 percent, amid significant growth in the proportion of Latino and mixed-race players. Though that barely chips away at the perception of the game as "white," it does signal change. And studies have found that signs of change—especially when perceived as a slippage in numbers or status—make white people nervous.

In 2008, after the US Census Bureau released a report projecting that people of color would make up more than 50 percent of the population by 2042, Yale psychologist Jennifer Richeson began researching white reaction to the "threat" of losing majority status. Her 2014 paper with Maureen Craig, replicated by numerous other studies, found that white participants who read about demographic changes showed greater preference for their own racial groups, expressed "more negative attitudes toward Latinos, Blacks and Asian Americans," and—significantly—increased their expression of racial bias.

Once elected president in 2016, Donald Trump repeatedly declined to condemn white supremacists and QAnon adherents, and indulged in racist rhetoric like telling four minority Congresswomen to "go back and help fix the totally broken and crime-infested places from which they came." During Trump's first three years in office, hate crimes in the US increased by nearly 21 percent; from 2019 to 2020, the FBI reported a 32 percent increase in incidents involving offender bias against the victim's race, ethnicity or ancestry. Hate crimes against Asians rose 77 percent, while the largest bias victim category—anti-Black, with 2,871 incidents—rose 49 percent.

The trend spilled across American sports. From 2015 to 2020, the number of documented racist acts against US athletes of color at the high school, college and professional level quintupled from 11 to 54. On November 11, 2020, the Nation United Foundation, a nonprofit affiliate of the majority-minority Nation United club lacrosse program, launched its own ongoing "Incident Report," detailing 15 major instances—from 2018 to 2020—in which "an act of racism in lacrosse has led to a substantial, damaging effect, including negative publicity, compromised safety, scholarship risk, and job loss." The dramatic spike—up from Jovan Miller's claim of "at least 20+" racial altercations from 2004 to 2018—made it easy to wonder if Trump's presidency had granted offending white players and fans a tacit green light. The increase might only reflect a new age of revelation via social media and, starting in 2013 with the Black Lives Matter movement, increased motivation to hold offenders accountable. Certainly, the racial problem in lacrosse—and anywhere else—didn't disappear when Trump exited the White House: In 2022, the University of Central Florida's Institute for Diversity and Ethics in Sport compiled 58 racist incidents in all US sports nationwide.

"Right now, lacrosse is just still very white," Mexico attackman Ernie Melero said in early 2021. "It's still okay to say these things and there being no consequences. There's not much of an outsider way of thinking to confront them and tell them that is not okay. Me being the only Latino at Tufts, and I'm sure for a lot of other Latinos in my shoes, a lot of Black kids in my shoes: You want to fit in so much that you let things slide, too, because you're like, *I don't want to be secluded* . . . But I didn't think some of the things they did or said were okay."

Before the 2018 World Championship, Melero was working full-time as a program manager of Harlem Lacrosse–Los Angeles, serving 150 to 200 kids, spending five days a week embedded in Walton Middle School in Compton. His instinct had been to let racial jibes "just roll off my back." His team's toxic experience in Israel changed that. "That Greece game definitely got me thinking in terms of my role and what I do for a living," Melero said.

In March 2021 he was still working for Harlem Lacrosse–LA, and coaching a Santa Monica–based, mostly white youth travel team, Berserkers, and had joined the coaching staff at majority-white Mira Costa High School in Manhattan Beach. "I'm around white kids all the time," he said. "How can I help them to not be as ignorant as some of these guys that we played in the World Championships? What can I do to push these kids to think about the world as a whole?"

Melero had no control over the racial makeup of the Mira Costa or Harlem Lacrosse teams. Berserkers was different. Figuring that only familiarity could dilute ignorance, he made a point of mashing up the rosters of his club team, blending poor, darker-skinned players in with the rich white ones.

"We take our kids from the inner city, and we have overnight trips down in San Diego with the Torrey Pines high school kids, Del Mar, Rancho Santa Fe," Melero said. "As important as it is for our kids to be mixed in with those kids, it's just as important for those kids to be around our Black and Latino kids and get a different perspective. Because, long-term, the more inclusion and mixing there is between the races, the better the sport is going to be."

SHORT-TERM? LACROSSE'S white majority seemed hardly capable of rapid change. Yet in one major instance, it did change. Whether this was due to enlightenment, embarrassment or a cynical reading of the zeitgeist isn't clear. But when confronted in the summer of 2020 with an injustice—and public relations debacle—of its own making, the sport's elite reversed course fast.

The crisis, paradoxically, was slow to develop. Though announced in December 2019, the fact that the Iroquois had not been invited to the 2021 World Games went all but unremarked upon for eight months. Partly, this was because the Haudenosaunee were preoccupied with a contentious overhaul of the Nationals board and its financial practices, governance of the women's team and preparation for the 2020 U-19 World Championship in Ireland. Then Covid-19 forced postponement of both tournaments for a year. World Lacrosse also mounted a backchannel effort to convince the Haudenosaunee that it did support their inclusion in the Olympics, but were pursuing a strategy of increments: Make no waves. Follow IOC guidelines that only recognize nations with UN recognition. Get lacrosse admitted to the 2028 Summer Olympics, *then* push for Iroquois inclusion.

But that approach depended on two factors: Iroquois trust and Iroquois silence. And Iroquois leaders didn't trust World Lacrosse. By mid-March 2020, Oren and Rex Lyons informed the federation that the Iroquois believed both World Lacrosse and US Lacrosse officials opposed their involvement in the Olympics—and would be taking the matter public. Their opening salvo arrived that month in an article, co-written by two Nationals officials for *Inside Lacrosse*, detailing the World Games 2021 snub and its role in boxing the Haudenosaunee out of any Olympic bid. It had no immediate effect. On April 2, when the World Games announced its postponement to 2022 due to Covid-19, the Iroquois were still not on the list of participants.

Then, in a display of social media's random nature and reach, the issue suddenly caught fire. After *Inside Lacrosse* reposted its piece on July 18, the Nationals retweeted it that night with a "call on colleagues, teammates and fans to support this Olympic Dream. It's time to raise the Haudenosaunee flag at the Olympics." Ensuing posts—feathered within the summer's overall racial justice tumult—kept the conversation bubbling. A day later Aidan Fearn, an 18-year-old midfielder of Mi'kmaq descent at The Hill Academy, Canada's preeminent prep lacrosse incubator, launched a petition on Change.org that demanded Iroquois participation at The World Games 2022 and called on the 10 invited lacrosse nations to boycott in support. World Lacrosse's initial response arrived later that night.

"For events conducted outside the auspices of World Lacrosse, such as international, multisport events, World Lacrosse does not determinate eligibility criteria," the organization said in a statement. It then described how England, Scotland and Wales, which operate at World Lacrosse events as individual entities, are required to combine for World Games and Olympic events as Team Great Britain. "Unfortunately," the statement concluded, "the Iroquois Nationals, as was the case in the 2017 World Games in Poland, do not meet the current eligibility criteria as established by the World Games."

For anyone aware that World Lacrosse had recognized—and benefited from—the Iroquois Nationals for 33 years, it came off like an abdication of responsibility; Fearn's petition would eventually gather 55,000 signatures. The statement confirmed two years of suspicion that, given a choice between the Olympics and the Haudenosaunee, World Lacrosse would readily forsake the latter. Now it was happening. As CEO Jim Scherr had warned, the sport was going "down the road without them."

Then, on the morning of July 24, 2020, two pivotal figures weighed in. Billionaire Joe Tsai tweeted:

```
I support the Iroquois Nationals to be in the 2022
World Games in Birmingham. I've studied the history
and there are strong precedents for the Iroquois
to be represented in competition recognized by the
International Olympic Committee.
```

Paul Rabil then tweeted:

```
Pledging my support and action for the inclusion of the
Iroquois/Haudenosaunee in all international lacrosse
competition. This is their game. #TogetherAsOne
```

Facing the choice of siding with a fellow governing body or rapidly gell-ing public sentiment, 39 minutes later US Lacrosse—led by longtime CEO Steve Stenersen, who, torturously enough, was also a World Lacrosse vice president—issued a statement calling the Nationals and the Haudenosaunee people "the very essence of lacrosse," and said the organization "stands firmly in support of the Iroquois Nationals' participation as a sovereign nation in international lacrosse competitions, including The World Games 2022."

On July 26, the Canadian Lacrosse Association chimed in louder, stand-ing "unequivocally in support" of Haudenosaunee participation in The World Games 2022, threatening boycott and calling for reconsideration of eligibility standards for the Olympic Games. "A World Championship of lacrosse, in any form, without the Haudenosaunee is not a World Championship," said Jason Donville, director of the CLA national teams. Now World Lacrosse's two most prominent members had publicly changed their minds.

By any measure, it was an astonishing turnaround. Timing mattered. Erupting amid a reckoning on racism against Black people in and out of the game, the World Games controversy fueled a fire already alight. And unlike slurred Black or Latino lacrosse players, whose lot offered no singular source or easy solution, the Haudenosaunee cause seemed both obvious and simple to fix. Native Americans invented the game, gave it to white people and fielded the third-best men's team in the world. The top eight were invited to Birmingham. Of course they should be there.

Among all the advocacy, however, no voice mattered more than Joe Tsai's. The Alibaba co-founder and owner of the Brooklyn Nets, finan-cially backing everything from World Lacrosse Championships to the new Premier Lacrosse League to Scherr's salary, was also indispensable to the game's Olympic hopes.

In 2017, Alibaba had agreed to pay $800 million to be an Olympic sponsor through 2028, the year of the Los Angeles Summer Games tar-geted by World Lacrosse. The musty term for the game's fading Baltimore establishment, the "Lords of Lacrosse," is barely heard anymore. But if any figure qualified for the title, it was the Taiwanese-born, Canadian billionaire lacrosse fanatic now living in Southern California. And few actions demon-strated Tsai's clout more clearly than the July 24 tweet he sent in support of the Iroquois Nationals' presence at The World Games and the Olympics. From then on, said then–Israel Lacrosse head Scott Neiss, the tone from World Lacrosse changed.

"Those same people that constantly were the source of negative language—'We've got to kick them out!'—were now using language supportive of them being in the Olympics," Neiss said. "The guy cutting their paychecks told them to."

To be fair, Scherr and Stenersen and World Lacrosse board members had begun preparing for Birmingham when "Grow the Game" and Olympic participation were the only goals. Because of that, Scherr said, he and the board assumed that everyone in lacrosse, including the Nationals, knew that the IOC didn't recognize the Iroquois and accepted their exclusion from Olympic-style competitions. "World Lacrosse should have understood the full impact of that," Scherr said, "but didn't."

Not only were the Iroquois prepared to challenge the World Games decision in court, but they had unexpected firepower. Two prominent North Carolina lawyers—Ripley Rand and Alex Buckley, who captained Tiffany's first team at Brown—represented them pro bono. In one of their first Zoom calls with World Lacrosse officials, Nationals officials were accompanied by Canadian attorney Howard Stupp, a former Olympic wrestler who had just retired after three decades as the IOC's director of legal affairs. Stupp was confident that the Haudenosaunee should and could compete in Birmingham, and signed on to advise on IOC matters. World Lacrosse had hired Scherr for his Olympic expertise and contacts. Stupp was just as wired in, if not more.

On July 29, 2020, World Lacrosse, the International World Games Association and the Games' Birmingham Organizing Committee announced that they were exploring "whether it is necessary to change the format for the lacrosse competition at the World Games 2022." Citing its adherence to eligibility criteria, the three bodies stated that they "also have inclusiveness among their key core values." They were now working to balance both priorities, "where special circumstances exist." A deal took only two weeks. On August 14, World Lacrosse issued a statement thanking World Games authorities "for their favorable response to our request to allow the Haudenosaunee Nation to compete in TWG 2022."

Only one obstacle remained: The eight-team men's field for the World Games had already been announced. For the Nationals to compete in Birmingham, one nation would have to withdraw. This was no easy ask: Sports people are notoriously selfish, especially when it comes to events that occur but once or twice in a career. The most obvious candidate was Ireland—12th ranked and invited to Birmingham only because Olympic rules forced superiors like

England and Scotland to combine; Puerto Rico and the Philippines were excluded because they were not yet full World Lacrosse members; and the Iroquois had been ignored. When Ireland Lacrosse CEO Michael Kennedy joined a late-night call on August 27 with Scherr—and then–World Lacrosse communications chief Darryl Seibel—he began by saying, "I know what you're going to ask."

By then, the 45-year-old Kennedy had spent three weeks canvassing the two dozen "heavy-lifters" of the Ireland program. From the start, there had been near-unanimous insistence—most notably from 2018 Ireland captain Aaron Cahill, who had grown up in the Syracuse area playing with and against the Onondaga—that the Irish should give up their place.

"And," Kennedy continued, "I'm going to make this very simple. We want to do whatever it takes to enable the Iroquois to compete. If it's eight teams only, we're ready to voluntarily vacate to make room."

Looking back years later—long after Ireland's extraordinary gesture had been called "inspiring" by Scherr and praised as a ray of graciousness in a graceless era, and Ireland Lacrosse became the first organization outside North America to receive a Musial Award for sportsmanship—Kennedy was still worried that the original intent had been misconstrued.

"Language is important," he said. "I didn't want to say, 'We're pulling out because we object.' We shouldn't have been invited in the first place. This was righting a wrong. I didn't want to be, like, the Great White Savior. In some interviews, I specifically used the words: 'They're taking back what is rightfully theirs.' Which, you know, kind of echoes land disputes and stuff like that. I wanted that to be the message, rather than 'Oh, we're magnanimous.'"

The Brooklyn-born Kennedy had fallen in love with the game as a boy growing up in Croton-on-Hudson, New York, and carried it with him when he moved to Ireland at 21. When asked why he thought the Haudenosaunee needed to be in Birmingham, Kennedy managed to say, "The Iroquois represent the soul of the game," before his voice thickened, then cracked. "Even after all this time, I get emotional about it," he said. "It's all very personal to me. I met my wife through lacrosse, we have two kids because of lacrosse, I became the CEO because of lacrosse, I became an international athlete because of lacrosse, I became a referee, a treasurer, a president, a coach—so much of what makes me the man that I am. I owe the game."

The official Nationals response was just as emotional: "We are storytellers, but today, we are without words as we contemplate the generosity of spirit shown by Ireland Lacrosse. All we can say is: You are in our hearts. You are part of the spirit of lacrosse. We will never forget that. *Nyawenha. Go Raibh Maith Agat.* Thank you."

The reinstatement of the Iroquois on September 2—and the resultant acclaim from inside and outside lacrosse circles—marked the end of a dramatic turning point. Now it didn't matter that the IOC didn't recognize the Haudenosaunee as a sporting nation. Now everyone knew that World Lacrosse's mission of making the sport an Olympic event, showcased at the 2028 Los Angeles Summer Games, could not proceed without the Nationals front and center.

Scherr makes no apologies for the pivot. Once the game's premier powers—and players—announced their outrage and support, his job as CEO was to read the room and adjust. Yes, he said, lacrosse's old guard had an "intolerance" for the Iroquois built up by three decades of contending with their "continual logistical problems." But the World Games controversy revealed "an evolution in attitude." Or, at least, an understanding that the old intolerance would no longer be tolerated.

"It helped World Lacrosse realize that, if were we to be the steward of the sport we're supposed to be and present our very best possible case for inclusion in the Olympic Games, we have to view the Iroquois Nationals as an asset, not a liability," Scherr said. "You could say, 'Oh, we did this because it was a noble and right thing to do.' Yeah. But we also did it because it's the most pragmatic thing to do."

However cold the calculation, the change was real. Amid the 2020 summer of mass racial protest, it mattered that the overwhelmingly white establishment of a traditionally white bastion reversed its attitude toward North America's first minority.

"Now the Iroquois fate is tied to lacrosse's fate," Israel's Scott Neiss said two months later. "That's been achieved. If lacrosse is going to be in the Olympics in '28, the Iroquois are going to be with it. The people that are advocating for lacrosse, the Olympics, have to—and are—leaning into the Iroquois as a positive toward the sport's inclusion in the Olympics. Not a negative. Not a black eye. That's the biggest win of 2020."

III

CROPS

L IKE THE REST of the world, the lacrosse community emerged from the Covid-19 shutdown in early 2021 primed for a reset. Months of bruising dialogue about the Black experience had everyone on high alert. The indispensability of the Iroquois had been proven like never before. Newly admitted Panama, the Dominican Republic and the US Virgin Islands had boosted World Lacrosse membership to 68 nations; South Africa was next. And the revamped pro game could suddenly do no wrong: After nimbly creating America's first successful "bubble" tournament in 2020, the Premier Lacrosse League signaled long-term viability that December by absorbing rival MLL. The pandemic left other sports feeling battered. Lacrosse considered itself improved.

But it wasn't that simple. In February 2021, a Marquette men's player was kicked off the team after repeatedly uttering the N-word on a social media post. A month later, a men's lacrosse game at Sewanee, a.k.a. "the University of the South," was halted by officials after students in the stands yelled racial slurs, including the N-word, at a team from Emmanuel College that included seven Black and numerous Indigenous, Latino- and Asian-American players. The perpetrators were never identified. Prominent Black lacrosse players expressed disappointment on social media. US Lacrosse issued a quick, if toothless, condemnation: "Playing a sport that you love should not result in having to endure harassment . . . We stand in support of the players from Emmanuel College, and are committed to doing our part to ensure that everyone feels welcomed and embraced in our sport."

For lacrosse, the episodes and response felt numbingly familiar. Indeed, throughout the spring of 2021, with the Virginia men hopping over the Covid gap year and grinding to a second straight NCAA title, it was easy to feel that the sport had picked up right where it had left off. If anything, lacrosse's cultural fault lines were now more defined, even institutionalized. On one hand the college game was still a traditional space appealing to its traditional base—well-off white families—in a sports-first venue largely free of social messaging and protest. On the other, in its third summer of play, the Premier Lacrosse League offered fans a wholly different sensibility—baldly liberal, stridently supportive of racial and sexual minorities.

That this reflected Paul Rabil's self-image is no accident. The PLL co-founder and prime salesman may not have been the best lacrosse player of the 21st century, but he's the most important, perhaps even irreplaceable in the sport's mission to become a mainstream phenomenon. Rabil knows this. But he has also consistently used his platform to advocate for the marginalized and rattle the macho jock ethos, whether it be sporting a cancer-fighting, "Woman Power" T-shirt in an Instagram post ("Woman power does not diminish my own; rather, it enriches us all"), or writing about cyberbullying and "non-heteronormative" sports culture after receiving a barrage of gay slurs prompted by his supportive Pride Day photo. ("No matter your sexual orientation, gender, race, religious affiliation or political views, people are people, and love is love. Tearing others down is never helpful.")

Still, on June 25, 2021, few of the fans bustling into Johns Hopkins's Homewood Field for a weekend of PLL games could have expected the radically different feel in lacrosse's Yankee Stadium, core of an old-line establishment in a Mid-Atlantic lacrosse galaxy informed by generations of lore, relationships, gossip and winning. Most had come because the retiring Kyle Harrison, at 38, was playing his last game on the hallowed turf, and Rabil, his old teammate, is the last in the line of Hopkins legends. The two men had led the Blue Jays to their last national championships, in 2005 and 2007, which, arguably, made Rabil's unapologetic bid to reengineer the game experience even more jarring.

Growing up in Montgomery Village, Maryland, one of the nation's most ethnically diverse areas, Rabil was one of the few whites in his basketball league; only in lacrosse did he find himself in the majority. That dynamic tilted at Hopkins, where the best player and captain was Harrison, and their friendship sensitized Rabil to the need for white allies. Then he came of age amid what he calls the two most "destructive" headlines in the game's history, the Duke lacrosse rape case and the murder of Yeardley Love, when the sport's image hit its nadir. Rabil conceived of the PLL not only as a nimbler and richer pro game, but a reboot, offering a striking change in emphasis, referencing lacrosse's Native American roots as not just exotica, but its philosophical core.

In its inaugural season the PLL had held land acknowledgments—honoring the field's original Native American owners—during a weekend of games in Albany, New York, and again in 2020 during the bubble tournament in Salt Lake City. Few fans experienced either. Rabil intended to rectify that for 2021. First, he acquired the world's most famous Indigenous player, the one who spoke most eloquently about lacrosse's spirituality. The whole point of the PLL's merger with the MLL, Rabil said, was to get Lyle Thompson. Now, in Thompson's first season, all 11 stops on the nationwide tour featured land acknowledgments—be it for the Cheyenne or Lenape or Ohlone—and each tribe was showcased on the oversized schedule posted on a tower near Homewood's main entrance. Next to it was a banner featuring Thompson's oversized, eight-paragraph explanation describing the forced removal of Indigenous people from their homelands ("The unjust treatment continues today"), calling for healing for all people of color, and making this entreaty:

> To all the non-Indigenous players and fans of the PLL: I invite you to take the time to learn the history of the land that we will not only be playing on but also the land you occupy in your day-to-day lives. I encourage you to support Indigenous movements and causes such as the #NODAPL (North Dakota Access Pipeline). In our way we say, "Water is Life."

It certainly was news to many there that, in attending a lacrosse game at Johns Hopkins, they were treading on land stolen from the Susquehannock, Nentego (Nanticoke) and Piscataway peoples. Most didn't expect to be forced—if only for a glancing second—to consider the environmental costs of Big Oil. The milling crowd featured much plaid, plenty of burly white men in sockless loafers, belts festooned with American flags. There was a Vineyard Vines banner and dozens of males wore impeccably faded polos with the trademark pink whale. But a handful of Black faces also peppered the stands; one Black father, tattooed and sporting long braids, sported a PLL T-shirt, complete with LGBTQ pride colors, reading, LACROSSE IS FOR EVERYONE. A Black teenager wore one reading, *UCK RACISM, with a lacrosse helmet in place of the F.

A few minutes before Friday night's opener, Lyle Thompson's face appeared on the stadium's video screen. He repeated his land acknowledgment and—as if to ensure that no one thought he was speaking solely for himself—the PLL public-address announcer followed by speaking of "respect for those who walked here before us" and the "Indigenous roots of the Creator's Game."

Down on the field, the game presented a slightly more diverse tableau than the usual college fare. Three Black players—Trevor Baptiste, Brent Adams and Romar Dennis—suited up for the Atlas, while the Whipsnakes were led by Seneca attackman Zed Williams and a Black PLL photographer roamed the sideline. The next afternoon, Kyle Harrison's last game at Homewood showcased an even greater example of his legacy. A clutch of young Black stars, all of whom used him as a role model, warmed up for the Redwoods-Chaos game: Isaiah Davis-Allen, Jules Heningburg, Dhane Smith, Myles Jones and Josh Byrne. More Black faces were in the stands.

Half an hour before the start, an announcement from the One Love Foundation began on the video screen: six minutes featuring the short life and killing of Yeardley Love; newsclips of police cars and mourning in Charlottesville; footage of her mother, Sharon Love, speaking about relationship violence and educating college kids on the signs of abuse. At the end, the place filled with reggae music, the ubiquitous strains of Bob Marley's "One Love."

Pro-Native, pro-women, pro-LGBTQ, anti-racist, anti-elitist: By the time the announcer officially rattled off Harrison's lifetime achievements and introduced him as "the first Black player to win the Tewaaraton" to a standing ovation, the PLL ethos was clear. A sweeping glance revealed lacrosse's constituency as still overwhelmingly white, but it was a whiteness that, for the moment, lacked the usual self-satisfaction, the kind provided by generations of comfort and money and cemented position; a whiteness repositioning itself as open, aware, tolerant. A familiar insurance name hung among the sponsor banners ringing the field, but in this context it read like a declaration: PROGRESSIVE.

The Redwoods lost, 11–9. Thicker, beard graying, Harrison had his one solid shot attempt blocked and barely figured in the contest. He didn't seem to mind that his final game at Homewood also represented his first-ever loss there; one of Hopkins's great winners always had a sharper perspective than most. His children and parents were present, sharing in all the affection. His father watched from the second floor of the Blue Jays' $10 million field house. Miles Harrison couldn't stop grinning as he sat amid the air-cooled luxury, the historic plaques and aura. He knew. In the longest game, generation to generation, his side won.

"SEE that flag?"

Oren Lyons was sitting by his son, Rex, in the cozy stadium at US Lacrosse headquarters north of Baltimore in Sparks, Maryland, just after noon on October 23, 2021. The Canada and Haudenosaunee women were playing on the field below. The Onondaga faithkeeper, 91, nodded across the playing field, in the direction of the three aluminum poles standing on the far side. Centered between the US stars-and-stripes and Canada's maple leaf, the purple-and-white standard of the Iroquois stirred gently in the gray autumn air.

"That took a lot of doing," Lyons said, "getting that flag up there."

Officially, this two-day gathering of the top three nations was a glorified test event, "World Lacrosse Super Sixes," the first chance for the sport's authorities to view and tinker with lacrosse's newest version at the highest level. Following the lead of cricket and rugby, a working group led by US Lacrosse's Steve Stenersen spent the previous three years crafting a shorter, smaller, faster, more unified game for men and women—six players to a side, 30-second shot clock, eight-minute quarters. Created to appeal to Olympic gatekeepers for the 2028 Summer Games, Sixes stresses speed over physicality, shooting over defense; in pace it resembles fast-break basketball more than classic field lacrosse. Oft described as box on grass, it thus seemed likely to help the Iroquois Nationals in their eternal quest to beat the two superpowers outdoors.

Lyons wasn't worrying the details. While the World and US and Canadian officials and players and coaches there focused on technical aspects, the former history professor had his eye on history. In the 19th century, when George Beers appropriated the Creator's Game for Canada and Americans embraced it as an elite pastime, lacrosse's Haudenosaunee inventors had no say. In the early 1930s, when Canadian hockey owners reshaped the game's contours to fit inside unused hockey arenas, lacrosse's inventors again were not consulted. And when Iroquois coach Brett Bucktooth was appointed to the six-person task force that drew up the formal rules for Sixes in December 2019, it almost felt like an insult. That same month the Iroquois Nationals had been left off the initial roster for the then–2021 World Games in Birmingham, where Sixes would make its debut.

But in the 13 months since a social media onslaught—and the support of Joe Tsai and Paul Rabil—forced the World Games to buckle and Ireland's team ceded its spot in Birmingham, the Iroquois said, World Lacrosse had treated them like full partners. For the first time ever, white people were conducting a new and dramatic overhaul of the Creator's Game, and the Haudenosaunee were involved, being heard, respected.

Opened in 2016, US Lacrosse's headquarters still carried a newish aura, as if waiting for the surrounding foliage to fill in. A monument space honoring the 70-plus lacrosse players killed on 9/11 stands on one end of the showcase field named for Denver coach Bill Tierney. A statue of Yeardley Love, frozen in mid-stride, was erected in 2020 near the flagpoles. Another 16-foot statue featuring two ancient Native players in bronze—titled *Creator's Game*—looms near the entrance.

The day is special for another reason. After 38 years, the Nationals organization has replaced the "Iroquois" label popularized centuries ago by the French, and for the first time both men and women are competing under their own name: Haudenosaunee. With just under four minutes left, a hawk—believed to be a messenger for the Creator—circled over the field.

"Oh," Oren said. "That's the best sign you could ever get."

There were others. Indeed, the mere presence of Lyons at the opening Sixes game signaled an advance not only in Haudenosaunee lacrosse, but in Haudenosaunee culture. Many traditional members of the confederacy remain opposed to women playing lacrosse—even with non-wooden sticks—and women on the Nationals have learned to live with public snubs and social media attacks. Lyons's position on this has always been less hard-line, but the Nationals co-founder remains the face of Longhouse conservatism and a prime interpreter of the lacrosse stick's "medicine." So when Haudenosaunee defender Cassandra Minerd glanced up from the field to see Lyons—along with Onondaga spiritual advisor Tracy Shenandoah—sitting there, she was stunned.

"That's when I knew: *Shoot, we're making change here*," Minerd said.

It had been a lifetime coming. Minerd, too, is Onondaga—Eel clan—and a kind of royalty: not only is she related to Lyons and Shenandoah, but her uncle is the Grand Council's supreme spiritual leader, Tadadaho Sidney Hill. Born in 1995, Minerd grew up in the Longhouse faith on the Onondaga Nation outside Syracuse, heard how Onondaga and Seneca clan mothers had derailed the women's national lacrosse program in 1987, was 10 when the program restarted with a semi-rogue sanction from the council at Six Nations of the Grand River. Her grandmother forbade her from touching even a plastic stick. But with her mom's blessing, Minerd secretly played youth lacrosse in nearby LaFayette, avoided all talk of lacrosse around her august relatives and never played catch where any of them could see. "I still don't even play catch down at my mom's house on the Nation," Minerd said in 2024. "I just get worried—because so many people don't like girls playing—that someone's going to come snap my stick in half on me."

In eighth grade, Minerd went public by playing on the girls' team at LaFayette Junior/Senior High School. The sight of her with a stick in the hallways sparked backbiting from Native peers, tumult within the family; even her sister said, "Girls shouldn't play lacrosse." Haudenosaunee had filled out LaFayette's boys' teams for generations. For the next four years Minerd was the LaFayette girls' lone Native; her most unqualified support came from white teammates. She went on to play four years at SUNY-Brockport, graduated, then earned a master's degree in environmental science.

All the while, Minerd never discussed lacrosse with her uncle, the Tadadaho, nor Lyons or Shenandoah—not even when she began playing, at 16, for the Haudenosaunee Nationals in 2011, not during or after she played every game and the Nationals finished seventh at the 2013 World Championship. It was just as well: The spiritual leaders at Onondaga aren't always skilled at hiding distaste. But starting in 2019, various elements combined to make clear that the Iroquois men needed the women's lacrosse program—perhaps for its survival—and vice versa.

For the Iroquois Nationals men, outside pressure to join forces first came from World Lacrosse, which, in its accelerating bid to make lacrosse an Olympic sport, stressed that gender equity would be a key factor for IOC decision-makers. Word, too, circulated that Nike—the main Nationals sponsor since 2006—was pushing a merger with the women's program as a condition of its sponsorship renewal. If Haudenosaunee men wanted to be part of the 2028 Summer Olympics in Los Angeles, the way was clear.

At the same time, Nike, along with influential figures within the confederacy, was also pressing for an overhaul in governance and finances for the men's program. By 2020, much of the Nationals administration from the 2018 World Championship was gone: Leo Nolan had replaced Ainsley Jemison as executive director, nine of 13 board members had been replaced, Rex Lyons had assumed—with Oren's blessing—his father's role as board spokesperson. In September, the nonprofit fundraising arm, Iroquois Nationals Development Group, was established, ensuring that the program would no longer be solely dependent on rich men like Smokin' Joe Anderson and Curt Styres, the Halifax Thunderbirds owner, who bankrolled the program's silver-medal run at the 2019 World Indoor Championship.

"If you're going to go to the Olympics, compete at that level, you can't be doing what we were doing," Rex Lyons said. "Top to bottom, there was a lot of internal stuff that needed to be cleaned up."

None of it, however, approached the crisis that would shatter the Haudenosaunee women's program. On January 23, 2020, a Wisconsin court convicted Six Nations faithkeeper Matthew Myke, 35, of repeated sexual assault of a 14-year-old girl in 2013. A member of the Iroquois Nationals 2003 U-19 and Onondaga Community College's 2006 national championship teams, Myke was known by many in the Haudenosaunee spiritual and sports community. Among some young Haudenosaunee women, Myke had—at best—a creepy reputation. According to one player and the team's current general manager, Claudia Jimerson, Myke had harassed or victimized some in the current Nationals player pool.

"I was 16 the first time he tried to talk to me, and he was already at least 10 years older than me," said defender Aryien Stevens, a Nationals player since 2011 and the first Seneca woman to sign a letter of intent to play Division I lacrosse, at Niagara. "We were at a powwow in Salamanca, and the categories in powwow are broken up by age. I was sitting there under my tent, and I had my card on that says, like, TEEN GIRLS, right on the front of my dress, and I was talking to my friends and I felt somebody tugging on my braid. I turned my head and he was just standing there looking at me. And he asked me to dance. I was like, 'No, I'm okay.' After that, he just wouldn't leave me alone. Everybody in our communities had a story about him. Any-time I was at Longhouse, he would be trying to find a way to get near me, or poke me in the sides, or was trying to message me on Facebook. This was all when I was underage."

In September of 2020, Myke was sentenced to 10 years in state prison and 10 years of additional extended supervision for his crime against the unidentified 14-year-old. Afterward, the Six Nations media outlet *Two Row Times* revealed that, before sentencing, 32 character-reference letters had been written for the purpose of gaining Myke leniency from the court. One, written and dated February 6, 2020, was signed by Haudenosaunee Nationals women's general manager Tia Schindler. In her letter, Schindler described Myke, a cousin, as "a good friend" and "good man" and "very passionate" about preserving Haudenosaunee language and culture.

The *Two Row Times* story contained a public link to the 32 support letters, soon spread across social media. After reading Schindler's letter, a growing group of current and former Haudenosaunee women players expressed concern to program officials and privately began circulating a petition demanding her removal as general manager. Yet through the team's October tryouts and the ensuing three months, Kathy Smith, the longtime executive director of the Haudenosaunee women's program, took no action. Schindler continued as GM. On February 5, 2021, Smith officially received the petition and its 18 signatures. Three days later, citing inaction by the five-woman Haudenosaunee board, the team's stated role as a safe space and the fact that "Matthew Myke has been a predator to players that have been apart [sic] of this team," Cassandra Minerd announced her resignation from the 2022 Nationals World Championship team.

"We have players that I know well who are sexual assault victims and you are going to sit there and allow Tia to continue to be General Manager?" she wrote in an email to the board. "You strive to empower women on our team yet you have someone who supports a rapist and an abuser who exploits women? Tell me how that makes any sense."

Minerd also posted news of her stand publicly on Instagram and Facebook. The same day, Aryien Stevens—citing the staggering rates of domestic and sexual abuse against Indigenous women, "myself being the 1 in 3 thats [sic] been sexually abused as a child"—also resigned from the program. Three days later, February 15, director Kathy Smith responded with a letter acknowledging Stevens's "pain," but informed both players that Schindler's future as GM would be determined in an undefined way by current and former players. Two other high-profile Haudenosaunee organizations had quickly apologized after learning their personnel had written letters in support of

Myke. Arguably the most front-facing Haudenosaunee women's organization, it seemed, intended to do and say nothing.

Minerd and Stevens, and others, also alleged a history of favoritism, bullying and lack of financial transparency by Haudenosaunee team management, but Schindler's letter—concrete and sensational—was impossible to ignore. It also presented the men with an opportunity. Influentials within Onondaga and the Iroquois Nationals men's program—including Rex Lyons, Mark Burnam and Minerd's uncle, Tadadaho Sidney Hill—had monitored the women's situation. Stated concerns included a "toxic environment created by team management," player safety and well-being. Unstated was the worry over a stain on the Haudenosaunee name just as its Olympic bid was gathering steam.

Up until this time, merger talks between the men's and women's programs had stalled. Now, the men launched a hostile takeover. On February 15 (the same day as Kathy Smith's response to Aryien Stevens), the nonprofit Iroquois Nationals Development Group sent the Nationals board a confidential plan to condemn the current women's staff and form a new program under the banner—and Grand Council sanction—of the Iroquois Nationals men, with full representation on the players' committee and Iroquois Nationals board of directors. The intent was not solely bureaucratic.

Making clear its break with a 1,000-year-old mindset, the Rex Lyons–directed proposal also sought to assure "the long overdue participation of women and [create] a more sound representation of the Haudenosaunee Community on the International Lacrosse stage." It framed the embrace of women's lacrosse as a symbolic first step: "A paradigm shift is required to dismantle structures that uphold violence and compromise the safety of Indigenous women and girls. These ideologies and actions, past and present, must be rejected. A new path forward is needed. In fact, it is demanded."

A hallmark of Haudenosaunee governance is its deliberate process of consensus, but from there matters moved with remarkable speed. Guided by voices aligned with the men's program, Minerd and Stevens co-wrote letters to both the Iroquois Nationals board and the Haudenosaunee Grand Council of Chiefs in Onondaga, formally requesting the disbanding of the current women's program and creation of a new one under their aegis.

Soon after, representatives from the Iroquois men's program petitioned the council at Six Nations of the Grand River. On April 5, 2021, the Grand River council revoked its 2006 sanction of the Haudenosaunee women's program. By mid-month the Iroquois Nationals had its new women's team up and running. The old program's five board members, executive director Kathy Smith, and general manager Tia Schindler were out. Covid restrictions, then, prevented the gathering of the Grand Council of Chiefs at Onondaga; instead, without approval from the confederacy's clan mothers and 50 chiefs, the Haudenosaunee women's team was de facto folded into the Iroquois Nationals men's organization under its original sanction of 1983.

On May 16, the new Iroquois Nationals women's team announced tryouts. But the controversy—combining hot-button issues like sexual abuse, crime, sports, money, Haudenosaunee politics and tribal definitions of male-female roles—didn't end. Friendships fractured. Emotion swamped subtleties. Some outright defended Matthew Myke, but many in the confederacy—while appalled by his acts or Schindler's letter—opposed what they perceived as a male, Onondaga power grab. It seemed dodgy that, after 37 years of, at best, ignoring women's lacrosse, the Iroquois Nationals now fancied themselves champions of women. On June 21, nine former Haudenosaunee Nationals women players issued a letter of protest to the Nationals board, stating that "it has been alarming to watch as the Iroquois Nationals promote #TogetherAsOne to the world, while simultaneously disempowering our women—a desecration to the very matrilineal society you claim to hold and respect."

As one of the letter's signatories—and Kathy's daughter—Katie Smith put it: "I still don't feel like they truly care about us women players. They needed us. They need us for World Lacrosse and the Olympics, and for the Nike sponsorship. That's why, all of a sudden in the past year, it's been this really big push to get their own program—really, by any means necessary."

Five days later, June 26 and 27, another lacrosse referendum was held at tryouts for the new Haudenosaunee Nationals women's team on the campus of Onondaga Community College. New Iroquois Nationals board member Claudia Jimerson, who had played on the 2013 World Championship squad with her daughter, Alie, was now the team's director of operations; Shaniece Mohawk had been named GM. For the first time in memory, players were not charged a fee, but nobody could predict the turnout. Opposing camps were dug in. And nobody could say how the traditionalists at Onondaga would react: The night before, word had it that some clan mothers—like the clan mothers who had derailed the program in 1987 by vowing to lie on the field—were coming to protest.

Neither Cassandra Minerd nor Aryien Stevens, also Longhouse raised, would dare play against the will of clan mothers. After just hearing the rumor, Minerd's body began to tremble. But when they walked out on OCC's field the next day, no clan mothers were waiting. No protest occurred. Necessities players had never seen under the old regime—free lunch, trainers to tape ankles, scrimmage pinnies—were made available. Most striking: 77 women had come out with sticks in their hands, the most in Nationals history.

"I remember looking at Aryien and being like, 'We did it,'" Minerd said. "The old program, we never had over 20 girls at a tryout, barely ever. Seeing 70 Native girls? I wish there was a picture of a drill: There were two lines, and they went all the way back to midfield. I saw Claudia after the first day and I said, 'Can you believe it?'"

FOUR MONTHS LATER, the opening "World Lacrosse Super Sixes" game at US Lacrosse headquarters ended with Canada beating the Haudenosaunee, 20–13. Someday, lacrosse historians will mark it as the coming-out party for the new Nationals women's program and the sport's first visible step toward the 2028 Olympic Games. October 23, 2021, should also be remembered for one woman's decision to take a stand against a North American crime spanning centuries. Selena Lasota, a Canadian citizen and once its rising star, walked off the field after her first appearance in a Haudenosaunee uniform. She had tallied three goals and three assists against her former teammates. "There's no way that I can represent Team Canada," she said. "Having Indigenous roots and being an Indigenous person, it's against all of my values if I was to play lacrosse with CANADA across my chest."

In 2015, the former Northwestern All-American had led Canada to an upset win in the final over the US and its first U-19 World Championship, was named to its 2017 senior national team and was expected to backbone the Canadian program for the next decade. But in college Lasota had been dismayed how, whenever she wrote papers about the mistreatment of Native Americans, her "powerhouse" history professors knew little of that history. During the pandemic's first onslaught, she was home in British Columbia, drawing closer to her Katzie First Nation roots. When society reopened, Lasota began working as a child and youth mental health counselor for British Columbia's Nuu-chah-nulth Tribal Council in the coastal town of Tofino.

Then ongoing revelations about Canada's long-shuttered "Indian Affairs" residential school system hit a grievous low. On May 27, 2021, news broke that the remains of 215 (later revised to 200) Indigenous children had been found on the former site of Canada's largest residential school in Kamloops, British Columbia. The discovery, unearthed by a researcher using ground-penetrating radar, raised the confirmed fatalities within the Canadian system—which lasted from 1880 to 1997, and was largely operated by the Catholic Church— to at least 4,000. Some victims were as young as three years old. That week, Lasota, 25, phoned Gary Gait, the general manager of Canada's women's national team and a British Columbia legend, to tender her resignation.

Within days, Prime Minister Justin Trudeau ordered Canada's flags to fly at half-staff (and would keep them there for the next five months); in June, another 933 graves were found buried on former school sites in British Columbia and Saskatchewan. In August, Canada committed $320 million to aid the excavation of burial sites and support survivors. (A year later the Pope would call the Canadian schools "a genocide," and issue a formal apology.) In lacrosse, PLL players were issued orange EVERY CHILD MATTERS helmet straps to highlight the issue; the indoor NLL issued EVERY CHILD MATTERS decals and warmup shirts. Once again, Lyle Thompson, playing with an orange ribbon in his hair, became the face and voice of Native pain for North America's sports public.

Lasota's defection didn't become known until the Haudenosaunee announced its Super Sixes roster October 9, and she would do nothing to explain it until issuing a statement three weeks after the tournament in Maryland ended. No other media requested comment, and Lasota didn't feel right addressing the Kamloops revelation unless asked. Indeed, her move seemed more like a personal trek, tied to her work in Tofino with second- and third-generation descendants of school survivors—and to revelations about her own family.

At the time of the Kamloops revelations, Lasota had discovered a personal narrative typewritten in 2001 by her Katzie grandmother, Lorain. It describes Lorain's life as a 10-year-old in a fish cannery in British Columbia in 1950, daughter of an alcoholic Indigenous mother and white father, hearing pretty white girls screaming, "go away you dirty little Indians," when she approached a gathering to eat strawberry shortcake. "Crying crying I ran to get away from the dirty little indians," Lorain wrote. "I was one of them. How could I feel such hurt?"

Lorain spent her days locked in a shack while her mom worked, cooking and diapering and doing everything possible to keep the confines and her little brothers, as Lasota put it, "so clean and so proper." As soon as she could, Lorain moved off the Katzie reserve. For the rest of her life, she tried to scrub away the "dirty" and erase her "Indian"-ness, carrying with her the same self-loathing imposed for a century on all the bodies in the schools and cemeteries, all the snipped ponytails and crushed languages and separated families, before and since.

"She did not want to be Indigenous. Like, she hated it," Lasota said. "That's a product of residential schools. That's a product of being stripped of your identity."

Three weeks before the Super Sixes, on September 30, 2021, Canada's first-ever National Day of Truth and Reconciliation, a group of school survivors led dozens on a two-mile march from the former site of a residential school in Tin Wis to the Tofino village green. Lasota walked with them. She watched adults like Grace Frank, a resident of two nearby schools from 1968 to 1972, reenact the verbal abuse delivered by white nuns onstage. "When I first went to residential school, I spoke my language and every time that I spoke my language I got strapped and whipped," Frank said afterward. "I have scars inside my hands and on my elbow. It was a living hell."

That only reinforced Lasota's decision, and eased any anxiety in competing against four of her former Canada teammates. Lining up for introductions with other Indigenous women in EVERY CHILD MATTERS shirts, wearing a Haudenosaunee jersey for the first time, felt full circle, like an embrace of everything her grandmother had been taught to deny. Lasota played with her usual ferocity, and a new lightness.

"It just feels like where I'm supposed to be," she said. "It makes me a happier person. Playing for a bigger reason, all of the unmarked graves that have been found: It takes the game out of the perspective of just winning and losing."

The next morning, Sunday, October 24, the Haudenosaunee women's team played Team USA on the showcase field at US Lacrosse headquarters. New Nationals women's director Claudia Jimerson—Cayuga, Bear clan—stood a few yards behind the Haudenosaunee bench, and began recounting all manner of history, program and personal: the year's "frenzy" over Matthew Myke, the team's death and resurrection, and the challenge now of assembling tryouts and competitions while figuring out finances and the new partnership with the Haudenosaunee men.

"There's growing pains still," Jimerson said of the new management team. "We're building a plane as we're trying to fly it: That's our motto right now."

Near the end of the third quarter, the USA was ahead, 14–5. Her daughter, Syracuse senior Jalyn Jimerson (sister Alie also played for the Orange), had scored once, and Jimerson was done rehashing the year's "ugly" details. Then she saw Lasota and midfielder Lois Garlow veering off the field toward her.

"Yo, Claudia," Garlow said. "They're saying some nasty stuff."

"He said, 'Get back on the island,'" Lasota said.

"Right there," Garlow said, pointing toward the American bench. "That piece of shit said that: 'Get back on the island.'"

The quarter ended, and all the Haudenosaunee players gathered near the bench. Both coaching staffs, World Lacrosse and game officials met on the neutral turf between benches. Five Haudenosaunee and five USA players met on the field. And for the next five minutes, instead of starting the fourth quarter, the Haudenosaunee-USA women's lacrosse game became a heated discussion about Native grievance and sensitivity, about language and humor and seeming white obliviousness; it became, in fact, another corner of Western culture roiled by the George Floyd era's yet-unsettled standards of racial discourse.

The controversy had started with a pregame hypothetical between a male US assistant coach and four American players—including goalie Rachel Hall—concerning the players they'd like to be stuck with on a desert island. The coach named three, and after Hall stopped Lasota's undefended, seemingly automatic shot with 1:12 left in the third quarter, the coach yelled, "You're back on the island!"

Lasota and Garlow, turning upfield near the USA bench, didn't hear it that way. "I thought he yelled, 'Go back to the island!'" Lasota said just after the game. "And I was like, *Are you kidding me? That's just outrageous.*"

To her and the rest of the Nationals, the phrase sounded like a reference to Lasota's home on Vancouver Island and echoed the dismissive racist chestnut "Go back to the rez." It also resonated as a dig at the Haudenosaunee name for North America: "Turtle Island." Lasota, primed by residential school horrors and her defection to the Haudenosaunee, became furious.

After hearing the explanation from the US staff, Jimerson told them about the Haudenosaunee's emotional year. She said Lasota's reaction was now common among her people, their nerves trip-wired for any hint of a slight. So, she asked, firmly, "Can you not say that?"

There was still a full quarter to play. Lasota would be facing off against former teammate Lindsey McKone, her partner in Northwestern's rebuild, just off another semifinal appearance at the 2021 NCAA Championship. The two waited at midfield, alone and talking and leaning on their sticks. McKone felt terrible. "She said she was so proud to be here and play and had so much joy—and then that moment just took it away from her," McKone said that afternoon. "It hurt to hear that, because I know how deeply she continues to be affected by all of this."

After the game, the US coach approached Lasota and apologized for any misunderstanding. Coming from him directly, the inside-joke explanation seemed reasonable, but nudged her only from outrage to uncertainty. When asked if she believes him, Lasota said, "I don't know." The damage was done. For many on the Haudenosaunee team, the incident just resurfaced, again, suspicions that no flag raising, no signs of acceptance, can fully overcome.

The US players discussed the Haudenosaunee afterward in the locker room. McKone—a white American child of wealth from Houston—said that most didn't get why the Native Americans instantly assumed the worst. But, she added, dismissing that as overreaction would be a mistake.

"For them to assume that means that there's a bigger issue in society," McKone said:

> We're wearing USA on our shirt and we represent a country that has horrible history with Indigenous people, and people of color in general. So it's almost embarrassing that that happened, too, because we're trying to represent who we are and our morals and trying to be as inclusive as possible. I feel so awful that that even had to be a conversation—but it does.
>
> None of us, on our side, have ever experienced that. And to see it and to experience it is something that I hope sticks with everyone. As in: I need to think about what I'm saying. I need to think about what I'm doing in my actions when in the position that we're in as white people.

A MONTH LATER and 240 miles south, in a packed classroom in tidewater Virginia, a group of young, proud, Black men gathered: the Hampton University lacrosse team. Here is where lacrosse had placed its splashiest bet on hope and change. The 2016 launch of Hampton University as the first Division I men's program at a historically Black university generated unprecedented publicity, including a two-hour blitz on ESPN before the season-opener that featured an endorsement from 80-year-old Jim Brown. "Hampton is exploring, educating and offering opportunities off the beaten path: that starts with lacrosse," Brown said then. "Where it ends, nobody knows, because there's so many things that the African American community have not had the opportunity to participate in. If lacrosse can be one that opens the door, then I'm all for it."

Hampton, too, happened to be ground zero for two resurgent cultural issues. In 2019 *New York Times* writer Nikole Hannah-Jones published her opening salvo in *The 1619 Project*, a controversial recentering of American history around the first arrival of African slaves that year, here at Point Comfort. In 1878, a year before founding the Carlisle Indian Industrial School, Captain Pratt had made the educational enclave for freed slaves the testing ground for his "kill the Indian and save the man" residential school system—and thus a crossroads of the continent's original sins. Hampton head coach Chazz Woodson's observation that "lacrosse is America" might have sounded like overkill, if not for when and where he said it: On Hampton's campus, two months after taking over the program.

Hampton is also where a pioneer's last act was about to unfold. More than 60 years after lacrosse's white establishment declared Jim Brown the greatest—and more than 50 after he became an embodiment of unapologetic Black power—his youngest son, Aris, was readying to play his first season for the Pirates.

The classroom held 33 players from Boston, Dallas, Baltimore, Iowa, Phoenix, Long Island, South Florida, Seattle, northern and southern California, Kansas City, Maryland, North Carolina. Two were white. They told of how they came to the game, early frustrations with the stick, why they chose Hampton. Most had choices. Shuttered by Covid in 2020 and again in 2021, the program remained a work in progress, and the best Black players—like their white peers—tend to gravitate to schools with a shot at the Final Four. The Hampton kid takes a longer view.

"To make history," said senior midfielder Ian Groom of Washington, DC, who ricocheted back to Hampton after a year at the University of Hartford. "There are a lot of small Black boys and girls who are looking at lacrosse and not seeing themselves. Obviously you might see Kyle Harrison or Myles Jones but, playing here, you get to show them that not only can one individual thrive, a whole team can thrive . . . and give them a beacon of light when it comes to lacrosse and what it can be. Not what it is."

Freshman midfielder Nathan Turner, who played for racially mixed Brooke Point High in Stafford, Virginia, said, "I knew it was going to be a safe environment for a lot of African American players. I just knew that this was going to be a place where I can fully express my Blackness."

Chazz Woodson, the former MLL star who co-founded the Black club team Nation United, had been hired on his third try at the Hampton job in July 2020. Returning to his hometown at last was sweet, but Hampton's Covid cancellation of its 2021 season left him without a team to coach. His first 16 months on the job were spent raising money, finding a conference, recruiting. It wasn't an easy sell. Since 2016 Hampton had won a total of just 12 games. All that newborn buzz was gone.

"Ultimately if this thing isn't successful, there's no story," Woodson said. "If this becomes a program that fades out, it just becomes a blip on the radar. Nobody's ever talking about it again."

The signing of midfielder Aris Brown caused a stir. After committing, Jim's son spoke of wanting to "make some history" and "change the culture of how lacrosse is looked at." But despite winning three conference titles at the tony Sierra Canyon School in Los Angeles, Aris wasn't a highly rated prospect, and in both his lanky, six-foot frame and soft-spoken manner, he radiated none of his dad's fierce physicality. He spoke of a tendency to play cautiously, to be too hard on himself, and of the lacrosse world's welcoming smallness.

Sixty-five years old when Aris was born, Jim Brown never pressed his son to follow in his footsteps. Aris grew up loving soccer. After first playing lacrosse in eighth grade, he would fling the ball back and forth with his father, receive the occasional tip. Aris always felt anxious when Jim would come to one of his games, "and he wouldn't even say anything. Just his presence, being there, I'd have to do really well. I didn't really want him to come to everything, because I didn't want that pressure." Some opponents taunted him about being Jim Brown's son, but the more mystifying cruelty came from parents in the stands.

Aris figured, maybe, on playing Division III somewhere. But a four-day stint with Nation United in Orlando introduced Aris to Black lacrosse ("a certain swag I hadn't seen before") and two Hampton commits. He signed on. Now, two years later, Aris was like most of his teammates in this study hall, still waiting to play his first college game. Fall practice was in full swing, but Covid restrictions had stunted campus life. The 2022 opener seemed far away.

In the classroom, Nathan Turner's mention of a "safe environment" prompted a question: "How many here have experienced a racial incident in this game?" Twenty-six of the 31 Black players instantly raised their hands. As they counted off, their collective expression read less like anger than resignation. When asked how many had white teammates come to their defense, only 13 Black hands went up.

Several detailed their various moments with the N-word or its variants during club or scholastic play. Nathan Turner spoke of how the insults came mostly from opponents, sometimes teammates: jabs about the jungle, words like "boy" and "cooner" and "monkey." Some told how the incident fueled them, how they said nothing and played harder, channeling rage into a sprint, a spun stick, a score. Pride, love of lacrosse, wouldn't let them walk away.

Questioned about the nation's "racial reckoning" since 2020, players universally responded with distrust. The impetus, they said, was not a desire to correct a great wrong. It was fear. Whites in authority were terrified of having their careers and reputation canceled. "People care about it because it was time to care about it: It was on the news every day," said sophomore midfielder Ethan Mitchell. "Companies now want to hire 'Diversity'? They didn't care about it two years ago . . . Now it's dying down. I don't think people care as much anymore."

Well before dawn the next morning, Chazz Woodson sat in a parking spot near Emancipation Oak, a tortured beauty with a 100-foot spread, deemed one of the world's great trees. During the Civil War, the Union Army maintained control of nearby Fort Monroe, and here established the "Great Contraband Camp" for escaped slaves. Legend has it that, in 1861, a Black teacher named Mary S. Peake began teaching freedmen, young and old, under the live oak's boughs. Two years later, before a crowd of former slaves, Lincoln's Emancipation Proclamation was read in the South for the first time.

Woodson backed up, eased through the gate and made the short drive to practice at Armstrong Stadium. He talked about the growth of Black faces in the game, social media making their voices heard like never before. And he believed that—for some—the white effort to bolster inclusivity is sincere.

Stadium lights blazed against black sky, under a moon in partial eclipse. Lacrosse goals squatted on the football field's 10-yard lines. Thirty-two

Hampton players passed and dodged out on the field, whipping balls through the slowly brightening air, running sprints from the 50-yard line to the five, giving the ancient Haudenosaunee game a different look. Their Black head coach was demanding more pace, yelling, "We're holding the ball too long! Move it!"

Aris Brown wasn't one of them. He was standing on the side, not practicing because of "stomach issues." Aris would end up spending the 2022 Hampton lacrosse season at home in Los Angeles, and the Pirates lost all 10 of their games. When he returned to campus the following fall, he tried again, but all his passion for lacrosse was gone. On May 18, 2023, a few weeks into Aris's internship with his father's old NFL team, Jim Brown, 87, would die in Los Angeles.

"Part of the reason I wanted to go back was because I wanted him to see me play," Aris said. "I talked to him about that, and ultimately he was like, 'This is your life. You're grown. You make the best decision for yourself.' That was great to hear, but it's always, like . . . I wish I would've been able to do that. That was one regret."

PART 2

THE LONG GAME

"Pope Francis has urged: 'Never again can the Christian community allow itself to be infected by the idea that one culture is superior to others, or that it is legitimate to employ ways of coercing others.' . . . In no uncertain terms, the Church's magisterium upholds the respect due to every human being. The Catholic Church therefore repudiates those concepts that fail to recognize the inherent human rights of indigenous peoples, including what has become known as the legal and political 'doctrine of discovery.'"
—Holy See Press Office, March 30, 2023

"This is what makes the World Championships. Yeah, the US and Canada will probably play the championship game again, but what happens with the Haudenosaunee is much more impactful. A group of people can't claim basketball. There's not a group of people who can claim football or wrestling; the Greeks, maybe, can claim the marathon. The roots of this game are given to us by the Indigenous people. And we can learn so much from them about the game, about the stick, about the ball. About the meaning."
—Quint Kessenich, former Johns Hopkins
All-American and ESPN commentator, June 16, 2023

I

TREATY BOUND

FOR NEARLY FIVE DECADES, a central piece of Tiffany family lore passed from family members to friends and the occasional reporter, from one generation to the next, with a mystery tied to its tail. The story of Brad's buffalo herd, the arrival of Oren Lyons at the front door, and the 11 head shipped to Onondaga to reunite, after 1,000 years, the nation with its spiritual brothers would be retold. The gorgeously detailed treaty between nation and family would draw the usual gasps. But the end was always vague: The Onondaga had pledged to repay the loan after six years by sending 11 buffalo back to the Tiffany ranch. They never appeared, and the conclusion seemed to be that the lead nation of the Haudenosaunee—forever insisting that the US honor the terms of its treaties, not least the annual payout of muslin under the 1794 Treaty of Canandaigua—didn't honor its most recent one.

For the Tiffany family, this was not due to welching on the part of Onondaga: Brad, as the story goes, decided—because his own herd was too large or out of sheer magnanimity or both—to free the Onondaga of their obligation. What was once a trade at some point in the late 1970s became a gift. This always seemed odd to Lars, knowing his dad to be a stickler on the details of a business deal. Indeed, in the years after Brad sold off his entire herd in 2001, he spoke of the transaction more as a loan, subject to being called in anytime. "Well," Brad told Lars more than once, "I guess they have 11 of my buffalo if I ever want some of 'em."

Such detail can seem trifling, considering that both the Onondaga and the Tiffanys view their buffalo exchange as a historical highlight and each other with high regard. But the Onondaga narrative is completely different. "We paid him back," Oren Lyons said. "We gave him 20 buffaloes back."

Lyons explained that this happened well after the treaty deadline fell in 1980, but he couldn't recall even the decade. Lars; his mother, Faith; and his brother, Peter, reiterated that the family never received 20 buffalo back from the Onondaga. Now the self-image of both parties was in question. The Tiffanys had proudly thought their dad's grant an act of generosity, one small symbolic reversal of a vast American wrong. The Onondaga—treaty sticklers, warrior proud—have no interest in being a white man's charity case. It seemed impossible for both to be correct.

Unlike Lyons and the Tiffanys, Vincent Johnson remained intimately involved with the Onondaga buffalo herd for the next 43 years. A member of the buffalo medicine society, Chief Johnson was on the Tiffany porch on New Year's Day, 1975, when the treaty was presented to Brad, and took charge of the herd, living within a stone's throw, in 1980. Johnson said that Brad Tiffany did not release the Onondaga from their treaty obligation. On one of Johnson's later visits to the ranch, Brad told him personally to alter the obligation. Now, the 83-year-old Johnson said, "The deal was: He asked us to give the buffalo to the other nations."

Brad told no one in his family of this verbal revision to the treaty terms; no new deerskin or paper was drawn up. Directing the Onondaga to instead distribute the 11 owed buffalo to the other five nations in the Haudenosaunee Confederacy may not, in his mind, have changed the original terms. But the Onondaga acted as if it did. According to Chief Johnson, they spent the next 42 years trying—under perceived new terms—to honor the Tiffany treaty.

It wasn't easy. An early attempt to send 26 buffalo to the Oneida in Canada, via North Dakota, fizzled because of botched paperwork. Disputes over the buffaloes' new pasturage derailed shipments to the Seneca at Allegany and the Mohawk at Akwesasne. Meanwhile, Onondaga's herd kept expanding, to its current estimate of 70 to 80 head, and became a vital part of Onondaga life. As a boy, Ji Thompson, Lyle's father, would help round up strays; as a boy, Lyle, as part of the reservation lawn-cutting crew, enjoyed seeing them ramble. Every year with the herd, Johnson held a buffalo ceremony and dance, attended by chiefs and clan mothers. "The buffalo are there," Johnson said. "We have a feast and they all come around us in a semicircle."

The beast's role as a food source toggles between spiritual and practical. Onondaga citizens can buy meat for the cost of butchery, $1 to $2 a pound.

Ten head were killed for the welcoming feast at the 2015 World Indoor Lacrosse Championship at Onondaga. In 2020, amid the economic strains brought about by the pandemic, 22 head—all descendants of Brad Tiffany's grant—were killed and distributed across the confederacy. "It's a gift that can't ever be measured," said Betty Lyons, president of the American Indian Law Alliance. "Especially during Covid . . . Because we fed the community with that meat, we shared it with other communities. It was a very rough time for everyone, so it gave an even deeper meaning."

Then on April 22, 2021—30-plus years past the deadline—the Onondaga at last honored the Tiffany treaty when it delivered 20 *dege-ya-gih* to the Seneca in Cattaraugus. Another 10 head, Johnson said, were sent to the Seneca in 2022, and then eight more—making for a total more than three times the treaty requirement. A matter of compound interest, perhaps.

SINCE HIS TIME with the Iroquois Nationals in Israel, Lars Tiffany had been focused on life in Charlottesville: recruiting; winning two NCAA titles; managing four dozen young, excitable men. After Brad's death in 2019, Lars retrieved the massive deerskin treaty from his dad's home and hung it by his bed. He tracked the Iroquois men's surprisingly weak, fifth-place performance (the Haudenosaunee women finished seventh) at the 2022 World Games in Birmingham, but the new Sixes discipline left him cold. Onondaga felt very far away.

Then, on September 14, 2022, the Nationals board of directors posted job openings for general manager, head coach and assistant coach of its men's team at the 2023 World Men's Field Championship in San Diego. Tiffany sent in a résumé and cover letter. Referencing Israel and his need to repay a debt to the Haudenosaunee for inspiring and making him "a better coach and father," he could not have been more clear.

"To be back with the Haudenosaunee as an assistant coach would be a tremendous affirmation of my mission," Tiffany wrote. "I intentionally write this previous sentence using the word 'assistant.' My head and heart both are convinced that a Native American serve as the leader and face of the team."

Two weeks later, Nationals board member Vince Schiffert phoned to offer the job of head coach. Tiffany stammered some. "Did you read my letter?" he said.

It wasn't the first time—and would hardly be the last—that Haudeno-saunee leadership left him puzzled. After the official announcement, through nine months of public tryout camps and roster cuts and Zoom sessions, much would be made of Tiffany's lifetime connection to the Onondaga, his prized wood stick, the buffalo herd. But in all that time none of his bosses with the Nationals, and no Onondaga elder, would mention that the treaty finally had been honored just two years before. That this was unintentional seems clear: When asked about the treaty, Oren Lyons answered instantly. Chief Johnson couldn't have been more eager to speak.

When the Haudenosaunee Nationals announced Tiffany's appointment as head coach for the 2023 World Championship on November 1, 2022, it was viewed by the greater lacrosse world as a great coup. No one in the field game could match his recent run—two straight NCAA Division I titles and a no-shame loss in the 2022 quarterfinals to unbeaten—and eventual champ—Maryland. Tiffany was, at that moment, the best coach in America. No previous Nationals coach had come close to winning even one NCAA championship. But there was one vocal dissenter.

Nationals attackman Austin Staats tweeted on the evening of February 2:

```
One thing I can't get my head around is having @HAU_
Nationals have white peoples lead us.
```

Coming after two quiet months, and drama-free tryout/training week-ends in Akwesasne, Buffalo and Albany, the tweet jolted Nationals management. A breakout star at the 2018 World Championship and No. 1 pick in the 2018 NLL draft, Staats, 25, had since emerged as a scoring force with the pro indoor San Diego Seals and the jewel of the next Haudenosaunee generation. The Mohawk from Six Nations of the Grand River, in Ontario, is also notoriously combustible. In 2021, Staats allegedly bit off the tip of an opponent's finger in a hotel brawl and was suspended by the Premier Lacrosse League for a year; after being reinstated in 2022, he played two games and quit. A relentless bull onfield, few athletes are more unpredictable off it.

Staats's tweet presented the Nationals new leadership with a telling test. Tiffany had been chosen—over 10 other candidates, including Albany head coach Scott Marr, Brock University head coach Vince Longboat and four other Native Americans—in part to upgrade the team's organization to Division I standards. Previous Nationals coaches had been shackled in team selection by political factors like tribal standing; player work commitments made tryouts and training optional. But Tiffany—in concert with Haudenosaunee general manager Darcy Powless and assistant coaches Chris Doctor, Longboat and Marr—required anyone who wanted to play in San Diego to commit to cutdown sessions in Buffalo and Albany and online Zoom meetings and chalktalks. The Nationals board had backed him on every directive.

That included the case of Chase Scanlan. Based solely on talent, the two-time All-American—and the youngest member of the 2018 team in Israel—belonged in the Haudenosaunee player pool. But, in April of 2021, Scanlan's Syracuse teammates—some showing public support for the One Love Foundation—refused to take the field with their leading goal scorer after he was accused of domestic abuse against his girlfriend. Soon to be jailed and charged, Scanlan left school, completed a 14-week domestic violence program and agreed to a plea deal requiring him to stay out of trouble through the spring of 2023, during the time frame that Tiffany was picking the team.

Otherwise insistent on deciding his 23-man roster, Tiffany asked the board to rule on Scanlan's candidacy. The vast majority voted against. "Very confirming," Tiffany said. "If I'd gotten different messaging about Chase Scanlan, I was prepared to tell them I can't be the coach anymore. I talked to Rex Lyons offline and said, 'Understand my position: Even if I wasn't adamant about violence against women, I'm at the University of Virginia. We had a man kill a woman here. I can't publicly survive if I'm part of an organization that is accepting Chase Scanlan.'"

Though impolitic, Staats's transgression nevertheless touched on a central question: Weren't the Nationals created in 1983 as a vehicle for Haudenosaunee sovereignty? The lone Native American to coach a Division I program—Bucknell's Sid Jamieson, a Cayuga—served as the program's first head coach from 1983 to 1986, and Mark Burnam, a Mohawk, equaled the Nationals' best-ever field performance in 2018. Since then, cultural identity had exploded as one of North America's defining issues, and the program changed its name from "Iroquois" to "Haudenosaunee." Staats, the son of a longtime Six Nations coach, was hardly alone in asking: Shouldn't the Indigenous now be led by the Indigenous? "There's a lot of people that said it," Burnam said.

Tiffany took Staats's tweet as a slam directed less at him than the Nationals 11-person board; again, he let them decide the response. Within hours four members, including Rex Lyons and executive director Leo Nolan, met Staats on a conference call. Powless said the board considered kicking him off the team. "We told our players: 'If you can't commit to us in the right kind of way and be good solid citizens . . . *Austin Staats*, get off your tangent about this,'" Nolan said. "He got the message and, hopefully, it'll make him a better person: Aim before you shoot. Think before you go off in a way that may not be the best thing for all of us."

Staats deleted the tweet soon after. Final cuts loomed. Ultimately, they decided on a warning: Any misstep could result in banishment from the Nationals for life. In his final phone call to Staats before naming the roster on March 7, Tiffany brushed off the tweet and focused on the game: "You're overweight," he told him. "Lose 20 pounds. Show you're committed. You're one of the 23, but if you're not ready to play? We'll play 22."

AT THE END OF March 2023, Pope Francis, after 530 years, renounced the Doctrine of Discovery. Tadadaho Sidney Hill said it was only a first step.

"This is the problem: somehow it got into the law," Hill said. "One thing you do learn of the US government is the separation of church and state. So here you have this law set down by the pope, this religion, and here they were taking it into their system and making it possible to do what they did to us. Making it alright. So rescinding it is one thing. Okay: that's a big gesture." But it resolved nothing. It did nothing to dissolve the layers of American case law and comment—like Justice Ruth Bader Ginsberg's majority opinion in the Supreme Court's 2005 majority opinion, in City of Sherrill v. Oneida Nation of New York, that rejected Native sovereignty over repurchased tribal lands—built upon the Doctrine. "It's progress," Hill said.

Since World Lacrosse's reversal on the Haudenosaunee in 2020 amid public pressure from Joe Tsai and Paul Rabil, lacrosse's dominant strains— Indigenous and white—seemed in the process of erasing George Beers's fingerprints, braiding into some new, possibly glorious, whole. That process gained a bonding momentum in August 2022, when the International Olympic Committee and the Los Angeles Organizing Committee named lacrosse to its shortlist of new sports to be considered for the 2028 Summer Olympics. It also set up a struggle over the soul of the sport. Because lacrosse's Olympic campaign is uniquely problematic—the IOC, following the lead of the United Nations, does not recognize the Haudenosaunee as a nation—it contains an open question: What if the Nationals are not eligible to compete? Complicating the matter is the fact that, for some Haudenosaunee, the Olympics are literally beside the point.

"When that bell rings?" Lyle Thompson said in April 2023:

I personally just don't care if lacrosse goes to the Olympics. Everyone wants to talk about it being a huge step in "Growing the Game." I could care less about the game growing if it doesn't come with the cultural values of it—and we're stepping so far away from that. Not with the [new Olympic discipline] Sixes: Lacrosse is lacrosse; if you have a stick you're playing the game. My thing is, at a professional level, at a youth level, at a college level, you're seeing lacrosse become like AAU basketball. It's a money grab.

Right from eight years old, a parent is looking at that kid as a scholarship. There's no cultural value in that. You go to a summer tournament, and you see showcases for the kid who wants to make their highlight tape. It's so far from what we know as the game of lacrosse. It's becoming the sport of lacrosse. It's becoming what kid is the best, what kid is the flashiest, what kid gets the most goals. I grew up with the same 12 kids playing almost every single tournament and all 12 of those kids had to throw a [long]pole in their hands, including me; had to play midfield, including me; had to play attack, including me. My dad didn't care about the winning and losing. He cared about our competitive nature. He didn't care who scored. He cared about what he was teaching us, the values that we were learning as lacrosse players.

By high school, Thompson said, he had absorbed them all: Respect. Playing with a good and clear mind. Passion. "Nowadays, you've got kids playing at the collegiate level who don't even know if it's their passion; it's *instilled* in kids. It's the same thing at a professional level, and it's really been hard for me to be participating. I mean, I'm playing in a professional world with players who make it really hard for me to enjoy the game. Their values don't honor the spirit of the game.

"You talk about Native Indigenous values? We personify everything, from the sun to the moon to the stick to this game. The game itself is energy—and I personify that energy. How do I honor that energy? How do I respect the spirit of this game? It's with my intention, and how I play the game. I don't want to go down in history as someone who won these championships or 'transcended' the game. I just want to be recognized as someone who honored the spirit of what that is: That ball of energy that we know as lacrosse. The Medicine Game. And I have a hard time seeing it being honored right now." Four weeks later, the 30-year-old Thompson—citing a need to focus on "myself, my family and my communities"—announced a sabbatical from Rabil's frenetic Premier Lacrosse League for 2023.

Thompson wasn't surprised by Austin Staats's tweet. He had heard the sentiment often. Indeed, a couple hours later his older brother, Jeremy—the Nationals senior statesman and one of Tiffany's tri-captains—said that he wished the Nationals board had named a Haudenosaunee like former Syracuse stars Cody Jamieson, Sid Smith or himself as head coach. "Should've been and could've been," Jeremy said. "They know what it takes to win at that level . . . It's a no-brainer."

Lyle disagreed. "You don't have to be Native to carry Indigenous values, and Lars embodies that. He has this spiritual connection and to be spiritual is to be present. It's to have a lot of gratitude. Our culture is all about respect and respect is to be mindful. He carries that."

Lyle also disagreed with his brother and like-minded others because he felt that they suffer from "a lack of understanding what we need to actually beat Canada and the US." He was referring to Tiffany's organizational skill and minutely planned practices, but the stated priority of beating Canada and the US—the logical goal for any other No. 3 team—represented a decided shift for the Haudenosaunee.

For 40 years Nationals management, led by Oren Lyons, had made clear that Haudenosaunee identity would trump nearly every other consideration. In 2006, two-time Iroquois head coach Ron Doctor, a Mohawk, quit 48 hours before the men's World Championship opener after the board—citing their lack of matrilineally descended bloodlines—declared his sons, Chris and Vince, ineligible to play. The insistence on using self-made passports derailed the Iroquois men's World Championship bid in 2010 and nearly again in 2018—but provided matchless publicity. Sovereignty, not winning, was the prime mission.

The use of Haudenosaunee passports overseas remained nonnegotiable. But Rex Lyons confirmed that the new, 11-member Nationals board had learned from its most recent controversy. They saw how popular outrage had forced World Lacrosse, after tacitly endorsing the shutout of the Nationals from the 2022 World Games, to backtrack: With the top eight teams invited, a competition without the No. 3 Haudenosaunee seemed indefensible. If that Olympic-sanctioned body could be embarrassed into reversing its ban on an Indigenous team, why not the Olympics themselves?

In short, the board realized that even in matters of identity, everybody loves a winner. The more the Nationals succeed—especially as David against the American Goliath—the better for Haudenosaunee nationalism. "Your standing is critical to the amount of empathy you get," Rex Lyons said. Otherwise, when it comes to considering the Haudenosaunee for the Olympics, "you could see [IOC members] saying, *Well, it's romantic but not really necessary.* They would love to be able to do that."

Considered in that light, choosing Tiffany was the no-brainer: The Olympics provide a platform for sovereignty like no other; beating the superpowers in San Diego would help Haudenosaunee to get there; he gave them the best chance. For nine months, Tiffany, the great American coach, would be serving as a great Native American tool.

"These guys are carrying the nationhood on their shoulders," Lyons said. "In a perfect world we definitely want to have Haudenosaunee coaches. But right now, we're going to give them the best, because we still have to be competitive. If we lose that? We wouldn't have the leverage that we have."

ON APRIL 30, 2023, a Sunday afternoon, No. 3 Virginia hosted No. 1 Notre Dame, and the stands and sidelines at trim and tidy Klockner Stadium were filled mostly with well-educated, economically set, white Christian Americans. It was UVa's 2023 Senior Day. The pregame video board boomed with testimonies from teary parents saluting their graduating sons. The national anthem played, and everyone rose as one and sang or hummed or just felt the fiery old words.

As the final recorded strains faded in the sunlight, and the cheering crowd made its clattering return to their seats, Lars Tiffany didn't move. He stood, half grin on his face and hand over heart, staring at the flag and hazy hills beyond. "The end of that song is a question mark, and that's always baffled me: '. . . the home of the brave?'" he later explained. "And I think about 'the brave,' as in the Native American brave. I get a little spiritual and think about the Monacan, the Powhatan—the Native people of this land, locally . . . spend a couple seconds thinking, *This is Native land.*"

It was a superb game. Virginia had already beaten Notre Dame that year, in South Bend, and now, in an even tighter defensive tussle, the Cavaliers were controlling matters early in the fourth quarter when the Irish cut the lead to 9–7. Tension mounted as the ball flew scorelessly for the next four minutes. Then came a time-out. Tiffany left the sideline, walked six feet behind the bench and began gulping a cup of water when he noticed his hickory longpole lying on the ground. Tiffany stood it back up in its honored spot beneath a stadium rail. His players waited. He shifted it left, right, making sure it wouldn't fall again.

The Cavaliers scored three straight, held on to win, 12–8. Afterward, Tiffany grabbed a duffel bag and his father's gift and walked out of the stadium, across campus to his car. Just before the parking lot, five white boys asked him to sign balls and programs. The smallest asked about the stick. Thus began a five-minute mini-lecture, Tiffany telling about the Haudenosaunee and how Alfie Jacques took six to nine months to craft it.

"Get a feel for it," he said. "You can feel this energy, the spirit of the stick."

"That's so sick," the boy said.

The exchange was one more of the day's little bonuses. Tiffany hadn't just beaten, for the second time that season, the nation's No.1 team, but also a coach with a far deeper claim on Virginia hearts. Son of former UVa lacrosse coach and athletic director Gene Corrigan, Notre Dame head coach Kevin Corrigan grew up in Charlottesville and played and coached under one of his father's successors, Jim "Ace" Adams. Kevin Corrigan—not Tiffany—had been UVa's first choice to replace Dom Starsia. Yet when Tiffany bumped into both Corrigan's mother, Lena, and Ace Adams's widow, Betty, after the win, they greeted him with warmth and hugs. The embrace of what he called "lacrosse royalty" left Tiffany beaming.

Now, up walked Starsia, accompanied by his daughters. Having just seen UVa's tall-tree defenders, Cade Saustad and Cole Kastner, shut down Notre Dame's dynamic Kavanagh brothers, Tiffany's mentor was sure Corrigan's Fighting Irish lacked the necessary firepower for a deep run in the upcoming NCAA tournament. "They don't have enough offense," Starsia said. "You can't say that, but I can: They just don't have enough offense."

Neither man understood, yet, that 2023 was not a year for the blue bloods. In the men's college game, Johns Hopkins's title drought would hit its 16th year, and archrival Syracuse—rebuilding under converted women's coach Gary

Gait—wouldn't even merit an invite to the NCAA tournament. The women's gold standard, Maryland, which last won a national championship in 2019, would again be supplanted by the likes of James Madison, Syracuse and, especially, 2021 champ Boston College, en route to its sixth straight NCAA final. And the original upstart, the program that first broke lacrosse out of its East Coast confines, would break back into the elite with a bang.

Northwestern head coach Kelly Amonte Hiller had rightly sensed, in late 2018, that her program had rekindled its founding fire. After Selena Lasota led the Wildcats back to the Final Four in 2019, they repeated the feat in 2021 and 2022. But emphatic losses in those three semifinals, including a gutting collapse—after holding a seven-goal lead with 9:16 left—against North Carolina in 2022, made it easy to conclude that the wilderness years had softened Amonte Hiller and Northwestern might never regain its merciless edge.

The missing element, it turned out, was Izzy Scane. After sitting out the entire 2022 season because of a torn knee ligament, the most prolific scorer—man or woman—in NCAA history scored five goals in the 2023 season-opener against Syracuse, and the Wildcats lost by a point. For the next game, Scane doubled her output; the Wildcats defeated Notre Dame, and didn't lose again all year. Powers old (Maryland) and new (Boston College, Michigan) were beaten, then beaten again. Vengeance was had over Northwestern's most recent tormentor, No. 1 North Carolina; Scane, as usual, led the way with four goals. Growing up in the non-lacrosse hotbed of Clarkston, Michigan, she had witnessed the early Northwestern dynasty and idolized Lasota. As a freshman, she mimicked the star senior's fearlessness and energy until it became her own.

Four years later, on May 28, 2023, all the culminations came at once. Entering the Final Four in Cary, North Carolina, Scane needed 10 goals to surpass—in just three full seasons—Lasota's Northwestern career record of 287. She had picked up six in the 15–7 romp over Denver in the semifinals, and three more by the end of third quarter of the final against Boston College. Then, with the Wildcats up by eight and 10:46 left to play, Scane, in one continuous motion, stripped the ball from BC midfielder Cassidy Weeks, scooped it up and—while being hammered to the ground—somehow flipped in her 99th goal of the year to break the program's single-season and career goal marks, cement the first of her two Tewaaraton Awards, and seal Northwestern's 18–6 win. Once the final horn sounded, Scane couldn't stop crying.

For Amonte Hiller, of course, winning her eighth national title 11 years after her seventh couldn't have been more gratifying; she called the in-between years challenging, humbling and "such a fun journey." For the game at large, the greater effect was a rebirth for lacrosse's frontier dynasty, a refreshed example for newly hatched programs like Pitt, Eastern Michigan, Xavier and Clemson. Indeed, Scane purposefully chose Northwestern so she could serve as a role model for her fellow hinterlanders.

Lacrosse's Midwest moment didn't end there. Like Northwestern, Notre Dame in 2023 was hardly an unknown quantity; Corrigan, the longest-tenured head coach in men's Division I, had produced top-20 seasons and All-Americans throughout his 35-year tenure, and led the Fighting Irish five times into the NCAA tournament's Final Four. But Notre Dame's two trips to the title game, in 2010 and 2014, ended in losses to Duke, and the program seemed stalled just outside the circle of elites. In 2022, despite winning a share of the ACC title and finishing the regular season ranked No. 4, Notre Dame had been notoriously snubbed for an at-large bid by the NCAA tournament committee and left out of the 18-team field.

The insult proved to be fuel of the highest octane. That day Irish midfielder Quinn McCahon dubbed the 2023 season a "vengeance tour," and though Corrigan tried softening that to "a quest, if you will," the result was predictably pointed. With eight starters, including the nation's top goalie, Liam Entenmann, turning in All-American campaigns, Notre Dame did everything possible to make the 2022 committee look stupid. It crushed five of its first six opponents, and beat presiding NCAA champ Maryland on the road, 13–12, in triple overtime. It dominated No. 1 Duke and No. 15 North Carolina twice. Its attack—led by brothers Chris and Pat Kavanagh, a playmaker supreme, and Jake Taylor and Eric Dobson—ripped through every regular season defense but Virginia's.

Then the Irish also proved Starsia wrong. After its second loss to the Cavaliers in Charlottesville, Corrigan's offense exploded with 18 goals against UNC and 20 in a first-round tournament win over Utah, then handled Johns Hopkins 12–9 to set up another showdown with UVa in the 2023 NCAA semifinal in Philadelphia on May 27. Still, the Cavaliers boasted the nation's top offense and all-time talent Connor Shellenberger. They again slowed up the Irish and held a two-goal lead with 2:40 left in the fourth quarter. The 32,107 fans in Philadelphia had reason to expect Virginia to win again. Then Tiffany's defense buckled.

Chris Kavanagh scored. Then Dobson, to make it 11–11. Virginia scored to grab back the lead with 52 seconds left, but Notre Dame sensed panic and knew where the holes were now. With 32 seconds left, a wide-open Jake Taylor spun and fired in a funky backhand twister to tie it again, 12–12. Tiffany jammed both hands against his head. The game spilled into overtime, the air thick with Irish momentum. Twenty-seven seconds later, captain Brian Tevlin sliced nearly unscathed through the Virginia defense, fired, and Notre Dame won.

Tiffany assumed blame, apologized for not winning another national title, pointed out that the program had taken strides beyond championships. "We're not focusing on bad behavior," he said. "We're not focusing on things that waste time. This group has sacrificed so much and transformed what it means to be a Virginia lacrosse player both on and off the field. It's been dramatic, the change there."

Two days later, on Memorial Day, Corrigan and Notre Dame rushed to a five-goal halftime lead, squandered it, then blew past longtime nemesis Duke, 13–9, to win the program's first national championship. Afterward, Corrigan spoke of all the title games he had lost, one as a player at Virginia in 1979, two as a coach. He spoke about his father's early role in establishing the NCAA lacrosse tournament, and the game's growth since. Notre Dame was now the third new Division I men's champion—with Denver and Yale—in eight years. Amonte Hiller had made Illinois lacrosse country. Now Indiana was, too.

II

SAN DIEGO

L ARS TIFFANY'S FATHER was a US Marine and served in the Korean War. A triangle frame in Tiffany's office holds the American flag that had been draped over Brad's casket. Back in 2019 it had been easy for Lars to say that he'd rather be an unpaid Iroquois assistant than the paid—$10,000—USA head coach; the issue was hypothetical. Now it was real: He, an American, would be leading its historic rival against his country at the 2023 World Men's Field Championship. "There are some conflicts," he said:

> It sends me back to having better empathy for the Civil War–era decision-making, when you're from the state of Virginia yet you went to West Point and here's this young nation at that point, 80 years old maybe. Do you defend the nation? Do you defend your true dirt roots? I had this wonderful opportunity to be in those men's and women's shoes and re-create that troubled decision-making.
>
> But there is no question in my mind that the loyalty is to the Haudenosaunee and the men and women I grew with, and the land I grew up upon, and the partnership we have because of my dad and the bison. That is much more meaningful to me than the nation that I'm a part of. It's the people. It's defined my spirituality. It's my best friends. I have no qualms.

Tiffany is hardly the Haudenosaunee's first American. One of the quiet ironies of the Nationals men's program has been its long dependence on US aid; since 1990, half of the Nationals field head coaches have been white men.

For Sixes at the 2022 World Games, they appointed Peter Milliman of Johns Hopkins. This is a necessity forced, of course, by history.

During their century-long estrangement from the game they created, Haudenosaunee focus turned to the welcoming milieu of box lacrosse and, at its highest level, semi-pro "Senior A" leagues in Canada. A few would end up starring for Syracuse, but generations had been cut off from the increasingly disciplined sets and defenses transforming field lacrosse at US universities. In the Nationals' first lopsided loss to Team USA in 1984—and in all 10 defeats since—that estrangement revealed itself, quarter by painful quarter.

The dramatic influx of Natives that began flowing into US colleges in the late 2000s dented the learning curve, but only at ground level. The only Haudenosaunee men's field coaches today are Chris Doctor, an assistant at Division I Sacred Heart University, and Longboat, the head coach at Brock University in St. Catharines, Ontario. Marty Ward, a member of Cherokee Nation, at Division II Florida Southern University, is the sole Native American head coach in the NCAA. Both the Haudenosaunee board and Tiffany hoped his appointment to be a tipping point. Wary of being derided as a "white savior," Tiffany told Nationals players and management from the start that 2023 would be his one head stint, that Longboat and Doctor and any aging Haudenosaunee stars with coaching ambitions should study his practice plans, speeches, play-calls and lineup decisions—and make them their own.

But that was long-term stuff. Tiffany's challenge for San Diego was the one faced and failed by every Nationals coach—including himself, as an assistant in 2018—for the last 40 years: defense. And that entailed tinkering with the Haudenosaunee mindset, an aesthetic born of spiritual practice, reinforced anytime a Medicine Game is called, passed down father to son. This doesn't mean the Haudenosaunee are incapable of superb field defense. Few cultures more celebrate the bone-crushing hit, and former Syracuse All-Americans Marshall Abrams and Sid Smith proved as smothering as anyone who ever wielded a longpole.

But, in truth, both were exceptions to the general Haudenosaunee attitude. Whether because of the imperative to "entertain the Creator," the dictates of box lacrosse's 30-second shot clock and its ban on longpoles, or the 100-year parade of legendary attackmen, Iroquois boys yearn and learn early to dazzle in tight spaces, flip no-look passes and fire behind-the-head shots. A common comparison holds that field lacrosse moves like soccer and box lacrosse like basketball, but the Native style would drive Coach K crazy. Haudenosaunee lacrosse loves to take chances. It needs to rush. Fans, of course, love it.

"It is just like street ball: there's structure, but not a whole lot," said Hiana Thompson, Lyle's next oldest brother. "Just like in our Medicine Games, where there could be 150 people on the field and it's hard to pick up the ball and run 10 steps. So you find ways. You create. I try to figure it out on the spot—how to get open or get guys open. The [American field] game is more structured and feels robotic, if you will: *Go out there and do this. Go to this spot.* That's the biggest difference."

Another Nationals problem, when it came to constructing a field team, was that mostly one kind of player would show up. Long before he became Tadadaho, Sidney Hill was a high-octane attackman at LaFayette High and Syracuse. "You weren't good unless you scored," said Hill, who, at 39, converted to defense for the Nationals debut at the 1990 World Championship. "The best players are thought of as the best scorers, so that's who came. A few of us said, 'Hey, we don't have defensemen, but somebody's got to pick up these longsticks.' So as far as true defensemen? We still have a problem with that."

Indeed, every Haudenosaunee roster since had been buffalo shaped: intimidatingly powerful up front, underdeveloped at the back. Meanwhile, despite the example of the NCAA's recently instituted shot clock (80 seconds in 2018, with a 60-second reset added in 2021), international field remained lacrosse's last bastion of timelessness. With no shot clock and continuous running time, stalling was common and miserly shooting a must and turnovers were mortal sins. In other words, it remained the slowest—and at times most boring—version of lacrosse, a perfect instrument to annoy the Creator, frustrate the Haudenosaunee ethos and expose the weakness of the Nationals' tiny talent pool. "We don't have the luxury of Canada and US, where we can pick 20 really good longpoles and 20 really good middies and defensive middies," said Lyle Thompson. "We have a boatload of offensive guys and then we have to nitpick what the team needs."

But with Tiffany's appointment, the message was sent: defense is now central. The following month in Buffalo, Zed Williams—the PLL's 2020 championship MVP—showed up at the first workout with a longpole. The sight alone provided a charge: Since being cut from the Nationals 2012 U-19 team, the 27-year-old Seneca had refused the program's every offer to play field. Now, not only was Williams on board, but one of the game's supreme offensive talents was volunteering to play defense for the first time. No one, including Tiffany, knew if Williams could learn fast enough. But few coaches have received a more striking endorsement.

Tiffany was the reason. During Williams's senior year at Virginia, something in his new coach's manner had showed him how to express his Native essence, connect with ancestors on the lacrosse field. "I needed some help pulling that emotional side, that spiritual side, that cultural side out of me," Williams said. "Because of that one year I had him, everything he's done for me, and the man he brought out of me? I'll do anything for him.

"To me, Lars cares more about the Native culture than a lot of Native people. I don't know who'll get mad, because it's a white guy and their whole race thing, but it's true. Lars genuinely cares about Native people and will stand up for Native culture and Native people more than Native people in our own community. You can see it."

In perhaps the clearest sign of changing priorities, the Nationals board also quietly relaxed its most unforgiving stand. Since inception, the Nationals had not only adhered to the FIL rule stipulating only three non–passport holders per roster, but strictly enforced the Haudenosaunee citizenship requirement of matrilineal descent. Teams had been decimated by the rejection of key players—like current assistant coach Chris Doctor—in 2006 and 2010. But for 2023, the board reduced its required number of Haudenosaunee passport holders from 20 to 17. Four of the remaining six slots went to Indigenous players with Ojibwe, Métis, Heiltsuk and Gwich'in heritage. Backup goalie Jack VanValkenburgh, whose Mohawk bloodline (like Chris Doctor's) descends from his father, was allowed.

But, practically, none was more important than defenseman Jacob Piseno, the UAlbany All-American who in 2023 was ranked second in Division I with 3.12 forced turnovers per game. Until taking a DNA test his junior year at Liverpool High, the Syracuse-born, 5-foot-7 Piseno had never heard of the Purépecha tribe of Mexico, never mind known that he had ancestry via his father. Like VanValkenburg, Piseno travels on a US passport. He also grew up in Onondaga County intrigued by the Iroquois mystique, which spiked when the Nationals became the only team to court him for their 2020 U-19 team.

"I want to stay with them for life now," Piseno said.

Gratitude isn't the only reason. Piseno also feels most at home with the Haudenosaunee mindset. "Yeah, I'm a defender, but we're pushing the ball; we're *all* offensive guys, even with six-foot poles," he said. "I didn't know I was Native my whole life, but that's why I am the player I am today. I've made that name as a jack-of-all-trades: I can play offense, defense, take a faceoff, go on the wing and block a shot. Having that in my blood—and finding it out while my high school career was ending—is the reason I started getting that feel. I really knew who I was, and where I came from."

The changes by the Nationals board didn't end there. Unlike previous World Championships, when Haudenosaunee prep work began just weeks—or even days—before their opening game, the 2023 Nationals were given eight months. The switch to transparent, nonprofit funding had paid off: Increased donations from Nike, as well as a $300,000 grant from Tamalpais Trust, a foundation funding Indigenous initiatives worldwide, and $100,000 apiece from the Mohawk and Seneca Nations, financed the three winter tryouts and training. Through the ensuing spring, when players were scattered with pro and college teams, Tiffany held monthly meetings on Zoom calls and tutored his defense with more than a dozen remote film sessions on the online chalk talk application ScoreBreak. Its $1,500 software fee might be petty cash to USA Lacrosse (annual operating budget: $23.5 million). Past Nationals teams would have done without.

"We were hand-to-mouth; as fast as we got it, it went out," said Rex Lyons. "We have money in the bank now. We're actually going to San Diego four days in advance to practice. That's unheard of. We've never done that before. We literally couldn't afford it."

ON THE MORNING of June 18, 2023, Father's Day, Lars Tiffany and his players found themselves walking a steep hill. The Haudenosaunee Nationals had arrived for the 2023 World Championship late the night before, frazzled and exhausted—not because of passport trouble, just the combination of a flight delay and missed connection that stretched nine hours of travel to 17. Then everyone woke in their dorm rooms at the University of San Diego to news that there would be no bus to practice. They started trudging the 15-minute route up Torero Drive.

With his hickory longpole in hand, Tiffany made a point of walking with Austin Staats. The two hadn't spoken much since Staats questioned Tiffany's hiring, but the Mohawk attackman had shown his commitment by losing the demanded 20 pounds. Tiffany talked. Staats smiled some and answered questions but, Tiffany said later that day, "he kept looking back behind him, and I almost wondered if he was hoping some other players would come up so the twosome would become a foursome. There's a bit of hesitation there still. But it's better."

Whatever the tension level, it had no impact on the team's upbeat first practice. Questions about readiness remained: Goalie Warren Hill and sniper Zach Miller hadn't played high-level field for many years; Lyle Thompson and Zed Williams had yet to arrive; sharpshooter Tehoka Nanticoke's ankle sprain wasn't healing. But the months of online prep, and the prospect of five days of bonding, film work and practice, had everyone almost giddy. "I think," said general manager Darcy Powless, watching from the sideline, "we'll be in the gold-medal game."

As always, the Nationals here would enjoy a status comparable only to Brazil in international soccer: everyone's second favorite team, historic, exotic, intrinsically cool. Fans and opponents would again take in the whipping braids, hear the Haudenosaunee screech alerting the Creator during warmups. But beneath the usual extraordinariness, the Nationals exuded a wholly new vibe. The drama was gone. The chronic disorganization was gone. Most striking, everyone involved kept talking about winning—beating the Americans, beating Canada, playing for gold. They sounded like an ordinary team.

Austin Staats had the potential to be the Nationals' most destructive or important element; though erratic off the field, few players radiate as relentless a will, as visceral a *joie de combat*. And though his coolness with Tiffany remained palpable, the slimmed-down Austin had been listening. He parroted the coach's line that the Haudenosaunee had to slow up and adapt the grindingly effective US style to have a chance. "Just trying to be more patient, right?" he said. "We need to cherish the ball. Cherish every possession and score when we get opportunities."

He spoke of Tiffany's "winning mentality," the fact that UVa had reached three of the last four Final Fours. And when asked about his preference for a Haudenosaunee head coach, Staats's face broke into a jack-o'-lantern grin. "Ah . . . I don't know," he said slowly. "Next question."

But his older brother didn't hesitate. At 30, Randy Staats is one of the pillars of the Haudenosaunee's golden generation; along with Lyle Thompson, Hill, Miller and Brendan Bomberry, he was part of the U-19 team that, in 2012, became the first—and only—Haudenosaunee field team to beat the US. The former Syracuse All-American was also one of the program's loudest, most influential voices, on and off the field.

"I don't think he should be the head coach," Randy said of Tiffany. "If we have assistants that are non-Native, that's fine."

Haudenosaunee talk about lacrosse has always centered on playing for the Creator's entertainment, healing, maintaining a "clear mind." For 40 years Nationals co-founder Oren Lyons had insisted: "It's not a sport. It's not a game." But the board's new focus—winning, to maintain political and popular leverage—forced a subtle change even in that longtime message. All year Rex Lyons had been stressing the distinction between the Haudenosaunee "secular game and spiritual game: They don't really live in the same space." Lacrosse remained a spiritual practice, but in San Diego it was about the scoreboard.

Randy Staats agreed. Against Tiffany's appointment for cultural reasons, he liked what it meant athletically. He planned to retire from field after this tournament, and didn't want to finish third again. His explanation was a reminder that the Nationals, no matter their piety, are young, proud, madly competitive men. Once the game clock started, the head coach's provenance wouldn't matter at all.

The Haudenosaunee men—the No. 2 power, behind only Canada—had beaten Team USA all seven times the two had played at previous World Indoor Championships. But Staats knows that box carries neither the symbolic tonnage nor the prestige of lacrosse's glamour game. Field is the lacrosse that fills stadiums with 40,000 fans each Memorial Day weekend, the game that had by 2023 spread to 86 nations. Field is where Johns Hopkins, Jim Brown, the Gait and Powell and Thompson brothers made their names. Field is the game of choice for the United States and the one stolen, in Haudenosaunee eyes, like the land by white men.

Asked what it would mean to beat the Americans here, for the first time on grass, Randy said, "If it was for a gold medal?" and suddenly couldn't speak. His eyes filled with tears. Thirty seconds passed in silence. "If there was a gold medal attached to it . . ." he began, then stopped again, staring at the ground.

Finally, Staats said softly, "It's bigger than this team. It would speak volumes to our people . . . where we come from, all that stuff. I shouldn't even be like this. But you think about it." He looked up, then.

"Can you imagine?"

THE OPENING CEREMONIES of any international competition, be it the Olympic Games or, in this case, the 2023 World Lacrosse Field Championship, is one of the few events where people gather ecstatically under national flags, briefly drop their guard, and agree to agree: Sports *is* our one common ground.

So it was inside Snapdragon Stadium early in the evening, June 21, 2023. Twenty-eight of the 30 playing nations—the US and Canada, prepping for the night's opener, waited in their locker rooms—assembled in the concrete-walled halls and ramps beneath the seats, some 750 players and coaches and staff waiting to march on field. Some stared at cellphones. But mostly the air was full of grins, chatter, players taking selfies. The mash of stereotypes was a lazy cartoonist's dream: kilted Scots, dreadlocked Jamaicans, sombrero-ed Mexicans, Dutchmen in all orange and Peruvians in knitted churros, Ugandans in untucked red-and-gold kikoy.

The parade started with Team Australia, everyone lined up alphabetically, shuffling forward, breaking into the perfect San Diego sunlight. Many waved. Some sang. Out went the Austrians in lederhosen, the Frenchmen in berets, the Haudenosaunee in purple ribbon shirts. Everyone carried an identifying sign, but the Nationals left theirs behind. For their first World Championship under their own name, someone in the organizing committee omitted an "A," misspelled it as TEAM HAUDENOSUNEE. Nanticoke led the way, instead, with Tiffany's wood stick.

They passed Joe Tsai chatting on the sideline. The day before the billionaire had been appointed chairman of Alibaba, and the following day his NBA team would host the NBA draft in Brooklyn. But he was also chair of this tournament's hosting committee and his son, Dash, was an attackman for Team Hong Kong. Tsai had just flown back in from China, making it to the stadium just in time.

After all the teams circled the stadium and gathered midfield, a train of speakers took the stage. The shift in messaging, from 2018 to now, was striking; the game's Indigenousness had been made central. Steve Newcomb, the Shawnee/Lenape scholar who helped spark the movement against the Doctrine of Discovery, opened with a land acknowledgment to the local Kumeyaay Nation. Haudenosaunee spiritual leader Tracy Shenandoah followed with a long blessing of the field. World Lacrosse president Sue Redfern reeled off a checklist of gratitude, capped by a singular shoutout to the Haudenosaunee. "Thank you," she said, "for the gift of the Creator's Game." Kumeyaay Nation birdsong dancers performed. USA Lacrosse CEO Marc Riccio, too, began his welcome by thanking the Haudenosaunee.

An hour later USA and Canada played what all figured was a preview of the final. Some 10,000 fans took in the familiar scene: Canada's Dillon Ward in goal, flanked by red-clad greats Curtis Dickson, Brodie Merrill and Jeff Teat; the Americans, coached again by John Danowski, populated by 2018 vets Trevor Baptiste, Michael Ehrhardt and the pair—Rob Pannell and Tom Schreiber—who combined to crush Maple Leaf dreams in the still-controversial last seconds in Israel. Again the two teams probed and parried with barely a shadow of difference between them; again it was compelling in the manner of two locked-up sumos. Which heavyweight, with the slightest of slips, the first lapse of concentration, would yield?

American faceoff dominance eventually had its way: Goals by Tiffany alums Charlie Bertrand and Ryan Conrad pried the US loose from a 4–4 tie in the third quarter, and after Brennan O'Neill added another, the action slowed to a crawl. Canada scored just once in the second half. "The international game is very strange," Danowski said after. "No shot clock: You're two men up, but you don't go to the goal. That's so against what we believe in, but you're just trying to win."

Indeed, the most rousing moment of the 7–5 US win came just afterward when, as if to confirm that their mutual loathing endures, the archrivals unleashed a bit of grabbing and shoving. "Gamesmanship: they know we're going to play one more time and they're trying to get in our heads," Pannell said. "We're not going to just sit there and take it."

The night's one big revelation was O'Neill, the lone collegiate player on the US roster. At 6-foot-2, 250 pounds, the 2023 Tewaaraton Award winner had looked nothing like a 21-year-old rookie playing his first-ever senior game. Even Danowski, who oversaw his three All-American years at Duke, didn't expect O'Neill to ravage the Canadian defense with three goals. But in a sense, even this was no surprise: Perhaps the most heavily recruited lacrosse player ever, the Bay Shore, Long Island, native was offered his first scholarship at 14. For the defending champs, there's never been a shortage of next ones.

Before the game, Nationals offensive coordinator Scott Marr, an assistant coach with Team USA in 2006, was standing on the sideline in his Haudenosaunee ribbon shirt, watching his old team warm up. The Nationals would be playing the US soon: He was no doubt scouting for some tendency or edge. Finally, after a few minutes, Marr had seen enough; he turned and hurried past, muttering.

"The only team," he said, "with their names on the back of their jerseys."

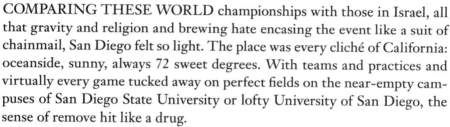

COMPARING THESE WORLD championships with those in Israel, all that gravity and religion and brewing hate encasing the event like a suit of chainmail, San Diego felt so light. The place was every cliché of California: oceanside, sunny, always 72 sweet degrees. With teams and practices and virtually every game tucked away on perfect fields on the near-empty campuses of San Diego State University or lofty University of San Diego, the sense of remove hit like a drug.

Two days later, even blocks away from one field at SDSU, the clamor of a crowd was already audible. Maybe 800 Team Mexico fans flanked the far side, and as ever provided wondrously outsized support. Bells rang. Sombreros crowned shouting faces; red-white-and-green flags flew; "Meh-Hee-Co!" chants started every time their team ran upfield. Though Italy led comfortably from start to finish, it never stopped; though they lost, 13–9, their players fed off the passion, and outplayed the Azzurri in the second half. When it was over, the entire team walked across the field to their loving fans, and together they shouted, "¡Viva México!"

This, too, is how San Diego was different from Israel. In 2018, the Mexican team, accompanied by a half-dozen family members, endured a miserable tournament marked by slurs like "wetback" and "beaner." Two players quit the sport. But here they were treated like a home team. The Mexican border is just 17 miles from downtown, and most of Team Mexico lives in America, if not Southern California, enduring personally the nation's ongoing debate over immigration. In 2023, an estimated 1,200 undocumented migrants, daily, crossed into San Diego County. The players viewed this tournament as a quiet way to honor the odyssey.

"We have a reminder of all those things we had to go through to live a different life, going through the border," Mexico midfielder Andres Patraca, the former president of Mexico's lacrosse federation, said after the game. "It's right here."

He pointed to the piece of string tied on his right wrist, after a meeting in which each player had related his personal history. "Everybody on the team has one," Patraca said. "This is the reason why we play. This is a reminder of what our families have been through to make us be able to be here. A lot of guys from this team had their families illegally in the States, and tried to fight and work and everything. We put this on the wrist just for ourselves."

One of those returning was midfielder Ernie Melero, whose late mother, Maria Elva, crossed somewhere near San Diego in 1990. Unlike in Israel, Melero said, Team Mexico had heard no slurs from opponents here. He also noted the many white stars who publicly backed their Black peers and the Haudenosaunee in the summer of 2020, and the new respect accorded to Native Americans at these Opening Ceremonies. But when asked if he believed the racial climate in lacrosse had improved, he balked.

"In a substantial manner, not yet," Melero said. "It's going to take a while. But definitely, there's steps in the right direction."

LATE ON THE AFTERNOON of June 24, 15 minutes before boarding the bus for their pool play showdown with Team USA, the Haudenosaunee Nationals gathered for a ritual. It is, arguably, the oldest in sports. Some variant unrolled centuries ago within the St. Lawrence lowlands, when hundreds ran and the ball was feathers wrapped in deerskin, and anytime the Nationals men played over the previous 40 years, and before their spectacular, tournament-opening win over England. It would happen six more times, before each game, in San Diego.

Players and coaches formed a large circle. No matter lineage or nation, Longhouse or Christian, Native or white: all took part. Tracy Shenandoah, a former player who had long traveled with the program, asked if anyone needed a specific type of healing. He produced a small pipe tamped with lit tobacco. Each National drew in a mouthful of smoke, passed it always to the right, released a cloud and waved it about head and shoulders. This was to open communication with spirits, the Creator. Then came a two-gallon blue plastic Igloo jug, the kind seen at every picnic, filled with "medicine"—water mixed with a ginseng-like solution. This was for protection against injury. Each National drank and rubbed the medicine on their hands and face and arms and chest.

Shenandoah then recited, in Onondaga language, a segment of the Thanksgiving Address, in gratitude for the land or trees or another blessing of nature. The Igloo jug traveled with the team on the bus. It then was placed just off the field near the Haudenosaunee bench, obscured by the usual giant orange sports vat. During games, players seeking fortification would occasionally hoist the Igloo for a drink, reapply it to skin. Some sprinkled Medicine water on their sticks.

Tiffany had revived another tradition. Just before the tournament, legendary Onondaga stickmaker Alfie Jacques died at 74. In his honor, Tiffany asked Zed Williams to play the first shift with his signature Jacques longpole. No serious player today uses wood (the Nationals last used one in 2014), and a defensive novice like Williams would only benefit from today's far lighter, scandium-shafted standard. He was also nervous about cracking Brad Tiffany's gift. Lars insisted. "I'm going to be buried with that stick," Tiffany said. "If it's broken? Alfie up in the Sky-World might be smiling more so."

Against Team USA, Williams again started with Tiffany's hickory in hand. Good karma ensued: Austin Staats, fresh off an absurd eight-goal, one-assist rampage in the 18–5 win over the Brits, opened the scoring 85 seconds in with a left-handed strike. Four minutes in, after a few probing cross-checks and a smack across the face mask of US star Matt Rambo, Williams exchanged the woodie for what the Haudenosaunee still call "plastic." Unknown to most, the 1–0 score represented just the second time, ever, that Haudenosaunee men had held a field lead on the US.

Before Israel, the Nationals practiced once. In the run-up here, the players not only drilled twice daily, but—contrary to the cliché about "Native time"—consistently hit the field 15 minutes early. In 2018, Marr would enter a huddle to draw up a play and five players would cut him off. Now, he said, "I speak and nobody says anything. Everybody's bought in." Out on the field against overmatched England, the Haudenosaunee indulged themselves in lacrosse's version of the "beautiful game": that riverine, multi-pass style prized by soccer and basketball purists. At such moments, as Quint Kessenich likes to say, the Haudenosaunee play the game in "cursive," while everyone else is reduced to block letters.

Now, against the USA, there were only traces of that, mostly when Randy Staats flipped a behind-the-back pass into dense traffic. It was as if the Haudenosaunee had downshifted to second gear. Setting picks, methodically cycling the ball, the Nationals dictated an American-style pace; Randy could hear the frustration as the minutes mounted: US players yelled, "They're lulling us to sleep!" Lyle Thompson scored two, USA's quicksilver Michael Sowers matched it, but Tiffany's staunch, Piseno-anchored defense held like never before. With nine minutes left in the third quarter, the Nationals led, 4–3.

Then came a moment of truth. In all 11 US victories since 1984, the Nationals never led this late, never came close; the Americans steamrolled every second half and won by an average of 14 goals. As if on schedule, the Haudenosaunee momentum seized up. Rambo easily beat a too-late Zed Williams off the right wing; Tiffany alum Ryan Conrad beat tiring goalie Warren Hill up high; 2018 MVP Michael Ehrhardt scythed a longpole goal from 15 yards out; Kieran McArdle popped in a too-easy left-hander. It was the usual American haymaker: "U-S-A!" chants filled the air. The Nationals staggered to the end of the third quarter, and looked no better early in the fourth: Jeremy Thompson losing every faceoff to T. D. Ierlan, Lyle frustrated by US defenseman J. T. Giles-Harris, Austin Staats laid out by an Ehrhardt high-stick to the throat. With 12 minutes to play, the US had a 7–4 lead—and every reason to think it was over.

"In years prior, 7–4? I don't think they would've come back," Rob Pannell, who scored seven in a rout of the Nationals in 2014, said later. "They would've just accepted: *Alright, we gave it our best shot.*"

But they didn't accept. With 11:27 left, Lyle Thompson, gamboling across the right wing, threaded a grass-cutter between six converging Americans—off one foot—to cut the lead to two. Three minutes later, Austin Staats lowered a shoulder 18 yards out and began churning goalward. With his ignominious fade from the PLL still lingering, the Mohawk attackman came to San Diego looking to show his peers "that I could still play field lacrosse." Now he juked once, twice. American Jack Rowlett charged forward. Staats leveled a hard shoulder to his chest, an elbow to the chin, flinging off 195 pounds of elite defenseman like a too-eager pup. He stepped back, whipsnapped as vicious an overhand as you'll ever see and cut America's lead to one. The Nationals bench leapt as if electrified. Haudenosaunee defiance had a new face.

Still, the US was the defending champ, famously cool when pressed. McArdle added two quick goals to widen the lead back to three, Jeremy

Thompson lost two more faceoffs, and Danowski had cushion enough to stall. The Nationals still didn't give. With 2:20 left and the Haudenosaunee man-up, they cycled the ball seamlessly around the perimeter, down to Austin Staats camped just outside the crease. Giles-Harris, the top American defender, was all over him. Staats backed in, pivoted, gave his stick enough of a shiver to freeze goalie Jack Kelly and plopped the ball in the back of the net.

The Americans hung on to win again, 9–7, but this one came with a caveat. A voice rose off the Haudenosaunee bench: "They know we can beat 'em!"

The following night, the Haudenosaunee played three-time champ Canada. The Nationals had lost all 14 of their previous outdoor meetings with the Canadians, by an average of 6.5 goals. Yet Oren Lyons, the Nationals co-founder, predicted, "We're going to beat them. We've got the best team here." This was his eighth field championship. He had never thought that before.

As they did with the defending champs, the Nationals matched the world's second-best team stride for stride into the third quarter; Randy fed Austin for an easy chip-in to tie matters at 4–4. Then came the avalanche, four Canadian goals, that in previous years would have left them buried. Again the Haudenosaunee rallied, held Canada scoreless in the fourth, and—powered by another relentless goal from Austin and a pair from Randy—clawed back the lead to one. They pushed frantically in the final minutes: Lyle Thompson missed on three choice opportunities; Zed Williams had both stick and ball checked loose on the final possession. Canada, too, barely escaped, 8–7. It was no fluke. The superpowers now had company.

"They are a completely different team than they were," Rob Pannell said. "They're playing smarter offensively; they know how to play together; they're possessing the ball, working the clock. Defensively, they've gotten a *lot* better. They are a contender. It's no longer USA-Canada. It's USA, Canada and Haudenosaunee."

AS THE NATIONALS ROLLED on through the week, cutting down Australia, Hong Kong and the rising program from Japan, there was no ignoring the irony. Tiffany was a major reason for the differences, and no one had thrived more in his careful, high-percentage system than those most opposed to his hiring. Austin and Randy Staats both say that theirs is a player-driven game, and they came to San Diego intensely motivated. But if the Haudenosaunee still wove the occasional breathtaking pattern, their signature play here was Austin firing from a standstill, or backing inexorably goalward. This took nothing from his skill. Few players combine such fearsome bulk with so supple a pair of hands; no one wades more effectively—even joyously—through hacking triple-teams, losing neither balance nor ball.

"Like a big bear," said Canada's Brodie Merrill. "Tough to crowd, tough to handle."

"So comfortable in the chaos," said the USA's Tom Schreiber. "Nobody plays like that."

On the eve of the Haudenosaunee rematch with Canada in the semifinals, Austin already had a stranglehold on the tournament scoring title and Randy led in assists. Leaner, faster and five years older, he knew his brother best, yet seemed to regard Austin as an unfathomable force of nature.

That the brothers remained standoffish with Tiffany mattered less and less, even to him. Like the rest, they had embraced the system, if not his attempts at inspiration. Indeed, the pep talks that spark dependable roars at UVa were received mostly in silence, along with Tiffany's love of four-dollar words. The use of "precipice," when discussing tactics during an early practice here, drew stares. For days, nobody responded whenever Tiffany opened the floor to questions; finally a National had one. "Coach," he said. "What does 'liberated' mean?"

"We all started laughing," says Jeremy Thompson. "But to be honest, a couple guys were happy he asked. They didn't know."

By the final weekend, the Nationals had grown comfortable enough to tease Tiffany ("I'm on the precipice," shouted attackman Kyle Jackson during their 10–5 quarterfinal win over Japan, "of being liberated!"). They were also exhausted. No one at the 2023 World Championship had run a rougher road—six games in six days, with one more looming against Canada; every other contender had been scheduled at least one day off before the semifinals. At this point, with the mission nearly accomplished, some knocking could be heard in the engine.

For months the Nationals had kept an unprecedented focus on the field, intent on batting away distractions and winning at least a silver medal. There had also been a backchannel agreement struck between World Lacrosse and Haudenosaunee management, based on their mutual ambition to play at the 2028 Summer Olympics. Concerned that another bout of infighting, like the World Games 2022 snub, would rattle the IOC, in 2020 World Lacrosse CEO Jim Scherr had urged the Nationals to, as they characterized it, "lay low"—especially on sticky IOC topics like sovereignty, or World Lacrosse trustworthiness—until the IOC made their decision. And so, off the field, too, the Haudenosaunee began operating more like an "ordinary" team.

But with the scheduling disparity in San Diego, the old extraordinariness began to rise. Coaches and trainers and board members talked about players risking injury. Players admitted weariness. Old hands speculated that maybe World Lacrosse *was* out to get them. The morning of the Japan game, Nationals co-founder and chairman Oren Lyons grumbled, "We're the only team playing without rest. I think it's designed so that we don't win. The US has had two days off."

That day, Tiffany and a Nationals attorney sent lengthy protest emails to World Lacrosse, essentially stating, *How can this happen?* In Pool A, the realm of top teams, both the US and Canada had two off days baked into their schedule, England and Australia had been given one day off apiece, and the Haudenosaunee had been given none. "They got a bit screwed: they're going to play Canada in the semis tomorrow and play seven straight games," Rob Pannell said. "That's brutal. If they'd had a day of rest, who knows? But they could still win. They showed that."

It was too late for any adjustment, but—as one World Lacrosse official pointed out—the championship schedule had been released February 2, more than four months before the championship, and Nationals management had never lodged a complaint. No Nationals coach or player mentioned concerns about the schedule; if anything, all seemed happy to play their first game two days later than the USA and Canada, with the time for more practice. Indeed, Haudenosaunee outrage might never have surfaced at all, but for the sudden realization that they actually could win.

Strikingly, the only Nationals unaffected by the heat, the schedule and this new spasm of aggrievement were Randy and Austin Staats. No Haudenosaunee more deserved a day off. But when Tiffany offered to rest them against lightly regarded Hong Kong, both refused. "We've got games to play: I'm not going to sit out," Austin said. "I'm playing for my community. I'm playing for my people. I can ice later."

The Nationals then crushed Hong Kong, 13–3, courtesy of the Staats brothers: Austin scored four goals and set up three more; Randy rang up a goal and three assists. Lyle and Jeremy Thompson, nursing sore shoulders, did take the day off, confirming the week's second surprise. For the first time in a decade, the first family of Indigenous lacrosse was not leading the Haudenosaunee effort. Jeremy, 36, had been getting consistently beaten at the faceoff X; banged-up Hiana, 35, was a secondary force on defense. And Lyle Thompson, the best of all, had been something of a mystery.

There had been brilliant flashes. Thompson is too great a talent to wholly disappear. But while the Staats brothers seized and capitalized on moment after clutch moment, Lyle looked increasingly adrift. His statistics were decent—though he wouldn't finish in the championship's top 10 in points, scoring or assists—but Thompson had been decidedly passive during the pool-play epics against the USA and Canada. For seven months, the Haudenosaunee had stated their mission: No more bronze. Only a gold or silver medal would do. Now, with Canada the last obstacle to the final, the need was clear. Thompson had to be great again. The Nationals needed to play the game of their lives.

Instead, almost immediately after the Haudenosaunee hit the Snapdragon Stadium field on June 29, it was clear that the pile-up of consecutive games, the fact—or maybe just the much-repeated idea—of fatigue, had caught up with them. A step slow, a split second late against the crisp Canadians, they played a lifeless and fatal first quarter, their worst of the week. Early in the second, with the Nationals down, 5–1, ESPN juxtaposed a fact box about their superstar—two-time Tewaaraton Award winner, one of the greatest field players ever—beside images of him pacing, scoreless, on the sideline. "Lyle Thompson, arguably the best player in the world," commentator Paul Carcaterra demanded, "*has* to make his presence felt."

Without outright asking what might be ailing him, the ESPN crew touched on the usual suspects: age, motivation, injury, Thompson's abrupt break from the PLL to focus on wife and family. He quieted all that with a shoulder-high strike from 30 feet, but it signaled no revival. Instead, Austin Staats stepped up in the fourth quarter to blister Canada with four goals, shine up the 12–7 loss and seal his emergence as the program's new leading man.

Watching Thompson trot off the field after, wondering if this was his golden generation's last, lost chance, the feeling rose again: that creep of white pity (*Poor Lo!*), a reminder that Native pride and spiritual need would—and should—plumb depths beyond outsider understanding. Throughout this 2023 campaign, Thompson appeared happy, no matter his disregard for the Olympics or weariness with the pros. He had raved so often about Tiffany and his fixes that he seemed content. But, now, Thompson's affect suggested something different. When asked, outside the locker room, if that was his last field game as a National, he was not surprised.

"I say yes, because it's just not my style of lacrosse," Thompson said. "It's very slow, it's very boring, and I care a lot about my passion to the game. The most important thing is joy. Yes, I feel a responsibility to represent my people at the world stage. But our job as attackmen is to slow the ball down and care for it—preciously. Which means: Slow your legs down, slow your mind down. My mind likes to be occupied. I think the game should be so fast that you don't have time to think about it. And this style of game? You can't have that mindset if you want to win."

By the time Tiffany emerged from the locker room, Team USA had begun its 11–2 dismantlement of Australia in the other semifinal. Cheers and whistles and grunts spilled up the tunnel as he walked toward the bus. He was carrying his wood stick, bottle of water in the webbing, a sheaf of papers. For the first time all week, Tiffany said, his defense couldn't hold. Their legs were shot.

"We had a chance for our time, and our legacy," Tiffany said. "We had a chance to really make a statement, to really do something special . . . And it's lost."

BUT IT WASN'T over. There was still one game to play, against Australia for the bronze medal the Nationals did not want. The loss of mission, a team-wide deflation, set in, reinforced by the now-despised schedule. Friday, June 30, was an off-day before the final: Too late, the Haudenosaunee would get their rest, had 48 hours to recover and recharge. The players could sleep in, be with family. They also had time to themselves.

Sixteen minutes after noon on July 1, the Nationals begin trickling onto the sun-washed field at Snapdragon Stadium. Randy Staats paused as he stepped out of the tunnel. "Ohh," he said, grinning. "My last field lacrosse game, ever."

Rex Lyons stood on the sidelines during warmups. He glanced back at Tiffany flipping balls to and fro, running the most basic of lateral footwork drills. "Look at that," he said. In 40 years with the Nationals, he had never seen defensemen practice that, let alone before a tournament's final game. Despite falling short of the gold medal game, the Tiffany hire had accomplished its greater mission—upgrading the operation, setting a new standard. The players committed like never before, with the greatest example being Austin Staats. "It is gratifying," Rex said. "His behavior on and off the field has been exemplary. That's all you can ask."

The day off seemed to do everybody good. The Haudenosaunee pried open a second quarter lead and cruised past Team Australia, 11–6, to win a third straight bronze medal. Marr's shift of Lyle Thompson to midfield had him running, mind busy, and it paid off with three loose and happy goals, one assist—and a backpedal. "It's an 80 percent chance this is my last one," Thompson said after the game. "I want to stay involved, because I know we can beat the US. I still want to help, whether it's coaching or selecting the team. Or I might come back as a middie."

Randy Staats served up five assists, raising his tournament-leading total to 17. His parents and wife and children came to see his field career end. "Especially to do it with my brother, that was amazing," he said. "It's like a happy funeral, you could say."

The Nationals operation was "1,000 percent" better than it was in 2018, Randy said. Total buy-in from the players made the Tiffany hire work, along with a great tournament from goalie Warren Hill. "Lars did a great job on the D-end, but as a group we're so tight and understand the game and know what we got to do and when.

"Hopefully, now, I can start a coaching role and still be involved. Because, you know, this team means . . ." Staats paused, eyes filling, voice catching, "more to me than a lot of things."

Austin scored three more to raise his tournament-leading tallies to 38 points and 30 goals, well ahead of number two; later in the day he was named the 2023 World Championship's Most Outstanding Attackman. In the handshake line at midfield, all the Nationals grinned and hugged the passing Aussies. Tiffany filed down with a word and hug for his players, toward the Staats brothers. He and Randy sidled into a quick embrace. But, just before Tiffany reached him, Austin broke out of the line, beelining past. Tiffany whipsnapped his neck to watch his star go, did another double-take, took two steps and stopped.

"Yeah, so Audie blows by me," Tiffany said 70 minutes later, sitting in his office outside the Nationals locker room. "And then I had to go find him, because he's one of the three selected for drug testing right now. And I'm a little nervous, because his reaction was, 'What happens if I fail?' That's instantly what he said. And I'm thinking, *That's about the worst reaction I think I've ever heard.*"

Five weeks earlier, when asked about beating the Americans, Oren Lyons had said, "We can beat anybody once we sober up. That's the last thing. I tell the guys: Don't pick up. And they're listening to that now, finally. It took 35 to 40 years. Indians drink a lot; we've got a reputation. You can't do that now."

Just two days earlier, Randy Staats had said of the team's veteran core— himself; Warren Hill; Lyle, Jeremy and Hiana Thompson; all playing for the Nationals since 2008, now going for their last hurrah—that they always tried to set an example, "doing it the way we think it should be done: not going out and partying, taking care of our bodies."

Tiffany wouldn't know, officially, for months that the sample Austin Staats provided would test positive for cocaine and marijuana. Nor that the sample given by a second Haudenosaunee, defenseman Oakley Thomas, would also test positive for the same substances—and that the punishment would include the stripping of Staats's award and statistics from tournament records and a three-month suspension for both players. Tiffany also was unaware that a positive drug test from the third selected National—Lyle Thompson, who tested negative—would have resulted in World Lacrosse rescinding the program's bronze medal. But he was already worried.

"I fear for our path to the Olympics with any kind of incident like that," Tiffany said of Austin Staats. "He did everything I asked of him. I just hope this drug test doesn't say: Well, maybe not *everything*. I mean, he's the best player in the world right now. Look what he can do sober. Look what he can do when he buys in and loses a little weight and eats the right things."

Austin needed to ingest eight bottles of water to produce his urine sample. By the time he finished, his teammates were up in the stands watching the second quarter of the US-Canada final, and he was the only player left in the locker room. He stepped into the shower, and for the next five minutes the sound of retching, raw fluid heaves, echoed throughout. Tiffany's head popped out of his office. He waited until Staats emerged, dried off, before approaching for one final effort.

"You're the best player in the world," Tiffany told him. "If nobody breaks out in this final, you're the MVP of this tournament."

Staats looked him in the eye and smiled. "Thanks, Coach," he said. The men hugged. Tiffany walked away grinning.

Austin was full of praise for "Coach Lars" and the Haudenosaunee defense. He wasn't interested in blaming the schedule. Asked how he was feeling, he smiled and said, "Perfect, right? We didn't play in the gold game, but we're bringing home a medal to our communities and showing the world that we're still here. And we're staying here."

LARS TIFFANY HAD it right: Before the US and Canada met for the 10th time for the World Field Championship final, no one in San Diego had outperformed Austin Staats. Midway through the second quarter with the US ahead, 3–2, the archrivals were so evenly matched, twin rosters stocked with cocky and driven all-timers, that another suffocating finish seemed fated. Yet somebody did break out, starting there: Brennan O'Neill beat sure–Hall of Fame goalie Dillon Ward for the second time with a running overhand. It set a pattern. All game O'Neill, who buckled Canada with a hat trick on opening night, kept providing the Americans room to breathe.

Canada scored twice to tie the game a third time at 4–4; O'Neill then rambled unhindered through two longpoles for his third score. A rising senior at Duke, and playing at midfield for the first time, O'Neill's newness itself seemed a weapon. It's as if the Canadians, faced with an unfamiliar, sneaky-fast element, hadn't had time yet to process and adjust. They came into the tournament ready for America's impeccable defense, its faceoff dominance, all the veteran stars. O'Neill was the difference. They couldn't stop him.

"He leaves me speechless," Danowski said on the field after. "I didn't see that coming today. When we needed somebody to put his foot in the ground, it didn't matter whether he was dodging a short stick or a longstick; he went to the rack. For a young guy to play that well—at this level, in this game—is incredible."

Thirty seconds after Canada's Dhane Smith cut the US's fourth-quarter lead to one, O'Neill launched himself goalward off the right wing. Planting just off the creaseline, he took a faceful of stick from the great Brodie Merrill while snaking his own through two other red jerseys. Now six Canadians converged, crushing O'Neill as his ball hit net. He lay face down in the grass an instant, rose, ambled off field like a steamroller seeking a place to park. After Josh Byrne brought Canada, for the last time, within one with five minutes left, on the next possession, O'Neill—again unassisted, again creating alone, again freeing himself with ease—orbited high, stepped back and launched another overhand from 30 feet to beat Ward for his fifth goal. It was the backbreaker, expanding the US lead to 9–7.

"Anytime you're playing for your country, you want to make your country proud—and you want to play with a lot of pride," O'Neill said after. "I just let the game come to me. It's nothing too crazy: Sometimes it falls your way, sometimes it doesn't and sometimes it just happens. The game came to me."

With two minutes left, the US began its stall, dodging and cycling the ball. On the American sideline, defensive midfielder Danny Logan roared a concise motto of athletic greed: "As much as we can!" He wasn't talking about goals, but about squeezing out more seconds of inaction, playing keep-away for as long as possible—before a referee finally made a subjective ruling of stalling—to eat up time. Only the international game allowed this: In every other iteration of lacrosse, college and pro, a shot clock would have made such delaying impossible. Few, then, knew they were witnessing another of the old world's last gasps.

Some arguing to keep lacrosse's international game shot clock–free were knee-jerk traditionalists. Some saw delaying as a way for new lacrosse nations to avoid discouraging blowouts. But sports has grown impatient: Even its greatest bastion of timelessness, Major League Baseball, introduced a pitch clock in 2023. And all week in San Diego, players and coaches dismissed chessboard lacrosse. Any sign of a stall touched off spectator eye rolls and boos; during Canada's first two-minute slowdown on the Haudenosaunee in the semifinal, a fan screamed, "You're ruining the game!" This is why World Lacrosse officials, hoping to seduce IOC hearts and votes, had invested its new Sixes discipline with a 30-second clock. This is why, a year hence, World Lacrosse members would overwhelmingly vote to introduce a shot clock to international field in 2026. Nobody, they understood, wants to see anyone win a championship for *possessing*.

In that sense, the classic field game felt particularly anachronistic in San Diego, right up to the moment, with 74 seconds left, when Canada pulled the goalie and Michael Sowers, perhaps the fastest man in the "fastest sport on two feet," sprinted past two gassed defenders and plopped the ball in to seal the championship, 10–7. Then American players and coaches rushed like kids onto the field. All the intangibles that make winning a gold medal for one's country the rarest of thrills—pride, camaraderie, patriotism—enveloped them.

Rob Pannell and Michael Ehrhardt, the heroes of 2018, met at midfield bellowing and crushed each other in a bear hug. At 34 and 32, respectively, both had just played their last World Championship. Injured most of the tournament, Ehrhardt didn't come close to replicating his MVP performance in Israel. Pannell again led Team USA in assists with 12. His first go-round, in 2014 in Denver, ended with Canada embarrassing the Americans on their home turf. Sometime here in San Diego, Pannell realized that redemption in 2018 wasn't enough. Only this second consecutive championship, pushing Canada firmly—and uncontroversially, this time—back into second place, could kill the sting for good.

Now Pannell could leave knowing that, in the American lacrosse galaxy, all had been set right. The game would change. Maybe new nations would rise up to challenge; maybe Sixes would become the next big thing. He walked away satisfied, and not because he was now the USA's all-time leading scorer. Here in San Diego, Pannell had seen the future.

"I think Brennan O'Neill is on his way," he said, "to breaking that record."

III

OLYMPIA

Tom Hayes didn't make it to San Diego. This saddened many. They know that few would have delighted more in the gathering and games than the Rutgers coaching icon and former International Lacrosse Federation president. And no one, over the last 40 years, had so consistently championed the themes dominating the 2023 World Championship: surging international growth, the embrace of Indigenous roots, optimism about the looming Olympics decision. Others had worked hard and long to expand the sport. Hayes worked harder, longer. He was expansiveness incarnate. He imbued the work with joy.

In January of 2021, at 81, Hayes's memory was sharp and his enthusiasm hummed. He had spoken again, then, of how a lacrosse stick is "magic"—the entire sport, actually—a quasi-spiritual framing rarely voiced by his fellow Long Island blue-collars or their prep-school rivals. Recounting how lacrosse got him into Penn State and enabled him to become the first in his family to graduate college, and how a college teammate's friend invited him to a party where US Air Force sergeant Hayes met his lifelong love, his words brimmed with gratitude. He never forgot the words of his Sewanhaka High coach, Bill Ritch: *You're gonna get a lot out of this sport. Make sure you put something back.* Not quite the Haudenosaunee Thanksgiving Address, but same idea.

In 1973, four years into his first head coaching job at Drexel, Hayes volunteered to chair the US Intercollegiate Lacrosse Association's nascent International Games Committee. To that point, there had been just one de facto men's world championship, contested in 1967 by the US, Canada,

Australia and England. When Australia hosted another invitational in 1974, Hayes organized the American program and team (which won its second world title), co-founded the International Lacrosse Federation and locked in the championship as a quadrennial event. The next decade was about consolidation, for Hayes in his new post at Rutgers, for the ILF in establishing rules for governance and hosting. Though the strongest advocate for admitting the Iroquois as a member nation in 1987, Hayes—still serving as Team USA's general manager, and shuttling from ILF vice president to secretary-treasurer to general delegate—had no greater plan for the game than basic maintenance.

Beyond barroom musings, few in lacrosse then—aside from Oren Lyons, who made his ambitions clear at the Nationals' 1983 debut—spoke much about a return to the Olympics. But in the late 1980s, Hayes began pushing the federation's focus to rapid expansion, keyed by overseas clinics and equipment grants. By the time his eight-year term as president ended in 2002, the ILF had grown to 18 member nations, including the Czech Republic, Japan, Sweden, the Netherlands, Argentina, Hong Kong and Italy. In 2004, at a strategic planning meeting in Denver called by his successor, ILF president Peter Hobbs, the Olympic mission was officially raised for the first time. Aside from knowing that the IOC required a unified men's and women's organization, "we had no idea," said then–ILF vice president Stan Cockerton, "what else we had to do."

The merger with the International Federation of Women's Lacrosse Associations, under the newly constituted Federation of International Lacrosse (FIL), became final in 2008. Now there were 30 lacrosse nations, and Hayes had been lured back as the FIL's development director, tasked with securing Olympic recognition. The first step was the easiest: In 2009, the FIL paid $5,000 in registration fees to become "WADA-compliant"—a signatory to the World Anti-Doping Agency code, subject to its Olympic-level testing regimes.

The next step was trickier. Like most in lacrosse, Hayes knew little about SportAccord—a Lausanne, Switzerland–based umbrella group best explained by its other name: Global Association of International Sports Federations. All Olympic and non-Olympic organizations, like the soccer behemoth FIFA, are part of SportAccord. Before any approach to the International Olympic Committee, conveniently based just down the road in Lausanne, lacrosse needed to join SportAccord. To apply, the FIL needed at least 40 member nations; in 2011, the addition of Hungary, Uganda, Israel and Russia made it

43. Without a staff, Hayes spent a year researching SportAccord, corralling all needed documents and audits and minutes and bylaws demanded in the 60-page application. The work was thankless. Many thought it would lead to nothing. "He just believed," said then–US Lacrosse CEO Steve Stenersen. "Certain steps in the process, he willed to happen."

In 2012, SportAccord accepted the FIL as its 106th member. Later developments would all feel like game-changers, but SportAccord was the breakthrough. For the first time nonbelievers began to see lacrosse's inclusion in the 2024 Olympics as achievable. *Lacrosse Magazine* named Hayes its 2012 Person of the Year, and the accompanying piece ended with the one-man gang, then 72, speaking for many.

"You've got to dream, right?" Hayes said. "I just hope I live long enough to see it."

NEXT CAME MEMBERSHIP in the International World Games Association, entrée to Olympic-style competition. Tired of paper, Tom Hayes and founding FIL official Ron Balls decided to piece together a slick video about lacrosse's past and present—men, box, NCAA, women, kids. Hayes had a crafty NYU film student, daughter of one of his former players, bring her skills biweekly to the Hayes home in northeastern Pennsylvania. Lacrosse was the last of four sports vying for IWGA membership at the 2013 SportAccord Convention in St. Petersburg, Russia, that May. The vast room was full of delegates, tired and chatty. Hayes flipped on the five-minute tape.

"All of a sudden the room gets quiet," Hayes said. "You'd be surprised how many sports people in the world have never seen lacrosse."

With that acceptance by the IWGA, it became clear that even an irrepressible old coach had limits. Winning over the IOC would take money, professionalism, insider knowledge. Hayes stepped down as FIL's development head in 2015, became something called "Olympic Vision Director." At some point that year, he got a call from his longtime Rutgers assistant and FIL development aide-de-camp, Bob DeMarco, in Taiwan running a clinic. All the Taiwan people were raving about Joe Tsai. "Think you could okay it for us to stop in Hong Kong and talk to this guy?" DeMarco asked. "Might be worth our while."

Hayes convinced Cockerton to okay the extra expense. The meeting in Tsai's skyscraper office overlooking Victoria Harbor lasted hours. Without DeMarco's call and Hayes's urging, Tsai might never have offered $2.5 million the following year to pay for FIL's first full-time CEO, which covered the hiring of a headhunting firm and a year-long global search, which, in 2017, landed new CEO Jim Scherr.

Scherr, 57, knew little about the game. He and twin brother Bill grew up in tiny Mobridge, South Dakota (pop. 4,174), as wrestling heroes, with sidelines in football, haybale stacking and rodeo. Only a half mile and the Missouri River separate Mobridge from the Standing Rock and Cheyenne River reservations, nations that don't play lacrosse. But in the former NCAA champion—and fifth-place finisher at the 1988 Seoul Olympics—who spent a decade as executive director of USA Wrestling before leading the USOC from 2003 to 2009, lacrosse now had a guide versed in Olympic bureaucracy and the five-ring logo's value. "It provides, perhaps, the largest platform in sports," Scherr said. "That builds your brand and legitimizes your sport to the world." Becoming a fully recognized Olympic sport also starts an annual flow of IOC dollars—anywhere from $200,000 to $1 million-plus—to each federation, opens up funding from national Olympic committees and provides entrée to prime training venues.

Like no one else at the FIL, Scherr also understood that the IOC was a bruised giant. Soccer's World Cup now equaled or surpassed the Olympics in passion, TV ratings and cultural heft. Humiliating withdrawals by Rome, Boston, Budapest and Hamburg from bidding to host the 2024 summer games, due to daunting costs, seemed proof that the Olympics were no longer worth the trouble. On September 13, 2017, the IOC awarded its 2024 and 2028 games to Paris and Los Angeles, respectively. They were the only bidders left.

Scherr thought introducing lacrosse into the 2024 or 2028 games was a reasonable goal. But when evaluating the FIL's rudimentary strategic plan before the board that same month, he was blunt. Admission to the Olympics would take much more than just sending a promotional video and lobbying attendees at SportAccord meetings. Rivals like cricket had already spent millions of dollars on similar campaigns. Lacrosse needed a half dozen full-time staffers now, and probably four more down the line. It needed more money, more social media impact, more of an attractive story to tell.

"We have 60 member nations, and hopefully, in the next five years we can get to 80 or 90 and within that the competitive spread has to be reduced," Scherr said in Israel in 2018.

Have to get more countries. Then? Surfing has 6.4 million people who'll tune in to the WSL professional event livestream—6.4 million! We've got 2,000 YouTube followers. So we've got to build a digital audience. We've got to build our world events. Got to build our capabilities, the capabilities of our member nations, grow the sport, close the competitive gap—all in the next four or five years.

Everybody thinks their sport should be in the Olympics. We have to convince the IOC that lacrosse is great and worthy, but we also have to understand what they need to make their product better. The Olympic Games has to remain relevant, has to reduce its cost and complexity so that more cities can bid on it—or any cities can bid on it. Can we bring an audience to the games, bring a sport that's cost-effective and drive revenues for them?

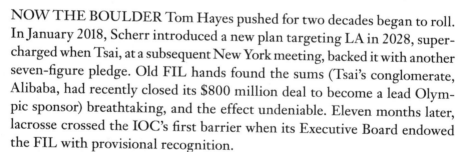

NOW THE BOULDER Tom Hayes pushed for two decades began to roll. In January 2018, Scherr introduced a new plan targeting LA in 2028, supercharged when Tsai, at a subsequent New York meeting, backed it with another seven-figure pledge. Old FIL hands found the sums (Tsai's conglomerate, Alibaba, had recently closed its $800 million deal to become a lead Olympic sponsor) breathtaking, and the effect undeniable. Eleven months later, lacrosse crossed the IOC's first barrier when its Executive Board endowed the FIL with provisional recognition.

Another two and a half years and a fivefold increase in World Lacrosse's anti-doping budget were needed to gain full IOC recognition. But by November of 2020, there had been enough winks and nods for Stenersen to tell Hayes that approval seemed a lock. "Make sure I get a suite," Hayes said of the celebration. "And there's a wheelchair and oxygen."

Two months later, at his home on a ridge in the Endless Mountains near Crystal Lake, Pennsylvania, Hayes was feeling upbeat. "Things are going good as long as we can keep everyone happy at the IOC," he said. "This thing with the Iroquois can be a real fly in the ointment." When asked, as lacrosse's longtime champion of both, about his feelings if the sport was forced to choose between the two, he said, "I would opt to have the Iroquois in the Olympics." But if the IOC refuses to allow the Iroquois, should World Lacrosse refuse to play in solidarity—or play on without them?

"It's a tough question, because you're damned if you do and damned if you don't," Hayes said finally. "I think we have enough people in international sport now . . . they would realize that if they want to have a better Olympics, the creator of the sport has to be involved."

ON JULY 20, 2021, with a vote at its 138th session in Tokyo, the IOC membership granted World Lacrosse full recognition. While not as sweet as an actual Olympic faceoff, Hayes still saw his sport hop the threshold. Eight months later, March 7, 2022, he died at the age of 82. "A true legend," World Lacrosse's then-president Sue Redfern called him. The federation's U-20 men's championship trophy bore his name. Rutgers played the rest of the season with TOM HAYES stitched onto every player's jersey nameplate. But his truest memorials would be the milestones passed, anticipation building, as lacrosse barreled toward its hoped-for Olympic return.

It was, for the moment, aiming at a temporary target. Traditionally, a sport's hope of admission to the Olympics core program began with an initial appearance as a "demonstration sport." Since ending that practice in 1992, the IOC updated its core program with successes like beach volleyball and snowboarding. Starting with the 2020 Olympics in Tokyo (with surfing, karate, baseball/softball, sports climbing and skateboarding), it also empowered each host city to add a one-time slate of sports with local, youth-oriented appeal. Given lacrosse's roots and recent boom, and its appearance at the first Los Angeles Olympics in 1932, Scherr figured the next American "host city" route as the fastest way in. More than 40 other eager sports federations figured the same.

The new Sixes discipline auditioned to Olympic eyes at the World Games 2022 in Birmingham, Alabama, from July 7 to 17. IOC president Thomas Bach visited midway through, watched competitions in boules, korfball, beach handball, ultimate frisbee—but not lacrosse. Other IOC observers, however, peppered lacrosse personnel with questions, took in Canada's twin championships in the men's and women's competition and noted the

Haudenosaunee Nationals' once-contentious, now-celebrated appearance as the first-ever Indigenous team at a World Games.

Three weeks later, in early August, the IOC and Los Angeles 2028 Organizing Committee named lacrosse and eight others—cricket, break-dancing, baseball/softball, flag football, karate, squash, kickboxing and motorsport—to the shortlist of candidates for LA28's host-city sports. The IOC, of course, would have final say. But the fact that all presentations would be made to—and vetted over the next year by—LA28 alone, made it clear that LA28 chairman Casey Wasserman would now be a pivotal figure in lacrosse history.

One day in October, Jim Scherr, Joe Tsai, Paul Rabil, Sue Redfern and Jane Lee—the Oxford-educated captain of Korea's national team and chair of World Lacrosse's Athletes Commission—gathered on a studio set in a Brooklyn production house to present, live via Zoom, lacrosse's multimedia case to a group of LA28 officials. Scherr, who had been part of a similar presentation by wrestling to the IOC in 2013 and sat in on many host-city bids for the USOC, walked out sure that lacrosse's presentation "could not have gone any better."

That Wasserman, the most important figure in the equation, purpose-fully watched none of the sports pitching that day didn't matter. Though lacrosse's panel—and even Wasserman himself—didn't quite know it yet, he was predisposed to their cause. This wasn't because of the game. Like Scherr, the 48-year-old Wasserman had little firsthand familiarity with lacrosse. But as the grandson of legendary Hollywood film mogul Lew Wasserman and CEO of an eponymous sports marketing and talent agency, the LA28 head prizes a vivid narrative arc, and is driven to make his games historically unique and emotionally powerful. The story of America's oldest team sport returning to the Olympics in Los Angeles, 96 years after its last appearance at a US games, dovetailed nicely with Wasserman's agenda.

Those around him also found Wasserman smitten with lacrosse's Haudenosaunee element, heard him call the prospect of their competing in LA "compelling" and "an incredible story." Neither IOC rules nor its horror of politics seemed a concern: Wasserman, a prominent fundraiser for the Democratic Party, had already proven himself happy to rattle that corner of the Olympic cage.

On June 19, 2020, amid the George Floyd protests, Wasserman had sent a letter to IOC president Thomas Bach supporting a growing demand that the IOC amend Rule 50 of its Olympic Charter—which, "to protect the neutrality of sport," since 1975 has barred all "political, religious or racial propaganda" from Olympic venues—and allow athletes to engage in anti-racist advocacy during the games. "Sport is not separate or clear of racism; it is a microcosm of our world where racism exists," Wasserman wrote. "I urge you to allow and encourage athletes to advocate against racism anywhere they can, including on and off the field of play."

A month after Wasserman's declaration, Bach answered that the Olympics cannot "descend into a marketplace of demonstrations." But, after consulting with 3,500 athletes, the IOC then relaxed its Rule 50 restrictions for the Tokyo Olympics in 2021, allowing participants to speak on sociopolitical issues at press conferences, in mixed zones and on social media; to display words like "peace" and "equality" (but not "Black Lives Matter"); and to take the field before competition with non-"disruptive" gestures that don't target "people, countries, organisations and/or their dignity."

Whether such softening signaled flexibility on an issue like Haudenosaunee inclusion, however, remained unclear. For admission to the IOC, a nation needs both recognition by an international body like the United Nations and its own National Olympic Committee, which itself requires participation in at least five internationally recognized sports. The Haudenosaunee have neither. The IOC once made exceptions for dependent territories like Guam, Puerto Rico and Hong Kong, but—after a much-publicized campaign for similar inclusion by Catalonia in the early nineties—closed that loophole in 1996.

In its bid, World Lacrosse made a point of stressing the sport's Haudenosaunee heritage. Scherr believes the dented Olympic brand could benefit from the Haudenosaunee example of "inclusion and excellence and perseverance." He also knows that the IOC is wary of any precedent that could spark similar quests by other Indigenous peoples. But "this is a unique circumstance that doesn't exist in any other sport," he said. "This is one people who essentially are sovereign in their own territory, as declared by the US and Canadian governments, that originated the game and still participate in it at the highest levels—against all odds."

He also stressed that World Lacrosse has little leverage to wield with the IOC. "All we can do is present," Scherr said. "We don't make the decision. We can present the very best possible case for why lacrosse should be in the Olympics and why the Haudenosaunee Confederacy should be part of that equation. We'll use all of our resources and influence to support that case. But that's all we can do."

OVER THE NEXT YEAR, as LA28 vetted the nine shortlisted sports, World Lacrosse waited in near silence. There was an occasional signal of encouragement, some technical questions about Sixes and Olympic qualifying. It seemed odd that no LA28—or IOC—observers showed up for the 2023 World Championship just two hours away in San Diego. Lacrosse folk decided to take that as a positive sign.

Still, the quiet on the Haudenosaunee front seemed curious. Since the World Games controversy first broke in 2020, the IOC had been aware that lacrosse's baggage included this singular administrative and political problem: Handled poorly, a public relations disaster was almost a certainty. The best way to avoid one, of course, would have been to reject lacrosse altogether—before announcing the shortlist. Instead, the IOC joined with LA28 in inviting the sport to apply, and the process churned on. The issue didn't appear to matter. Scherr knew better. But if Olympic officials weren't going to raise it, World Lacrosse wouldn't go out of its way to remind them.

Hence, the Haudenosaunee agreed to maintain a low profile—and follow Scherr's lead—during the Olympic process. Hence, the Haudenosaunee decision to refrain from stirring up the kind of outrage that forced their admission to the World Games in 2022. Hence, Scherr's low-grade panic when he learned that a Haudenosaunee delegation, led by Tadadaho Sidney Hill and Oren and Rex Lyons, were meeting with Biden administration officials at the White House on July 24, 2023. His worst fear: a press conference featuring Haudenosaunee demands for Olympic recognition and White House support. Few things annoy the IOC more than meddling politicians, grandstanding American politicians in particular. A public ultimatum could well scuttle lacrosse's chances.

To the Haudenosaunee, the private, hour-plus meeting with Tom Perez, senior advisor to President Joe Biden and Director of Intergovernmental Affairs, and others wasn't just about lacrosse. Because its independence prevents a diplomatic relationship via the Bureau of Indian Affairs, the

Confederacy seizes on any chance to meet with US officials for dialogue—
to "polish the covenant chain."

Before Rex Lyons stepped into the ornate confines of the old "Secretary of War" suite, Scherr contacted him to ask what was happening. Lyons
explained the larger purpose, assured Scherr that there would be no incendiary statements by the Haudenosaunee about the IOC. "We have no interest
in doing that," Lyons said later, paraphrasing his response. "We understand
we need World Lacrosse as a partner. We're not here to make it harder for
you to help us. But we're also in charge of our destiny. We've got to do things
for ourselves. Things that you cannot do."

But the Olympics was, in fact, the reason White House Director of
Tribal Affairs PaaWee Rivera had initiated the sitdown, the reason for Rex
Lyons's attendance and the reason the Haudenosaunee delegation walked in
toting a six-foot hickory longpole. Perez, a lacrosse dad who kept statistics
for his daughter's travel team and remains a fan, knew that the sport was
poised on the doorstep of the 2028 Olympics, and that the Haudenosaunee
sought White House support to compete as a sovereign nation. "That really
excited me," Perez said later. "Going into the meeting it was a no-brainer,
in my mind, and certainly a no-brainer in PaaWee's mind. There was never
any persuading that anyone had to do."

Instead, Rex Lyons found himself in the odd position of stressing cau-
tion, asking the Biden administration to follow their lead to avoid rattling
the IOC. Much of the meeting was devoted to Nationals history and laying
out the timeline ahead—the cutdown of the shortlist by LA28, the multiple
IOC hurdles after. "We just wanted to set the table," Lyons said. But he also
made clear that, if lacrosse did get into the Olympics, the Haudenosaunee
would be asking for public backing. To seal matters, Oren, 93, gifted Perez
the lacrosse stick.

Just as important, news of the meeting never leaked. In early September 2023 Scherr said that he had fielded no sticky questions, felt no negativity
at all, on the Haudenosaunee issue from either LA28 or the IOC. And later
that month, an LA28 official with knowledge of the process confirmed that,
over the past year, the organizing committee, too, had received no pushback
on the Haudenosaunee issue from the IOC.

"We haven't yet, because we haven't pushed it yet," the LA28 official
said. "The way the IOC works, it's one thing at a time. You try and boil the

ocean and their head explodes. Once [lacrosse] is in, we have all the leverage and we can force this on them. I think."

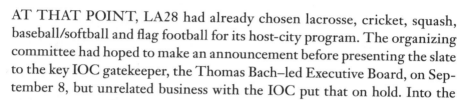

AT THAT POINT, LA28 had already chosen lacrosse, cricket, squash, baseball/softball and flag football for its host-city program. The organizing committee had hoped to make an announcement before presenting the slate to the key IOC gatekeeper, the Thomas Bach–led Executive Board, on September 8, but unrelated business with the IOC put that on hold. Into the vacuum rumors flew.

The delay fed fears of eroding support, a dreaded October surprise. But for the Haudenosaunee, Tiffany's concern that Austin Staats's failed drug test might hurt their Olympic quest proved unfounded. Few actually knew it happened. Long after the International Testing Agency reported an "adverse analytical finding" of marijuana and cocaine in the urine samples collected from Staats and Nationals teammate Oakley Thomas on July 1, the sport maintained its traditional quiet on illicit drug use. World Lacrosse made no announcement when the ITA issued its official notification September 6, nor when Staats (after verifying that the substances were ingested on the off-day, and thus not regarded as performance-enhancing) accepted a three-month suspension, nor when it revoked his Most Outstanding Attackman and All-World awards and wiped out his San Diego statistics. Staats's abrupt withdrawal two days later from the 2023 Mann Cup Final, Canada's senior A box championship, was explained by the Six Nations Chiefs only as a "personal matter."

When, on January 24, 2024, the ITA finally announced the suspension of one of lacrosse's biggest stars for admitted drug use, it smacked of old news: Staats's punishment had ended seven weeks before. None of the sport's top publications and websites mentioned it. Haudenosaunee Nationals officials, too, announced nothing. When asked, board member Rex Lyons admitted that his post-test conversation with Staats didn't inspire much confidence.

"I don't know if they're going to be looking at us hard, because the Olympics are coming, but I kind of welcome this," Rex Lyons said. "It makes it obvious: if you want to be one of us, you've got to be in your right mind and doing the right things or you're going to be down the road. It's embarrassing as it is. Here's the problem, too: You tell a guy, 'This is horrible behavior. What's wrong with you?' Then he goes and makes All-World and he's rolling his eyes at you, like, *Look how I behaved and I'm still the best in the world.* I don't know if the dots are connecting yet for him."

Meanwhile, Wasserman's original list for the host-city sports remained unscathed. Well before the second scheduled reveal, on October 7, World Lacrosse knew that it had survived the cut. "When we talk about having the most compelling sports program and the greatest collection of athletes in the history of the world—which it will be in 2028—lacrosse is an important piece," Wasserman said. "We're thrilled with it."

LA28's choices went before the IOC's Executive Board just prior to the 141st IOC Session in Mumbai on October 13. Approval by that 15-member body all but ensured admission; the IOC member countries generally follow the board's lead. LA28 presented the five-sport program to the Executive Board as an unbreakable whole. Contrary to rumor, the board didn't push to edit the number or kind of sport. It also made no issue, when asking about lacrosse, of Haudenosaunee eligibility.

On Friday, October 13, Bach announced the Executive Board's approval of the five-sport slate at a press conference. "Lacrosse Sixes" was named third, and Bach paused dramatically for the audience in India before finishing with ". . . and cricket." As one of the globe's most popular sports, cricket dominated the questioning in the ensuing 50-minute press conference. The one time that Bach addressed lacrosse, he said that it—like squash and flag football—reflected a specific part of American culture and sports culture. He didn't refer to Baltimore preps or Long Island blue-collars or the booming women's game. Bach only said, "If you look at lacrosse, this is the sport . . . if I may say so—of the First Nations of the US."

One formality remained: approval from the full IOC membership. Three days later, on October 16, LA28 addressed the body in a hotel ballroom in Mumbai. Wasserman began with an impassioned speech detailing his Ukrainian Jewish heritage, the massacre in Israel on October 7, the slaughter and the hostages taken. "Unfortunately, the Olympics are not immune to the times we live in," he said. "At its worst, it is a platform for hate to express itself on the world stage, and we will always remember the 11 members of the Israeli Olympic team who were taken hostage and murdered in Munich. But at its best, it is an opportunity for the sport to show the world a better path."

The LA28 report lasted nearly 34 minutes. After pivoting to its host-city program, it stressed lacrosse's Sixes discipline, the game's rapid American growth, its Indigenous roots. Before the final vote, Bach opened the floor to questions. The Pakistani delegate complained about the "political content" in Wasserman's speech; the French delegate, whose first Olympics were at Munich in 1972, rose to support it. During the brief Q&A, no one asked about lacrosse.

When Bach asked for a show of hands in support of the five new host-city sports, nearly all went up. When he asked for those against, Bach said, "Is there more than one? Is somebody too shy? Two. Two against. Any abstentions? Two or three. Anyway, abstentions are not being taken into account. Then . . . the proposal is approved."

Early Monday morning in the US, Steve Stenersen—two-time national champion at North Carolina, the US Lacrosse founding president and World Lacrosse VP who led the development of Sixes—was awakened by the ping of a text. "We're LA bound!" Scherr wrote. "It's official!"

"The achievement I'm most proud to be a part of," Stenersen, who left the sport in 2022, said. "We all were texting each other and the first thing everybody said was 'THINKING OF TOM . . . CAN'T BELIEVE HE'S NOT HERE TO SEE IT . . .' It was heartbreaking. But I'm convinced he knew it was going to happen. He didn't see it with his own eyes, but he believed it."

THE NATIONALS ORGANIZATION posted its official response the following day.

"The Haudenosaunee (Confederacy of Six Nations), as originators of the game of lacrosse, are incredibly pleased with the return of lacrosse to the Olympics," the statement began. Executive Director Leo Nolan called the news "exciting and humbling." Congratulations and thanks were offered to all who made it possible. There was a reminder that a Haudenosaunee team had won a bronze medal at the 1904 Olympics and been allowed to play again in a qualifying tournament for the first Los Angeles games in 1932.

"We welcome this opportunity to build upon that historic legacy, and we have been heartened by the support from the Los Angeles 2028 Committee for our inclusion," it said in closing. "We would be thrilled to be involved in the games."

By then, Wasserman had publicly expressed support of the Haudenosaunee, stating his intent to "find a solution to allow them to compete" and his understanding that this was "not a simple decision" for the International Olympic Committee. Both were messages to Lausanne, and notable for their measured tone; the Nationals and LA28 were hoping to start a friendly negotiation. But the IOC's reply wasn't friendly. It sounded like a slammed door.

"Only national Olympic committees recognized by the I.O.C. can enter teams for the Olympic Games in accordance with the Olympic Charter," the International Olympic Committee said in a statement issued October 19. "This means it is up to the two NOCs concerned (USA and Canada)—in coordination with World Lacrosse and the National Federations concerned—to decide if they include athletes from Haudenosaunee in their respective teams depending on the passport they hold."

WILL THEY make it? As it has been for the Nationals so often before, as it has been for the Six Nations for centuries, that is the Haudenosaunee question now for the 2028 Olympics in Los Angeles. Though the North American locale precludes the kind of airport drama that nearly locked the Nationals out of Israel, the IOC's current stance means that Haudenosaunee passports—the citizenship they assert, the sovereignty they proclaim—will again be the deciding issue.

But there is a major difference. After the IOC approved the admission of lacrosse, powerful allies began lining up publicly behind the Nationals' quest. Five years before LA's Opening Ceremony, Olympic players like Wasserman actively joined the work of sorting options, charting the course with the best odds of getting the Haudenosaunee in there, too. "Given the history of the sport and its founding origins: it's a unique opportunity," Wasserman said. "If we were doing the Olympics and lacrosse in a different country, I'm not sure I'd be saying that. I understand the complications, but that doesn't mean it's not an interesting idea: to see if there's a pathway."

The preferred IOC route was dismissed early. The Haudenosaunee had neither the resources nor time nor will to meet the prerequisites (participation in five sports recognized by international federations; UN-confirmed nationhood) for a national Olympic committee in time for 2028. The IOC's other stated option—Haudenosaunee players trying out for USA or Canada—on its face seems an insult. "I would never play for Canada or the US," said Lyle Thompson. But many Nationals grew up dazzled by the Olympic mystique and also carry US or Canadian passports. Even former Haudenosaunee National Alie Jimerson, the daughter of the women's team's current director, opted to play for Team Canada at the 2017 and 2022 World Championships. Should the Haudenosaunee be shut out, a roster spot with the colonial powers would still lend the lone Mohawk or Seneca an unmatched platform to promote or protest.

In early conversations with those backing the Haudenosaunee, most coalesced around a solution resembling the Refugee Olympic Team. For the 2016 Olympics in Rio de Janeiro, the IOC sponsored 10 athletes from South Sudan, the Democratic Republic of Congo and Ethiopia, to highlight the plight of stateless millions worldwide. Competing under the Olympic flag, the Refugee Team became one of Rio's clear successes, a boost to the Olympic image. It also set the tone for another boundary-breaking initiative in 2018, when the IOC unified the North and South Korean women's hockey teams for the Winter Games in Pyeongchang. Such extranational moves from the avowedly apolitical organization sparked speculation that Thomas Bach was bucking for a Nobel Peace Prize. Showcasing the world's Indigenous peoples, via the Haudenosaunee, would fold nicely into such a campaign.

By September of 2023, all the immediately affected entities—World Lacrosse, LA28, the US Olympic and Paralympic Committee and the Canadian Olympic Committee—expressed support for the IOC to grant the Haudenosaunee a one-time exemption from IOC rules for inclusion in 2028. All agreed that Wasserman should spearhead the campaign. However, no established pathway exists within the IOC to pursue such an exemption. Both the Refugee Team and Korea's unified hockey team were created from the inside out. There is no recent precedent for an outside entity like the Haudenosaunee to lobby for entry, and no IOC procedure for a federation like World Lacrosse to make a formal request.

Also, the Haudenosaunee weren't embracing the idea. Even before the IOC publicly reinforced its hard line, Nationals officials were reiterating theirs. Sovereignty remains a core reason for the team's existence, and walking into any Olympic Opening Ceremony beneath a Haudenosaunee flag remains the mission. "It would be a recognition on the biggest global platform that there is," said Rex Lyons. Whenever an established state like the UK or Australia or Israel recognized the Haudenosaunee passport—affirming the Native credo "we are still here"—it represented a win bigger than any game. To have the IOC do the same, before a television audience of billions, would be titanic.

Complicating everything is a potential roadblock that, at least publicly, almost everyone ignored. Any Olympics is a sporting event, first, involving qualification processes that run years in advance. The men's and women's tournaments approved by the IOC for 2028 feature just six teams. World Lacrosse's working idea was to divide that geographically: two teams from the Americas, two from Europe and two from Asia. With the host US guaranteed entry, that presumably leaves one spot for either Canada and the (as yet unallowed) Haudenosaunee to fight over. And even if World Lacrosse succeeds in its hope of expanding the fields to eight teams, the Nationals are no lock: Sixes, so far, has proven to be their weakest discipline. As of mid-2024, the Haudenosaunee men stand fifth in the World Sixes rankings, the Haudenosaunee women seventh.

With qualification tournaments for the 2028 Olympics expected to begin sometime in late 2026, then, hard questions will need answers by late 2025. Might the IOC soften and grant the Haudenosaunee an exemption before then? If so, what if the Haudenosaunee don't qualify? Would LA28 and the IOC carve out a ceremonial spot for the Nationals in the tournament? What if the IOC does not grant an exemption, and the Haudenosaunee are barred from entering qualification? Might LA28 seek a creative way to involve them in the games regardless?

No real progress was expected, however, until after the 2024 Summer Olympics in Paris. Then came a bombshell: The Haudenosaunee's summer meeting in the White House paid off.

On December 6, 2023, in remarks declaring a "new era of self-determination" and "respect for tribal sovereignty," President Joe Biden announced his support for the Nationals' inclusion at the 2028 Olympics "under its own tribal flag." His endorsement carried none of the tangible benefits of the day's bigger news—an executive order that expanded Indigenous access to, and authority over, federal funding. But Biden's words, onstage before the 11th White House Tribal Nations Summit, invested the marginal IOC affair with presidential import. More than 228 years after

George Washington signed the Treaty of Canandaigua, his 45th successor had polished the covenant chain with the Haudenosaunee to a high gleam.

Among the packed audience of more than 400 Native leaders at the Department of the Interior sat Haudenosaunee Tadadaho Sidney Hill, Nationals executive director Leo Nolan, and Seneca chief Roger Hill. They waited through 10 minutes of Biden's recounting of Indigenous communities that "still live in the shadows of the failed policies of the past," his work directing "the largest direct federal investment ($32 billion) in tribal nations ever," his appointment of Interior Secretary Deb Haaland as the nation's first-ever Native cabinet secretary. Biden spoke about his new executive order, his restoration of Trump-gutted protections for tribal lands. They knew what was coming. It still was startling to hear the American president, over the next 90 seconds, make the case for lacrosse:

> *The game brought tribes together, a force for peace, friendship and healing. The Six Nations players are still among the very best in the world. And as a point of personal privilege, I know about this because I went to Syracuse University, long the home of a powerhouse lacrosse program. And, I might add, my daughter was a first-rate lacrosse player in high school, and my niece was an [high school] All-American . . . so we have a little knowledge of lacrosse in our family . . .*
>
> *This fall, it was announced that lacrosse will once again be an official Olympic sport. And the Six Nations team asked to compete under its own tribal flag. And today, I'm announcing my support for that request.*
>
> *Their ancestors invented the game. They perfected it for a millennia. Their circumstances are unique, and they should be granted an exemption to field their own team at the Olympics.*

The audience of Native American leaders broke into raucous applause. It didn't take long for Biden's words to have an effect. Within hours, Canada's sports minister, Carla Qualtrough, issued a similar call. "When lacrosse returns to the Olympics in the 2028 games," she said, "I hope to see the Haudenosaunee Nationals qualify and compete under their own flag." Ten days later, a poll of 1,229 likely voters found that 66 percent of Americans—including firm majorities of Republicans and Independents—agreed that the IOC should allow Haudenosaunee participation in the 2028 Olympics.

At breakfast the morning after Biden's remarks, Rex Lyons showed his father video of the ceremony on his cellphone. "There we were at the top of the top: He was singing our praises, rallying for our sovereignty, that we should be able to compete under our own flag," Rex said. "No president's ever said that." Oren Lyons had been fighting for Native rights forever, it seemed, nearly 60 years of explaining and traveling, of grinding losses and barely visible progress. He never was much for celebrating, because the work didn't end. Another conference or crisis or obstacle always loomed.

But after the Biden video clip ended, Rex saw it: his dad taking stock for once, enjoying the win. "Jeez," Oren said, allowing a half grin. "There it is. Real success."

STILL, IT COULD all go for naught. All of it—the presidential clout, the public sympathy, the rich and influential supporters—could well smash against an IOC stone wall that leaves the Haudenosaunee Nationals locked out of the 2028 Olympics. Certainly, Biden's words prompted no immediate give; in the ensuing months, LA28's cockiness about leveraging IOC needs and Thomas Bach's ego dissolved. Wasserman vowed to keep seeking a solution, but failure, too, is an option. What then?

The easy answer, of course, is that the game will go on, just as it went on after the Nationals missed the men's World Championship in 2010 and the U-19 women's World Championship in 2015. The easy answer is that whatever nations are welcomed in LA will be delighted to take part in lacrosse's return to the Olympics for the first time in 80 years. World Lacrosse's mission was never intended to be all-or-nothing. In 2010, when Haudenosaunee inclusion was even more unlikely, the federation's 39 nations voted overwhelmingly to pursue the Olympics. Its membership has more than doubled since, but aside from the US and Canada—representing constituencies awash in residential school revelations, whose players have formed close bonds with Onondaga, Mohawk and Seneca teammates—few seem conflicted. "I think the members would still, today, vote to pursue Olympic inclusion," Scherr said.

Still, the US and Canada are the sport's role models, and—with their governments—many prominent Americans and Canadians stand in emphatic support of the Haudenosaunee cause. Few want to speculate on the worst-case scenario: Olympic lacrosse without the game's originators. But on his final day as Nationals coach in San Diego, Lars Tiffany did say that if the American team goes into the 2028 Olympics without the Nationals, USA Lacrosse should be shamed into removing the bronze *Creator's Game* statue outside its headquarters. Others think that the US, Canada—indeed, the entire sport—should follow Ireland's example, defer to the Haudenosaunee and not play at all.

"I say we don't go," said Hampton head coach Chazz Woodson, a former USA Lacrosse board member. "I say that understanding there's major ramifications: If we don't go, [lacrosse in the Olympics] probably doesn't happen ever again. But that would be the right thing to do."

Lacking that stand, one outcome seems wholly predictable. If a lacrosse championship is held at the 2028 Olympics without the Haudenosaunee Nationals, there will be fierce criticism. In the lead-up to the games, nearly every mainstream media piece will mention the game's originators and their absence. Haudenosaunee leaders and players will display outrage and cite tragic history; commentators and columnists and famous names will lambaste the IOC. The narrative framing all but builds itself. "Here we are, refugees in our Turtle Island, and they're stealing our game again?" Rex Lyons said. "I can just see the headlines."

In the broadest sense, the IOC has little hope of winning a war of public opinion. Its history of bribery scandals and sportswashing of repressive regimes makes it a perfect foil: the latest in a 536-year-old line of corrupt elites to deem the Indigenous unworthy. But it's also true that, no matter the controversy, the IOC is always saved the instant that games start and athletes begin winning and losing and crying. No matter how fun and fast, lacrosse in LA figures to be marginalized by glamour events like swimming, gymnastics and track and field. By the end, the entity most afflicted by a Haudenosaunee absence would be lacrosse itself.

My understanding of that came sideways, at a time when positions on both sides were hardening. In mid-December 2023, a week after Biden's endorsement, I was speaking with Kyle Harrison about the progress of African Americans in lacrosse; since 2020, the total of Black men playing Division I had risen from 115 to 133, the total of women from 110 to 120. I asked if they were in a better place now.

"Yes," Harrison said. "The Black player is not alone. Black players clearly have other allies that are Black and allies that are other ethnicities;

there's a unification. Do I think the overall Black experience as a lacrosse player is better? We have a lot of work to do still. The racial incidents, when you look on social, haven't stopped. When you talk about the N-word, kids getting that on the field: That stuff hasn't stopped. We've got a long way to go, and we're committed to the effort."

Then he added, "It's a really important time for our sport. We've got to get our stuff together. Because, in my mind, we're relaunching this sport to the world in 2028. This is going to be what we are to everyone else. And it should be good."

Harrison is right. Like few events, an Olympics is the ultimate coming-out party, one that not only mints new athletic stars, but enables the host city—and often host country—to reintroduce itself as a global player. In the same way, the 2028 Summer Games in Los Angeles is the greatest opportunity in a century for the continent's oldest sport to rebrand itself, to transform what we think about when we think about lacrosse.

The game is recovering still from the Duke rape fiasco and the killing of Yeardley Love. Like nothing else, those searing experiences spilled lacrosse into the zeitgeist and—despite all exceptions—vacuum-packed its popular image as a hermetic American subculture of rich and entitled, East Coast and white, boozing, careless laxbros. Since 2020, though, Olympic ambitions and racial politics have forced a makeover of the sport's image from within. "Meet the New Era of Lacrosse," declared the opening 2023 salvo in a sport-wide campaign to double US participation to four million. Six players—Australian, Haudenosaunee, American, Canadian, British and Jamaican—were displayed. Three were women. Three were of color. Three of the six keywords deployed: "Modern. Approachable. Equitable."

The message: Lacrosse is no longer the exclusive game of excitable white boys, a totem of upper-class arrival. Lacrosse is diverse, international, a sport for strivers. But if the lacrosse in Los Angeles in 2028 is played without the Haudenosaunee, any claim of openness will ring hollow. The image will revert to form. The product presented, day after day, will seem more reiteration than relaunch; the game will be dominated as ever by white people, while its locked-out creators cry foul. At best, it will be seen as just one flashy diversion among dozens. At worst, it will be decried as appropriation in excelsis, the same old story.

But since America is a place where the least likely thing can still happen, alternatives can be considered. If the Haudenosaunee men and women are included in the 2028 Olympics, nothing will better signal that lacrosse is, indeed, now equitable to all. Their presence for the entire fortnight would make the sport about something far bigger than competition. It would be a stand-in for Indigenous peoples worldwide. It would provide a symbolic acknowledgment—if not the righting—of the oldest American wrong. Native peoples will never get all their land, all the lost lives, back. Before an audience of billions, though, they would reclaim their game.

That this could only be accomplished via a partnership with the game's white establishment, completing a process begun 40 years ago, would be something to celebrate. Suddenly, the sport of red cups and Range Rovers would be a model for racial redress. When White House official Tom Perez—son of Dominican emigres, former secretary of labor—was asked why he thinks having the Haudenosaunee Nationals at these Olympics is important, lacrosse itself barely rated a mention.

"I used to participate in a program called 'Facing History and Ourselves,' in which we spend time understanding that the most important dependent clause in the Constitution is the first: 'We the People, *in order to form a more perfect union*,'" Perez said. "[It is] about facing our history—the good, the bad, the ugly. We have a number of moral Achilles' heels in our nation's admittedly imperfect journey to form a more perfect union. Our historic mistreatment of our tribal communities is certainly one of those at the top of the list.

"This is a quintessential example of a sport that provides a remarkably important teachable moment to our nation. I've already put on my list to go to the 2028 Olympics, and I only want to do two things: I want to go get my picture taken with the confederacy when they're walking [in the Opening Ceremony], and I want to go to the first lacrosse game for the men and the women. Then I want to go to the medal ceremony when they win."

Few foresee the least likely scenario happening. But because I've come to agree with Chazz Woodson's belief that lacrosse reflects America, I like to imagine that if the Haudenosaunee are locked out, the sport will refuse to play. I like to imagine the American and Canadian and other players—be they English or Japanese or Israeli or Australian or Czech—not showing up for the first game, or sitting down in protest on an Olympic field, then streaming out of the grounds to meet the Nationals in some public park. The Olympics has its own history of activism and racial breakthrough: Jesse Owens dominating Hitler's 1936 games in Berlin; Tommie Smith and John

Carlos raising fists in Mexico City in 1968; Aboriginal Australian gold medalist Cathy Freeman waving her people's flag at the 2000 games in Sydney. This would be another.

Maybe it would start with a Thanksgiving Prayer. Then a new kind of Medicine Game: Hundreds of men and women wielding hickory or plastic, bumping hips, first team to score three wins. Then the Haudenosaunee begin a chant, taken up by all: *We are still here!*

I like to imagine it. Lacrosse would become a cultural phenomenon, a light not a mirror, awash in street credibility and crossover appeal. Here, some would say, is what the Olympics should be about and too often isn't. Here is what America should be, needs to be: A truly open playing field. Where anyone can take part. Where everybody can win.

ACKNOWLEDGMENTS

Work on this book began in early 2018 and consumed the next six years. It wasn't planned, yet the timing proved impeccable. Much of this, of course, is because lacrosse's Haudenosaunee question, Olympic mission and new pro league all bubbled to a head amid the era's racial and cultural tumult. But my immersion in the sport also flanked the pandemic, which cemented a new reality in major American sports coverage. Journalists with the NBA, NFL, Major League Baseball, Olympics and pro tennis complained of ever-withering access to players and personnel, the economic demand for clickbait stories on the most famous names, a looming and seemingly unstoppable irrelevance. Few seemed happy.

Lacrosse country proved to be nothing like that. From the start, I found myself welcomed with a near-universal grace and patience, and a startling openness to critical thinking about the game's virtues and problems. With but a few exceptions, players, coaches and officials at the high school, club, collegiate, pro and international level submitted to interviews—some 370 overall—and allowed an access that media working other sports can only imagine. I was unwittingly lucky with my earliest contacts—Nationals co-founder Oren Lyons and longtime U.S.A. Lacrosse CEO Steve Stenersen—both of whom saw the project's value, submitted for years to endless queries and chats, and made extraordinary efforts to vouch for, and connect, me with key people. Though leaders of historic archrivals, the two shared much in perspective and sense of humor, and I'm grateful for their generosities.

In that same vein, Oren's son and successor Rex Lyons, University of Virginia head coach Lars Tiffany, and Albany head coach Scott Marr took great pains to field my endless—and often elementary—questions, and opened up their personal and professional histories with rare candor. I thank them for their toughness and trust.

Any outsider—or journalist, in the words of Janet Malcolm, "not too stupid or full of himself"—understands the need for a guide. Throughout, I've been guided here by the wisdom, reportage and meticulous fact-checking of Baltimore-based writer and editor Corey McLaughlin, whose elegant prose has graced *USA Lacrosse* magazine, *Baltimore* magazine and the *Baltimore Banner* for nearly two decades. The moments when Corey corrected fact and interpretation, opened a new line of thought, or improved the contents of these pages (i.e., when he saved me from myself) are countless. Lacrosse (and Baltimore) is lucky to have him.

This project was never meant to be comprehensive. As an exploration of prevailing lacrosse themes in the early 21st century, it necessarily took shape according to breaking events, shifting lines of inquiry, my own sense of story. Compared with other sports, the lacrosse bookshelf is narrow, and deep studies of, say, the men's and women's dynasties at the University of Maryland, modern Canadian lacrosse history, Gary Gait, and the rollicking box universe beg still to be written. But essential texts do exist and, for me, proved invaluable. Anyone seeking the most exhaustive—yet elegant—account of Indigenous, Canadian and American lacrosse history must first turn to Donald M. Fisher's *Lacrosse: A History of the Game*. Thomas Vennum's *American Indian Lacrosse: Little Brother of War* provides an unparalleled survey of Indigenous lacrosse origins and lore, and introduced me—indelibly—to the evolution of Alexander Pope's "Lo" into a term of white condescension. And the writings of Indigenous (Dakelh, Nak 'azdli Whut'en) historian Allan Downey, particularly his book, *The Creator's Game: Lacrosse, Identity, and Indigenous Nationhood* and 2012 article, "Engendering Nationality: Haudenosaunee Tradition, Sport and the Lines of Gender" greatly informed my understanding of the tensions informing the modern Haudenosaunee game.

For further research into George Beers's original rules, I'm indebted to Dave Stewart-Candy at the Canadian Lacrosse Hall of Fame, Natalie Ralph at Library and Archives Canada, as well as the work and aid of Canadian historians Don Morrow and Christina Burr. Archivist Joe Finn at the National Lacrosse Hall of Fame and Museum in Sparks, Maryland, couldn't have been more generous with his resources and interpretations. Thanks also to Jane Klain, for access to the archive in The Paley Center for Media in New York City, and William Miller, reference librarian at my hometown Ferguson Library in Stamford, Connecticut, for help above and beyond. The late Bill Tanton, dean of American lacrosse writers and clear-eyed exemplar of the Baltimore style, helped with contacts and research questions. Lisa Romano Moore, with the Onondaga Historical Association, provided vital information and images.

The lifeblood of this kind of work flows through interviews. Those who did much to expand my understanding of the Haudenosaunee include Freeman Bucktooth, Brett Bucktooth, Tadadaho Sidney Hill, Betty Lyons, Carol Patterson, historians Michael Oberg and Laurence M. Hauptman, Mark Burnam, Curt Styres, Ansley Jemison, G. Peter Jemison, Brendan Bomberry, Ji and Dee Thompson, Randy Staats, Leo Nolan, Sid Jamieson, Jeremy Thompson, Lyle Thompson, Hiana Thompson, Jake Piseno, Claudia Jimerson, Tia Schindler, Gayle Kelley, Quint Kessenich, Darcy Powless, and Joe Solomon. Any error of misinterpretation or fact, of course, is mine alone.

In their willingness to grapple with often sensitive narratives, I am forever grateful to Selena Lasota, Aryien Stevens and Cassandra "Bean" Minerd, George Barrow, Devon and Chuck Sherwood, Chazz Woodson, Dom Starsia, Miles and Kyle Harrison, Donnie Brown, Fred Opie, Nabil Akl, the entire Hampton University men's lacrosse team, Daniela Eppler, Ernie Melero, Andres Axkana Patraca, Joe Anderson, Timothy Gonzales, Jules Heningburg, Scott Neiss, Kyle Hartzell, Joe Cowan, Shamel Bratton, Willie Scroggs, Faith Corwin, Zed Williams, Max Seibald, Ryan Conrad, Josh Offit, Jovan Miller, Chad Toliver, Mark Ellis, Tina Sloan Green, John Danowski, Rob Pannell, Paul Rabil, Tom Perez, Howdy Myers's granddaughter Kit Donnelly, Dan Kraft, Justin Guterding, Matt Holman, DeMaurice Smith, Casey Carroll and Stan Cockerton.

Though perhaps less evident, others whose wisdom and knowledge greatly inform this work include: Roy Simmons Jr., Roy Simmons III, Gary Gait, Canada's Geoff Snider, David Gross, USC women's head coach Lindsey Munday, Frank Kelly III, Yochanan Katz, Doug Gansler, Bill Lewis, Brian Holman, Trevor Baptiste, Paul Katsiaunis, A.B. "Buzzy" Krongard, Ireland Lacrosse's Michael Kennedy, Margot Putukian, Steele Stanwick, David Lasday, Brian Reilly, Heather Higginbottom, George Baldassare, Jacqueline and Bria Cook, Jacob Silberlicht, Monique Brown, Alex Smith, Kyle Sweeney, Adam Ghitelman, Aris Brown, Elijah Hayes-Miller, Steele Downing, Joe Tsai and Lindsey McKone.

Three vital interview subjects died before publication: Former Rutgers head coach Tom Hayes, Onondaga stickmaker Alfie Jacques and Onondaga Chief Vincent Johnson. All were outsized figures with an infectious spiritual connection to their respective fields—be it the "magic" of lacrosse, the craft of the wooden lacrosse stick or Haudenosaunee kinship with the buffalo. The story told here would not be possible without their cooperation, but, book aside, I was just one of thousands enriched by their soulful, joy-filled understanding of the truly important.

At World Lacrosse, first thanks must go to England lacrosse pioneer Ron Balls, a key figure in the admission of the Haudenosaunee in 1987, who generously excavated and shared his memories and documentation of that historic process. The patient cooperation of Christy Cahill and Jim Scherr cannot be overstated. At USA Lacrosse, Brian Logue and the great Ann Kitt-Carpenetti instantly laid a foundation of professionalism and humanity that never betrayed a crack. Joe Favorito, with the National Lacrosse League, was—as always—a rock of professionalism.

The great and good Don Van Natta Jr., investigative pillar at ESPN and champion of longform writing at his weekly, *The Sunday Long Read*, somehow managed to fit in a vital and penetrating first read, and improved all he surveyed with his sharp ear, eye and blade. I am grateful for his steady hand, and friendship.

At Grove/Atlantic, executive editor George Gibson, whose sensibility, pencil and work ethic seem to be transported from some earlier, more elegant age, saw the possibilities here first, and never wavered. My thanks to him, Grove editorial aces Emily Burns, managing editor Mike Richards, John Mark Boling and founder Morgan Entrekin, are eternal. Literary agent Andrew Blauner, stunningly, has been working my corner for two decades now. They don't come any better.

Fiction has its clichéd writer in a garrett, wrestling alone with a vision. But along with the kindness of strangers, nonfiction depends on the support of friends and colleagues, those who provide fuel with a word, a question or, simply, enthusiasm for your strange, amorphous, glacially moving beast. For their selfless help, knowing or not, over the last seven years, I thank Bruce Schoenfeld, Marilyn Price, Sue Price, Chuck Lane, Jessica Blau, John Drescher, the great Farrell Evans, Drew Lawrence, Joel Drucker, Budd Mishkin, Thomas Oberdorfer, Seth Wickersham, Dave and Katherine Martin, and Laura and Chris Scalzo. At *Sports Illustrated*, Terry McDonell greenlit my early forays into lacrosse, and Steve Cannella kept the flame alive. Dean Robinson's stubborn curiosity proved invaluable. Molly McCloskey's last-minute suggestion ended up gold.

Once again, of course, no one provided more unwavering support or endurance than Jack Price, Adelaide Price, Walker Price and, most of all, Fran Brennan. Families take the hardest hit during any book marathon, and seven years is a long road. Thank you for racing alongside, and propping me up, the entire way.

NOTES

Preamble

ix **Once confined to**: Fisher, Donald M. *Lacrosse: A History of the Game* (Baltimore: Johns Hopkins University Press, 2002), 156; "Growing Fast Elsewhere, Lacrosse Is Still the Island's Game," Beller, Peter C., *New York Times*, June 5, 2005, Section LI, 14.

ix **"We're in the process"**: Tierney, Bill, author interview, December 11, 2018.

ix **a thousand years**: "The Native American Origins of Lacrosse," Kennedy, Lesley, *History.com*, April 23, 2024.

x **For more than a century**: Fisher, 71.

x **Plans for a new type of professional league**: "Paul Rabil's Premier Lacrosse League Launches," DaSilva, Matt, *US Lacrosse Magazine*, October 22, 2018.

x **mission to become part of the Olympic Games**: "With Olympics Ongoing, Federation of International Lacrosse Continues Push for Lacrosse Inclusion," McLaughlin, Corey, *LaxMagazine.com*, August 18, 2016.

x **Everything—from field dimensions to length of games**: "Olympic Lacrosse Rules Take Shape," Wilson, Connor, *Lacrosse All Stars*, March 20, 2019, https://laxallstars.com/olympic-lacrosse-rules-take-shape/.

x **expanding opportunity for women**: "Women's Lacrosse Sets the Pace for Continued Growth," Leytham, Tammy, *SportsEvents Media Group*, May 15, 2023.

x **talent pool skews predominantly white**: "NCAA Demographics Database," https://www.ncaa.org/sports/2018/12/13/ncaa-demographics-database.aspx.

x **a religious practice fashioned by Indigenous Americans**: Downey, Allan. *The Creator's Game: Lacrosse, Identity, and Indigenous Nationhood* (Vancouver, BC: UBC Press, 2018), 42, 81–83, 154–155.

x **"You have the great athletes"**: Tierney, author interview.

xi **the game's originators**: Downey, 20; Fisher, 61–62.

xi **a wood stick is a sacred gift**: Downey, 190–195.

xi **overtaken by mass-produced versions**: Downey, 166.

xi **"The lacrosse stick"**: Tierney, author interview.

xi **In 1969**: Brown, Donnie, author interview, July 13, 2019.

xi **"They said"**: Ibid.

xi **In 1979**: Marr, Scott, author interview, February 24, 2021.

xi **early modern**: "First Generation STX Lacrosse Sticks—The 1970's," http://www.oldschoollaxfreak.com/STX-Lacrosse---The-1970-s.html.

xii **"I still have that feeling today"**: Marr, author interview, November 29, 2018.

xii **In May the Tar Heels upset mighty Johns Hopkins**: "UNC Grabs Lacrosse Title," Greenberger, Neil H., *Charlotte Observer*, May 31, 1981, D1.

xii **met Hopkins in the 1982 NCAA final and won again**: "Defense Is Tar Heels' Ticket Again," *Charlotte News*, May 31, 1982, 16C.

xiii **UNC football was ranked in the nation's top five**: "September 19, 1983 AP Football Poll," http://collegepollarchive.com/football/ap/seasons.cfm?appollid=560.

xiii **Legendary basketball coach Dean Smith**: "Dean Smith Free at Last," *Asheville Times*, March 30, 1982, 14.

xiii **A freshman named Michael Jordan**: "Jordan Saw Vision Of Win," *Asheville Times*, March 30, 1982, 14.

xiii **There was no UNC women's team then**: "Carolina: 2020 Women's Lacrosse," http://goheels.com/documents/2020/2/21/2020WLAXMediaGuide.pdf, 17.

xiii **The men's roster was all white**: "2009 UNC Men's Lacrosse Media Guide," 38.

xiii **hailed as the best lacrosse player ever**: "Lacrosse Coaches Still Talk About Football Star," *Charlotte Observer*, April 28, 1984, 3E.

xiii **Brown's late-1950s run at Syracuse University**: Ibid.

xiii **for another 24 years**: "The Most Influential Figures in Black Lacrosse History," Simpkins, Brian, *USA Lacrosse Magazine*, February 4, 2021.

xiii **no avoiding lacrosse's private school network**: "Murder At UVA: George Huguely, Yeardley Love, And Lacrosse's Worst Case Scenario," Sharp, Andrew, *SBNation*, May 6, 2010; "Public vs. Private," Brennan, Fran, *Washington Post*, May 22, 2006.

xiii **the epithet "laxbro"**: "What's a Lax Bro? Don't Ask a Lax Bro," Randall, Eric, *The Atlantic*, June 5, 2012.

xiv **the most celebrated Black player since Jim Brown**: "Diversifying Lacrosse Still Work in Progress," Ricardi, Alisha, *ESPN.com*, February 27, 2011.

xiv **lacrosse's equivalent of the Heisman Trophy**: "Tewaaraton Award: History of the College Lacrosse Honor," Harris, Janie, *NCAA.com*, February 26, 2024.

xiv **mushroomed by 79 percent**: Beller.

xiv **From 2001 to 2005**: 2017 US Lacrosse Participation Survey, https://cdn3.sportngin.com/attachments/document/114e-1909590/Lacrosse_Participation_2017_Survey.pdf.

xiv **in 2005 the Northwestern women**: "Northwestern Wins Women's Crown," *Northwest Herald* (IL), May 23, 2005, C2.

xiv **On March 14, 2006**: "DNA Tests Ordered for Duke Athletes," Khanna, Samiha, Blythe, Anne, *News & Observer* (NC), March 24, 2006, 1.

xiv **"a bunch of hooligans"**: "Duke Puts Lacrosse Games on Hold," Blythe, Anne, Stancill, Jane, *News & Observer* (NC), March 29, 2006, 13.

xiv **Nine of the 47 players**: "2006 Men's Lacrosse Roster," http://goduke.com/sports/mens-lacrosse/roster/2006.

xiv **"I sympathize for the team"**: "Duke Scandal Hits Home, Nine Blue Devil Players Are From the D.C. Area," Dillon, Liam, *Washington Post*, April 1, 2006.

xv **Duke lacrosse players had incurred**: "The Damage Done," Price, S.L., Evans, Farrell, *Sports Illustrated*, June 26, 2006, 83.

xv **The accused would be declared innocent and the accuser a liar**: On November 13, 2024, Crystal Mangum stated in an online interview, "I testified falsely against them by saying that they raped me when they didn't, and that was wrong." https://www.letstalkwithkat.com, released December 11, 2024; "Accuser in Duke Lacrosse Rape Case Admits That She Lied," Edwards, Jonathan, *Washington Post*, December 15, 2024, A11.

xv **Sources in the players' camp**: Price and Evans, 76.

xv **Others confirmed that another white player**: Ibid.

xv **The victim of assault by one of the accused**: "Wolves in Blazers and Khakis," Fisher, Marc, *Washington Post*, July 13, 2006, B1.

xv **Ryan McFadyen's post-party email**: Price and Evans, 82.

xv **"kerosene"**: Ibid.

xv **The Blue Devils lacrosse season was canceled**: Ibid.
xv **the team's one Black member**: Price and Evans, 80.
xv **"But as soon as I got to Duke"**: Price and Evans, 82.
xv **Many Duke players were private school products**: "2006 Men's Lacrosse Roster," http://goduke.com/sports/mens-lacrosse/roster/2006.
xv **Long Island's oft-overlooked blue-collar pipeline**: Ibid.
xvi **Brian Loftus, the father**: Price and Evans, 77.
xvi **"Wanted"-style flyer**: Price and Evans, 76.
xvi **He hadn't even attended the party**: Ibid.
xvi **"Without a scholarship"**: Price and Evans, 77.
xvi **saved as many as 18 lives**: "Parents grieve 9/11 hero son 'Man in the Red Bandanna' Welles Crowther," Scarborough, Chuck, *NBC 4 New York*, September 11, 2023.
xvi **Cornell's poetic All-American Eamon McEneaney**: "Remembering Eamon McEneaney: Cornell's Wild Irish Rose," *Lacrosse Magazine*, September 2011.
xvi **Dozens of other lacrosse players, coaches and relations died**: "Lacrosse Remembers: In Honor of Those in Our Community Who Perished on 9/11," http://www.usalacrosse.com/news-media-blog/lacrosse-remembers-honor-those-our-community-who-perished-911.
xvi **"Every lacrosse coach came into my house"**: Price and Evans, 77.
xvii **wired into Wall Street**: "Wall Street Remains Occupied by Lacrosse Bros," Trotter, J.K., *The Atlantic*, May 23, 2013.
xvii **annual pay rarely topping $60,000**: "Paul Rabil of the Philadelphia Wings Becomes Lacrosse's First Million Dollar Man," Flannery, Jim, *Bleacher Report*, April 2, 2013.
xvii *World Lacrosse Championships have been held every four years since 1974*: "Spin Right and Shoot Left," McPhee, John, *New Yorker*, March 23, 2009.
xvii **Since the 1970s**: "Oren Lyons, Onondaga Nation," National Native American Hall of Fame, http://nativehalloffame.org/oren-lyons/.
xviii **His public identities neatly merged in 1983**: "Native Bidaské (Spotlight) with Oren and Rex Lyons," *Native News Online*, May 1, 2022.
xviii **Perhaps as early as 1,100 A.D.**: Kennedy.
xviii **codified the rules by Victorian standards**: Beers, W. G. *Lacrosse: The National Game of Canada* (New York: W.A. Townsend & Adams, 1869).
xviii **in 1880**: "The Creator's Game," Schilling, Vincent, *American Indian*, Spring 2021, http://www.americanindianmagazine.org/story/the-creators-game; Downey, 69–74.
xviii **"We are *allies*"**: Lyons, Oren, author interview, January 17, 2010.
xviii **On May 3, 2010**: "2nd-Degree Murder," Koon, Samantha, *Daily Progress* (VA), A1.
xviii **"culture"**: "When Peer Pressure, Not a Conscience, Is Your Guide," Roberts, Selena, *New York Times*, March 31, 2006, D1.
xix **Most of his adult life**: Jacques, Alfie, author interview, June 14, 2010.
xix **It started with a walk in the woods**: Ibid.
xix **James Naismith couldn't make lacrosse work indoors**: "The Olden Rules," Wolff, Alexander, *Sports Illustrated*, November 25, 2002.
xix **precursor of nearly every game on a rectangular patch**: Wood, J.G. *The Modern Playmate* (London: Frederick Warne and Co., 1870), 74–91.
xx **"You make the stick from the *living* part of the tree"**: Jacques, 2010.
xx **United Kingdom refused to recognize Iroquois travel documents**: "Iroquois Team Still Hopes to Make Trip to Britain," *Press & Sun-Bulletin* (NY), July 16, 2010, 4B.
xx **sensational details of George Huguely's behavior**: "Former Lovers Detail Volatile Relationship," Koon, Samantha, *Daily Progress* (VA), February 10, 2012, A1.

xx **the Iroquois' first-ever field win**: "Iroquois Beat Team USA for First Time Ever," McLaughlin, Corey, *LaxMagazine.com*, July 17, 2012.

xx **a bronze-medal finish for the first time**: "Iroquois Dominate Australia to Reach Podium," Burns, Sean, *LaxMagazine.com*, July 19, 2014.

xx **admission of the Iroquois**: "A History of Iroquois National Lacrosse," Camara, Lena, http://iroquoisnationals.com/the-iroquois/a-history-of-iroquois-nationals-lacrosse/.

xxi **the 2014 death of Michael Brown**: "Officer Kills Ferguson Teen," Thorsen, Leah, Giegerich, Steve, *St. Louis Post-Dispatch*, August 10, 2014.

xxi **the first Division I program**: "It's Real," McLaughlin, Corey, *Lacrosse Magazine*, November 2015, 42–45.

xxi **"convicts"**: "Social Media Posts, Reactions Raise Social Concerns Among Lacrosse Players, Coaches," Foy, Terry, Kinnear, Matt, *InsideLacrosse.com*, December 31, 2017.

xxi **hastily deleted post**: "Virginia Tech Women's Team Video Provides Latest Example of Lacrosse's Diversity Problem," Grossman, Evan, *New York Daily News*, March 27, 2018.

xxi **"only ones" . . . "serious discussion" . . . "inclusion, diversity and what is acceptable behavior"**: Ibid.

xxi **"LaxCon 2018,"**: "4 Cool New Things at LaxCon, Team USA Box Notes + PHOTO BLAST!," Conwell, Ryan, *Lacrosse All Stars*, January 23, 2018, https://laxallstars.com/4-cool-new-things-laxcon-team-usa-box-notes-photo-blast/.

xxi **"We still have the image"**: Stenersen, Steve, author interview, January 19, 2018.

xxii **in a conference room**: Stenersen, Steve, e-mail to author, March 22, 2021.

xxii **"at least 20+" . . . "racial altercations"**: "Dear Lacrosse . . .," Miller, Jovan, JoviNation23, http://jovination23.wordpress.com/2018/02/01/dear-lacrosse/, February 1, 2018.

xxii **"Everybody keeps asking"**: Miller, Jovan, author interview, September 29, 2020.

xxii **"Nobody"**: Harrison, Kyle, author interview, August 8, 2019.

xxii **The convention**: "Speaker Schedules | US Lacrosse," January 3, 2018, http://www.uslacrosse.org/events/convention-and-fan-fest/speaker-schedules.

xxii **"The most diverse"**: Kemp, Troy, author interview, January 20, 2018.

xxii **Confederate statues were coming down**: "Felonies to Be Dropped in Case of Confederate Statue Toppling," Drew, Johnathan, *The Associated Press*, January 12, 2018.

xxii **"Unite the Right"**: "Students Demand Uva Prioritize Safety," Bragg, Michael, *Charlottesville Daily Progress* (VA), August 20, 2017.

xxiii **The opioid epidemic**: *Drug Overdose Deaths: Facts and Figures*, National Institute on Drug Abuse, http://www.drugabuse.gov/drugs-abuse/opioids/opioid-overdose-crisis, April 1, 2020.

xxiii **Census projections**: "It's Official: The U.S. Is Becoming a Minority-Majority Nation," Wazwaz, Noor, *U.S. News & World Report*, July 6, 2015.

xxiii **Two months later**: Grossman.

xxiii **"Lacrosse is America"**: Woodson, Chazz, author interview, September 29, 2020.

xxiii **"white privileged game"**: Ibid.

xxiv **for the first time since 1948**: *The Official Report of the Organizing Committee for the XIV Olympiad* (London, 1948), 532–533.

xxiv **in October of 2023**: "L.A. Names Coveted Five Provisional Sports It Wants to Add for 2028 Olympics," Wharton, David, *Los Angeles Times*, October 9, 2023.

xxiv **IOC rules—and fear**: "Lacrosse at the Olympics Gives Indigenous Communities a Chance to See Their Sport Shine," Pells, Eddie, *Associated Press*, October 19, 2023.

xxiv **And though all the game's powers**: "Pro Lacrosse Season Begins as Sport's Leaders Eye Olympics," Kekis, John, *Associated Press*, June 4, 2022.

xxiv **President Joe Biden**: "President Joe Biden and the White House support Indigenous lacrosse team for the 2028 Olympics," Pells, *Associated Press*, December 6, 2023.

xxiv **It was the largest and last tournament of its kind**: "World Lacrosse Championship Comes to a Thrilling and Controversial End," Rosen, Armin, *Tablet Magazine*, July 23, 2018.

Part 1
I. The Battle of Toronto Airport

5 **A seaside city founded in 1927**: "Straus Square: Rededication Ceremony, June 18th, 1998," *Straus Family Newsletter*, August 1998; "Thank God Natan Missed the Boat," *Rationalist Judaism*, October 1, 2013; "The Story of the City of Netanya," http://www.torah-box.net/news/news/the-story-of-the-city-of-netanya_1445.html, May 3, 2020.

5 **one of the largest international sporting events in its history**: 2018 FIL World Lacrosse Championship program, Kaplan, Arik, letter, 10.

6 **Holiday Inn Express**: Jemison, Ansley, author interview, November 11, 2020; "Bronze at World's, Gold in Travel," Mohawk, Shaniece, *Smolax.com*, September 4, 2018.

6 **Six Nations**: "The 6 Nations of the Iroquois Confederacy," Wallenfeldt, Jeff, *Britannica.com*; Lyons, Oren, author interview, January 17, 2010.

6 **"snakes"**: "Haudenosaunee—'People Who Build a House,'" Hudson River Valley Institute, https://www.hudsonrivervalley.org/Haudenosaunee.

6 **Haudenosaunee**: "Haudenosaunee: People of the Longhouse," Roberson Museum, Binghamton, N.Y., http://roberson.org/project/haudenosaunee-people-of-the-longhouse/.

6 **15 months**: Cockerton, Stan, Federation of International Lacrosse president, letter to Neiss, Scott, April 14, 2017.

6 **in 2010 and 2015**: "Media Release: Iroquois Nationals Have Not Withdrawn from Championships," Onondaga Nation website, July 17, 2010, http://www.onondaganation.org/news/2010/media-release-iroquois-nationals-have-not-withdrawn-from-championships/; "Iroquois U19 Women Withdraw From WLC," Wilson, Connor, *Lacrosse All Stars*, July 10, 2015, https://laxallstars.com/iroquois-u19-women-withdraw-from-wlc/.

6 **a Nationals women's team**: "Women's Field History," World Lacrosse, https://worldlacrosse.sport/events/womens-field-history/.

6 **The three-dozen-strong**: "Iroquois Nationals Name 2018 FIL World Men's Championship Team," *NDNSports*, July 10, 2018, https://www.ndnsports.com/iroquois-nationals-name-2018-fil-world-mens-championship-team/.

6 **Canadian and Israeli ministers**: "The Iroquois Nationals Lacrosse Team's Incredible Journey to Israel," Chernick, Ilanit, *Jerusalem Post*, July 12, 2018.

6 **sport's decade-old governing body**: "Men's and Women's International Lacrosse Groups Merge," Weaver, John, *Baltimore Sun*, September 4, 2008.

7 **long-ago All-Americans**: "Paul Carcaterra: Lacrosse Analyst and Reporter/College Football Reporter," ESPN Press Room website, https://espnpressroom.com/us/bios/carcaterra_paul/; "Quint Kessenich: Lacrosse Analyst/College Sports Reporter," ESPN Press Room website, https://espnpressroom.com/us/bios/kessenich_quint/.

7 **"Some of the ownership . . ."**: Carcaterra, Paul, author interview, July 11, 2018.

7 **"Months ago!"**: Kessenich, Quint, author interview, July 11, 2018.

7 **The FIL had officially decided**: "Vision Statement," 2018 FIL World Lacrosse Championship program, 14.

7   **in May 2017**: "Jim Scherr Named First Federation of International Lacrosse CEO," World Lacrosse website, May 24, 2017, http://worldlacrosse.sport/article/jim-scherr -named-first-federation-of-international-lacrosse-ceo/.

7   **soon rebrand itself**: "Lacrosse Launches New Name and Logo at Sport Accord Summit as It Continues Olympic push," Mackay, Duncan, *Inside the Games*, May 5, 2019.

7   **the IOC follows**: "Gaming the State System," Kron, Josh, *Foreign Policy*, August 22, 2021.

8   **"After '10"**: Scherr, Jim, author interview, July 14, 2018.

8   **"I mean, I was having"**: Balls, Ron, author interview, July 13, 2018.

8   **The Iroquois are a confederation of six**: Wallenfeldt.

8   **6.8 million Indigenous people**: "Facts for Features: American Indian and Alaska Native Heritage Month: November 2018," United States Census Bureau, census.gov, October 25, 2018.

8   **anywhere from 30,000 to 45,000**: "The American Indian and Alaska Native Population: 2010," Norris, Tina, Vines, Paula L., Hoeffel, Elizabeth M., 2010 Census Briefs, January 2012, Table 7, 17.

8   **Until about 1700**: Hämäläinen, Pekka. *Indigenous Continent: The Epic Contest for North America* (New York: Liveright, 2022), 205–208.

8   **"Foremost in war"**: Parkman, Francis. *The Conspiracy of Pontiac and the Indian War after the Conquest of Canada*, Vol. I (Boston: Little, Brown, 1895), 7.

9   **Though they once controlled**: Hämäläinen, 165–166, 181, 183–186.

9   **The original confederacy**: Barr, Daniel P. *Unconquered: The Iroquois League at War in Colonial America* (Westport, CT: Praeger, 2006), 78, 85.

9   **predated the United Nations by at least 375 years** . . . : Graymont, Barbara. *The Iroquois in the American Revolution* (Syracuse, NY: Syracuse University Press, 1972), 14–15.

9   **"democratic principles"**: United States. Select Committee on Indian Affairs. H. R. Res. 331 (1988).

9   **"acquire fresh strength and power,"**: "How the Iroquois Great Law of Peace Shaped U.S. Democracy," Hansen, Terri, PBS website, December 13, 2018, http:// www.pbs.org/native-america/blog/how-the-iroquois-great-law-of-peace-shaped-us -democracy.

9   **"It would be a very strange thing"**: "Native Americans Are the Foundation of America," Milloy, Courtland, *Washington Post*, November 23, 2021.

9   **George Washington's starving troops**: "Oneida: Our Ways, Historic Timeline, American Revolution," Oneida Nation website, http://oneida-nsn.gov/our-ways/our -story/historic-timeline/american-revolution/.

10 **"If the Oneidas"** . . . : Lyons, Oren, author interview, November 28, 2018.

10 **Steelwork on high**: "A Mohawk Trail To the Skyline; Indian Ironworkers Return, Lured by Building Boom," Leduff, Charlie, *New York Times*, March 16, 2001.

10 **"Native Americans are"**: *Broken Promises: Continuing Federal Funding Shortfall for Native Americans* (Washington, D.C.: U.S. Commission on Civil Rights, 2018), 1.

10 **dialed a number**: Balls, author interview; Lyons, author interview, January 17, 2010.

10 **the first Indigenous people**: Camara, Lena, "A History of Iroquois National Lacrosse," http://iroquoisnationals.com/the-iroquois/a-history-of-iroquois-nationals-lacrosse/.

11 **"the English"**: Lyons, author interview, January 17, 2010.

11 **"Just cannot trust them"**: Lyons, author interview, November 28, 2018.

11 **"In one sense"**: Balls, author interview.

11　**"the Membership"**: Ibid.
12　**On July 4, 2018**: "Open Letter: Palestinians Urge Iroquois Nationals to Withdraw from Lacrosse Championships in Israel," BDSmovement.net, July 4, 2018.
12　**"As Indigenous peoples"**: Ibid.
12　**"We said that our overall issues"**: Lyons, author interview, November 28, 2018.
12　**Another Iroquois no-show**: "Iroquois Nationals Reject Palestinian Request to Boycott World Lacrosse Championship in Israel," Faris, Nick, *National Post*, July 11, 2018; Balls, author interview.
13　**"We would've been done"**: Lyons, author interview.
13　**This vibe**: Mark Burnam, author interview, July 12, 2018.
13　**declared its opposition**: Jemison, Ansley, author interview; Waterman, Denise, author interview, July 15, 2018; Burnam, Mark, author interview.
13　**the Grand Council had not once**: Ibid.
14　**On May 14**: "Israel Kills Dozens at Gaza Border as U.S. Embassy Opens in Jerusalem," Halbfinger, David M., Kershner, Isabel, Walsh, Declan, *New York Times*, May 14, 2018.
14　**On June 6**: "Argentina Cancels Soccer Game against Israel amid BDS Campaign," *Associated Press*, June 6, 2018.
14　**On June 13**: "UN General Assembly Urges Greater Protection for Palestinians, Deplores Israel's 'Excessive' Use of Force," United Nations, June 13, 2018, https://news.un.org/en/story/2018/06/1012162.
14　**when Jemison showed up**: Jemison, author interview.
14　**the Haudenosaunee Grand Council there**: "Government," Haudenosaunee Confederacy website, https://www.haudenosauneeconfederacy.com/government/.
14　**Each nation is divided**: "Clan System," Haudenosaunee Confederacy website, https://www.haudenosauneeconfederacy.com/clan-system/.
14　**Clan mothers nominate**: "Haudenosaunee Guide for Educators," National Museum of the American Indian: Education Office, 2009, 3.
14　**the Great Law of Peace**: Ibid, 2; "Oren Lyons: An Extraordinary Life," Burns, M.C., *Central New York Magazine*, January–February 2011, 49.
14　**operates by consensus**: "Guide for Educators," 3.
14　**And on that day**: Lyons, Oren, author interview, November 28, 2018; Burnam, author interview, July 12, 2018.
14　**Jemison and others**: Jemison, author interview.
14　**had been part of the Under-19 team**: McLaughlin, June 17, 2012.
15　**At the 2014 World Championships**: "Iroquois Dominate Australia to Reach Podium," Burns, Sean, *LaxMagazine.com*, July 19, 2014.
15　**pressed the Iroquois to keep quiet**: Neiss, Scott, author interview, November 3, 2020.
15　**"I was getting a bit of a gag order"**: Jemison, author interview.
15　**in 2002, a Hamas suicide bomber**: "Ten Years after Passover Blast, Survivors Return to Park Hotel," Friedman, Matti, *Times of Israel*, March 27, 2012.
15　**Deloris "Dee" Thompson, mother,**: Thompson, Deloris, author interview, November 30, 2018.
15　**The Nationals 13-member board**: "Iroquois Nationals: Board of Directors," https://iroquoisnationals.com/board-of-directors/.
15　**issued a new, neither-nor resolution**: Jemison interview; Waterman, author interview.
15　**four pulled out**: Ibid.
15　**to fill their roster slots**: Ibid.
16　**"Go," Jemison said**: Burnam, author interview, July 12, 2018.

16 **Israeli immigration**: Neiss, author interview.
16 **"We will have the ability"**: Neiss, email, April 19, 2017.
16 **Neiss's interest**: Neiss, author interview.
16 **"If they don't come"**: Kraft, Dan, author interview, November 5, 2020.
17 **In 2015**: Neiss, author interview.
17 **"They don't like"**: Ibid.
17 **"relevant ministries/agencies"**: Lasday, David, email received from Anthony Hinton, Deputy Head of Mission, Embassy of Canada in Israel, April 9, 2018.
17 **one-time waiver**: "Iroquois Lacrosse Team Cleared to Travel by America—Then Blocked by Britain," MacAskill, Ewen, *Guardian*, July 14, 2010.
17 **hosted a ceremony**: "Remarks to Commemorate the Canandaigua Treaty," Higginbottom, Heather, Deputy Secretary of State for Management and Resources, Washington, D.C., February 22, 2016.
17 **protected 1.35 million acres**: "About the Monument," Bears Ears Inter-Tribal Coalition website, http://www.bearsearscoalition.org/about-the-monument/.
18 **Trump reversed Obama's efforts**: "Trump Signs Orders Advancing Keystone, Dakota Pipelines," Holland, Steve, *Scientific American*, January 24, 2017.
18 **"Pocahontas"**: "Trump Calls Warren 'Pocahontas' at Event Honoring Native Americans," Vitali, Ali, *NBC News*, November 27, 2017.
18 **slashed the Bears Ears footprint**: "President Trump Significantly Reduces Size of Two National Monuments," Winston & Strawn LLP, Winston's Environmental Law Update blog, December 7, 2017.
18 **4,000-page report**: *Honouring the Truth, Reconciling for the Future*, Truth and Reconciliation Commission of Canada, 2015.
18 **"forgiveness of the Aboriginal peoples"**: Trudeau, Justin, *Statement by Prime Minister on Release of the Final Report of the Truth and Reconciliation Commission*, Ottawa, Ontario, December 15, 2015.
18 **applied for the Nationals**: Neiss, author interview.
18 **dug into his Rolodex**: Kraft, Dan, author interview.
19 **including $6 million**: "Patriots Owner Kraft to Donate $6 Million for Israel's First American Football Stadium," *Algemeiner*, February 9, 2017.
19 **As backup**: Neiss, author interview.
19 **El Al officials**: Ibid.
19 **Though renowned**: "Joseph Tsai," *Forbes* Profile, http://www.forbes.com/profile/joseph-tsai/.
19 **one of his great triumphs**: "Joe Tsai #19 Yale Bulldogs," posted August 31, 2016, by Craig Lunde, YouTube, 3:02, http://www.youtube.com/watch?v=FeTGte0VECw.
19 **as benefactor of**: "Tsai Lacrosse Field House Opens for 2021–22 Athletic Season," YaleBulldogs.com, November 2, 2021; "Joe Tsai Buying National Lacrosse League Expansion Team in Las Vegas," Soshnick, Scott, Novy-Williams, Eben, *Sportico*, May 26, 2021; Tsai, Joe, author interview, March 25, 2020.
19 **Even before the Nationals**: Tsai, email to author, March 26, 2020.
19 **goes into "withdrawal"**: Tsai, interview.
19 **one-page email to Trudeau**: Tsai, email to author.
20 **also forwarded Trudeau an email**: Kraft, author interview.
20 **"We could practice"**: Tiffany, Lars, author interview, November 10, 2019.

20 **Team USA's roster**: "U.S. Men's National Team 2018 Roster Announced," *Inside Lacrosse*, January 7, 2018, https://www.insidelacrosse.com/article/u-s-men-s-national -team-2018-roster-announced/51055.

20 **set just the week before**: "Iroquois Nationals Name 2018 FIL World Men's Championship Team," NDNSports, July 10, 2018.

20 **"One practice"**: Tiffany, author interview.

21 **he offered the team's president**: Jemison, author interview.

21 **renowned human rights lawyer**: "Irwin Cotler—A Champion of Justice," The Irwin Cotler Institute—Democracy/Human Rights/Justice, Tel Aviv University, https://cotler .tau.ac.il/irwin-cotler-bio/; "The Cotler Family's Fight against the 'Vicious Circle' of Antisemitism," Kay, Barbara, *National Post*, September 24, 2023.

21 **"fantasy" document**: "Passport Impasse Keeps Haudenosaunee Home," *LaxMagazine .com*, July 24, 2015.

21 **But when the two spoke by phone**: Neiss, author interview.

21 **was sure the team**: Thompson, Lyle, author interview, July 12, 2018.

22 **"What's going on in Israel"**: Faris.

22 **fabric-swabbed**: Mohawk.

22 **US and Canadian passports**: Neiss, author interview.

22 **Kraft blew up**: Ibid.

22 **For five more hours**: Ibid; Thompson, Neiss, author interviews.

22 **found in his bag**: Neiss, author interview; Jemison, author interview.

23 **"We made it"**: Iroquois Nationals 2018, (@iroqnats2018), Twitter (now X) July 12, 2018, http://twitter.com/iroqnats2018/status/1017354274987266050?ref_src =twsrc%5Etfw

23 **"Lo, the Poor Indian!"**: "An Essay on Man: Epistle 1," line 99, Pope, Alexander, (London, 1733–34), http://rpo.library.utoronto.ca/content/essay-man-epistle-i.

23 **a New York sportswriter**: Vennum, Thomas. *American Indian Lacrosse: Little Brother of War* (Baltimore: Johns Hopkins University Press, 2008), 278.

23 *Humanitarians may weep*: "Custer! More about the Black Hills—And the Indians," *Bismarck Tribune* (ND), June 17, 1874, 1.

24 **"Whoooooooooo!"**: ESPN2 television broadcast, July 12, 2018.

24 **nine of the 12**: "Men's Field History," World Lacrosse, http://worldlacrosse.sport/events /2023-world-lacrosse-mens-championship/history/.

24 **172–63**: "Haudenosaunee men's national lacrosse team," Wikipedia, http://en.wikipedia .org/wiki/Haudenosaunee_men%27s_national_lacrosse_team.

24 **This US squad**: "U.S. Men's National Team 2018 Roster Announced," *InsideLacrosse .com*, January 7, 2018; Flannery.

24 **hired Duke head coach John Danowski**: "College Roundup," *Baltimore Sun*, November 24, 2015.

24 **"One day to go over"**: Thompson, author interview.

25 **many anointing *him* the game's best**: "The Many Talents (And Surprising Modesty) of Tom Schreiber," McLaughlin, Corey, *US Lacrosse Magazine*, January 16, 2018.

25 **"Doesn't need to"**: ESPN2 broadcast, July 12, 2018.

25 **Netanya Stadium**: "Netanya Stadium," Soccerway, http://us.soccerway.com/venues /israel/winner-stadium/v16717/.

25 **only since 2011**: "Israel Takes Center Stage as Host of Biggest International Lacrosse Event in History," Drucker, David, *Jerusalem Post*, July 12, 2018, 8.

25   **"From a programming"**: Shroff, Anish, author interview, July 11, 2018.

26   **co-Tewaaraton winners in 2014**: "Native American Brothers Share Tewaaraton," *Daily Progress* (VA), 8.

26   **five inches and 35 pounds**: "The Real World Can Wait: Ehrhardt Has Sights on Another Gold Medal," DaSilva, Matt, *USA Lacrosse Magazine*, November 3, 2022; "Lyle Thompson," Georgia Swarm roster, 2018.

27   **"They went out there"**: Gonzales, Timothy, author interview, January 27, 2021.

27   **"Listen: Our talent pool"**: Marr, Scott, author interview, July 20, 2018.

27   **from 2011 to 2015**: University at Albany, State University of New York men's lacrosse rosters, 2011–2015, ualbanysports.com.

27   **"Red Burnam kept"**: Marr, author interview.

II. Faithkeepers

28   **most prominent Indigenous**: "Oren Lyons," National Native American Hall of Fame.

28   **He has**: "Oren Lyons, Lacrosse, Enshrined 1988," Greater Syracuse Sports Hall of Fame, http://www.greatersyracusesportshalloffame.com/oren-lyons; *What's My Line?*, CBS, February 14, 1960; "On the Birthday of John Lennon, Oren Lyons Remembers a Friend," Kirst, Sean, *Syracuse.com*, March 22, 2019; "What Onondaga Faithkeeper Oren Lyons Said at Muhammad Ali's Funeral," Benny, Michael, *CNYCentral.com*, June 10, 2016.

28   **before all that**: "Oren Lyons Is Inducted in the 2008 Native American Athletic Hall of Fame," Lyons, Sue, OnondagaNation.org, December 17, 2008.

28   **since at least 1976**: Balls, Ron, International Lacrosse Federation/Federation of International Lacrosse meeting notes, compiled November 21, 2018; English Lacrosse Union correspondence to Carr, Clive, ILF Secretary, September 9, 1976.

28   **"recognized as a"**: Balls, ILF meeting notes.

28   **suggested that his old teammate**: Lyons, Oren, author interview, January 17, 2010.

28   **"We don't have a field team"**: Ibid.

29   **three of Simmons Jr.'s players**: "Iroquois in Lacrosse Festival," Forbes, John B., *New York Times*, June 5, 1983, Section 5, 10.

29   **indoor, or "box," lacrosse**: Fisher, Donald M., *Lacrosse: A History of the Game* (Baltimore: Johns Hopkins University Press, 2002), 157.

29   **created its lacrosse league**: "Murder Ball in the Box," Vesilind, Priit J., *Sports Illustrated*, September 3, 1973, 40.

29   **"North American Native Warriors"**: "The Nations in 1980," Holroyd, Steve, *Crosse-Check, The Magazine*, September 21, 2019, https://crossecheck.com/author/laxmavn/page /8/.

29   **the ILF board agreed**: Balls, ILF meeting notes, December 6, 1980.

29   **"kind of snuffed out"**: Simmons Jr., Roy, author interview, 2010.

29   **a bid to take part**: Balls, ILF meeting notes, July 13, 1980, and December 6, 1980.

29   **a confrontation erupted**: Balls, author interview, July 13, 2018; Hayes, Tom, author interview, January 5, 2021; Patterson, Carol, author interview, February 25, 2021.

29   **Lacrosse's first Hall of Fame**: Stenersen, Steve, Tanton, Bill, email interviews, February 2021.

29   **Budnitz, an all-time**: "'Buzzy' Budnitz: A Great Salesman for 'a *Great* Sport,'" Siegel, Eric, *Baltimore Sun*, June 13, 1982, E1.

29 **Patterson**: "John W. Patterson Jr., 74, Lacrosse Star, Coach," *Baltimore Sun*, July 2, 2000, 27; "John W. Patterson Jr., 74, Dies; a Legend in World of Lacrosse," Michelmore, Bill, *Buffalo News*, C-8.

30 **hustled in to separate**: Hayes, author interview; Balls, author interview.

30 **"there was prejudice"**: Balls, author interview.

30 **necessary sanction**: Lyons, Oren, author interview, November 28, 2018.

30 **"The Iroquois Nationals"**: Balls, ILF meeting notes.

30 **Even partnered with**: Lyons, author interview, January 17, 2010; Patterson, Carol, author interview; Michelmore,, "John W. Patterson Jr., 74, Dies."

30 **"Lacrosse International '83"**: "Lacrosse Feast Brings Brown to Baltimore," Tanton, Bill *Evening Sun*, June 8, 1983.

30 **astounding comebacks in lacrosse history**: "A Startling Comeback by Syracuse," Candel, Mike, *Newsday* (NY), May 29, 1983, 7/Sports.

30 **"Your team is getting"**: "The Iroquois Nationals Lacrosse Story," Lyons, Oren, *Florida Lacrosse News*, September 29, 2015, http://floridalacrossenews.com/uncategorized/the -iroquois-nationals-lacrosse-story/.

30 **"He's my cousin"**: "Syracuse, Canada triumph," Jackson, James, *Baltimore Sun*, June 10, 1983, C8.

30 **28–5 . . . 22–14**: Ibid; "Syracuse is International Titlist," Jackson, James, *Baltimore Sun*, June 13, 1983, C4.

31 **appearances at the Olympics**: *The Official Report of the Organizing Committee for the XIV Olympiad*.

31 **"You need eight teams"**: "Struggling to Compete in a Game They Created," Miller, Stephen, *Democrat and Chronicle* (NY), June 11, 1983, 8C.

31 **pre-1984 Olympic Games tourney**: "Pow-Wow to Precede Jim Thorpe Event," Escalante, Virginia, *Los Angeles Times*, June 7, 1984, Part IX, 9.

31 **seven-week Native relay**: "Thorpe Memorial Native Games Held," *Associated Press*, July 22, 1984; Lyons, "Iroquois Nationals Lacrosse Story."

31 **Nationals came loaded**: "Haudenosaunee Men's National Lacrosse Team," Wikipedia, http://en.wikipedia.org/wiki/Haudenosaunee_men%27s_national_lacrosse_team.

31 **score of 54–30 . . . England, 10–9**: Ibid.

31 **At the ILF meetings**: ILF meeting, July 21, 1984, Whittier, California.

32 **"It was very emotional"**: Hayes, author interview.

32 **five-game goodwill tour**: Balls, author interview; Lyons, Oren, author interview, January 17, 2010.

32 **To smooth their path**: Balls, author interview.

32 **"I'm really tired"**: Patterson, Carol, author interview.

32 **In October 1985**: Balls, ILF meeting notes, Hilton Hotel, New Brunswick, New Jersey, October 12 and 13, 1985; "Star Spangled," Grauer, Neil A., *Evening Sun*, July 6, 1990; "Iroquois Nationals Won't Wait Four More Years," Sexton, Joe, *Post-Standard* (NY), July 12, 1986.

32 **"This is an original American game"**: "Lacrosse: All-American Game," Lipsyte, Robert, *New York Times Magazine*, Section 6, 28, June 15, 1986.

32 **He truly considered**: Hayes, author interview.

32 **Hall of Fame coaching run**: "Thomas Hayes," National Lacrosse Hall of Fame, Inducted 1989.

33 **jailed for brawling**: Hayes, author interview.

33 **"I always felt"**: Ibid.

33   "competitive affiliate": Balls, ILF meeting notes, Hilton Hotel, New Brunswick, New Jersey, October 12 and 13, 1985.

33   In July 1986 . . . : Balls, ILF meeting notes, Varsity Stadium and Four Seasons Hotel, Toronto, Canada, July 13, 1986.

33   "inside" the Canadian camp: Lyons, author interview, January 17, 2010.

33   even to her: Patterson, author interview.

33   became unstuck: Balls, ILF meeting notes, Alma Lodge Hotel, Stockport, Cheshire, England, November 20 and 22, 1987.

33   contemporaneous notes: Balls, Ron, ILF/FIL meeting notes, compiled November 21, 2018.

33   dialed up: Balls, author interview, July 13, 2018; Lyons, Oren, author interview, January 17, 2010.

34   "everybody's agreed": Balls, Ron, author interview, July 13, 2018; Lyons, Oren, author interview, January 17, 2010.

34   "Full nation": Lyons, January 17, 2010.

34   "We're in": Burnam, Mark, author interview, November 20, 2020.

34   130: Burnam, Mark, interview, *The Fred Opie Show* podcast, March 10, 2018, https://www.fredopie.com/sports/2018/3/10/img-academy-coach-mark-burnam.

34   "We put it out": Ibid, 13:30–16:02.

35   $1,200 for travel: Vennum, 292.

35   original design based: "Flag Holds High Promise of Peace," Kirst, Sean, *Post-Standard* (NY), November 19, 2003.

35   repurposed the Haudenosaunee: Lyons, Oren and Lyons, Rex, author interview, October 23, 2021.

35   makeshift studio: Lyons, Rex, author interview, October 23, 2021; Burnam, author interview.

35   "You're the host": Jamieson, Sid, "The Missing Link" lecture, 2018 US Lacrosse National Convention, Baltimore, MD, January 20, 2018.

35   "You have to understand": Hayes, author interview, January 5, 2021.

35   "just overwhelming": Hill, Sidney, author interview, April 6, 2023.

36   a $35,000 donation: Fisher, 299.

36   inaugural game against Canada: "U.S. Lacrosse Team Wins Easily, Ups Record in Australia to 3–0," Grauer, Neil A., *Evening Sun*, July 9, 1990.

36   "call it 'kill snakes'": Burnam, author interview, November 20, 2020.

36   "Custer's Last Stand": Opie, Fred, author interview, November 17, 2020.

36   Nationals, 26–10: "Showing of Pride For the Iroquois," Pennington, Bill, *New York Times*, July 16, 1990, C2.

36   "They were whining": Burnam, author interview.

37   mid-tournament clinic: Pennington, "Showing of Pride."

37   "We the Original People": Balls, author interview.

37   "When you say 'Indians, Native Americans'": Jacques, Alfie, author interview, June 14, 2010.

38   "Get the animals": "The Gathering of the Tribes," Seabrook, John, *New Yorker*, September 7, 1998.

38   "They look like": Harrison, Kyle, author interview, August 8, 2019.

38   legendary goal against Siena: "Ty Thompson Crazy Goal," UAlbany Sports, YouTube video, 0:17, http://youtu.be/taeYvikbXWc?si=mS3NcNpltI3766hj.

39   "Their body control": Bratton, Shamel, author interview, September 6, 2019.

39 **$25,000** Iroquois Nationals source, author interview, July 2018; **"hefty"**: Rex Lyons, author interview, April 15, 2023.

39 **first major passport controversy**: "UK Won't Let Iroquois lacrosse Team Go to Tourney," Gross, Samantha, *Associated Press*, July 14, 2010.

39 **"You cannot buy"**: Abrams, Percy, author interview, 2010.

39 **director James Cameron**: Ibid.

39 **"They pulled a bait and switch"**: Ibid.

39 **"It is a win"**: Bucktooth, Brett, author interview, 2010.

40 **Championship in Prague**: "Haudenosaunee: World Silver Medalist," Tsadeyohdi, Onondaga Nation website, June 29, 2011, http://www.onondaganation.org/news/2011/haudenosaunee-world-silver-medalist/.

40 **inventive routing**: Schindler, Tia, author interview, December 4, 2020.

41 **"honor the Creator"**: Jamieson, Sid, "The Missing Link," lecture at 2018 US Lacrosse National Convention, January 20, 2018.

41 **"They said, 'Well'"**: Scherr, Jim, author interview, October 23, 2021.

41 **"Let me answer"**: Balls, author interview, July 13, 2018.

42 **"Run to the nearest gas station"**: Jemison, author interview, November 11, 2020.

42 **"deer-in-headlights"**: "Dialed In: Your Lacrosse Fix, Wednesday, July 18," Schneider, Megan, *USA Lacrosse Magazine*, http://www.usalacrosse.com/magazine/dialed-your-lacrosse-fix-wednesday-july-18.

42 **"like a bear"**: Shroff, Anish, ESPN2 broadcast, July 12, 2018.

42 **five straight faceoffs**: "US Offense Finds Groove in Win over Inspired Iroquois," *USA Lacrosse Magazine*, July 12, 2018, http://www.usalacrosse.com/magazine/us-offense-finds-groove-win-over-inspired-iroquois.

42 **"hate that shit"**: Danowski, John, author observation, July 12, 2018.

42 **"I saw a lot"**: Gonzales, Timothy, author interview, January 27, 2021.

43 **"Twenty-four hours ago"**: Thompson, Lyle, interview, July 12, 2018.

43 **"I'm still looking"**: Ibid.

43 **"There's a lot of people"**: Ibid.

III. He Is Flying Over Us

44 **"Scalplock," explained Oren**: "Pride of a Nation," Price, S.L., *Sports Illustrated*, July 19, 2010, 71.

44 **As a junior**: "Thompson Brothers Make History in 2014," Donahue, Mark, *Lacrosse All Stars*, June 10, 2014, https://laxallstars.com/thompson-brothers-make-history-2014/.

45 **win the Tewaaraton Award twice**: "Men's Recipients," Tewaaraton Foundation, http://tewaaraton.com/winners/.

45 **indoors and field**: "Lyle Thompson: Face of Lacrosse Candidate," McMichael, Craig, *Lacrosse All Stars*, December 30, 2022, https://laxallstars.com/lyle-thompson-face-of-lacrosse-candidate/.

45 **"I don't even know"**: Harrison, author interview.

45 **"Such a good combination"**: Stanwick, Steele, author interview, March 19, 2020.

45 **His father, Jerome**: "Thompson Family's 'Symbol of Pride,'" Vock, Casey, *Inside Lacrosse*, October 2010, https://www.insidelacrosse.com/article/mag-archives-thompson-family-s-quot-symbol-of-pride-quot-/18862.

45 **"I'd have a hard time"**: Lyons, Oren, author interview, November 28, 2018.

46   **names get famous**: Price, *Sports Illustrated*, 2010.

46   **1930s**: Root, Christopher P. "An Examination in the Evolution of Iroquois Lacrosse" (master's thesis, State University of New York, Buffalo State College, 2016), 57.

46   **155-pound "mosquito"**: "'I Knocked Down Jim Brown,'" Poliquin, Bud, *Post-Standard* (NY), republished March 14, 2008, http://www.onondaganation.org/news/2008/i-knocked-down-jim-brown/.

46   **"the place went wild"**: Simmons Jr., author interview.

46   **"I still don't"**: Thompson, Dee, author interview, November 30, 2018.

46   **"The way we play"**: Thompson, Ji, author interview, November 30, 2018.

47   **"They Bump Hips"**: "History," Onondaga Redhawks website, https://redhawkslax.com/history/.

47   **"that anciently discharged social tensions"**: Fenton, William N. *The Great Law and the Longhouse: A Political History of the Iroquois Confederacy* (Norman: University of Oklahoma Press, 1998), 27.

47   **Handsome Lake's Longhouse religion:** "The Code of Handsome Lake," Bonaparte, Darren, http://mohawkvalleymuseums.us/writing-series/the-code-of-handsome-lake/.

47   **staged to "cheer"**: Fenton, 116.

47   **"You'll be playing again"**: Lyons, Oren, author interview, January 17, 2010.

47   **Each spring, at Onondaga**: Jacques, author interview.

47   **"The mecca"**: Ibid.

47   **"The ball is the medicine"**: Lyons, Oren, author interview.

47   **"The wooden stick"**: Lyons, Rex, author interview, November 28, 2018.

48   **"calls" for a Medicine Game . . . "comes to" the needful man**: Thompson, Jerome "Ji," author interview.

48   **"You kind of feel"**: Ibid.

48   **"clear mind"**: Ibid.

48   **Mohawk, Wolf clan**: Ibid.

49   **"when I get committed"**: Ibid.

49   **estimates of Longhouse adherents**: Clairmont, Don. *Aboriginal Policing in Canada: An Overview of Developments in First Nations* (September 2006).

49   **During the American Revolution**: "Big Idea 5: Native American Soldiers and Scouts," Liberty Exhibit, Museum of the American Revolution, Philadelphia, http://www.amrevmuseum.org/big-idea-5-native-american-soldiers-and-scouts.

49   **lucrative business: casinos**: "State of Play, New York: All Casinos," American Gaming Association website, http://www.americangaming.org/state/new-york/; "Tuscarora Nation of North Carolina," https://tuscaroranationnc.com/.

49   **"morally opposed to casino"**: "Haudenosaunee Statement on High Stakes Gambling," Hill, Sidney, Tadadaho, 2005, http://www.onondaganation.org/government/policy/haudenosaunee-statement-on-high-stakes-gambling/.

50   **"territorial map of the Iroquois"**: "Two Row Wampum Renewal Campaign," Neighbors of the Onondaga Nation, Syracuse, N.Y., 2013, https://honorthetworow.org/.

50   **Onondaga control 14 seats**: "Chiefs," Onondaga Nation website, http://www.onondaganation.org/government/chiefs/.

50   **no formal representation**: "Haudenosaunee Guide for Educators," National Museum of the American Indian.

50   **"does not pay"**: "Today," Onondaga Nation website, http://www.onondaganation.org/aboutus/today/.

50   **US Census**: "About Us," Onondaga Nation website; "Onondaga's Say: That's Not Us in Your Census," McAndrew, Mike, *Syracuse Post-Standard* (NY), March 21, 2001; United States Census Bureau data, Onondaga Nation Reservation, NY.

50   **gave $6 million in housing grants**: "HUD Tries to Give Away Federal Money, but Onondaga Says No Thanks," Weiner, Mark, Syracuse.com, March 9, 2015.

50   **Offered $800,000**: Ibid.

50   **also about independence**: Ibid.

51   **"Are you nuts"**: Lyons, Oren, author interview, January 17, 2010.

51   **"hungry for a lot"**: Thompson, Ji, author interview.

51   **Onondaga, Wolf clan**: Thompson, Deloris, author interview.

51   **defied the US government**: "Why Dennis Banks Matters," Native America: A History website, November 6, 2017, http://michaelleroyoberg.com/current-events/why-dennis -banks-matters/.

51   **Ji and Dee married**: Thompson, Deloris and Thompson, Ji, author interview.

51   **family moved to Akwesasne**: Ibid.

51   **play for the Akwesasne Thunder**: Vock, "Thompson Family's 'Symbol of Pride."

51   **"moon time"**: Schindler, Tia, author interview, August 13, 2020.

51   **"We weren't allowed"**: Thompson, Jeremy, author interview, October 23, 2021.

51   **"Women do pick up"**: Thompson, Dee, author interview.

52   *Gaä Gwa Gyehe*: Vock; Thompson, Lyle, author interview, November 26, 2018.

52   *Susquehanna*: Ibid.

52   *Giaehgwaeh*: Thompson, Lyle, author interview.

52   *Deyhahsanoondey*: Ibid.

52   **highest rates**: Dickerson, Daniel et al, "American Indians/Alaska Natives and Substances Abuse Treatment Outcomes: Positive Signs and Continuing Challenges," *Journal of Addictive Diseases* 30 (January 2011): 63–74.

52   **"people that we were around"**: Thompson, Ji, author interview.

52   **"Even if they were"**: Thompson, Dee, author interview.

52   **"Get through"**: Thompson, Ji, interview.

52   **No running water, electricity**: Thompson, Ji, interview. "A Symbol Of Family And Tradition For 4 Iroquois Brothers," Littlefield, Bill, *Only A Game*, WBUR, June 2, 2017.

53   **"We kind of forced ourselves"**: Thompson, Ji, interview.

53   **learning disabilities**: *The Medicine Game*, directed by Lukas Korver, (Lincoln, NE: Vision Maker Media, 2013).

53   **failed three times**: Ibid.

53   **about 12 percent**: Ibid.

53   **"easy switch"**: Thompson, Lyle, author interview.

53   **"Kill the Indian, and save the man"**: "Past," The Carlisle Indian School Project website, http://carlisleindianschoolproject.com/past/.

53   **American network**: "US Indian Boarding School History," National Native American Boarding School Healing Coalition, https://boardingschoolhealing.org/education/us -indian-boarding-school-history/; "Legacy of Trauma: The Impact of American Indian Boarding Schools Across Generations," Lajimodiere, Denise K., *PBS.org*, October 20, 2023, http://www.pbs.org/native-america/blog/legacy-of-trauma-the-impact-of-american -indian-boarding-schools-across-generations; "War Against Children," Levitt, Zach, Parshina-Kottas, Yuliya, Romero, Simon, Wallace, Tim, *New York Times*, August 30, 2023.

53 **Canada's counterpart**: "Canada's Residential Schools Were a Horror," Mosby, Ian, Millions, Eric, *Scientific American*, August 1, 2021.

54 **"I do not recall"**: Standing Bear, Luther. *My People the Sioux* (Boston, New York: Houghton Mifflin Company, 1928), 141.

54 **"Our hair was part"**: Thompson, Lyle, author interview, April 5, 2019.

54 **"protection medicine"**: Ibid.

54 **braiding each other's hair**: *The Medicine Game*.

54 **through a car window**: Ibid.

54 **his "bad twin"**: Thompson, Jeremy, author interview, Spring 2010.

55 **"smoking up"**: *The Medicine Game*.

55 **"It was some kind of healing"**: Thompson, Dee, author interview.

55 **"I was at this age"**: Thompson, Lyle, author interview, November 26, 2018.

55 **Nearly one in ten**: "1 in 10 Native American Deaths Alcohol related," *Associated Press*, August 28, 2008.

55 **Kent Squire-Hill**: "Squire-Hill guilty of second-degree murder," Horn, Greg, *Kahnawake News*, December 3, 2010.

55 **28 percent . . . 17 percent**: "Native American Students in Higher Education," Postsecondary National Policy Institute, November 2023.

55 **"always thinking back home"**: Thompson, Jeremy, author interview, Price, *Sports Illustrated*, July 19, 2010, 70.

56 **"But another coach?"**: Desko, John, author interview; Price, *Sports Illustrated*, July 19, 2010, 70.

56 **first score with the Orange**: "Question Mark in 2009 Becomes Instant Offense in 2010 for Syracuse Lacrosse," Rahme, Dave, *Post-Standard* (NY), February 26, 2010.

56 **Haudenosaunee Promise Scholarship**: "The Haudenosaunee Promise at the College of Professional Studies," Syracuse University, http://professionalstudies.syracuse.edu/tuition-aid/scholarships-grants/haudenosaunee-promise/.

56 **the 12.6 scholarships allowed**: "Your Complete Guide to Men's Lacrosse College Scholarships," NCSA College Recruiting, http://www.ncsasports.org/mens-lacrosse/scholarships.

57 **95 goals and 56 assists**: "Miles Thompson," University at Albany men's lacrosse roster, 2014.

57 **one play against Cazenovia**: "2009 4 25 Cazenovia at Lafayette 3rd Quarter 8 11 Lyle Thompson Scores Amazing," Zabek, Joe, YouTube video, 1:11, http://www.youtube.com/watch?v=of14BDzhif0.

57 **Ji made it clear**: Thompson, Ji, author interview.

57 **"Scottie," Ralph said**: Marr, author interview.

57 **never been to Onondaga**: Ibid.

58 **lost his longtime girlfriend his junior year**: "Jeremy Thompson," Syracuse men's lacrosse roster, 2011, http://cuse.com/sports/mens-lacrosse/roster/jeremy-thompson/7903.

58 **"held back as a player"**: Thompson, Jeremy, author interview, April 14, 2023.

58 ***"I don't want to go there"***: Thompson, Lyle, author interview.

58 **showed real interest**: Ibid.

58 **Orange's disinterest . . .**: Simmons III, Roy, author interview, November 30, 2018.

58 **"all they did was send me one letter"**: Thompson, Lyle author interview.

58 **never did earn his diploma**: Thompson, Lyle, author interview, November 26, 2018.

58 **"It came down to"**: Ibid.

58 **Marr went all in . . .** : Thompson, Lyle, author interview; Marr, author interview; University at Albany men's lacrosse roster, 2011, http://ualbanysports.com/sports/mens-lacrosse/roster/2011.

59 **"Have You Ever Seen the Rain?"**: Thompson, Ji, author interview.

59 **"If I'd turned around"**: Ibid.

59 **One night in August . . .** : Marr, Scott, author interview, November 29, 2018.

59 **Native pictures and books all around**: Ibid.

59 **putting him in a paddy wagon**: Ibid.

60 **diagnosed with bipolar I disorder**: Ibid.

60 **"what the game is"**: Ibid.

60 **"minimum requirement"**: NCAA Eligibility Center Quick Reference Sheet, 2011–12, NCAA Division I Sliding Scale Core Grade-Point Average/Test-Score; Marr, Scott, author interview.

60 **"not going to make it"**: Marr, author interview.

60 **"I needed trigonometry"**: Thompson, Lyle, author interview, July 12, 2018.

61 **one of Lyle's faceoff moves**: Akl, Nabil, author interview, May 28, 2020.

61 **baby slept in a drawer**: Thompson, Lyle, author interview, November 26, 2018.

61 **five wins and 11 losses**: University at Albany men's lacrosse schedule and results, 2012, http://ualbanysports.com/sports/mens-lacrosse/schedule/2012.

61 **"No fuckin' *way*"**: Marr, author interview.

61 **16–15, in double overtime**: "UAlbany Men's Lacrosse Upsets #13 Syracuse, 16–15, in Double Overtime to Kick Off 2013 with a Bang," University at Albany Athletics, http://ualbanysports.com/news/2013/2/17/206457613.aspx.

61 **113 points in 18 games**: "Lyle Thompson," University at Albany men's lacrosse bio, 2015, http://ualbanysports.com/sports/mens-lacrosse/roster/lyle-thompson/5505.

62 **"controlled chaos" . . . "spaghetti" . . .** : "Syracuse Defense Prepares to Face Lethal, Unpredictable Albany Attack, Top Scorer Lyle Thompson," Grossman, Connor, *Daily Orange* (NY), April 1, 2015.

62 **Zed Williams**: "Student Spotlight: Native American Lacrosse Star Forges His Own Bold Path to UVA," White, Jeff, *UVA Today*, April 19, 2016.

62 **Zach Miller and Frank Brown**: Denver men's lacrosse roster (2013–2016), https://denverpioneers.com/sports/2018/6/6/mens-lacrosse-archives; Hobart men's lacrosse roster (2013–17), https://hwsathletics.com/sports/mens-lacrosse/roster.

62 **joined him in Denver**: "Brendan Bomberry Mastering Life, Lacrosse with Denver Pioneers," Chambers, Mike, *Denver Post*, February 21, 2017.

62 **"We still, to this day"**: Simmons III, author interview.

62 **"But they still didn't win one"**: Ibid.

63 **"Go back to the Rez"**: Thompson, Lyle, author interview.

63 **"about my hair"**: Ibid.

63 **"wagon burners"**: Marr, author interview.

63 **two more children**: Thompson, Lyle, author interview.

63 **"like everyone else"**: Ibid.

63 **"What [Lyle]'s done"**: "Albany's Lyle Thompson has become the face of college lacrosse," Lee, Edward, *Baltimore Sun*, February 5, 2015.

64 **Lyle and Miles graduated**: Thompson, Lyle, author interview.

64 **"different person"**: Marr, author interview.

64 **"contemptuous"**: *More Than a Word*, Little, John and Kenn, Media Education Foundation, 2017, http://go.mediaed.org/more-than-a-word.

64   "CAUCASIANS": "Lyle Thompson's Evolution From Shy Star to Influential Voice," Kinnear, Matt, *Inside Lacrosse,* December 15, 2016, https://www.insidelacrosse.com /article/lyle-thompson-s-evolution-from-shy-star-to-influential-voice/36665.

64   "It's dehumanizing": Thompson, Lyle, author interview.

65   Dakota Access oil pipeline: "Key Moments In the Dakota Access Pipeline Fight," Hersher, Rebecca, *NPR: The Two-Way,* February 22, 2017.

65   "bunch of lacrosse people": Thompson, author interview.

65   Standing Rock reservation: *NPR.*

65   Lyle retweeted the support . . . retweeted updates: Lyle Thompson (@lyle4thompson), Twitter (now X), October 28, 2016 to November 23, 2016, https://twitter.com /lyle4thompson.

65   "I had to be there": Thompson, Lyle, author interview.

65   On the afternoon of November 20: Marr, author interview; Thompson, Lyle, author interview.

66   En route: Thompson, Lyle, interview.

66   hold a Medicine Game: Ibid.

66   The next morning: Ibid.

66   "completely disrespected": "Lyle Thompson, Scott Marr Visit Standing Rock, Host Medicine Game," Kinnear, Matt, *Inside Lacrosse,* November 22, 2016, https://www.insidelacrosse .com/article/lyle-thompson-scott-marr-visit-standing-rock-host-medicine-game/36571.

67   "Stand for what you believe in": Thompson, Lyle, interview.

67   "It had a purpose": Marr, author interview.

68   "ethnically cleansed": Faris.

68   "honoring Israel": "Iroquois Nationals Going to Israel Despite Calls to Boycott World Lacrosse Championships," Brake, Justin, *APTN News,* July 11, 2018, https:// www.aptnnews.ca/national-news/iroquois-nationals-going-to-israel-despite-calls-to -boycott-world-lacrosse-championships/.

68   "Excuse my ignorance": Thompson, Lyle, Instagram message, July 8, 2018.

68   Akl, then a law student: Akl, author interview.

69   "Israel is generally": Akl, Instagram message, July 8, 2018.

69   "I don't hate": Akl, author interview.

70   "This is their Medicine Game": Ibid.

70   He educated me": Thompson, Lyle, author interview.

70   "I don't think it's *ever*": Ibid.

Part 2

I. The Lonely Sons of Simeon Moss

73   injured by a grenade: "IDF officer moderately wounded by grenade during Gaza riots," *Times of Israel,* July 13, 2018.

74   "National Institute for Sports Excellence": "About the Wingate Institute located in Netanya, Israel," International Jewish Sports Hall of Fame, http://www.jewishsports .net/wingate_institute.htm.

74   regional qualifiers: "World Lacrosse Championship Comes to a Thrilling and Controversial End," Rosin, Armin, *Tablet Magazine,* July 23, 2018.

74   non-passport holders: "For a Shot at World Championship, Maryland Lacrosse Players Follow Family History to Nontraditional Nations," Lee, Edward, *Baltimore Sun,* July 12, 2018.

74 **FIL's guidelines**: Federation of International Lacrosse (FIL) Player Eligibility Criteria, agreed on at FIL General Assembly, July 10, 2018.

74 **"a further exception"**: FIL Player Eligibility Criteria, July 10, 2018.

75 **"Help me"**: "Israel Lacrosse World Games," Gonzales, Timothy, GoFundMe, http://www.gofundme.com/f/5g5zoow.

75 **"the stick is magic"**: Hayes, Tom, author interview, January 5, 2021.

75 **kill himself**: Gonzales, author interview, January 27, 2021.

76 **"shoot myself, 100 percent"**: Ibid.

76 **"18 years of my life in prison"**: Ibid.

76 **"The moment I started"**: Ibid.

77 **"never stay down long"**: Hylen, Scott, author interview, March 7, 2021.

77 **field tourney in Lake Tahoe**: Gonzales, author interview.

77 **soccer and American football**: Patraca, Andres Axkana, author interview, January 18, 2021.

77 **In 2009, while studying**: Ibid.

77 **"going to be my life"**: Ibid.

77 **"You were *there*"**: Ibid.

78 **23rd in Denver . . .**: "FIL World Championships Final Update," University of Michigan Athletics, July 14, 2014, http://mgoblue.com/news/2014/7/14/fil_world_championships_final_update.

78 **"no idea the impact"**: Patraca, author interview.

78 **Virginia bred . . .**: Haas, Andrew, author interview, March 23, 2021.

78 **"*Mexicanos, al grito de Guerra*"**: "The National Anthem of Mexico," August 31, 2013, http://imagine-mexico.com/the-national-anthem-of-mexico/.

78 **"Hymn to Liberty"**: "The Greek National Anthem and Its Meaning," Chrysopoulos, Philip, *Greek Reporter*, October 28, 2023.

78 **"big difference for us"**: Patraca, author interview.

78 **Zacharopoulos would be playing**: "At 17, Homegrown Elias Zacharopoulos Makes Greece Debut," Meyer, Justin, *Lacrosse All Stars*, August 13, 2018, https://laxallstars.com/elias-zacharopoulos-greece-debut/.

79 **Joe Boulukos, 34**: "Joe Boulukos (2016)—Hall of Fame,"—Cornell University Athletics, 2016, http://cornellbigred.com/honors/hall-of-fame/joe-boulukos/580.

79 **scored 10 in one loss**: "Lewnes Ties School Record With Ten Goals, But UMBC Rally Halted in 15-14 OT Loss to No. 5 Albany," UMBC Athletics, April 30, 2016, http://umbcretrievers.com/news/2016/4/30/4_30_2016_2209.aspx.

79 **"You guys swim across?"**: Gonzales, author interview.

79 **deriding his braids**: Ibid.

79 **"give them the toothbrushes"**: Ibid.

79 **"at least three times," he and the rest**: Patraca, author interview.

79 **Greek team's "racial comments"**: Haas, author interview.

79 **"insult us as a nation"**: Patraca, author interview.

79 **"that made us lose our mind"**: Ibid.

79 **"Stay down, beaner"**: Gonzales, author interview.

80 **singularly gracious: "you're a good team"**: Melero, Ernie; author interview, March 1, 2021; Haas, author interview.

80 **said they heard no slurs**: Buckley, Mark, author interview, December 1, 2023; Luxion, Steve, author interview, December 1, 2013.

80 **contest was the "most heated"**: Luxion, author interview.

80 **"could well have happened"**: Buckley, author interview.

80 **"nothing really happened"**: Melero, author interview.

80 **Simon Cataldo, a special education**: "A Message From Our Founder," Cataldo, Simon, September 6, 2016, http://www.harlemlacrosse.org/blog/2016/9/2/a-message-from-our -founder.

81 **Alliance has since expanded**: "Urban Lacrosse Alliance," USA Lacrosse, http://www .usalacrosse.com/urban-lacrosse-alliance.

81 **embedded full-time in underserved**: "Our Model," Harlem Lacrosse, http://www .harlemlacrosse.org/model.

81 **In 2008, 92 percent**: *NCAA Student-Athlete Ethnicity Report, 1999–2000–2008–09*, Zgonc, Erin (Indianapolis: National Collegiate Athletic Association, February 2010), 46.

81 **figure dropped to 82 and 83 percent**: "NCAA Demographics Database," National Collegiate Athletic Association, December 13, 2018, http://www.ncaa.org/sports/2018 /12/13/ncaa-demographics-database.aspx.

81 **participation in the US grew by 227 percent**: "Total number of participants in lacrosse in the United States from 2001 to 2018," Statista, December 8, 2022, http://www.statista .com/statistics/490367/lacrosse-total-participation-us/.

81 **more than doubled to 13.6**: "NCAA Demographics Database," National Collegiate Athletic Association.

81 **"such a white space"**: Melero, author interview, March 1, 2021.

81 ***After hitting an all-time high**: *Sports, Fitness, and Leisure Activities Topline Participation Report* (Laurel, MD: Sports & Fitness Industry Association, 2024), 34.

82 **The first, defenseman Fred Opie**: "The Most Influential Figures in Black Lacrosse History," Simpkins, Brian, *USA Lacrosse Magazine*, February 4, 2021.

82 **not a single racial comment**: Opie, Fred, author interview, November 17, 2020.

82 **"only Black guy on the team? Lonely"**: Ibid.

82 **his final stat line**: "US Offense Finds Groove in Win over Inspired Iroquois," *USA Lacrosse Magazine*, July 12, 2018, http://www.usalacrosse.com/magazine/us-offense-finds -groove-win-over-inspired-iroquois.

82 **Baptiste became only the sixth**: "Trevor Baptiste '14, At the Top of His Game," Morristown Beard School, http://www.mbs.net/powerfully-prepared/~board/profiles/post /at-the-top-of-his-game-trevor-baptiste-14.

82 **"you won is because you got"**: Baptiste, Trevor, author interview, July 18, 2018.

83 ***"these guys have my back"***: Ibid.

83 **In his first game**: "Freshman Trevor Baptiste can stick it to DU foes on faceoffs," Chambers, Mike, *Denver Post*, February 21, 2015.

83 **last game of his freshman**: "Pioneers Win First Men's Lacrosse Title," University of Denver Athletics, May 25, 2015.

83 **"dominated that much"**: Seibald, Max, author interview, July 17, 2018.

83 **"I'm happy with it"**: Baptiste, author interview.

83 **in 1939**: "Rutgers Jay-Vee Stickmen Click," *Central New Jersey Home News*, May 4, 1939, 24; "Princeton Ten Compiles Early Lead to Win on Neilson Field," *Central New Jersey Home News*, May 21, 1939, 10; "Rutgers Indians Conquer Lehigh Easily. 14 to 3," *Central New Jersey Home News*, April 9, 1939, 19; "Rutgers Takes Lacrosse Test," *Asbury Park Press*, April 2, 1939, 10; Harrison Jr., Miles, Silverman, Chip. *Ten Bears* (Positive Publications, 2001), 43.

83 **part of his junior year**: "Army Stickmen Rout Rutgers," *Central New Jersey Home News*, May 12, 1940.

83 **before quitting**: "Moss, Simeon," Piehler, G. Kurt, Holyoak, Sandra Stewart, Cooper, Melanie, Rutgers Oral History Archives, May 2, 1997, http://oralhistory.rutgers.edu /alphabetical-index/interviewees/30-interview-html-text/371-moss-simeon.

83 **"only thing that I know about anything"**: Ibid.

84 **against all academy custom**: "Harvard Students May Go to F.D. on Discrimination," *Boston Globe*, April 9, 1941.

84 **2.3 percent of navy personnel**: "African American Sailors in the U.S. Navy, A Chronology," Naval History and Heritage Command, http://www.history.navy.mil/browse -by-topic/diversity/african-americans/chronology.html.

84 **"seagoing bellhops"**: "Segregation in the Navy," Hegranes, Emily, *Naval History*, February 2021, http://www.usni.org/magazines/naval-history-magazine/2021/february /segregation-navy.

84 **fear of race riots**: "Students, Teachers Blast Ban Against LaCrosse Player," Davis, Paul Daniel, *Pittsburgh Courier* (PA), April 19, 1941.

84 **could not take the field with a "colored man"**: Gup.

84 **after some initial resistance**: Davis.

84 **forfeit the game**: "Harvard to Tolerate No Racial Discrimination," *Boston Globe*, April 21, 1941, 6.

84 **"We were guests"**: Gup.

84 **600 signatures**: Ibid.

84 **on April 17, First Lady Eleanor Roosevelt**: "Mrs. F.D. Wires Harvard Council on Negro Player," *Boston Globe*, April 18, 1941.

85 **no longer tolerate**: *Boston Globe*, April 21, 1941, 6.

85 **commander in chief had been paying attention**: Goodwin, Doris Kearns, *No Ordinary Time* (New York: Simon & Schuster, 1994), 249.

85 **historic executive order**: Executive Order 8802, Fair Employment Practice in Defense Industries, Roosevelt, Franklin D., June 25, 1941.

85 **Wesley A. Brown became the first** : "Naval Academy Breaks Ground on Wesley Brown Field House," United States Navy, Jarvis, Matt, March 28, 2006.

85 **Albert F. Lewis**: "Souvenirs of Sport," MacDonald, D.A.L., *Montreal Gazette*, February 27, 1890.

85 **not the sole**: Hayes, Tom, author interview.

86 **"finest midfield man I've ever seen"**: "Keeping Posted," Reddy, Bill, *Post-Standard* (NY), January 10, 1956.

86 **"At that time, maybe 175 pounds"**: Simmons Jr., Roy, author interview, April 24, 2020.

86 **never thrown a discus**: "Schwartzwalder Won't Let '53, '55 Take His Mind Off '54 Challenges," Fox, John W., *Press and Sun-Bulletin* (NY), September 21, 1954.

86 **Brown later joked**: "'The truest All-American I've ever seen,'" Kekis, John, *Associated Press*, May 22, 2005.

86 **"Jim Brown rule"**: "Dobbin Given Stick Award," *Baltimore Sun*, December 16, 1956; Finn, Joe, National Lacrosse Hall of Fame archives, author inquiry, June 9, 2021; Many people have claimed that Brown inspired the rule making it illegal to hold the stick next to your body to keep the ball from being dislodged. However, the rule prohibiting this was not added to the college rule book until 1973, and Brown's senior year was 1957. Rule XI, Section 2, F (2) states, "A player shall not hold his stick in close proximity to his body with the express purpose of preventing an opponent from the opportunity of dislodging the ball." Today, the prohibition falls under Rule XI, Section 11 of the NCAA men's rule book, which states in part, "A player in possession of the ball who holds the crosse against any part of the body, thus preventing the normal dislodgment of the ball, is illegally withholding the ball from play."

86   **"best stickhandler we ever had"**: Simmons Jr., Roy, author interview.

87   **"People down South"**: Ibid.

87   **spring schedule**: "Jim Brown Victory Key In 2-Sport Afternoon," *Star-Gazette* (NY), May 19, 1957.

87   **Syracuse won, 24–4** . . . : "Why Harvard's Lewis Picked Lacrosse Ahead of Baseball," Roberts, Ernie, *Boston Globe*, April 16, 1956.

87   **May 18, 1957, after a two-year absence**: "Jim Brown Victory Key In 2-Sport Afternoon."

87   **North-South All-Star Game**: "Stick Leaders Tag Brown No. 1 Great," Tanton, William, *Evening Sun* (MD), June 8, 1957, 10.

87   **"think they invented"**: Simmons Jr., author interview, April 24, 2020.

87   **"scored one goal underhanded"**: "Jim Brown's Best Sport," Vecsey, George, *New York Times*, March 19, 1984, Section C, 6.

88   **"greatest lacrosse player I ever saw"**: Ibid.

88   **career-ending "blaze of glory"**: Tanton, 10.

88   **conceding him the all-time title**: Ibid.

88   **in the stands that day, too**: Ibid.

88   **"Brown was a man among boys"**: "The Big Question," *Johns Hopkins Magazine*, April 2002, http://pages.jh.edu/jhumag/0402web/bigques.html.

88   **"in my mind he's the greatest"**: Simmons Jr., author interview.

88   **"giant Negro athlete"**: Tanton, 10.

89   **"fire-breathing, chocolate-colored monster"**: "Why Jim Brown Matters," Layden, Tim, *Sports Illustrated*, October 6, 2015.

89   **tendency by white people to subconsciously assign**: "Study: People See Black Men as Larger and More Threatening than Similarly Sized White Men," Lopez, German, *Vox*, March 17, 2017.

000 **Simmons Jr. says he heard plenty of abuse**: Simmons Jr., author interview, September 24, 2020.

89   **Brown later conceded**: "In the Seats and on the Field, Lacrosse Finds New Faithful," Thamel, Pete, *New York Times*, May 26, 2005, Section D, 7.

89   **received more congratulatory notes**: Ibid.

89   **"like a special fraternity"**: Ibid.

90   **twisted walk of Wilmeth Sidat-Singh**: "A Not-So-Proud Moment in Syracuse University History: One of Earliest Black Quarterbacks in College Had to Pretend He Wasn't Black," Case, Dick, *Post-Standard* (NY), February 12, 2012.

90   **prime advisor in high school**: Vecsey, 6.

90   **"did not want Black athletes"**: "SPORTS WORLD SPECIALS: The Greatest Ever," Thomas Jr., Robert Mcg., *New York Times*, June 6, 1983.

90   **"You racists . . . fuck you"**: Brown, Jim and Delsohn, Steve. *Out of Bounds* (New York: Zebra Books, 1989), 40.

90   **sleeping or skipping drills he found useless**: Greene, John Robert, Baron, Karrie A. *Syracuse University: The Tolley Years, 1942–1969* (Syracuse University Press, 1996), 139–140.

90   **"I was tired of him"**: Ibid.

90 **"pretty white co-ed"**: Brown and Delsohn, 121.

90 **"One afternoon"**: Ibid.

91 **proven his color-blindness in 1954**: "A Conversation With Oren Lyons," Sten-ersen, Steve, Muller, Kira, Logue, Brian, *US Lacrosse*, November 27, 2020, http://www
.usalacrosse.com/magazine/conversation-oren-lyons.

91 **"only encouraging voice"**: Brown, Jim and Cope, Myron. *Off My Chest* (New York: Doubleday), 120.

91 **"greatest man I have ever known"**: "'My Teams Are Collages,'" Lidz, Franz, *Sports Illustrated*, March 26, 1984.

91 **a scholarship, and the two men**: Simmons Jr., author interview, April 24, 2020; "Jim Brown Named the Inaugural Tewaaraton Legend," February 2010, http://www.fredopie
.com/sports/2010/02/jim-brown-syracuse-walk-on.html.

91 **hotel out of town**: "Moment of Truth," Smith, Gary, *Sports Illustrated*, July 26, 1999.

91 **First Baptist Church in Elmira**: "Thousands Honor Davis At Funeral," *New York Times*, May 22, 1963.

91 **"introduce you to my favorite coach"**: Simmons Jr., Roy, author interview, April 24, 2020.

92 **the maneuverings of Ken Molloy . . .** : Kekis; "Jim Brown's Formula for Fun: Practice Lacrosse, Play Football," *Press and Sun-Bulletin* (NY), March 4, 1957.

92 **Black businesses and wealth**: Brown and Delsohn, 59.

92 **became known as the Black Economic Union**: "Our Story," Black Economic Union, http://blackeconomicunion.org/about-us.

93 **"I'm sure finances and exposure"**: "Lacrosse's Changing Face: Game Gaining Black Acceptance, Participation with Growth of Youth Programs in Urban Areas," Preston, Mike, *Baltimore Sun*, May 19, 1993.

93 **Maryland midfielder Len Spicer**: University of Maryland Sports Information Depart-ment, author inquiry, May 20, 2021; Joe Finn, National Lacrosse Hall of Fame archives, author inquiry, May 19, 2021; University of Maryland men's lacrosse roster, 1970, http://
umterps.com/sports/mens-lacrosse/roster/1970.

93 **casually announced that Joe Carlton**: "Hopkins Stickmen Beaten But Unbowed, Eye Crown," Chevalier, Jack, *Baltimore Sun*, April 1, 1966, 26.

94 **"Nobody knew what happened"**: Cowan, Joe, author interview, December 2022.

94 **Carlton, who became a doctor of neurology**: "Accolades for 13 Amazing TCP Teach-ers," McGill University, Health e-News, February 27, 2020, http://healthenews.mcgill
.ca/accolades-for-13-amazing-tcp-teachers/.

94 **"didn't know what to do"**: Cowan.

94 **"wanted me to go out for lacrosse"**: "Oral history of Ernest Bates '58," Johns Hopkins University oral history collection, Warren, Mame, October 11, 1999.

II. The Shadow Game

95 **"just looking at the skin"**: Harrison, Miles, author interview, July 13, 2019.

95 **Black America's "Talented Tenth"**: Du Bois, William Edward Burghard. "The Tal-ented Tenth" in *The Negro Problem: A Series of Articles by Representative American Negroes of Today*. Edited by Washington, Booker T. (United States: J. Pott, 1903), 33–75.

95 **Forest Park . . . QB**: "Harrison Does It All For Foresters," Shane, Larry, *Evening Sun* (MD), March 29, 1967, C6; Harrison, Miles, author interview.

95 **Sophomore year, he picked up**: Harrison, Miles, author interview.

96　**during peak "white flight"**: "Baltimore Trying to Stem Decades-Long Disappearing Act," McFadden, David, *Associated Press*, December 29, 2018.

96　**at Forest Park, Harrison estimates**: Harrison, author interview.

96　**invited him for a recruiting visit**: Ibid.

96　**"Held onto it"**: Ibid.

96　**"Folks that look like him"**: Harrison, Kyle, author interview, December 15, 2023.

97　**began agitating for a lacrosse program**: "Memories of Lacrosse at Morgan," Ewell, Christian, *Baltimore Sun*, May 28, 2001.

97　**"another All-MSA defenseman"**: "All-M.S.A. Lacrosse Team," *Baltimore Sun*, June 11, 1967, 34.

97　**"Nobody knew it was time"**: Ibid.

97　**"team has a lot of pride"**: "Something New For Morgan; Lacrosse Is In The Air," Hargrove, Larry, *Evening Sun* (MD), March 25, 1970.

97　**"swaggish clothing store"** . . . : "Morgan State Lacrosse: The Stepchild Finally Grows Up," Hersh, Phil, *Evening Sun* (MD), April 30, 1975, E1, E5.

97　**"Diner Guys"** . . . : "Much Ado About Nothing," Price, S.L., *Vanity Fair*, March 2012, 330–337, 386–389; Silverman, Chip, *Diner Guys* (New York: Birch Lane Press, 1989).

97　**the Bears went 4–3**: "Bears Open Stick Season Against Swarthmore Today," Fischer, Albert B., *Baltimore Sun*, March 20, 1971.

98　**"Looking at my *waist*"**: Harrison, Miles, author interview.

98　**"called one of us that, the game changed"** . . . : Ibid.

98　**"extension of the civil rights movement"**: Ewell.

98　**22 goals and 16 assists for 38 points**: "Lacrosse Scoring, State Scoring Leaders," *Baltimore Sun*, May 17, 1971.

99　**"Ultimate Affirmative Action Bowl"**: Harrison and Silverman, *Ten Bears*, 153.

99　**"'Spics, Tonto and Crazy Horse'"**: Ibid.

99　**"He's a superman"**: "Jackson Five (Not Rock Group) Spurs Morgan Stick Team," Klingaman, Mike, *Evening Sun*, March 30, 1972.

99　**on March 8, 1975** . . . : "Bear Ten Upends Generals in Opener," *Baltimore Sun*, March 9, 1975.

99　**stopped 25 shots**: Ibid.

99　**"That was no upset or fluke"**: Harrison and Silverman, 230.

100　**distracted by the Atlantic Coast Conference**: "Morgan Ready To Join Top 10 Of Lacrosse," Hersh, *Evening Sun*, March 18, 1975.

100　**"tooting my horn"**: Sherwood, Chuck, author interview, July 14, 2021.

100　**"See, you guys?"**: Ibid.

100　**"We proved," Silverman said**: *The Morgan Lacrosse Story*, David, Luke, Maryland Public Television, September 7, 2021.

100　**"In a four-block radius"**: Carter, Lloyd, author interview, December 7, 2021.

100　**"never placed in front of us"**: Ibid.

101　**most of his $1,500 salary**: Hersh, *Evening Sun*, March 18, 1975.

101　**game-winner 90 seconds into overtime**: "Morgan Ten Edges Irish," *Baltimore Sun*, March 21, 1981.

101　**Loyola beat the Bears that day, 25–8**: "Men's Lacrosse History vs. Morgan State University from April 24, 1971-May 6, 1981," Loyola Athletics, http://loyolagreyhounds .com/sports/mens-lacrosse/opponent-history/morgan-state-university/296.

102　**"You always run into another player"**: Brown, Donnie, author interview.

102   **erroneously, as revealed decades later**: "After 36 Years in Prison For 'Georgetown Jacket' Murder, 3 Men Are Exonerated At Last," Wamsley, Laurel, *NPR*, November 26, 2019.

102   **King convinced school volunteer Earl Banks**: "Lacrosse to La Rescue," Bishop, Morin, *Sports Illustrated*, June 1, 1987.

103   **an average of 800 fans**: "Unusual Pursuit Bears Fruit in Harlem Park," Preston, Mike, *Baltimore Sun*, April 14, 1987, 1D, 6D.

103   **"Indians and preppies"**: Stenersen, Steve, author interview, January 19, 2018.

103   **applied for a $134,000 grant**: "Lacrosse Spurs Inner-City Youths onto Goals," Bomster, Mark, *Baltimore Sun*, November 29, 1992.

103   **all-Black midfield, the "Soul Patrol"**: "Blaxers Blog: The Inside Story of Hobart's Historic 'Soul Patrol,'" *US Lacrosse Magazine*, November 20, 2020, http://www.usalacrosse .com/magazine/blaxers-blog-inside-story-hobarts-historic-soul-patrol.

103   **"old guard, the 'Lords of Lacrosse'"**: Preston, "Lacrosse's Changing Face," May 19, 1993.

104   ***"and be that horrible"***: Brown, Donnie, author interview.

104   **cover, in 1978, of the NCAA lacrosse guide**: "Lombard Wins Middle School Title, 11-1 Hall of Fame Classic," Brown, Doug, *Baltimore Sun*, June 18, 1993.

104   **"answering the prayer that I prayed"**: Brown, Donnie, author interview.

104   **Carter reconnected with old Morgan teammates**: "Like Father, Like Son," Satterfield, Lem, *Baltimore Sun*, May 31, 2006, 4Z.

104   **Hero's lacrosse league**: Carter, author interview, December 7, 2021.

105   **"He had everything"**: Ibid.

105   **Medlin as "little-noticed"**: "Medlin Gets 3 goals in Losing Effort," Frainie, Mike, *Baltimore Sun*, June 4, 2001.

105   **"They just ignored him"**: Carter, author interview.

105   **Blax Lax, Inc.**: Ibid.

106   **"kids weren't getting recruited"**: Ibid.

106   **"My dad played lacrosse"**: Harrison, Kyle, author interview, August 8, 2019.

106   **"Big poster of him wearing"**: Ibid.

106   **"larosse was my worst sport"**: Ibid.

106   **"wearing And1 basketball shorts"**: Ibid.

107   **"lacrosse seems the best sport available"**: Ibid.

107   **"I was just super lucky"**: Ibid.

107   **"You know the answer"**: Harrison, Miles, author interview, July 13, 2019.

107   **"That's so uncomfortable"**: Harrison, Kyle, author interview, August 8, 2019.

108   **"should've worn that number there"**: Harrison, Kyle, author interview, December 15, 2023.

108   **Blue Jays went 55–6 and never lost at home**: Johns Hopkins men's lacrosse schedule/ results, 2002–2005, http://hopkinssports.com/sports/mens-lacrosse/schedule.

109   **"icebreaker, or the game winner"**: Rabil, Paul, author interview, July 21, 2018.

109   **"12 of them standing there"**: Harrison, Kyle, author interview, August 8, 2019.

109   **2005 NCAA semifinals**: "In the Seats and on the Field, Lacrosse Finds New Faithful," Thamel, *New York Times*, May 26, 2005, Section D, 7.

110   **The triumph completed**: "Johns Hopkins Wins First Lax Title in 18 years," *Associated Press*, May 30, 2005.

110   **celebration barbeque at the Chesapeake Bay home**: Harrison, Miles, author interview.

110   **"make you an honorary Blue Jay"**: Ibid.

110   **for him was a framed montage**: Ibid.

111   **would end being a career-long deal**: "Kyle Harrison '01," friendsbalt, YouTube, May 21, 2020, http://www.youtube.com/watch?v=8GCzmqcrZIE.

111   **Beats Electronics customized headphones**: "Kyle Harrison Custom Dr. Dre Beats Headphones," Rabidou, Ryan, *Inside Lacrosse*, August 6, 2013, http://www.insidelacrosse .com/article/kyle-Harrison-custom-dr-dre-beats-headphones/12143.

111   **he was, indeed, "super-lucky"**: Harrison, Kyle, author interview.

112   **majority-Black town of Norview**: Woodson, Chazz, author interview, June 24, 2020.

112   **"I got some odd looks"**: Ibid.

112   **"how many other outliers"**: Ibid.

112   **accepted as insiders**: Opie, Fred, author interview, November 17, 2020.

113   **"make a choice at that moment"**: Woodson, Chazz, author interview.

113   **". . . all standing there. They heard it"**: Ibid.

114   **"It's important for two reasons"**: Sherwood, Chuck, author interview, May 14, 2006.

114   **"Social Disaster"**: "What Does a Social Disaster Sound Like?," *Duke Chronicle*, April 6, 2006, http://today.duke.edu/showcase/mmedia/pdf/socialdisasterad.pdf.

114   PLEASE COME FORWARD: "The Damage Done," Price, S.L. and Evans, Farrell, *Sports Illustrated*, June 26, 2006, 76.

114   **"a great sense of 'Screw you'**: Wood, Peter, author interview, Spring 2006.

114   **sure the writer**: Ibid; "Big Men On Campus," Boyer, Peter J., *New Yorker*, August 27, 2006.

115   **"Entitlement is at the heart"**: "Lacrosse Afflicted by Sense of Entitlement," Steele, David, *Baltimore Sun*, March 30, 2006.

115   **"most vile players in his depiction"**: "Lacrosse Team Out of Control," Sheehan, Ruth, *News and Observer* (NC), April 3, 2006, B1.

115   **"entitlement and lack of accountability"**: "Blue Wall of Silence," Wolff, Alexander, *Sports Illustrated*, April 10, 2006.

115   **"new definition of the word 'teamwork'"**: "Wrong Time for Team Unity at Duke," Brennan, Christine, *USA Today*, March 29, 2006.

115   **"privileged players of fine pedigree"**: "When Peer Pressure, Not a Conscience, Is Your Guide," Roberts, Selena, *New York Times*, March 31, 2006.

116   **"bunch of lacrosse players raping a Black girl"**: "Duke Lacrosse Investigation Focus Of Durham DA Candidate Debate," WRAL News, April 12, 2006, http://www.wral .com/story/156778/.

116   **"Are these teammates racist?"**: Sherwood, Devon D., author interview, July 10, 2021.

116   **his time playing at Long Island's Baldwin High**: Sherwood, Devon D. *Give Me A Sporting Chance: Accessibility To Sport: African Americans And The Game of Lacrosse*, Master of Arts in the Liberal Studies Program, Graduate School of Duke University, 2011, 7.

116   *but they let me be me*: Sherwood, Devon D., author interview.

116   *dressed differently; this was the hip-hop era*: Ibid.

117   **thanking a Black dancer's "grandpa for my fine cotton shirt"**: Wolff.

117   **"an absolute shame" to abolish**: Sherwood, Chuck, author interview.

117   **Fifteen years later, he still didn't know**: Sherwood, Devon D., author interview.

III. Wiggle, Please

118 **innocent—not merely, "not guilty"**: "Charges Dropped In Duke Case; Players Are Pronounced Innocent," *Associated Press*, April 12, 2007, http://goduke.com/news/2007 /4/12/860161.aspx.

118 **Nifong a "rogue prosecutor"**: Ibid.

118 **career detoured to Division II Bryant College**: "Former Duke lacrosse coach Pressler hired by Bryant," *Associated Press*, August 6, 2006.

119 **"As seniors, they were simply the best"**: "The Boy Wonders of Lacrosse," Thamel, Pete, *New York Times*, June 3, 2007.

119 **"I'm thinking we'll be fine"**: Bratton, Shamel, author interview, September 6, 2019.

120 **"Best Recruiting Class Ever?"**: *Inside Lacrosse* 10, no. 7 (2007).

120 **"In the end"**: "Dazzling Duo," Czapnik, Dana, *Inside Lacrosse* 10, no. 7 (2007).

120 **"You want a can't-miss story?"**: Ibid.

120 **"a very heavy threat of violence"**: Bratton, author interview.

120 **at a June birthday party**: Ibid; Thamel, *New York Times*, June 3, 2007.

121 **in 1994 to John Christmas and Will Barrow**: "A Milestone for Diversity within Lacrosse," Weaver, John, *Baltimore Sun*, March 24, 2008.

121 **Hofstra . . . 2004 Empire Challenge**: "Locals Display Talents in Empire Challenge," Bessen, Jeffrey, *Suffolk County News* (NY), July 8, 2004; "Most Valuable Player, Timothy M. O'Brien MVP Award," Empire Challenge, Boomer Esiason Foundation, http://www .empirechallenge.com/most-valuable-player.

121 **football drills in UVa lax shorts**: Bratton, Shamel, author interview.

121 **"chance to be great"**: Harrison, Kyle, author interview, August 8, 2019.

121 **"thing after thing was happening"**: Ibid.

122 **first all-Black offensive midfield**: Weaver.

122 **"There's major significance here"**: Ibid.

122 **South American-born**: Barrow, George, author interview, June 11, 2021.

123 **steering him toward the riches**: Ibid.

123 **"Dad, you know nothing about lacrosse"**: Ibid.

123 **He seemed content**: Ibid.

123 **14–4**: "2007–08 Men's Lacrosse Schedule," University of Virginia Athletics, http:// virginiasports.com/sports/mlax/schedule/season/2007-08/.

123 **"really humble, like my wife"**: Barrow, author interview.

124 **"What can I do for you?"**: Bratton, Shamel, author interview.

124 **Starsia famously made "connections"**: Starsia, Dom, author interview, November 11, 2019.

124 **intellectually disabled twin daughters**: "Coach Unifies Job, Family," *Daily Press* (VA), May 28, 1994, https://www.dailypress.com/1994/05/28/coach-unifies -job-family/.

124 **"little bit standoffish"**: Starsia, Dom, author interview.

124 **"volatile relationship" that flared**: Ibid.

124 **"may not love her as much"**: Ibid.

124 **"happy guy"**: Bratton, Shamel, author interview.

124 **"Will was fine, his regular self"**: "Milestone, Life Lessons Move Starsia," Clemmons, Anna Katherine, *ESPN.com*, March 2, 2010.

124 **"spoke by cellphone around 12:30 p.m."**: Barrow, author interview.

124   "come down and talk to the professor?": Ibid.

125   "what time": Bratton, Shamel, author interview.

125   "Will's gone": Ibid.

125   Later that evening, sometime around 8 p.m.: Barrow, author interview.

125   found dead in his apartment: "Lacrosse Star Barrow's Death Stuns U.Va.," *Richmond Times-Dispatch* (VA), November 25, 2008; "Lacrosse Player's Memory Lives On Through Record-Breaking Fundraiser," Reid, Whitelaw, University of Virginia, December 2, 2021.

126   had a titanic argument: Starsia, author interview.

126   "I guess it was a tough night": Barrow, author interview.

126   "some kind of relationship thing": Bratton, Shamel, author interview.

126   "irrelevant data point": Barrow, author interview.

126   As far as he knows, Will: Ibid.

126   "I'm unique in how I deal": Ibid.

126   CDC reported 36,035 suicides: "Suicide Data and Statistics," CDC Suicide Prevention, htts://www.cdc.gov/suicide/facts/data.html.

126   third-leading cause among young people: "Suicide Data Page: 2008," McIntosh, John L., Ph.D., American Association of Suicidology, September 13, 2011.

127   "It's been . . . it's been great": Ibid.

127   participation was up 28.5 percent: "Lacrosse Scores as Participation Grows Over 100% in Past Decade," Ryan, Thomas J., SGB Media, June 24, 2009, http://sgbonline.com/lacrosse-scores-as-participation-grows-over-100-percent-in-past-decade/.

127   Patriots coach Bill Belichick: "Belichick Charged to See Lacrosse Tourney," Mchugh, Eric, *Patriot Ledger* (MA), May 22, 2008.

128   Headline: "The dream": "The dream (or fantasy) of black lacrosse," Cortes, Ryan, Shroff, Anish, *The Undefeated*, May 26, 2016.

128   mother . . . segregated Mississippi: Miller, Jovan, author interview, September 29, 2020.

128   "I was really confused": Ibid.

128   fan yelling . . . ejected: Ibid.

128   first Black All-American since Jim Brown: "Syracuse Lacrosse Player Jovan Miller Joins Jim Brown in an Exclusive Orange Club of Two," Rahme, Dave, *Post-Standard* (NY), June 17, 2010.

128   "never go to Syracuse. Ever": Miller, author interview.

129   joked that he should dress up as "Radio": Ibid.

129   threatened to "put my hands": Ibid.

129   "Whatever, dude" was the reply: Ibid.

129   "Never got an apology": Ibid.

129   being "that one little dot": Ibid.

130   "Yes: syracuse is still across our chest": Ibid.

130   "Here's the number one thing": Kemp, Troy, author interview, January 20, 2018.

130   *due to the dominating numbers*: Sherwood, Devon D., *Give Me a Sporting Chance*, 50.

130   only Hampton University had a Black head coach: "NCAA Demographics Database"; "Chazz Woodson, Men's Lacrosse," Hampton University Athletics, http://hamptonpirates.com/sports/mens-lacrosse/roster/coaches/chazz-woodson/1483.

130   five had Black coaches: "NCAA Demographics Database."

131   years . . . at Syracuse "a nightmare": Cortes and Shroff.

131   used the term "colored": "As Lacrosse Grows, the Diversity of Players Remains Largely Unchanged," Cohen, Michael, *New York Times*, May 24, 2013.

131   Jenkins asked for an apology: Ibid.

131   brushed off his request: "Inside the Lack of Racial Diversity in Lacrosse," Liberman, Matt, *Daily Orange* (NY), April 22, 2019.

131   that he apologized, "right away": Ibid.

131   "wrong" and "inappropriate" . . . "I meant it in a good way": Cohen.

131   "I am sometimes myself confused": Ibid.

131   as the sport's "angry Black man": Miller, author interview.

132   say, 'Ah we're just being edgy'": Gross, David, author interview, July 27, 2021.

132   "expect to be Kaepernick, 10 years before": Miller, author interview.

132   tweet: "be offended": Miller, Jovan (@jovination23), Twitter (now X), October 25, 2013.

132   "I'm not going to knock anybody": Miller, Jovan, author interview.

133   "I came to the decision": Woodson, Chazz, Facebook, October 26, 2012, http://www .facebook.com/OfficialChazz/posts/497422713610285.

133   Miller offered to give away: "Black Lacrosse Player Boycotts Equipment Company Over 'Ninja, Please' Slogan, Threatens To Retire," Gartland, Dan, *Deadspin*, November 8, 2012, http://deadspin.com/black-lacrosse-player-boycotts-equipment-company -over-5958909/.

133   "you've got to be realistic": Gross, author interview.

134   apologizing to "anyone who was offended": "When Marketing Goes Awry: #NinjaPlease," Wilson, Connor, *Lacrosse All Stars*, November 9, 2012, http://laxallstars .com/when-marketing-goes-awry-ninjaplease/.

134   agreed to return: "Miller Ends Boycott, Plans Return to MLL in 2013," DaSilva, Matt, *LaxMagazine.com*, December 5, 2012.

134   "had to work through that": Miller, author interview.

134   "'think about playing in another league'": Miller, author interview.

135   coach Mike Cerino over his play: Gross, author interview.

135   Cerino agreed, saying: Cerino, Mike, author interview, September 16, 2021.

135   "White-balled": Miller, author interview.

135   "make sure these actions are not repeated": Ibid.

135   Washington, DC's, Wilson High: "College Lacrosse is 86 Percent White. This High School Team Is Showing What Diversity Could Do for the Sport," Dougherty, Jesse, *Washington Post*, April 18, 2017.

135   introduced to the game: Stallworth, Thomas, author interview, January 20, 2018.

135   "play with this . . . *nervousness*": Ibid.

136   "flight school: *huge* culture shock": Ibid.

136   "challenge you to name five": Ibid.

136   "What if we put 'em all on the same team?": Ibid.

136   launched the Sankofa: "Woodson, Harrison Launch Sankofa Lacrosse For Brown, England Scrimmages," Brown University Athletics, October 8, 2013, http://brownbears .com/news/2013/10/8/10_8_2013_3568.

137   Hampton University announced: "Breaking: Hampton to Add Men's Lacrosse for 2016," Foy, Terry, *Inside Lacrosse*, May 5, 2015, https://www.insidelacrosse.com/article /breaking-hampton-to-add-men-s-lacrosse-for-2016/31989.

137   "chiefed up": Carter, author interview, December 7, 2021.

137   **written a proposal to the Hampton administration**: "Hampton Lacrosse: It's Real," McLaughlin, Corey, *Lacrosse Magazine*, October 2015.

137   **No one knew that he had an enlarged heart**: Ibid.

137   **Carter could hear Verina Crawford crying**: Carter, author interview.

138   **"Ms. Crawford, you believe in God?"**: Ibid.

138   **general interest meeting at Hampton**: Ibid.

138   **Fifty students attended**: McLaughlin.

138   **"And you're the coach"**: Carter, author interview.

139   **Hampton lacrosse had zero scholarship money**: Ibid.

139   **"I would just say, 'Thank you, Jesus'"**: Ibid.

139   **ESPN came to town**: "How a History-Making Lacrosse Team Is Challenging a Sport's Lily-White Image," Graham, Latria, *Guardian*, April 22, 2016.

139   **Harvey agreed**: Carter, author interview.

139   **"Well, where's the Disney movie?"**: Ibid.

139   **"changing the way the game looks"**: Stallworth, author interview.

140   **No more than 75 percent**: Ibid.

140   **"believe lacrosse really should look like"**: Woodson, author interview, September 29, 2020.

140   **"a team of *Me*'s"**: Harrison, Kyle, author interview, August 8, 2019.

140   **looser, a bit "angry"**: Ibid.

140   **what Troy Kemp calls "wiggle"**: Kemp, author interview.

140   **"Fast-paced, athletic"**: Harrison, Kyle, author interview.

140   **only part of the mission**: "Inspiring Diversity Through Elite Level Lacrosse," Nation United Lacrosse, http://nationunitedlc.com/#faqs.

141   **"We came for the same thing"**: Kemp, author interview.

141   **named president of Charm City Youth Lacrosse**: "Transition Game," McLaughlin, Corey, *Baltimore*, March 2019.

141   **a new travel team, "Charm Nation"**: Ibid.

141   **in 2023, Harvard grad**: "Isaiah Dawson: Investment Banking Analyst at Morgan Stanley," LinkedIn, August 28, 2024, https://www.linkedin.com/in/isaiah-dawson-954388166/.

141   **"Incident Report" served as a database**: "Nation United Launches Virtual Portal to Gather, Catalog, Racist Incidents," *US Lacrosse*, November 11, 2020.

141   **"Our goal is to educate the ignorant"**: Stallworth, author interview.

142   **"That's what it takes: intent"**: Ibid.

142   **Haas got a bad feeling**: Haas, Andrew, author interview, March 23, 2021.

142   **"definitely" complained about being slurred**: Melero, Ernie, author interview, March 1, 2021; Haas, author interview.

142   **"Bermuda was horrid"**: Gonzales, Timothy, author interview, January 27, 2021.

143   **"never dealt with racism more"**: Ibid.

143   **"couldn't be more thankful"**: Ibid.

143   **"I have such a connection"**: Ibid.

Part 3

I. Jerusalem

148   **the last 24 hours**: "Rocket & Mortar Attacks Against Israel by Date (2001—Present)," Jewish Virtual Library, http://www.jewishvirtuallibrary.org/palestinian-rocket-and-mortar-attacks-against-israel.

148 **Ten Lost Tribes of Israel**: "Are the American Indians of Israelite Descent?," Jews for Judaism, http://jewsforjudaism.org/knowledge/articles/are-the-american-indians-of -israelite-descent.

149 **papal bull, the "Doctrine of Discovery"**: "The Doctrine of Discovery, 1493," The Gilder Lehrman Institute of American History, http://www.gilderlehrman.org/history -resources/spotlight-primary-source/doctrine-discovery-1493.

149 **By 1600, perhaps as many as 56 million**: Koch, Alexander, Brierley, Chris, Maslin, Mark M., Lewis, Simon L., "Earth System Impacts of the European Arrival and Great Dying in the Americas after 1492," *Quaternary Science Reviews*, 207, (March 1, 2019): 13–36.

149 **"We've got a lot of Christian Indians"**: Lyons, Oren, author interview, November 28, 2018.

149 **Newcomb and . . . Birgil Kills Straight**: "The 1493 Doctrine of Discovery: An Inter-view with Steven Newcomb, Shawnee/Lenape," Marsh, Amy Hadden, *Sopris Sun*, June 7, 2023.

149 **Longhouse faith codified**: Bonaparte.

150 **Deganawidah "the Peacemaker"**: "Peacemaker: I Come with Good Tidings from the Chief of the Sky," Great Spirit Mother, http://great-spirit-mother.org/_/peacemaker_i _come_with_good_tidings_from_the_chief_of_the_sky.htm.

150 **"Peacemaker's journey . . . part of our history"**: Thompson, Lyle, author interview, November 26, 2018.

151 **commemorating the Treaty of Canandaigua**: "Treaty of Canandaigua, 1794," Smith-sonian National Museum of the American Indian, transcript: originally published in *Indian Affairs: Laws and Treaties*, Kappler, Charles J., 1904, digitized by Oklahoma State University; National Archives.

151 **lawn of the Ontario County Courthouse**: "Commemoration of the Canandaigua Treaty," Ganondagan State Historic Site, http://www.ganondagan.org/canandaigua -treaty-commemoration.

151 **"significant today"**: Oberg, Michael, author interview, June 3, 2020.

151 **Seneca lands at the Treaty of Big Tree**: Oberg, Michael. *Peacemakers: The Iroquois, the United States and the Treaty of Canandaigua, 1794* (New York, Oxford: Oxford University Press, 2016), 142.

151 **controls 7,300 acres**: "FAQ," Onondaga Nation, http://www.onondaganation.org/land -rights/faq/.

151 **acres had been reduced to 32**: Hauptman, Laurence M. *The Iroquois In The Civil War: From Battlefield to Reservation* (New York: Syracuse University Press, 1993), 148–149.

152 **"pretty faithless"**: Oberg, author interview.

152 **violated or broken some 368 treaties**: Kappler, Charles J. *Indian Affairs: Laws and Trea-ties, Vol. I* (Washington: Government Printing Office, 1904), Compiled December 1, 1902; DeLoria, Jr., Vine. *Behind the Trail of Broken Treaties: An Indian Declaration of Independence* (University of Texas Press, 2010); "Native Rights Are Human Rights," Zotigh, Dennis, *Smithsonian Voices, National Museum of the American Indian*, December 9, 2021.

152 **build Pennsylvania's Kinzua Dam**: "Dam-Building and Treaty-Breaking: The Kinzua Dam Controversy, 1953–1958," Rosier, Paul A., *Pennsylvania Magazine of History and Biography*, October 1995; "Treaty of Canandaigua Remains a Powerful Symbol of Native Sovereignty," Whitefield, Autumn, *Indian Country Today*, July 22, 2011; "Kinzua Dam: 50 years of Flood Control, Memories," Myers, Valerie, *Erie Times-News* (PA), Septem-ber 13, 2015.

152 **"a contract based on shared interests"**: "Remarks to Commemorate the Canandaigua Treaty," Higginbottom, Heather, Deputy Secretary of State for Management and Resources, Washington, D.C., February 22, 2016.

152 **George Washington Covenant Belt**: "George Washington Belt," Onondaga Nation, http://www.onondaganation.org/culture/wampum/george-washington-belt/; "Canandaigua Treaty Belt," Wampum Belt Archive, http://www.wampumbear.com/W _Canandaigua%20Treaty%20Belt.html.

152 **together holding the belt**: "222nd Annual Canandaigua Treaty Ceremony," Schilling, Vincent, *Indian Country Today*, February 25, 2016.

152 **handed thick folds of white muslin**: Higginbottom, Heather, author interview, August 21, 2019.

152 **US will pay out, "yearly forever"**: Smithsonian National Museum of the American Indian; National Archives.

152 **payout evolved into its present form**: Bouchard, Kimberly A. "Treaty Cloth of the Six Nation of New York," Freedom of Information Act request response, United States Department of the Interior, Bureau of Indian Affairs, Eastern Regional Office, September 4, 2019.

153 **in the form of medium-grade muslin**: Ibid.

153 **Seneca allotment ended up about three feet long**: Jemison, G. Peter, author interview, November 9, 2020.

153 **"It comes in a truck"**: Lyons, Oren, author interview.

153 **transfer the $1,800**: "Fund Distribution Process," U.S. Department of the Interior, Indian Affairs, http://www.bia.gov/sites/default/files/dup/assets/as-ia/obpm/2-OTS%20 -%20Settlements%20-%20Claims%20and%20Treaty%20Obligations.pdf.

153 **BIA's Eastern regional office—now in Nashville**: "BIA Eastern Office to Move to Nashville," Adams, Jim, *Indian Country Today*, September 12, 2018.

153 **"my one yard, allotted to me"**: Jemison, author interview.

153 **"domestic dependent nations"**: *Cherokee Nation v. Georgia*, 30 U.S. (5 Pet.) 1 (1831), Library of Congress, March 18, 1831.

154 **"It's about implementing our sovereignty"**: Lyons, Rex, author interview, November 19, 2020.

154 **"coming through on treaty promises"**: Thiele, Raina, author interview, August 25, 2021.

154 **"The inherent right of self-government"**: "Aboriginal Lands Claims Defy Timely Resolution," WikiLeaks, unclassified cable, August 21, 2009, http://wikileaks.org/plusd /cables/09OTTAWA643_a.html; "Canada, Natives Locked in Uneasy Dance over Self-Governance," Carlson, Kathryn Blaze, *National Post*, July 24, 2011.

155 **By 2021, the Black Hills settlement**: "The Battle for the Black Hills," Estes, Nick, *High Country News*, January 1, 2021.

155 **"Power concedes nothing without a demand"**: Douglass, Frederick, "West India Emancipation Speech," Canandaigua, New York, August 3, 1857, University of Rochester Frederick Douglass Project, http://rbscp.lib.rochester.edu/4398.

155 **"the size of a postage stamp"** . . . : Jemison, author interview.

155 **Whitney Museum of American Art**: Ibid; "Artists: G. Peter Jemison, 1945—," Whitney Museum of Art, http://whitney.org/artists/18539.

155 **Mohawk artist Carla Goodleaf Hemlock**: "Treaty Cloth Shirt," National Museum of the American Indian, http://americanindian.si.edu/collections-search/object/NMAI _408047; "Hemlock's Treaty Cloth Shirt Gets New Home in Smithsonian," Goodleaf,

Terence, *Kahnawake News*, 2013, http://kahnawakenews.com/hemlocks-treaty-cloth
-shirt-gets-new-home-at-smithsonian-p1608-1.htm.

156 **"We got one back, baby!"**: Jemison, Ansley, author interview, July 16, 2018.

156 **got married**: Jemison, Ansley, author interview, November 11, 2020.

156 **"Dish with One Spoon"**: "Peace Between Nations," *A Treaty Guide for Torontonians*,
http://talkingtreaties.ca/treaties-for-torontonians/dish-with-one-spoon/peace-between
-nations.

156 **"cradle of three major religions"**: Jemison, Ansley, author interview, November 11,
2020.

157 **glitzy opening on June 20**: "Kraft Family Sports Campus Opens in Jerusalem," Sturm,
Uriel, *Jerusalem Post*, June 20, 2017.

157 **welcoming words to a crowd**: "Inaugurating new fields, Patriots' Kraft Puts Jerusalem
football in End Zone," Steinberg, Jessica, *Times of Israel*, June 20, 2017.

157 **the site of Deir Yassin**: "Palestinian Pasts in the Present," Davis, Rochelle, *CCAS
Newsmagazine*, Center for Contemporary Arab Studies, Georgetown University, June 6,
2024, https://ccas.georgetown.edu/2024/06/06/palestinian-pasts-in-the-present/.

157 **"The fields bring people from all tribes"**: Steinberg.

158 **beacon of anti-violence and anti-racism**: "Fan Owned Hapoel Katamon Look for
Tolerance in Fractious Jerusalem," *AFP*, April 9, 2018.

158 **The Iroquois Nationals lined up**: "Iroquois Nationals Visited Jerusalem to Do a
Lacrosse Coexistence Practice . . .," ndnsports.com, July 17, 2018, http://www.facebook
.com/watch/?v=1734837726623547.

158 **"come together as a group"**: Ibid.

158 **"eating from the same dish"**: Ibid.

158 **"Our women are very important"**: Ibid.

158 **Near the end of his eight-minute talk**: Ibid.

159 **"The most important thing"**: Ibid.

159 **"Left to our own devices"**: Lyons, Oren, author interview, January 17, 2010.

160 **"We should have offered them Manhattan"**: "Tradition Failed the Iroquois In a
Lacrosse Skirmish With the Champs," Lidz, Franz, *Sports Illustrated*, July 25, 1983.

160 **"we get our land back, right?"** *Spirit Game: Pride of a Nation* (One Bowl Productions,
2017).

160 **battle his evil twin, Sawiskera**: White, Louellyn. *Free to Be Mohawk: Indigenous Education at the Akwesasne Freedom School* (University of Oklahoma Press, 2015), 29.

160 **showdown between Animals and Birds**: Calder, Jim, Fletcher, Ron. *Lacrosse: The
Ancient Game* (Toronto: Ancient Game Press, 2011), 31.

160 **"The Animals are the bear, the deer"**: Jamieson, Sid, US Lacrosse National Convention, Baltimore, Maryland, January 20, 2018.

161 **"tupperware"**: Lyons, Oren, author interview, January 17, 2010.

160 **"The Great Tree of Peace"**: "Oren Lyons the Faithkeeper," interview by Moyers, Bill,
July 3, 1991, American Archive of Public Broadcasting, http://americanarchive.org
/catalog/cpb-aacip-754a309a31f.

162 **Edmund Wilson gained access**: "Apologies To The Iroquois," Wilson, Edmund, *New
Yorker*, October 9, 1959.

162 **"It's not even your real business"**: Lyons, Oren, author interview, November 19,
2020.

162 **"Is this not worthy of compassion?"**: Thwaites, Reuben Gold. *The Jesuit Relations
and Allied Documents: Travels and Exploration of the Jesuit Missionaries in New France*,

1610–1791 (Cleveland: The Burrows Brothers Company, 1897), 185, originally published by de Brebeuf, Jean, in *Le Jeune's Relation of 1636*.

163 **On June 4, 1763**: The date of the Attack at Michilimackinac is disputed. Contemporaneous accounts say June 4, 1763; modern accounts say June 2 of the same year.

163 **King George III's birthday**: Vennum, Thomas, *American Indian Lacrosse: Little Brother of War* (Baltimore: Johns Hopkins University Press, 2008), 93.

163 **flying through the fort's open gates . . .**: Armour, David A., *Attack At Michilimackinac 1763: Alexander Henry's Travels and Adventures in Canada and the Indian Territories between the years 1760 and 1764* (Mackinac Island, Michigan: Mackinac State Historic Parks, 1971), 57; Vennum, 95.

163 **"Nothing could be less liable"**: Armour.

163 **"carried us into the woods"**: "Etherington, Entrenched in Mackinaw," Harburn, Todd E. *Essence of Emmet: A Four-Part Historical Series about Emmet County, Michigan.* Mackinac State Historic Parks, 19, http://www.emmetcounty.org/wp-content/uploads/2022/04/EssenceOfEmmetPart1.pdf.

163 **tomahawks**: Vennum, 101.

163 **"a crowd of Indians within the fort"**: Armour.

164 **"hatchets hid"**: Harburn; Beers, 74.

164 **major part of the sport's white narrative**: Fisher, Donald M.,*Lacrosse: A History of the Game* (Baltimore: Johns Hopkins University Press, 2002), 1.

164 **falsely retailed to the British public as a victory**: Wood, J.G, *The Modern Playmate* (London: Frederick Warne and Co., 1870), 76.

164 **Cherokee played a two-stick version**: Vennum, pgs. 39–41, 76; Beers, 12.

164 **Great Lakes games featured**: Vennum, 79–81, 321–24.

164 **Haudenosaunee in the northeastern woodlands**: Vennum, pgs. 69, 79, 80–82, 324–27.

164 **hence the city of La Crosse, Wisconsin**: "Historical Essay: La Crosse, Wisconsin, Origin of La Crosse, Wisconsin," Wisconsin Historical Society, http://www.wisconsinhistory.org/Records/Article/CS9524.

164 **Eastern Algonquins somewhere between**: Fisher, 18.

164 **"Right here," he said**: Lyons, Oren, author interview, November 28, 2018.

165 **"crib sticks"**: Lyons, Rex, author interview, November 19, 2020.

165 **and the confederacy broken**: "Big Idea 5: Native American Soldiers and Scouts," Museum of the American Revolution, http://www.amrevmuseum.org/big-idea-5-native-american-soldiers-and-scouts.

165 **"total destruction and devastation"**: "General George Washington's Original Orders to General James Clinton Assigning Him to Help Lead the Sullivan Expedition Against the Iroquois," May 24, 1779, Raab Collection, http://www.raabcollection.com/presidential-autographs/washington-iroquois.

165 **On April 21**: Egly Jr., T.W., *History of the First New York Regiment 1775–1783* (Portsmouth, New Hampshire: Peter E. Randall, 1981); "List of Revolutionary War Battles for 1779," American Revolutionary War, http://revolutionarywar.us/year-1779/.

166 **Without consulting or even mentioning**: Jasanoff, Maya, *Liberty's Exiles: American Loyalists in the Revolutionary World* (New York: Vintage Books, Random House, 2011), 189–198.

166 **led by war chief Joseph Brant**: Jasanoff, 16, 189–198.

166 **Fort Stanwix in 1784**: Jasanoff, 193; Samuel Kirkland Papers, Hamilton and Kirkland College, Burke Library, http://wardepartmentpapers.org/s/home/item/37042.

166 **Fort Harmer in 1789**: Transcribed Treaties and Conventions Advised and Ratified by the Senate. (RG46) (M200, roll 2), National Archives, http://wardepartmentpapers.org /s/home/item/39742.

166 **By 1829, the number of Native Americans:** "Removal of the Indians," Cass, Lewis, *North American Review*, January 1830, pgs. 62–64; http://www.teachushistory.org /indian-removal/resources/indian-populations-1830.

166 **"I have met the last of the Iroquois"**: de Tocqueville, Alexis. *Democracy in America* (London: Saunders and Otley, 1835–1840).

166 **Jackson signed . . . Indian Removal Act**: "President Andrew Jackson's Message to Congress 'On Indian Removal,' December 6, 1830, National Archives, http:// www.archives.gov/milestone-documents/jacksons-message-to-congress-on-indian -removal.

166 **"the intelligence, the industry, the moral habits"**: "December 3, 1833: Fifth Annual Message to Congress," UVA Miller Center, http://millercenter.org/the-presidency /presidential-speeches/december-3-1833-fifth-annual-message-congress.

167 **Oneida began emigrating to Wisconsin**: "Oneida History: Life in New York," Milwaukee Public Museum, http://www.mpm.edu/content/wirp/ICW-156.

II. The Whaleness of the White

168 **19-year-old lacrosse goalie named W. George Beers**: Beers, W. George, *Lacrosse: The National Game of Canada* (New York: W.A. Townsend & Adams, 1869), preface, xi.

168 **the eye of the Prince of Wales**: Cornwallis, Kinahan. *Royalty In the New World: Prince of Wales in America* (New York: M. Doolady, 1860), 97–99; Beers, x, 135, 222.

168 **"determined and excited"**: Beers, x-xi.

168 **"Grand Display of Indian Games"**: Morrow, Don. *A Concise History of Sports in Canada* (Toronto: Oxford University Press, 1989), 47; Fisher, 25.

168 **first game against whites in 1844**: "Timeline of the Indigenous History of Lacrosse," *Canadian Press*, March 13, 2021.

169 **Beers wrote up a foundational pamphlet**: *The Game of Lacrosse* (Montreal: M. Longmore Co., 1860); *Montreal Gazette*, September 15, 1860; "The Process of Evolution of Competitive Sport: A Study of Senior Lacrosse in Canada, 1844 to 1914," Burr, Christina A. (master's thesis, University of Western Ontario, 1986), Appendix A: 255; "Beers, William George," West, J. Thomas. *Dictionary of Canadian Biography*, Vol. 12, University of Toronto: Universite Laval, 2003, https://www.biographi.ca/en/bio/beers _william_george_12E.html; "Lacrosse," Adamski, Barbara K., Marshall, Tabitha, *The Canadian Encyclopedia*; August 7, 2013, Fisher, 25.

169 **"We are British Indians"**: Phillips, Alan. *The Living Legend: The Story Of the Royal Canadian Mounted Police* (Boston, Toronto: Little, Brown and Company, 1954–55), 298.

169 **"ever trusted"**: Utley, Robert M. *The Last Sovereigns: Sitting Bull and the Resistance of the Free Lakotas* (University of Nebraska Press, 2020).

169 **Sitting Bull and his people collided again**: Fisher, 23.

169 **"Indian, who plays mainly by instinct"**: Beers, vii.

169 **"sensible, thoroughly civilized people cannot"**: Beers, 55.

170 **"gentle savage turned to us"**: Beers, 205.

170 **"No Indian must play in a match for a white club"**: Beers, 254.

170 **"National Game of Canada"**: Fisher, 26.

170 **"paradoxical fascination with the "noble savage"**: Fisher, 27.

170 **July 1867**: Beauvais, Johnny. *Kahnawake: A Mohawk Look at Canada and Adventures of Big John Canadian* (Montreal: Techno Couleur, 1985); Beers, xiii; Downey, 56.

170 **"dressed in their blue and red drawers"**: Wood, 77.

170 **"Canadian Gentlemen Amateurs"**: Fisher, 30; Vennum, 269.

170 **"conduct "war dances" and wear "Indian" regalia**: Vennum, 268–269.

170 **"We hope you"**: Downey, 67; "Letters from W.G. Beers concerning Massiah's Appointment as Agent for Touring Teams—1876, Christopher William Massiah fonds, IM 29-C171, file I, Reference no. R7445-0-6-E, Library and Archives of Canada.

171 **"very pretty to watch"**: "The Lore of Lacrosse," Tobin, Suzanne, *Washington Post*, October 2, 1998; National Lacrosse Hall of Fame.

171 **1880 . . . :** Vennum, 271–276, 292.

171 **Canada barred the Iroquois**: Ibid; Downey, 42–54.

171 **"exterminate"**: "Report of the Secretary of the Interior, communicating, in compliance with a resolution of the Senate, a letter from the Commissioner of Indian Affairs, with copies of communications received from the agents of the department in California, in relation to debts contracted by them," Senate Executive Document No. 104, 32nd Congress, 1st Session, 1852; University of Oklahoma College of Law Digital Commons, http://digitalcommons.law.ou.edu/cgi/viewcontent.cgi?article=8384&context=indianserialset.

171 **"the only good Indians"**: "Theodore Roosevelt Timeline," Addressing the Statue exhibition, American Museum of Natural History, New York, http://www.amnh.org/exhibitions/addressing-the-statue/timeline.

172 **"Kill every buffalo you can!"**: Kappler, 980–988; Butler, Sir W.F. *Sir William Butler: An Autobiography* (London, Constable, Ltd., 1911), 97.

172 **great Sioux warrior Crazy Horse**: "George Kills in Sight Describes the Death of Indian Leaders Crazy Horse," *History Matters*, George Mason University, http://historymatters.gmu.edu/d/64.

172 **In 1879, Richard Henry Pratt opened**: "Past," The Carlisle Indian School Project, Conestoga, Pennsylvania, http://carlisleindianschoolproject.com/past/.

172 **"ethnocide"**: Lyons, Oren, author interview, April 3, 2019.

172 **The first Haudenosaunee passport**: "Six Nations Council Will Accept British Subjects as Arbitrators," *Ottawa Citizen*, January 8, 1923.

172 **In September he sailed to London**: "Returns Home After Trip to See The King," *Ottawa Journal*, September 3, 1921.

173 **Deskaheh traveled to Geneva**: "Iroquois Indian Chief in Geneva Colorful Figure," *Calgary Herald*, September 10, 1923.

173 **"figure of romance"**: Ibid.

173 **"heroic and pathetic reading"**: "Our London Correspondence," *Guardian* (London), August 8, 1923.

173 **returned home exhausted in early 1925**: "Four Chosen to Continue Indian Fight," *Democrat and Chronicle* (NY), August 17, 1925.

173 **his great-uncle Jesse Lyons**: "The Citizenship Act of 1924," Onondaga Nation, http://www.onondaganation.org/news/2018/the-citizenship-act-of-1924/; "Onondaga Chief Will Inaugurate Robinson Route," *Cornell Daily Sun* (NY), November 8, 1943.

173 **on March 5, 1930**: Lyons, Oren, author interview, January 17, 2010; "Oren Lyons," North American Indigenous Athletics Hall of Fame, http://www.naiahf.org/oren-lyons.

173 **He recalls a chief**: Lyons, Oren, author interview, January 17, 2010.

173 **reject it, overwhelmingly**: Philp, Kenneth. *Indian Self Rule: First-Hand Accounts of Indian-White Relations from Roosevelt to Reagan* (Utah State University Press, 1995); Hauptman, Laurence M. *The Iroquois and the New Deal* (Syracuse University Press: 1981), 57–61.

174 **"I started out in the field"**: Lyons, Oren, author interview, November 28, 2018.

174 **national magazine *MacLean's* wondered**: "Can Lacrosse Come Back?," Roxborough, Henry H., *MacLean's*, 1929; Wilson, Jason, Reid, Richard M. *Famous For a Time: Forgotten Giants of Canadian Sport* (Toronto: Dundurn Press, 2023).

174 **Westchester Polo Club staged games**: Fisher, 53–54.

174 **New York University and Manhattan College in 1877**: "Lacrosse," *Brooklyn Daily Eagle*, November 23, 1877, 3; "Lacrosse," *New York Daily Herald*, November 23, 1877, 5; "NYU Men's Lacrosse," New York University Men's Lacrosse Team, http://nyulacrosse.tripod.com/.

174 **teams formed at Princeton, Columbia, Yale**: Fisher, 66.

174 **John Flannery**: *New York Times*, August 24, 1878; Fisher, 55.

174 **Baltimore got its first taste**: *Baltimore Sun*, November 25, 1878, 1; Fisher, 72.

175 **first intercollegiate championship**: "Lacrosse History," Hall of Fame & Museum, USA Lacrosse, http://www.usalacrosse.com/lacrosse-history.

175 **Crescent Athletic Club of Brooklyn**: "The Epic Rise and Fall of Bay Ridge's Once Most-Important Institution," heyridge.com, April 21, 2017.

175 **Johns Hopkins played its first game**: Fisher, 73.

176 **"not in a class with the college twelves"**: "Hopkins Team Will Get Rest," *Baltimore Sun*, May 25, 1932.

176 **1932 elimination tournament**: USA Lacrosse.

176 **Syracuse coach Laurie D. Cox**: Fisher, 81, 170, 173–174.

176 **Onondaga star Clinton Pierce**: *Syracuse Daily Orange*, April 17, 1931, April 16, 1932.

176 **box lacrosse circuit in the summer of 1931**: Fisher, 157–158.

177 **Jay Silverheels, who played Tonto**: Fisher, 224.

177 **clubs sprung up**: Fisher, 223.

177 **manly proving ground . . . closer in spirit**: Fisher, 226; Downey, 167–174.

177 **"I was out of my element"**: Simmons Jr., Roy, author interview, April 24, 2020.

177 **"Every Sunday I went out there"**: Ibid.

178 **Mohawk Angus Thomas**: Lyons, Oren, author interview, January 17, 2010.

178 **"anxious to play him, test this guy out"**: Ibid.

178 **"Get out of my way, Lee!"**: Ibid.

178 **"You're going to be a good goalie"**: Ibid.

178 **3,000 feet up, his parachute failed**: Logue, Stenersen, Muller interview, November 27, 2020; "Oren Lyons: An Extraordinary Life," Burns, M.C., *Central New York Magazine*, January–February 2011, 51–52.

178 **Onondaga box team . . . three-year winning streak**: "At The Post," Lewis, Grace, *Post-Standard* (NY), June 22, 1954.

179 **"I was the second Indian to play at Syracuse"**: Lyons, Oren, author interview, January 17, 2010.

179 **fought for Simmons**: Ibid; "LSU and Syracuse Renew Old Boxing Rivalry in Sugar Bowl," *Town Talk* (LA), December 28, 1955, 8; "Louisiana State Boxers Defeat Syracuse, 6 to 2," *Democrat and Chronicle* (NY), December 29, 1955.

179 **"a legitimate C"**: Lyons, Oren, author interview.

179 **"little" Oren Lyons set up like a goalie"**: *Troy Record* (NY), May 12, 1956; *Lebanon Daily Times* (PA), May 9, 1957.

179 **"Just about long enough"**: Simmons, Jr., author interview.

179 **Lyons set a collegiate record with 274 saves**: "Nears Lacrosse Mark," *Philadelphia Inquirer* (PA), May 24, 1957.

179 **still stands**: Lyons made 274 saves in 13 games for Syracuse in 1956, a "collegiate record" at the time. Lyons' 21 saves per game average that season is higher than Paul Bishop's NCAA-era 19.2 average (307 saves in 16 games) in 1972, listed in Syracuse's men's lacrosse media guide as the program's individual record for saves in a season. "1956 Men's Lacrosse Schedule," Syracuse Athletics: http://cuse.com/sports/mens-lacrosse /schedule/1956; Syracuse 2023 Men's Lacrosse Media Guide, "Individual Records,"pg .102, http://cuse.com/documents/2023/2/13/2023_Men_s_Lacrosse_Media_Guide.pdf.

179 **him and Simmons Jr. as co-captains**: *Ithaca Journal* (NY), April 29, 1958.

179 **Lyons was named All-American**: "Chief Oren Lyons, Lacrosse, 1956–1958," Syracuse Athletics, http://cuse.com/sports/2006/9/26/lyonslaxbio.

179 **"the best I have ever coached"**: "Orange Lacrossers Face Army," *Post-Standard* (NY), May 18, 1957.

180 **"You must know who you are"**: "Oren Lyons—'We Are Part of the Earth,'" Sacred Land Film Project, October 10, 2011, http://www.youtube.com/watch?v=bSwmqZ272As; "The Value of a Single Leaf and the Oneness of All," Muse, Stephen, Holy Transfigura- tion Orthodox Church, January 2, 2022, https://orthodoxcolumbus.org/the-value-of-a -single-leaf-and-the-oneness-of-all/#_ftn1; Lyons, author interview.

180 **Norcross Greeting Card Company**: "Oren Lyons: Wisdom Keeper," Hope, Marjorie, Young, James in Whitefield, Freddie. *Visionaries: The 20th Century's 100 Most Important Inspirational Leaders* (White River Junction, Vermont: Chelsea Green Publishing Co., 2007), 165; Burns, M.C., 54.

180 **joking about his Native name**: "What's My Line?," CBS, February 14, 1960; Burns, 54.

180 **release, to his adoption**: Lyons, Oren, author interview, November 28, 2018; Burns, 57.

181 **"I was a runner for the nation"**: Lyons, Oren, author interview, May 22, 2023.

181 **American Indian Movement (AIM), begun in 1968**: "The American Indian Move- ment, 1968–1978," Abbott, Frankly, Digital Public Library of America, https://dp.la /primary-source-sets/the-american-indian-movement-1968-1978; "Occupation Of Alcatraz: 30-Year Anniversary of Indian coup," Fimrite, Peter, *San Francisco Chronicle*, November 19, 1999.

181 **Oren Lyons often in the thick of it**: There are some in the Six Nations who criti- cize Lyons for the instances, over the decades, when mostly white media sources have referred to him as an Onondaga "chief." Partly this is due to his public stature and partly because Lyons, at times, has tacitly allowed it. In 1971, when he appeared with Yoko Ono on the nationally syndicated "David Frost Show" to protest a highway expansion on Onondaga land, he was called "Chief Lion" in TV listings and by Ono on stage. In 1987, as the first witness in a Congressional select committee hearing celebrating the Iroquois Confederacy, Lyons was introduced by Senator Daniel Inouye as "Chief of the Onondaga Nation" and thanked at the close of his testimony as "Chief Lyons." When I first met him, in 2010, Lyons introduced himself as "Faithkeeper," but, when asked if he was a chief, said, "Yeah, we're chiefs," and explained that faithkeepers are essentially "sub-chiefs." In the years since, though, he consistently described himself as a faithkeeper and runner. His clearest explanation came in 2023: "Faithkeeper is a partner to the chief, who doesn't work alone," Lyons said. "They're partners. And

with the other Indian nations—Seneca or Tuscarora or any other ones—then you're a sub-chief. But those are English terms, European terms. All those terms have Indian language to it that means almost entirely different from just the word, 'Chief.' That's European. We didn't say, 'chief' before that. *Hoyaneh* is what we say. You know what that means? 'He Keeps the Peace.' See how different that is?"

181 **On November 1, 1972**: "A Half-Century after Siege, a Native American Is Set to Oversee Indian Affairs," Hedgpeth, Dana, *Washington Post*, January 25, 2021; Lyons, Oren, author interview, April 3, 2019.

181 NATIVE AMERICAN EMBASSY: Hedgpeth.

182 **"The place was barricaded"**: Lyons, Oren, author interview, April 3, 2019.

182 **"It's a good day to die"**: Hedgpeth.

182 **"I could smell gasoline"**: Lyons, Oren, author interview.

182 **"no spare tire"**: Ibid.

182 **$66,650 in small bills was procured**: "The Trail Of Broken Treaties: A March on Washington, D.C., 1972," *Rising: The American Indian Movement and the Third Space of Sovereignty*, Spring 2020, William & Mary Muscarelle Museum Of Art, https://muscarelle.wm.edu/rising/broken-treaties/.

182 **during the siege of Wounded Knee**: *Voices From Wounded Knee, 1973: In The Words of the Participants* (Mohawk Nation: Akwesasne Notes, 1974).

183 **statement of support from the Grand Council of Chiefs**: Ibid, 94–97.

183 **Two months later, Lyons**: "Shoot-Out Feared: Indian Chiefs Ask Action," *Post-Standard* (NY), May 3, 1973.

183 **"We have not asked you to give up your religion"**: *Voices*, 95

183 **"fence system of the United States"**: *Voices*, 97.

184 **"What do you do with those buffalo?"**: Lyons, Oren, author interview, November 28, 2018.

184 **"What took you so long?"**: Ibid; "Indians Kept the Faith And Buffalo Are Back," Keegan, Marcia, *Parade*, May 14, 1978.

184 **National Bison Range in Montana**: "New York Indians See Bison's Return As a Sign of Renewal and Hope," *New York Times*, March 4, 1978, 23. Tiffany, Lars, author interview, November 10, 2019; Keegan.

184 **largest buffalo enclave east of the Mississippi**: Ibid.

184 **By the late 19th century**: Hornaday, William T. *The Extermination of the American Bison* (Smithsonian Institution, 1889).

184 **An 1806 account**: Ashe, Thomas. *Travels In America, Performed in 1806* (London, 1808), 47–49.

184 **narrative has been dismissed as exaggeration**: Adams, Henry. *History of the United States* (New York: Charles Scribner's Sons, 1891), 1:54.

184 **within a few decades bison bones and a skull**: *New York State Museum, 67th Annual Report, 1913* (Albany: The University of the State of New York, 1915), transmitted to the Legislature, March 12, 1915.

184 **"They were here"**: Lyons, Oren, author interview, May 22, 2023.

185 **Korean War Tiffany dropped out of high school**: Tiffany, Lars, author interview.

185 **Scotch N' Sirloin**: Tiffany, Lars, author interview; "Scotch N' Sirloin: How it all began 50 years ago (photo essay)," Weaver, Teri, *Syracuse.com*, April 11, 2017.

185 **"Sizzler, Outback Steakhouse . . . knockoffs"**: Tiffany, Lars, author interview.

185 **"no part of a piece of paper"**: *New York Times*, March 4, 1978.

186 **a taste for sassafras tea**: Ibid.

186   **"Eleven got on the truck"**: Tiffany, Lars, author interview.

186   **treaty, hand-painted by Lyons**: Ibid.

186   **"It's a spiritual feeling"**: Keegan.

187   **"hard pressed for survival"**: *New York Times*, March 4, 1978.

187   **"different side of my dad"**: Tiffany, Lars, author interview.

187   **Until, one day, it wasn't**: Ibid.

187   **"Crying and crying and crying"**: Ibid.

188   **"really bothered me, killing the animals"**: Ibid.

188   **Geneva for the first-ever**: *Akwesasne Notes*, 9, no. 5, (December 1977), https://cendoc
      .docip.org/collect/cendocdo/index/assoc/HASH014b/77b7b9ea.dir/Akwesasne%20
      Notes%20Vol.9%20n5%201977.pdf#search=%22passports.

188   **"Discrimination Against Indigenous Populations in the Americas"**: "A Documen-
      tary History of the Origin and Development of Indigenous Peoples Day: Part 1, The
      Geneva Conference, 1977," Curl, John, Indigenous Peoples Day, https://ipdpowwow
      .org/Archives_1.html; Burns, M.C., 144; Lyons, Oren, Mohawk, John, Barreiro, Jose.
      Basic Call to Consciousness, Akwesasne Notes, Native Voices, 2005.

188   **"declaration for the four-footed"**: *Akwesasne Notes* (December 1977); *Call to Con-
      sciousness*; Smith, Huston. *A Seat at the Table: Huston Smith In Conversation with Native
      Americans on Religious Freedom* (Berkeley and Los Angeles: University of California
      Press, 2006), 163.

188   **standing ovation in 1992**: "Chief Oren Lyons' December 1992 Address to the United
      Nations," Southern Methodist University, December 10, 1992. Published, March 24,
      2012, https://s2.smu.edu/twalker/orenlyo4.htm.

188   **Indian Gaming Regulatory Act . . .** : Indian Gaming Regulatory Act, S.555–100th Con-
      gress (1988)(enacted).

189   **By 1996, 177 different ones**: "Profile of Indian Gaming," Gandhi, Natwar M., United
      States General Accounting Office, Washington, D.C., August 20, 1996, https://www
      .gao.gov/assets/ggd-96-148r.pdf.

189   **in 1990, a shootout**: "Timeline: Oka Crisis (Kanesatake Resistance), Canadian Ency-
      clopedia, Historica Canada, https://www.thecanadianencyclopedia.ca/en/timeline/oka
      -crisis.

189   **The Haudenosaunee is philosophically opposed**: "Haudenosaunee Statement On
      High Stakes Gambling," Hill, Sidney, Tadadaho, Onondaga Nation, http://www
      .onondaganation.org/government/policy/haudenosaunee-statement-on-high-stakes
      -gambling/.

190   **"Are you nuts?"**: Lyons, Oren, author interview, January 17, 2010.

190   **Fred Opie, the first Black man**: "Making the Team," *Daily Item* (NY), February 11,
      1990.

190   **"Do you know why we're here?"**: Opie, Fred, author interview, November 17, 2020.

191   **"same tactic of Malcolm X"**: Ibid.

191   **"like a Tommie Smith"**: Ibid.

191   **White Boy and the Wagonburners**: Lyons, Rex, author interview, November 28, 2018;
      "The Band," The Ripcords, http://www.fabulousripcords.com/the-band.html.

191   **As a young man**: Burns, 54.

192   **"I was pretty much a garbage head"**: Lyons, Rex, author interview, March 8, 2022.

192   **"Me and his dog"**: Lyons, Oren, author interview, November 28, 2018.

192   **than any other ethnic group**: "Key Substance Use and Mental Health Indicators in
      the United States: Results from the 2023 National Survey on Drug Use and Health,"

Substance Abuse and Mental Health Services Administration, U.S. Department of Health and Human Services, July 2024, 13, 10, 26, tables B.4B, B. 8B, B.13B.

192 **"You're spiritually bankrupt"**: Lyons, Rex, author interview.

192 **"That saved my life"**: Ibid.

192 **"I need you to sit up, one more time"**: Ibid.

192 **"I'm like tempered steel"**: Ibid.

III. Money Ball

193 **growing to $41.9 billion**: " NIGC: Record 2023 Shows Adaptability and Resilience of Native American Gaming" Fletcher, Robert, iGamingBusiness.com, June 28, 2024.

193 **In early 2012, Oren Lyons phoned**: "Onondaga Nation Legend Oren Lyons Brings Lacrosse Back to Origins," Fortier, Sam, *Daily Orange* (NY), September 23, 2015.

193 **40,000-square-foot field house**: Lyons, Oren, author interview, November 28, 2018.

194 **additional $3.75 million**: Lyons, Oren, author interview.

194 **"I'm rooting for the Iroquois"**: *Spirit Game: Pride of a Nation.*

194 **expected role reversal**: Ibid.

194 **refused to present their documents**: Ibid, interview with Lyons, Betty, President, American Indian Law Alliance, Onondaga Nation.

194 **labeled the school system "cultural genocide"**: Truth and Reconciliation Commission of Canada. *Honouring the Truth, Reconciling for the Future*, 2015.

195 **"a stretch to claim all the benefits"**: Carlson.

195 **one of 71 "fantasy passports"**: "Passport Impasse Keeps Haudenosaunee Home," *LaxMagazine.com*, July 24, 2015; "More Problems with Tribal Passports," native.america.news, September 8, 2011.

195 **Canadian government has pressed Peru**: "My Six Nation Haudenosaunee Passport Is Not a 'Fantasy Document,'" Hill, Sid, *Guardian* (London), October 30, 2015.

196 **vain attempt to confront Pope Francis**: "Onondaga Nation Members Felt Disrespected During Pope Francis Visit in NYC," Buckshot, Sarah, Moses, *Syracuse.com*, September 25, 2015.

196 **ceremonial Tadadaho headdress**: Hill, Sidney, author interview, April 6, 2023; *Spirit Game: Pride of a Nation*; Buckshot.

196 **"We hear a lot this week"**: *Spirit Game: Pride of a Nation.*

197 **"it can't take a political position"**: Lyons, Rex, author interview.

197 **reversed course in 2003 . . .**: "Reversal for Fortune: N.Y. Cayugas Drop-Anti-Gaming Stand," Adams, Jim, *Indian Country Today*, April 11, 2003.

197 **Tonawanda band of Seneca and Tuscarora**: Ibid.

197 **28-year-old dissident Joe Anderson**: "Bingo Debate Divides Tuscarora Reservation," Bonfatti, John F., *Associated Press*, August 20, 1987.

197 **opened another high-stakes bingo parlor**: "Indians, Too, Debate Gaming," Andriatch, Bruce, *Democrat and Chronicle* (NY), April 21, 1994; *Democrat and Chronicle* (NY), August 29, 1993; *Star-Gazette* (NY), March 15, 1994.

197 **"Baptists" in chief's clothing**: Anderson, Joe, author interview, November 27, 2018.

198 **"Tradition is nice"**: "Entrepreneur Uses Wits, Roots to Dodge Tax Laws," Gladwell, Malcolm, *Washington Post*, April 15, 1995.

198 **loans totaling $40,000**: "Embattled Falls Mayor finds His Life Has Become an Open Book: The FBI Probe into Vince Anello's Financial Dealings with 'Smokin' Joe' Anderson Has Been the Talk of the Town," Herbeck, Dan, Norheim, Gail, *Buffalo News*, October 21, 2005.

198 **$50,000 fine**: "'Smokin Joe' Anderson Hit with $50,000 Fine, but Avoids Jail Time and Probation," Pfeiffer, Rick, *Niagara Gazette*, February 24, 2011.

198 **New York was closing a deal**: "State Pays $25 Million for Smokin' Joe's Niagara Falls Properties," Prohaska, Thomas J., *Buffalo News*, August 15, 2018.

198 **"It's just the size of it"**: Lyons, Rex, author interview, November 28, 2018.

198 **$25,000 . . . $40,000**: Iroquois Nationals source, author interview, July 2018.

198 **$25,000**: Anderson, Joe, author interview.

199 **$51,000 check for the tickets**: Ibid.

199 **"Lacrosse is important"**: Ibid.

200 **"I'm just finding out"**: Lyons, Oren, author interview, November 28, 2018.

200 **"I would've said no"**: Ibid.

200 **"I was that close to never playing lacrosse"**: Tiffany, Lars, author interview, November 10, 2019.

200 **white and Indigenous students at LaFayette High**: "Hall of Fame Class of 2021: Carl 'Ket' Weist," Upstate Lacrosse Foundation, http://www.upstatelacrossefoundation.org/hall-of-fame/carl-ket-weist/; "The 50th Season Celebration and Review," LaFayette Central School District, April 25, 2009, http://www.lafayetteschools.org/teacherpage.cfm?teacher=715.

201 **sixth-graders as managers**: Tiffany, Lars, author interview.

201 **1983 NCAA championship at Rutgers**: Ibid.

201 **"ran around war-whooping"**: Ibid.

201 **Lars became the first white man**: Ibid; Lyons, Oren, author interview.

200 **"Lars Tiffany"**: Starsia, Dom, author interview, November 11, 2019.

202 **Tiffany played three years for him**: "Lars Tiffany," Virginia Athletics, http://virginiasports.com/coach/lars-tiffany/.

202 **trauma ward at Crouse-Irving Memorial**: Johnson, Vincent, author interview, June 13, 2023; Corwin, Faith, author interview, May 18, 2023.

202 **"Don't you recognize me?**: Ibid.

203 **fake name of Luke Warmwater**: Tiffany, Lars, author interview.

203 **"showboating and trash-talking"**: Ibid.

203 **"okay if you incite the Mohawks"**: Ibid.

203 **Tiffany sold his herd**: "Bradford Tiffany: 1933–2019," *Syracuse.com*, http://obits.syracuse.com/us/obituaries/syracuse/name/bradford-tiffany-obituary?id=15336869.

203 **"felt like I was being called home"**: Tiffany, Lars, author interview.

204 **"got a very measured report"**: Lyons, Oren, author interview, November 28, 2018.

204 **"just float after I talk to him"**: Tiffany, Lars, author interview.

204 **"The USA team could ask me"**: Ibid.

205 **"Imagine the '92 Dream Team"**: Gurenlian, Greg, author interview, July 15, 2018.

205 **"They robbed our game from us"**: "Sacred Sport. Native Americans Look to Recapture Lacrosse Glory," Hayes, Marcus, *Syracuse Herald-Journal* (NY), April 9, 1992.

206 **Canadian Lacrosse Association . . . standoff**: "'Brazen Union-Busting': Canadian Lacrosse Association Threatens to Use Replacement Players at World Championships," Russell, Andrew, Robinson, Megan, *Global News*, May 4, 2018.

206 **Canada's 2014 world title was dedicated**: 'Legends Never Die,' McLaughlin, Corey, *US Lacrosse*, September 2014, pg. 40.

207 **"in more ways than people can even understand"**: Snider, Geoff, author interview, July 19, 2018.

207 **"This team is something worth fighting for"**: Ibid.

207 **Dave Huntley, the pioneer of Canada's field renaissance**: "Remembering Dave Huntley Four Years After His Death," Foy, Terry, *InsideLacrosse.com*, December 18, 2021.

207 **"saw more in me than I saw in myself"**: Snider, Geoff, author interview.

207 **Twenty-two of the 23**: "Canada Names 23-Player Roster for 2018 FIL World Championship," *USALacrosse.com*, http://www.usalacrosse.com/magazine/canada-names-23 -player-roster-2018-fil-world-championship.

208 **"the back-and-forth"**: Rabil, Paul, author interview, July 15, 2018.

209 **Rule 75.3 of the FIL field rulebook**: "Rules of Men's Field Lacrosse," World Lacrosse, May 2021, ver 1.0, 62, https://worldlacrosse.sport/wp-content/uploads/2021/05/Mens -Rules-2021-23-May-2021-V1.0-1.pdf.

209 **"They were desperate"**: Gurenlian, Greg, author interview.

210 **"We rolled over, and started going palms up"**: Ibid.

210 *"It's not a war"*: Burnam, Mark, author interview, July 16, 2018.

Part 4
I. Because You Killed Her

213 **"It's always got that stigma"**: Seibald, Max, author interview, July 17, 2018.

213 **Hewlett, Long Island**: "Hewlett Honors a Humble Athlete," Bessen, Jeff, *LI Herald*, April 26, 2021; "Cornell's Seibald Blazes Lacrosse Trail from Small Long Island Town," Armstrong, Kevin, *Sports Illustrated*, May 22, 2009; Seibald, author interview.

213 **As a pro he was a five-time**: "Seibald '09 Opens Doors for Others through Lacrosse," Simpson, Lauren, Cornell Athletic Communications, April 23, 2021, http://cornellbigred .com/news/2021/4/20/mens-lacrosse-alumni-spotlight-max-seibald-09.aspx.

213 **"The worst is the 'laxbro'"**: Seibald, author interview.

214 **highest levels of binge drinking**: "NCAA National Study on Substance Use Habits of College Student-Athletes," NCAA Research, June 2018, 10, http://ncaaorg.s3.amazonaws .com/research/substance/2018RES_SubstanceUseFinalReport.pdf.

214 **use of cocaine**: Ibid, 22.

214 **narcotic pain medication**: Ibid, 29.

214 **"notably higher than other sports"**: "Rates of Excessive Drinking among Student-Athletes Falling," NCAA.org, July 22, 2014, http://www.ncaa.org/news/2014/7/22/rates -of-excessive-drinking-among-student-athletes-falling.aspx.

214 **227 percent participation growth**: "Total Number of Participants in Lacrosse in the United States from 2001 to 2018," Statista, http://www.statista.com/statistics/490367 /lacrosse-total-participation-us/.

214 **"Two kids in my class at Cornell"**: Seibald, author interview.

214 **"There's two ends to it"**: Ibid.

214 **his freshman roommate, John Decker**: "John Decker, 30, analyst and athlete who battled addiction," Cook, Bonnie L., *Philadelphia Inquirer*, January 30, 2016.

215 **"happened last week"**: Seibald, author interview.

215 **first college athlete suspended for drinking**: "Lacrosse Player Suspended for Drinking of 3.2 Beer," *Evening Standard* (PA), April 13, 1933.

215 **"you will see alcohol. Lots of alcohol"**: "For Lacrosse Parents, a Tragedy Too Familiar," Reimer, Susan, *Baltimore Sun*, February 24, 2012.

215 **"It's part of the culture"**: Bratton, Shamel, author interview, September 6, 2019.

215 **"Alcohol and lacrosse have gone hand in hand"**: "Yeardley Love's Murder Shines Light on Domestic Violence, Alcohol Abuse, and Lacrosse," Hess, Amanda, *Washington*

City Paper, May 6, 2010; "Scrutiny falls on U-Va. lacrosse," Bonesteel, Matt, de Vise, Daniel, Smith, Meg, *Washington Post*, May 5, 2010.

216 **"pull over and go to a liquor store"**: Holman, Brian, author interview, December 9, 2018.

216 **With graduation rates topping 90 percent**: "Trends in NCAA Division I Graduation Rates," NCAA Research, December 2023, https://ncaaorg.s3.amazonaws.com/research /gradrates/2023/2023D1RES_GSRTrends.pdf.

216 **"So in one part"**: Tierney, Bill, author interview, December 11, 2018.

216 **"Everything that happens off the field—the bonds"**: Offit, Josh, author interview, December 3, 2018.

217 **Overall, significant blocs**: "National Survey on Drug Use and Health," Substance Abuse and Mental Health Services Administration, 2022, http://www.datafiles.samhsa .gov/dataset/national-survey-drug-use-and-health-2022-nsduh-2022-ds0001.

217 **2023 NCAA Abuse Survey again revealing**: "Current Findings on Student-Athlete Substance Use: NCAA Student-Athlete Health and Wellness Study (January 2024), NCAA Research, http://ncaaorg.s3.amazonaws.com/research/wellness/Jan2024RES _HW-SubstanceUseRelease.pdf.

217 **Tierney saw plenty of it as a player**: Tierney, author interview.

217 **"It just bred on each other"**: Holman, author interview.

217 **"It certainly is concerning"**: Putukian, Margot, author interview, January 4, 2022.

217 **Certain schools can't—or won't—afford the cost**: "Drug Testing in Schools: Policies, Practices, and Association With Student Drug Use," Institute for Social Research (Ann Arbor, Mich.: The University of Michigan, 2003), 1; "Costs Minimized Cal Poly Drug Testing," Wilson, Nick, *Fresno Bee* (CA), August 20, 2014, B1.

218 **schools, which included lacrosse powers Cornell**: "Banned Substances/Nutrition," Cornell University Athletics, http://cornellbigred.com/sports/2007/7/11/ComplianceSA .aspx.

218 **Brown**: "University Athletic Department Drug and Alcohol Policy," Brown University, http://brownbears.com/sports/2018/4/27/compliance-drugalcoholpolicy.

218 **Yale**: "2023–2024 Student-Athlete Handbook," Yale University, https://yalebulldogs .com/sports/2023/7/19/2023-2024-student-athlete-handbook.aspx.

218 **He preferred Denver's policy**: Tierney, author interview.

218 **"There's no incentive"**: Offit, Josh, author interview.

218 **"When's the beer party?"**: Tiffany, author interview, November 10, 2019.

218 **"It's cultural. We've bred it"**: Holman, author interview.

219 **Sales of lacrosse gear**: "Year After Scandal, a Sport Thrives," Thamel, Pete, *New York Times*, May 28, 2007.

219 **Participation . . . had tripled since 1999**: Ibid.

219 **had risen 70 percent**: Ibid.

219 **Hobart midfielder Warren Kimber IV**: "N.J. Student at Hobart Found to Have Died of overdose," *Philadelphia Inquirer*, May 13, 2009.

219 **former . . . Towson State midfielder Drew Pfarr**: "Drew Charles Pfarr," *Baltimore Sun*, July 31, 2009.

219 **former . . . Massachusetts attackman Kevin Glenz**: "Former Lynbrook Teacher Raising Money for Film About Son's Heroin Addiction," Doyle, Heather, Patch.com, August 11, 2015; Glenz, Larry. *Forgiving Kevin: A Son's Addiction Becomes a Father's Greatest Teacher* (BalboaPress, 2011).

219　the sport was only tracking a national trend: "Drug Overdose Deaths in the United States, 1999–2015," Hedegaard, Holly, Warner, Margaret, Minino, Arialdi M., National Center for Health Statistics Data Brief No. 273, February 2017.

219　"tackle this immense, complex, dark side": "Lasagna: Drug Use Survey a Wakeup Call," Lasagna, Peter, *Inside Lacrosse*, March 2010.

220　"secret" undergraduate drinking societies: "All About UVA Secret Societies," *Charlottesville Guide*, May 25, 2024, http://charlottesville.guide/blog/uva-secret-societies/.

220　traditions like the "four-year fifth": "U-Va. Takes Aim at Alcohol-Based Tradition," Sipress, Alan, *Washington Post*, November 15, 1998.

220　From 1990 to 1998 alone, 18 Uva students: Ibid.

220　no program landed more talent: Tierney, author interview.

220　"I always thought alcohol was an issue here": Hess; Bonesteel, de Vise, Smith, *Washington Post*, May 5, 2010.

220　"what I lived with all the time: the fear": Starsia, Dom, author interview, November 11, 2019.

220　"Can you please let the kid drink?": Ibid.

220　"He kind of trusts kids": Stanwick, Steele, author interview, March 19, 2020.

221　Final Four 13 times . . . career victories, 375: "Dom Starsia: Head Coach (1993–2016), University of Virginia Athletics, http://virginiasports.com/coach/dom-starsia/.

221　Starting in 1999, he empowered his teams: "Friends Saw Multiple Sides of UVa's Huguely," *Daily Progress* (VA), May 23, 2010.

221　not once in his 24 years on campus: Starsia, Dom, author interview.

221　"I have a lot of respect": Barrow, George, author interview, June 11, 2021.

222　14-1: "Bocklet's Career Day Helps No. 1 Virginia Cruise to Victory Over Robert Morris," Virginia Athletics, May 1, 2010, http://virginiasports.com/news/2010/05/01/bocklet -s-career-day-helps-no-1-virginia-cruise-to-victory-over-robert-morris/.

222　Drinks flowed afterward: "UVA Lacrosse Players Had 'Rocky Relationship' Before Killing," Lavoie, Denise, *Associated Press*, April 26, 2022; "George Huguely Trial: Excessive Alcohol Consumption a Recurring Issue," *ABC News*, February 10, 2012.

222　Wintergreen Resort: "George Huguely and Yeardley Love: Love, Death, and Lacrosse," Jaffe, Harry, *Washingtonian*, June 1, 2011.

222　meandered into Boylan Heights: "Boylan Heights Bar at Center of U.Va. Drinking Scene," Johnson, Jenna, Flaherty, Mary Pat, *Washington Post*, February 21, 2012.

222　"We were drinking pitchers of beer": Bratton, Shamel, author interview, September 6, 2019.

222　Seven other Cavalier players: "Eight U-Va. Lacrosse Players Have Been Charged with Alcohol-Related Offenses During Their Careers at the School," Bonesteel, Matt, de Vise, Daniel, Smith, Meg, *Washington Post*, May 6, 2010.

222　played minimally in his final game: "Virginia 18, Robert Morris 9: Boxscore," http:// rmucolonials.com/sports/mens-lacrosse/stats/2010/virginia/boxscore/73#individual -stats.

223　"He's not complicated": "Trial of Lacrosse Player in Girlfriend's Death Begins," Sampson, Zinie Chen, *Associated Press*, February 8, 2012.

223　"Huguely had no constraints": Offit, Josh, author interview.

223　Galliher & Huguely: Jaffe.

223　*Washingtonian* magazine described him as a "party boy": Ibid.

223　He and George V's mother, Marta, divorced: Ibid.

223   **demanded her phone number** . . . : "University of Virginia Murder Suspect Led a Privileged Life," *Associated Press*, May 6, 2010.

223   **described him as "upbeat"**: Ibid.

223   **never emerged from a secondary role**: "The Complex Life of Murder Suspect George Huguely" *Baltimore Sun*, May 23, 2010; "Suspect Tells Police Details of U.Va. Lacrosse Death," *Daily Press* (VA), May 5, 2010.

223   **North Carolina . . . 40-foot yacht, the *Reel Deal***: *Baltimore Sun*, May 23, 2010; Jaffe.

223   **policewoman . . . Rebecca Moss**: Ibid.

223   **"I'll kill all you bitches"**: Jaffe.

224   **Huguely argued with his father**: "Dad of Lacrosse Murder Suspect Once Called Cops on Son," *ABC News*, May 3, 2010.

224   **UVa officials said they didn't know**: "Under Law, U. of Virginia Was Never Told of Lacrosse Player's Violent Past," Corbin, Cristina, *Fox News*, May 6, 2010, https://www.foxnews.com/us/under-law-u-of-virginia-was-never-told-of-lacrosse-players-violent-past; "Frequently Asked Questions (FAQ)," Clery Center, http://www.clerycenter.org/faq.

224   **university policy required Huguely**: "Teammates Accuse UVA Suspect of Attacking Sleeping Student," Stabley, Matthew, *NBC4 Washington*, May 8, 2010, https://www.nbcwashington.com/news/local/teammates-accuse-uva-suspect-of-attacking-sleeping-student/2095804/.

224   **teammates took to calling him "Fuguely"**: *Baltimore Sun*, May 23, 2010.

224   **"Sweet dreams, punk"**: *Baltimore Sun*, May 23, 2010.

224   **downplayed it as a minor scuffle**: Ibid.

224   **North Carolina midfielder Michael Burns**: "Officer Describes Beaten, Bruised Lacrosse Player," *WBAL-TV 11*, February 9, 2012, http://www.wbaltv.com/article/officer-describes-beaten-bruised-lacrosse-player/7072509; "George Huguely Trial: Other Man Saw Yeardley Love in Violent Choke Hold," *ABC News*, February 9, 2012, http://abcnews.go.com/US/george-huguely-trial-yeardley-loves-man-witnessed-violent/story?id=15546816.

224   **"I can honestly say"**: Ibid.

224   **scared that she couldn't breathe**: *ABC News*, February 9, 2012.

224   **"Alcohol is ruining my life"**: "George Huguely Trial: Huguely Had 'No Intent' to Kill, Was a 'Stupid Drunk,' Defense Says," *ABC News*, February 18, 2012, http://abcnews.go.com/US/george-huguely-trial-huguely-intent-kill-stupid-drunk/story?id=15744836.

224   **an "on and off again" relationship**: *ABC News*, February 9, 2012.

225   **On April 27, Love**: "Details Emerge in UVA Murder: Violent Arguments Days Before Love Died," *ABC News*, August 19, 2010, https://abcnews.go.com/US/TheLaw/uva-lacrosse-player-yeardley-love-struck-george-huguely/story?id=11437672; "Understanding the First Week of the George Huguely Murder Trial," Means, Senlin, *C-VILLE Weekly*, February 14, 2012; Jaffe.

225   **hooked up with Love the night of the choking**: Senlin.

225   **"I should have killed you"**: "Huguely, George W. v. Woodson, John A., Warden, Virginia Circuit Court of the City of Charlottesville, Crim. No. 11-102-1, 12, January 19, 2016, http://d33byq9npfy6u9.cloudfront.net/2/2016/01/2016-01-19-First-Habeas-Petition-Final.pdf; "Huguely Files Habeas Corpus Petition," Provence, Lisa, *C-VILLE Weekly*, January 27, 2016, http://www.c-ville.com/huguely-files-habeas-corpus-petition.

225   **"youre so fucked up"**: Ibid.

225 **Huguely was drinking by 9 a.m.**: *ABC News*, February 10, 2012
225 **unable to play the final nine holes**: Ibid.
225 **44.5 drinks**: "'Fuller Truth:' Love v. Huguely Hearing Presents New Version of Yeard-ley's Death," Provence, Lisa, *C-VILLE Weekly*, July 26, 2016, https://www.c-ville.com /fuller-truth-love-v-huguely-hearing-presents-new-version-yeardleys-death.
225 **"He just drank all day"**: Starsia, author interview.
225 **five foot six**: "Yeardley Love's Legacy Lives On, 10 years After Her Death, by Empow-ering Millions to Identify Abuse," Merrill, Elizabeth, *ESPN.com*, May 3, 2020.
226 **Love was drinking, too**: *ABC News*, February 10, 2012.
226 **Her blood alcohol level**: "Huguely Jury Gets Texts; Defense Begins," *WBAL-TV 11*, February 15, 2012, http://www.wbaltv.com/article/huguely-jury-gets-texts-defense -begins/7072586.
226 **flurry of unanswered messages**: Ibid.
226 **11:45**: Huguely, George Wesley v. Clarke, Harold W., Memorandum Opinion, U.S. District Judge Cullen, Thomas T., CASE No. 7:20CV30021, December 21, 2020, http:// casetext.com/case/huguely-v-clarke.
226 **At about 11:40 he walked the 70-plus steps**: Huguely v. Clarke, Cullen opinion; Jaffe.
226 **Love's bedroom door was locked**: Huguely v. Clarke, Cullen opinion; Jaffe.
226 **Huguely kicked it open**: "FULL George Huguely Interrogation Tape," WVIR TV NBC 29, True Crime Review, http://www.youtube.com/watch?v=ZbymVdJwY88; "George Huguely Trial Update: Jury Asks to See Yeardley Love's Bedroom Door, Part of Wall," *CBSNews.com*, February 22, 2012; Jaffe.
226 **Love shrank from him**: WVIR TV NBC 29, True Crime Review.
226 **grabbed Love by the shoulders and shook**: Ibid; "Huguely's Statement Brings Tears to Jurors, Families, and George Huguely," Snook & Haughey, P.C., February 10, 2012, http://www.snookandhaughey.com/news/huguelys-statement-brings-tears-to-jurors -families-and-george-huguely/.
226 **her nose began to bleed**: Huguely v. Clarke, Cullen opinion.
226 **struggling on the floor**: Ibid; WVIR TV NBC 29, True Crime Review.
226 **threw Love's body on the bed, grabbed her laptop**: Ibid.
226 **"very, very loud"**: Huguely, George Wesley vs. Commonwealth of Virginia, Rec-ord No. 1697-12-2, pg. 560–561, March 4, 2013, http://casetext.com/case/huguely-v -commonwealth.
226 **2:15 a.m.**: Ibid.
226 **Her right eye was blackened and swollen shut**: "Murder Trial of UVA Lacrosse Player Set to Begin," *Baltimore Sun*, February 5, 2012.
226 **She had bruising on her cheeks, cuts**: "Medical Experts Describe How Yeardley Love Died," WJZ Baltimore, February 13, 2012, http://www.cbsnews.com/baltimore/news /murder-trial-of-ex-university-of-virginia-lacrosse-player-enters-week-2/.
226 **cause of death . . . blunt force trauma**: "Trauma cited in Yeardley Love's death," *Asso-ciated Press*, February 15, 2012; "Coroner: Signs of suffocation present," *Associated Press*, February 13, 2012; "Medical testimony: Yeardley Love's brain injury caused by blunt force trauma," *CBS News/Associated Press*, February 14, 2012, https://www.cbsnews.com /news/medical-testimony-yeardley-loves-brain-injury-caused-by-blunt-force-trauma/; "George Huguely Trial: Yeardley Love's Brain Hemorrhaged from Force," *ABC News*, February 14, 2012, http://abcnews.go.com/US/george-huguely-trial-yeardley-loves -brain-hemorrhaged-force/story?id=15584424.
226 **began questioning Huguely**: WVIR TV NBC 29, True Crime Review.

227 **In minutes he would be cuffed and charged**: "Lacrosse Player George Huguely Charged in Fellow U-Va. Student Yeardley Love's Death," Flaherty, Mary Pat, Johnson, Jenna, *Washington Post*, May 4, 2010, A1; "When Your Son is Charged With 1st Degree Murder: One Mother Speaks Out," Ludwig, Robi, LinkedIn.com, September 30, 2016, http://www.linkedin.com/pulse/when-your-son-charged-1st-degree-murder-one -mother-speaks-ludwig/.

227 **would be found guilty**: "Ex-Lacrosse Player Gets 23 years in U.S. Prison for Murder," Shulleeta, Brandon, *Reuters*, August 30, 2012.

227 **"She's dead. You killed her, George"**: WVIR TV NBC 29, True Crime Review.

227 **"How the fuck is she dead?"**: Ibid.

227 **"you killed her"**: Ibid.

227 **rendered them forever "like seven-year-olds"**: Starsia, author interview.

228 **cancer metastasized**: Ibid.

228 **"Way to go, Dom"**: Ibid.

228 **sleep next to him**: Ibid.

228 **"these life-altering experiences"**: Ghitelman, Adam, author interview, October 23, 2021.

229 **"business as usual"**: "Virginia Lacrosse Welcomes Return to Action," Kurz Jr., Hank, *Associated Press* in *Herald-Palladium* (MI), May 16, 2010.

229 **seal the 14-12 win**: "UVa Remembers Teammate in Victory," *Associated Press*, May 16, 2010.

229 ***"Do you believe in life after love?"***: Ibid.

229 **diagnosis was intense anxiety**: "Virginia Lacrosse Coach Dom Starsia Sticks to His Methods in Wake of Tumultuous Year," Yanda, Steve, *Washington Post*, February 18, 2011.

229 **return as coach the following year**: "Coach Dom Starsia will Return as Coach of the Virginia Lax Team in 2011," Thurston, Trent, *C-VILLE Weekly*, June 5, 2010, https:// www.c-ville.com/Coach_Dom_Starsia_will_return_as_coach_of_the_Virginia_Lax _team_in_2011/.

230 **"Just firing me"**: Starsia, author interview.

230 **$29.45 million civil lawsuit**: "Yeardley Love's Mother Sues Lacrosse Coaches Over Daughter's Death," *ABC News*, May 4, 2012.

230 **suit was quietly withdrawn**: "Love Family Drops Wrongful Death Lawsuit Against Huguely," Smith, Ruth Serven, *Daily Progress* (VA), August 8, 2018.

230 **"It's a scary profession in that way"**: Tierney, author interview.

231 **In 2006, UVa crushed opponents**: "In Final, Virginia Lacrosse Team Has Eye on Victory and Legacy," Thamel, Pete, *New York Times*, May 29, 2006; "Men's Lacrosse Faces UMass for National Title," Virginia Athletics, May 28, 2006, http://virginiasports .com/news/2006/05/28/men-s-lacrosse-faces-umass-for-national-title/.

231 **On paper, the Cavaliers headed**: "Men's Lacrosse Ranked No. 2 in the Nation in Three Preseason Polls and No. 1 in a Fourth," Virginia Athletics, February 13, 2011, http://virginiasports.com/news/2011/02/13/men-s-lacrosse-ranked-no-2-in-the-nation -in-three-preseason-polls-and-no-1-in-a-fourth/.

231 **"blatantly disrespectful to the Love family"**: "Virginia Lacrosse Player Bray Malphrus Is Always Looking for Ways to Improve His Team," Swezey, Christian, *Washington Post*, May 20, 2011.

231 **"strictest, most stringent rule"**: Yanda.

231 **Saturday night**: Bratton, Shamel, author interview.

232 **"I never intended"**: Starsia, author interview.

232 **"we'd rather you not be out"**: Bratton, Shamel, author interview.

232 **"Good or bad or indifferent"**: Ibid.

232 **Adam Ghitelman was suspended**: "Virginia Lacrosse Tops Drexel Thanks to Backup Goalkeeper Rob Fortunato's Key Saves," Yanda, Steve, *Washington Post*, February 19, 2011.

232 **joined the Brattons in at least one transgression**: Bratton, Shamel, author interview.

232 **North Carolina's Outer Banks**: Ibid.

232 **Stony Brook game was the Brattons'**: Ibid; "Brattons' Senior Year Takes Downward Turn," Marcus, Steven, *Newsday* (NY), April 30, 2011.

233 **"a distraction" for Mount St. Mary's**: Bratton, Shamel, author interview.

233 **Then, on March 26**: "2010–11 Men's Lacrosse Schedule," Virginia Athletics, http://virginiasports.com/sports/mlax/schedule/season/2010-11/.

233 **the team boarded the bus**: Bratton, Shamel, author interview.

233 **Shamel had admitted**: Ibid.

233 **attend a funeral on Long Island**: "Shamel Bratton Dismissed from Virginia Men's Lacrosse Team; Team Votes to Suspend Rhamel Bratton Indefinitely," Swezey, Christian, Yanda Steve, *Washington Post*, April 29, 2011.

233 **"It ultimately came from the coaches"**: Stanwick, Steele, author interview, March 19, 2020.

233 **best defender, Matt Lovejoy**: "UVa Lax: Final Thoughts From Baltimore," White, Jeff, Virginia Athletics, May 31, 2011, http://virginiasports.com/news/2011/05/31/uva-lax-final-thoughts-from-baltimore/.

234 **"We're ready to go"**: Starsia, author interview.

234 **doubled down on the zone defense**: "Virginia vs. Cornell lacrosse: Cavaliers Reach Final Four With Record-Setting Win for Coach Dom Starsia," Swezey, Christian, *Washington Post*, May 21, 2011.

234 **"kind of limping in"**: Stanwick, author interview.

234 **"The zone"**: Ghitelman, author interview.

234 **"addition by subtraction"**: "The Rise. The Fall. The Future: A Lacrosse Magazine Exclusive with the Bratton Brothers," Censer, Joel, *Lacrosse Magazine*, September 2011, 38–45.

234 **Briggs . . . O'Reilly**: "Virginia Attackman Nick O'Reilly Suspended for 2012 Season," *InsideLacrosse.com*, November 22, 2011.

235 **"It's almost better"**: Bratton, Shamel, author interview.

235 **"I'm so sorry"**: Starsia, Dom, author interview.

235 **"It's heartbreaking"**: Stanwick, author interview.

II. One Every Year

236 **opioids—an "epidemic"**: "Vital Signs: Overdoses of Prescription Opioid Pain Relievers—United States, 1999—2008," Centers for Disease Control and Prevention, November 4, 2011, https://www.cdc.gov/mmwr/preview/mmwrhtml/mm6043a4.htm.

236 **40 deaths daily**: Ibid.

236 **Native Americans were nearly 50 percent more likely**: "Tribes Reach Landmark $665 Million Settlement with J&J, Opioid Distributors," Kornfield, Meryl, *Washington Post*, February 2, 2022, A6.

236 **one in 20**: Centers for Disease Control and Prevention, November 4, 2011.

236 **more than quadrupled**: "QuickStats: Rates of Deaths from Drug Poisoning and Drug Poisoning Involving Opioid Analgesics—United States, 1999–2013," Centers for Disease Control and Prevention, Morbidity and Mortality Weekly Report, January 16, 2015, http://www.cdc.gov/mmwr/preview/mmwrhtml/mm6401a10.htm.

236 **drug manufacturers like Purdue Pharma**: "Opioid Manufacturer Purdue Pharma Pleads Guilty to Fraud and Kickback Conspiracies," U.S. Department of Justice, Office of Public Affairs, November 24, 2020, http://www.justice.gov/opa/pr/opioid-manufacturer -purdue-pharma-pleads-guilty-fraud-and-kickback-conspiracies.

236 **Male high school athletes**: "Painfully Obvious: A Longitudinal Examination of Medical Use and Misuse of Opioid Medication Among Adolescent Sports Participants," Veliz, Philip, Epstein-Ngo, Quyen M., Meier, Elizabeth, Ross-Durow, Paula Lynn, Boyd, Carol J., McCabe, Sean Esteban, *Journal of Adolescent Health*, March 2014, https://www.ncbi .nlm.nih.gov/pmc/articles/PMC3943832/; "How Painkillers Are Turning Young Athletes Into Heroin Addicts," Wertheim, L. Jon, Rodriguez, Ken, *Sports Illustrated*, June 18, 2015.

236 **second wave from 2010 to 2013**: "The Opioid Crisis in the United States: A Brief History," Congressional Research Service, November 30, 2022.

237 **Kings Park High star Thomas Ventura**: "Ventura: Don't Let Another Child Be Lost to Heroin," Ventura, Linda, *Newsday* (NY), February 8, 2014.

237 **Huntington Beach High attackman Tyler Macleod**: "H.B. Calls for Action After Teen's Suspected Heroin OD Death," Fletcher, Jaimee Lynn, Jow, Lauren, *Orange County Register* (CA)., October 3, 2012.

237 **Alex Bement was a sophomore defenseman**: "Alexander C. 'Alex' Bement, a Natural Athlete Who Excelled at Lacrosse and Coaching Middle school and High School Players, Dies," Rasmussen, Frederick N., *Baltimore Sun*, June 30, 2019.

237 **"Main Line Takeover Project"**: "Main Line Drug Dealer Timothy Brooks Sentenced to Jail," Fiorillo, Victor, *Philadelphia* magazine, February 3, 2015.

237 **"notoriously an alcohol- and drug-use sport"**: "American Boy Fall Brawl Raises Funds for Addicts, Families," Feil, Justin, *US Lacrosse*, October 16, 2019.

237 **slowing growth rate . . . declining attendance**: "As Lacrosse Rises, Its Final Four Falls Fast," Schonbrun, Zach, *New York Times*, May 22, 2015.

238 **synthetic opioid fentanyl**: Congressional Research Service, November 30, 2022.

238 **"kept you high all day"**: "How One D.E.A. Agent Cracked a Global Fentanyl Ring," Palmer, Alex W., *New York Times Magazine*, October 16, 2019.

238 **rocketed from 32 kilograms to more than 270**: Ibid.

238 **Only two milligrams**: "Facts About Fentanyl," United States Drug Enforcement Administration, https://www.dea.gov/resources/facts-about-fentanyl; "'If You Can See It, It Can Kill You,'" Jackson County Combat Prevention, http://www.jacksoncountycombat .com/818/Get-The-Fentanyl-Facts.

238 **In March 2015**: "DEA Issues Nationwide Alert on Fentanyl As Threat To Health And Public Safety," United States Drug Enforcement Administration, March 18, 2015, https://www.dea.gov/press-releases/2015/03/18/dea-issues-nationwide-alert-fentanyl -threat-health-and-public-safety.

238 **Between 2013 and 2017**: "The Fentanyl Failure," Higham, Scott, Horwitz, Sari, Zezima, Katie, *Washington Post*, March 13, 2019.

238 **Prince in 2016, Tom Petty in 2017**: "Music's Fentanyl Crisis: Inside the Drug That Killed Prince and Tom Petty," Browne, David, *Rolling Stone*, June 20, 2018.

238 **Angels pitcher Tyler Skaggs**: "The Desperate Hours: A Pro Baseball Pitcher's Fentanyl Overdose," Wharton, David, Fenno, Nathan, *Los Angeles Times*, June 27, 2024.

238 **killed Alex Bement**: "Harm Reduction Might Have Saved My Son's Life," Bement, Liz, June 10, 2021, http://www.loveinthetrenches.org/post/harm-reduction-might-have -saved-my-son-s-life.

238 **Late Sunday morning, April 24, 2016**: Metropolitan Police Department of the District of Columbia, Public Incident Report, CCN #16064218, Lyons, Tisha, responding officer, Second District, April 24, 2016, 14:32 (time of report).

238 **"worked on the decedent"**: Ibid.

238 **cause of death was acute intoxication**: Adams, Cheryle E., Special Assistant to the Chief Medical Examiner, Office of the Chief Medical Examiner, Washington, D.C., email to author, October 31, 2018.

238 **Senior Night . . . Cooper Field**: "Joe Bucci's Five Goals Not Enough in 8-7 Loss to Virginia on Senior Night," Georgetown Athletics, April 23, 2016, http://guhoyas.com /news/2016/4/23/Joe_Bucci_amp_8217_s_Five_Goals_Not_Enough_in_8_7_Loss_to _Virginia_on_Senior_Night.aspx.

239 **limited by injury**: NCAA lacrosse source; "Ed Blatz fondly remembered as a player and a person," Herzog, Bob, *Newsday* (NY), April 25, 2016.

239 **possible overdose due to "a combination"**: "Georgetown Lacrosse Player Dies," Zovak, Juliana, *Georgetowner*, April 26, 2016, http://georgetowner.com/articles/2016 /05/03/georgetown-lacrosse-player-dies/; "Police Confirm Death at 33rd & O Streets NW," Devaney, Robert, *Georgetowner*, May 3, 2016, https://georgetowner.com/articles /2016/05/03/police-confirm-death-33rd-o-streets-nw/.

239 **family declined to speak . . . determined to respect their privacy**: When contacted by the author on July 18, 2019, Blatz's father—Ed Blatz, Sr.—declined to comment and asked that nothing be written about his son. Georgetown head coach Kevin Warne declined an interview request through a university spokesperson, email response on September 23, 2020.

239 **But Ed Blatz was beloved**: "LI's Edward Blatz Jr., a Lacrosse Player at Georgetown, Dies at 21," Sarra, Gregg, *Newsday* (NY), April 24, 2016.

239 **"Eddie brought light"**: Guterding, Justin, author interview, December 6, 2018.

239 **Maryland defenseman Tim Muller**: "Former Hoya Blatz Honored by Many," Lee, Edward, *Baltimore Sun*, March 16, 2017.

239 **on his way to practice, and broke down sobbing**: Guterding, author interview; Lee.

239 **Guterding had never scored an OT game-winner**: Guterding, author interview; "Duke's Justin Guterding seeks elusive lacrosse title," Herzog, Bob, *Newsday* (NY), February 10, 2018.

240 **"he was laughing down at me"**: Ibid.

240 **On May 4, 2016**: "Cause of Student Death: Swept Under the Rug?," *Georgetowner*, May 4, 2016, http://georgetowner.com/articles/2016/05/04/cause-student-death-swept -under-rug/.

240 **at least one was another lacrosse player**: In its Public Incident Report, D.C. police said a Georgetown player, and two other individuals, found Blatz's body and called 911. When contacted on February 22, 2023, the player declined to speak about the incident. When contacted on March 8, 2023, a Georgetown player who, multiple sources say, received medical treatment the night of Blatz's death, called that night "extremely challenging" and declined to comment.

240 **"Georgetown University is so tight-lipped"**: *Georgetowner*, May 4, 2016.

240 **"survive in the dark, not so much in the light"**: Ibid.

240 **printed only one brief paragraph**: "Sports Digest: Georgetown Men's Lacrosse Player Dies," *Washington Post*, D2, April 25, 2016.

240 **changed their uniform numbers**: Lee.

241 **unreported cause. Publicly**: Ibid.

241 **"an emergency too critical to ignore"**: Lasagna.

241 **Georgetown University asked all student athletes**: "Viewpoint: An Undue Weight on Athletes," Thomas, Caroline, *Hoya*, January 8, 2017, http://thehoya.com/opinion /viewpoint-an-undue-weight-on-athletes/.

241 **new, far more stringent**: Ibid; "Case Study: Georgetown University," http://www .drugfreesport.com/case_studies/test-case-study/; "Editorial: For Athletes, Rehabilitation Over Repercussions," *Hoya*, January 31, 2017, http://thehoya.com/opinion/editorial -for-athletes-rehabilitation-over-repercussions/.

241 **"building culture"**: "Men's Lacrosse I GU Looks to Revitalize Team Culture," Cavacos, Elizabeth, *Hoya*, February 14, 2017, http://thehoya.com/sports/mens-lacrosse-gu-looks -to-revitalize-team-culture/.

241 **In October 2018**: Adams, email to author, October 31, 2018.

241 **"was a complete shock"**: Guterding, author interview.

242 **22, only when 14 wasn't available**: Guterding, author interview, October 23, 2021.

242 **"which I hate saying"**: Guterding, author interview, December 6, 2018.

242 **"Same thing"**: Ibid.

242 **"like, you hear one every year"**: Ibid.

243 **"You're *not* going to Virginia"**: Starsia, author interview.

243 **Williams grew up fiercely close**: Williams, Zed, author interview, January 20, 2022; "Strength of the Wolf: How Zed Williams Brought Joy to His Family," Rice, Nelson, *US Lacrosse*, September/October 2020.

243 **Muscogee midfielder Justin Giles**: "Justin Giles: Stick and Ball Game," as told to Hamilton, Matt, *US Lacrosse*, April 2019.

243 **first glimpse . . . home visit**: Starsia, author interview.

243 **"needed more than that"**: Williams, Zed, author interview.

244 **"a proper email"**: Ibid.

244 **habit of avoiding direct eye contact**: Starsia, author interview.

244 **flip phone**: Williams, Zed, author interview.

244 **"I don't see"**: Starsia, Dom, author interview.

244 **"they were all very welcoming"**: Williams, Zed, author interview.

245 **father, Daniel, died of diabetes**: Ibid; Rice.

245 **a bachlor's degree in drama**: Williams, Zed, author interview; Starsia, author interview; Rice.

245 **"if he wasn't there"**: Williams, Zed, author interview.

245 **"We want to make a change"**: Starsia, author interview; Littlepage, Craig, author interview, June 19, 2023.

245 **Give me one more year**: Starsia, author interview.

245 **"people didn't care"**: Williams, Zed, author interview.

245 **demanded a new three-year contract**: Starsia, author interview.

245 **Conflicting reports**: "After a Week of Uncertainty, Dom Starsia Out as Virginia Men's Lacrosse Coach," Wallace, Ava, *Washington Post*, May 23, 2016.

246 **"*tough sheriff?*"**: Tiffany, author interview.

246 **"level of accountability"**: Littlepage, author interview.

246 **civil lawsuit against Huguely**: "Civil Trial to Begin in 2010 Death of UVA Lacrosse Player," Lavoie, Denise, *Associated Press*, April 23, 2022.

246 **$15 million**: "Jury Awards $15M in Damages in UVA Lacrosse Player's Killing," Lavoie, Denise, *Associated Press*, May 2, 2022.

246 **"It was to make a point"**: "A $15 Million Award, and Some Legal Closure, for Yeardley Love's Family: 'I Just Feel Like She's with Me,'" Marbella, Jean, *Baltimore Sun*, May 5, 2022.

246 **Yet, on June 3, 2016**: "Interested Party Sharon D. Love's Opposition to Plaintiff's Second Motion for Summary Judgment," Chartis Property Casualty Company v. Huguely V, George W., Murphy III, Andrew, Murphy, Marta, Love, Sharon D., United States District. Court for the District of Maryland, Greenbelt Division, Civil Action No.: 13-cv-01479 DKC.

246 **"interested party" brief**: Ibid, 20; "Victim's Mother Backs Huguely's Version of Fatal Encounter," Vieth, Peter, *Virginia Lawyers Weekly*, June 17, 2016.

247 **"so intoxicated that he lacked the capacity"**: "Interested Party Sharon D. Love's Opposition," Blumberg, Neil, M.D., 6.

247 **"zero tolerance for drugs"**: Tiffany, author interview.

247 **Starsia was the first to suggest**: "Of Love and Lacrosse: A Conversation with Dom Starsia and Lars Tiffany," Lambrecht, Gary, *US Lacrosse*, September 24, 2019.

247 **"a little awkward"**: Starsia, author interview.

247 **put him up . . . Kip Turner, too**: Ibid.

248 **orientation barbeque**: Ibid.

248 **Tiffany kicked him off the team**: Tiffany, author interview; "Virginia Lacrosse: Senior goalkeeper Matt Barrett Arrested for Drug Possession," Darney, Caroline, *Streaking the Lawn*, August 25, 2016.

248 **Starsia has never accepted**: Starsia, author interview.

248 **"The culture of Virginia lacrosse"**: Tiffany, Lars, author interview, May 1, 2023.

248 **random tests on a dozen athletes**: Tiffany, author interview, November 10, 2019.

248 **"I'll sign the transfer papers"**: Ibid.

248 **"when he yelled he flipped out"**: Williams, Zed, author interview.

248 **"two-week period where we all tried out"**: Ibid.

III. Builders

249 **entrepreneur David Neeleman**: Holman, author interview; "Crosse Fit," Coon, John, *Continuum*, University of Utah, spring 2019, http://attheu.utah.edu/facultystaff/crosse -fit/.

249 **Starsia turned the job down**: Starsia, author interview.

249 **Holman himself said no, twice**: Holman, author interview.

250 **self-described "turnpike guy"**: "How a Bunch of 'Turnpike Guys' are Giving the US Men's Lacrosse Team a Distinct New York Mentality," Vaccaro, Chris, *The Athletic*, July 11, 2018.

250 **"cowfucker"**: Marr, Scott, author interview, July 19, 2018.

250 **"a modern-day Johnny Appleseed"**: "Coach Myers Implants His Mark in Lacrosse As He Leaves Hofstra," Vecsey, George, *New York Times*, June 1, 1975.

250 **Moran's Sewanhaka High teammate**: Hayes, Tom, author interview, January 5, 2021.

250 **first Division I school west of the Mississippi**: "Denver Wins First Lacrosse Title as Tierney Complete Turnaround," Novy-Williams, Eben, *Bloomberg*, May 25, 2015; "A Win for the West," McLaughlin, *US Lacrosse*, July/August 2015.

250 **born in 1951 and raised in Levittown**: "2009 Person of the Year Interview," DaSilva, Matt, *Lacrosse Magazine*, December 2009.

250 **"I was 'head assistant'"**: Tierney, author interview.

251 **Willie Scroggs**: "Hall of Fame Inductees: William Scroggs," USA Lacrosse, http://www.usalacrosse.com/player-profile/william-scroggs.

251 **Waverly in inner-city Baltimore**: Scroggs, Willie, author interview, November 15, 2021.

251 **met her while an army MP at Pearl Harbor**: Ibid; "Scroggs Leaves a Legacy of Leadership, Service at Carolina," *University Gazette*, The University of North Carolina at Chapel Hill, April 1, 2014.

251 **shaking down an 82-year-old pharmacist**: Ibid; "'Shakedown' Probe Starts," *Baltimore Sun*, June 5, 1953; "Ober Fires Policeman," *Baltimore Sun*, October 24, 1953.

251 **stitch London Fog raincoats**: Scroggs, author interview; *University Gazette*, April 1, 2014.

251 **smashed the glass on a door**: Ibid; "Ex-Policeman Held After Row," *Evening Sun* (MD), December 11, 1961.

251 **"kill my mother with a gun"**: Scroggs, author interview.

251 **wrestled the gun away**: Ibid.

251 **"I hardly saw him after that"**: Ibid.

252 **George Young**: "George Young | Pro Football Hall of Fame," http://www.profootballhof.com/players/george-young/.

252 **"Catch Us If You Can"**: Scroggs, author interview.

252 **"It's Mister Scroggs to you"**: Ibid.

252 **He never spoke**: Ibid.

252 **"a wonderful human being"**: Ibid.

253 **Henry "Chic" Ciccarone**: Ibid; "He's Put Hop into Hopkins," Marshall, Joe, *Sports Illustrated*, May 12, 1975.

253 **"You didn't want that job at Princeton"**: Scroggs, author interview.

253 **Ciccarone fired him, then took him back**: Ibid.

253 **North Carolina hired the 31-year-old**: "Scroggs Is Named UNC lacrosse Coach," *Baltimore Sun* (MD), June 8, 1798.

253 **perfect transitional figure**: Marshall.

253 **made suits for presidents**: "Henry E. Ciccarone, 97, Naval Academy Tailor," *Baltimore Sun*, March 1, 2004.

253 **elope in Las Vegas**: "A Century of Excellence," Lidz, Franz, *Sports Illustrated*, April 25, 1983.

253 **wrote the book on the game**: Scott, Bob. *Lacrosse: Technique and Tradition* (Baltimore, London: The Johns Hopkins University Press, 1976).

253 **"Would you rather be Babe Ruth in Yankee Stadium?"**: Cowan, Joe, author interview, December 12, 2022.

254 **1979 Ciccarone recharged the Blue Jay mystique**: "Johns Hopkins Remains No. 1 in Lacrosse," Forbes, John B., *New York Times*, April 10, 1979, Section C, 17.

254 **first undefeated and untied season in 38 years**: "2005 Men's Lacrosse Season-Ending Notebook," Johns Hopkins Athletics, July 21, 2005, http://hopkinssports.com/news/2005/7/21/2005_Men_s_Lacrosse_Season_Ending_Notebook.aspx.

254 **22-game winning streak**: "N. Carolina, Hopkins Vie In Title Bid," Greenberger, Neil H., *Washington Post*, May 30, 1981.

254 **That year's player revolt**: "New Boy On an Old Block," *Sports Illustrated*, March 30, 1981.

254 **UNC lacrosse had already died once, in 1954**: 2020 Carolina Men's Lacrosse Record Book, pg. 4.

254 **Not one high school in North Carolina**: Scroggs, Willie, author interview; *Sports Illustrated*, March 30, 1981; "N. Carolina's Title a Promising Sign for Lacrosse Future," Tanton, Bill, *Evening Sun* (MD), June 4, 1981.

254 **"athletic scholarships"**: "Two St. Mary's Lacrosse Players Win Full Scholarships," O'Malley, Pat, *Evening Sun* (MD), February 9, 1983; "Massacre On a Muddy Plain," Underwood, John, *Sports Illustrated*, April 23, 1962.

254 **All-Metro first team**: *Sports Illustrated*, March 30, 1981; "UNC Lands Stars," Tanton, *Evening Sun* (MD), June 6, 1979; "Twelve Make All-Metro Stick Team: Five Lacrosse Stars Bound for Carolina," Klingaman, Mike, *Evening Sun* (MD), C8.

254 **"With one or two more recruiting years like that"**: Tanton, June 6, 1979.

254 **17 Baltimore stars had migrated to Chapel Hill**: Tanton, June 4, 1981.

254 **clean Kenan Stadium after football games**: Scroggs, author interview; *Sports Illustrated*, March 30, 1981.

254 **"I've never met anybody like Willie"**: Sears, Tom, author interview, November 15, 2022.

254 **"I don't know that anybody really knows him"**: Ibid.

254 **"Play like the Indians play"**: Scroggs, author interview.

254 **"We were run-and-gun"**: Voelkel, Peter, author interview, November 15, 2022.

254 **"played possum"**: Scroggs, author interview.

256 **rampage through the 1981 season . . .** : North Carolina Men's Lacrosse Media Guide, http://goheels.com/documents/2021/10/7/2002_Media_Guide.pdf.

256 **"looked like old-timers, but played that way, too"**: "N. Carolina Overpowers Mount Washington Ten," *Baltimore Sun* (MD), March 29, 1981, C2.

256 **"a warning to Johns Hopkins"**: Ibid.

256 **"Now it's up to us"**: Scroggs, author interview.

256 **Gary Waters**: Ibid; Waters, Gary, author interview, November 20, 2022.

256 **nine one-handed pushups**: Scroggs, author interview.

257 **"It's not going to be easy"**: Ibid.

257 **firing a short-barreled cannon**: "Syracuse Plugs Its Ears in Preparation for Hopkins' Annoying Pep Band," Rahme, Dave, *Syracuse Post-Standard* (NY), March 14, 2008; *Baltimore Sun* (MD), March 1, 1981, pg. 33.

257 **"I always felt like I was out of place there"**: Holman, author interview.

257 **"You want it? I'll take it"**: Scroggs, author interview; Cowan, author interview, December 12, 2022.

257 **"Does that mean they forfeit"**: Scroggs, author interview.

257 **into the sunshine for the 2 p.m. faceoff**: "1981 NCAA Lacrosse Championship North Carolina vs Hopkins," Colucci, Ryan, YouTube, April 16, 2020, http://www.youtube.com/watch?v=lfvcRH_ZRmg.

258 **Up went his middle finger**: Scroggs, author interview.

258 **the referees disallowed last-second Hopkins goals**: "UNC Gives Lacrosse Southern Flavor," Snyder, Dutch, *Evening Sun* (MD), June 1, 1981; "Disputed Goals Mark End of Jays' Dynasty," Snyder, Cameron C., *Baltimore Sun* (MD), May 31, 1981.

258   **felt like a score**: Snyder; "The Heels Get Their Feet In The Door," *Sports Illustrated*, June 8, 1981.

258   **Scroggs agrees that it should have been a goal**: Scroggs, author interview.

258   **no access to the TV replay** . . . : YouTube, http://www.youtube.com/watch?v=lfvcRH _ZRmg.

258   **Backup midfielder Doug Hall**: Snyder.

258   **Ciccarone went haywire**: Ibid.

259   **"But I guess it took a Hopkins man"**: Ibid.

259   **"It was devastating"**: Holman, author interview.

259   **"Nobody wanted Hopkins to win four in a row"**: Greenberg, Mark, author interview, August 15, 2019.

259   *Evening Sun* **columnist Bill Tanton**: "Men's Lacrosse Record Book," Johns Hopkins Athletics, pg. 116., http://hopkinssports.com/documents/2019/3/7/Print_Version_3_7 _19_.pdf.

260   **"Hallelujah!"**: Tanton, *Evening Sun* (MD), June 4, 1981.

260   **1982 regular season at Homewood**: "North Carolina Wins 2nd Lacrosse Crown," Cramer, Gary, *Charlotte Observer* (NC), May 30, 1982, D1.

260   **playing against themselves**: Simmons Jr., Roy, author interview, September 24, 2020.

260   **"Man, I'll never forget that"**: Simmons Jr., author interview, April 24, 2020.

261   **"a completely different animal"**: Holman, author interview.

261   **"collages"**: "'My Teams Are Collages,'" Lidz, Franz, *Sports Illustrated*, March 26, 1984.

261   **"*John* Hopkins"**: Simmons Jr., Roy, author interviews, September 24, 2020 and April 24, 2020.

261   **"Blue Jay blue"**: Simmons, Jr. Roy, author interview, September 24, 2020; "A Season That Changed the Game: In 1983, Syracuse University Lacrosse Upstarts Began a Dynasty," Kirst, Sean, *Syracuse.com*, May 23, 2008.

261   **at the half** . . . **blazing May sun**: "The Legend of Syracuse Lacrosse Started with Miracle Comeback of 1983," Kramer, Lindsay, *Syracuse.com*, May 19, 2020; Lidz, March 26, 1984.

261   **tossing his stick in the air**: Holman, author interview.

262   **greatest comeback in the history of the NCAA championship**: Cantel, Kramer, Kirst; "Syracuse Coach Savors Title Victory over Jays," Jackson, James H., *Baltimore Sun* (MD), May 30, 1983.

262   **"I think you're good enough now"**: Simmons Jr., author interview, September 24, 2020.

262   **would die of a heart attack**: "Henry Ciccarone, Lacrosse Coach, 50," *New York Times*, November 19, 1988, Section I, 10.

262   **beer distributorship**: "Hall of Fame Inductees: Henry Ciccarone," USA Lacrosse, http://www.usalacrosse.com/player-profile/henry-ciccarone.

262   **Blue Jays alum Don Zimmerman** . . . : "Zimmerman Replaces Ciccarone at Hopkins," Stewart, John W., *Baltimore Sun* (MD), October 4, 1983, C8.

262   **"Hopkins was the mecca"**: Voelkel, author interview.

263   **"then it spread and now, my God"**: Simmons Jr., Roy, author interview, April 24, 2020.

263   **It stunned him to later hear that Bob Scott**: Scroggs, author interview.

263   **"They didn't want me, Mom"**: Ibid.

263   **impersonal card in response. An interview**: Ibid.

264 **everything worked out for the best**: "Few Words, Many Deeds, All for Love," Jared, Scott, UNC University Relations, March 28, 2014, http://www.unc.edu/posts/2014/03/28/few-words-many-deeds-all-for-love/.

264 **"I always designate it for the football program"**: Scroggs, author interview.

264 **"We had never seen lacrosse like this"**: Holman, author interview.

264 **"hugs and kisses"**: "Syracuse Doesn't Have to Look Far in Recruiting," Bonnell, Rick, *Syracuse Herald-Journal* (NY), June 22, 1983, 24.

265 **"It's 40 seconds"**: Burnam, Mark, author interview, September 21, 2020.

265 **"It caught everybody completely off-guard"**: Simmons III, Roy, author interview.

265 **"Is Syracuse still playing 'spaghetti'?"**: Tierney, Bill, author interview.

265 **the soon-outlawed"Air Gait"**: "At Least the U.S. Still Can Stick It to the World in Lacrosse," Tanton, Bill, *Evening Sun* (MD), June 27, 1990, B2.

265 **"I finally beat you at *your* game"**: Simmons Jr, Roy, author interview, April 24, 2020.

266 **1992 season, Syracuse lost three scholarships**: "NCAA Places Restrictions on Five Athletic Programs (from the Archive)," *Syracuse.com*, October 1, 1992; "Colleges: N.C.A.A. Calls a Two-Year Foul on Syracuse," Rhoden, William C., *New York Times*, October 2, 1992, Section B, 7.

266 **"excessive" financial aid from 1988 to 1991**: "NCAA: Orange Out of Tourney; The Penalties, Violations," *Associated Press*, October 2, 1992.

266 **would be stripped of their national title**: "Men's Lacrosse: Championship History," NCAA.com, http://www.ncaa.com/history/lacrosse-men/d1.

266 **The organization found that**: "SU Releases Report on Lacrosse," *Syracuse Herald-Journal* (NY), December 8, 1993, D1.

266 **return the 1990 national championship trophy**: "The Visible, Invisible Legacy of the 1990 Syracuse Lacrosse Team," Grossman, Evan, *Vice*, February 18, 2016.

266 **"Well, the Friends of Syracuse Lacrosse"**: Simmons Jr., author interview.

266 **roadtripped as a high school freshman**: Tiffany, author interview.

267 **Bill Tierney left Baltimore**: "Notebook," Jackson, James H., *Baltimore Sun* (MD), June 18, 1987, 7D.

267 **"This Will Never Work"**: Tierney, author interview, 11/1/23.

267 **As if taking the reins from . . . Pete Carril**: Ibid.

268 **Tierney's "Princeton defense" spread**: "The Man Who Dared to Slide from the Crease," Miller, Wyatt, PremierLacrosseLeague.com, May 29, 2024; "A Dreamer. A Square Peg in a Round Hole. Bill Tierney Exiting Coaching With Cupboard Full," Kinnear, Matt, *InsideLacrosse.com*, January 7, 2023.

268 **"He was the ultimate lacrosse manager"**: Tiffany, author interview.

268 **$65,000 a year**: Tierney, author interview.

268 **"at the place you beat?"**: Ibid.

268 ***It will never be your program***: Ibid.

269 **"I'm fearful of that"**: Ibid.

Part 5

I. We Can Do It

273 **championships since 1982**: "Women's Field History," World Lacrosse, http://worldlacrosse.sport/events/womens-field-history/.

273 **From 1998 to 2018**: "NCAA Sports Sponsorship and Participation Rates Report (1956–57 through 2022–23)," NCAA, 40, 79.

274 **"I wish the men's sport"**: Offit, Josh, author interview, December 3, 2018.
274 **"freeze-tag" element**: "Gary Gait: Women's Lacrosse New Rules Create a 'Totally Different' Game," Alvarez, Nick, *Daily Orange* (NY), January 30, 2018.
274 **"as if on the jet of a fountain"**: "Spin Right and Shoot Left," McPhee, John, *New Yorker*, March 23, 2009.
274 **Now nearly 60 percent**: "National Center for Education Statistics," Table 303.70. Total Undergraduate Fall Enrollment in Degree-Granting Postsecondary Institutions, by Attendance Status, Sex of Student, and Control and Level of Institution: Selected Years, 1970 through 2031 (2023–2031 Projected), http://nces.ed.gov/programs/digest /d23/tables/dt23_303.70.asp; "What Does It Mean that Women Now Dominate Higher Education?," Gordon, Rebecca, *ScheerPost*, June 11, 2022; "Colleges Have a Guy Problem," Thompson, Derek, *Atlantic*, September 14, 2021.
274 **Part of the shift is due to Title IX**: "Education Amendments of 1972," United States Public Law No. 92-318, 86 Stat. 235, June 23, 1972, 373, http://www.govinfo.gov/content /pkg/STATUTE-86/pdf/STATUTE-86-Pg235.pdf; "50 Years of Title IX: Then And Now," Mertens, Maggie, *Sports Illustrated*, June 2022, 28–31.
274 **According to the 1979 policy interpretation**: "A Policy Interpretation: Title IX and Intercollegiate Athletics," U.S. Department of Education, Federal Register, Vol. 44, No. 239, Rules and Regulations, December 11, 1979.
275 **effort to exempt college football failed**: "Colleges Mystified by Title IX Fund Rules," White Jr., Gordon S., *New York Times*, December 15, 1978, A: 27.
275 **In 1972 . . . today, the total tops 3 million**: "Title IX at Age 50," Tugend, Alina, *New York Times*, April 27, 2022.
275 **most clearly in soccer**: "Once an 'Easy Way Out' for Equality, Women's Soccer Is Now a U.S. Force," Petri, Alexandra E., *New York Times*, June 27, 2022, Section A: 1; NCAA Sports Sponsorship and Participation Rates Report, 8, 90.
275 **more Division I women's teams than men's**: NCAA Sports Sponsorship and Participation Rates Report, 37, 38.
275 **"We're stalled"**: Offit, Howard, author interview, October 30, 2018.
275 **Its coach, Janna Kaufman**: "Goucher Graduate Janna Kaufman Set To Coach Israel In The 2019 European Championship Gold Medal Game On Thursday," Goucher Athletics, July 24, 2019, http://athletics.goucher.edu/sports/wlax/2018-19/releases /20190724cnn5xt.
275 **Attacker MacEllen McDonough**: "Israel Heartbroken at Not Being Included in 2024 Women's Worlds, But Determined to Keep Growing Game," Levi, Adam, *InsideLacrosse .com*, April 17, 2024; "MacEllen McDonough," Jacksonville University Athletics, http:// judolphins.com/sports/womens-lacrosse/roster/macellen-mcdonough/2328.
276 **San Diego State defender Julia Masias**: "Coaches We Love: Julia Masias," Triad Athletes, http://triadathletes.com/blogs/lifestyle/coaches-we-love-julia-masias; "Julia Masias," San Diego State Athletics, http://goaztecs.com/sports/womens-lacrosse/roster /season/2018/player/julia-masias.
276 **That woman's nickname is "Killer"**: "Killer Instinct," Lochary, Clare, DaSilva, Matt, *Lacrosse Magazine*, December 2008, 43.
276 **"wonderful game, beautiful and graceful"**: Lumsden, Louisa Innes. *Yellow Leaves: Memories of a Long Life* (Edinburgh: William Blackwood & Sons, 1933); "History of Lacrosse at St Leonards," http://www.stleonards-fife.org/index.asp?MainID =4382.
277 **In the spring of 1890**: Ibid; Fisher, 147.

277 **"Whether the game"**: *St Leonards Gazette*, June 1890; "History of Lacrosse at St Leonards," http://www.stleonards-fife.org/index.asp?MainID=4382.
277 **no physical contact and no hard boundaries**: Fisher, 147–48, 200.
277 **Clubs formed in London. American graduates**: Fisher, 147.
277 **Rosabelle Sinclair**: "About: History," The Bryn Mawr School, http://www.brynmawrschool.org/about/history.
277 **In 1941, the first intercollegiate women's lacrosse game**: "Roots: The History of Women's Lacrosse," posted March 31, 2021, by Premier Lacrosse League to YouTube, March 31, 2021, http://www.youtube.com/watch?v=8X08uTZQ8dY.
277 **"feminine"**: Fisher, 147–148, 200; "Local Women Eye U.S. Title: National Feminine Lacrosse Tourney To Open Today," Turner, Frances, *Baltimore Sun* (MD), May 30, 1941, pg. 14; "Girls, Too, Study At Famous College," *Leader-Post* (SK, Canada), November 14, 1940.
277 **under the headline "The Tough Game"**: Cover of *Sports Illustrated*, April 23, 1962.
277 **story contained an authoritative primer**: "Massacre on a Muddy Plain," Underwood, John, *Sports Illustrated*, April 23, 1962, 36–39.
278 **Lacrosse is a game for girls, too**: Ibid.
278 **In 1976 the Blue Jays women**: "A Taste for Victory," Blackburn, Maria, *Johns Hopkins Magazine*, June 2004.
278 **in 1974 Tina Sloan Green**: "Tina Sloan Green, a Pioneer in Every Sense of the Word," USA Lacrosse, http://www.usalacrosse.com/magazine/tina-sloan-green-pioneer-every-sense-word; "Roots of Resistance: The Origins of the Black Women in Sport Foundation and the Politics of Race and Gender," Rahim, Raja Malikah, Liberti, Rita, *Women in Sports and Physical Activity Journal*, 2023, Vol. 31, No. 2, pgs. 55–62.
278 **Temple's rare institutional commitment**: "UNCP Mourns Loss of Former Chancellor Dr. Joseph B. Oxendine," UNC Pembroke, April 15, 2020, http://www.uncp.edu/news/uncp-mourns-loss-former-chancellor-dr-joseph-b-oxendine; "Peter Liacouras, President Who Transformed Temple, Dies," Whelan, Aubrey, Babay, Emily, *Philadelphia Inquirer*, May 13, 2016.
278 **Quietly set the school's standard**: "Tina Sloan Green, passionate pioneer," Hunt, Donald, *Philadelphia Tribune*, February 4, 2010; Temple Lacrosse 2024 Record Book, 3, 13, 14.
278 **ten straight Final Fours**: Multiple non-contemporary sources say Temple reached 11 straight national semifinals under Sloan Green through 1990, but contemporaneous newspaper accounts show a streak of 10 beginning in 1981, with Temple losing to UMass 7-4 in the quarterfinals of the 1980 national women's lacrosse tournament; "For The Record," *Baltimore Sun* (MD), May 10, 1980, B7. In 1981, Temple lost to Ursinus 11-8 in the national semifinals and beat Harvard 8-6 in the third-place game; "Lacrosse," *Baltimore Sun* (MD), May 16, 1981, B9; "Lacrosse," *Baltimore Sun* (MD), May 18, 1981, C9.
278 **three Division I national championships**: Under Sloan Green, Temple won NCAA Division I women's national titles in 1984 and 1988 and the Association of Intercollegiate Athletics for Women (AIAW) Division I championship in 1982. The AIAW, founded in 1971, administered women's collegiate national championships—covering different divisions—that were a precursor to NCAA-governed national championships for women's sports. Temple beat Maryland 3-2 for the 1982 AIAW Division I title; beat Maryland again, 6-4, for the 1984 NCAA D-I title, and defeated Penn State 15-7 to cap a 19-0 national championship season in 1988.
279 **"It's a disappointment"**: Sloan Green, Tina, author interview, February 15, 2024.

279 **Under head coach Janine Tucker**: Blackburn.

279 **All eight Stanwick children**: "The Stanwicks, One of the First Families of Lacrosse, Find the Ties That Bind," Sugam, Matt, *New York Times*, April 23, 2015.

279 **"Baltimore is still a hot spot"**: Stanwick Burch, Sheehan, author interview, August 20, 2020.

279 **Cindy Timchal**: "Cincy Timchal: Head Coach," United States Naval Academy, http://navysports.com/staff-directory/cindy-timchal/150.

280 **"I was pretty skeptical"**: Amonte Hiller, Kelly, author interview, December 14, 2018.

280 **anyone figuring that Gait**: "Gary Gait to Be Named Next Syracuse Men's Lacrosse Coach," Croston, Samantha, *Sports Illustrated*, June 6, 2021.

280 **equally between soccer and lacrosse**: "Amonte Has Amore For Lacrosse, Soccer," Goff, Steven, *Washington Post*, October 21, 1992.

280 **"Once Gary started coaching, it was over"**: Amonte Hiller, author interview.

280 **grandfather**: Ibid.

280 **forced him to retire. The family survived**: Ibid; "This Blackhawk Is All Blue-Collar," Johnson, K.C., *Chicago Tribune*, January 19, 2000.

280 **Kelly's older brother Tony**: "Go West, Young Lady," Wertheim, L. Jon, *Sports Illustrated*, May 12, 2008.

280 **Thayer administrators tried to withdraw her aid**: Amonte Hiller, author interview.

280 **"the Kneebreaker"**: "Game Changer," Stein, Anne, *Northwestern* magazine, spring 2013.

280 **waitressing at Jake's Seafood**: Amonte Hiller, author interview.

281 **"My parents couldn't afford it"**: Ibid.

281 **one of the recruits**: Goff, October 21, 1992.

281 **After she committed to Maryland**: Lochary, DaSilva.

281 **named All-American**: Wertheim.

281 **Amonte headed back to New England**: Lochary, DaSilva; Amonte Hiller, Kelly, author interview.

281 **assistant coach Scott Hiller**: "Scott Hiller: Assistant Coach," Northwestern Athletics, http://nusports.com/sports/womens-lacrosse/roster/coaches/scott-hiller/3387.

281 **even Cindy Timchal couldn't make that work**: "NU, Navy Women's Lacrosse Coaches Forever Linked," Hersh, Philip, *Chicago Tribune*, March 24, 2012.

281 **clear Title IX play**: Amonte Hiller, author interview.

281 **men's fencing in 1941**: Lochary, DaSilva.

281 **starting salary of $45,000**: Amonte Hiller, author interview.

281 **with the marching band**: Ibid.

282 **Ashley and Courtney Koester**: "Northwestern Lacrosse's Dynasty Is Dead. Long Live the Dynasty," Goren, Ben, *InsideNU.com*, May 15, 2016; Wertheim, May 12, 2008.

282 **"Do you know what lacrosse is?"**: Amonte Hiller, author interview.

282 **emailed a heartfelt missive**: Ibid.

282 **allowed to go in the crease**: Ibid.

282 **And I'm like, *I believe you***: Munday, Lindsey, author interview, November 7, 2018.

282 **improved to 8-8 in 2003**: "Year-By-Year Results/NCAA Tournament History," Northwestern Athletics, Lacrosse Record Book, 10.

282 **In the run-up to the 2004 season**: "Lacrosse Magazine Releases 2004 Preseason College Rankings," Old Dominion University Athletics, December 15, 2003.

282 **Preseason polls for 2005**: "League Champs Grab Preseason No. 3 in Poll (Women's lacrosse)," *Daily Northwestern*, January 10, 2005.

282 **21-0**: Northwestern Athletics, Lacrosse Record Book, 10; "Kelly Amonte Hiller's U20 Coaching Staff a Reflection of Her Legacy," Mayer, Beth Ann, *USA Lacrosse Magazine*, August 5, 2024.

283 **"We were so used to seeing a certain kind of player"**: Kalkstein, Brittany, author interview, July 11, 2019.

283 **"competitive cauldron" . . . April Heinrichs**: "Anson Dorrance's Competitive Cauldron," Duke, JJ, *Our Game Magazine*, January 29, 2016.

283 **new and edgy vein**: "Amonte Hiller's Guide to Building a National Champion," Reynolds, Lauren, *ESPN.com*, July 19, 2006.

283 **When her players wore flip-flops**: "White House footwear fans flip-flop kerfuffle," *Associated Press*, July 22, 2005; "Lacrosse players defend flip-flops," *Associated Press*, July 19, 2005.

283 **first women's lax program to play in shorts**: Stein.

283 **helped spur ever-younger recruitments**: Lochary, DaSilva.

284 **nickname, "the Evil Empire"**: Wertheim, May 12, 2008; Goren.

284 **headlined "Killer Instinct"**: Lochary, DaSilva.

284 **Her first star, Kristen Kjellman**: Wertheim, May 12, 2008.

284 **two-time Tewaaraton Award winner**: Harris.

284 **consecutive championships streak ended at five**: Northwestern Athletics, Lacrosse Record Book.

284 **new coach Joe Amplo**: "Gearing Up," Jenkins, Chris, *Marquette Magazine*, Spring 2013, 23.

284 **a raise and five-year contract**: "Former Teammates Go Against Each Other in Lacrosse Final as Coaches," Hersh, Philip, *Chicago Tribune*, August 23, 2021.

284 **next best option: clones**: "Kelly's Coaching Tree," *Northwestern* magazine, spring 2013.

285 **in 1998 Howard became**: "Women's Lacrosse Team Tells Of Obstacles Encountered in Becoming NCAA, Varsity Sport," Edwards, Derrick S., *The Hilltop* (Howard University student newspaper), April 17, 1998, B4; "Laurie Podmilsak: Head Women's Lacrosse Coach," Palm Beach Atlantic University bio, http://pbasailfish.com/sports/womens -lacrosse/roster/coaches/laurie-podmilsak/1927.

285 **In 1984**: Oxendine, Joseph B. *American Indian Sports Heritage* (Lincoln: University of Nebraska, 1995), 294; "Engendering Nationality: Haudenosaunee Tradition, Sport, and the Lines of Gender," Downey, Allan, *Journal of the Canadian Historical Association*, 23, no. 1 (2012): 337.

286 **menstrual cycle, or "moon time"**: "We Got Next: Rise of the Haudenosaunee," Schneider, Megan, *Lacrosse Magazine*, September 2, 2014; Schindler, Tia, author interview, August 13, 2020; Sunseri, Lina. *Being Again of One Mind: Oneida Women and the Struggle for Decolonization* (Vancouver: University of British Columbia Press, 2011), 130; Downey, 341.

286 **When public high schools**: "Engendering Nationality . . .," Downey, 333.

286 **clan mothers representing**: Downey, 338–340.

286 **"My heart broke into a thousand pieces"**: "Cradle of a Sport Has Crossed the Gender Line," Berg, Aimee, *New York Times*, May 13, 2007.

286 **Pete Sky, a stickmaker**: "Onondaga Chief Peter Sky Passes at 82," Powless, Lynda, *Turtle Island News*, November 12, 2014.

286 **Tia Smith, took part**: Schindler, Tia, author interview, August 13, 2020.

287 **Still, before 1995**: Ibid.

287 **"I just grew up watching the guys play"**: Ibid.

287 **she tried out for Team Canada**: Ibid.

287 **2002 Miss Indian World beauty pageant**: "Canadian is Crowned Miss Indian World," Hunter, Troy, *Ontario Birchbark*, 1, issue 5 (2002): 11; Schindler, Tia, author interview.

287 **Cup of Nations**: "Tight Spot for Iroquois," Crandall, Kate, *Baltimore Sun* (MD), July 2, 2005, C1; Berg.

287 **embraced its 11th member nation**: Berg.

287 **In 2007, Tuscarora goalie Amber Hill**: Schneider; Berg.

287 **2007 U-19 world championship**: Schindler, Tia, author interview; "IFWLA U19 2007," Haudenosaunee Statistics, Roster, Schedule, Pointstreak.com, http://pointstreak.com/stats/pro/teamschedule.html?teamid=90273&seasonid=2094.

288 **Four years later, at 32**: Schindler, Tia, author interview; Schneider.

288 **"have a place to play"**: Schindler, Tia, author interview.

288 **"As long as the women"**: Lyons, Oren, author interview, January 17, 2010.

288 **sparked a mix unknown**: "How Haudenosaunee Women are Overcoming Stigma to Earn a Place in Lacrosse," *CBC Radio*, February 16, 2018; "Haudenosaunee Women Fighting To Change Societal Norms," Hamilton, Matt, *US Lacrosse Magazine*, November 6, 2020; Schindler, Tia, author interview; Schneider.

288 **Her introduction to lacrosse**: Lasota, Selena, author interview, March 31, 2020; "Northwestern's Selena Lasota is the Unlikeliest of Lacrosse Superstars," Bushnell, Henry, Gernon, David, *SB Nation: Inside NU*, April 16, 2015.

288 **"I didn't really need to be protected"**: Lasota, Selena, author interview, March 31, 2020.

289 **took her to work fishing tuna**: Ibid.

289 **Katzie First Nation**: Ibid; "Freshman Selena Lasota Takes Circuitous Route to Northwestern Lacrosse," Hersh, Philip, *Baltimore Sun* (MD), February 4, 2015.

289 **"a different feeling of strength"**: Lasota, author interview.

289 **Team BC's U-19 women's field squad**: Bushnell, Gernon; Hersh.

289 **at the 2012 President's Cup**: Ibid; Lasota, author interview.

290 **including the game-winner in overtime**: Bushnell, Gernon.

290 **fledgling program at USC**: "USC Set to Open Inaugural Season With Northwestern," *usctrojans.com*, February 7, 2013.

290 *We're not a powerhouse anymore*: Amonte Hiller, author interview.

290 **urged to have more of a "killer instinct"**: Lasota, author interview.

290 **"lost a lot of my personal values"**: Ibid.

290 **After digging through old notes**: Amonte Hiller, author interview.

291 **"perceived *everything* coming from us as pressure"**: Ibid.

291 **"completely different" head coach**: Lasota, author interview.

291 **Lasota unleashed a record-tying, 22-goal tear**: "2019 Women's Lacrosse Roster: Selena Lasota," Northwestern Athletics, http://nusports.com/sports/womens-lacrosse/roster/selena-lasota/8195.

291 **"Selena changed the entire sport"**: McKone, Lindsey, author interview, October 24, 2021.

291 **McKone grew up amid wealth**: Ibid.

292 **"No, I'm not a winner right now"**: Amonte Hiller, Kelly, author interview.

292 **"But I *know* it's coming"**: Ibid.

II. Strong Island

293 **Herzlia's Shefayim kibbutz**: "Kibbutz Shefayim," http://www.kibbutzvisit.com/listing /kibbutz-shefayim/.

293 **Winner of three NCAA championships**: "John Danowski: Head Coach," Duke Athletics, https://goduke.com/sports/mens-lacrosse/roster/coaches/john-danowski/5030.

294 **"One of the best men"**: Wolf, Jordan, author interview, July 13, 2018.

294 **Phil Jackson, the NBA coaching great**: Tierney, author interview, December 11, 2018.

294 **"Don't talk to me!"**: Holman, Marcus, author interview, July 13, 2018.

294 **unprecedented No. 2 ranking**: "Hofstra Sweeps 2006 All-CAA Men's Lacrosse Awards," Hofstra Athletics, May 4, 2006.

294 **pew at St. Kilian's**: Danowski, John, author interview, July 15, 2018.

294 **team culture, off-field behavior, discipline**: "Duke Fell Into Right Coach to Revive Lacrosse," Vaughn, Peter, *News and Observer* (NC), May 10, 2015, B1.

294 **"Not once"**: Danowski, author interview.

295 **familiarity with Duke's course catalogue**: Vaughn.

295 **"He was like our team rabbi"**: Sherwood, Devon, author interview, July 10, 2021.

295 **"What's pissing you off today? . . . What makes you happy?"**: Vaughn.

295 **plastic lawn chairs**: "The Miracle on the Mediterranean (and the Making of a Gold Medalist," DaSilva, Matt, *US Lacrosse Magazine*, September/October 2018.

295 **"I wanted to deliver that for them"**: Danowski, author interview.

295 **his son Matt forever suspect adult authority**: Ibid.

295 **"We trusted no one"**: Ibid.

296 **"So I'm still leery"**: Ibid.

296 **Crescent Athletic Club**: *beyridge.com*, April 21, 2017.

296 **number of Long Island high schools**: "High School Sports; Lacrosse Booms on Long Island As 37 High Schools Field Teams," *New York Times*, April 22, 1964.

296 **"The opportunity is such"**: "Myers In Line For New Post," *Baltimore Sun* (MD), February 7, 1950.

296 **Anne leapt from the midpoint of the 29th Street Bridge**: "Wife Of Coach Killed In Plunge," *Valley Times* (CA), November 9, 1950; "Woman Killed As She Falls From Bridge," *Baltimore Sun* (MD), November 9, 1950; "Wife of LI Athletic Exec Dies in Plunge," *Newsday* (NY), November 9, 1950.

297 **1955 Class B**: "Coach Myers Implants His Mark in Lacrosse As He Leaves Hofstra," Vecsey, George, *New York Times*, June 1, 1975.

297 **A decade after Myers arrived**: "They're Not Going to Like It in Maryland," *Sports Illustrated*, May 4, 1970.

297 **By 1975 the number approached 100**: Vecsey.

297 **police officer Ronnie Kloepfer**: "One For Fallen NYPD Hero: Cop-FDNY Lacrosse Game to Aid Victims," *New York Daily News*, November 19, 2001; "Adelphi Athletics Remembers 9/11 Heroes," Adelphi Athletics, September 8, 2021.

297 **"Man, I wish I was there"**: McMahon, Timothy, author interview, July 16, 2018.

298 **"They're Not Going to Like It in Maryland"**: *Sports Illustrated*, May 4, 1970.

298 **"you'd better be as tough"**: Offit, Howard, author interview.

298 **"fellow "turnpike guys""**: "How a Bunch of 'Turnpike Guys' Are Giving the US Men's Lacrosse Team a Distinct New York Mentality," Vaccaro, Chris, *The Athletic*, July 11, 2018.

298 *taking a cab right now*: Wolf, Jordan, author interview.

299 **"But the amount of money"**: Danowski, John, author interview.

299 **His own father, Ed Danowski**: "Coach Follows His Father While Leading His Way," Vecsey, George, *New York Times*, June 1, 2010.

299 **quarterback, led East Meadow**: Ibid; "If They Could Only Can 8 Great Plays," Kornheiser, Tony, *Newsday* (NY), October 19, 1970, 55.

299 **"I regret it to this day"**: Danowski, John, author interview.

299 **"very embarrassed about the end of my career"**: Ibid.

299 **"Most unselfish player I've ever had"**: Hayes, Tom, author interview, January 5, 2021.

299 **record for assists**: "2023 U.S. Men's Staff: John Danowski," USA Lacrosse, http://www.usalacrosse.com/player-profile/john-danowski.

300 **Gone were the gratuitous**: Holman, Brian, author interview, December 9, 2018.

300 **Duke won 15 of them**: "Weekend Preview: Big Ten Play, Happy Hour Lacrosse and More," *InsideLacrosse.com*, March 30, 2018.

300 **"We had this saying"**: Guterding, Justin, author interview.

300 **In the spring of 2006**: "The Damage Done," Price, S.L., Evans, Farrell, *Sports Illustrated*, June 26, 2006; Carroll, Casey, author interview, October 17, 2022.

301 **first-team All-American**: "2014 Men's Lacrosse Roster: Casey Carroll," Duke Athletics, https://goduke.com/sports/mens-lacrosse/roster/casey-carroll/3090.

301 **Serving was always the intent**: "Casey Carroll's Homecoming Season," McLaughlin, Corey, *Lacrosse Magazine*, April 2014; Carroll, author interview, November 16, 2021.

301 **dominated the college game**: "National Champions: NCAA Men's Lacrosse Championships," United States Intercollegiate Lacrosse Association, http://usila.org/sports/2015/10/27/GEN_1027151106.aspx.

301 **renamed to honor Lt. Raymond Enners**: "About Ray Enners and the Award," http://www.rayennersaward.com/about.php.

301 **Army lacrosse player killed in action in 1968. Navy's**: Ibid.

301 **soon-to-be SEAL Brendan Looney**: "Remembering Brendan Looney," Navy Athletics, September 25, 2010, http://navysports.com/news/2010/9/25/Remembering_Brendan _Looney; "Navy: Brendan Looney," Travis Manion Foundation, http://www.travismanion .org/fallen-heroes/lt-brendan-looney-usn/.

302 **the goal nets at Hopkins' Homewood**: "Their Sacrifice Will Not Be Forgotten," McLaughlin, Corey, Johns Hopkins University, November 11, 2022, https://hub.jhu .edu/2022/11/11/hopkins-lacrosse-memorial-wall-cordish-center/.

302 **The Hopkins contingent includes**: Ibid.

302 **three became SEALs, three marines and one a Ranger**: Danowski, author interview.

302 **Syracuse captain Rorke Denver**: "Ultimate Warrior," *Lacrosse Magazine*, November 2014, 19; "Rorke Denver Named Keynote Speaker at US Lacrosse Convention," *US Lacrosse*, December 11, 2014.

302 **Tad Stanwick**: "The Stanwick Way," Smith, Dean, *Pressbox* (MD), February 17, 2014; "Special Ops Pipeline," White, Matt, *Lacrosse Magazine*, November 2014.

302 **Bray Malphrus**: White.

302 **Army Sgt. Jimmy Regan**: "Jimmy Regan To Be Immortalized," Johnson, Elizabeth, *Manhasset Press* (NY), August 2, 2017; "Fallen LI Soldier a 'Friend to Everyone,'" Epstein, Reid J., *Newsday* (NY), February 11, 2007.

302 **news, Carroll again decided to enlist**: McLaughlin, April 2014.

303 **Hansen said, "We'll keep an eye out"**: Carroll, author interview.

303 **For the next four weeks**: McLaughlin.

303 *Who the fuck do you think you are?*: Carroll, Casey, author interview.

303   **During his four-and-a-half-year hitch**: Ibid; McLaughlin.
303   **Travis Manion, Looney's best friend**: "Marine from Bucks Is Killed in Combat in Iraq," *Morning Call* (PA), May 1, 2007.
303   **captain Roslyn Schulte**: "2006 Graduate Killed in Afghanistan," Van Winkle, John, U.S. Air Force Academy Public Affairs, July 13, 2009, http://www.usafa.af.mil/News /Article/429193/2006-graduate-killed-in-afghanistan/.
303   **Arlington Cemetery next to Manion**: "Best Friends Buried Side-by-Side in Arlington National Cemetery," Norman, Nancy, NBC4 Washington, October 4, 2010.
303   **"the skills and mind set"**: Denver, Rorke, Henican, Ellis. *Damn Few: Making the Modern SEAL Warrior* (New York: Hachette Books, 2013), 109.
303   **most likely to stick**: "Study Points SEAL recruiters toward Athletes," Steele, Jeanette, *San Diego Union-Tribune* (CA), March 15, 2010.
304   **men's lacrosse roster, like a platoon**: McLaughlin.
304   **Carroll acknowledges**: Carroll, author interview.
304   **"It's one of the more humbling sports"**: Ibid.
304   **On the afternoon of May 31, 2010**: Ibid.
305   **"The names on the jerseys"**: Carroll, author interview, October 17, 2022.
305   **"Old Man"**: "Former Army Ranger Carroll Again Leads Duke Lacrosse Defense," Klingaman, Mike, *Baltimore Sun* (MD), May 23, 2014.
305   **blew out the anterior cruciate ligament**: "Duke's Casey Carroll Tears ACL, Will Miss 2013 Season," *SB Nation: College Crosse*, January 31, 2013.
305   **"I could just see it in his eyes"**: Class, Deemer, author interview, November 19, 2018.
305   **Wells Fargo in Charlotte undercut his fitness**: McLaughlin.
306   **"What I would do for one more day"**: Carroll, author interview.
306   **On February 8, 2014**: McLaughlin.
306   **third-best defenseman**: Klingaman, May 23, 2014.
306   **He addressed the team before every game**: Ibid.
306   **irresistible storyline**: "Veteran Salutes Slain Soldier on Battlefield, Lacrosse Field," *CBSNews.com*, May 21, 2014.
306   **"would fit better on Monday's stage than Carroll"**: Klingaman.
306   **then the impossible happened**: "Duke's Carroll Completes a 10-Year Odyssey," Moore, Roger, *NCAA.com*, May 26, 2014; "Swezey: Casey Carroll's 'Hollywood Story' Ends With NCAA Title on Memorial Day," Swezey, Christian, *InsideLacrosse.com*, May 27, 2014.
306   **"Hugging them . . . they are always so special'"**: Carroll, author interview.

III. The Money Game

308   **killed by sniper fire**: "IDF Names Aviv Levi, 21, as Soldier Killed by Hamas Sniper," Ahronheim, Anna, *Jerusalem Post*, July 21, 2018.
309   **sixth straight meeting in the final**: "Canada, United States Advance To World Lacrosse Men's Championship," DaSilva, Matt, USALacrosse, June 30, 2023.
309   **"it's not about '14"**: Rabil, Paul, author interview, July 15, 2018.
310   **tournament's Most Valuable Player**: "From VP to MVP: Team USA's Michael Ehrhardt," Logue, Brian, USA Lacrosse, August 31, 2018.
310   **Ehrhardt's side hustle**: Ibid; Ehrhardt, Michael, author interview, January 19, 2023.
310   **Drafted seventh overall**: "Two Former Flyers Picked in 2014 MLL Draft," Walter, Geoffrey, *Patch.com* (Mineola, NY), January 14, 2014.

310   **"More of a glorified summer league"**: Ehrhardt, author interview.
310   **Fifty hours of the week**: Ibid.
310   **rest of the time he was a pro lacrosse player**: Ibid.
311   **"million-dollar man"**: "Paul Rabil, Lacrosse's Million-Dollar Man," Soshnick, Scott, *Bloomberg*, April 4, 2013.
311   **"less than ten guys"**: Seibald, Max, author interview, July 17, 2018.
311   **Then another email would ping in**: Ehrhardt, author interview.
311   **guided by US assistant Tony Resch**: Ibid.
311   **the first rumblings of a revolution**: Ehrhardt, Michael, author interview.
311   **failing in their attempt to buy—for $35 million**: *Fate of a Sport* (ESPN Films, Matt Tolmach Productions, Uninterrupted, Time and Room, Cloverhill Pictures, August 29, 2022); "A Barnstorming Lacrosse Champ Starts a League of His Own," Winfrey, Graham, *Inc. Magazine*, March 2023.
312   **spent two decades cultivating beltway contacts**: "The Fighter," Trotter, Jim, *Sports Illustrated*, February 21, 2011.
312   **"never seen anything like it"**: Smith, DeMaurice, author interview, November 15, 2018.
312   **Riverside Baptist School**: "NFLPA Head DeMaurice Smith Enjoying Son Alex's Lacrosse Career at Maryland," Lee, Edward, *Baltimore Sun* (MD), April 5, 2019.
312   **took it up in seventh grade**: Smith, DeMaurice, author interview.
312   **"pick up the phone and call us anytime"**: Ibid.
313   **Alex. Brown & Sons**: "Alex. Brown: History," http://www.alexbrownbranches.com/baltimore/history.asp.
313   **A.B. "Buzzy" Krongard**: "For Lacrosse Devotees, All Roads Lead to Baltimore," Green, Andrew A., *Baltimore Sun* (MD), May 24, 2003; "Alex. Brown Picks Chief Executive: Alvin B. Krongard Takes Helm of Investment Firm," Frank, Peter H., *Baltimore Sun* (MD), July 24, 1991; "200 Years Come Down To a Moment of Timing," Knight, Jerry, *Washington Post*, April 8, 1997; "'Buzzy' Krongard Gets CIA's No. 3-Ranked Job," Atkinson, Bill, *Baltimore Sun* (MD), March 17, 2001.
313   **punched a great white shark in the jaw**: Krongard, Buzzy, author interview, February 3, 2023.
313   **"Why don't you come to Alex. Brown?"**: Krongard, Buzzy, author interview.
313   **"A great pipeline"**: Greenberg, Mark, author interview, August 15, 2019.
313   **Baltimore's "lacrosse mafia"**: Green.
313   **"Wall Street lacrosse mafia"**: "Wall Street's Lacrosse Mafia," Wachter, Paul, *Bloomberg Businessweek*, March 22, 2012.
314   **"The only way"**: "On Lacrosse Fields, a Battered Bank Is Still a Player," Evans, Kelly, *Wall Street Journal*, April 3, 2008.
314   **Tierney estimates that more than 140**: Ibid.
314   **"hundreds"**: Offit, Howard, author interview.
314   **Sol Kumin came aboard**: "Exaggerator Owner Sol Kumin, a Former Hopkins Lacrosse Player, Can Party in Baltimore Like the Old Days," Shaffer, Jonas, *Baltimore Sun* (MD), May 21, 2016.
314   **"Thousands"**: Sweeney, Kyle, author interview, February 2, 2023.
314   **Gotham lacrosse summer league in 2007**: Evans.
314   **dominated the league's 16 men's teams**: Sweeney, author interview.
314   **but the Tuesday night games at Columbia didn't stop**: Evans.
314   **"When I'm looking at résumés"**: Lewis, William, author interview, July 25, 2019.

314 **"There is nothing close to black power"**: "The Most Powerful Black Executives in America," Daniels, Cora, Sutro, Martha, *Fortune*, July 22, 2002.
315 **merged two white and wealthy sub cultures**: "Wall Street Remains Occupied by Lacrosse Bros," Trotter, J.K., *Atlantic*, May 23, 2013.
315 **"The money is in what happens next"**: Woodson, Chazz, author interview, September 29, 2020.
315 **more than a dozen Yale alums on its floor**: Reilly, Brian, author interview, July 24, 2019.
315 **"I didn't even know what 'finance' was"**: Class, author interview.
315 **internship after his junior year at Barclays**: Ibid.
315 **"That's why so many lacrosse guys"**: Ibid.
316 **65-hour workweeks took an instant toll**: Ibid.
316 **more than $100,000 . . . $8,500**: Ibid.
316 **RBDC Lacrosse**: "How Sharpshooter Ryan Brown Played His Way Onto Team USA," USA Lacrosse, http://www.usalacrosse.com/magazine/how-sharpshooter-ryan-brown -played-his-way-us-team.
316 **In the year after leaving Barclays**: Class, author interview.
316 **fell for the eighth straight year**: "Major League Lacrosse: League Attendance," Point-streak.com, htts://pointstreak.com/prostats/attendance.html?leagueid=323&seasonid =18259.
317 **"I haven't had a regret"**: Class, author interview.
318 **"I've gotten yelled at a few times"**: Schreiber, Tom, Team USA post-game press conference, July 21, 2018.
318 **clear discrepancy**: DaSilva, *US Lacrosse Magazine*, September/October 2018; "U.S. Wins World Lacrosse Gold with 9-8 Win over Canada," *US Lacrosse*, July 23, 2018.
318 **"Chaos, pretty much"**: Mearns, Randy, Team Canada post-game press conference, July 21, 2018.
319 **phantom penalty that forced the fatal turnover**: "Last-Second Goal Secures Title," *Baltimore Sun* (MD), July 22, 2018.
319 **"We didn't feel that we were offside"**: Mearns, Randy, post-game press conference, July 21, 2018.
319 **"It's a shame that the game"**: Schreiber, post-game press conference.
319 **"We're grateful that we did win"**: Ibid; Danowski.
319 **"with time still on the clock"**: "FIL Confirm Controversial World Championship-Winning Goal Was Scored Within Regulation Time," Morgan, Liam, *insidethegames .biz*, July 29, 2018.
319 **"I'll add to that"**: Mearns, post-game press conference.

The New World

Part 1
I. Tewaaraton

325 **On October 22, 2018 . . . NBC . . . $25,000**: "Can a New Barnstorming, Player-Centric Lacrosse League Serve as a Template for Other Sports," Reiter, Ben, *Sports Illustrated*, November 16, 2018; "Is This Pro Lacrosse's Moment? This Star Is Betting Everything on It," Cotto, Andrew, *New York Times*, July 18, 2019.

325 indoor NLL average of $ 19,000: "National Lacrosse League Commissioner Optimistic About the Growth of the Sport," Koehler, Kristy, *The Gauntlet* (University of Calgary), November 20, 2018.

325 health care and an undisclosed equity stake: "Paul Rabil's Premier Lacrosse League Launches," DaSilva, Matt, *USA Lacrosse Magazine*, October 22, 2018.

325 MLL defectors: "Premier Lacrosse League Announces 140-Plus Player List," *Inside-Lacrosse.com*, October 22, 2018.

325 "I was ready to hang up the cleats": Ehrhardt, Mike, author interview, January 19, 2023.

325 "a bit of the Kevin Bacon": Smith, DeMaurice, author interview, November 15, 2018; "Rabil's PLL Secures First Round Of Investors; League Gains Momentum," *Sports Business Journal*, October 23, 2018.

326 "non-endemic" and "monthly actives": "Full Transcript: Investor and Lacrosse Player Paul Rabil on Too Embarrassed to Ask," *Recode*, June 18, 2018.

326 Ten yards had been cut: "PLL Announces New Rules For 2019 Season," *LaxAllStars.com*, May 29, 2019.

326 McKnight, a former All-American attackman: "We the Players: The Making of a Pro Lacrosse Revolution," McLaughlin, Corey, *US Lacrosse*, May/June 2019.

326 Soon aboard were former Hopkins players: "Wall Street's Lacrosse Fraternity Backs Rabil's New League," Soshnick, Scott, Boudway, Ira, *Bloomberg*, October 22, 2018; McLaughlin.

326 former Cornell attackman Mike Levine: "CAA Co-Head of Sports Mike Levin Joins Board of Directors," Premier Lacrosse League, May 1, 2023, https://premierlacrosseleague.com/articles/caa-co-head-of-sports-mike-levine-joins-premier-lacrosse-league-board-of-directors.

326 would join its front office as a financial analyst: *Sports Business Journal*, October 23, 2018; "Paul Rabil, Investors and Players Reflect on 5th Anniversary of PLL's First Game," Shore, Phil, *USA Lacrosse*, May 31, 2024.

326 154th-richest man in the world: Cotto; Bloomberg Billionaires Index, February 12, 2019.

326 Tsai himself: Tsai, Joe, author interview, March 25, 2020.

327 Tsai's father, Paul: "Biography of Paul Tsai," Paul Tsai China Center, Yale Law School, http://law.yale.edu/china-center/about-us/biography-paul-tsai.

327 Getting called "chink": Tsai, author interview.

327 "One of the most devastating": Ibid.

327 "to this day I actually thank": Ibid.

327 Teamed with: Ibid; Reilly, author interview; Gansler, Doug, author interview, October 30,2018.

327 Tsai scored: "Joe Tsai #19 Yale Bulldogs," posted August 31, 2016, by Craig Lunde, YouTube, 3:02, http://www.youtube.com/watch?v=FeTGte0VECw.

327 Alibaba co-founder Jack Ma in 1999: "Inside Alibaba: Vice Chairman Joe Tsai Opens Up About Working With Jack Ma And Jonathan Lu," Flannery, Russell, *Forbes.com*, January 8, 2014.

327 $600-a-year salary: *Acquired* podcast, season 3, episode 5, "Alibaba," September 23, 2018, http://www.acquired.fm/episodes/season-3-episode-5nbspalibaba.

327 In 2015, well before: Hayes, author interview, January 5, 2021; Cockerton, Stan, author interview, October 27, 2023.

327 Its annual operating budget: Cockerton, author interview.

327 **In Coquitlam, Canada, he met over dinner**: Ibid; Hayes, author interview; Kelly III, Frank, Tamulonis, Bill. *Influence and The Creator's Game* (Furniture Press Books, 2023), 311–314; Kelly III, Frank, contemporaneous notes, texted to author October 26, 2023.

328 **guaranteed FIL $250,000 a year**: Hayes, author interview.

328 **"You've never seen so many grown men cry"**: Cockerton, author interview.

328 **"you know the guy's genuine"**: Hayes, author interview.

328 **"I'm baffled why the NHL is so big"**: Tsai, author interview.

328 **Tsai sees no way**: Ibid.

329 **"I'm afraid probably not"**: Ibid.

329 **After years of explosive growth**: "Number of Participants in Lacrosse in the United States from 2006 to 2018," Statista; "Lacrosse's Surge in Popularity Is No Surprise," Paha, Jason, Sports Planning Guide, http://sportsplanningguide.com/lacrosse-is-growing/.

329 **provisional recognition to the FIL. "I can't think"**: "Welcome to the World: IOC Recognizes FIL," Logue, Brian, *US Lacrosse*, November 30, 2018.

329 **World Games—a quadrennial festival**: Logue.

330 **"go down the road without them . . ."**: Scherr, Jim, author interview, July 14, 2018.

330 **"They need to understand"**: Ibid.

330 **"We will always be"**: Thompson, Lyle, author interview, November, 26, 2018.

330 **On January 12, 2019**: "After Racist Taunts, Lacrosse Star Lyle Thompson Stands for his Heritage," Price, S.L., *Sports Illustrated*, April 17, 2019.

330 **"Let's snip the ponytail right here!"**: Price, April 17, 2019; "Thompson Target of Insensitive Remarks at Wings Game Saturday," Hamilton, Matt, *USA Lacrosse*, January 13, 2019.

330 **"It was disgusting"**: Guterding, Justin, author interview, October 23, 2021.

331 **"cut your hair? Or do we have to scalp you?"**: Thompson, Lyle, author interview, April 5, 2019.

331 **Thompson tapped out a pair of tweets**: Price, April 17, 2019; "Thompson Target of Insensitive Remarks at Wings Game Saturday," Hamilton, Matt, *US Lacrosse Magazine*, January 13, 2019.

331 **Three minutes later Brendan Bomberry**: Bomberry, Brendan, (@Leftybombz21), "Great game and atmosphere @NLLwings but it was overshadowed by your in game announcer's comments towards my teammates," Twitter (now X), January 12, 2019, 9:41 p.m., http://twitter.com/Leftybombz21/status/1084279203145699331.

331 **"at the professional level"**: Thompson, Lyle, author interview, April 5, 2019.

331 **Within 12 hours**: Hamilton; "Philadelphia Wings In-Game Announcer Apologizes for Racially Insensitive Remarks," *Canadian Press*, January 13, 2019.

331 **apologized, saying his words**: *Canadian Press*, January 13, 2019; "Announcer Apologizes for Remark; Team, League Vow Discipline," *Associated Press*, January 13, 2019.

331 **Wings fired him the next day**: Price.

332 **announced an immediate launch**: Ibid.

332 **"We fly together"**: Ibid.

332 BACK THE BRAID: Price.

332 **"so much good came of it"**: Thompson, Lyle, author interview.

332 **#DrawTheLine**: "#DrawTheLine Campaign Calls For Lacrosse Players to Take a Stand," *InsideLacrosse.com*, April 3, 2019.

332 **The same weekend of the braid incident**: Carpenetti, Ann, USA Lacrosse, email to author, March 17, 2023.

332 **made that course mandatory**: "Kyle Harrison: Building a Future for Everyone," Harrison, Kyle, *Lacrosse Playground*, June 19, 2019.

332 **NLL did the same**: "National Lacrosse League and US Lacrosse Partner To Bring Cultural Awareness," *NLL.com*, June 25, 2019.

332 **"This has brought the lacrosse community"**: Thompson, Lyle, author interview.

333 **saying, "I love you"**: Tiffany, Lars, author interview, November 10, 2019.

333 **a stroke, on January 28, 2019**: "Bradford L. Tiffany," *Press and Sun-Bulletin* (NY), February 3, 2019, 19A.

333 **burial had to wait for spring**: Tiffany, author interview.

333 **A year earlier, Brad had asked**: Ibid; Solomon, Joe, author interview, November 2, 2021.

333 **"like a gift from the other side"**: Tiffany, Lars, author interview.

333 **"Tofu Tiffany"**: Tiffany, author interview.

333 **"stick was built to be played with"**: Ibid.

334 **"give you an ulcer"**: "For Tiffany, There's No Slowing Down," Counts, Ron, *Daily Progress* (VA), March 17, 2017.

334 **lacrosse-only carve out**: Tiffany, author interview.

334 **He began "Cultural Thursdays"**: "Less Partying Has Led to More Winning as Lars Tiffany Has Rebuilt U.Va. Lacrosse," Barber, Mike, *Richmond Times-Dispatch* (VA), May 5, 2019.

334 **"It was intense and crazy"**: Conrad, Ryan, author interview, March 29, 2023.

334 **finished 8-7. In 2018**: "How Virginia Returned to the Pinnacle of College Lacrosse," Lambrecht, Gary, *US Lacrosse*, July 23, 2019.

334 **In August of 2018**: Tiffany, author interview, May 1, 2023.

335 **"We were now on double-secret probation"**: Ibid.

335 **"It wasn't easy, frankly"**: Conrad, author interview.

335 **agreement to swear off alcohol**: Ibid; Tiffany, author interview, May 1, 2023.

335 **"Absolute validation"**: Tiffany, author interview.

335 **openly about substance abuse**: "American Boy Fall Brawl Raises Funds for Addicts, Families," Feil, Justin, *US Lacrosse Magazine*, October 16, 2019.

336 **American Boy Fall Brawls**: Ibid.

336 **in 2021, overdose deaths**: "U.S. Overdose Deaths In 2021 Increases Half as Much as in 2020—But Are Still Up 15%," CDC National Center for Health Statistics, May 11, 2022, http://www.cdc.gov/nchs/pressroom/nchs_press_releases/2022/202205 .htm.

336 **NCAA's 2023 Abuse Survey**: "Current Findings on Student-Athlete Substance Use," NCAA Student-Athlete Health and Wellness Study, NCAA Research, (January 2024), 14, 15, 24, 32, 35, 57, 58.

336 **intended as "a healing"**: Tiffany, author interview, November 10, 2019.

336 **"It meant a lot"**: Dziama, Matt, author interview, March 27, 2023.

336 **2019 NCAA tournament, Tiffany's Haudenosaunee talisman**: "'A Gift From Your Father': How a Wooden Stick Brings Perspective to Virginia," Shannon, Geoff, *Inside-Lacrosse.com*, June 17, 2019.

337 **"he was telling the world"**: Lyons, Betty, author interview, April 23, 2023.

337 **until attackman Ian Laviano**: "No. 3 Seeded UVA Upends No. 2 Seeded Duke In Two Overtimes, 13-12," VirginiaSports.com, May 25, 2019; "Cavaliers' Revival Continues with Comeback to Send Them Back to Title Game," Gutierrez, Matthew, *Washington Post*, May 26, 2019, D4.

337 **Tiffany won his first NCAA championship**: "Virginia Lacrosse Beats Yale to Win the 2019 National Championship," Staats, Wayne, *NCAA.com*, May 28, 2019.

337 **National Museum of the American Indian**: "National Museum of the American Indian Architecture Fact Sheet," National Museum of the American Indian, July 2014.

338 **members of DC's University Club**: "Tewaaraton Award," The University Club, Washington, D.C., http://www.universityclubdc.com/tewaaraton.

338 **Sidney Hill presented the trophy**: "Sculptor Puts Essence of Lacrosse in Trophy," Stiehm, Jamie, *Baltimore Sun* (MD), June 6, 2001.

338 **first female Tewaaraton finalist of Indigenous descent**: Tewaaraton Foundation, author query.

338 **Haudenosaunee Thanksgiving Address**: "2019 Tewaaraton Award Ceremony," streamed live on May 30, 2019, by Lacrosse All Stars, YouTube, 2:31.41, http://www.youtube.com/watch?v=zDVrRroCXeQ.

339 **World Lacrosse would unveil**: "Is This the Way to Introduce Lacrosse to the Rest of the World?," *USA Lacrosse Magazine*, October 2019.

340 **"It was really deliberate"**: Lyons, Rex, author interview, April 15, 2023.

340 **By that November**: "U.S. Selected for 2021 World Games Competition," *USA Lacrosse Magazine*, December 4, 2019.

340 **"If the Iroquois aren't"**: Tiffany, author interview, November 10, 2019.

340 **"Lacrosse without Native Americans?"**: Ibid.

340 **Three weeks later, December 4, 2019**: *USA Lacrosse*, December 4, 2019.

II. An Awful Roar

341 **"the pandemics are coming"**: Lyons, Oren, author interview, November 28, 2018.

341 **canceled its basketball tournaments and all spring sports**: "NCAA Announces Cancellation of Spring Sports Championships," Nazar, Jake, *SB Nation: College Crosse*, March 12, 2020; "A Year of COVID-19: What Was Going On in the US in March 2020," Pereira, Ivan and Mitropoulous, Arielle, *ABC News*, March 4, 2021.

341 **On the morning of March 8**: "Racist Incident Prompts Men's Lacrosse Probation, Coach Termination and BSU Activism for Greater Accountability," Gieger, Olivia, De Rosa, Natalie, *The Amherst Student*, March 27, 2020.

342 **condemning their racial language as "revolting"**: Ibid.

342 **December 2018 party**: "Men's Lacrosse Members Involved in Racist Incident," Chen, Shawn, *The Amherst Student*, March 11, 2020.

342 **transphobic comments made by other players**: "Amherst College Places Men's Lacrosse on Probation, Fires Coach for Racist Incident," Walfish, Josh, *Daily Hampshire Gazette* (MA), March 21, 2020.

342 **"deeply troubling cases"**: Gieger, De Rosa, March 27, 2020.

342 **Jon Thompson was fired**: "Breaking: Amherst Parts Ways With Jon Thompson, Team Will Not Play in 2021 Postseason," *InsideLacrosse.com*, March 20, 2020.

342 **Then, on May 25, 2020**: "How George Floyd Was Killed in Police Custody," Hill, Evan et al, *New York Times*, May 31, 2020.

342 **"Black Lives Matter"**: "How Black Lives Matter Reached Every Corner of America," Burch, Audra D.S. et al, *New York Times*, June 13, 2020.

342 **weekly online Zoom series**: "Overtime: A Candid Discussion of Racism in Lacrosse," *LaxAllStars.com*, June 10, 2020; "OVERTIME—A Candid Discussion on Racism in

Lacrosse. EPISODE I," posted on June 11, 2020 by Mattie H, YouTube, 1:44.37, http://youtu.be/pOgffxCQlbA?si=pa-YXOlS1A4mjP_5.

343 **"It was my sport"**: "Overtime: Episode II—The Womens Game, OVERTIME—A Candid Discussion on Racism in Lacrosse," posted on June 17, 2020 by Mattie H, YouTube, 1:23.30, http://www.youtube.com/watch?v=DGV_2MICFY0.

343 **On June 2**: "Marquette Rescinds Offer of Admission to Lacrosse Player Over Snapchat Post on George Floyd's Death," Shastri, Devi, *Milwaukee Journal Sentinel* (WI), June 2, 2020.

343 **A month earlier, on May 6**: "Premier Lacrosse League Announces PLL Championship Series," PLL press release, May 6, 2020.

343 **Behind the scenes**: *Fate of a Sport.*

343 **"We stand united"**: Premier Lacrosse League statement, Rabil, Paul, Rabil, Mike, Facebook.com, Twitter.com, Instagram.com, June 1, 2020.

344 **"The time is now"**: "Kyle Hartzell | Pat Young—A Conversation on Race in Lacrosse," posted on June 8, 2020 by US Lacrosse, YouTube, http://youtu.be/bHEHMZvSq3I?si =QX-TKLneKscwKuMV.

344 **"difficult—but positive—conversations"**: Harrison, Kyle, author interview, December 15, 2023.

344 **in 2013 in reaction to the acquital**: "This Day in History: July 13, 2013: The Hashtag #BlackLivesMatter First Appears, Sparking a Movement," History.com, http://www .history.com/this-day-in-history.

344 **nuclear family structure**: "BLM Site Removes Page on 'Nuclear Family Structure' Amid NFL vet's Criticism," Miller, Joshua Rhett, *New York Post*, September 24, 2020.

345 **support plummeted from 37 to 16 percent**: "Support for Black Lives Matter Has Decreased since June but Remains Strong among Black Americans," Thomas, Deja, Horowitz, Juliana Menasce, Pew Research Center, September 16, 2020; "Black Lives Matter Support Drops 12 percent Over Summer, Poll Finds," Eustachewich, Lia, *New York Post*, September 17, 2020.

345 **Only 13 of the PLL's 154 players**: "Taking A Stand," *Inside Lacrosse*, September 2020, http://www.insidelacrosse.com/article/september-issue-in-their-words-/56795; Black Lacrosse Alliance (@BLAlliance_), "If you cheer for us in there, stand with us out here," Twitter (now X), July 25, 2020, 1:57 p.m., http://twitter.com/BLAlliance_/status /1287084614364758016; "Premier Lacrosse League Announces Rosters for Upcoming PLL Championship Series," Premier Lacrosse League, July 2, 2020, https:// premierlacrosseleague.com/articles/premier-lacrosse-league-announces-rosters-for -upcoming-pll-championship-series.

345 **The spark was hearing Wiley**: Hartzell, Kyle, author interview, November 14, 2023.

345 **tried to convince objectors**: Heningburg, Jules, author interview, November 8, 2023; Harrison, Kyle, author interview, December 15, 2023.

345 **"Very charged times"**: Heningburg, author interview.

346 **"stark opposition"**: Black Lacrosse Alliance (@BLAlliance_), "We, The Black Lacrosse Alliance, stand with @_TyWarner5 and unapologetically support his message. Please take the time to hear him and the players perspective," Twitter (now X), August 17, 2020, 2:23 p.m., http://twitter.com/BLAlliance_/status/1295426098688401410.

346 **"dumb" comments**: Hartzell, Kyle, author interview, November 14, 2023.

346 **"It was a difficult time"**: Ibid.

346 **"I have a very close friend"**: Heningburg, author interview.

346 **NBA was offering its players 29 options**: "With the Words on Their Backs, NBA players Take a Stand," Wallace, Ava, *Washington Post*, July 30, 2020.

346 **"me as the bad guy"**: *Fate of a Sport.*

346 **some two dozen**: *Inside Lacrosse Podcasts*, "8/4 Pro Podcast: Knockout Round," American City Business Journals, August 4, 2020, 57:10–58:48, http://podcasts.apple.com/us/podcast/8-4-pro-podcast-knockout-round/id601462524?i=1000487074808.

347 **publicly explained their objection**: Ibid; Black Lacrosse Alliance statement on Twitter, August 17, 2020.

347 **"MLL Four"**: "MLL's Black Players Stand Together, Demand Action on Diversity," *InsideLacrosse.com*, August 13, 2020; author interview, Ellis, Mark, November 3, 2023; author interview, Toliver, Chad, November 3, 2023.

347 **MLL social media feeds were not posting messages**: Ibid.

348 **"candid, and at times, painful discussion"**: Brown, Alexander (@MLLCommish), Twitter (now X) July 23, 2020, 12:27 p.m., http://x.com/MLLCommish/status/1286337248691204096?ref_src=twsrc%5Etfw.

348 **"This culture hasn't changed"**: Toliver, Chad, author interview.

348 **Major League Lacrosse . . . the most prominent casualty**: "MLL Cancels Saturday's Semifinals, Denver-Boston to Play Sunday at 2 p.m. on ESPN," *InsideLacrosse.com*, July 25, 2020; "Premier Lacrosse League Merges with Major League Lacrosse," Roberts, Daniel, *Yahoo! Finance*, December 16, 2020; *Fate of a Sport.*

348 **swallowed the MLL whole**: "Paul and Mike Rabil lead efforts to merge the PLL & MLL in 'Fate of a Sport,'" posted on August 29, 2022 by ESPN, YouTube, 3:09, http://www.youtube.com/watch?v=tcSs92Gp4xA.

348 **Toliver suspected**: Toliver, author interview.

348 **"bad blood" between the two leagues**: Heningburg, author interview.

349 **"Black lacrosse is very small"**: Ellis, author interview.

349 **"offer to play in the PLL and I didn't"**: Ibid.

349 **On July 26, 2020**: "No Racism Allowed: Sweet Lax's 'Zero Tolerance' Policy After July 26 Incident," DaSilva, Matt, *US Lacrosse*, November 3, 2020.

349 **Mexico women's coach Daniela Eppler**: Eppler, Daniela, author interview, August 9, 2020.

349 **titled "The Denial"**: "Overtime Episode 8—The Denial," *LaxAllStars.com*, August 5, 2020, http://laxallstars.com/overtime-episode-8-the-denial/.

350 **"It's hard raising"**: Schindler, Tia, Overtime Episode 8, August 5, 2020.

350 **"Just based on"**: Eppler, Overtime Episode 8.

350 **"beaners"**: Ibid.

350 **"Players Against Hate"**: "About Us: Our Story," Players Against Hate, http://playersagainsthate.org/our-story/; "Second Annual Players Against Hate Charity Game in Laurel," Sumner, Ben, *Capitals Outsider*, July 8, 2023.

351 **database compiled nearly 100 reports**: "Players Against Hate Crossing Out Racism in Youth Sport," D'Agostino, Alex, Monumental Foundation, http://www.monumentalfoundation.org/article/2022-players-against-hate.

351 **declined from 89 to 83 percent**: NCAA Demographics Database.

351 **In 2008, after the US Census Bureau**: "Minorities in U.S. Set to Become Majority by 2042," Roberts, Sam, *New York Times*, August 14, 2008.

351 **Her 2014 paper**: "On the Precipice of a 'Majority-Minority' America: Perceived Status Threat from the Racial Demographic Shift Affects White Americans' Political Ideology,"

Craig, Maureen A, Richeson, Jennifer A., *Psychological Science* 25, no. 6 (June 2014), 1: 189–197.

351 **telling four minority Congresswomen to "go back"**: "Trump tells Dem Congresswomen: Go back Where You Came From," Quilantan, Bianca, Cohen, David, *Politico*, July 14, 2019.

351 **During Trump's first three years**: "FBI: Hate Crime Incidents Rose 2.7% in 2019," Farivar, Masood, *VOA News*, November 16, 2020.

351 **the number of documented racist acts**: "Lapchick: The Year in Racism and Sports," Lapchick, Richard, *ESPN.com*, January 24, 2017; "Acts of Racism in Sports Rise, but So Do Efforts to Educate," Lapchick, *Sports Business Journal*, March 29, 2021.

351 **ongoing "Incident Report"**: "Nation United Launches Virtual Portal to Gather, Catalog, Racist Incidents," *US Lacrosse Magazine*, November 11, 2020.

352 **58 racist incidents**: "Racist Incidents in High School Football Spark Talks and Programs," Brunt, Cliff, *Associated Press*, December 22, 2022.

352 **"still very white"**: Melero, Ernie, author interview, March 1, 2021.

352 **"That Greece game"**: Ibid.

352 **"I'm around white kids all the time"**: Ibid.

352 **"We take our kids from the inner city"**: Ibid.

353 **postponement to 2022**: "The World Games in Birmingham Postponed Until 2022," Logue, Brian, *USA Lacrosse*, April 2, 2020.

353 **reposted its piece on July 18**: "Iroquois Nationals: Fighting for the Olympic Dream," Wong, Brian A, McDonough, Aileen, *InsideLacrosse.com*, July 18, 2020; originally appeared in March 2020 print issue of *Inside Lacrosse*.

353 **that night with a "call on colleagues"**: "World Lacrosse, Iroquois Nationals Issue Statement in Wake of Call for World Games Inclusion," Foy, Terry, *InsideLacrosse.com*, July 24, 2020.

354 **A day later Aidan Fearn**: "Petition Calls on 10 countries to Boycott 2022 World Games over Iroquois Nationals Exclusion from Lacrosse," Morgan, Liam, *Insidethegames.biz*, July 25, 2020.

354 **"For events conducted outside"**: Foy, July 24, 2020.

354 **"I support"**: Tsai, Joe (@joetsai1999), Twitter (now X), July 24, 2020, 11:06 a.m, http://x .com/joetsai1999/status/1286679159951876096?ref_src=twsrc%5Etfw.

354 **"Pledging my support"**: Rabil, Paul (@PaulRabil), Twitter (now X), July 24, 2020, 11:22 a.m, https://x.com/PaulRabil/status/1286683082536259589.

355 **"the very essence of lacrosse"**: "US Lacrosse Statement on Iroquois Nationals and the World Games," *US Lacrosse*, July 24, 2020.

355 **"unequivocally in support"**: "Lacrosse Association Pushing for Inclusion of Iroquois Nationals at World Games," McDougall, Allana, *APTN*, July 27, 2020.

355 **Alibaba had agreed to pay $800 million**: "Alibaba Olympics Sponsorship Deal Said to Be Worth $800 Million," Panja, Tariq, Wang, Selina, Satariano, Adam, *Bloomberg*, January 19, 2017.

356 **"Those same people"**: Neiss, Scott, author interview, November 3, 2020.

356 **"World Lacrosse should have understood"**: Scherr, Jim, author interview, October 23, 2021.

356 **Ripley Rand and Alex Buckley . . . Howard Stupp**: "Alex Buckley and Ripley Rand Help Secure International Win for Iroquois Nationals Lacrosse Program," Womble Bond Dickinson, September 8, 2020.

356 **On July 29**: "Joint Statement From The International World Games Association, World Lacrosse and The World Games 2022 Birmingham Organizing Committee," Twitter (now X) World Lacrosse (@WorldLacrosse), July 29, 2020, 11:48 a.m., http://twitter.com /WorldLacrosse/status/1288501599971627009.

356 **On August 14, World Lacrosse**: "They Gave the World the Creator's Game. Now They're Fighting to Be Allowed to Play," Whitepigeon, Monica, *Native News Online*, August 24, 2020.

357 **"I know what"**: Kennedy, Michael, author interview, April 26, 2023.

357 **the Irish should give up their place**: "Ireland Vacates Spot in 2022 World Games to Make Way For Iroquois," *InsideLacrosse.com*, September 2, 2020.

357 **called "inspiring" by Scherr**: "Ireland Lacrosse Voluntarily Withdraws from TWG 2022," World Lacrosse press release, September 2, 2020.

357 **"Language is important"**: Kennedy, author interview.

357 **"We are storytellers"**: "Friendship between Ireland, Tribes Lives on in Lacrosse" Walker, Dalton, *Indian Country Today*, September 15, 2020.

358 **"intolerance" for the Iroquois built up**: Scherr, author interview, October 23, 2021.

358 **"most pragmatic thing to do"**: Ibid.

358 **"That's the biggest win of 2020"**: Neiss, author interview.

III. Crops

359 **68 nations**: "United States Virgin Islands becomes 68th member of World Lacrosse," Palmer, Dan, *Insidethegames.biz*, November 10, 2020.

359 **Marquette men's player**: "Marquette Responds to Another Racist Social Media Incident; One Student Removed from Men's Lacrosse Team," Shastri, Devi, *Milwaukee Journal Sentinel* (WI), February 16, 2021.

359 **Sewanee**: "Racial Slur Taunting at Lacrosse Match: University Response," Lytle, Leslie, *Sewanee Mountain Messenger* (TN), March 18, 2021.

359 **"Playing a sport that you love"**: "US Lacrosse Statement on Racial Incident at College Lacrosse Game," *US Lacrosse*, March 16, 2021.

360 **"Woman power does not diminish"**: Rabil, Paul (@PaulRabil) "I come from, have been shaped by, and deeply admire women. Woman power does not diminish my own; rather, it enriches us all," Twitter (now Xd) December 29, 2017, 12:23 p.m., http://twitter .com/PaulRabil/status/946793774679773185.

360 **prompted by his supportive Pride Day photo**: "Straight Lacrosse Player Paul Rabil Posts LGBT Pride Message,Gets Attacked for It, Stands Up against Bullying," Buzinski, Jim, *OutSports*, July 16, 2017.

360 **Harrison, at 38, was playing his last game**: "Harrison Coming Full Circle," Lee, Edward, *Baltimore Sun* (MD), June 21, 2021.

361 **"destructive" headlines**: Rabil, Paul, author interview, January 12, 2022.

361 **Native American roots as not just exotica:** Ibid.

361 **land acknowledgments**: "Why Professional Lacrosse Is Swapping East Coast Elitism for Land Acknowledgments," Lauer, Alex, *InsideHook*, May 3, 2021.

361 **get Lyle Thompson**: *Fate of a Sport.*

362 **He didn't seem to mind**: "Kyle Harrison's Last Dance," Rice, Nelson, *USA Lacrosse*, August 25, 2021.

363 **$10 million field house**: "New Facility a Monument to Winning Tradition of Johns Hopkins Lacrosse," Rienzi, Greg, *Johns Hopkins Gazette*, March 2013.

363 **"That took a lot of doing"**: Lyons, Oren, author interview, October 23, 2021.
363 **"World Lacrosse Super Sixes"**: "363 Goals, 385 Minutes: Looking Back at World Lacrosse Super Sixes," USA Lacrosse press release, October 27, 2021.
364 **appointed to the six-person task force**: "World Lacrosse Governance Working Group," World Lacrosse meeting minutes, August 11, 2020.
364 **"best sign you could ever get"**: Lyons, Oren, author interview.
364 **"*Shoot, we're making change here*"**: Minerd, Cassandra, author interview, January 23, 2024.
365 **"I still don't even play catch"**: Ibid.
365 **In eighth grade, Minerd went public**: Ibid.
365 **SUNY-Brockport**: "Current Sloan Indigenous Graduate Fellows," State University of New York College of Environmental Science and Forestry, http://www.esf.edu /nativepeoples/graduate-partnership/current-fellows; "Cassandra Minerd (Onondaga): The Good Medicine of Playing Lacrosse at SUNY Brockport and on the World Stage," Ninham, Dan, *NDNSports.com*, September 29, 2021.
366 **Iroquois Nationals Development Group**: "Iroquois Nationals Establish a Nonprofit," Iroquois Nationals Development Group press release, September 25, 2020.
366 **"If you're going"**: Lyons, Rex, author interview, April 15, 2023.
366 **On January 23, 2020**: "Convicted Child Rapist Worked with Indigenous Youth on Six Nations as Late as 2019," Garlow, Nahnda, *Two Row Times*, January 24, 2020.
366 **2003 U-19 and Onondaga Community College's 2006 national**: "Haudenosaunee Men's National Under-19 Lacrosse team," Wikipedia, http://en.wikipedia.org/wiki /Haudenosaunee_men%27s_national_under-19_lacrosse_team; "2006 Men's Lacrosse Roster: 18, Matt Myke," Onondaga Lazers, https://onondagalazers.com/sports/mens -lacrosse/roster/matt-myke/443.
366 **"the first time he tried to talk to me"**: Stevens, Aryien, author interview, January 22, 2024.
367 **Myke was sentenced**: "Faithkeeper at Sour Springs Longhouse Sentenced to 20 Years in Prison for Child Rape," *Two Row Times*, September 16, 2020.
367 **dated February 6, 2020**: Ibid; "Reference Letters Matt Myke," Clerk of Circuit Court, Brown County, WI, Case 2016CF001728, Document 87, Filed August 28, 2020, 3.
367 **public link to the 32 support letters**: *Two Row Times*, September 16, 2020, http://drive .google.com/file/d/1W9YGs2274CFOVv-Pt6xRwoLp4TJmGLUJ/view.
367 **Smith officially received the petition**: Haudenosaunee Lax, (@HaudenosauneeLx), "HNWL (Haudenosaunee Nationals Women's Lacrosse) finally received a petition that had been in existence since the Fall of 2020 from the Iroquois Nationals on February 5, 2021, not from the petitioners themselves," Twitter (now X), June 25, 2021, 12:33 p.m., http://twitter.com/HaudenosauneeLx/status/1408463432035274754.
367 **"Matthew Myke has been a predator to players"**: Minerd, email to Haudenosaunee Board, February 8, 2021, 9:57 a.m.; Minerd, author interview.
367 **The same day**: Stevens, author interview; Iroquois Nationals Development Group, Fearn, Terrelyn, et al., letter to Iroquois Nationals Board of Directors, February 15, 2021.
367 **acknowledging Stevens's "pain"**: Smith, Kathy, Haudenosaunee Nationals Board of Directors, letter to Stevens, Aryien, February 15, 2021.
367 **Two other-high profile Haudenosaunee organizations**: "Removal of General Manager Sparks New Beginning for Haudenosaunee Women's Nationals Field Team," *Two Row Times*, April 21, 2021.

368 "toxic environment created by team management": Iroquois Nationals Development Group letter, February 15, 2021.

368 sent the Nationals board a confidential plan: Ibid.

368 "long overdue participation of women": Ibid.

368 formally requesting the disbanding: Minerd and Stevens, letter to Haudenosaunee Grand Council, March 3, 2021; Minerd, author interview.

368 April 5, 2021: Lyons, Rex, author interview, January 30, 2024.

369 By mid-month the Iroquois Nationals: "Iroquois Nationals Announce Women's Nationals Lacrosse Program," Two Row Times, May 19, 2021; Lyons, Rex, author interview, January 27, 2024.

369 On May 16, the new Iroquois Nationals: Two Row Times, May 19, 2021.

369 On June 21, nine former: Haudenosaunee Lax (@HaudenosauneeLx), "This letter comes from former Haudenosaunee Nationals Women's Lacrosse (HNWL) players . . .," Twitter (now X), June 25, 2021, 12:33 p.m., http://twitter.com/HaudenosauneeLx/status /1408463432035274754.

369 "I still don't feel": "Haudenosaunee Women's Lacrosse Team Disbanded—Let's Talk Native #547," Let's Talk Native with John Kane, posted July 13, 2021, by Let's Talk Native TV, YouTube, 17:50-18:10, https://youtu.be/b5RMaLsiR7Q.

369 another lacrosse referendum was held at tryouts: Minerd, author interview; Stevens, author interview; "Iroquois Nationals Women's Program Evaluations, June 26–27 'New Location: Onondaga Community College,'" Facebook, June 11, 2021; Haudenosaunee Nationals (@HaudenosauneeNationals), "Women's Tryout Hype Video," Facebook.com, July 27, 2021, http://fb.watch/usz9ndQdJK/.

370 began to tremble: Stevens, author interview; Minerd, author interview.

370 Most striking: 77 women: Jimerson, Claudia, author interview, October 24, 2021.

370 "We did it": Minerd, author interview.

370 first appearance in a Haudenosaunee uniform: "Selena Lasota Headlines Iroquois Nationals' World Lacrosse Super Sixes Roster," DeJohn, Kenny, USA Lacrosse, October 11, 2021.

370 "There's no way that I can represent Team Canada": Lasota, Selena, author interview, October 23, 2021.

370 named to its 2017 senior national team and was expected: "Selena Lasota Leads Canada to First-Ever U-19 World Championship," Northwestern Athletics, August 1, 2015; "Trio of Wildcats Named to Canada's 2017 Women's World Cup Roster," Kelley, Kyle, Northwestern Athletics, October 19, 2016.

371 On May 27, 2021: "Grief, Sorrow after Discovery of 215 Bodies, Unmarked Graves at Former B.C. Residential School Site," Potenteau, Doyle, Global News, May 28, 2021.

371 tender her resignation: Lasota, author interview.

371 another 933 graves: "182 Unmarked Graves Discovered Near Residential School in B.C.'s Interior, First Nation Says," Migdal, Alex, CBC News, June 30, 2021; "Canada Discovers 751 Unmarked Graves at Former Residential School," Cecco, Leyland, Guardian (London), June 24, 2021.

371 In August Canada committed $320 million: "Ottawa Pledges $320 Million to Search for Residential School Graves and Support Survivors," Canadian Press, August 10, 2021.

371 EVERY CHILD MATTERS: "Every Child Matters: PLL Players Educate and Advocate for Victims of Residential Schools," Lacrosse Playground, August 11, 2021; "NLL Teams

Will Wear 'Every Child Matters' Decal This Season," *TorontoRock.com*, September 30, 2021.

371   **Lasota's defection didn't become known until**: Haudenosaunee Nationals Lacrosse (@NAU_Nationals), "We are proud to announce the women that will compete at @worldlaxsport Sixes in Sparks, MD! #TogetherAsOne," Twitter (formerly X), October 9, 2021, 1:57 p.m., http://twitter.com/HAU_Nationals/status/1446897639463792640.

371   **Lasota had discovered a personal narrative**: Lasota, author interview, October 23, 2021.

372   **Lorain spent her days**: Ibid.

372   **On September 30, 2021**: "Tla-o-qui-aht Organizes March in Tofino to Commemorate Residential School Survivors and Victims," Renwick, Melissa, *Ha-Shilth-Sa*, September 30, 2021.

372   **"When I first went to residential school"**: Ibid.

372   **"It just feels like"**: Lasota, author interview.

373   **"There's growing pains still"**: Jimerson, author interview, October 24, 2021.

373   **"I thought he yelled"**: Lasota, author interview, October 24, 2021.

374   **"It hurt to hear that"**: McKone, Lindsey, author interview, October 24, 2021.

374   **"For them to assume"**: Ibid.

375   **including a two-hour blitz on ESPN**: "ESPN's 'Journalism Showcase'—February 12, 2016," ESPN Front Row, February 12, 2016.

375   **"Hampton is exploring"**: "Video: Jim Brown on Significance of Hampton Lacrosse," *InsideLacrosse.com*, February 16, 2016; Brown, Jim (@JimBrownNFL32), "Way to go @_HamptonU on being the 1st HBCU to play Div 1 lacrosse . . . ! Honored to share my story . . . @SportsCenter," Twitter (now X) February 13, 2016, 11:21 p.m., http://twitter.com/JimBrownNFL32/status/698723797696794624.

375   **in 1878, a year before founding**: "Samuel Chapman Armstrong," *Encyclopedia Virginia*, Virginia Humanities, http://encyclopediavirginia.org/entries/armstrong-samuel-chapman-1839-1893/.

375   **his youngest son, Aris**: "Aris Brown, Son of Legendary Jim Brown, Commits to Play Lacrosse at Hampton University," WTKR-3 Hampton Roads | Northeast NC, May 6, 2020.

375   **They told of how they came**: Hampton University men's lacrosse players, author interviews, November 17, 2021.

376   **third try at the Hampton job**: Woodson, Chazz, author interview.

376   **"Ultimately if this thing isn't successful"**: Ibid.

376   **"and he wouldn't even say anything"**: Brown, Aris, author interview, November 17, 2021.

376   **"a certain swag I hadn't seen before"**: Ibid.

377   **In the classroom, Nathan Turner's mention**: Hampton University men's lacrosse players, author interviews.

377   **"People care about it because"**: Mitchell, Ethan, author interview, November 17, 2021.

377   **Emancipation Oak**: "The History Behind Hampton's Fort Monroe," McLeod, Nia Simone, *Urban Views RVA*, August 13, 2019.

377   **He talked about the growth of Black faces in the game**: Woodson, author interview, November 18, 2021.

378   **"Part of the reason"**: Brown, Aris, author interview, February 21, 2024.

Part 2
I. Treaty Bound

381 **Brad, as the story goes**: Tiffany, Lars, author interview, November 10, 2019; Corwin, Faith, author interview, May 18, 2023.

381 **"if I ever want some of 'em"**: Tiffany, Lars, author interview.

382 **"We paid him back"**: Lyons, Oren, author interview, May 22, 2023.

382 **Johnson said that Brad**: Johnson, Vincent, author interview, June 13, 2023.

382 **"The deal was"**: Ibid.

382 **"The buffalo are there"**: Ibid.

383 **Ten head were killed for the welcoming feast**: "World Indoor Lacrosse Championship Set for Onondaga Nation," Donahue, Mark, LaxAllStars.com, April 7, 2015.

383 **"a gift that can't ever be measured"**: Lyons, Betty, author interview, April 3, 2023.

383 **Then, on April 22, 2021**: "Twenty Onondaga Dege•yá'gih (Bison) are Transferred to Gakwi:yo—Seneca Farms," Onondaga Nation, April 26, 2021.

383 **2022 World Games in Birmingham**: "Results of The World Games: The World Games 22, Birmingham (USA), Sixes Lacrosse," theworldgames.org.

383 **résumé and cover letter**: Tiffany, letter to Nolan, Leo, September 26, 2022.

383 **"better coach and father"** . . . **"To be back"**: Ibid.

383 **"Did you read my letter?**: Tiffany, author interview, May 1, 2023.

384 **After the official announcement**: "Lars Tiffany Named Head Coach of Haudenosaunee Nationals," DeJohn, Kenny, *USA Lacrosse*, November 2, 2022.

384 **"One thing I can't get my head around"**: Staats, Austin (@Top_ched83), Twitter (now X), February 2, 2023 (since deleted).

384 **No. 1 pick**: "Austin Staats: #83, Forward, San Diego Seals," National Lacrosse League, http://www.nll.com/players/14307/austin-staats.

384 **In 2021, Staats**: "Lacrosse Player Matt Gaudet Allegedly Has His Finger Bitten Off by Austin Staats," Hookstead, David, *Daily Caller*, June 7, 2021; "Lacrosse Community Says Pro Lax Bro Has Part Of His Finger Bitten Off By Another Lax Bro In A Hotel Fight," Kinsey, Joe, *Outkick*, June 7, 2021.

384 **Tiffany had been chosen**: Tiffany, author interview.

385 **But, in April of 2021**: "SU Lacrosse Players Condemn Domestic Violence with Support of One Love Foundation," Majumder, Arabdho, *Daily Orange* (NY), May 4, 2021; "Syracuse Star Chase Scanlan Involved in 'Domestic' Police Call before Suspension; DA Investigating," Libonati, Chris, Dowty, Douglass, *Post-Standard* (NY), April 28, 2021; "Ex-Syracuse Lacrosse Star Chase Scanlan 'Back on Track' to Have Abuse Charges Dismissed after Screwup," Dowty, Douglass, *Post-Standard* (NY), January 25, 2022.

385 **"Very confirming"**: Tiffany, author interview.

385 **"There's a lot of people that said it"**: Burnam, Mark, author interview, June 12, 2023.

386 **"*Austin Staats*, get off your tangent"**: Nolan, Leo, author interview, April 3, 2023.

386 **"Show you're committed"**: Tiffany, author interview.

386 **Pope Francis, after 530 years**: "Joint Statement of the Dicasteries for Culture and Education and for Promoting Integral Human Development on the 'Doctrine of Discovery,'" Holy See Press Office, March 30, 2023.

386 **"This is the problem"**: Hill, Sidney, author interview, April 6, 2023.

386 **Supreme Courts's 2005 majority opinion**: *City of Sherrill vs. Oneida Indian Nation*, 544 U.S. 197, 2005.

386 **"It's progress"**: Hill, author interview.

386   **August 2022**: "Lacrosse Is on a Shortlist to Be Added for 2028 Olympics in Los Angeles. Leaders of the Sport are Optimistic," Lee, Edward, *Baltimore Sun* (MD), August 9, 2022.

387   **"It's a money grab"**: Thompson, Lyle, author interview, April 14, 2023.

387   **"You talk about Native Indigenous values?"**: Ibid

388   **Four weeks later**: "Lyle Thompson Stepping Away From PLL For 2023 Season," DeJohn, Kenny, *USA Lacrosse*, May 15, 2023; "Questions—and Motivation—Abound as Haudenosaunee Begin 2023 World Lacrosse Championship," Foy, Terry, *InsideLacrosse .com*, June 23, 2023.

388   **Thompson wasn't surprised**: Thompson, Lyle, author interview.

388   **"Should've been"**: Thompson, Jeremy, author interview, April 14, 2023.

388   **"You don't have to be Native"**: Thompson, Lyle, author interview.

388   **"a lack of understanding what we need"**: Ibid.

388   **In 2006, two-time Iroquois head coach**: "Being Inventors of Lacrosse Doesn't Mean that Playing It Will Come without Problems," MacGregor, Roy, *Globe and Mail*, July 13, 2006.

388   **learned from its most recent controversy**: Lyons, Rex, author interview, June 24, 2023.

389   **"Your standing is critical"**: Ibid.

389   **"nationhood on their shoulders"**: Ibid.

389   **"The end of that song"**: Tiffany, author interview.

390   **Kevin Corrigan**: "Ousted UVa Coach Starsia Talks about Search and State of the Program," Doughty, Doug, *Roanoke Times* (VA), June 27, 2016; "Notre Dame Coach Kevin Corrigan: 'I Will Continue In That Role,'" Foy, Terry, *InsideLacrosse.com*, June 8, 2016.

390   **"lacrosse royalty"**: Tiffany, author interview, April 30, 2023.

391   **Final Four**: "Year-by-Year Results/NCAA Tournament History," Northwestern Athletics, Lacrosse Record Book, 10.

391   **gutting collapse**: "No. 4 Northwestern Collapses against No. 1 North Carolina, Loses Third Straight NCAA Semifinal," Varnes, Charlotte, *Daily Northwestern* (IL), May 29, 2022.

391   **After sitting out**: "Northwestern's Izzy Scane to Miss 2022 Season Due to ACL Injury," *USA Lacrosse*, December 5, 2021; "Izzy Scane's Journey Back to the Height of Lacrosse," Higuchi, Kikue, *NUSports.com*, March 29, 2023.

391   **May 28, 2023**: "As Scane Chases Her Scoring Record, Selena Lasota is Still Making an Impact," Siegel, Austin, Northwestern Athletics, May 26, 2023.

392   **"such a fun journey"**: Amonte Hiller, Kelly, NCAA championship postgame press conference, WakeMed Park, Cary, N.C., May 28, 2023.

392   **led the Fighting Irish**: "Kevin Corrigan: Baumer Family Head Men's Lacrosse Coach," Notre Dame Athletics, http://fightingirish.com/coach/kevin-corrigan-2/.

392   **snubbed**: "The Committee Got it Wrong: Notre Dame Lacrosse," Tenant, Michael, *LaxAllStars.com*, May 10, 2022.

392   **"vengeance tour"**: McCahon, Quinn (@qmccahon), "It's a vengeance tour next year for @NDLacrosse We will be back even better than before . . . ," Twitter (now X), May 9, 2022, 2:06 p.m., http://twitter.com/qmccahon/status/1523726130322481152.

392   **"a quest, if you will"**: Corrigan, Kevin, NCAA quarterfinal postgame press conference, Navy-Marine Corps Memorial Stadium, Annapolis, MD, May 21, 2023.

392   **Philadelphia on May 27**: "Notre Dame Men's Lacrosse Beats Virginia 13-12 in Epic OT Semi-Final game," *SB Nation: One Foot Down*, May 27, 2003.

393 **"We're not focusing"**: Tiffany, NCAA semifinal postgame press conference, Lincoln Financial Field, Philadelphia, May 27, 2023.

393 **first national championship**: "Notre Dame Wins First Men's Lacrosse Title with Defeat of Duke," Timanus, Eddie, *USA Today*, May 29, 2023.

393 **Afterward, Corrigan spoke of all the title games**: Corrigan, Kevin, NCAA championship postgame press conference, Lincoln Financial Field, Philadelphia, May 29, 2023.

II. San Diego

394 **"There are some conflictions"**: Tiffany, Lars, author interview, May 1, 2023.

395 **Peter Milliman of Johns Hopkins** : "JHU's Peter Milliman To Serve As Head Coach Of The Iroquois Nationals Lacrosse Team At The World Games," Rienzi, Greg, *Johns Hopkins Magazine*, Fall 2021.

395 **sole Native American head coach in the NCAA**: "Marty Ward: Head Men's Lacrosse Coach," Florida Southern Athletics, http://fscmocs.com/staff-directory/marty-ward /40; "Marty Ward: Cherokee," North American Indigenous Athletics Hall of Fame, http://www.naiahf.org/team-1/marty-ward/cherokee.

395 **derided as a "white savior"**: Tiffany, Lars, author interview.

396 **"like street ball"**: Thompson, Hiana, author interview, April 15, 2023.

396 **before he became Tadadaho**: "Sid Hill: Hall of Fame Class of 2023," Upstate Lacrosse Foundation, http://www.upstatelacrossefoundation.org/hall-of-fame/sid-hill/.

396 **"You weren't good unless you scored"**: Hill, author interview.

396 **80 seconds in 2018, with a 60-second reset**: "Men's Lacrosse Adds 80-Second Shot Clock," Johnson, Greg, NCAA.org, September 13, 2018; "60-second Shot Clock Reset Approved in Men's Lacrosse," Johnson, Greg, NCAA.org, July 21, 2021.

396 **"We don't have the luxury"**: Thompson, Lyle, author interview.

397 **"I needed some help"**: Williams, Zed, author interview, April 25, 2023.

397 **But for 2023**: Tiffany, author interview, May 1, 2023.

397 **Until taking a DNA test**: Piseno, Jacob, author interview, March 21, 2024.

397 **"stay with them for life"**: Ibid.

398 **nonprofit funding**: Lyons, Rex, author interview, April 15, 2023.

398 **$100,000 apiece**: "Mohawks Contribute to Haudenosaunee Nationals Lacrosse Path to the Olympics," Sommerstein, David, North Country Public Radio, July 26, 2022; Lyons, Rex, author interview.

398 **ScoreBreak**: Tiffany, Lars, author interview.

398 **"money in the bank now"**: Lyons, Rex, author interview.

399 **"he kept looking back"**: Tiffany, Lars, author interview, June 18, 2023.

399 **"gold-medal game"**: Powless, Darcy, author interview, June 18, 2023.

399 **"cherish the ball"**: Staats, Austin, author interview, June 18, 2023.

399 **"Next question"**: Ibid.

400 **"I don't think"**: Staats, Randy, author interview, June 18, 2023.

401 **"Can you imagine?"**: Ibid.

401 **appointed chairman**: "Alibaba Group Announces Chairman and CEO Succession Plan," Alibaba Group press release, June 20, 2023, http://www.alibabagroup.com/en -US/document-1607836456397570048/.

402 **"very strange"**: Danowski, John, author interview, June 21, 2023.

402 **the 7-5 U.S. win**: "United States Opens World Lacrosse Championship with 7-5 Win over Canada at Snapdragon Stadium," Carter, Ivan, *San Diego Union-Tribune*, June 21, 2023.

402 **"Gamesmanship"**: Pannell, Rob, author interview, June 21, 2023.

403 **13-9**: "Mexico vs. Italy Men's World Lacrosse Championship 2023 Pool play," posted August 4, 2023, by Team Zebra World Lax archives, YouTube, 1:35.24 http://www.youtube.com/watch?v=gKTt8KSVMvk.

403 **undocumented migrants, daily**: "300,000 Have Unlawfully Crossed the Border between San Diego and Tijuana in 2023," Rivera, Salvador, *Border Report*, December 22, 2023.

404 **"We have a reminder"**: Patraca, Andres, author interview, June 23, 2023.

404 **"not yet"**: Melero, Ernie, author interview, June 23, 2023.

405 **Alfie Jacques died at 74**: "Master Lacrosse Stick Maker Alfie Jacques Passes on Tradition before Dying," Maracle, Candace, *CBC News*, July 1, 2023, https://www.cbc.ca/news/indigenous/alfie-jacques-onondaga-haudenosaunee-traditional-wooden-lacrosse-stick-1.6889893.

405 **"going to be buried with that stick"**: Tiffany, author interview, June 23, 2023.

405 **eight-goal, one-assist rampage**: "'It's Poetry'—The Haudenosaunee Put on an Incredible Display in Opening Win," World Lacrosse, June 23, 2023.

405 **"nobody says anything"**: Marr, Scott, author interview, June 23, 2023.

406 **"In years prior"**: Pannell, Rob, author interview, June 24, 2023.

406 **"still play field lacrosse"**: Staats, Austin, author interview.

407 **hung on to win again**: "USA Answers Haudenosaunee Challenge as Men's Championship Heats Up on Day Four," World Lacrosse, June 24, 2023.

407 **8-7 . . .**: "Canada vs. Haudenosaunee: Box Score," World Lacrosse, June 25, 2023, http://www.worldlax2023.com/sports/mlax/2023-24/boxscores/20230625_hlfy.xml.

407 **"completely different team"**: Pannell, author interview.

408 **"Like a big bear"**: Merrill, Brodie, author interview, June 25, 2023.

408 **"So comfortable in the chaos"**: Schreiber, Tom, author interview, June 28, 2023.

408 **"couple guys were happy"**: Thompson, Jeremy, author interview.

409 **"We're the only team playing without rest"**: Lyons, Oren, author interview, June 28, 2023.

409 **"They got a bit screwed"**: Pannell, author interview.

409 **"I can ice later"**: Staats, Austin, author interview, June 27, 2023.

409 **crushed Hong Kong**: "Hong Kong, China at Haudenosaunee: Box Score," World Lacrosse, June 27, 2023, http://www.worldlax2023.com/sports/mlax/2023-24/boxscores/20230627_4nli.xml.

410 **though he wouldn't finish**: "Men's Championship Statistical Leaders," World Lacrosse, July 1, 2023, http://worldlacrosse.sport/article/statistical-leaders/.

410 **12-7 loss**: "Haudenosaunee at Canada: Box Score," World Lacrosse, June 29, 2023, http://www.worldlax2023.com/sports/mlax/2023-24/boxscores/20230629_ldu0.xml.

411 **"I say yes"**: Thompson, Lyle, author interview, June 29, 2023.

411 **11-2 dismantlement**: "Canada, United States Advance To World Lacrosse Men's Championship Final," DaSilva, Matt, *USA Lacrosse*, June 30, 2023.

411 **"We had a chance"**: Tiffany, author interview, June 29, 2023.

412 **"It is gratifying"**: Lyons, Rex, author interview, July 1, 2023.

412 **third straight bronze medal**: "Haudenosaunee Claim Bronze With Emphatic Win," *Two Row Times*, July 5, 2023.

412 **"80 percent chance"**: Thompson, Lyle, author interview, July 1, 2023.

412 **"happy funeral"**: Staats, Randy, author interview, July 1, 2023.

412 **"I'm a little nervous"**: Tiffany, Lars, author interview, July 1, 2023.

413 **"once we sober up"**: Lyons, Oren, author interview, May 22, 2023.

413 **"should be done"**: Staats, Randy, author interview, June 29, 2023.
413 **test positive for cocaine and marijuana**: "Haudenosaunee Nationals Lacrosse Player Austin Staats Accepts a 3-Month Period of Ineligibility," International Testing Agency press release, January 24, 2024.
413 **defenseman Oakley Thomas**: "Haudenosaunee Nationals Lacrosse Player Oakley Thomas Accepts a 3-month Period of Ineligibility," International Testing Agency press release, January 24, 2024.
413 **"I fear for our path"**: Tiffany, author interview, July 1, 2023.
414 **"Perfect, right?"**: Staats, Austin, author interview, July 1, 2023.
414 **midfield for the first time**: "How the U.S. Team Culture Brought Out the Best in Brennan O'Neill," DaSilva, Matt, *USA Lacrosse*, July 3, 2023; "O'Neill's MVP Performance Lifts USA to 11th World Championship," DaSilva, *USA Lacrosse*, July 2, 2023.
414 **"He leaves me speechless"**: Danowski, John, postgame interview, Snapdragon Stadium, San Diego, CA, July 1, 2023.
415 **"Any time you're playing"**: O'Neill, Brennan, postgame interview, Snapdragon Stadium, San Diego, CA, July 1, 2023.
415 **introduce a shot-clock**: "World Lacrosse to adopt shot clock in international field lacrosse," World Lacrosse press release, July 26, 2024.
415 **seal the championship, 10-7**: DaSilva, July 2, 2023.
416 **"Brennan O'Neill is on his way"**: Pannell, author interview.

III. Olympia

417 **lacrosse stick is "magic"**: Hayes, Tom, author interview, January 5, 2021.
417 **In 1973**: Ibid.
418 **18 member nations**: "Nations and Member Growth," 2018 FIL World Lacrosse Championship program, 16.
418 **"we had no idea"**: Cockerton, Stan, author interview, October 27, 2023.
418 **The merger**: "Men's and Women's International Lacrosse Groups Merge," Weaver, John, *Baltimore Sun*, September 4, 2008.
418 **"WADA-compliant"**: Sciacca, Joseph, Independent Auditor's Report for the years ended December 31, 2010 and 2009, Federation of International Lacrosse, August 2, 2011, pg. 8.
418 **part of SportAccord**: "One Man's Mission," Forman, Matt, *Lacrosse Magazine*, December 2012, 40.
419 **"He just believed"**: Stenersen, Steve, author interview, April 15, 2024.
419 **"got to dream, right?"**: Forman, 43.
419 **slick video . . . 2013 SportAccord Convention**: Hayes, author interview.
419 **"room gets quiet"**: Ibid.
419 **acceptance by the IWGA**: "IWGA Welcomes New Members," *The Daily: Your Guide to the Saint Petersburg SportAccord Convention*, May 28, 2013, 2.
420 **Hayes convinced Cockerton**: Hayes, Tom, author interview; Cockerton, Stan, author interview.
420 **wrestling heroes, with sidelines**: "Scherr and Scherr Alike," Neff, Craig, *Sports Illustrated*, September 14, 1988.
420 **"It provides"**: Scherr, Jim, author interview, July 14, 2018.
420 **On September 13, 2017**: "IOC Makes Historic Decision by Simultaneously Awarding Olympic Games 2024 to Paris and 2028 to Los Angeles," International Olympic Committee, September 13, 2017.

421   **"We have 60 member nations"**: Scherr, author interview, July 14, 2018.
421   **provisional recognition**: "FIL Receives Provisional Recognition by the International Olympic Committee," Federation of International Lacrosse press release, November 30, 2018.
417   **"Make sure"**: Hayes, author interview.
421   **"Things are going good"**: Ibid.
422   **On July 20, 2021**: "Historic Moment for Lacrosse: International Olympic Committee Grants Full Recognition to World Lacrosse," World Lacrosse press release, July 20, 2021.
422   **died at the age of 82**: "Rutgers Coach Tom Hayes was a Lacrosse Giant with a Global Reach, but Personal Touch," Kinney, Mike, *NJ.com*, March 19, 2022.
422   **"A true legend"**: "Remembering Legendary Coach, Administrator Tom Hayes," World Lacrosse, March 7, 2022.
422   **IOC president Thomas Bach**: "IOC President Back Meets Athletes During Visit to World Games," Shefferd, Neil, *insidethegames.biz*, July 14, 2022.
422   **shortlist of candidates**: "LA28 Shortlists Nine Sports for Olympic Games Inclusion," Livingstone, Robert, *GamesBids.com*, August 4, 2022.
422   **"could not have gone any better"**: Scherr, author interview, April 16, 2024.
424   **"Sport is not separate"**: "L.A. Olympic Officials Ask IOC to Allow Athlete Protests," Wharton, David, *Los Angeles Times*, July 31, 2020; "L.A. Olympic Chair Wasserman Asks IOC President to Repeat Rule That Bars Advocacy," Soshnick, Scott, *Sportico*, July 31, 2020.
424   **"descend into a marketplace"**: "IOC Chief Bach Says Olympic Games Cannot Be 'Marketplace of Demonstrations,'" *Reuters*, October 24, 2020; "The Olympics Are about Diversity and Unity, not Politics and Profit. Boycotts Don't Work," Bach, Thomas, *Guardian*, (London) October 23, 2020.
424   **relaxed its Rule 50**: "The Tokyo Olympics Has Relaxed Its Rules On Athlete Protests—To A Point," Wamsley, Laurel, NPR, July 23, 2021.
424   **"unique circumstance"**: Scherr, author interview, October 23, 2021.
425   **"But that's all we can do"**: Ibid.
425   **White House on July 24, 2023**: White House Office of Intergovernmental Affairs, author inquiry, April 22, 2024.
426   **ask what was happening**: Scherr, author interview, April 29, 2024; Lyons, Rex, author interview, September 6, 2023.
426   **"really excited me"**: Perez, Tom, author interview, April 30, 2024.
426   **"set the table"**: Lyons, Rex, author interview.
427   **"adverse analytical finding"**: International Testing Agency press releases, January 24, 2024.
427   **"personal matter"**: "Six Nations Chiefs' Bench Depth Leads to Another Mann Cup Win," Laskaris, Sam, *Windspeaker.com*, September 18, 2023.
427   **"I don't know if they're"**: Lyons, Rex, author interview, April 11, 2024; contacted personally and via the San Diego Seals for comment, Staats did not respond.
428   **"lacrosse is an important piece**: Wasserman, Casey, author interview, May 1, 2024.
428   **"Lacrosse Sixes" was named third**: USA Lacrosse Magazine, (@USALacrosseMag), "BREAKING: IOC Executive Board accepts @LA28 proposal to add lacrosse to 2028 Olympics, subject to final vote at upcoming IOC Session in Mumbai," Twitter (now X), October 13, 2023, 6:15 a.m., http://twitter.com/USALacrosseMag/status /1712773969663656121.

428 **"First Nations of the US"**: "IOC Board Approves Five New Sports for 2028 Olympic Games in Los Angeles," *Associated Press*, October 13, 2023.

428 **"Olympics are not immune"**: "Bach Says Added-Term Discussions are Personal; New LA28 Sports to Rely on Pro Leagues; Wasserman's Declaration for Ukraine and Israel," Perelman, Rich, *Sports Examiner*, October 17, 2023.

429 **"The achievement I'm most proud"**: Stenersen, author interview.

429 **"incredibly pleased"**: "Haudenosaunee Rejoice as Lacrosse is Included in 2028 Olympics," *Two Row Times*, October 18, 2023.

429 **"exciting and humbling"**: Ibid.

429 **"We welcome this opportunity"**: "The New Pinnacle: Lacrosse, The Olympic Movement And LA28," DaSilva, Matt, *USA Lacrosse*, January 31, 2024.

430 **"find a solution to allow them to compete"**: Ibid; "LA28 Boss Casey Wasserman Talks MLB Players, Indigenous Lacrosse Team," Novy-Williams, Eben, *Sportico*, October 13, 2023.

430 **"This means it is up to"**: "Lacrosse Is Coming to the Olympics. Will Its Inventors Be There?," Mather, Victor, *New York Times*, October 19, 2023; "Haudenosaunee Deserves a Lacrosse Team of its Own at the 2028 Olympics," Newberry, Paul, *Associated Press*, October 20, 2023; "The Haudenosaunee Nationals' Quest to Play under Their Own Flag at the Olympics," Foresta, Mathew, *Guardian* (London), February 28, 2024. https://www.theguardian.com/sport/2024/feb/28/the-haudenosaunee-nationals-quest-to-play-under-their-own-flag-at-the-olympics.

430 **"founding origins"**: Wasserman, Casey, author interview, May 1, 2024.

431 **"I would never"**: Thompson, Lyle, author interview, November 26, 2018.

431 **Haudenosaunee National Alie Jimerson**: "Road to Worlds: Alie Jimerson—More than a Game," Lacrosse Canada, June 21, 2022.

431 **Refugee Team became one of Rio's**: "IOC Refugee Olympic Team Rio 2016," http://olympics.com/ioc/refugee-olympic-team-rio-2016.

431 **North and South Korean women's hockey**: "When North Joined South: The Story Of The Unified Korean Olympic Ice Hockey Team," Waleik, Gary, *Only a Game*, January 10, 2020.

431 **"recognition on the biggest global"**: Lyons, Rex, author interview, September 6, 2023.

432 **six teams**: "Lacrosse's Return to the Olympics: Q&A," World Lacrosse, November 1, 2023, http://worldlacrosse.sport/article/lacrosses-return-to-the-olympics-qa/.

432 **World Sixes rankings**: "World Rankings," World Lacrosse, http://worldlacrosse.sport/the-game/world-rankings/.

432 **On December 6, 2023**: "Remarks by President Biden at the White House Tribal Nations Summit," Department of the Interior, Washington, D.C., December 6, 2023.

433 **"still live in the shadows"**: Ibid.

433 **"The game brought tribes together"**: Ibid.

433 **raucous applause**: "Watch again: Biden speaks at White House Tribal Nations Summit," posted December 6, 2023, by *The Independent*, YouTube, December 6, 2023, http://www.youtube.com/watch?v=vva49v27RT0, 40:36.

433 **"I hope to see the Haudenosaunee Nationals"**: "Canada's Sport Minister Supports Haudenosaunee Bid to Play Lacrosse at 2028 Olympics," Chidley-Hill, John, *Toronto Star*, December 6, 2023.

433 **66 percent of Americans**: "Americans Want to See the Haudenosaunee Nationals in the Olympics," Data For Progress, December 20, 2023.

434 **"No president's ever said that"**: Lyons, Rex, author interview, April 11, 2024.

434 **"Real success"**: Ibid.

434 **"I think the members"**: Scherr, author interview, April 16, 2024.

435 **should be shamed into removing**: Tiffany, author interview, July 1, 2023.

435 **"I say we don't go"**: Woodson, Chazz, author interview, November 18, 2021.

435 **"refugees in our Turtle Island"**: Lyons, Rex, author interview, April 11, 2024.

435 **115 to 133, the total of women from 110 to 120**: NCAA Demographics Database.

435 **"The Black player is not alone"**: Harrison, Kyle, author interview, December 15, 2023.

436 **"Meet the New Era of Lacrosse"**: "Meet the New Era of Lacrosse," World Lacrosse, October 26, 2023, http://worldlacrosse.sport/article/meet-the-new-era-of-lacrosse/; "Leading Lacrosse Organizations Join Forces in Elevate28 with Shared Goal of Doubling U.S. Participation in the Sport to 4 Million Annual Players by 2030," World Lacrosse press release, October 31, 2023.

437 **"most important dependent clause in the Constitution"**: Perez, author interview.

437 **Jesse Owens dominating**: "Berlin 1936 Olympic Games," Encyclopedia Britannica, http://www.britannica.com/event/Berlin-1936-Olympic-Games.

437 **Tommie Smith and John Carlos**: "Those Raised Fists Still Resonate, 50 Years Later," Grigsby Bates, Karen, National Public Radio, *Code Switch*, October 16, 2018.

438 **Aboriginal Australian gold medalist Cathy Freeman**: "Cathy Freeman's Sydney 2000 Gold was a Moment of Ecstasy at a Time of National Reckoning," Birch, Tony, *Guardian* (London), January 23, 2024.

INDEX

Abernethy, Syd, 127
Aboriginal Australians, 18, 31, 37, 156, 438
Abrams, Marshall, 56, 395
Abrams, Percy, 39
Abrams, Pierce, 56
Adams, Brent, 362
Adams, Hank, 182
Adams, Sylvan, 19
Afghanistan, 302, 303
agreement of 1701, 156
Aharon, Shai, 158
Aharoni, Ido, 17
Aiontonnis, Jean-Baptiste, 170–171
Akl, Nabil, 60–61, 68–70
Akwesasne, 13, 21, 195
Akwesasne Mohawk Casino, 193
Akwesasne Thunder (box lacrosse team), 51
Alabama football, 93
Albrecht, Sarah, 285
Alcatraz occupation (1969–1971), 181
alcohol use. *See also* drug use
    culture of lacrosse and, 214–219
    of Indigenous Americans, 10, 52, 54–55, 191–192
    of Jeremy Thompson, 54–55
    Longhouse ethics against, 50, 166, 189
    survey of lacrosse players, 214
    violent incidents involving, xviii, 222, 224–227, 334–335
Alex, Joe, 97
Alexis, Lucien, Jr., 84–85
Alford, Harry, 108
Algonquin, 6, 164
Ali, Muhammad, 40, 46, 98
Alibaba, 355, 401, 421. *See also* Tsai, Joe
Alleyne, Kris, 347
American bison. *See* buffalo
American Boy (Megale), 335
American Boy Fall Brawl, 336
American Indian Law Alliance, 383
American Indian Movement (AIM), 51, 181–183
American Revolution, 9–10, 49, 165–166, 169
Amherst University lacrosse, 341–342
Amonte Hiller, Kelly, 280–285, 289–292, 391–392, 393
Amplo, Joe, 284, 298
Anderson, Joe, 197–200, 366
Anderson, Wallace "Mad Bear," 197
Anello, Vince V., 198
Anishinaabe, 31, 156

anti-Black violence, xxi, 10, 132, 331, 342, 343, 344. *See also* Black lacrosse; racism in lacrosse culture
Arapaho, 31
Arbery, Ahmaud, 342, 343
Argentina lacrosse, 14, 76, 418
Army Rangers, 302–303, 304, 306–307
Ashe, Arthur, 100
Ashe, Thomas, 184
Assimilation. *See also* cultural genocide; violence against Indigenous Americans
    of Indigenous children, 18, 53
    in lacrosse culture, 112, 130, 136
    US policy on, 154, 172
Atlanta Blaze (MLL team), 315
Aust, Alex, xxi
Australia lacrosse
    at 2018 World Championships, 206
    at 2023 World Championships, 401, 407, 411, 412
    Hayes and, 417–418
    on Nationals in ILF, 33
Australia World Championships (1990), 33, 34–37
Austrian lacrosse, 401

Bach, Thomas, 422, 423, 427, 428, 431
baggatiway, 163
ball-and-stick marathons, 162–163
Balls, Ron, 8, 10–11, 37, 41, 327, 419
Baltimore, Maryland, xxi, 47, 96–98, 101–106, 174–175, 250, 298
Banks, Dennis, 51, 181, 182–183
Banks, Earl, 102–103
Baptiste, of Caughnawaga, 168
Baptiste, Trevor, 42, 82, 83, 309, 317, 345, 362, 402
Barak Netanya (lacrosse team), 274, 275–276
Barkat, Nir, 157
Barrett, Matt, 248
Barrow, George, 123, 124–125, 126, 127
Barrow, Will, 121, 122–127, 221
baseball, xix, 40, 93, 174, 422, 423, 427
basketball, xix, 100, 106–107, 221, 258, 275
Bates, Ernest, 94
Battle at Little Bighorn, 169
BDS (Boycott, Divestment and Sanctions) movement, 12, 15, 43, 68, 156

beach volleyball, 422
Bears Ears National Monument, 17, 18
Beers, W. George, 168–170, 175, 205, 363
Beijing Olympic Games (2008), xvii
Beitar Jerusalem, 158
Belichick, Bill, 127, 194
Belisle, Mitch, 310
Bell, Tyson, 206
Bellecourt, Clyde and Vernon, 181
Bement, Alex, 237, 238
Berlin Olympics (1936), 191, 437
Bermuda lacrosse, 142–143
Bernhardt, Jake, 26, 42
Bertrand, Charlie, 402
Biden, Joe, xxiv, 425–426, 432–433
binge drinking. *See* alcohol use
Bingham, William, 84, 85
bingo, 197
Birmingham World Games (2021/2022), 329, 339, 340, 354, 355, 356–357, 364, 383, 422–423
Black Economic Union, 92
Black Hills settlement, 154–155, 172
Black lacrosse. *See also* anti-Black violence; racism in lacrosse culture; *names of specific persons and teams*
    BLM and, 343–349
    coaches, 102, 130n, 278–279
    hostile incidents against, x
    players, x, 81, 82, 92–93, 95–96, 102–106, 127, 435–436
Black Lacrosse Alliance, 345–346, 348
Black Lives Matter movement, xxi, 64, 331, 342, 343–349, 352, 424
Blatz, Edward, Jr., 238–242
Blax Lax, Inc., 105
Boggs, Patton, 312
Bomberry, Brendan, 62, 331
Boots, Francis, 182
Boulukos, Joe, 79
boxing, 40
box lacrosse, 29, 51, 176–177, 193–196, 364, 395–396
braid, 44, 330–332. *See also* hair
Brant, Joseph, 166, 167
Bratton, Rhamel, 119–122, 123–125, 127–128, 232–235
Bratton, Shamel, 39, 119–122, 123–126, 127–128, 231–235
Brazil Olympics (2016), 431
breakdancing, 423
Brebeuf, Jean de, 162
BRIDGE initiative, 80–81, 105
Briggs, Colin, 234

Brine Lacrosse, 36
Brodhead, Richard, 114, 117
"Broken Promises" (US
    Commission on Civil
    Rights), 10
Brooks, Timmy, 237, 335, 336
Brown, Aris, 375, 376, 378
Brown, Donnie, xi, 101–102
Brown, Frank, 62, 332
Brown, Jim, x, xiii, 28, 46, 85–94,
    375, 378
Brown, Kenny, 103–104
Brown, Michael, xxi
Brown, Ryan, 42, 205, 309
Brown, Wesley A., 85
Brown University lacrosse, 112–113,
    202, 334
Bruce, Louis, 181
bubble tournament (2020),
    343–344, 348, 359, 361
Buckley, Alex, 356
Bucktooth, Brett, 39, 364
Bucktooth, Freeman "Bossy," 99
Budnitz, Emil "Buzzy," 29–30
buffalo, 171–172, 184–188, 381–383
Buffalo Bowmans (lacrosse team),
    177
Buffalo Medicine Society, 184–185,
    186, 202, 382
Bureau of Indian Affairs, 153, 181,
    425–426
Burnam, Mark "Redman," 13, 23,
    27, 29, 31, 199, 385
Burnett, Michael, 258
Burns, Michael, 224–225
Byrne, Josh, 309, 362

Cahill, Aaron, 357
Caldor, Tom, 263
Calico Treaty. See Treaty of
    Canandaigua (1794)
Cameron, James, 39
Canadian history with Indigenous
    people, 168–172
Canadian lacrosse, 168–178. See also
    Indigenous lacrosse history;
    Team Canada
Canadian Lacrosse Association, 33,
    206, 355
Canassatego, 9
Carcaterra, Paul, 7, 25
Carlisle Indian Industrial School,
    53, 54, 172, 173, 375. See also
    forced removal; residential
    boarding schools
Carlos, John, 98, 191, 437–438
Carlton, Joe, 93–94, 96
Carril, Pete, 267
Carroll, Casey, xvi, 300–307
Carter, Lloyd, 100, 101, 104–105,
    137–139
casino gambling, 49–51, 166,
    188–190, 193, 286
Cataldo, Simon, 81
Cathers, Edmund, 58

Catholic Church, 149, 196, 371
Caughnawaga (Kahnawake),
    168–170
Cayuga, 8, 49, 50, 189, 190, 197.
    See also Iroquois Confederacy
Chamberlain, Wilt, 89
Charlotte Hounds (MLL team),
    310, 311
Charm City Youth Lacrosse, 106,
    135, 141
Chartis Property Casualty,
    246–247
Cherokee, 8, 164, 166, 395
Cherry, Stan, 97
Chester, Raymond, 97
Cheyenne, 31, 361
Chicago Machine (MLL team),
    124
"Chief Wahoo" (cartoon), 64
Choctaw, 166
Christianity, 49, 149, 150, 197
Christmas, John, 108, 109, 121
chronic traumatic encephalopathy
    (CTE), 126
Ciccarone, Henry, 216, 253–254,
    258–259, 260, 262
City of Sherrill v. Oneida Nation of
    New York, 386
clans, 14, 51, 52, 160
Class, Deemer, 315–317
Cleveland Browns (football team),
    86, 91
Cleveland Indians (baseball team),
    64, 65
Clinton, Hillary, xx, 39
clutching, 86
cocaine, 52, 192, 214, 217, 237–238,
    241, 248, 334, 336, 413, 427.
    See also drug use
Cockerton, Mark, 317, 327–328
Cockerton, Stan, 418
Conrad, Ryan, 334, 402
Cook, Jeff, 257
Cooper, Polly, 9
Cooper, Roy, 118
Corrigan, Kevin, 336, 390, 393
cosmology, 160–162, 185. See also
    spirituality
Costabile, C. J., 304
Cotler, Irwin, 21
Cottle, Dave, 58
Covid-19 pandemic, 341, 342, 348,
    359, 375, 376, 383
Cowan, Joe, 257, 263
Cox, Laurie, 46, 176
Craig, Maureen, 351
Crawford, Michael, 137–138
Crazy Horse, 172
Creator's Game (statue), 364, 435
Crescent Athletic Club, 175, 296
cricket, 420, 423, 427, 428
Crowley, Kevin, 208
Crowther, Welles, xvi
Cullors, Patrisse, 344
cultural appropriation, 38, 64, 436

cultural genocide, 172, 194, 331.
    See also assimilation; genocide;
    violence against Indigenous
    Americans
Cummings, Gail, 278
Custer, George, 23, 169
Custom Act (Canada), 195
Cutrone, Frank, 121
Czech Republic lacrosse, 418

Dakota, 31, 154–155
Dakota Access Pipeline, 18, 65–67,
    361
Danon, Dan, 18
Danowski, Ed, 299
Danowski, John
    coaching career of, 24, 82,
    204–205, 293–296, 298–300, 305
    at World Championship games,
    249–250, 402
Danowski, Matt, 207–208, 294, 317
Davis, Clarence "Tiger," 98
Davis, Damien, 108
Davis, Ernie, 91
Davis-Allen, Isaiah, 347, 348, 362
Dawson, Brian, 136
Dawson, Isaiah, 135, 141
Decker, John, 214–215
Declaration on the Rights of
    Indigenous Peoples, 154, 188
Deganawidah, 150
Deir Yassin, 157
DeMarco, Bob, 419–420
democratic principles, 9, 37, 166
Democratic Republic of Congo, 431
Dennis, Romar, 362
Denver, Rorke, 302, 303
Denver World Lacrosse
    Championships (2014), xx, 15,
    40, 77–78
Dermer, Ron, 18
Deskaheh, 172–173, 188
Desko, John, 56, 128, 129–130, 131
Dey Hon Tshi Gwa' Ehs, 46–47
Dickson, Curtis, 205, 208, 309, 317,
    319, 402
discrimination, 10, 84–85, 138. See
    also racism in lacrosse culture
"Dish with One Spoon," 156–157,
    158
Dixon, Mark, 121
Dobson, Eric, 392, 393
Doctor, Chris, 385, 388, 395, 397
Doctor, Ron, 388
Doctor, Vince, 388
Doctrine of Discovery, 149, 196,
    386, 402
domestic violence. See abuse; murder
    case (2010); sexual abuse
Dominican Republic lacrosse, 359
Donville, Jason, 355
Dorrance, Anson, 283
Doty, Paul, 254
Douglass, Frederick, 155, 190
#DrawTheLine campaign, 332

drinking. *See* alcohol use
drug overdose, 214, 217, 219, 236–239, 335, 336
drug testing, 217–218, 248, 412–413, 418, 421, 427–428
drug use, 10, 191–192. *See also* alcohol use
  cocaine, 52, 192, 214, 217, 237–238, 241, 248, 334, 336, 413, 427
  fentanyl, 238, 240–241, 336
  marijuana, 214, 217, 237, 248, 334, 336, 413, 427
  opioids, xxiii, 55, 236–238
  survey on lacrosse players, 214
Druid Lacrosse Club, 175
Dubin, Steve, 261
Du Bois, W. E. B., 95
Duckett, DeWitt, 102
Duke University lacrosse, xiv–xv, xvi, 116–117, 118–119, 120, 294–295, 300–306
Duke University lacrosse rape case (2006), xiv–xv, xvi, 113–116, 117–119, 293
Durham, North Carolina, xiv–xvi

Eccles, Derrick, 61
Ecuador lacrosse, 329
Education Amendments Act (1972), xiv, 274–275
Ehrhardt, Michael, 24, 26, 309–311, 316, 325, 346, 402, 416
Elliott, Ann, 285
Ellis, Mark, 347, 348, 349
Elva, Maria, 404
Emancipation Proclamation, 377
Emery, Val, 135
Emmer, Jack, 99
England lacrosse, 170–171, 276, 357, 405
England World Lacrosse Championships (2010), xviii, xx, 7, 15, 39, 40
England World Lacrosse Championships (2017), 6, 11, 17
English Lacrosse Association, 170
enslaved persons, 122, 149, 155, 375, 377. *See also* slavery
Entenmann, Liam, 392
Eppler, Daniela, 349
erasure of Haudenosaunee, xx–xxi, 9–10, 330–331
Eruzione, Mike, 115
Erwin, Benson, 110
ESPN, 6, 7, 25, 128, 375
Etherington, George, 163, 164
Ethiopia, 431
ethnocide, 172, 194. *See also* assimilation; genocide
Evans, David, 119
Every Child Matters movement, 371, 372

Fearn, Aidan, 354
Federation of International Lacrosse (FIL), 6–7, 28, 206, 327–329, 339n, 418. *See also* International Lacrosse Federation
Federico, Mike, 254
fentanyl, 238, 240–241, 336. *See also* drug use
Fenton, William N., 47
Field World Lacrosse Championships. *See* World Lacrosse Championships
FIL Championships
  (2010), 6, 7, 8
  (2015), 6
financial careers and lacrosse, xvi–xvii, 312–317, 325–327
Finnerty, Collin, xv, 119
First Stick program, 80–81
fishing traditions, 289
Fitzgerald, Cantor, xvi
flag, 35
flag football, 423, 427
Flannery, John, 174–175
Florida Launch (MLL team), 135
Floyd, George, 331, 342, 343, 345, 373. *See also* Black Lives Matter movement
FOGO strategy, 83
football, xix, 86, 252, 264
forced removal, 18, 53, 166–167, 169, 172, 361. *See also* Carlisle Indian Industrial School; land theft; residential boarding schools
Fort Harmer, 166
Fort Michilimackinac massacre, 163–164
Fort Monroe, 377
Fort Stanwix, 166
Fowlkes, Joe "Flaky," 104
Francis (pope), 196, 379, 386
Frank, Grace, 372
Freedom School, Akwesasne, 51
Freeman, Cathy, 438
French, Dean, 196
French and Indian War (1754–1763), 163–164

Gait, Gary, xiii, 36, 111, 208, 280, 390–391
Gait, Paul, xiii, 36, 111
Galloway, John, 25, 208, 210, 317
gambling, 49–51, 166, 188–190, 193, 286
Garlow, Lois, 373
Garza, Alicia, 344
genocide, xxi, 149, 166, 171–172, 371. *See also* violence against Indigenous Americans
  cultural, 172, 194, 331
George III (king), 169, 172
Georgetown University lacrosse, 238–242, 279

George V (king), 173
George Washington Covenant Belt, 152, 155
Georgia Swarm (NLL team), 330, 332
Gersuk, Ashley, 282
Ghitelman, Adam, 120, 228, 232
Gibson, Althea, 100
Giles, Justin, 243
Giles-Harris, J. T., 406, 407
Ginsberg, Ruth Bader, 149, 386
Glenz, Kevin, 219
Gonzales, Timothy, 27, 42, 73, 75–77, 79, 142
Gore, Al, 194
graduation rates, 10, 216
Grand Council. *See* Haudenosaunee Grand Council of Chiefs
Grand Marnier Foundation, 36
Great Law of Peace, 14, 150, 156
Great Sioux Nation, 154–155. *See also* Sioux
Great Tree of Peace, The (Lyons), 161–162
Greece lacrosse, 74, 78–80, 142, 352
Greenberg, Mark, 254, 259, 313
Greenberg, Sara, 18
Greenwood, Jimmy, 110
Groom, Ian, 375–376
Gross, David, 133
Gurenlian, Greg "The Beast," 205, 209, 210
Guterding, Justin, 239–240, 241–242, 300
Gwich'in, 397

Haaland, Deb, 433
Haas, Andrew, 78, 142
hair, 44, 53–54, 330–332
Halifax Thunderbirds, 366
Hall, Dickie, 97
Hall, Rachel, 373
Hampton University lacrosse, xxi, 137–139, 374–378
Handsome Lake, 47, 49, 149–150, 151, 166, 189
Hannah-Jones, Nikole, 375
Hansen, Tyler, 302–303
Hapoel Katamon F. C., 158
Harjo, Susan Shone, 182
Harlem Lacrosse-Los Angeles, 352
Harrison, Kyle
  Barrow and, 121
  BLM and, 345, 348
  lacrosse career of, xiv, 82, 105, 106–111
  on Lyle Thompson, 45
  MLL career of, 132
  on Nationals playing style, 38
  on Nation United, 140
  on racism in lacrosse culture, xxi, xxii, 106, 107–108
  retirement of, 360, 362–363

Harrison, Miles, Jr., xxii, 95–98,
    106, 108, 109, 110, 363
Hartzell, Kyle, 344, 345, 346
Harvard University lacrosse,
    84–85, 135, 174, 175, 281
hate crimes, 12, 351. *See also under*
    violence
Haudenosaunee
    1701 agreement of, 156
    on casino gambling, 49–50
    colonial America history and,
        165–167
    FIL's recognition of, 339n
    flag of, 35, 363
    history of nation, 8–10
    IOC on, 423–427
    lacrosse's origins and, xi, xviii,
        xix, xx–xxi, 46–49, 158,
        164–167, 336–339
    McPhee on, xvii
    names of, xi, 6, 364
    sovereignty of, xviii, 6–8, 11, 17,
        30, 151–154, 172–173, 353,
        386–389, 425–426
    territorial description of, 50, 151
Haudenosaunee Constitution, 14
Haudenosaunee Grand Council
    of Chiefs
    on AIM protest, 183
    on establishing Nationals, 30
    on gambling, 49–50, 189–190
    as model, 9
    on Nationals 2018 participation,
        13, 14
    on women's lacrosse, 285–286,
        368–369
Haudenosaunee Nationals (lacrosse
    team)
    1984 Olympic showcase, 31
    1985 England games of, 32
    1990 team tryouts for, 34–35
    at 2014 World Championships, xx
    at 2018 World Championships,
        xxiv, 5–8, 11–16, 18–27, 41–42,
        147–152
    at 2023 World Championships,
        394, 398–416
    establishment of, xviii, 28–31
    ethos of, 40–41
    existence of, 10
    FIL Championships and, 6
    financing of, 196–200
    heritage rules of, 35, 388, 397, 398
    ILF membership of, 10–11,
        31–33, 171
    Jerusalem tour of, 147–148,
        156–159
    media attention of, 37–38
    Nike sponsorship of, 39
    Olympic hopes of, xxiv, 329–330,
        429–434
    playing style of, 38–39, 395–397,
        399–401
    pregame ritual of, 404–405

Tiffany as coach of, 383–386,
    394–395
white head coaches and, 394–395
women's team, 6, 285–288
World Games and Olympics
    exclusion of, 329–330, 339–340,
    353–356, 430
World Games inclusion of,
    356–358
Haus, Will, 26
Hayes, Tom, 29, 31–33, 75, 250,
    417–422, 429
head trauma, 126
Healy-Silcott, Karen, 349–350
Hemlock, Carla Goodleaf, 155
Heningburg, Jules, 345, 346, 362
Hero (organization), 104
heroin, 214, 219, 236, 237. *See also*
    drug use
Higginbottom, Heather, 152
Hill, Isaac, 45
Hill, Oliver, Sr., 46
Hill, Rick, 30, 35
Hill, Roger, 433
Hill, Shawny, 330–332
Hill, Sidney
    award presentation by, 338
    on gambling, 49–50
    lacrosse career of, 31, 35, 36,
        396
    on Pope Francis and Doctrine of
        Discovery, 196, 386
    at White House events, 425, 433
Hill, Warren, 14, 26, 399, 412
Hiller, Scott, 281
Hobbs, Peter, 418
hockey, xix, 174, 176, 328, 350–351,
    364, 431
Hofstra University lacrosse, 31,
    121, 250, 278, 284, 285, 294,
    296–299
Hogan, Chris, 326
Holman, Brian, 215–216, 217,
    218–219
Holman, Marcus, 249–251, 259,
    294, 309
Holman, Matt, 342–343, 349
Holmes, Stanley, 102
Holocaust, 12
Hong Kong lacrosse, 19, 74, 401,
    407, 409, 418
"Hound Dog" (song), 38
Howard University lacrosse, 135,
    285
Howell, Jay, 120, 121
Howell, Zach, 119–121
HSBC, xvii
Huguely, George, xviii–xix, xx, 125,
    222–227, 246–247
Hungary lacrosse, 418
Huntley, Dave, 207
Huron (tribe), 164
Huyghue, Ryland, 122
Hylen, Scott, 76–77

I Am Charlotte Simmons (Wolfe), 115
Indian Act (Canada), 172
Indian Appropriations Act (1871),
    153–154
Indian Citizenship Act (1924), 154
Indian Gaming Regulatory Act
    (1988), 188–189
Indian Removal Act (1830), 18,
    166–167
Indian Reorganization Act (1934),
    154, 173
Indigenous lacrosse history, xi,
    xix, xviii, xx–xxi, 46–49, 158,
    162–167, 168–172, 175–177,
    276–277. *See also* Canadian
    lacrosse
indoor lacrosse. *See* box lacrosse
Indoor World Lacrosse
    Championships. *See* World
    Lacrosse Championships
infant mortality, 10
Inside Lacrosse (publication),
    353–354
integration, 92
International Federation
    of Women's Lacrosse
    Associations, 418
International Lacrosse Federation.
    See also Federation of
    International Lacrosse (FIL)
    establishment of, 417
    Nationals membership to, xx,
        10–11, 28, 31–33, 171
International Olympic Committee,
    xxiv, 7–8, 329, 339n, 386, 417–
    438. *See also* Olympic Games
International Testing Agency, 427
International World Games
    Association, 356, 419. *See also*
    The World Games
Ioannou, Nicolas, 80
Iraq War, 302, 303
Ireland lacrosse, 297, 356–358,
    364, 435
Iroquois (tribe). *See* Haudenosaunee
Iroquois Confederacy, 8–10,
    151–153, 164–167. *See also names*
    of specific tribes
Iroquois Lacrosse Association, 203
Iroquois Nationals. *See*
    Haudenosaunee Nationals
    (lacrosse team)
Iroquois Nationals Development
    Group, 366, 368
Israeli-Palestinian conflict, 12,
    13–14, 15, 68–70, 73, 147–150,
    157, 308
Israel lacrosse, 275, 418
Israel Lacrosse Association, 6, 15, 19
Israel World Lacrosse
    Championships (2018), xxiv,
    5–8, 11–16, 18–27, 41–42, 68,
    70, 74–75, 142–143, 308–310
Italy lacrosse, 297, 418

Jackson, Andrew, 18, 166–167
Jackson, Kyle, 408
Jackson, Wayne, 97, 104
Jacques, Alfie, xix, xx, xxii, 37, 333, 338, 405
Jacques, Louis, xix
Jamieson, Cody, 56, 129, 388
Jamieson, Sid, 35, 160–161, 385
Japan lacrosse, 407, 409, 418
Japan World Lacrosse Championships (1994), 37
Jay Treaty (1794), 172
Jemison, Ansley, 14, 16, 17, 20, 22, 42, 151, 156–159
Jemison, G. Peter, 151, 155
Jenkins, Drew, 129, 131
Jerusalem tour, 147–148, 156–159
Jimerson, Alie, 431
Jimerson, Claudia, 366, 369, 372
Jimerson, Jalyn, 373
Jimerson, Johnson, 15, 26
Jim Thorpe Memorial Pow-Wow and Native Games, 31
Johns Hopkins University lacrosse, xii, xiv, 29–30, 106–111, 175–176, 260–264
Johnson, Arthur, 138
Johnson, Harold, 35
Johnson, James, 202
Johnson, Tim, 35
Johnson, Vincent, 186, 202, 382
Jones, Myles, 362
Jordan, Michael, xiii, 46
Judaism, 49, 158

K18 line (STX), 111
Kaepernick, Colin, 132, 134
Kane, John, 68
karate, 422, 423
Katagas, Anthony, 80
Katzie First Nation, 289, 370, 371–372
Kaufman, Janna, 275–276
Kavanaugh, Chris, 390, 392, 393
Kavanaugh, Pat, 390, 392
Kelly, Jack, 407
Kemp, Troy, xxii, 130, 140
Kennedy, John F., 91
Kennedy, Michael, 357
Kennedy, Ted, 183
Kessenich, Quint, 7, 24, 262, 318
Keyes, David, 18
kickboxing, 423
Kills Straight, Birgil, 149
Kimber, Warren, IV, 219
Kimbers, Ben, 97
King, Earl, 102
King, Martin Luther, Jr., 92, 97
kinship, 160
Kinzua Dam, 152
Kirwan, Sean, 334
Kivlen, Chris, 57
Kjellman, Kristen, 282, 284
Kloepfer, Ronnie, 297

Knute, Derek, 80
Kocis, Scott, 119
Koester, Ashley and Courtney, 282
Korea lacrosse, 423
Korean War, 178, 394
Kraft, Dan, 16, 18–19, 22
Kraft, Robert, 16, 18–19, 20, 22, 157
Kraft Family Sports Complex, 19, 157
Krongard, A. B. "Buzzy," 313
Kumeyaay, 402
Kumin, Sol, 314, 326

La Crosse, Wisconsin, 164
Lacrosse Foundation, 102
lacrosse historical origins. See Indigenous lacrosse history
Lacrosse International '83, 30
lacrosse sticks. See sticks and stickmaking
Lacrosse: Technique and Tradition (Scott), 253
Lakota, 31, 154–155, 182–183
land acknowledgments, 361, 389, 402
land reclamation, 197
land theft, 166–167, 181. See also forced removal; treaties
language programs, 51, 56
Lasagna, Peter, 219
Lasday, David, 17
Lasota, Selena, 288–292, 338, 370–374, 391
Lasota, Steve, 289
Latino lacrosse players, x, 81, 352. See also names of specific players
Latvia lacrosse, 142
Lawlor, Darren, 261
lax, as term, xiii–xiv
laxbro persona, xiv, xv, 203, 213–214, 222, 237, 293, 436. See also whiteness
LaxCon, xxi–xxii, 138
L. C. C. Radotin, 274
League of Nations, 173. See also United Nations
Lecky, Hakeem, 129, 131
Lee, Jane, 423
Lenape, 361
Levine, Mike, 326
Lewis, Albert F., 85
Lewis, William, 314–315
life expectancy, 10
Littlepage, Craig, 245–247
little war (two-stick lacrosse), 164
Loftus, Brian, xvi
Logan, Danny, 415
Longboat, Vince, 384, 385, 395
Longhouse faith, 47, 49, 149–150, 151, 166, 189–190, 338–339, 365. See also spirituality
Long Island Athletic Club, 297
Long Island lacrosse, 296–299
Looney, Brendan, 301, 303

Los Angeles Olympics (1932), 171, 422, 429
Los Angeles Olympics (2028), xxiv, 7, 355, 386, 422–437
Los Angeles Organizing Committee (LA28), 386, 422–430
lottery, 193
Love, Sharon, 230, 246–247, 362
Love, Yeardley, xviii, 221–222, 224–227, 246–247, 364
Lumsden, Louisa, 276–277
Lyons, Betty, 337, 383
Lyons, Ike, 176
Lyons, Jesse, 173, 175–176
Lyons, Oren
  on 2018 World Championships, 13
  activism of, xvii–xviii, 28, 181–182, 183–184, 188, 190–191
  alcoholism of, 191
  on alcohol use, 413
  on Anderson's contribution, 199–200
  on BDS letter, 12
  on braid, 44
  buffalo treaty of, 184–188
  coaching career of, 10–11
  development of lacrosse program and, 28–30
  early life of, 173–174
  on ethnocide, 172
  as faithkeeper, xvii, 341
  family of, 179
  ILF membership and, 31–34
  lacrosse career of, 28, 178–180
  on lacrosse origins, 164–165
  on Medicine Games, 47
  meeting with Biden, 425, 434
  military service of, 178
  on spirituality, 159–160, 161–162
  on symbolic moments, 363, 364
  on treaty cloth, 153
Lyons, Rex
  alcohol and drug use of, 191–192
  on cultural roles, 165
  on IOC and World Games, 388–389
  lacrosse career of, 31, 36, 191, 192
  as Nationals board leader, 366
  on sovereignty, 154
  on sticks, 47–48
  at White House events, 425, 433–434

MacLeod, Tyler, 237
Madalon, Matt, 237
Major League Lacrosse, 111, 124, 132–135, 325, 347–348, 359. See also Premier Lacrosse League (PLL); US Lacrosse
Malcolm X, 191
malnutrition, 18
Malphrus, Bray, 120, 231
Manion, Travis, 303

Mann Cup, 427
Marcus, Jon, 326
marijuana, 214, 217, 237, 248, 334,
    336, 413, 427. *See also* drug use
Marr, Scott, xi–xii, 20, 27, 57–62,
    66, 403
Marshall, John, 153
Martin, Carolyn, 342
Martin, Trayvon, 344
Maryland Scholastic Association,
    95–96
Masias, Julia, 276
Mathis-Crawford, Verina, 137
matrilineality, 9, 14, 158, 369.
    See also women's power
McCahon, Quinn, 392
McCallie School, 130
McDonough, MacEllen, 276
McEneaney, Eamon, xvi
McFadden, Owen, 93
McFadyen, Ryan, xv
McKnight, Drew, 326
McKone, Lindsey, 291–292, 374
McMahon, Angela, 284
McMahon, Corey, 297
McMahon, Kieran, 297
McPhee, John, xvii, 274
Means, Russell, 181, 182
Mearns, Randy, 318–320
medicine, lacrosse play as, xi, 46
Medicine Games. *See also*
    spirituality
    history of, 46–47, 162–167
    Marr's vision of, 59
    modern players on, 47–48, 51
    Nationals on, 149
    at Standing Rock, 65–66
Medlin, Shawn, 105
Megale, Larry, 335–336
Megale, Shea, 335
Melero, Ernie, 78, 80, 81, 142,
    352, 404
Men's World Lacrosse
    Championships. *See* World
    Lacrosse Championships
mental health, 59–60, 75–77, 126.
    See also suicide
Merrill, Brodie, 402, 408, 414
Messi, Lionel, 14
methadone, 236
Métis, 18, 397
Mexico City Olympics (1968), 98,
    121, 191, 437–438
Mexico lacrosse, 77–80, 142–143,
    350, 403–404
military service and lacrosse,
    301–306. *See also names of
    specific wars*
Milke, Mark, 195
Miller, Jovan, xxii, 127, 128–130,
    131–135
Miller, Kari, 286
Miller, Kyle, 206
Miller, Mike, 58

Miller, Zach, 62, 399
Milliman, Peter, 395
Minerd, Cassandra, 364–365,
    367–368, 370
Miss Indian World, 287
Mitchell, Ethan, 377
Mitchell, Hohnegayehwahs,
    338–339
MLL Four, 347–348
Mohawk, 8. *See also* Iroquois
    Confederacy
    1860 lacrosse exhibition of,
        168–169
    in 1904 Olympics, 171
    during the American Revolution,
        49, 165–166
    Calico Treaty and, 153
    employment of, 10
    on gambling, 189, 193
    honors by, 338
    support of Nationals, 398
    territorial description of, 50
Mohawk, Shaniece, 369
Mohawk Institute, 194
Mohawk language, 51
Mohawk Nation Council of Elders,
    338
Molloy, Kenneth, 90, 92
Monacan, 389
Montreal Athletic Association, 175
Montreal Lacrosse Club, 168–169
Moore, Joe, 129
Moore, Woody, 121
Moran, Richie, 250, 254
Morgan State University lacrosse,
    96–101, 105, 135, 285
Morris, Robert, 336
Morrow, David, 132
Moss, Simeon, 83–84
motorsport, 423
Mount Washington Lacrosse Club,
    175, 256, 313
Mueller, Chris "Rocky," 256
Muller, Tim, 239
Munday, Lindsey, 282, 285, 290
murder case (2010), xviii–xix,
    221–227
Murphy, Charlie, 59
muslin, 152–153, 154, 155–156, 381
Myers, Howard "Howdy," 250, 284,
    296–297
Myke, Matthew, 366–369, 372

N7 Fund, 65
Naismith, James, xix
Nanticoke, Tehoka, 26, 42–43,
    62, 399
National Buffalo Association, 185
National Day of Truth and
    Reconciliation, 372
National Football League Players
    Association, 312
National Lacrosse Association of
    Canada, 170, 171

National Lacrosse League (NLL),
    111, 330–332
National Museum of the American
    Indian, 337–338
Nationals. *See* Haudenosaunee
    Nationals (lacrosse team)
"Nations" indoor championships,
    29
Nation United (lacrosse program),
    xxi, xxii, 139–142, 351, 376
Nation United Foundation, 351
Native American Graves
    Protection and Repatriation
    Act (1990), 155
Native American Heritage Month,
    65
Navajo, 8, 18
Naval Academy, 84, 85, 202, 301, 303
Navy SEALs, 302, 303–304
Neiss, Scott, 15, 16–17, 18, 355–356,
    358
Nentego (Nanticoke), 361
Netanya, Israel, 5, 15. *See also*
    Israel World Lacrosse
    Championships (2018)
Netherlands lacrosse, 418
Neville, Colin, 326
New Balance, 132
Newby, Anthony, 101
Newcomb, Steven, 149, 402
Newhouse, Jon, 61
Nifong, Michael, xiv, xv, 116, 118
Nike, 39, 65, 111, 160, 198, 365–366,
    398
#NinjaPlease campaign, 132–135
Nolan, Leo, 366, 386, 429, 433
North Korea, 431
Northwestern University lacrosse,
    281–285, 289–292, 391–392
Notre Dame lacrosse, 62, 101, 140,
    239, 243, 290, 304, 306, 335,
    389–390, 392–393
N-word, xxi, xxiii, 89, 98, 113,
    128, 342, 359. *See also* racism
    in lacrosse culture; violence
    against Black people

Oakes, Richard, 181
Obama administration, 17, 18, 152
Oberg, Michael, 151
offender bias, 351
Offit, Howard, 275, 298
Offit, Josh, 216–217, 274
Ohlone, 361
Ojibwe, 163, 397
Olympic Games. *See also*
    International Olympic
    Committee
    (1904), 171, 429
    (1932), 171, 422, 429
    (1936), 191, 437
    (1968), 98, 121, 191, 437–438
    (1984), 31
    (2000), 438

(2008), xvii
(2016), 431
(2018), 431
(2020), 422
(2024), 420, 432
(2028), xxiv, 7, 355, 386, 422–437
early lacrosse appearances in, 31,
    171, 175
Haudenosaunee Nationals and,
    329, 339–340, 353–358, 389
lacrosse's mission to go to, x,
    xxiv, 7, 329, 386–387, 418–429
Oneida, 8, 9–10
during American Revolution, 49
federal funding for, 50, 152–153
on gambling, 189, 193
territorial description of, 50, 151
See also Iroquois Confederacy
O'Neill, Brennan, 402–403, 414, 416
O'Neill, Michael, 257
One Love Foundation, 246, 362, 385
Onondaga, 8, 10, 14. See also
    Iroquois Confederacy
during the American Revolution,
    49
buffalo herd of, 184–187, 381
as cultural caretaker, 165, 180
on gambling, 189, 193
identity of, 50–51
support of Nationals by, 196–197
territorial description of, 50, 151
Onondaga language, 56
Onondaga Nation Reservation,
    xix, 13
Onondaga Nation School, 56
Onondaga Red Devils (lacrosse
    team), 174
Onondaga Reservation, 49
Opie, Fred, 36, 82, 112, 190–191
opioid epidemic, xxiii, 55, 236–238.
    See also drug use
O'Reilly, Nick, 234
Orozco-Cohen, Tlaloc, 78
Ostrander, Anthony, 61
overdoses. See drug overdose
Overtime: A Candid Discussion of
    Racism in Lacrosse (Holman),
    342–343, 349
Owens, Jessie, 191, 437
OxyContin, 55, 214, 219, 236
Ozaagii, 163

Palestinian-Israeli conflict, 12,
    13–14, 15, 68–70, 73, 147–150,
    157, 308
Panama lacrosse, 359
pandemics, 341
Pannell, Rob, 42, 205, 206, 309, 311,
    317–318, 402, 416
Paris Olympics (2024), 420, 432
Parkman, Francis, 8–9
Passports. See also sovereignty
at 2015 World Championships,
    194–195

Canada on "fantasy passports," 195
disputes, 6–7, 11, 16–17, 21–22,
    32, 39, 388
first Haudenosaunee, 172–173
paternalism, 153
Patraca, Andres Axkana, 77–78
Patterson, Carol, 33, 285
Patterson, Kim, 37
Patterson, Wesley, 28, 30
Peacemakers: The Iroquois, the
    United States and the Treaty of
    Canandaigua, 1794 (Oberg), 151
Peake, Mary S., 377
Perez, Tom, 425, 426, 437
Pfarr, Drew, 219
Philadelphia Wings (NLL team),
    330, 331–332
Philippines lacrosse, 204, 357
Pierce, Clinton, 176
Pietramala, Dave, 107–108, 111
Pine Ridge Reservation, 182–183
Piscataway, 361
Piseno, Jacob, 397–398
Players Against Hate initiative,
    350–351
police brutality, xxi, 10, 132, 331,
    342, 343, 344. See also violence
    against Black people
Pomper, Max, 124
Pontiac's War, 163–164
Pope, Alexander, 23
population statistics, 8, 50, 329
Powell, Casey, 111
Powell, Mikey, 111
Powell, Ryan, 111
Powers, Mike, 261
Powhatan, 389
Powless, Darcy, 385, 399
Powless, Gaylord, 46
Powless, Irving, Jr., 46, 186
Powless, Irving, Sr., 180
Powless, Neal, 205
Powless, Ross, 46
Prague Indoor World
    Championships (2011), 40
Pratt, Richard Henry, 53, 172, 375
pregame ritual, 404–405
Premier Lacrosse League (PLL)
    absorption of MLL, 359
    BLM movement and, 343–349
    establishment of, 325–326,
        360–361
    ethos of, 332, 361–363
President's Cup, 51, 289
Pressler, Mike, xv, 118, 230, 295
Preston-Laurent, Eboni, xxii
Princeton University lacrosse, 85,
    108, 175, 267–268
Printup, Emmett, 31
professional team names as slurs, 64
protests, 51, 65–67, 98, 132–134,
    181–183
Puerto Rico lacrosse, 204, 357
Purdue Pharma, 236

Purépecha, 397
Putukian, Margot, 217

Quaker religion, 150, 151. See also
    Christianity
Qualtrough, Carla, 433
Quinn, Larry, 255, 262

Rabil, Mike, 312, 326, 348
Rabil, Paul
    on 2014 loss, 309
    attempt to buy MLL, 311–312
    on BLM, 343–344
    on Haudenosaunee in
        international competition,
        xxiv, 354
    lacrosse career of, 24, 82, 83, 206,
        208, 360
    Premier Lacrosse League of, 325,
        360–361
racism in lacrosse culture, xx–
    xxiv. See also N-word; violence
    against Black people; violence
    against Indigenous Americans;
    whiteness
    BLM and, 342, 343–347
    Brown and, 88–91
    Holman's series on, 342–343, 349
    initiatives against, 80–81, 140–142
    Melero on, 81, 352–353
    Miller and, 128–129
    Moss on, 83–84
    reporting on prevalence of,
        350–352
    Sherwood on, 130–131
    Sloan Green on, 279
    slurs against Black players, 342,
        349–350, 359
    slurs against Mexican players, 79,
        80, 142–143, 350, 403
    slurs against Thompsons, 63,
        330–331
    slurs by Greek team, 79–80
    Woodson on, 112–113
Ralph, Bill, 57
Rambo, Matt, 405, 406
Rand, Ripley, 356
rape, 18, 113. See also Duke
    University lacrosse rape case
    (2006)
RBDC Lacrosse, 316
Red Arrow, Mikko, 31
Redfern, Sue, 402, 422
Red Power, 51, 181–183. See also
    sovereignty
Reese, Cathy, 292
Refugee Olympic Team, 431
Regan, Jimmy, 302, 303, 305, 306
Reilly, Brian, 315, 327
relay of tribal nations (1984), 31
residential boarding schools, 53,
    172, 194, 331, 371–372, 375. See
    also Carlisle Indian Industrial
    School; forced removal

resiliency, 27, 35–36
Riccio, Marc, 402
Rice, Jean-Baptiste "Big," 170
Richeson, Jennifer, 351
Rivera, PaaWee, 426
Robinson, Jackie, 40, 83, 88, 93
Rochester Knighthawks (lacrosse
      team), 191, 198
Roosevelt, Eleanor, 84–85
Roosevelt, Franklin D., 85, 173
Roosevelt, Theodore, 171
Rubeor, Ben, 124
rules
   of IOC, 423–424, 430
   in lacrosse, 86, 169, 170, 209
Russia lacrosse, 418
Rutgers University lacrosse, 32, 299
Ruth, Babe, 46, 253
Ryan, Anthony "Merc," 104, 105

S.A.C. Capital, xvii, 314
Sanderson, Chris, 206–207
San Diego World Lacrosse
      Championships (2023), 394,
      398–416
Sankofa Lacrosse Alliance,
      136–137, 140
Sauk, 163
Sawiskera, 160
scalplock, 44. See also braid
Scane, Izzy, 391–392
Scanlan, Chase, 15, 385
Scherr, Jim, 7, 8, 41, 330, 354,
      355–358, 420–421, 424–425
Schindler, Gewas, 287–288
Schindler, Tia, 350, 367
Schmidt, Jerry, 277
scholarships, 56, 64, 81, 338
Schreiber, Tom, 25, 42, 309, 318,
      326, 402, 408
Schulte, Roslyn, 303
Schmucker, Marie, 278
Schwartz, Homer, 110
Schwartzwalder, Ben, 90, 91, 92
Scotland lacrosse, 74, 357
Scott, Bob, 88, 93–94, 110,
      252–253, 262
Scroggs, Willie, 251–255, 257–258,
      263–264
Seaman, Tony, 268
Sears, Tom, 254, 255–258
Seibald, Max, 83, 213–215, 311
Seligmann, Reade, 119
Seminole, 166
Seneca, 8. See also Iroquois
      Confederacy
   during the American Revolution,
      49
   on gambling, 189, 193, 197
   support of Nationals, 398
   territorial description of, 50
September 11, 2001 attacks, xvi,
      xvii, 297, 364
seven generations concept, 188, 341

sexual abuse, xiv–xv, xvi, 53,
      366–367
Shefayim Kibbutz, 293
Shellenberger, Connor, 392
Shenandoah, Edward, 46
Shenandoah, Leon, Sr., 30, 45, 51,
      180, 186
Shenandoah, Leroy, 46
Shenandoah, Tracy, 364, 402,
      404–405
Sherwood, Chuck, 82, 100, 114,
      116, 117
Sherwood, Devon, xv, 116–117,
      130–131, 295
Shroff, Anish, 25, 42
Sidat-Singh, Wilmeth, 90
Silverman, Howard "Chip," 97, 98
Simmons, Roy, III, 62
Simmons, Roy, Jr., 28, 30, 46, 61,
      86–88, 177–178, 260–266
Simmons, Roy, Sr., 90–92
Sinclair, Rosabelle, 277
Sioux, 18, 65–67, 154–155, 164,
      169, 361
Sitting Bull, 169
The 1619 Project (Hannah-Jones),
      375
Sixes, 363–364, 370–374, 387, 395,
      416, 422, 425, 428, 429, 432
Six Nations at Grand River. See also
      Iroquois Confederacy
   creation of reserve, 49
   on gambling, 189
   reserve description, 6, 13, 14
Six Nations Chiefs (lacrosse team),
      20–21, 29
skateboarding, 422
Sky, Gloria, 286
Sky, Pete, 286
slavery, 99, 149, 346, 377. See also
      enslaved persons; violence
      against Black people
Sloan Green, Tina, 103, 278–279
slurs. See N-word; racism in
      lacrosse culture
smallpox, 165
Smith, Alex, 312
Smith, Dean, xiii
Smith, DeMaurice, 312, 326
Smith, Dhane, 362
Smith, Harry, 177
Smith, Kathy, 367, 369
Smith, Katie, 369
Smith, Roger "Buck," 287
Smith, Shannon, 285
Smith, Sid, 56, 129, 287, 395
Smith, Tia, 286–287
Smith, Tommie, 98, 121, 191,
      437–438
Snibbe, Dick, 84
Snider, Geoff, 207, 208–209, 309
snowboarding, 422
soccer, 11, 14, 158, 281, 420
softball, 422, 423, 427

Solomon, Joe, 201, 202
Solomon, Travis, 30, 56, 201, 203
Sotiropoulos-Lawrence, Loukas, 79
Sour Springs Longhouse, 15
South Africa lacrosse, 359
South Korea, 431
South Korea lacrosse, 142
South Sudan, 431
sovereignty, xviii, 6–7, 7–8, 11,
      17, 30, 151–154, 172–173, 353,
      386–389, 425–426. See under
      Haudenosaunee; passports;
      Red Power
Sowers, Michael, 406, 415
Spencer, Danielle, 289
Spencer, Pat, 339
Spirit of Protection (Nike line), 65
spirituality, 49, 149–150, 160–162,
      338–339. See also cosmology;
      Longhouse faith; medicine,
      lacrosse play as; Medicine
      Games
SportAccord, 418–419
sports climbing, 422
Sports Illustrated (publication),
      277–278, 298
squash, 423, 427
Squire-Hill, Kent, 55
Staats, Austin
   at 2023 World Championships,
      399, 406, 407–408, 409, 410,
      412, 414
   drug testing of, 413, 427–428
   playing style of, 26
   Tiffany and, 384–386
Staats, Randy
   at 2023 World Championships,
      400–401, 406, 407, 409, 411,
      412, 413
   lacrosse career of, 14, 26, 290
Stallworth, Christian, 135–137,
      140, 142
Stallworth, Thomas, 135–136
Standing Bear, Luther, 54
Standing Rock Indian Reservation,
      65–67
Standing Rock Sioux, 18, 65–67.
      See also Sioux
Stanwick, Coco, 279
Stanwick, Covie, 279
Stanwick, Sheehan, 279
Stanwick, Steele, 45
Stanwick, Tad, 302
Stanwick, Wick, 279
Starsia, Dom
   Barrow and, 124
   coaching career of, 202, 230–231
   family of, 227–228
   firing of, 245–246
   intimidation of, 120
   on lacrosse's substance problem,
      215, 220–221, 242–243
   on Notre Dame offense, 390
   suspensions by, 232–235

on Thompson brothers, 58
Williams and, 243–245
Steele, David, 114–115
steelwork, 10
Stenersen, Steve, xxi–xxii, 102, 103, 355, 419, 429
Stevens, Aryien, 366, 367, 370
sticks and stickmaking
checks at game of, 209
of Haudenosaunee, xi
by Jacques, xix, xx, 333, 338
by Patterson, 30
Rex Lyons on, 47–48
sacredness of, xi
women's menstruation and, 51, 286
St. Paul High School sex tape scandal, 114–115
Straus, Nathan, 5
Stuart, Alexander H. H., 171
Stupp, Howard, 356
STX (brand), 111, 332
Styres, Curt, 198, 366
substance abuse. *See* alcohol use; drug use
suicide, 125–126, 219, 221. *See also* mental health
surfing, 421, 422
Susquehannock, 361
Sweden lacrosse, 418
Sweeney, Kyle, 314
Sydney Olympic Games (2000), 438
Syracuse Red Devils (lacrosse team), 177
Syracuse University, xiii
lacrosse program of, 28–29, 46, 56–58, 85–87, 127–130, 176, 179
rivalry with Hopkins, 260–264
student population of, 55, 89–90

Tadadaho, 49–50, 152, 338
Taft, William Howard, 175
Taiwan lacrosse, 19, 328
Talented Tenth, 95
Tamalpais Trust, 398
Tanton, William "Bill," 88, 259–260
Taylor, Breonna, 342, 343
Taylor, Jake, 392, 393
Taylor, Megan, 339
Team British Columbia, 289
Team Canada
at 2017 World Championships, 431
at 2018 World Championships, 204–210, 309–311, 317–320
at 2022 World Championships, 431
at 2023 World Championships, 407, 414–416
Team USA
2010 season, xviii, xx
at 2018 World Championships, xxiv, 5–8, 11–16, 18–27, 41–42, 68, 70, 73–75, 142–143, 204–210, 293, 309–311, 317–320

at 2023 World Championships, 400, 401, 402–403, 409, 411, 414–416
budget of, 398
at LA28, 430–431, 435
record of, 24, 400
Teat, Jeff, 205, 208, 309, 402
Temple University lacrosse, 278–279
Ten Bears (Harrison), 109
tennis, 93, 100
Tevlin, Brian, 393
Tewaaraton, 47, 338
Tewaaraton Award, xiv, 62, 106, 110, 213, 337–340, 362, 391, 402
Tewaaraton Foundation, 338
"They Bump Hips," as name for lacrosse, 46–47, 158
Thiele, Raina, 154
Thomas, Angus, 46, 178
Thomas, Oakley, 413, 427
Thompson, Amanda, 60, 61, 63
Thompson, Deloris "Dee," 15, 51
Thompson, Godehaot, 61
Thompson, Jeremy, 23, 44, 45, 51–58, 129, 406–407, 409
Thompson, Jerome "Hiana," Jr., 44, 51–56, 396
Thompson, Jerome "Ji," Sr., 44, 45, 48–49, 51–54, 382
Thompson, Jon, 342
Thompson, Lyle, xx
2012 win, 14
at 2023 World Championships, 406, 407, 409, 410–411
activism of, 64–67, 371
career of, 44–45
children of, 61, 63
college lacrosse of, 61–63
description of, 44
early life of, 51
family of, 51–56
on hair, 54
on Israel-Palestine conflict, 21, 43, 150
lacrosse play of, 57
name of, 52
on Olympics, 330, 387
on PLL, 361–362
schooling of, 52, 53, 60, 64
scouting of, 57–58
slurs against, 330–331
on spirit of the game, 387–388
World Championships and, 6, 24, 25, 26
Thompson, Miles, xx, 26, 44, 45, 51–62, 64
Thompson, Ty, 27, 38, 58, 61
Thornton, Big Mama, 38
Thorpe, Jim, 86
Tierney, Bill
coaching career of, 40, 250–251, 267–269
on Danowski, 294

on lacrosse's appeal, x–xi, 63
on lacrosse's rise, ix
on lacrosse's substance problem, 216, 217, 218, 230
USA Lacrosse field named for, 364
Tierney, Seth, 111, 298
Tiffany, Bradford, 184–187, 203, 332–333, 381–383, 394
Tiffany, Lars
at 2018 World Championships, 158–159
on buffalo treaty, 185, 186–188, 381–382, 383
coaching career of, 20, 26, 203–204, 247–248, 268, 333–337, 383–384, 394–401
as coach of 2023 World Championships, 394, 398–416
hickory stick of, 333, 336–337, 338, 405
lacrosse career of, 200–203, 266–267
on lacrosse's substance problem, 218, 413
Timchal, Cindy, 279–280, 284
Tisha B'Av, 308–309
Title IX (1972), xiv, 274–275, 276, 278, 285
Tocqueville, Alexis de, 166
Tokyo Olympics (2020/21), 422, 424
Toliver, Chad, 347–348
Tometi, Opal, 344
Trail of Broken Treaties, 181
Trail of Tears, 167
treaties, 10, 17, 39, 151–155, 381. *See also* land theft
treaty cloth, 152–153, 154, 155–156, 381
Treaty of Big Tree (1797), 151
Treaty of Canandaigua (1794), 151–155, 166, 381, 433
Trudeau, Justin, 18, 20, 371
Truman, Harry, 85
Trump administration, 18, 22, 67, 132, 157, 351, 352
Truth and Reconciliation Commission (Canada), 18, 194
Tsai, Joe, xxiv, 19–20, 326–329, 354–356, 401, 419–420, 421
Tucker, Janine, 279
Turner, Nathan, 376, 377
Turning Stone Casino, 193
Tuscarora, 8. *See also* Iroquois Confederacy
during American Revolution, 49
federal funding and, 50
on gambling, 189, 190, 197
territorial description of, 50

Uganda lacrosse, 418
Ukraine lacrosse, 329
United Nations, 7, 9, 14, 188, 190–191, 386–387, 430–431

Unite the Right rally (2017), xxii–xxiii
University of Albany (SUNY Albany), 57–62
University of North Carolina lacrosse, xii, 253–260, 300
University of Utah, 249
University of Virginia lacrosse, xviii, 119–125, 219–221, 227–235, 242–243, 333–337, 389–393
Urban Lacrosse Alliance, 81
USA Lacrosse (team). *See* Team USA
US Army Corps of Engineers, 152
US Commission on Civil Rights, 10
US Department of Housing and Urban Development, 50
US Intercollegiate Lacrosse Association, 87, 301, 417
US/USA Lacrosse (organization). *See also* Major League Lacrosse; Premier Lacrosse League (PLL); Team USA
cultural competency initiatives of, xxii, 332
diversity initiatives of, 80–81, 105
exclusion of Nationals, 353–358
on racism in lacrosse, 359
on Warrior Sports campaign, 133–134
US National Amateur Lacrosse Association, 175
US Olympic Committee, 7
US Virgin Islands lacrosse, 359
Ute, 31

Van Orman, Ray, 175–176
VanValkenburgh, Jack, 397
Ventura, Thomas, 237
veterans. *See* military service and lacrosse
Vicodin, 236
Victoria (queen), 170–171, 174, 276
Vietnam War, xvi, 238, 301, 302
violence against Black people, xxi, 10, 132, 331, 342, 343, 344, 345, 373. *See also* racism in lacrosse culture; slavery
violence against Indigenous Americans, xxi, 149, 166, 171–172, 194, 331, 371. *See also* assimilation; forced removal
violence against women. *See* Love, Yeardley; Myke, Matthew; sexual abuse
Virginia. *See* University of Virginia lacrosse
Virginia Tech lacrosse, xxiii
Voelkel, Peter, 255, 258, 262–263

Walker, John, 108, 109
Walker-Weinstein, Alicia, 285
Wall Street. *See* financial careers and lacrosse
wampum belts, 152, 155, 156, 158, 173
Ward, Dillon, 205, 309, 318, 402, 414
Ward, Marty, 395
war declarations, 178
Warne, Kevin, 241
Warren, Elizabeth, 18
Warrior Society, 189, 197
Warrior Sports (brand), 132–134
Washington, Booker T., 92
Washington, DC, xiii–xiv
Washington, George, 9, 151, 152, 165, 433
Washington Redskins (football team), 64–65
Wasserman, Casey, 423–424, 428–430
Waterman, Paul, 35
water protectors, 65–67
Waters, Gary, 256
Webster, Marvin, 97
Weist, Carl, 200
Westchester Polo Club, 174
Western Shoshone, 31
West Point lacrosse, 85, 301
white flight, 96
Whiteley, Mitch, 313
whiteness, xxii, 80–81, 93–94, 100, 362. *See also* laxbro persona; racism in lacrosse culture
white supremacy, xxii–xxiii. *See also* slavery; violence against Black people
Wiley, Marcellus, 344
Williams, Carla, 335
Williams, McRae, 242
Williams, Serena and Venus, 93, 120
Williams, Zed, 62, 243–245, 248, 334, 362, 396–397
Willson, Russell, 84, 85
Wilson, Edmund, 162
Wingate Institute for Physical Education, 73–74
Wolf, Jordan, 294, 298, 316
women's lacrosse. *See also names of specific persons, universities, and teams*
development of, 276–287
Haudenosaunee Nationals, xxi, 6, 285–288, 365–374
Israel 2018 games of, 274
players, xiv, x
special rules of, 289
success and explosion of, 273–276
women's power
Haudenosaunee Nationals and, 365–369
matrilineality of clans, 9, 14, 158
during menstruation, 51, 286

Women's World Lacrosse Championships. *See* World Lacrosse Championships
Wood, Peter, 114
Wooden, John, 284
Woodson, Chazz, xxii, xxiii, 108, 111–113, 132, 140, 315, 375, 376, 435
World Anti-Doping Agency (WADA), 418
World Cup, 11, 14, 420
World Games, 329–330, 339–340, 339n, 340, 353–358, 364, 383, 422–423. *See also* International World Games Association
World Lacrosse (organization), xxiv, 339, 353, 421–425, 434
World Lacrosse's Athletes Commission, 423
World Lacrosse Championships, xvii, 339n. *See also* Indoor World Lacrosse Championships
(1967), 82
(1982), 29
(1990), 33, 34–37
(1994), 37
(1998), 37
(2002), 37
(2003), 37
(2007), 37
(2010), xviii, xx, 7, 15, 39, 40, 434
(2011), 40
(2012), 14–15
(2013), 365
(2014), xx, 15, 40, 77–78, 195, 204
(2015), 7, 193–196, 434
(2017), 6, 11, 17
(2018), xxiv, 5–8, 11–16, 18–27, 41–42, 68, 70, 73–75, 142–143, 308–310, 317–320
(2019), 198–199, 340, 366
(2022), 422–423
(2021/2022), 329, 339, 340, 354, 355, 356–357, 364, 383, 422–423
(2023), 394, 398–416
World Lacrosse Super Sixes, 363–364, 370–374
World Trade Center attacks (9/11/01), xvi, xvii, 297, 364
World War I, 178, 302
World War II, 12, 174, 178, 302
Wounded Knee occupation (1973), 182–183
wrestling, 420

Yale University lacrosse, 19, 57, 218, 315, 327, 337, 393

Zacharopoulus, Elias, 78
Zimmerman, Don, 262, 267